PEOPLE BUILDING PEACE II

A project of the European Centre for Conflict Prevention
(Utrecht, Netherlands)

Financially supported by the Swedish International Development Agency
(Sida), the Austrian Development Agency, and the Ford Foundation

PEOPLE BUILDING PEACE II

SUCCESSFUL STORIES OF CIVIL SOCIETY

edited by
Paul van Tongeren, Malin Brenk, Marte Hellema,
and Juliette Verhoeven

LYNNE
RIENNER
PUBLISHERS

BOULDER
LONDON

Published in the United States of America in 2005 by
Lynne Rienner Publishers, Inc.
1800 30th Street, Boulder, Colorado 80301
www.rienner.com

and in the United Kingdom by
Lynne Rienner Publishers, Inc.
3 Henrietta Street, Covent Garden, London WC2E 8LU

Library of Congress Cataloging-in-Publication Data
People building peace II : successful stories of civil society / edited
by Paul van Tongeren . . . [et al.].
  (A project of the European Centre for Conflict Prevention)
  Includes bibliographical references and index.
  ISBN 1-58826-358-4 (hardcover: alk. paper)
  ISBN 1-58826-383-5 (pbk. : alk. paper)
1. Pacifism. 2. Peace movements. 3. Civil society. 4. Pacifism—Case studies.
5. Peace movements—Case studies. 6. Civil society—Case studies. I. Title:
People building peace two. II. Tongeren, Paul van. III. European Centre for
Conflict Prevention. IV. Series.
JZ5560.P462 2005
303.6'6—dc22

                                                 2005000412

British Cataloguing in Publication Data
A Cataloguing in Publication record for this book
is available from the British Library.

Printed and bound in the United States of America

    The paper used in this publication meets the requirements
  ∞ of the American National Standard for Permanence of
    Paper for Printed Library Materials Z39.48-1992.

5 4 3 2 1

Contents

Foreword, Kofi Annan   xi
Acknowledgments   xiii

Introduction, *Paul van Tongeren, Malin Brenk, Marte Hellema,*
    and Juliette Verhoeven   1

Part 1 Reflections
1   Weaving the Web: Civil-Society Roles in Working with
     Conflict and Building Peace   7
     Catherine Barnes

        Personal Story: Kay Rala Xanana Gusmão   25

2   Discourses on Peace Practices:
     Learning to Change by Learning from Change?   29
     Cordula Reimann and Norbert Ropers

3   Effective Regional Networks and Partnerships   45
     Andrés Serbin

4   UN–Civil-Society Interactions: Working Together for Peace   59
     John Clark

5   The War on Terror: Effects on Civil-Society Actors in the
     Field of Conflict Prevention and Peacebuilding   71
     Kevin P. Clements

6   People Building Peace: Key Messages and Essential Findings   83
     Paul van Tongeren, Juliette Verhoeven, and Jim Wake

Part 2 Themes and Cases
7   Women: Using the Gender Lens   97
     Lisa Schirch and Manjrika Sewak

        Personal Story: Queen Noor   108

7.1   Women Breaking the Silence:
         The Athwaas Initiative in Kashmir   111
7.2   The Other Clan: Save Somali Women and Children   117
7.3   Women Weaving Bougainville Together: Leitana Nehan
         Women's Development Agency in Papua New Guinea   122
7.4   The Fate of Disappeared Children: The Grandmothers
         of the Plaza de Mayo in Argentina   127
7.5   Women's Peace Activism in West Africa:
         The WIPNET Experience   133
7.6   Leaving Lebanon: The Four Mothers Movement in Israel   141

8   Youth: Protagonists for Peace   147
      L. Randolph Carter and Michael Shipler

8.1   Picking Up the Pieces: Jamaa in Burundi   157
8.2   And a Child Shall Lead: The Children's Movement for
         Peace and Return to Happiness in Colombia   162
8.3   Young Kosovars Help Themselves:
         The Kosovar Youth Council   167

9   The Media: Reaching Hearts and Minds   175
      Francis Rolt

      Personal Story: John Marks   185

9.1   Changing Attitudes Through Children's Television:
         Nashe Maalo in Macedonia   187
9.2   *Operation Fine Girl* Exposes Sexual Violence:
         WITNESS in Sierra Leone   193
9.3   Unsung Heroes: Studio Ijambo in Burundi   200

10   Faith-Based Organizations:
       The Religious Dimensions of Peacebuilding   209
       Douglas Johnston

10.1 Struggling for a Just Peace: Naga Churches in
         Northeast India   219
10.2 The Pastor and the Imam:
         The Muslim-Christian Dialogue Forum in Nigeria   226
10.3 Step by Step on the Way to Peace:
         The Dhammayietra Peace Walk in Cambodia   233
10.4 Restoring the Power of Speech:
         The REMHI Initiative in Guatemala   239

11   Education That Makes a Difference   245
       Tricia S. Jones

       Personal Story: David Hamburg   255
11.1 Food, Education, and Peacebuilding:
         Children's Learning Services in Sierra Leone   257

11.2 Committed to Building Peace:
     The City Montessori School in India   264
11.3 Uniting Children During War: *Sawa*-UNICEF in Lebanon   269
11.4 Managing Conflict at School: The Ohio Commission
     on Dispute Resolution and Conflict Management
     in the United States   275

12 The Arts and Peacebuilding: Using Imagination and Creativity   283
   John Paul Lederach

12.1 Using Creative Arts to Deglamorize War:
     Peacelinks in Sierra Leone   293
12.2 Artistic Responses to the Siege of Sarajevo:
     The Cellist and the Film Festival in Bosnia-Herzegovina   301

13 The Peacebuilding Potential of Local Businesses   309
   Nick Killick and Canan Gündüz

13.1 Brokering Peace and Building the Nation:
     The National Business Initiative in South Africa   321
13.2 A Profitable Peace: The Confederation of British Industry
     in Northern Ireland   327
13.3 Planting Peace: Philippine Business for Social Progress   332

14 Diasporas: Untapped Potential for Peacebuilding in
   the Homelands   339
   Abdullah A. Mohamoud

14.1 Fear and Hope in Acholiland: Kacoke Madit in
     Uganda and the United Kingdom   348
14.2 Contributing to Peace at Home:
     The Berghof Foundation in Sri Lanka   354

15 Civilian Peacekeepers: Creating a Safe Environment
   for Peacebuilding   363
   Tim Wallis and Claudia Samayoa

15.1 An Experiment at Mixing Roles:
     The Balkan Peace Team in Croatia and Serbia/Kosovo   369
15.2 Protecting the Protectors:
     Peace Brigades International in Colombia   376
15.3 Human Shields to Limit Violence:
     Witness for Peace in Nicaragua   382
15.4 Grassroots and South-South Cooperation:
     Bantay Cease-fire in the Philippines   388

16 Development: No Development Without Peace,
   No Peace Without Development   395
   Malin Brenk and Hans van de Veen

16.1 Peace Aid: Norwegian Church Aid in Mali   409
16.2 A Journey Toward Peace:
        St. Xavier's Social Service Society in India   414

17 Early Warning and Early Response: Preventing Violent Conflicts   421
    Takwa Zebulon Suifon

        Personal Story: Max van der Stoel   433

    17.1 Managing Conflicts by Phone:
            The Mobile Phones Network in Northern Ireland   435
    17.2 Working with the Local Wisdom: The National Council
            of Churches of Kenya Peace Program   441

18 Traditional and Local Conflict Resolution   449
    Jannie Malan

    18.1 Clan Elders as Conflict Mediators: Somaliland   459
    18.2 Revitalizing Tradition to Promote Reconciliation:
            The Gacaca Courts in Rwanda   466

19 Dialogue-Based Processes: A Vehicle for Peacebuilding   473
    Edward (Edy) Kaufman

    19.1 Engaging the "Other":
            The Nansen Dialogue Network in the Balkans   488
    19.2 Building Trust, Promoting Hope: The Families Forum
            Hello Peace Project in Israel and Palestine   495
    19.3 Creating Expertise: The Oxford Research Group in
            the United Kingdom   501
    19.4 Inside the Revolution of Roses: Georgia   507
    19.5 Taking the Constitution to the People:
            The Citizens Constitutional Forum in Fiji   512

20 Campaigning to Create Awareness:
    How to Influence People and Change the World   519
    Rebecca Peters

    20.1 Never Again: The Archdiocese of São Paulo and
            the World Council of Churches in Brazil   528
    20.2 Making a Difference: The International Women
            Building Peace Campaign   533
    20.3 Fighting Corruption: The Clean Election Campaign
            in Kenya   540
    20.4 Rage Against the Regime: The Otpor Movement in Serbia   545
    20.5 Protests Stop Devastating Nuclear Tests: The Nevada-
            Semipalatinsk Anti-Nuclear Movement in Kazakhstan   552
    20.6 Lessons from Campaigns of the 1990s:
            Innovations in Humanitarian Advocacy   558

21 Civil Society: Participating in Peace Processes   567
  Celia McKeon

  21.1 A Nonthreatening Approach to Peace:
      The Community of Sant' Egidio in Mozambique   576
  21.2 Facilitating a Mutual Deescalation Process:
      Quakers and the Peace and Reconciliation Group in
      Northern Ireland   582
  21.3 Engendering the Peace Process in West Africa:
      The Mano River Women's Peace Network   588
  21.4 Small Steps Toward Reconciliation: The Joint Committee
      for Democratization and Conciliation in Moldova   594
  21.5 A Second Way: Grupo Maryland Between Peru and Ecuador   600

22 Disarmament, Demobilization, and Reintegration:
    Not Only a Job for Soldiers   607
  Sami Faltas and Wolf-Christian Paes

    Personal Story: Oscar Arias   617

  22.1 Former Rebels Use Market Forces to Achieve Their
      Social Ideals: New Rainbow in Colombia   619
  22.2 Transforming Arms into Ploughshares:
      The Christian Council of Mozambique   623
  22.3 Fruits of War: Homies Unidos in El Salvador and
      the United States   630

23 Reconciliation: Challenges, Responses, and the Role of Civil Society 645
  Hizkias Assefa

    Personal Story: Desmond Tutu   645

  23.1 From Saying "Sorry" to a Journey of Healing:
      National Sorry Day in Australia   647
  23.2 Listen to Understand: The Listening Project in Croatia 654
  23.3 The Spirit of Caux: Moral Re-Armament and Initiatives
      for Change in Switzerland   661
  23.4 Dialogue Spices Peace: Baku Bae in Indonesia   667

Index   673
About the Book   693
About the Global Partnership for the Prevention of Armed Conflict 695
About the European Centre for Conflict Prevention   697

Foreword

Kofi Annan

Even though states remain the building blocks of the international system, there are real limits to what states can achieve on their own, particularly in our era of globalization and interdependence. Fortunately, networks of nongovernmental organizations now embrace virtually every level of organization—from the village community to global summits—and almost every sector of public life—from the provision of microfinance and the delivery of emergency relief supplies to environmental and human rights activism.

The presence of civil society strengthens the legitimacy, accountability and transparency of intergovernmental decisionmaking. And effective partnerships among civil society, governments, and international organizations are vital if our world is to mount effective collective responses to evolving threats to people everywhere. Those threats include not just civil and interstate conflict, terrorism, and weapons proliferation, but also poverty, disease, and environmental destruction.

Since its founding, the United Nations has joined hands with civil society in a range of fields—from policy development and advocacy to program design and implementation. The importance of this relationship has grown in the past decade, and it is vital that this is reflected in the procedures for interaction between the UN and civil society. That is why, in 2003, I established a panel, led by the former president of Brazil, Fernando Henrique Cardoso, to make recommendations to strengthen the organization's engagement with civil society groups. I have commended the panel's report to the General Assembly, together with my own observations, and I hope that its recommendations will receive the careful attention and action they deserve.

Nowhere is close engagement with civil society more important than in the task of preventing violent conflict. Indeed, some years ago, when I said that the international community had to move from a culture of reaction to a culture of prevention, I called for an international conference of local, national, and international nongovernmental organizations on conflict prevention. I am very pleased that, in response, the conference of the Global Partnership for the Prevention of Armed Conflict is taking place in July 2005. I have high hopes for this conference, and I look forward to working with member states and civil society to ensure that its outcomes are reflected in concrete follow-up steps.

In this book, readers will find a treasure trove of ideas on what civil society can do to help build peace, and on how effective partnerships with governments and international organizations can be forged. They will also draw inspiration from the stories of civil society groups working in countries all over the world. This collection shows how good intentions can be turned into good, and effective, deeds. I am therefore glad to commend it to a wide global audience.

Kofi Annan
Secretary-General of the United Nations

Acknowledgments

This book is one of the major outcomes of the Global Partnership for the Prevention of Armed Conflict. Numerous individuals and organizations worldwide provided their advice, insights, and support in shaping the project, providing feedback on draft texts and assisting in the identification and selection of the cases. The book represents the involvement and ideas of many more persons than those whose names are mentioned as authors. We are indebted to all of them. This publication has been made possible through the strong dedication of many people, and we would like to extend our sincere thanks to all involved. The editors also wish to express a special and deep debt of gratitude to the authors of the chapters and inspiring cases without whom there would not have been a publication.

The book would not have been possible without generous grants from several funding sources. We are grateful to the Swedish International Development Agency (Sida), the Austrian Development Agency, and the Ford Foundation for providing financial support.

Throughout this process, we were guided by the members of our editorial board, who gave useful comments and encouragement. We are very grateful for the constructive input of Gus Miclat (the Philippines), Lisa Schirch (U.S.), Andrés Serbin (Argentina), and George Washira (Kenya). During a meeting on issues and themes of the Global Partnership for the Prevention of Armed Conflict in December 2003, the structure and approach of the book was discussed with a broader group of experts. We are very thankful for the input and inspirational guidance that we received from Catherine Barnes (UK), Lee Habasonda (Zambia), Raya Kadyrova (Kyrgyzstan), Andrei Kamenshikov (Russia), Edy Kaufman (Israel), George Khutsishvili (Georgia), Fatoumatta M'boge (Ghana), Sue LeMesurier (UK), Gus Miclat (Philippines), Tatjana Popovic (Serbia), and Tore Samuelsson (Sweden).

Hundreds of cases were presented to us from all around the world, and we are indebted to all regional initiators of the Global Partnership, key experts, and lead organizations who took time out of their busy schedules to send us relevant information of stories from people working for peace, to recommend authors, and to comment on the write-up of cases.

The reflection and introduction chapters were reviewed critically by several experts and practitioners. This often led to enriched texts, and we are very grateful for the constructive input of the reviewers and thank the authors for their flexibility and willingness to revise their chapters.

The journalistic office Bureau M&O (Environment and Development Productions), based in Amsterdam, provided an invaluable service in editing the cases and some of the chapters. We thank Jos Havermans, Niall Martin, Fitzroy Nation, Bram Posthumus, and Jim Wake. Special thanks go to Hans van de Veen for coordinating this editing process and for his constructive advice and input in the overall development of the book.

We are very grateful for the support from our colleagues at the European Centre for Conflict Prevention. In particular, we thank Guido de Graaf Bierbrauwer for his continuous advice and moral support and Pieter Schultz for cross-checking references. Last but not least, we are extremely grateful to several interns for their constructive assistance. They were instrumental in organizing and writing the report of the content meeting, collecting information about inspiring cases, providing background research, and compiling resource information. We thank Charlotte Crockett, Gerinke Fountain, Danny van Geel, Niklas Hansson, and Franka Oluji for their efforts and assistance in producing this book.

While thankful for all the support we received, we assume full responsibility for the publication.

* * *

The editors would like to dedicate this book to Peter Meyer Swantée, who passed away as the book went to print. Peter Meyer Swantée was one of the cofounders of the European Centre for Conflict Prevention and a very committed board member, who served as treasurer for a number of years. We are very appreciative of his dedication to our work and grateful for his support throughout the years.

—*The Editors*

Introduction

Paul van Tongeren, Malin Brenk, Marte Hellema & Juliette Verhoeven

"Instead of continuing to weep in frustration we should pick up the phone, hear the voices, and continue onward with renewed hope, knowing that there's someone to talk to, that the cycle of bloodshed can be brought to an end." —A user of Hello Peace

"I think it teaches us to dream big and act boldly. A small group of peace activists, most with church connections, with little money and no time to waste created a thriving citizens' movement" —Michael L. Westmoreland-White about Witness for Peace

"You ask me am I crazy for playing the cello, why do you not ask if they are crazy for shelling Sarajevo?" —Vedran Smailovic, the cellist who, when twenty-two of his fellow citizens were killed in the early days of the siege of Sarajevo, responded by taking his cello to the spot of the massacre and playing for the following twenty-two days in their honor. It was a gesture that inspired not only the people of Sarajevo, but the entire caring world.

These are a few quotes from the several successful cases of civil-society activities included in this publication. They comprise, in a few words, the message of the whole publication: That, in order to effectively prevent and resolve the violent conflicts of today, all stakeholders, from the grassroots to the international levels, need to be included in developing and implementing such strategies throughout the entire conflict cycle. Most importantly, peacebuilding from below—by civil-society actors—works and is needed for any peace process to succeed. This is, by no means, a new revelation. However, while much literature is available on Track One negotiations, international military interventions, peacekeeping missions, and even more theoretically, on the need to include civil society in different parts of the peace process, there is still a gap in the literature mirroring the successful contributions that civil society is already making in conflict prevention and peacebuilding. This publication fills this gap by showing that people on the ground, ranging from women, youth, and faith-based organizations to artists and the media, can make and already have made a positive difference in many of the conflict areas around the world. Civil-society organizations and nongovernmental organizations—CSOs and NGOs, as they are commonly called—although not a substitute to Track One actors, should therefore be seen as a necessary and irreplaceable complement to the activities of governments and intergovernmental organizations in the field of conflict prevention and peacebuilding.

Setting the Stage

The so-called war on terrorism draws attention away from the reality in which we live today: Of the thirty-four countries that are the furthest away from achieving the UN Millennium Development Goals, twenty-two are currently or were recently affected by conflict. The new world order, envisaged after the collapse of the Soviet Union, rapidly dissolved into a series of brutal civil wars in which thousands have been killed and millions more displaced. Driven by short-term pressures and lack of political will, many governments usually respond too late. The costs of squandered resources have been great and the scars of human misery will take generations to heal.

Nevertheless, there are currently thousands of individuals and organizations outside governments and intergovernmental organizations that are working for peace around the world. These people are achieving important results, but unfortunately the work that they do is not often given the acknowledgment it deserves. Therefore, we believe that the time has come to raise the profile of the people who are working to achieve peace on the ground in conflict areas around the world.

The Need for Change

The international community, as it is embodied by the UN, has too often proved ineffective when faced with the harshest realities of world conflicts. Given that the nature of conflicts has changed, shifting from interstate to intrastate, so must the strategies to solve them change. There has likewise been a growing interest in civilian forms of conflict prevention and peacebuilding, even among governments and international organizations. The UN secretary-general has, for example, spoken of the need to shift from a "culture of reaction" to a "culture of prevention," and many other organizations, including the European Union and the Organization for Security and Cooperation in Europe, have responded to the call.

Linked to this shift is the importance of CSOs. Although political leaders across the world are becoming increasingly aware of civil society's potential to anticipate and resolve its own tensions, the scope and magnitude of civil societies' activities in this field are still not fully recognized. Too often it seems that governments are reluctant to admit nonstate actors into the business of peace and security.

Despite this reluctance, successful work in conflict prevention and peacebuilding by civil society is already taking place on the ground as community leaders, women's groups, academics, journalists, and businessmen initiate and involve themselves in activities with results that have, at times, extended beyond that of soldiers and diplomats.

The Global Partnership for the Prevention of Armed Conflict

In 2002, the European Centre for Conflict Prevention (ECCP) initiated a civil-society process to generate a global agenda for the prevention of armed and violent conflicts, in response to the UN secretary-general's 2001 *Report on the Prevention of Armed Conflict.*

The Global Partnership for the Prevention of Armed Conflict (GPPAC) was formed to build a new international consensus on the prevention of violent conflict and peacebuilding and to support a shift from reaction to prevention. Fifteen regional processes comprise the fabric of the initiative and will develop separate action agendas to reflect principles and priorities for their regions. Building from these regional agendas, the GPPAC has developed a Global Action Agenda and worked toward a global civil-society conference at UN headquarters in July 2005, and a long-term network of people and organizations committed to peacebuilding and conflict prevention. The publication currently in your hands is also one of the main outcomes of the Global Partnership and is based on the valuable input from organizations facilitating different regional branches of the GPPAC and other lead organizations in this field.

Process and Challenges

The idea of this book arose about three years ago, when the Global Partnership provided us with an excellent opportunity to publish a follow-up to the first People Building Peace publication entitled *People Building Peace: 35 Inspiring Stories from Around the World* (1999). This book presented for the first time a broad overview of grassroots successes in this field from different countries and continents. The publication is still in great demand by NGOs, training institutes, and other organizations whose work touches on conflict prevention and peacebuilding.

The worldwide scope of the Global Partnership provided an excellent opportunity to work with different grassroots organizations and to collect the local stories that had, in many cases, never previously been documented. Seizing this opportunity, this book project was discussed several times within the Global Partnership as well as with external experts.

The challenges we have faced during the process of developing this publication have been many. Once the idea was launched, we sent out initial requests to all of our regional partners in the Global Partnership, as well as to lead organizations in this field, asking for their stories. The responses were overwhelming and we had soon collected over three hundred cases from all over the world. Our biggest challenge therefore became developing a selection process based on criteria such as regional spread, sustainability, innovation, and a clear impact to end up with a more manageable number of cases. During this process it also became clear that, to fully raise the voices of these people working on the ground, we needed to provide them with the opportunity to write the cases themselves. Although the proposal was very well received by the organizations in question (about two-thirds chose to write the cases themselves), this led to another main challenge. For the first time, many of the organizations involved were not only required to reflect on and objectively assess their own work, but they likewise had to build the capacity within their own organizations to document their successful cases.

For the editors, this strategy also presented the tremendous challenge of working with over eighty authors in the very short time span that was dedicated to the publication process. There was also the challenge of balancing these unknown cases with better known, and often published, ones to show the great variety of activities in which civil society is currently involved in this field.

Despite, and probably because of, all these challenges, the publication process has been extremely interesting and rewarding.

This Publication

This book aims to celebrate the work of individuals and organizations working for peace around the world by showcasing and promoting their inspiring and successful stories. The formula of this book is the same as its predecessor, *People Building Peace: 35 Inspiring Stories from Around the World.* The first part of the publication gives an overview of the current state of affairs, latest trends and developments in peacebuilding, and ways forward in relation to civil society, the UN, and other international organizations.

The second part of the publication contains a series of chapters going more deeply into determining the roles of nine key groups of civil-society actors and sectors and clearly formulating eight tools, approaches, and strategies that these actors have at their disposal throughout the different phases of the conflict cycle.

Each thematic section begins with a brief overview of the issues at stake, all of which were written by leading experts and practitioners from this field. Linked to each introduction are case studies of how people successfully can and have made a difference in the field of conflict prevention and peacebuilding. These cases are intended to raise the profile of people working for peace from different parts of civil society, in different regions, and on different levels. In several of these chapters, valuable contributions from more controversial civil-society actors such as diaspora, faith-based leaders, and the media are highlighted. This is to show that, contrary to much of the current literature and discussions that most often focus on the negative role these groups can play in conflict situations, many of these civil-society actors are engaged in extensive conflict prevention and peacebuilding activities seldom acknowledged inside and outside this field. By showing the "other side," we hope to rectify that negative image. Furthermore, we hope to stimulate more peacebuilders to work with these groups of powerful but often neglected individuals and sectors and to create a stronger "peace constituency" in different conflict areas.

Only if we involve all stakeholders will we be able to build sustainable peace, bringing the cycle of bloodshed to an end. The stories in this publication shows a variety of successful activities by civil-society actors working toward this end. By bringing them to you in this accessible format, we hope that you will enjoy reading this book as much as we have enjoyed making it.

PART I

Reflections

1

Weaving the Web:
Civil-Society Roles in
Working with Conflict and Building Peace

Catherine Barnes

Outsiders can never make peace for others; people and societies must create their own systems for working through their differences. While governments must play a crucial role in this process, the people are the key to long-term conflict transformation—with outsiders potentially playing important supportive and enabling roles. Through the process of engaging with each other, people can determine how they will live in the world they share and give consent to the process through which they agree to be governed. This act of making and keeping agreements in all realms of life and the willingness to coexist and engage peacefully and, occasionally, even joyfully is at the center of the roles played by civil society in working with conflict.

"Civil society" resists easy definition, especially when discussing it as a global development. Every society has its own distinct forms of social organization, cultural and political traditions, as well as contemporary state and economic structures—all of which are central to the development of civil society and shape its specific features. Most broadly understood, however, *civil society* refers to the web of social relations that exist in the space between the state, the market (activities with the aim of extracting profit), and the private life of families and individuals. Interlinked with the concept of civil society is the idea of social capital: the values, traditions, and networks that enable coordination and cooperation between people. Therefore these concepts have qualities associated with relationships, with values, and with organizational forms.

Civil society takes form through various types of association. Ranging from officially constituted institutions to small, informal community groups, these associations give expression and direction to the social, political, spiritual, and cultural needs of members. By reflecting diverse interests and values, they enable the articulation, mobilization, and pursuit of the aspirations of the different constituent elements within a society. Figure 1.1 illustrates many—though not all—of the types of groupings that can potentially comprise civil

7

Figure 1.1 Civil Society—Diverse Sectoral and Organizational Forms

society. Some would contest the inclusion of some of these groupings as a part of civil society, more narrowly defined. Yet all have played important roles in responding to conflict, as illustrated in this volume. What becomes clear is that civil society is far more than public-benefit nongovernmental organizations (NGOs). NGOs with technical-professional skills do, however, play an important role in providing services, promoting change, and working with conflict.

As a concept, civil society rose to prominence globally during the 1990s. This was, in part, as a result of agendas articulated by international NGOs. It was also a response to initiatives of donor agencies that aspired to support the development of this independent space within societies in transition from various forms of authoritarian rule. Transnational and global civil society has developed powerfully over the past two decades, as is discussed further below. Along with this has been a rapid expansion in civil-society organizations (CSOs) explicitly aimed at working with conflict. This significance of civil society in general and its role in conflict in particular have been recognized by the United Nations in recent reports and resolutions.

There are significant variations in how theorists define civil society and view its functions. Many incorporate a normative quality to their definition and view it as the space for cultivating "civic" values and practices. It is also seen as the space for cultivating values of "civility" in the public realm, in which power is mediated by constitutionalizing relations between different groups within society. In this view, civil society can be distinguished from patrimonialism: personalized power relations operating through alliances organized around patron-client relations that underpin social, political, and economic organization.

Some stress the political role of civil society, viewing it as the space for cultivating processes through which citizens engage in public life by channeling their interests and aspirations through peaceful deliberative processes. Civil society interfaces with the state through parliamentary institutions (with parliamentarians often seen as serving a bridging role as the elected representatives of civil society), through various forms of policy dialogue, and even through direct displays of power through protest movements and activism. Furthermore, civil-society groups can help to monitor and constrain the arbitrary exercise of state power and, increasingly, the behavior of private businesses and even multinational corporations. Therefore, civil society enables different groupings in society to debate differences, reach compromise, form priorities, and—sometimes—develop consensus on a higher common purpose.

Civil society does not, however, replace the state. At its worst, an authoritarian government can constrict—or even crush—the functioning of civil society through methods that violate human rights. Yet it is difficult for civil society to thrive amidst lawlessness and widespread violence. A flourishing civil society typically depends on the security and predictability provided by an effective democratic state that is controlled by a government that ensures the rule of law and policies that respond to the needs of the population. If these conditions are not present, people—through civil-society organizing—strive to create the elements of self-governance and security. In some cases, communities have striven to create these conditions amidst state failure, as has been seen in parts of Somalia. In so doing, people are re-creating the basis for democratic government, which rest on the consent of the governed. Thus civil society and democratic states are highly complementary and even interdependent.

Polarized Communities, the Challenge of "Uncivil" Society, and the Power of Dialogue

Most people, most of the time, do not want to be a part of wide-scale violence. Many will, however, engage in or condone violence when they do not see alternatives or are so inflamed with a burning sense of injustice that violence is considered necessary as a remedy or for protection. In these cases, civil-society actors can be central to the mobilization and escalation of war. Intellectuals, traditional authorities, and religious leaders may provide the rationale and moral justification for violence; educational institutes and the media can shape perceptions of what is going on and advocate war as the answer; civic associations and political parties may mobilize their members for the war effort. Thus civil-society groups can be a factor in war as well as a force for peace.

A maximalist conception of civil society recognizes this plurality because it is a manifestation of the range of opinion, interests, and values that exist within a society. In some contexts, there may be deep divisions within the society that are, in turn, reflected in and shaped by polarized CSOs. Some CSOs promote causes that are incompatible with internationally agreed norms and principles, such as those promoting exclusionary or other hate-based ideologies

Modalities for Engagement Between Civil Society Organizations and Governments

Civil-society organizations (CSOs) responding to conflict need to deliberate and analyze the values and political positioning that characterize their relationship with the state, so as to engage more effectively, ethically, and strategically. They should strive to be:

- Complicit—as citizens and as organizational groups embedded in a country's civil society, we are party to the decisions that our governments make in our name
- Contractual—when CSOs implement government policies and programs through their work, often by receiving funding from governments
- Contributing—through participation in policy dialogue and recommendations for appropriate responses to specific situations or issues
- Complementarity—working in parallel as separate/autonomous entities within the same system of issues and relationships
- Contesting/Confronting—when CSOs challenge government actions, priorities, and behaviors

Note: This framework was developed by the participants in the Global Partnership for the Prevention of Armed Conflict London "Brainstorming" meeting of 3 December 2003, with key inputs from Andy Carl and Simon Fisher.

or those tolerating (or even endorsing) tactics based in violence or oppression. There are also dominant elements in society that may use various forms of coercive power—sometimes executed through state institutions—to maintain their privilege and promote their interests at the expense of other groups, of future generations, or of the environment as a whole. While most would argue that armed groups are not a part of civil society per se, these groups are often supported by elements in civil society that champion the cause and view armed struggle as legitimate—further indicating the fuzzy lines around the "civility" of some CSOs.

A diverse and thriving civil society is nevertheless one of the crucial underpinnings for strengthening the capacity of societies to manage conflict peacefully. This is particularly true when individuals are members of multiple groups, each of which addresses different aspects of their concerns—such as their communal identity, vocational interests and hobbies, social and political values, and neighborhood environment. These cross-cutting memberships across CSOs create "bridging social capital": the dense networks that are a powerful force integrating society and minimizing the potential for polarization along any specific divide.

Ultimately, the state belongs to its people; CSO engagement in addressing problems that could generate conflict strengthens long-term social and political development of the country. Civil society is a potentially powerful force that can mobilize either to escalate conflict or to facilitate its resolution. Governments that attempt to suppress the aspirations voiced through civil society tend to provoke a struggle to meet those needs through other means, including violent resistance. Any long-term strategy for prevention needs to be rooted in creating cultures of peace. In the meanwhile, it is important to engage antagonistic civil-society actors in dialogue processes capable of working through differences, developing common ground, and transforming perceptions distorted by fear, misunderstanding, and hatred.

Engaging with Conflict and Preventing War

The potential for conflict exists in all aspects of human social life. Most broadly understood, conflict occurs when two or more parties (individuals or groups) have—or *perceive* that they have—incompatible goals and this perception of incompatibility shapes their attitudes and behaviors toward each other. Many people think of conflict as intrinsically negative. However, conflict typically emerges from real issues and seemingly contradictory interests, thus revealing underlying problems that need to be addressed to keep the system of relationships dynamic and strong. The way people respond to conflict makes the difference between it becoming a force for destruction or being a catalyst for constructive change. Sometimes people respond by seeking to avoid the problem or trying to suppress it. Sometimes people use aggression or even violence against those they see as creating the problem or blocking their goals. Yet it is also possible to engage with conflict through peaceful processes. This can help those involved to address the causes and to repair relationships that have been weakened by anger, fear, and hatred; thereby helping to transform the situation that gave rise to the conflict.

Conflict is typically entwined with processes of change. Conflict can be embraced as a way of working proactively toward social-change goals and is an intrinsic feature of the struggle for justice. Many activists have sought to surface conflict so that problems that are being suppressed or ignored can be put on the agenda and addressed. While this is sometimes done through armed movements and the use of violence, there is a long and well-developed tradition of peaceful protest, nonviolent direct action, and other activism. This distinction points to the importance of channeling conflict through peaceful processes capable of delivering constructive change. Historically, civil-society activism has been one of the most powerful resources for these processes, as famously demonstrated in the nonviolent movements led by Gandhi in ending colonial rule in South Asia or by Martin Luther King, Jr., in the struggle against racism and for civil rights in the United States.

Thus many CSOs do not seek to prevent conflict per se; instead they aim to prevent war and deal with the consequences of violence. This is particularly important in an era when noncombatant civilians are increasingly the focus of war—with estimates of civilian deaths counting for approximately 75 percent of all casualties (UN Secretary-General 2001a). Forcible displacement and massacres; the targeting of women and children and abduction of children as soldiers; environmental destruction and economic collapse creating profound impoverishment; and the legacies of crippling bitterness, fear, and division are some of the many reasons why civil-society actors are compelled to use their energy and creativity to find alternatives to violence, end wars, and prevent them from starting or reoccurring.

At its most comprehensive, prevention aims both to prevent and impede violent conflict and to build a just and sustainable peace by transforming underlying causes of conflict. The Carnegie Commission on Preventing Deadly Conflict developed this idea into the distinction between *structural prevention* (strategies to address root causes) and the *operational prevention* (strategies to impede the emergence, escalation, and spread of violence). The UN secretary-general, in his 2001 *Report on the Prevention of Armed Conflict,* subsequently adopted these concepts and they have become cornerstones of the framework for thinking about conflict prevention internationally.

Multiple Arenas for
CSO Roles in Prevention and Peacebuilding

In a globalizing world, preventing war and armed conflict and building sustainable peace require strategies that address structural causes of conflict, many of which may be inherent in the global system. It also needs partnerships between civil-society actors at the local, national, regional, and global levels with governments, intergovernmental organizations (IGOs), and potentially businesses. In addressing this challenge, there seem to be three basic orientations that motivate civil-society groups to work on conflict-related issues, as illustrated in Figure 1.2.

First, there are preexisting civil-society groups—such as women's organizations or faith-based groups—that do not consider working on conflict as part of their core focus but who feel compelled to respond to the challenge that

Figure 1.2 Civil Society Orientations to Working on Conflict Issues

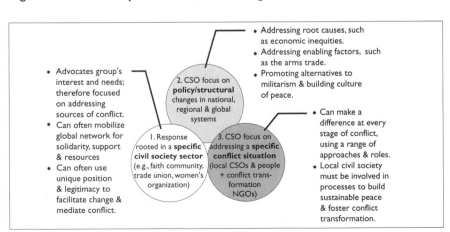

conflict and war poses for their constituents. Their involvement may be motivated in part to ensure that their core concerns are addressed; they often highlight key issues that should be addressed in processes to address the conflict. For example, women's organizations may aim to ensure that women's needs are met and women are represented at the negotiating table. These sectoral CSOs often call upon others in their wider networks to extend solidarity, thus helping to mobilize resources and make a powerful contribution to raising awareness. Second, as described in the next subsection, there are CSOs that aim to address underlying structural problems that give rise to conflict in general through efforts aimed at policy reform and systems change, yet who are not directly focused on efforts to resolve or transform specific situations of conflict. Third, there are groups that are focused primarily on responding to specific conflict situations. Their role is the focus of the remainder of this chapter.

Global Civil Society: Addressing Systemic Causes of War and Conflict

A global civil society is emerging with the growth of communications technology. There are many substantive reasons for its expansion: the failure of governments to respond effectively to global challenges, such as the environment; the growing concern for the situation of people elsewhere, as witnessed in the human rights movement; and feelings of solidarity in the face of common threats, such as concern about the implications of the concentration of power in transnational corporations. For many, it is a reaction to growing inequality of power and the increasing discrepancy between economics and governance, whereby the effects of increasingly interdependent markets are not counterbalanced by effective global regulatory mechanisms.

The ability of nonstate actors to set a compelling agenda—particularly on environmental, social, and, to a lesser extent, economic and security issues—has been a significant force in shaping global responses to key structural problems. Some have remarked that public opinion has become "the second superpower." Although CSOs do not have the legal, political, or military power of states, they have the power to persuade, to propose solutions rooted in their analysis of the problems, and to influence by example and by the integrity of their moral voice. Governments and corporations are more likely to listen when they perceive that CSOs have the support of large numbers of people who want change.

Global civil society has played a key role in mobilizing campaigns aimed at policy change. The important roles played by civil-society groups and the citizens they mobilized in support of the Climate Convention, the International Campaign to Ban Landmines, the movement for the International Criminal Court, to raise awareness of HIV/AIDS, and to reduce the debt burden are a few examples on successful CSO campaigning initiatives. Some of the campaigns have specifically targeted factors that enable armed conflict, such as the effort to ban the trade of conflict or "blood" diamonds that funded militias and ongoing efforts to regulate the trade of small arms and light weapons.

Globalization and Conflict: Challenges for Structural Prevention

Many have observed that economic globalization simultaneously brings economic growth in some places while weakening economies and whole states in others. This process is coupled with growing social polarization between the "haves" and the "have-nots." The economic restructuring of the 1980s and 1990s was based on liberalization. International financial institutions prescribed structural adjustment in exchange for much needed loans to indebted countries, thereby opening domestic markets, ending government subsidies and other protection for domestic businesses, and reducing government spending, including social spending. Liberalization has resulted in what the United Nations Development Program terms the "ascents/descents" pattern of development. In many cases, preexisting inequalities have widened: those who were already strong in the marketplace have been able to accumulate proportionately more wealth; whereas those who were already economically vulnerable have experienced intensified exclusion. This is widely understood as a significant root cause of conflict. The likelihood that this conflict will be expressed in violent revolts is increased when peoples' aspirations are frustrated because of this relative disparity and the government is seen as unresponsive or oppressive—rather than being triggered by the experience of grinding poverty.

Another factor contributing to the feasibility of armed insurgencies is that governments do not have full control over regulating cross-border economic interactions. The growing "shadow globalization" of illicit trade gives increasingly lucrative incentives to criminal networks capable of transferring whatever goods can be profitably traded: from timber to diamonds, to drugs, to weapons, to human beings. This provides the channels through which "war economies" operate—thus helping to both sustain the resources needed by fighting groups (whether state or nonstate actors) and providing the incentives that motivate some to engage in armed conflict. This is achieved by linking local resources to global networks and otherwise exploiting the adaptive power of networks made possible through globalization.

In addition to campaigns targeting specific policy matters, there are global protest movements to address the issues raised by economic globalization and the challenges raised in the wake of 9/11, such as the global peace movement's mass mobilization in 2003 against the war in Iraq.

In addition to analyzing the economic and institutional structures that generate conflict and policy responses to change them, there is a need to transform deeply embedded attitudes and patterns of relationships between groups of people that give rise to violence. Countless CSOs throughout the world—independently or together with governments and IGOs—work toward creating the longer-term foundations for sustainable peace. This includes a focus on peace education and conflict resolution life-skills, demilitarization, gender equality, fulfillment of human rights, promoting equitable and sustainable development, and human and environmental security.

Given the significance of transnational civil society as a force for change, it is perhaps not surprising that problems have arisen. There are often imbalances between those in the "center" and those on the "periphery" of access to resources and power. This dynamic plays out in terms of who is able to determine the agenda for change and whose voices are heard in decisionmaking and social-change initiatives. Within some international NGO coalitions, there is a tendency for the Northern/Western partners to assume a dominant voice and thus set agendas that respond to their perceptions of problems in ways that might not reflect the views and goals of Southern/Eastern partners. Some have also critiqued the ways in which these initiatives have imposed demands on governments in the South and the East—such as through advocating aid conditionality and sanctions. They are troubled that externally imposed prescriptions on national policy undermine democratic processes by making the government more accountable to external forces—especially international financial institutions and powerful foreign governments—than to the domestic population.

Roles of CSOs in Responding to Specific Conflicts and Wars

The UN secretary-general has made it clear that the primary responsibility for responding to conflict rests with local actors. CSOs rooted in conflict-affected communities are crucial to this equation. While they often work in partnership with civil-society actors from other parts of the world, who help to support their efforts, the most crucial efforts are made by those within the societies concerned. Civil-society groups bring a number of important qualities for responding to specific cases of conflict. In general:

- Their independence—and, in some cases, the unique status they hold because of their perceived expertise, integrity, or moral authority—enables them the freedom to act swiftly and flexibly
- CSOs often rely on innovative, creative, and noncoercive strategies to persuade people to engage in peaceful processes based on dialogue and deliberation to address problems and reconcile relationships
- CSOs can act when—for various reasons—official actors are immobilized (often related to mandates, lack of political will, or the implications conveyed by their official status). This can include the capacity to talk to those in militant movements in order to clarify conflict issues and explore opportunities for entry into negotiation processes
- CSOs can improve communication and relationships by fostering interaction across conflict divides through informal exchanges and joint projects. While they can facilitate dialogue between the protagonists in armed struggle, CSO-led processes are often focused on helping ordinary people to articulate what they really need and then helping to find a common ground from which they can work to establish peaceful coexistence

- By mobilizing "people power," CSOs can put pressure on decision-makers to reach a peaceful settlement. They can push for policies and practices designed to address root causes of conflict.
- CSOs can bear witness to violations in powerful ways that undermine the moral authority and legitimacy of abusers, sometimes stimulating conditions that lead to the collapse of regimes over the long term. They can routinely monitor events and generate attention when violations occur or agreements are unfulfilled.

These qualities and others are deployed in countless ways that are appropriate to the context at different stages in the development of a conflict. There are barriers that must be overcome to play these roles effectively. How can the range of actors in a society feel that they have the capacity to make a difference and play an effective role in shifting the emerging conflict dynamics—especially if they are themselves mobilized/polarized along conflict divides? What is the basis of their influence? How do they access decisionmakers? How do they engage with the wider population to mobilize people not only to stop the violence but also to create a better society?

CSO Involvement in Structural Prevention and Responding to Conflict

In much the same way as transnational civil-society efforts seek to address key challenges within the global system, CSOs in a particular country are often at the forefront of addressing problems in their own society. Many aim to address sources of structural violence and to promote human security through initiatives for social and economic development, human rights monitoring, promoting the rule of law, and preventing environmental degradation, among other challenges. Through participation in political processes, policy dialogue, monitoring, advocacy campaigns, and protests they help to make governments and state structures more responsive to the needs of their citizens.

CSOs can also play important roles in helping to alleviate social tensions and conflict. They work both to challenge racism, xenophobia, and discrimination and to promote tolerance and a culture of peace. Person-focused methodologies—such as prejudice-reduction workshops and interfaith dialogue—can complement efforts to address discrimination through policy reform and structural change. Often these initiatives are focused on youth, who may have greater capacities for change than older generations. Summer camps, integrated schools, and exchange programs can all promote what has become known as "next generation work."

In many parts of the world, there are efforts to strengthen local capacities to mediate conflict and manage differences through conflict resolution training, mediation services, and dialogue facilitation. For example, the Kyrgyz Republic–based NGO Foundation for Tolerance International has trained and supported community mediators in villages in the often volatile Ferghana Valley, where there are frequently disputes over water rights and economic resources that can spark escalating wider tensions. By focusing on the local dimension of conflict, these mediators can help to provide alternatives to violence.

CSO Roles in Addressing the Escalation of Violence and Emergence of War

Civil-society actors do not need to be passive bystanders in situations of emerging and ongoing conflict. Their roles in delivering humanitarian aid and other services aimed at relieving suffering are well known. However, when sufficiently empowered, CSOs can help change the conflict dynamics, as well as to address its consequences. This is often most effectively achieved through partnerships with others, including IGOs, governments, and international CSOs.

Early warning of emerging crises through monitoring, analysis, and communication strategies to raise awareness and generate attention. International human rights organizations, such as Amnesty International, have played this role notably for decades and have been joined by others, such as International Crisis Group. The knowledge of local people is especially valuable. They are aware of events as they are unfolding and are acutely sensitive to signs of preparations for war. Too often, however, they have no mechanisms to effectively inform the world and their knowledge is not factored into decisionmaking processes of international organizations with responsibility for peace and security. In West Africa, however, a new partnership has been evolving between the West African Network for Peacebuilding—which has local CSO members throughout the region—the regional organization the Economic Community of West African States (ECOWAS) and the UN Office for the Coordination of Humanitarian Affairs, who have signed a memorandum of understanding to develop a joint early warning system for the region.

Mobilizing political will, developing options and strategies for response. Civil-society groups can analyze the situation, formulate recommendations, and engage in policy dialogue to address conflicts. They have to be skilful to ensure that their voices are heard. This can be done through coordinated lobbying and raising awareness among domestic and international audiences. Much more can be done to strengthen civil society's capacities in this area by fostering networks to mobilize rapid responses. Yet there are cases where it has been done on an ad hoc basis—such as when a global coalition of CSOs mobilized in 1999 to focus international attention on the violence in East Timor and helped to ensure that an international protection force was deployed to uphold the results of the referendum on independence.

Developing and strengthening constituencies for peace. Those involved in armed conflict often justify their actions by claiming to represent popular causes or on the basis of their authority as governments. Civil-society actors committed to exclusively peaceful means often challenge this by demonstrating that public opinion rejects military approaches. Through raising public awareness and education about alternatives, they generate public support. Some of the effective methods for creating a new atmosphere stem from peace media, art projects, concerts, and other creative ways of reaching out to the wider public. Sometimes efforts involve mass protests at the use of military force or demonstrations in favor of peace processes. Either way, they can reveal that there are significant constituencies for peace, which can be a persuasive force in altering the responses of governments and armed groups.

Facilitating communication, generating alternatives, and building relationships. Transforming the relationship between adversaries is often necessary before a lasting cooperative relationship on functional issues can be established. While this most often is a long-term and complex process, one of the common methodologies for fostering this change is through dialogue-based processes. Activities through which dialogue can occur include: trainings, exchanges, problem-solving workshops, and peace commissions. Often they involve some element of joint analysis, in which members of groups in conflict discuss the causes and dynamics of conflict—seeking to understand the other's perspectives—and explore potential ways of addressing it. These kinds of methods can be designed as one-off events. Increasingly common, however, is the recognition that dialogue forums and processes may need to be sustained as longer-term processes.

Violence reduction, peace monitors, and zones of peace. It is very difficult for people to build peace when they feel threatened or under attack. Those who want to wreck a peace process tend to escalate violence targeted against civilians. Conventional state security forces have an important role in protection; yet too often they are a part of the problem. To address these problems, numerous communities created peace monitors to act as witnesses and mediators. For example, in South Africa, the National Peace Accord provided the architecture of structures for people's involvement in violence prevention. Thousands of peace committees were formed to mediate disputes and monitor demonstrations and other activities that might degenerate into violence. The committees coordinated their work with the political parties and with the security forces and held them accountable for their actions. In a context where civilian populations are frequently massacred, some communities—including many in Colombia and the Philippines—have responded to violence by negotiations with armed forces to declare their communities as neutral, demilitarized "zones of peace."

Civil-Society Roles in Peacemaking and Political Negotiations

Peace processes—and especially the political negotiations to reach peace agreements—are a unique opportunity for creating the bridge to lasting social and political change. They offer opportunities to create an agreed road map toward the future by addressing the underlying issues generating conflict, developing new "rules of the game," and transforming relationships among antagonists. Those who participate in negotiations can determine the substantive and procedural agreements that can lead to structural changes in the state and governance system, human rights, security, and development policies. Therefore, it matters how the process is structured and who gets to participate in it.

Developing a vision for the future. It is often remarked that "unless you know where you want to go, it is unlikely that you will get there." Sustainable peace processes need to be about more than finding ways to end the fighting; they also need to start societies on the path toward a more equitable and peaceful future. To do this, it is important to engage in public deliberation about what kind of society they want to create. Looking back on sustained peace processes, it is possible to identify moments where public visioning was facilitated by large-scale public initiatives. In the early 1950s, a Congress of the People was held in South Africa. First, ordinary citizens in thousands of community meetings across the country were asked the open-ended question: "What needs to change in South Africa for you to enjoy full and abundant lives in terms of country, community, and individual?" Then the congress of delegates chosen by their community drafted the Freedom Charter to articulate not just what they opposed but also what they stood for. It shaped the development of political thinking, formed the foundations for a prodemocracy movement, and influenced the negotiations in the 1990s.

Track Two dialogue. Using their unofficial and low-key status, CSOs can facilitate dialogue involving those close to government leaders and armed opposition groups. These processes often involve participants connected with the political negotiations and/or who can effect change at the grassroots level and support social reconciliation. It often takes time before the ideas, relationships, and personal changes that develop through these processes manifest into significant social and political change. Yet key figures from processes as diverse as those in Guatemala, Northern Ireland, South Africa, Tajikistan, and Sri Lanka all look back on their experience in Track Two dialogue and in conflict resolution training workshops and claim it to be a turning point in how they perceived the conflict. It helped them to develop ideas for how to address the conflict issues and to develop constructive working relationships with counterparts previously perceived as enemies. Often these experiences occurred prior to a sustained political negotiation process and were a significant factor in why negotiators could engage constructively in talks once conditions became ripe.

Creating a "pragmatic peace" at the local level. Peacemaking goes far beyond reaching a political agreement between the main parties; often it is necessary to make peace between those who live side by side and have nowhere else to go. Even when national-level peace processes are stalled or nonexistent, local communities can act to address the issues that generate conflict and escalate violence locally. In northern Mali, negotiations to end a secessionist insurgency and the transition to democratic governance had created the context for peace but did not secure it. However, a series of self-led community meetings were held to build consensus on how to tackle issues that were within their capacity to address. They addressed many of the factors that were generating conflict and created a united front against those who used violence to promote their cause or position. Once the peace process was fostered at the very local level, the broad popular consensus secured the transition to sustainable peace.

Shaping the negotiating agenda to ensure it addresses root causes and participating in the negotiations process, directly or indirectly. There are a number of processes, including those in Guatemala, Northern Ireland, and South Africa, where civil-society activists have asserted the right of the wider public to participate in the negotiated processes to shape their country's future. In so doing, they were able to influence the shape of the process, the negotiating agenda of issues addressed, the substantive agreements reached, and their implementation. In most cases they brought the talks process further into the public sphere, enabling a wider range of people to contribute suggestions and follow the negotiations—including women and those from marginalized groups. With greater transparency, the public was better able to understand and potentially accept the reasons for the compromises reached. Furthermore, the processes marked a historic moment of change in each country and helped to establish the value of public debate and democratic processes as the legitimate response to conflict.

Consolidating Peace and Preventing Reoccurrence of War

Peace processes are typically unfinished and imperfect. Conflicts are not transformed by agreements alone; they also need a commitment to address ongoing problems through political means. A sense of public ownership of the process becomes crucial at this stage. If the public and organized civil society have been excluded from the process or believe that it has not addressed their real needs, they are less likely to work actively toward its implementation. Without a broad public constituency in support, there are few safeguards against those who want to derail the agreement.

Civil society can play important roles in raising awareness and educating the public about the agreement itself. They can also be crucial for consolidating support. In Northern Ireland, the public was asked to vote on whether to accept the agreement. It was assumed that this would basically be a procedure for rubber-stamping the agreement—after all, if the competing political parties agreed, would not the public as well? Yet it was soon apparent that a huge chasm had opened between those who drafted the agreement and the population as a whole. Nonpartisan peace activists responded by organizing a "Yes" campaign. Within six weeks, the majority of the population voted in favor of it. In so doing, they gave a massive impetus for political compromise, which has helped to sustain the process through many years of difficulty.

Yet agreements on paper mean very little if people are still suffering from the consequences of war and if the inequities that gave rise to it are left unaddressed. This is where sustained financial, technical, and political support are crucial. Appropriate international aid, combined with determined government efforts, are needed to facilitate the rehabilitation of war-affected communities and help ensure that everyone experiences a peace dividend. This can be strengthened through the involvement of local and international CSOs in policy analysis as well as program implementation and service delivery.

Furthermore, this is a time when CSOs need to resume efforts to ensure structural prevention—encouraging good governance, reconstruction, and development; mediating social conflict; promoting human rights, and other efforts to build a culture of peace. CSOs can play an especially important role in addressing the challenges of fostering transitional justice processes and enabling the potential for long-term reconciliation.

The Limits of Involvement
The previous sections have concentrated on exploring the many contributions that civil society can make to transforming conflict. Yet it is rarely possible for CSO initiatives to be able to achieve peace on their own. Governments and other political actors—especially those who make decisions over the deployment of military force—are often decisive. Intergovernmental and multilateral organizations also have tremendous political, technical, and other resources they can bring to processes of working with conflict. CSOs often have limits in the scope of the conflict dynamics they can address, such as:

- Few are able to effectively deal with the political economy of war—i.e., the greed that leads armed forces to have a stake in keeping the war going—although there are promising global campaigns that are trying to address these factors systemically
- Many CSO initiatives are depoliticized and, in their efforts to restore peaceful interaction between people, fail to link issues of justice, human rights, and equity that often drive the conflict. They may also fail to address the very real dynamics of political power that sustain conflicts as a tug-of-war for dominance
- CSOs start initiatives that are beyond their skills and capacities. They may make the situation worse by escalating danger, exacerbating divisions and tensions, and/or through reinforcing prejudice. They may not be able to sustain initiatives that have been started, leading to missed opportunities and/or disempowering cynicism because raised expectations are dashed
- Too often, CSO initiatives are too small and too isolated to make the kind of difference that is needed in these urgent life-or-death conditions. They may also divert attention away from the most urgent or strategically important concerns. There is a need to be more strategic, with better coordination for long-term change through processes that are aimed at outcomes, as well as on the integrity of the process itself

- Sometimes the legitimacy of CSO initiatives is questioned, especially when it is unclear to whom they are accountable and what they are trying to achieve. Sometimes they are criticized for being insufficiently linked to real constituencies and responding to their concerns. At other times, suspicions are aroused by insufficiently transparent communication about what they are doing and why. Even though this may be more due to misunderstanding than malfeasance, it can undermine confidence and generate suspicion in fragile political environments

There are also challenges concerning how CSOs work among themselves, such as:

- While effective partnerships can be a powerful resource for peace, too often there are destructive dynamics in "insider" and "outsider" relationships. Local civil-society peacebuilders rooted within conflict-affected communities can find their efforts displaced or undermined by outsiders (whether NGOs, IGOs, or donor agencies) who implicitly or explicitly impose their own agendas and values, introduce inappropriate initiatives, and potentially further entrench conflict through an insufficiently nuanced understanding of the situation and opportunities to make change
- Too often, CSOs fail to communicate among themselves and may even compete for the scarce resources available to undertake their initiatives. This can lead to a lack of coordination and coherence so that, instead of building momentum for peace, efforts are dispersed and potentially less effective

Toward Partnerships for Peace
While it is rare for grassroots efforts to transform wider systems of conflict and war, it is also not possible for these wider systems to be transformed without stimulating changes at the community level. Therefore, many analysts and practitioners agree with John Paul Lederach's observation that there is a need to build peace from the bottom up, the top down, and the middle out. Yet the methodologies for crossing the scale barrier, simultaneously and in a coordinated manner, are not well developed. Therefore the key seems to be in negotiating dynamic and strategic partnerships.

Primary responsibility for conflict prevention rests with national governments and other local actors. Greater ownership is likely to result in a more legitimate process and sustainable outcomes. The primary role of outsiders is to create spaces and support inclusive processes that enable those directly involved to make decisions about the specific arrangements for addressing the causes of conflict. Outsiders should help to build on the capacities that exist and avoid actions that displace and undermine homegrown initiatives or that promote short-term objectives at the expense of long-term prevention. Based on a collaborative understanding of the sources of conflict and the factors that continue to generate it, people based elsewhere can seek to address some of the causes that are located elsewhere in the conflict system (such as arms suppliers in third countries or policies promoted by foreign governments that further escalate war).

Partnerships for peace may be the antidote to systems and networks sustaining war. Yet to achieve this potential, we need to acknowledge the legitimacy of CSOs in peace and security matters and to strengthen official recognition of their roles in the conflict prevention partnership. This can then be operationalized through stronger mechanisms and resources for interaction between IGOs, CSOs, and governments in order to institutionalize the capacity for prevention.

It is likely, however, that efforts to shift to a culture of peace and to prioritize prevention over crisis management will be sustained only when there is widespread awareness among the general publics around the world that common security cannot be obtained through the barrel of a gun; instead, we can best work toward sustainable peace through collective efforts at meeting basic human needs and strengthening systems for managing differences peacefully.

Catherine Barnes is an independent consultant working in support of peacebuilding initiatives through facilitation, training, and research. She is an advisor to the Global Partnership for the Prevention of Armed Conflict and an associate of Conciliation Resources. She holds a doctoral degree in conflict analysis and resolution from George Mason University and has authored publications on peace processes, minority rights, and specific conflict situations around the world.

Selected Bibliography

Anderson, Mary, and Lara Olson. 2003. *Confronting War: Critical Lessons for Peace Practitioners.* Online at: http://www.cdainc.com/rpp/archives/2003/01/confronting_war.php.

Austin, Alex, Martina Fischer, and Norbert Ropers, eds. 2004. *Transforming Ethnopolitical Conflict: The Berghof Handbook* (Wiesbaden: VS Verlag).

Barnes, Catherine, ed. 2002. *Owning the Process: Public Participation in Peacemaking.* Accord 13 (London: Conciliation Resources, 2002). Online at: http://www.c-r.org/accord.

Burbidge, John E. 1997. *Beyond Prince and Merchant: Citizen Participation and the Rise of Civil Society* (Brussels: Institute of Cultural Affairs International).

Carnegie Commission on Preventing Deadly Conflict. 1997. *Preventing Deadly Conflict: Final Report with Executive Summary* (New York: Carnegie Commission on Preventing Deadly Conflict).

Clark, John D. 2003. *Worlds Apart: Civil Society and the Battle for Ethical Globalisation* (Bloomfield CT: Kumarian Press Inc.).

Conflict Research Consortium. n.d. "Intractable Conflict Knowledge Base Project," University of Colorado. Online at: http://www.beyondintractability.org.

Fisher, Simon, Dekha Ibrahim Abdi, Jawed Ludin, Richard Smith, Steve Williams, and Sue Williams. 2000. *Working with Conflict: Skills and Strategies for Action* (London: Zed Books).

Fitzduff, Mary, and Cheyanne Church, eds.. 2004. *NGOs at the Table: Strategies for Gaining Influence* (Lanham, MD: Rowman & Littlefield Publishers).

Lederach, John Paul. 1997. *Building Peace: Sustainable Reconciliation in Divided Societies* (Washington, DC: United States Institute of Peace Press).

United Nations Secretary-General. 2001a. *Report to the Security Council on the Protection of Civilians in Armed Conflict* (S/2001/331). Online at: http://www/un/org.
———. 2001b. *Report on the on Prevention of Armed Conflict* (A/55/985–S/2001/574). Online at: http://www.un/org.
United Nations. 2004. *We the Peoples: Civil Society, the United Nations, and Global Governance*. Report of the Panel of Eminent Persons on United Nations–Civil Society Relations, June (New York: United Nations, A/58/817).
United Nations. N.d. *UNDP and Civil Society Organisations: A Policy of Engagement*. Online at: http://www.undp.org/cso.

PERSONAL STORY:
"A Vital Force"—Kay Rala Xanana Gusmão

When reflecting on the theme of civil society's role in conflict prevention and peacebuilding, I am again reminded that the struggle for Timor-Leste's right to self-determination and independence was also fought by various components of civil society both inside and outside of the country.

During our struggle, the role of the Catholic Church in Timor-Leste was critical in providing a voice and a sanctuary for the many victims of the brutal military occupation. The clandestine network, consisting of students, lay people, public servants, women, teachers and youth, was the backbone of the resistance.

On the international scene, Timor-Leste at one stage had the largest worldwide solidarity movement, advocating for an end to the violence and for peace in the territory. These bands of dedicated, ordinary citizens of the world united their efforts to pressure their respective governments in support of an independent Timor-Leste.

Five years have gone by since the historical referendum in August 1999, and two years since independence was officially declared. Timor-Leste has gone through three critical phases in the space of five short years: emergency humanitarian period, transitional period and now reconstruction and development.

In each of these phases, the role of civil society can never be underestimated. In each of these phases, the crying need to build peace and prevent further conflict was foremost in the mind of every Timorese.

It is the desire of every Timorese to live in peace and to never again experience the pain and destruction that war brings. Indeed, it is only in situations of war that we feel the need for peace, for a tranquility of spirit.

During our twenty-four-year-long difficult struggle, we learned to love peace and dialogue.

Peace, reconciliation, understanding and harmony between citizens are fundamental conditions for political stability and economic and social progress in our country.

Without stability and peace, there would not be democracy; there would not be progress.

Reconciliation has peace as its fundamental objective. Reconciliation entails breaking away with the environment of conflict.

The Timorese leadership, then under the umbrella organization, CNRT (National Council for Timorese Resistance), of which I was president, recognized from the very beginning that reconciliation was a fundamental need for a future independent Timor-Leste, to build peace in our society and thus avoid further conflict. Therefore, maximum attention was afforded to this process.

However, reconciliation is more than just forgiving and moving away from the past. Reconciliation is a long process, demanding from each and every Timorese, the courage to admit our mistakes and to forgive. Reconciliation between ourselves and with our former enemies is instrumental in consolidating the peace that we Timorese fought so long and hard to achieve.

Very early on, I defended that no-one should hold bitterness towards their enemies; they too, were merely instruments of a system, which oppressed them as it did us.

A few years ago, not long after we achieved our freedom, I was touring around the country visiting all the villages as part of the promise I made upon my return to Timor-Leste.

Everywhere was destruction; everywhere the cries and pain of the victims could be heard. Village after village—men, women and children gathered together and told me their stories. On one particular, exhausting night, where I was overwhelmed with the grief the many widows; all demanding justice for their suffering, an old man approached me and asked if he could speak. He stood before his fellow villagers and in a clear, steady voice, devoid of any emotion, he raised his badly twisted arms and declared

"If putting my tormentor in jail means regaining the use of my hands, then I demand justice, here and now. But what use is there in seeking justice if it will not make any difference to my life?"

This poor, simple villager expressed the heart of the policy that the Timorese leadership had been advocating all along—that there could be no real everlasting peace, without reconciliation; that our independence would mean nothing if we could not bring peace and tranquility to the daily lives of our people, if we could not promise them a future free of further conflict.

Still the government alone could not transmit this policy into action on the ground. It needed the support of civil society.

It is the policy of the Timorese State to pursue the avenue of reconciliation and dialogue both in the domestic and international scene. With every effort made at the highest level, a complimentary one was made on the ground.

As President of the Republic, I am continuing this policy through two critical programs: Open Presidency and National Dialogue.

Open Presidency is where the president comes to the people, and listens to their concerns and provides information where possible. Its objective is to reduce tension, through the exchange of information on the current processes and difficulties the people are facing. It is a preventative measure of conflict.

National Dialogue is another means of conflict prevention as it provides a forum for bringing issues of national interest to public debate. It brings conflicting parties together and gathers feedback from the general public.

Both programs are conducted with the invaluable support of civil society groups.

The goodwill talks between the governments of Timor-Leste and Indonesia have been complimented on the ground with traditional methods of post-conflict resolution such as public confession and apology, led by civil society. A Commission on Truth and Reconciliation (CAVR) was established to provide a platform for addressing past wrongs. CAVR, consisting of members of all segments of civil society, has conducted community based reconciliation nationwide and as a result, has succeeded in enabling ex-militias to reintegrate into their communities and for the most part, for those communities to continue with life in the normal way. Alongside these local dispute resolution initiatives is the need for national healing. Many Timorese want answers from those who caused their loss and suffering. With answers people can start the healing process and close the horrible chapter in their lives and finally be able to live in tranquility and with peace of mind.

As with its current role in peacebuilding, civil society will continue to be an important actor in ensuring peace and stability in Timorese society. Civil society should continue to play a role in helping to strengthen the democratic institutions, in helping the Timorese state lay the foundations of the rule of law, in helping to meet the social needs of the people. Civil society can be a vital force to check and balance the actions of the government by denouncing corruption, lack of transparency and other acts contrary to the interest of the people, to ensure that they are in line with the universal values and principles of freedom, democracy and prosperity.

Kay Rala Xanana Gusmão led the East Timorese Resistance Movement from 1978 until he was captured and sentenced to seven years in a Jakarta prison, followed by house arrest. He was released in 1999 after the UN-sponsored referendum, in which Timor-Leste chose independence from Indonesia. On 14 April 2002, Xanana Gusmão was elected president of the Democratic Republic of Timor-Leste.

2

Discourses on Peace Practices:
Learning to Change by Learning from Change?

Cordula Reimann and Norbert Ropers

"Would you tell me, please, which way I ought to go from here?"
"That depends a good deal on where you want to get to."
— Lewis Carroll, *Alice's Adventures in Wonderland*

One of the favorite topics in the second half of the 1990s was to reflect on the importance of nongovernmental organizations for active participation in the area of conflict prevention and transformation. Comparative advantages and shortcomings were listed and it was argued that a new "culture of peace" should be established, including a broad-based alliance of government actors, international organizations, nongovernmental organizations, and other civil-society organizations. Critics responded by questioning the weight and political legitimacy of civil-society organizations by outlining the darker sides of the expanding "humanitarian interventionism" of the 1990s.

One decade later the involvement of civil-society organizations in the field of conflict prevention and transformation is no longer a matter for principled discussion. Now the attention is on how to assess and improve the quality of the work, how to enhance the internal networking as well as the cooperation with other actors. There is a widespread impression that the sum of civil-society organization activities on conflict prevention and transformation has left the pioneer phase and has started to consolidate itself as a field of its own.

How far the field of conflict prevention and transformation has moved from the pioneer phase to a phase of consolidation is dependent on the criteria used. At least three benchmarks are regularly mentioned in this respect: (1) the quantitative and qualitative impressive *growth* of civil-society organizations (CSOs) active in this field, (2) the *mainstreaming* of conflict prevention and conflict sensitivity into the work of donor agencies, government institutions, and international NGOs, and (3) the establishment of associations formulating and representing common interests of CSOs involved in this field (which could be defined as "trade organizations").

The growth rate is impressive, but it reflects such a diversity of actors that it is difficult to assess how far its multiplication can also be interpreted as an indication of the ideas of conflict prevention and transformation taking root within the respective societies. Efforts of mainstreaming might be more revealing, but they are not necessarily linked to the involvement of CSOs. In many cases it just means the creation of special administrative units or procedures for handling conflict-related topics within existing governmental or intergovernmental agencies. If and how far this also leads to a more proactive involvement of CSOs is an open question (see below the important difference between CSOs working on the input or output side of political decisionmaking).

The most interesting indicators might therefore be the activities of "trade organizations" and other initiatives to reflect on the state of the art in and perspectives for the field of conflict prevention and transformation. This is also the reason why we have chosen the concept of "discourses on peace practice." It helps us to describe the status of the field of conflict prevention and transformation with respect to the involvement of CSOs.

This discourse approach is informed by the idea that social actors co-constitute the social reality through engaging in discussions about the meaning of activities, interactions, ideas, and perceptions. Through participating in such discourses, the actors are not only contributing to an intellectual exercise, they are also starting to co-constitute a kind of "collective identity." This is what we mean when using the term *we* for the collective of practitioners, scholars, activists, trainers, consultants, etc., involved in conflict prevention and transformation, particularly from the perspective of CSOs. The introspection into the state of our field then becomes a question of who participates in which discourses, and what the insights and implications are from these discourses.

Obviously it is not possible to elaborate all relevant discourses here in which peace practitioners and scholars are currently involved. Therefore we would like to concentrate on those that predominantly shape its overall development. The first observation in comparison to the state of the field ten to fifteen years ago in this respect is that the very legitimacy and rationale of conflict prevention and transformation with the help of CSOs is no longer an issue. The discourses today are rather on questions of how to enhance the quality, efficiency, and impact of this type of peace work. Yet there are also some issues that have accompanied and will continue to accompany the field because they are part of the complex political agenda of dealing with contradictory and dynamic violent conflicts.

We would like to differentiate in detail between three clusters of discourses on peace practices:

1. Discourses on social change and justice
2. Discourses on cooperation and networking, and
3. Professionalization discourses

These are closely intertwined and together constitute the emerging framework of conflict prevention and transformation (see Figure 2.1).

The guiding questions throughout this chapter will be:

- How far and why has conflict prevention and transformation as a field learned to change, grow, and mature?
- What are the remaining analytical and political obstacles and challenges in conflict prevention and transformation?

Discourses on Social Change and Justice

One of the roots and driving forces within the peace practice field is the movement to overcome the destructive mode of violence and war to address conflicts. In this respect the field is closely related to the secular project of the "civilization of conflict" and to the vision of *si vis pacem, para pacem* ("If you want peace, prepare for peace") instead of *si vis pacem, para bellum* ("If you want peace, prepare for war") (see Senghaas 2004). With the "mainstreaming" of conflict prevention and transformation into the international realpolitik, this normative dimension was somewhat marginalized. One concrete expression of this organizational development was when, in the 1990s, the traditional peace movement and pacifist discourses were taken over by newly established conflict resolution organizations such as International Alert, Saferworld, and the International Crisis Group.

This situation has dramatically changed since 9/11 and the subsequent international "war on terror." This campaign of the Bush administration seems

Figure 2.1 Discourses on Peace Practices

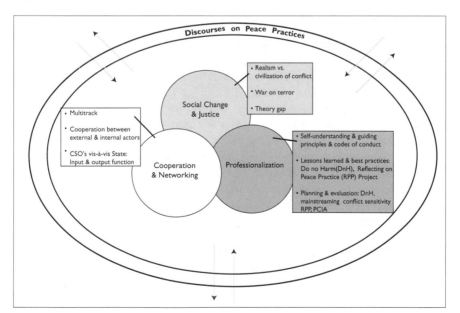

to have united a heterogeneous and diverse field of peacebuilding and development actors: it has not only united them in their reservation if not outright rejection of the fast-growing remilitarization of U.S. foreign policy and the misuse of development and humanitarian aid on the grounds of antiterrorism. It has also led to a revitalization of the normative references to their noncoercive peacebuilding work as the only acceptable and successful alternative to long-lasting peace processes and structures.

The net outcome is a highly diverse field of peace practice in which principled approaches to nonviolent conflict prevention and transformation do coexist with pragmatic strategies of making the best use of a mix of measures and instruments. What is clearly underdeveloped in this situation are endeavors to explore and discuss in detail how far these approaches are complementary or mutually incompatible with each other. This is also a lacuna for many CSO activities at the macropolitical level: should they, and in which way can they, play a constructive role within the often Machiavellian political power struggles to prevent or end wars and to negotiate peace agreements? A similar lacuna also exists with respect to the interaction between CSOs working on the basis of different mandates (e.g., as advocacy and movement CSOs or as service-providing CSOs) and in different realms (e.g., in conflict transformation, security studies, human rights, or development).

Another area of discourse centers on the interface and interaction between activities promoting relationship building, empathy, trust, and confidence on the one hand, and those promoting the publication of and accountability for human rights violations, good governance, and pluralism on the other. More recently, this field of tension has been discussed under "transformative approaches versus conditionality." The conditionality approach makes the safeguarding of individual human rights and pluralism a fundamental precondition for peace processes. Yet the transformative approach does not make their safeguarding the prime condition, but considers the most effective way of promoting human rights to engage with all actors in a critical-constructive process of dialoguing and capacity building.

This tension is a fascinating revitalization of the 1970s and 1980s debate on the policy in the West vis-à-vis the Soviet Union and its allies, i.e., that between the followers of the "change through rapprochement" approach and those arguing for the "no concessions without civil rights improvements" approach.

The fundamental question behind many of these debates about the best way to achieve conflict prevention and transformation is: What are the underlying theories of social change? Most actors involved in conflict prevention and transformation work with rather implicit theories of social change and justice. Largely unstated and hidden visions of social change and justice guide the practice of conflict prevention and conflict transformation. The evidence put forward by the Reflecting on Peace Practice project (Anderson and Olson 2003) highlights that most organizations still lack a clear and solid understanding of their "peace vision" for the country they are working in/on, as well as of the causal assumptions that could lead toward the realization of this peace vision. The implication is that it is difficult to make any statement about the macropolitical impact of those programs and projects apart from assessing their concrete output and outcome (number and profile of participants, mode of interaction, etc.).

This debate, sometimes described as the "theory-gap discourse," arises from time to time, most recently in the Reflecting on Peace Practice project and in the Utstein Study, a comparative evaluation study of a group of bilateral donors (Smith 2003). It is still an open question as to whether their conclusions will lead to a stronger overall strategizing in this field.

The theory gap discourse seems dispersed and to have lost its analytical urgency and focus. Instead, one can observe the emergence of discourses on single-focused aspects of conflict prevention and transformation, such as on a highly elaborated body of research and reflection on reconciliation and transitional justice with highly normative questions being at the center of much of the debate.

One area in which the theory gap was successfully reduced is that dealing with the causes of conflict. This was particularly due to the debate on whether "greed or grievance" is the more convincing explanations for the outbreak and endurance of internal conflicts (Berdal and Malone 2000). The result was that each conflict has its own biography and will comprise a different combination of psychosocial and political grievances, as well as of socioeconomic factors. One of the professional standards in the field after this debate is the need for having a sound conflict analysis before any strategy for intervention is elaborated.

Discourses on Cooperation and Networking

One of the key discourses at the beginning of the emergence of CSOs specialized in conflict prevention and transformation centered on the existence of several tracks of engaging parties into dialogues, problem-solving workshops, capacity-building projects, and joint peace processes. The "multitrack" idea was probably the single most successful concept toward creating a legitimate space for the work of CSOs, particularly in the framework of ethnopolitical conflicts. Furthermore, it has also inspired the need for differentiating the conflict issues as well as the transformation process, leading to multi-issue and multi-phase conceptualizations. More challenging were the discussions on how to link the various tracks with each other and to design and organize a mutually supportive division of labor between different tracks in "peace constituencies."

In the meantime, the discussion has further elaborated these challenges. The two most debated issues are now the interaction and cooperation between different groups of actors (independent from their belonging to the same or different tracks), and second, the creation of frameworks for integrating the contribution of different actors.

The classical dimension of cooperation relates to the one between the realm of states, including international organizations, and the realm of civil society. One of the observations that have been made here is that the capacity of both sides to contribute successfully to conflict prevention and transformation is to an impressive level dependent on each other. Another observation is that they influence each other in a complex way through mutual inputs and outputs. To understand these mechanisms, it is helpful to make use of an interesting model to differentiate between four functions of civil society that are related to the historical development of statehood in the Western tradition. Table 2.1 uses this differentiation to identify the conflict transformation potential of civil society and CSOs.

The CSOs working in these areas are either primarily movement-style and advocacy-oriented organizations, or they are service-providing agencies. In the former case, they concentrate mainly on the input side of politics and try to influence political decisionmaking. In the latter case, they operate chiefly on the output side of politics, at least insofar as political authorities determine the conditions under which they work and decide on their resource allocation. This is obviously an ideal-typical differentiation, but it helps to understand the complex interaction between the two realms and the need to balance the composition of CSOs to ensure a complementary relationship with governmental and international agencies.

If the conflict-related work of CSOs is primarily located in the output sphere, e.g., by providing humanitarian or development aid, there is the danger

Table 2.1 Civil Society Discourses and Their Potential for Conflict Transformation

Theoretical Tradition Mainly Attributed to	Its Understanding of Civil Society	Its Potential Contribution to Conflict Transformation
Locke (1632–1704)	Affirm an independent social sphere as a safeguard against arbitrary action by the state	Offer protection against the excesses of arbitrary state power and foster the establishment of the rule of law on a lasting basis
Montesquieu (1689–1755)	Promote social networks as a counterweight to a central political authority	Promote the growth of "acquired"—rather than "ascribed"—social affiliations, and of overlapping memberships, thus countering the scission of society along lines defined by ethnic characteristics
De Tocqueville (1805–1859)	Political socialization of citizens, through which the habit of democratic behavior is acquired	Foster an open, discursive approach to conflicts, because citizens, having undergone the relevant political socialization, are used to dealing with differences
Habermas (1929–)	Create a public space for disadvantaged interests, given the ossified power-based structure of political systems	Provide through various forums and channels a favorable framework for the articulation of interests that are otherwise suppressed or disadvantaged, and foster the emergence of shared values

Source: Based on Merkel/Lauth, 1997

that their agenda is dominated by considerations within the realm of states, probably without a sufficient reflection of power political implications. In some cases, CSOs in particular emphasized issues on the input side, e.g., in the areas of lobbying for the banning of antipersonnel landmines or through establishing early warning mechanisms. However, to be effective it is obvious that they need to be integrated into the agendas of national and international governmental agencies and organizations.

The second most important issue of cooperation relates to that among different CSOs in this field. In light of tough competition over limited funding and despite all rhetoric about the need for burden sharing, many CSOs still prioritize self-preservation over true and meaningful cooperation and coordination. This is even more paramount in light of the ever-increasing number of outsider actors getting involved in other people's conflicts and engaged with insider parties. External organizations often dominate the relationships with internal partners—in terms of financial and organizational resources as well as with respect to setting the agenda.

In fact, strategic, co-owned, and joined-up conflict transformation initiatives among external and internal CSOs and governments still are more the exception than the norm. Some argue that they are first and foremost accountable to the donors and their interests and to a lesser degree to their beneficiaries and their needs. As a matter of fact, most actors in conflict prevention and transformation continue to be dependent on funding from national or international donor agencies or government ministries. In this scenario, what room do CSOs have to develop and implement an independent political agenda?

This raises an issue that has found growing attention in the most recent past: How can meaningful partnerships be established between external and internal actors, including the donor community (IPA/WSP International 2004)? Many CSOs are interested in facilitating long-term processes of social change. Yet most donors are thinking in terms of concrete and representable results in order to satisfy their respective constituencies, to serve their strategic national interests, and to be visible and influential among the donor community.

Despite this, there are also encouraging signs. The Peacebuilding Forum 2004 of the International Peace Academy and WSP International has generated a set of sound proposals for improving the coordination and interaction among the internal and external actors separately, as well as the dialogue between them. How far these recommendations will be implemented depends very much on the determination of CSOs to spell out their vision, their assumptions of social change and justice, more explicitly and proactively. Furthermore, on the side of the donors, it calls for a more flexible, long-term-oriented, and risk-taking approach.

Apart from the issue of cooperation between different actors, the other crucial topic is the development of a joint framework that allows the actors to organize their cooperation according to a common understanding of the conflict, its implications, and the sharing of strategic goals. Robert Ricigliano (2003) has emphasized that too often collaboration is just a secondary consideration that is brought in because of pragmatic or cost-related calculations and implemented in the form of subcontracting. His argument is that for effective cooperation it is necessary to develop a common "theory of action" and to work toward Networks of Effective Action (NEA). Such NEA should bring actors together in a conflict zone across the various divisions in a "chaordic fashion" (decentralized decisionmaking, self-organizing, and flexible in form). Ideally it would bring together three types of peacebuilding interventions in the areas of political, social, and structural transformation.

According to all experiences in the field, the network idea is indeed the key for establishing a sound and sustainable infrastructure of CSOs working for peace. In our assessment, one of the key preconditions for establishing effective networks is the availability of actors with facilitation capacities and skills who are willing to serve and are accepted in that function and can also mobilize resources for the institutional capacity building of other members in the network. These functions can be provided by one member (who should then, because of conflicting interests, not be a competitor for funding provided for other members in the network) or through sharing among several members.

Other variations of the network idea are focused on enhancing the capacities of all stakeholders to a conflict with respect to all key issues (e.g., the organization of an inclusive peace negotiation process; the identification of a viable power sharing arrangement; the organization of security-enhancing measures; the management of development and rehabilitation efforts; and the elaboration of an adequate mechanism for reconciliation and transitional justice).

Professionalization Discourse

As a clear sign of a steady professionalization and standardization, the field has increasingly engaged in questions of lessons learned and best practices, and particularly with respect to self-understanding and guiding principles, planning, and assessment. These questions are best understood to be inter-related and highly interwoven.

Self-Understanding and Guiding Principles

As indicated above, the complex and multifaceted nature of violent conflicts calls for nongovernmental and governmental actors and strategies of different quality and quantity working together. Given the variety of actors and strategies, the field of conflict prevention and transformation has so far been reluctant to explicitly define itself and come to a common understanding of its underlying values and principles. Most actors take for granted their conflict transformation work being value-based, rooted in the projects of enlightenment and the "civilization of conflict."

Additionally, many actors have come to recognize the need to frame their work in principles of impartiality/multipartiality, cooperation, transparency, accountability, and legitimacy over the last couple of years. Many organizations followed the examples of the International Committee of the Red Cross, International Alert, Search for Common Ground, and developed codes of conduct.

The development of these made the formerly largely implicit and hidden value-based guiding principles of conflict transformation actors more explicit. While bringing into the open largely implicit ethics of conflict prevention and transformation work, the debate on guiding principles also made the self-understanding of CSOs more open for critical debate and scrutiny.

How far did the consciousness of common ethics led to a meaningful, different practice? It has to remain an open question as to how far the actors in the field of conflict prevention and conflict transformation interpret and operationalize guiding principles of accountability, impartiality, and legitimacy in any comparatively similar and systematic way—both within and among CSOs. What does it mean, for example, for a conflict transformation organization to be impartial or multipartial in the face of highly asymmetric and fluid conflict dynamics and parties such as those in Sri Lanka? The point here is not so much that different CSOs should come up with similar interpretations of their guiding principles. What matters more is that CSOs consciously and openly assess how they project their interpretation of impartiality/multipartiality on the changing conflict setting and conflict stakeholders.

While most guiding principles first and foremost focus on the outreach work with partner organizations, beneficiaries, and donors, the key challenge

---

Search for Common Ground's Operating Practices

Make long-term commitments. Avoid "parachuting" (dropping into a conflict for a short visit). Use a continuing presence to develop a knowledge base and to build networks of relationships on all sides of the conflict.

Use an integrated approach. Work simultaneously on multiple levels and on multiple fronts, while striving for societal conflict transformation.

Become engaged in order to see the possibilities. Conflicts are extraordinarily complex, and it takes profound engagement in order to start to understand them. Although we conduct assessment missions before undertaking any new program, we strive to remain flexible to adapt to the changing environments in which we operate.

Be social entrepreneurs. Look for problem solvers and creative thinkers who, from a shared vision, can develop finite and achievable projects. Continuously develop new tools and approaches.

Become immersed in local cultures. Work with and build on individuals' and communities' knowledge, wisdom, and creativity. Partner with local peacebuilders to strengthen their ability to transform their own conflicts.

Practice cooperative action. Dialogue is a necessary but insufficient means to change attitudes and behaviours. Wherever possible, work with parties in conflict to help them not only understand their differences but also to act on their commonalities.

remains how to apply and implement the guiding principles within the organization and its respective team. What does it mean to be truly impartial/multipartial in a highly asymmetric and continuously changing conflict setting in terms of the organizational and team development? How can CSOs implement internally what they preach externally?

Not only do most organizations struggle with "other people's conflicts," they also have to address their own internal team and organizational conflicts. In fact, in many local CSOs the dynamics of the conflict are well reflected in the dynamics of the team and its organizational development.

The review of the institutional structures of CSOs suggests that many actors of conflict prevention and transformation struggle to understand and act upon both the conflict-related and organization-related dynamics and changes. The "web of outside and inside interpersonal conflicts" raises crucial questions of organizational and team development, which so far have been largely sidelined in the field. As a first step, CSOs have to understand themselves as "learning organizations" making organizational capacity building and team development one of its priorities. This requires not only conflict and communication skills development, but regular mentoring and coaching by staff who operate in a highly stressful, dynamic, and contradictory conflict setting. Struggling to address both the organization-related and conflict-related changes could mean for many organizations nothing less than a painstaking and time-consuming exercise being open to regularly revising working priorities and reforming organizational structures. The biggest challenge here is how to improve and mainstream organizational and team development in the conflict prevention and conflict transformation work.

Planning and Assessment

Much of the critical introspection of the last couple of years went hand in hand with the development of "new" conflict-sensitive approaches and frameworks. The two best-known and widely implemented approaches to date are outlined in *Do No Harm* (Anderson 1999) and *Peace and Conflict Impact Assessment* (Berghof Handbook Dialogue Series), with the Do No Harm approach leading to the most radical rethinking of Western development and humanitarian aid in conflict settings in the mid and late 1990s. This approach mainly targeted development and humanitarian aid aimed at preventing the negative, conflict-escalating effects of conflict interventions and strengthening the conflict-deescalating effects and factors. In recent years, pressures of accountability on CSOs and donors provoked a stronger emphasis on impact assessment such as Peace and Conflict Impact Assessments.

While the Do No Harm approach focused very much on how single development and humanitarian aid projects can prevent negative effects (working *in* conflict), the debate on Peace and Conflict Impact Assessments put center-stage how development can explicitly generate positive impacts on macro-level peace dynamics and factors (working *on* conflict). In reality, the difference between applying the Do No Harm and Peace and Conflict Impact

International Alert's Principles
for Conflict Transformation Work

Primacy of people in transforming conflicts. We believe that genuine conflict transformation is only possible with the participation and involvement of those most affected by the conflict.

Humanitarian concern. Our primary motivation is the alleviation of human suffering and our engagement in situations of violent conflict is driven principally by concern for the societies and peoples at risk from such conflicts.

Human rights and humanitarian law & principles. We are committed to the principle and practice of promoting human rights in our work in situations of violent internal conflict. We urge compliance with international humanitarian law & principles and respect for human rights amongst all parties to the conflict.

Respect for gender and cultural diversity. We respect the dignity and cultural diversity of all peoples and we make no discrimination on grounds of nationality, race, class or gender or religious, cultural or political beliefs. We recognize and endeavor to build upon the capacities of people to resolve their own conflicts and we support the distinctive peacemaking roles of women in societies affected by violent conflict.

Impartiality. We endeavor to be inclusive in our work, seeking access to the relevant parties to the conflict. We do not take sides in conflicts and we derive guidance from our adherence to the principles outlined in this Code, which we strive to advance in appropriate ways at all times.

Independence. We are an independent organization, free to formulate policies and operational strategies in accordance with our legally registered aims and the principles expressed in this Code.

Accountability. We are morally responsible to those whom we seek to assist and accountable to those with whom we work. We are bound by UK Charity Law through our trustees and accountable through regular reporting mechanisms to our donors. As a means of enhancing accountability, we endeavor to be open and transparent in our work.

Confidentiality. Whilst endeavoring to be open and transparent, we are committed to maintaining confidentiality in situations where the effectiveness of our programs or the security of our staff and partners may be at risk. Furthermore, we believe that, in most cases, conflict transformation work is best done discreetly.

Partnerships. We are committed to working in collaboration and complementarily with individuals, organizations, governments and other institutions that can contribute to the prevention and resolution of conflict. In particular, we believe sustainable conflict transformation is dependent upon effective co-operation with individuals and organizations within conflict-affected societies.

Institutional learning. We are committed to building up our collective pool of knowledge, institutional memory and experience through undertaking regular reviews and evaluations of our work and developing the skills of all our staff. Furthermore, we endeavor to share the lessons we learn with relevant individuals and organizations who may benefit from them and, in turn, learn from the experiences and knowledge of others.

Assessment frameworks has always been a blurred and fine one, with both approaches often lumped together under "conflict sensitivity," or more confusingly under "conflict analysis."

At present, both Do No Harm and Peace and Conflict Impact Assessment approaches are increasingly used as planning, monitoring, and assessment procedures for conflict-sensitive projects. As far as planning and assessment procedures are concerned, there is a trend toward standardization and all-in-one universally applicable tool kits on the one hand, and tailor-made tool kits for individual organizations on the other. At the same time, some development organizations such the German agency Deutsche Gesellschaft für Technische Zusammenarbeit (GTZ) offer comprehensive tool kits where one can pick and choose the appropriate tools (Leonhardt 2001), while other organizations such as the Swiss Agency for Development and Cooperation offer a step-by-step procedure.

The challenge remains as to how to mainstream conflict sensitivity in one's organizations' project-cycle management in times of limited funding, lack of conflict knowledge, and the organizational complexities resulting from simultaneously mainstreaming gender, HIV/AIDS prevention, environmental issues, and conflict sensitivity. Evidence shows that training in different conflict-sensitive methodologies like Do No Harm is crucial, but remains futile if not linked to the concrete experience of staff, structural, and organizational changes. The biggest challenge here is how to successfully transfer and translate individual learning into the wider organizational learning process.

What the debates on Do No Harm, Peace and Conflict Impact Assessment, and the more recent Reflecting on Peace Practice project have in common is the realization that even well-intended and planned conflict interventions have not been effective or relevant to the conflict context, while some interventions had a negative, conflict-aggravating impact.

While Do No Harm puts vital questions of effectiveness on the agenda, the discussion on the Peace and Conflict Impact Assessment and Reflecting on Peace Practice projects took the debate further by also focusing on questions of the relevance and impact of peacebuilding work. Much of this discourse is still in the "test phase." Fundamental challenges and questions remain. The following ones seem the most pressing and paramount.

How to measure impact. The debates on both the Reflecting on Peace Practice project and Peace and Conflict Impact Assessment highlighted the challenge to measure the impact of peacebuilding work on the macropolitical level. Given that conflicts embody nonlinear, fluid, and contradictory processes and structures, how are we to trace linear causation/causal relationships between activities and outcomes? How to measure process-oriented relationships and confidence building, both being very much at the core of most conflict transformation work? Current practice highlights of most donors and agencies show that while considering Peace and Conflict Impact Assessment as increasingly technocratic procedures measuring impact, many fall into the trap of measuring (and proving) outcomes only. It is still up for debate as to how far

CSOs, as an immediate result of a Peace and Conflict Impact Assessment, have improved their performances through a purposeful learning and changing process.

How to identify accurate and meaningful indicators of impact. What are meaningful indicators for processes initiated by conflict transformation actors? The debate on both Peace and Conflict Impact Assessment and the Reflecting on Peace Practice project generate some criteria that have broken into meaningful indicators. The debate on whether these indicators should be context-specific or generally applicable is still ongoing. It also raises the more general question if there should be, as some demand, standardized internationally agreed-upon planning, assessment, and evaluation criteria. Most importantly, the debate highlights the real need to spell out the clear strategic objectives of a project, against which indicators should be assessed.

What kinds of tools are most usable for measuring impact? Clearly, the debate on effectiveness, impact, and relevance fostered the analytical knowledge and conflict-sensitive planning, strategizing, and assessment within the field. While there has been progress on sophisticated conflict analyses and risk assessments, analytical frameworks and tools for measuring impact are still embryonic. Some favor the idea of "peace auditing" methodologies to assess CSOs in terms of peacebuilding impacts, asking questions on their identity and values, relationships and linkages, and programs. The need remains for creative and innovative methods such as "scenario building" to be further developed and implemented. Other fresh impetus may come from game and

---

Reflecting on Peace Practices

Reflecting on Peace Practice (RPP), by the Collaborative for Development Action and the Life and Peace Institute was initiated in 1999 as a follow-up of the Do No Harm approach and the Local Capacities for Peace project. It involves a number of agencies that specifically work on conflict; that is, those agencies that undertake intergroup mediation, reconciliation, peace education, conflict management, conflict transformation and other approaches to reducing the dangers of conflict.

Its purpose is to analyze experience at the individual program level across a broad range of agencies and contexts and its goal is to improve the effectiveness of international efforts to help in "other people's conflicts."

The RPP has developed some preliminary tools for looking at the effectiveness of conflict mitigation programs, which are laid out in *Confronting War: Critical Lessons for Peace Practitioners* (Mary B. Anderson & Lara Olson with assistance from Kristin Doughty, 2003.

Note: For more information, see RPP's website: www.cdainc.com/rpp/publications/confrontingwar/ConfrontingWar.pdf.

chaos theory. Both offer a different perspective from the cause-and-effect logic that underpins impact assessment.

How to identify success. The Reflecting on Peace Practice project makes clear that while most actors in conflict prevention and conflict transformation are able to identify negative impacts, most struggle how to identify "success" in their work.

The overarching challenge is how the field of conflict prevention and transformation, while becoming a "professional peace industry," can retain its critical edge: How can we continue to work on long-term social change without being co-opted by short-term donor work priorities? Again, this dilemma is not easily reconciled, but stresses the real imperative to be more explicit about the heavily value-loaded work and to self-critically challenge one's own "open and hidden agenda" of conflict prevention and transformation.

Conclusion

The field of conflict prevention and transformation is shaped by an unchanged high level of frozen stalemates, violent struggles, fragile cease-fires, and precarious peace processes. It is furthermore characterized by a changing multiplicity of discourses that aim to address the changing challenges and the unchanged high expectations from donors and partners, on the one hand, and the changing limitations of the work on the other.

The field has learned to change and achieved substantive progress with respect to its professionalism and the elaboration of networks and multitrack structures and processes. The main challenge is to learn from change and to link its impressive record of learned experiences with the need to reflect more systematically on the theoretical and highly political underpinning of its own work.

Peace and Conflict Impact Assessment

The discourse on Peace and Conflict Impact Assessment (PCIA) stresses the need for a thorough analysis of the conflict context. From this develops a methodology for the assessment and evaluation of peace and conflict impact that offers a framework for peacebuilding. However, under the label PCIA we find quite different concepts and approaches. For some users, PCIA is a tool set that is applied for program planning, while others regard it as a framework for evaluation and cross-country comparison. Similarly, some view it as a method to contribute and monitor the contribution of an intervention to peacebuilding, while others use PCIA for screening the impact of a conflict on the project itself.

Note: For more information, see Berghof Handbook Dialogue Series: http://www.berghof-handbook.net/articles/pcia_complete.pdf.

Cordula Reimann is senior researcher and program coordinator for the Centre for Peacebuilding (KOFF)/Swiss Peace Foundation (Bern). The Centre for Peacebuilding's objective is to strengthen Switzerland's capacities in civilian peacebuilding by providing information, training, advisory services, and platform activities.

Norbert Ropers is director of the Berghof Foundation for Peace Support (Berlin) and director of the Berghof Foundation Sri Lanka Office (Colombo). The Berghof Foundation supports the Sri Lankan peace process through providing capacity-building, dialoguing, and problem-solving opportunities for all principal stakeholders.

This chapter is dedicated to Werner Lottje (1945–2004), a German pioneer in the field of human rights work through conflict prevention and conflict transformation, who has inspired both of us immensely with his vision and passion.

Selected Bibliography

Anderson, Mary B. 1999. *Do No Harm: How Aid Can Support Peace—or War* (Boulder, CO: Lynne Rienner Publishers).

Anderson, Mary B., and Lara Olson. 2003. *Confronting War: Critical Lessons for Peace Practitioners* (Cambridge, MA: Collaborative for Development Action Inc.). Online: http://www.cdainc.com/rpp/publications/confrontingwar/ConfrontingWar.pdf.

Berdal, Mats, and David M. Malone, eds. 2000. *Greed and Grievance: Economic Agendas in Civil Wars* (Boulder, CO: Lynne Rienner Publishers).

Boyer, Glaucia Yoshiura. 2004. "Internal and External Actors and the Quality of Their Dialogue in Post-Conflict Countries." Background paper for Peacebuilding Forum, 7 October, New York City. Sponsored by WSP International and International Peace Academy's Security-Development Nexus Program.

Fitzduff, Mari, and Cheyanne Church, eds. 2004. *NGOs at the Table: Strategies for Influencing Policies in Areas of Conflict* (Lanham, MD: Rowman & Littlefield and International Development Research Centre. A project of the International Peace Academy).

IPA/WSP International and International Peace Academy's Security-Development Nexus Program. 2004. "Building Effective Partnerships: Improving the Relationship Between Internal and External Actors in Post-Conflict Countries." Peacebuilding Forum conference document, 7 October.

Lauth, Hans-Joachim, and Wolfgang Merkel, eds. 1997. *Zivilgesellschaft im Transformationprozess* (Mainz, Germany: Institut für Politikwissenschaft).

Leonhardt, Manuela. 2001. "Konfliktbezogene Wirkungsbeobachtung von Entwicklungsvorhaben." (Eschborn, Germany: Deutsche Gesellschaft für Technische Zusammenarbeit [GTZ]). Online: http://www.gtz.de/crisisprevention/deutsch/leonhardt2.htm.

Ricigliano, Robert. 2003. "Networks of Effective Action: Implementing an Integrated Approach to Peacebuilding." *Security Dialogue* 34, no. 4 (December) (Sage Publications).

Senghaas, Dieter. 2004. "The Civilization of Conflict: Constructive Pacifism as a Guiding Notion for Conflict Transformation," in Alex Austin, Martina Fischer, and Norbert Ropers, eds., *Transforming Ethnopolitical Conflict: The Berghof Handbook* (Wiesbaden, Germany: Berghof Research Center for Constructive Confict Management and VS Verlag).

Smith, Dan. 2003. *Getting Their Act Together: Towards a Strategic Framework for Peacebuilding* (Oslo: International Peace Research Institute, Overview Report of the Joint Utstein Study of Peacebuilding).

Swiss Agency for Development and Cooperation (SDC). 2004. "Konfliktsensitives Programm-Management. Ein Konzept zur Verankerung der Konfliktperspektive im Programm-und Projektmanagementzyklus der DEZA." (Bern: SDC).

3

Effective Regional Networks and Partnerships

Andrés Serbin

While globalization garners much attention around the world, organizations at local and regional levels are reacting to the trend by strengthening regional ties. Regional civil societies are emerging that reflect and embrace specific regional interests. In the field of conflict prevention and peacebuilding, networks and partnerships established at the regional level can play important roles by interacting with local actors as well as governments, international organizations, and intergovernmental agencies.

As the process of globalization has established itself ever more firmly, new opportunities have emerged around the world for organizations and civil-society networks operating at the regional level. These regional entities are uniquely positioned to forge links to civil-society activities at the national and local levels, on the one hand, and to global initiatives on the other. This is particularly true for regional networks engaged in conflict prevention and peacebuilding.

Regional networks and regional partnerships, including those involving governments, subregional and regional organizations, and local and regional civil-society networks, are becoming crucial actors in early warning, early response, and conflict management. However, to date, the links between those working at the local level with local expertise and those working at the regional or global level have generally been weak. These links can be strengthened by creating formal mechanisms that facilitate coordination and cooperation between individuals and organizations engaged in conflict prevention and peacebuilding at these various levels.

A Changing Global Dynamic
Since the end of the Cold War, the world has been changing rapidly. Social, economic, and political relations have been undergoing a dramatic change. Technology has enabled connections that were not possible until recently; the

breakdown of the bipolar world dominated by the Soviet Union and the United States has changed the way states, regions, nongovernmental entities, and individuals interact with each other; and the preeminence of the nation-state is being transformed. Globalization, is the word most often used to refer to these processes—a kind of shorthand for a range of significant changes in the world order. One result of globalization has been that the centers of power and decisionmaking are more widely distributed than they had been in the past (a situation contested by such recent events as the war in Iraq), and that actors at all levels within the international community—subnational, national, regional, transnational, and international—are increasingly capable of asserting global influence.

Within this framework, global civil society—all those individuals and organizations operating independently of governments and international organizations—has come to play an increasingly prominent role. Even the renewed attention to security issues in the wake of the 9/11 attacks on the United States cannot halt this more fundamental shift in global relations. Global civil society is enormously rich and diverse, and engaged at all levels, from the village to the international. Among those players active in global civil society—and with growing importance in view of this changing global dynamic—are those that together are coalescing into what may be described as "regional civil societies" all over the world.

"Regionness" and Civil Society

To some extent, in fact, the globalization process has elicited a response in the form of regionalization: not only governments but also civil society at the local and regional levels are coming together in response to a perception of vulnerability and exclusion and the sense that local and regional autonomy has been sacrificed as a result of globalization. Where civil-society organizations (CSOs) see shared interests and goals, they are forging links and creating networks that traverse national boundaries, with the aim of addressing crucial regional issues. Each of these networks will have its own particular dynamic, its own agenda, and its own strategies.

To the extent that these processes are undertaken with the specific intent of strengthening regional identity and the mechanisms of regional interaction and cooperation (rather than for specific goals associated with the objectives and programs of the organizations themselves), we can speak of a trend toward "regionness." Here, we see partnerships among CSOs, civil-society networks, national governments, and regional intergovernmental organizations. These regional partnerships are involved, among other things, in the identification, preservation, and strengthening of regional common goods, including, significantly, conflict resolution and the construction of a culture of peace.

Thus those engaged in the effort to build a more equitable, peaceful, people-oriented global community need to understand that what occurs at the regional level is of vital importance. The dynamics at the regional level are also crucial to the maintenance and strengthening of cultural diversity and pluralism, particularly in view of the pressures toward conformity and uniformity associated with globalization. In each region and country, civil society expresses itself uniquely, and conflict prevention has its own distinct characteristics and dynamics. Those working on global initiatives need to recognize and respect these regional differences if the aim is to implement conflict prevention strategies that are appropriate in specific cultural, social, and geopolitical contexts.

Presently, many of the most pressing issues on the international agenda are issues that merit the attention not only of states, but also of nonstate actors with their own specific concerns and interests. These actors, operating in various civil-society networks and as representatives of independent organizations, have gained considerable credibility and influence in recent years. One result is that issues that once were local concerns—respect for human rights and the rule of law (including, especially, international law) and adherence to democratic practices—are issues addressed in the international arena.

Still, the implications of the simultaneous emergence of global and civil societies, on the one hand, and this "new regionalism" on the other, have been largely overlooked. There have been limited attempts to understand the linkages between globalization and regionalization, and there has been little interest in how these linkages might affect networks and other types of interaction at the regional level.

New Synergies

The linkages formed between civil-society initiatives at the regional and global levels create new synergies that contribute to the democratization and increased influence of citizens in international decisionmaking processes. CSOs and networks are gradually developing new forms of "citizen diplomacy" on both the global and the regional levels. These groups are monitoring governmental agencies, international organizations, and multilateral forums and call on them to better manage the process of globalization and to act in the interests of common citizens. Through citizen diplomacy, civil society exerts pressure from the bottom up, overcoming the usual democratic deficits inherent to international processes, and broadening and strengthening democracy.

The recently established Global Partnership for the Prevention of Armed Conflict (GPPAC) is an example of just such an effort to forge links between global and regional civil-society processes and initiatives in order to create and exploit synergies in the field of conflict prevention and peacebuilding. It is not the only initiative under way where the aim is the coordination of regional initiatives on a global level, but, with an agenda focused squarely on the prevention of war, violent conflict, and peacebuilding, it can become one of the most relevant to the lives of the citizens of the world.

The Global Partnership embraces a global vision, but its base consists of fifteen regional networks providing the necessary inputs to forge a global action agenda on conflict prevention and peacebuilding. This bottom-up structure allows for the expression and pursuit of different cultural and political ways of dealing with violent conflict. It also results in a partnership that is pluralistic, interactive, and accountable—an example of how a civil-society initiative may articulate local, regional, and global concerns without disregarding the particular traits and dynamics of each region.

Think Globally, Focus Regionally

Currently, much work in the field of conflict prevention tends to focus on global actors. However, focusing on UN agencies, powerful governments, and intergovernmental organizations (INGOs) is not sufficient when dealing with conflict prevention on the ground. Regional networks and initiatives, with strong links to the grassroots at the community level, are crucial for any global peacebuilding process, particularly when dealing with subregional or regional conflicts.

Often, the root causes of a conflict can be traced to regional factors—historical, political, economic, and geographic in nature. At the same time, local conflicts can become regionalized as they spill across borders (Sriram and Nielsen 2004: 3). To manage such conflicts, then, it is only logical to involve not only the international organizations (be they intergovernmental or civil society), but also regional and subregional organizations and networks with strong links to local and community-based organizations. Such regional players can have a significant role not only in early warning and early response, but also in crisis management on the ground. It is, therefore, important to build partnerships that bring CSOs together with governmental, intergovernmental, subregional, and regional organizations. This is all the more important in view of the fact that CSOs often have a better knowledge and understanding of the regional political and cultural dynamics, greater capacity to analyze local developments, and well-established (and sometimes extremely complex) links with contending local parties.

Regional actors will often be capable of more effective conflict prevention interventions and peacebuilding than outside agencies that may be perceived with mistrust or suspicion by regional and local actors, and which, in any case, may lack the knowledge and expertise of local and regional players. As Zoe Nielsen notes (2004: 181) in addressing conflict in the Horn of Africa, "Regional and subregional organizations may be better placed to act, because some governments are more open to intervention by their peers than by organizations or governments that have no link to the region."

However, regional actors may also be perceived as too partial, or may be identified too closely with one of the contending parties. Nevertheless, there are numerous examples of regional entities that have effectively intervened to manage conflict—sometimes more effectively than external actors. These include regional organizations such as the Organization of American States (OAS) in Latin America and the Caribbean, the Intergovernmental Agency on Development (IGAD) in the Horn of Africa, or the Economic Community of West African States (ECOWAS) in West Africa; groups of "friends" such as

The Global Partnership for the Prevention of Armed Conflict

This partnership was established in June 2003 in the Netherlands. The incentive came from UN secretary-general Kofi Annan's report *The Prevention of Armed Conflict* (2001), in which he "urge[s] NGOs with an interest in conflict prevention to organize an international conference of local, national, and international NGOs on their role in conflict prevention and future interaction with the United Nations in this field" (Recommendation 27).

The Global Partnership for the Prevention of Armed Conflict (GPPAC) is formed to build a new international consensus on the prevention of violent conflict and peacebuilding. It is pursuing its goals and activities through fifteen regional processes, which comprise the fabric of the initiative and will develop action agendas to reflect principles and priorities for their region. Regional initiators, who collectively govern the direction of the GPPAC through an International Steering Group, facilitate the regional processes. An International Secretariat, currently hosted by the European Centre for Conflict Prevention, serves the global process.

The GPPAC is working toward the creation of a sustainable network of people and organizations committed to conflict prevention and peacebuilding. In the line of the recommendations in the report of the Panel of Eminent Persons on Civil Society and UN Relationships (the Cardoso Panel), in which the panel recommends the UN to forge multistakeholder partnerships to deal with global issues, the GPPAC aims to include governments, regional and multilateral organizations, and the United Nations in this partnership and to invent or improve mechanisms for interaction between these actors and civil society.

The Global Conference at the UN Headquarters in July 2005, "From Reaction to Prevention," serves as the launching point for the Global Action Agenda, outlining conflict prevention principles, policies, and practices to be adopted by civil-society organizations, the UN system, and governments worldwide.

The GPPAC aims to support a shift from reaction to prevention through the following goals:

- To create a sustainable network of individuals and groups committed to prevention and peacebuilding at global, regional, and national levels. Strong regional networks are crucial as there is a host of small organizations active in this field and it is important that they know what others are doing, what their strengths and capacities are, and how they can best work together. Unfortunately, regional networks in the field of conflict prevention and peacebuilding are virtually nonexistent in a number of regions—as was a global network until the GPPAC was forged
- To articulate and work toward the implementation of a policy change agenda, as articulated in the series of Regional Action Agendas and in the Global Action Agenda that will strengthen the effectiveness of conflict prevention and peacebuilding
- To generate and mobilize diverse public constituencies around the world who are informed about the need for prevention and peacebuilding and the important role of civil society in achieving it and who actively support human security as an alternative to militarism

Note: For more information, see http://www.gppac.net.

the Contadora Group during the Central American crisis in the 1980s or the Group of Friends intervening in the conflict between Ecuador and Peru in the 1990s; and regional "zones of peace" promoted by national governments or regional integration initiatives in South and Central America.

However, few of these regional initiatives, even if successful, have been based on CSO participation or developed in partnership with CSOs. Instead, they have generally tended to be predominantly governmental or intergovernmental, conceived basically from above and often ignoring the knowledge, expertise, and commitment that CSOs and local, grassroots organizations can bring. They have also tended to be reactive, acting in response to emerging crises or conflicts, and focusing on conflict mediation, management, or resolution, or on postconflict peacebuilding. Very few of them have focused on conflict prevention as such, and very few even tried to engage local and grassroots CSOs. Instead, they have operated primarily at the macro level, where general agreements on policies and goals may be achievable, but where effective strategies for conflict prevention or the establishment of early warning systems are rarely formulated or implemented, and which, at any rate, proceed without the benefit of local expertise or commitment. This is unfortunate.

How Civil-Society Organizations Fit In

If early warning systems were established at the national level and coordinated on a subregional or regional level through regional civil-society networks, they could serve as important elements in a larger effort to implement proactive preventive measures from the bottom up. With the involvement and commitment of CSOs, it would then be possible to warn other actors and to encourage them to take preventive action at an early stage. Such partnerships could play especially useful roles responding at an early stage to local conflicts where there is a very real risk of regional spillover.

Several recent developments in West Africa show, as Catherine Barnes (2004) observes, that it is possible to channel grassroots CSO involvement in early warning and conflict prevention into highly flexible, creative initiatives that promote dialogue and mobilize across a broad cross-section of society. Furthermore, it is possible to build broader partnerships with governmental or international organizations in order to promote positive change, address conflict, and reduce violence and, especially (if not explicitly), to develop social capital and strengthen democratic norms and procedures.

Barnes cites John Katunga, of the Nairobi Peace Initiative-Africa, who observed that civil-society actors can play an important role in two ways: by channeling information to appropriate international and/or governmental actors capable of dealing with conflict; and also by offering reassurance to local communities by providing accurate and reliable information about what is going on and, if appropriate, advising local actors.

CSOs with roots in conflict-affected communities may be able to shape appropriate strategies and policies to deal with local tensions and conflicts, particularly when they have the recognition and support of a broader network

The UN, the OAS, and CSOs
in Latin America and the Caribbean

There is a general perception that the Organization of American States (OAS) is consistently and proactively involved in responding to conflict throughout Latin America and the Caribbean, with the UN most often playing a secondary role to the OAS and state actors. Interestingly, however, the OAS frames its engagement as promoting democratization and human rights rather than as promoting peace and security or preventing conflicts per se.[1] This is also perhaps one of the reasons why the language of "prevention" and "peacebuilding" is unfamiliar to many in the region. What is also true is that CSO engagement with OAS peace initiatives is very limited. The OAS does acknowledge civil-society organizations (CSOs) and regional networks, particularly those related to human rights issues, and consults them as well, but these networks nonetheless have little influence or involvement in conflict prevention or peace processes. Once a conflict has been settled, CSOs are invited to contribute to postconflict reconstruction, as has occurred on several occasions in Central America, or to support the activities of UN peace forces, as in the recent crisis in Haiti. However, in general, both regional and local CSOs have only limited involvement on the ground and their roles are usually restricted to the regional macro level, where dialogue and interaction with governments or the OAS bodies may occur.

Additionally, as the experience of the CRIES (Coordinadora Regional de Investigaciones Económicas y Sociales—Regional Coordination for Economic and Social Research) shows, Latin American governments and the OAS are disinclined to seriously consider CSO perspectives and recommendations on conflict prevention. Clearly, building an effective partnership linking local and regional CSOs and CSO networks, governments, and intergovernmental organizations will require a long and sustained process.

Through a regional initiative led by the CRIES and commissioned by the Citizens' Diplomacy Forum, Latin American and Caribbean CSOs and networks have, in recent years, begun to strengthen their networking and advocacy capacities in the field of regional and global security, peacebuilding, and conflict prevention. With the establishment of the Global Partnership for the Prevention of Armed Conflict (GPPAC), CSOs at the regional level have been able to forge stronger links and improve coordination with other relevant regional and global actors. Furthermore, CSOs are also laying the foundations for a more fundamental transformation of conflict management, which has, in most cases in Latin America, been more about conflict resolution and conflict mediation than conflict prevention, and viewed as a matter exclusively within the purview of governments.

Note: For more information see www.cries.org.

of partners committed to the peaceful resolution of conflicts and the strengthening of democratic institutions. However, if outside actors are perceived to be attempting to impose external solutions on the local parties, the credibility of the local CSOs may be undermined. In other words, external expertise and guidance, while crucial to these processes, should not be allowed to hinder the internal, local dynamics that are themselves integral to meaningful, firmly based, sustainable change.

Linking Bottom to Top: Essential Partnerships

The effectiveness of local grassroots/community-based organizations working on the ground can be enhanced when they are supported by wider regional CSO networks. These local organizations have solid knowledge of the local environment, and they are familiar with the local actors and cultural norms. The wider CSO networks can help to establish communication channels and links with more powerful outside actors, such as governmental agencies, INGOs, or intergovernmental regional organizations, and assist in the analysis of any specific measure or initiative. It follows, then, that conflict prevention initiatives can be made more effective when broad partnerships are established between local CSOs, larger CSO networks and INGOs, and governmental and intergovernmental agencies on a regional level.

In fact, as part of a global initiative for conflict prevention and peacebuilding, these partnerships can be considered essential building blocks. The implication, then, is that such partnerships should not be established on an ad hoc basis, but rather in a more formal process, through consultation, research, and networking, in order to create formal mechanisms that bring CSOs into deliberative, interactive, and consultative processes and allow for the design and implementation of collectively agreed strategies (Barnes 2004). At the same time, it is crucial that institution building and reform take place to assure the successful implementation of long-term strategies of conflict prevention that effectively address the root causes of future conflicts (Sriram and Nielson 2004: 156).

As Barnes notes in this regard, it is important to take into account that:

- Regional and subregional prevention mechanisms are most likely to be effective if they develop according to the needs of the area and respond to the existing patterns of regional conflict dynamics. The implication is that they do not necessarily have to reflect already existing structures
- Mechanisms may be developed under the auspices of a regional or subregional organization, or under the auspices of the UN, or be developed collaboratively, depending on what capabilities already exist on the ground. Consistent with the subsidiarity principle, the UN should fill in gaps in a complementary and additive manner
- The engagement of local and regional CSOs and networks and the exploration of mechanisms for appropriate ongoing cooperation and partnerships should be priorities. In areas of the world where existing regional organizations are more closed, the UN can play an important role by opening up space for CSO involvement in dialogue on conflict-related issues and strategies

• The establishment of advisory councils on conflict should be considered, with the participation of local and regional CSOs, governmental agencies, and regional organizations

A broad cross-section of civil-society actors should be involved in these processes, with representation from local networks, regional CSOs and networks, academia, the media, and religious organizations. The international community has a role to play as well, particularly by channeling development assistance to conflict prevention initiatives (Sriram and Nielsen 2004: 11).

Interregional Cooperation

There is, beyond these regional partnerships, a place for interregional cooperation as part of this global process. Such cooperation, in the form of the sharing experiences and the exchanging information, collaborative research and networking, and the development of joint strategies, can contribute significantly not only to the global process but also to interregional initiatives and CSO dialogue. This has occurred with interregional collaboration between the North American, Latin American, and Caribbean Global Partnership regional net-

---

Interregional Cooperation in the Americas

There are two Global Partnership for the Prevention of Armed Conflict (GPPAC) regional networks in the Americas: one for North America and one for Latin America and the Caribbean. Each region is enormously complex and interregional cooperation does not, therefore, address specific conflict situations, but rather areas where "added value" can be reasonably expected as the result of collaboration. Interregional collaboration must also take into account the high demands on resources and time required for ongoing regional and country-level activities. Taking these constraints into consideration, the following objectives were identified:

• The creation and strengthening of links between civil-society organizations (CSOs) working in the areas of security and conflict prevention in the Americas
• The systematic sharing of knowledge and information between the North American and Latin American and Caribbean CSO regional initiatives in the context of the GPPAC
• The comparison of the regional experiences of CSOs in conflict prevention, contributions to joint research activities, and cooperation on additional activities beyond the scope of the global initiative
• The promotion of dialogue between CSOs in the Americas and regional institutions in order to strengthen initiatives throughout the Americas focusing on conflict prevention, conflict resolution, peacebuilding, and security

works. These initiatives are particularly relevant when dealing with powerful governmental actors or with regional organizations, consolidating resources and expertise to further advocacy and dissemination activities, or developing joint strategies to influence policies, policymakers, government officials, or parties to a conflict.

The Regional Networking Imperative

In the spring of 2004 the European Centre for Conflict Prevention organized the European Conference on the Role of Civil Society in the Prevention of Armed Conflict in the framework of the Global Partnership. At Dublin Castle in the Republic of Ireland, the 230 participants who work actively in the field of conflict prevention and peacebuilding in Europe adopted the "Dublin Action Agenda on the Prevention of Violent Conflict." Several of the issues in the agenda point to the importance with which GPPAC views networking. The agenda calls for a "new partnership for prevention between civil society, governments, and IGOs." It further states:

> Effective conflict prevention requires the creation of collaborative, strategic partnerships for prevention at the national, regional, and international level. CSOs can undertake initiatives that government officials cannot and are well placed to mobilize wider societal support for prevention. The effectiveness of this partnership hinges on official legitimacy of CSOs that are representative and accountable in peace and security matters; recognition of their roles in the conflict prevention partnership; and the mechanisms and resources to fulfill their potential operationally.

In this chapter, the focus has been especially on how those partnerships can be forged at the regional level. As civil society continues to expand, the possibilities for effective regional partnerships should continue to grow. It can only be hoped that the influence of these networks will expand as well, and that the outcomes will produce a tangible reduction in armed conflict.

Andrés Serbin is full professor (ret.) at the Central University of Venezuela, director of the Center for Global and Regional Studies in Argentina (CEGRE), and the current executive president of the Regional Coordination for Economic and Social Research (CRIES), an organization that holds the general secretariat of the Citizens' Diplomacy Forum in Latin America and the Caribbean, a wide network of regional civil-society organizations and networks.

Note

1. The focus of regional organizations varies greatly: whereas OAS frames its engagement as promoting democratization and human rights rather than as promoting peace and security or preventing conflicts per se, other regional organizations such as Association of Southeast Asian Nations (ASEAN) focus more on security and order.

Understanding Networks

In these early years of the twenty-first century, networks are ubiquitous. They appear in various forms, from well structured with high-tech features, to interrelated decentralized units, to barely visible, loose, and informal. They can appear all of a sudden and then disappear as soon as their function has been fulfilled, or they can endure for long periods of time.

Such networks may be formed for various reasons:

- To promote cooperation based on complementary interests and objectives, especially when there is a scarcity of means
- To facilitate the exchange of information and experience when the issues or tasks at hand are complex
- To realize the benefits of economies of scale through collective learning, analysis, and implementation
- To avoid duplication of efforts and identify skills gaps
- To maximize the impact of an intervention, particularly when engaged in advocacy and lobbying
- To expand outreach and have a presence or impact at various levels of society
- To draw on a range of skills, opinions, and insights.

In the area of peacebuilding and conflict transformation, networks fulfill an obvious need to connect people from different areas, backgrounds, and ideologies. Networks are becoming a favored organizational form wherever a broad operational field is involved (e.g., where links are being made between different regions, or between the grassroots and higher levels of society), where problems or themes are so dynamic that rigid structures are not suitable, and where loose ties are preferable to formal organizational bonds. All these features are well known in areas of violent conflict.

There is no single way to classify networks, but most peacebuilding networks can be distinguished by their function, theme, or topic. Examples include networks focusing on human rights, democratic movements, or marginalized groups, or networks of professionals engaged in research and/or the application of conflict transformation and mediation skills. These networks all exist to facilitate the exchange of information and the process of learning, to coordinate and cooperate on policy and practical issues, and/or to formalize interactions and connections between different groups in order to increase their collective impact.

Some networks exist more to serve the needs of their members than to project outwardly. Within such "passive" networks, the primary objectives are likely to be the sharing of information and experience (see Table 3.1 below). Moving along an axis, other activities might include facilitating dialogue, or providing expertise. "Active" networks are focused more on the outside world, engaging in advocacy and lobbying, for example, or going beyond that to proactive engagement in early warning, for example, or actual interventions to prevent or resolve conflict. The more passive the network, the less that will be required from the members in terms of commitment, and the less formal the structure that will be required. A highly engaged, proactive network demands high levels of commitment from its participants, and a more formalized structure.

(continues)

Understanding Networks (continued)

Table 3.1 Functions of Networks

Engagement with outside	Functions	Characteristics
Passive	Sharing information and experience Facilitating dialogue Providing expertise	Less commitment required Loose informal network

	Advocacy, Lobbying and
	  Campaigning
	Early warning
	Coordination between member
	  groups
	Collective interventions	

Proactive		High level of commitment required More formalized structure

Networks, by definition, have a relatively loose organizational structure. However, that does not mean that a network can exist without some guidance and some delegation of responsibilities. In fact, in many cases, the strength or weakness of a network is proportional to the strength or weakness of the network's coordinating body. Furthermore, in most cases that means that a secretariat should be established and supported with adequate funding and facilities. Even in widely distributed, informal, decentralized networks, there needs to be a delineation of authority and responsibility, or some tasks will be left undone, while others may be duplicated.

While networking offers benefits and advantages over other approaches to organizing and advocacy, it presents particular difficulties and challenges as well. One of the strengths of the network, for example, is that a broad cross section of nongovernmental organizations (NGOs) can participate. However, within certain NGO sectors, particularly among organizations working in development or providing humanitarian assistance, where impartiality is a vital credential, there is an inherent reluctance to engage with networks that may be perceived as too "political." Creating a broad network drawing on various NGO sectors may also be difficult because there are great differences in the organizational cultures of the large international NGOs and the smaller and more informal local and regional NGOs.

Because the network is, in a sense, a multiheaded beast, one of the serious challenges it will face is to establish for itself a public voice that is clear, sufficiently assertive, and representative of the shared vision of all the network's members. Reaching consensus on positions with respect to specific issues can be exhausting and frustrating work. Moreover, the members of the network may discover that, as the profile of the network grows, their own profiles will be diminished. If, by virtue of its own success, a network saps the strength of its members, it will not be able to sustain its success for long.

(continues)

Understanding Networks (continued)

Both of these considerations suggest that for maximum effectiveness, there may be limits to the size, breadth, and diversity of a network. The instinct of networkers is to be inclusive, to draw in all who have an interest and will be capable of making a contribution. However, if a network is so broad that virtually nothing distinguishes those who join from those who remain outside, there is not likely to be much depth of commitment or much of a common agenda to which all can agree.

There is at least one more caveat for networkers that should not be ignored: networking costs a great deal of time, money, and energy. No one should think that because the load is shared, it is lighter. Furthermore, while everyone in the network is expected to contribute, the benefits of participation will not be evenly distributed. Some will be "net payers," investing much in human resources and possibly funds, while others will be "net receivers." The returns, of course, are not just in terms of resources, but also in terms of experience, information, public recognition, access, etc. As such, they are difficult to measure.

Because networking is based on connecting various interests, experiences, and behaviors in pursuit of a common goal, networks are full of inherent tensions. For example, the various participants in the network have come together because they have complementary objectives. However, each participant also has a unique agenda, and those agendas will not always be parallel. In fact, where organizations and individuals are engaged in similar work, they may well be competing for support from the public, the media spotlight, and funds. Balancing this tension between complementarity and competition is a constant challenge in networking. Effective networking demands, in the end, that the participants acknowledge and accept that tensions will exist and attempt to manage rather than eliminate these tensions.

Networks can assume a variety of forms. Ideally, the institutional form of a network is the product of its function and the context. Three models predominate:

1. The "spiderweb" model—a strongly centralized network with a central secretariat and circles emanating from the center, often at various levels. There may be links between the various levels as well, but the primary linkage is back to the center.
2. The "fishnet" or "cell structure" model—there is no central coordinating body. Instead, each member shares in the coordinating responsibilities, and each member maintains and coordinates relationships with those in closest proximity.
3. The "chain" model—actors are linked to each other in a line, where actions or information can be passed along, or an end objective can be achieved by carrying out consecutive steps along a chain. The chain model is fragile, since it is rendered ineffective if a break occurs anywhere along the chain.

Note: This text has been excerpted and adapted from an unpublished paper by Fulco van Deventer (director of I/C Consult), with additional information drawn from an unpublished paper by Paul van Tongeren and Guido de Graaf Bierbrauwer; and from the European Centre for Conflict Prevention's "Lessons Learned on Networking" (2002).

Selected Bibliography

Barnes, Catherine. 2004. "UN-CSO Interaction in Conflict-Affected Communities." GPPAC Discussion Paper, September. Online: http://www.gppac.org.

European Centre for Conflict Prevention. 2002. "Lessons Learned on Networking: On National and International Levels and Interactions of NGOs with Governments," in Anneke Galama and Paul van Tongeren, eds., *Toward Better Peacebuilding* (Utrecht: European Centre for Conflict Prevention).

Global Partnership for the Prevention of Armed Conflict. 2004. "European Conference on the Role of Civil Society in the Prevention of Armed Conflict: Conference Report."

Nielsen, Zoe. 2004. "Implications for Conflict Prevention," in Chandra Lekha Sriram and Zoe Nielsen, eds., *Exploring Subregional Conflict: Opportunities for Conflict Prevention* (London and Boulder, CO: Lynne Rienner Publishers).

Rusu, Sharon. 2001. "Principles and Practice of Conflict Early Warning." *CSD Conflict, Security, Development* 1, no: 2.

Sriram, Chandra Lekha, and Zoe Nielsen. 2004. "Why Examine Subregional Sources and Dynamics of Conflict?" in Chandra Lekha Sriram and Zoe Nielsen, eds., *Exploring Subregional Conflict: Opportunities for Conflict Prevention* (London and Boulder, CO: Lynne Rienner Publishers).

4

UN–Civil-Society Interactions: Working Together for Peace

John Clark

The coming years will see a growing role for civil society, the private sector, parliamentarians, and local authorities in the United Nations and other forums of global governance. This chapter argues that these organizations should engage to the fullest extent possible with the myriad groups who purport, with varying authenticity, to speak for the people. This will, however, not be without controversy. The main tension will concern the role of policy-oriented civil-society organizations.

While World War II still raged, twenty-six governments came together to found a new organization that might ensure a world without future war and foster development. The charter establishing the United Nations (UN) was agreed to by this small gathering, but in the name of all humanity—hence its resounding first few words: "We, the Peoples." None questioned whether this group, many of whom represented undemocratic governments, had the right to speak for the world's people. Universally, citizens were tired of wars that they paid for by their blood and taxes.

Things are very different today. While most governments are democratically elected now and are more powerful in many ways (including militarily), their remit to speak for "we the peoples" is more contested. This is becoming a clear feature of twenty-first-century politics as myriad groups have emerged who purport, with varying authenticity, to speak for the people. Governments vary as to how attentive they are to these voices, though even the least democratic are not entirely deaf to them. The dilemma for an international organization such as the UN is the degree to which it should have its own mechanisms to engage with these voices or leave it to its member states.

This chapter argues that the UN and other international organizations should engage to the fullest extent possible, short of making reasonable governments feel that their unique right to define the basic policies of those organizations has been usurped. Governments must retain the lead in tackling global issues; and their citizens will suffer if there are no forums where they can negotiate with their peers on collectively addressing a shared global agenda. On the other hand, they must recognize that other stakeholders are vital for this agenda, and there are compelling reasons for opening avenues for both listening to and working with them. A global organization must have clear global standards. It should work as much as possible in the same way throughout the world—hence it makes no sense to engage closely with civil society in some countries but not others.

Why Other Voices Have Become More Powerful

The discussion concerning the UN becoming a more outward-looking institution, engaging with civil society and others beyond its formal membership of governments, is not essential because this is the direction of fashion or political correctness. It is because the world has changed in the decades since its birth and the UN can only tackle today's global priorities effectively by broadening its appeal. There are four sets of global changes of relevance.

First is the rise of *stakeholder power*. Large corporations, religious leaders, leading media channels, and others have immense inherent power today because of their economic, political, and social muscle. Some governments resist this tide (for example by controlling the media, muzzling free expression, and dominating production) but it is increasingly clear that they do so at the long-term expense of their nations.

Second is the *democratization of information*. The Internet has leveled the playing field regarding access to information. People—especially the young and the more politically active—increasingly draw on web-based resources. Since these are "scale free" (their costs do not rise according to demand), it is no longer necessary to be rich to inform what people know and how they think. This contributes to rising cynicism about governments, large corporations, and others who shape the world we live in, and heightens trust in civil-society organizations (CSOs) and others who provide these independent information sources.

Third, there are *realities of governance*. The 191 nation-states who comprise the UN today have vastly different global footprints; the "one nation–one vote" principle no longer reflects how power is really shared. The control of other bodies by the largest economies is equally problematic. Hence shifting coalitions, depending on the issue, have emerged to counterbalance the vast inherent power of the United States and European Union.

Fourth, of course, there are the *forces of globalization*. New technology, transnational capitalism, and increasing acceptance of market forces have dramatically shaped today's power balance. Large corporations and the U.S. government are among the obvious winners, but so too are organizations within civil society who have pioneered global activism (Clark 2003). However, it is also increasingly apparent that today's pressing problems are often global in origin and hence require global responses. This applies equally to the AIDS pandemic, drugs trade, climate change, the world water crisis, and terrorism. These issues have often been put on the global agenda by civil society.

These phenomena combine to present an important lacuna in policymaking: while a great deal of the substance of politics has become global (trade, economics, climate change, HIV/AIDS, SARS, terrorism, etc.), the process of conventional politics has not. Its main institutions—elections, political parties, and parliaments—remain rooted at the national level, and hence the gap. CSOs, on the other hand, are well able to adapt to working in strong global organizations and networks (Cardoso Panel 2004).

This means that democracy now means more than the right of citizens to vote every few years for politicians to represent them across the spectrum of political matters. Such representative democracy has become diminished as disenchantment with electoral politics spreads. The more politically active citizens today are increasingly able to take part in participatory democracy as well. By joining nongovernmental organizations (NGOs), pressure groups, social movements, protests, etc, they are entering directly the debates that most interest them.

In traditional democracy, we are grouped according to where we live; our neighborhoods form the constituencies for which we elect our parliamentary representatives. The range of political parties often assumes that our class and income, and the locality where we live, are the determinants of our politics. Participatory democracy is changing the geography of politics. It allows us to aggregate differently—with others who share our burning concerns wherever they live. In other words, communities of neighborhood are being supplemented by communities of interest—and, thanks to modern information and communications technologies, such communities can be global as easily as local.

What These Changes Mean for the United Nations

Not only does a new agenda confront international organizations reflecting these new global challenges, but their modus operandi must also change. Today's political realities necessitate that they respond to concerns of all main stakeholders, not just governments, and that they also recognize the practical contributions those stakeholders can make to tackling the new priorities. As CSOs that focus on concerns of the politically and economically weak have multiplied and become more powerful, issues of inclusion, trust, and individual security have become more prevalent.

These new imperatives have been recognized in numerous UN resolutions and speeches by UN leaders, but fine words mean little unless backed by comparable actions. Often these pronouncements have not born fruit for two reasons. First, member states are reluctant to share power with CSOs; this is especially so for developing countries who already think their power in the UN has weakened while that of the United States and Europe has become unassailable. Ironically, those with the weakest democratic traditions are often first to point out that CSO leaders are mostly unelected. Second, the UN has not invested to ensure a constructive engagement with civil society, especially at the country level where CSOs find that, contrary to the rhetoric about dialogue and partnership, resident missions are often unresponsive to them and are sparing with information about forward plans—hence there is little opportunity in practice for CSOs to help shape those plans.

Unless the UN changes the institutional culture by encouraging openness, rewarding staff efforts to work closely with civil society, and investing resources to make this possible, progress will be slow. This will be disappointing to NGOs and others in civil society for whom the UN is a vitally important organization, but it will also be damaging to the UN itself. It will find that its ability to negotiate international agreements that have traction will diminish unless it can foster growing public demand for such treaties and high public respect for the UN's role in nurturing them. This requires good relations with leading actors in civil society, the media, and political life.

The imperative to work in new ways has been well demonstrated by the International Campaign to Ban Landmines. As evidence mounted about the terrible human cost of antipersonnel mines and other devices, various efforts were made through UN channels to promote a ban on their use in the 1970s and 1980s. These failed to bear fruit because a number of powerful governments resisted them. Hence in 1992 an informal coalition began to form of NGOs, religious groups, academics, and others—backed by a growing body of supportive governments, particularly Canada. The latter convened two exceptional conferences that led to the adoption of a treaty banning landmines in 1996. This treaty has now been ratified by 143 governments (as of October 2004). Although this remarkable campaign deservedly won the Nobel Peace Prize in 1997, it has not yet secured the prize it truly seeks—the universal ban. The United States still refuses to sign the treaty, as do China, Russia, India, and others. However, what is pertinent to our present discussion is that the breakthrough came as a result of an ad hoc global policy network of NGOs and governments (not conventional UN channels) that took the issue outside UN forums, and only brought it back to the UN once sufficient support for the treaty had been achieved. For the UN to be fully relevant in the future, it must become able to service such iterative and informal processes directly. (See Chapter 20.6.)

This way of working is not entirely new for the UN. Indeed, it has been a characteristic of the "big conferences" tackling major global issues in the last twelve years. These helped shape an emerging set of cosmopolitan political rules and norms transcending national sovereignty—especially in areas of human rights, gender relations, and the environment. Although some governments resist these trends, the UN has recognized that constructive and strategic engagement with civil society is a vital weapon for facing its main challenges today. A UN that is more attuned to global public opinion, that is strongly connected with leading CSOs, and that can broker dialogue with all relevant stakeholders is better able to succeed in those challenges and strengthen global governance. In short, there is a symbiosis: civil society is strengthened by opportunities the UN offers, but this gives a new raison d'être that in turn empowers the UN and enhances its relevance.

A vital aspect of this development is to strengthen civil society's involvement in deliberative processes at the country level, not just in headquarters. This demands a cultural shift throughout the UN group of agencies to see local CSOs as vital to policymaking, not just as potential operational partners. The UN's regional commissions have a pivotal role in making this happen by orchestrating regional deliberative processes and acting as an intermediary between the specialized agencies and the UN's global policy process. The experience of the UN Economic Commission for Europe in engaging civil society in the Aarhus Convention (on "Access to Information, Public Participation in Decision-Making and Access to Justice in Environmental Matters") is an interesting example to learn from. The regional commissions could also help encourage uniformly high standards of civil-society engagement and could help facilitate CSO applications for UN accreditation from developing countries.

Tackling Conflict

In no other field is engagement with civil society more vital than in the field of conflict and security. The characteristics of the issues addressed by the UN Security Council today are radically different from those of earlier decades. Conflicts tend to be intrastate, rather than between states; they involve developing countries, rather than rich ones (with some notable exceptions); 75 percent of casualties are civilians, whereas in the UN's early days 90 percent of casualties were combatants; their origins often lie in ethnic or sectarian divides, rather than national politics; and the Security Council increasingly focuses on threats other than armed conflicts, including global public health threats. Furthermore, the global public is much better informed and less tolerant of collateral human suffering.

Whereas "old" conflicts were well understood by diplomats and specialists in political science, this new agenda requires much more on-the-ground knowledge, new skills of social and cultural analysis, the active involvement of communities and their leaders, links to vulnerable groups, bridges into mainstream development processes, and new ways of working. Humanitarian NGOs and other categories of civil society often have strong (sometimes unique) insights into these new needs. Hence the Security Council has become increasingly receptive to information and analysis from civil society—through informal meetings (particularly through the so-called Arria formula meetings between the Security Council and invited experts on the topic at hand).

Although this engagement—as well as dialogue between NGOs and member states in their capitals—is important, very few from conflict-affected countries get a chance to brief the Security Council on their experience and concerns. There are sometimes council field missions that may meet with local NGOs, but this practice is still very rare.

How the United Nations Can Enhance
Its Relations with Stakeholders

The present UN secretary-general, Kofi Annan, is well aware of these challenges and has identified enhancing relations with civil society and others as one of his main reform goals. His early efforts in this regard, however, revealed the many political difficulties. To give guidance on this path, he commissioned a Panel of Eminent Persons on Civil Society and UN Relationships—chaired by Fernando Henrique Cardoso, the former president of Brazil, and comprising twelve distinguished people from diverse geographic and sector backgrounds. What follows is a summary of the panel's main proposals, contained in its report (Cardoso Panel 2004).

The so-called Cardoso Panel's starting observation was that today's multilateralism is different from that of thirty years ago, when governments would come together to debate an emerging issue and build sufficient consensus for a treaty that international organizations would be responsible for implementing. Today, it is increasingly likely that a civil-society movement and crescendo of public opinion puts a new issue on the global agenda; next, some likeminded governments take up the cause and start pressing for global action; together with the civil-society protagonists, they form an ad hoc coalition on the issue that builds public and political support for global action through iterative processes of public debate, policy dialogue, and perhaps pioneering action to demonstrate how the issue can be tackled. Such global policy networks have shaped responses to issues as diverse as landmines, poor-country debt, climate change, affordable treatment for AIDS, and gender relations. These networks generate a set of cosmopolitan values and norms that transcend national boundaries and spawn operational partnerships for tackling the issues. Hence—like it or not—civil society is as much part of global governance today as governments are. To adapt to this new multilateralism, the UN must continue evolving from a rather inward-looking institution to an outward-looking, networking organization.

Governments should not see this as threatening. They and CSOs play different roles; one is no substitute for the other. Civil society is an arena for policy debate, not decisionmaking. Yes, it greatly influences governments—where governments truly embrace democracy and civil society has full rights (the three freedoms—of expression, assembly, and association). It furthermore successfully advances citizens' concerns so long as the media are free and objective. CSOs, however, focus on specific causes, not overall political programs; this is both their strength and weakness. Aggregated, civil society presents a huge array of diverse interests, not an alternative governing blueprint. We still need state and local governments to balance the competing demands and construct an overall policy framework.

This analysis led the panel to suggest that the UN should be guided in its reforms in this area by the four key imperatives or paradigm shifts that follow.

Reinterpret Multilateralism to Mean Multiconstituencies

The way multilateral agendas are shaped has changed—with civil society bringing new issues to the global agenda and governments taking effective actions not by consensus but through multiconstituency coalitions of governments, civil society, and other groups. Increasingly iterative processes of public debate, policy dialogue, and pioneering action are the way to redress problems. The UN should explicitly adopt this important mode of multilateralism, and use its convening power to create multiconstituency forums, open formal

UN forums to all actors necessary to solve critical issues, and regularize the use of a range of participatory modes such as public hearings.

Realize the Full Power of Partnerships

Multistakeholder partnerships have emerged as powerful ways of getting things done and closing the implementation gap by pooling the complementary capacities of diverse actors. Achieving the Millennium Development Goals (MDGs) and other global targets demands a UN that is proactive and strategic in catalyzing new partnerships, incubating emerging ones, and investing in developing necessary staff skills and resources.

Link the Local with the Global

The deliberative and operational spheres of the UN are separated by a wide gulf, hampering both in all areas from development to security. A closer connection between them is imperative so that local operational work contributes to the global goals and global deliberations are informed by local reality. The UN needs to give priority to enhancing its relationship with civil society at the country level. On the development side this implies prioritizing relations in field offices. On the security side, it means strengthening informal engagement of the Security Council with civil society.

Help Tackle Democracy Deficits and Strengthen Global Governance

The new configurations of the twenty-first-century political landscape, described above, pose critical challenges for traditional mechanisms of global governance. They demand changes in the UN not just by engaging civil society in policy-making at all levels, but also by enhancing the role of parliamentarians and local authorities in the deliberative process on pressing global issues.

The box on the following page gives a summary of some of the Cordosa Panel's specific proposals. The full report is available on the panel's website: http://www.un.org/reform/panel.htm.

Strengthening the UN's Response to Conflict

The Cardoso Panel urged deepening of the links the Security Council has made in recent years with CSOs. This could be even more important for smaller (nonpermanent) council members, who mostly have few specialist advisors. The object should be to systematize relations and extend them beyond the New York–based CSOs and large international humanitarian NGOs with New York offices, in particular to include more voices from communities who directly experience the security issues focused on by the council. This requires better planning of meetings with CSOs, providing longer lead time and providing travel assistance for field-based participants (identified in consultation with the main humanitarian and human rights NGOs and the UN Secretariat). The panel further urged that the council more regularly use field missions and ensure that these engage with civil society—perhaps sometimes including a civil-society leader in the mission to help interpret the communities' perception of the issues to council members.

Key Proposals of the Panel of Eminent Persons on Civil Society and UN Relationships

Shift from a "fixed slate" approach. The United Nations (UN) has tended, through its emphasis on admitting to its deliberative processes primarily those nongovernmental organizations (NGOs) who have been accredited by an intergovernmental committee, to prioritize engagement with a fixed set of NGOs on all issues. Instead it should engage with actors most relevant to the issue at hand (be they NGOs, private-sector organizations, local authorities, or others). The responsible stakeholder networks focusing on those issues, rather than intergovernmental committees, should determine who speaks and who attends.

Establish a new "civil society and partnership tsar." A new high-level bureau should be established in the Secretary-General's Office to help create critical mass for enhanced engagement. This would steer the UN's relations with civil society, parliamentarians, local authorities, the private sector, and others—making sure there are appropriate balances between these sectors. It would also catalyze institutional culture changes toward an outward-looking organization.

Open the General Assembly (GA) and its committees and special sessions to civil society. At present, accredited NGOs only have formal rights to engage with the UN Economic and Social Committee (ECOSOC). This restriction is historic and no longer defensible. The GA is the overarching UN forum and hence should also be enriched through carefully structured inputs from civil-society organizations (CSOs) and others.

Reform and depoliticize the accreditation processes. Some accreditation process will still be needed, but this should be reformed to: (1) allow entry to the GA as well as ECOSOC, (2) emphasize the technical merits of those applying, rather than political factors, and (3) become swifter and more transparent. The panel-proposed mechanism hinges on a review of applications by a secretariat body (not as at present by a special intergovernmental committee), drawing on the experience of staff throughout the UN system who work most closely with CSOs. Recommendations on accreditation would then be presented in a consolidated report for intergovernmental approval, but specific applications would only be discussed at this level when deemed problematic. This process should be taken up in an existing committee of the GA (probably the General Committee) so that accreditation is not overemphasized and that it is considered alongside other organizational issues.

Enhance the UN Security Council's links with civil society. It should expand the growing practice of holding informal consultations with CSOs but should broaden this to include CSOs from the affected countries—not just those based in New York. The practice of Security Council field missions should be expanded, and these should always include meetings with civil-society organizations. Commissions of enquiry after council-mandated operations should also become the norm, ensuring opportunities for civil society to contribute to these.

(continues)

Key Proposals of the Panel of Eminent Persons on Civil Society and UN Relationships (continued)

Strengthen links with parliamentarians. The UN should convene "global public policy committees" on the most pressing issues to provide a link between standing committees relevant to those issues in a wide range of state governments. As with their national-level counterparts, these would take evidence from a range of experts, forward policy proposals, and scrutinize progress on past agreements.

Revive multiconstituency forums. Governments have decided that the "big conference" has been an overused tool. Perhaps—but it should not be completely abandoned. Used sparingly, it can help foster global norms on emerging policy issues. Smaller, more politically predictable events—public hearings—can also be staged to bring all relevant stakeholders together for reviewing progress on meeting globally agreed goals, especially the Millennium Development Goals.

Focus at the country-level. The UN should appoint civil-society and partnership specialists at the country level to help UN offices in the country strengthen their engagement.

Establish a fund to enhance Southern civil-society engagement with the UN and to promote innovations in partnerships. At present, Northern CSOs dominate processes of engagement with the UN. While many do a good job in representing Southern CSOs, the latter generally want the chance to engage directly. Also at present, while examples of partnerships abound, these are often little more than implementation contracts. Experience shows that more holistic approaches can add much greater value and should be developed fully. To address these challenges requires new sources of "venture funding," for which a special donor-financed trust fund should be set up.

Note: For more information see http://www.un.org/reform/panel.htm.

The panel also suggested experimental Security Council seminars on complex upcoming issues. These would be open to all UN ambassadors, and would receive evidence from expert witnesses (such as special rapporteurs and academics). It also suggested that the Security Council and the secretary-general initiate independent commissions of inquiry after major UN operations under council mandates (such as the Kosovo Commission). These would both include and take evidence from civil-society leaders.

The Path Ahead

The report of the panel was issued in June 2004. Although most responses from civil society have been positive, others (particularly some of the New York lobbyists) have voiced concerns.[1] In September 2004 the UN secretary-general issued a response to the panel's report (UN Secretary-General 2004) in which he urged member states to adopt many of the panel's proposals, including strengthening the dialogue of the Security Council with civil society, and announced a number of measures that he had decided to take, as chief executive, to implement the panel's proposals. These steps included establishing a trust fund to enhance the capacity of CSOs in developing countries to engage more systematically with the UN; identifying a civil-society focal point person in resident missions to coordinate the UN system's work and dialogue with civil society at the country level, guided by country-level UN–civil society advisory groups; and opening a partnership office in his cabinet to provide institutional leadership in strengthening relations with the full cast of actors important to the UN beyond its formal membership—especially civil society, the private sector, parliamentarians, and local authorities.

The panel's report and Kofi Annan's response were submitted to the General Assembly. As of late 2004, there had been a preliminary GA debate (4–5 October 2004), but no conclusion on those proposals that require member state approval.

Undoubtedly, the coming years will see a growing role for civil society, the private sector, parliamentarians, and local authorities in the UN and other forums of global governance. However, this will not be without controversy. Many in civil society resent the growing clout of large corporations—especially as hard-pressed international organizations increasingly seek funding and operational links with major companies. Similarly, central governments tend to resist the shifting power toward local authorities. Furthermore, as matters of foreign policy come to dominate politics, parliamentarians resent their relatively weak voice in international forums.

The main tension, however, will concern the role of CSOs. As Jody Williams said of the sector, when accepting the Nobel Peace Prize on behalf of the International Campaign to Ban Landmines: "We are a superpower!" It is true. Even the most powerful governments find that CSO pressure forces them to be more accountable and often to moderate their policies, and corporate chief executive officers are routinely challenged to demonstrate "corporate social responsibility."

Superpowers, however, are inevitably resented. The clear ascendancy of policy-oriented CSOs has led to increasingly aggressive challenges from governments, corporations, the establishment media, and others. Questions are increasingly asked about who elects the CSOs. To whom are they accountable? How can they prove they speak with authenticity for particular constituencies or on specific issues? What is their level of integrity? Such concerns are certainly surfacing in the debate now under way about the implementation of the panel's proposals.

John Clark was staff director for the Panel of Eminent Persons on UN–Civil Society Relations. He now works in the East Asia Region of the World Bank, where he formerly headed the NGO/Civil Society Unit. The views expressed in this chapter are purely his, and are not to be ascribed to the World Bank or the UN.

Note

1. Concerns relate to issues such as: (1) the proposed shift of NGO accreditation from a special purpose committee of the ECOSOC to the General Committee of the General Assembly could lead to greater control of NGOs by member states. The panel proposed this for precisely the opposite reason. A similar approach works well for accreditation to "big conferences." Furthermore, if, as the panel suggested, civil society is granted access to the General Assembly—the principal organ of the UN—not just to ECOSOC, an accreditation process would need to facilitate this; and (2) the proposed bureau in the Office of the Secretary-General for guiding the UN's relations with all actors beyond member states might enhance the access of the private sector and might contaminate UN-CSO relations. This is an outdated concern. Links with the private sector cannot be ignored today (although they must be entered with caution). The panel stressed, however, that such engagement must not be at the expense of its links with CSOs, and does not bestow special access privileges on commercial firms. Hence it suggested that a single office having oversight of the UN's relations with the whole constellation of potential partners and interlocutors could ensure that all external relations fit an overall strategy, dictated by the needs of the organization and its mission.

Selected Bibliography

Amnesty International: http://www.amnesty.org.

Cardoso Panel. 2004. *We the Peoples: Civil Society, the United Nations and Global Governance.* Panel of Eminent Persons on UN–Civil Society Relations, UN General Assembly, A/58/817, 11 June.

Cardoso Panel: http://www.un.org/reform/panel.htm.

Clark, John. 2003. *Worlds Apart: Civil Society and the Battle for Ethical Globalization* (Bloomfield, CT: Kumarian Press; London: Earthscan).

Conference of NGOs in Consultative Relationship with the UN: http://www.ngocongo.org.

Gaventa, J., et al. 2002. "Making Rights Real: Exploring Citizenship Participation and Accountability." *IDS Bulletin* 33, no. 2 (April).

Held, D. 2000. "The Changing Contours of Political Community," in B. Holden, ed., *Global Democracy: Key Debates* (London: Routledge).

Hertz, N. 2001. *The Silent Takeover: Global Capitalism and the Death of Democracy* (London: William Heinemann).

Kaldor, M. "Civilizing Globalization: The Implications of the 'Battle in Seattle'." *Millennium* 29 (January).

Nelson, J. 1996. *Business as Partners in Development: Creating Wealth for Countries, Companies, and Communities* (London: Prince of Wales Business Leaders' Forum).

Nelson, P. 1995. *The World Bank and Nongovernmental Organizations: The Limits of Apolitical Development* (Basingstoke, England: Macmillan).

Oxfam International: http://www.oxfam.org.

Stakeholder Forum: http://www.stakeholderforum.org.

UN Department of Economic and Social Affairs: NGO Section: http://www.un.org/esa/coordination/ngo.

UN Department of Public Information: http://www.un.org/dpi/ngosection.

UN Non-Governmental Liaison Service: http://www.un-ngls.org.

UN Secretary-General. 2004. Response to the Cardoso Panel Report, September. Online at: http://ods-dds-ny.un.org/doc/UNDOC/GEN/N04/507/26/PDF/N0450726.pdf?OpenElement.

World Federalist Movement: http://www.wfm.org.

World Federation of United Nations Associations: http://www.wfuna.org.

5

The War on Terror:
Effects on Civil-Society Actors in the Field of
Conflict Prevention and Peacebuilding

Kevin P. Clements

The "war on terror" and the way in which it is manifesting itself nationally, regionally, and globally is having adverse and deleterious effects on the capacity of civil-society organizations all around the world to work with and across a range of political movements (both legitimate and illegitimate) in order to prevent violent conflict and to develop institutional mechanisms that make the resort to terrorist violence less likely. It is important, however, that the field of conflict prevention and peacebuilding maintains its commitment to a radical humanism and human security is given priority over state security so that no one is dehumanized and demonized on grounds of race, religion, or political ideology.

It was President George W. Bush who—after 11 September 2001—declared that he would "direct every resource at our command, every means of diplomacy, every tool of intelligence, every instrument of law enforcement, every financial influence, and every necessary weapon of war to the disruption and to the defeat of the global terror network" (Luck 2003: 163). In other words, terrorism moved right to the top of the U.S. foreign and defense policy agendas and was framed as the "threat to American and world peace." It was analyzed and interpreted primarily as a military and security issue rather than a criminal problem.

The UN Security Council, on 12 September 2001 in Resolution 1368 and again in Resolution 1373, recognized "the inherent right of individual and collective self-defense" as a legitimate response to terrorism. Resolution 1373 was a Charter VII resolution that applied to the whole UN membership and required extremely tough criminal, financial, and administrative measures aimed at individuals and entities supportive of, or involved in, terrorism.

This resolution and the proclaimed right to self-defense against terror have resulted in the collapse and conflation of many diverse and different terrorist movements into a single "global terror network" and a rapid expansion of state security institutions—especially intelligence and military institutions.

71

These institutions have generated a difficult environment for a range of humanitarian, human rights, and conflict resolution civil-society organizations (CSOs) around the world.

In recognition of this difficult environment, Resolution 1373 was balanced by Security Council Resolution 1456 of 20 January 2003, which instructed member states to ensure "that any measure taken to combat terrorism comply with their obligations under international law . . . In particular international human rights, refugee, and humanitarian law." According to the Human Rights Watch's briefing paper of 10 August 2004, the United States and the UN Counter Terrorism Executive Directorate have been more interested in the enhancement of national capacity to counteract terrorism than they have been in ensuring that states are in compliance with international humanitarian and human rights law (Human Rights Watch 2004). This has resulted in the application of national counterterrorist laws that have been used against many legitimate democratic and civil-society actors.

In Egypt, for example, the government asked the UN to accept a definition of terrorism that was so broad it makes almost any critic of the government susceptible to political repression (Human Rights Watch 2004: 8). This was also the case in Uzbekistan, where individuals can be arrested for preparing and distributing material containing "treats to public security and public order" or the creation, direction, or participation in religious extremism, separatism, fundamentalism, or other banned organizations (Human Rights Watch 2004: 9).

The Internal Security Act of Malaysia is another piece of legislation that creates a political chill over the activities of many legitimate organizations and makes open and transparent conflict resolution problematic. This piece of legislation has been used for many years to imprison a wide variety of governmental critics. The Internal Security Act can be used to "detain persons with a view to preventing them from acting in any manner prejudicial to Malaysia's national security, maintenance of essential services, or the economic life of Malaysia, or as a preventive measure" (Human Rights Watch 2004: 10).

These particular measures are only the most remarkable. The so-called right to self-defense against terrorism, for example, has also been used by Russia to justify military actions against Chechens and by the United Kingdom to detain suspects without trial (although the Law Lords in the British House of Lords are now raising questions about the legitimacy and acceptability of the UK's counterterrorist legislation in terms of basic conceptions of human rights and civil liberty). China, similarly, has used the right to self-defense to justify coercive action against Muslims in Xinxiang; the Philippine government has employed it against separatist movements in Mindanao and the Nepalese government against the Maoist insurgency in Nepal. Other states have invoked UN Resolution 1373 to justify and heighten internal surveillance and in many instances illegal mistreatment of "aliens." Conflicts that in other circumstances might have been viewed as "normal politics" or legitimate acts of self-determination or resistance against arbitrary and dictatorial rule have also fallen under the terrorist rubric.

Conceptions of Terror

Before evaluating exactly how the war on terror is having such negative effects, it is worthwhile to ask the question of how to define a terrorist. There are high levels of subjectivity in the definition of who is a terrorist or what is a terrorist act. Many of the attempts to define this term have been made in the context of groups that specific governments consider politically threatening, rather than in terms of clearly defined or specific terrorist acts. The United Nations, for example, has been unable to develop a satisfactory definition of terrorism even though it has been trying to do so for the last seven years. However, the panel's report on "Threats, Challenges and Change" describes the elements that a definition of terrorism should include, which is a step toward just such a definition (UN General Assembly 2004).

Some Definitions of Terrorism

The Oxford English Dictionary defines a terrorist as:
"Anyone who attempts to further his views by a system of coercive intimidation" as "a member of a clandestine or expatriate organization aiming to coerce an established government by acts of violence against it or its subjects."

The U.S. Federal Bureau of Investigation regards terrorism as:
"The unlawful use of force or violence against persons or property to intimidate or coerce a government, the civilian population, or any segment thereof, in furtherance of political or social objectives" (Barnaby 2001: 12).

Paul Wilkinson, in his 1986 book on the subject, says:
"What distinguishes terrorism from other forms of violence is the deliberate and systematic use of coercive intimidation" (Wilkinson 1986: 26).

The British government, in its attempt to define terrorism officially in the British Terrorism Act of 2000, defines terrorism as:
"The use or threat of action where the use or threat is designed to influence the government or to intimidate the public or a section of the public, and the use or threat is made for the purpose of advancing a political, religious, or ideological cause. Action falls within the Act if it involves serious violence against a person, involves serious damage to property, endangers a person's life other than that of the person committing the action, creates a serious risk to the health or safety of the public or a section of the public, or is designed seriously to interfere with or seriously to disrupt an electronic system" (Stationary Office, 2000: 3).

Rich Rubenstein defines terrorism as follows:
"Terrorism is violence by small groups claiming to represent massive constituencies and seeking by 'heroic' provocative attacks to awaken the masses, redeem their honor, and generate an enemy over reaction that will intensify and expand the struggle" (Rubenstein n.d.: 1).

(continues)

Some Definitions of Terrorism (continued)

As *Ambassador Philip C. Wilcox* put it:

"This problem of a definition masks a deeper problem of the need to resolve the grave conflicts that give rise to terrorism. We need an international consensus on definition in order to isolate and eliminate all sympathy and support for terrorism but we can't reach this definition unless we work harder to deal with the underlying conflicts. Let's face reality. So as long as there are weak, oppressed, and aggrieved people and groups who can find no redress, there will be terrorism, and what for one man is a terrorist, will continue to be another's freedom fighter. Of course, there will always be terrorists whose causes have no merit and who must be defeated. I do not recommend, however, that we give up trying to win a consensus that terrorism is an unacceptable political weapon under any circumstances. In the search for a more peaceful, humane, and civilized world, we need to keep trying to absolutely de-legitimize terrorism in favor of more civilized forms of political action" (Wilcox 2002: 2).

Irrespective of what definition is employed, it is clear that terrorist threats and acts do have a capacity to induce fear within communities and states. It is important, however, to focus attention on issues of their probability and lethality as well if we are to develop a realistic assessment of the dangers posed by terrorist activity. One of the interesting consequences of the international response to the Asian tsunami has been a recognition of the greater real dangers posed by natural disaster rather than terrorist threat. It is also important that we do not just accept Western definitions of terror. Individuals in a variety of non-Western states have quite different concepts of terrorism.

There is, for example, the daily existential terror faced by those without food, shelter, or basic security. Then there is the unpredictable terror generated by those who feel powerless and marginalized and who utilize violent tactics against more powerful entities as tools in asymmetric warfare. This is an example of bottom-up terrorism.

There is pathological terror inflicted to gratify the sadistic or psychopathic inclinations of some severely disturbed individuals. Then there is the terror inflicted by state systems on their own citizens or the citizens of other countries. When citizens fear arbitrary arrest, torture, imprisonment, and death, they are experiencing top-down terrorism. Powerful military machines also generate terror when they inflict suffering on innocent civilians in pursuit of military objectives. Each one of these conceptions of terror will generate its own distinctive politics as individuals seek to avoid and or challenge what they perceive to be the sources of their own terror.

Good Versus Evil

The words "terror" and "terrorism" assumed popular currency during the French Revolution. In this context, terrorism referred to state-sponsored top-down efforts to rule and govern through terror. It is important to remember this original historic understanding of terrorism—as noted above, states can and do terrorize their own citizens and those of other nations when it suits them to do so. If, as many argue, terrorism is the deliberate targeting of civilian populations for political or ideological purposes, then it is clear that states are as likely to engage in terrorist acts as much as nonstate actors.

Individuals and political movements that cannot realize their political objectives through nonviolent political means will always have violence as an option. The challenge facing the world community and CSOs interested in nonviolent problem solving, therefore, is how to:

- Discourage disaffected groups from embracing terrorism, or
- Deny them the means for pursuing such action, and
- Stimulate collaborative activities that negate the impact of terrorist activity and ensure the arrest, trial, and imprisonment of the perpetrators of terrorist acts.

A broader question has to do with whether the language currently used in the war on terror generates communications that encourage it. Somewhat paradoxically, for example, using military language in response to terrorism tends to disempower civil-society actors from assuming responsibility for delegitimizing terror and terrorist tactics. Indeed, militarized language and military responses to terrorist activities will tend to perpetuate militarized and violent resistance with higher levels of violence and terror.

The war on terror—despite being a contradiction in itself because you cannot fight an abstract noun—rests on a division of the world into good and evil, civilized and barbarian, terrorist and counterterrorist. This divisive discourse generates real problems for those CSOs who are much more interested in highlighting connections rather than divisions, bridges rather than fault lines, and inclusive rather than exclusive concepts of community.

The End of Soft Power

From the end of the Cold War until 2001, the world community (as reflected in a wide variety of regional and global institutions) focused considerable attention and energy on "soft power" (Nye 2004: 4–5); on the consolidation of relationships between peoples as well as states; on the development of human as opposed to national security; on collaborative problem solving rather than adversarial competition; and on the expansion of international legal and institutional regimes.

One of the most negative consequences of 9/11 and the enunciation of a never-ending war against terror has been a renewed emphasis on state security;

on the assertion and application of power and a strengthening of military capacity; on unilateralism and national exceptionalism as opposed to multilateralism; and an inclination to focus on the politics of fear rather than the politics of trust. This environment makes it more difficult to reassert the central importance of resilient civil-society and state systems. It also makes nonviolent humanitarian engagement—before, during, and after violent conflict—more difficult.

Civil-society actors, faced by the prospect of the United States and its allies waging a never-ending, unwinnable war against terror, have to counter some extremely powerful dynamics in order to focus attention on nonmilitarized ways of dealing with terrorist acts. Much of the national legislation dealing with terror has resulted in a draconian tightening of immigration laws and procedures, increased use of surveillance mechanisms, infringements of privacy, challenges to civil liberties and the rule of law, and a deepened division of the world into "them" and "us." The fact that most of these measures are not having a particularly positive impact on the incidence of terrorist activity is further cause for concern.

The Effects of the War on Terrorism

Just what is the grand plan? Is there any evidence that the declaration of a never-ending war against terrorism and specific wars aimed at regime change

---

Terrorism's Impact on U.S. Civil Society

After 11 September 2001, the U.S. government created the Patriot Act to bolster its security. The Patriot Act allows for greater surveillance of civilians and civil-society groups, and prevents U.S. citizens from interacting with individuals and groups identified by its government as "terrorists." The Patriot Act has negatively affected the ability of U.S. civil society to mediate or facilitate dialogues between armed groups around the world. Those working in Nepal, Sri Lanka, or the Philippines, for example, can no longer communicate legally with many of the armed rebel groups in their regions because they have been identified as terrorists, and there is no distinction between those the U.S. is fighting, such as Al Qaeda, and those who may be fighting a repressive government in their home country. Civil-society groups also face tight new restrictions in how they receive donations and spend their money, as the Patriot Act aims to ensure that terrorist efforts are not supported through donations to civil-society groups. Some civil-society actors face personal hardships under the Patriot Act because it allows for high levels of surveillance, long detainments without charges or legal assistance, and other sanctions on civil-society actors such as being listed on "no fly" lists that prevent individuals from traveling by air.

Note: By Lisa Schirch, associate professor of peacebuilding at Eastern Mennonite University's Masters in Conflict Transformation Program: The United States.

in Afghanistan and Iraq are having their intended positive effects, or are they an overreaction to terrorist threat and generating more malign than benign consequences? In particular, what have been its impacts on CSOs committed to peace and justice?

Many people feel that the war in Iraq has diverted resources that might have been directed to dealing with the root causes of terrorism and its specific manifestations. It has certainly done huge reputational damage to the United States and its closest allies in Europe and in the Middle East. The war on terrorism and the war in Iraq have also generated a major transatlantic rift (Benjamin et al., 2004).

Second, the U.S. decision to invade Iraq has resulted in a very significant battering of the United Nations as the legitimate global agency for managing global threats to peace.

Third, the Security Council's resolution on the right to self-defense has resulted in a wide variety of different countries using the war on terrorism as a means of centralizing power and dramatically challenging the legitimate civil and political rights of individuals, groups, and social movements. Thus 9/11 has had far-reaching effects both on national and international politics. Most of these effects have not been beneficial for constitutional democracy or world order.

Despite the manifest failure of military solutions in Iraq and Afghanistan to deliver stability and security, political leadership in the West (especially within the United States, Australia, and the UK) remains committed to the privileging of their state security institutions (departments of defense, the military, and intelligence agencies) as the primary and leading response to terrorist and other threats to security. There has been a very deliberate discounting of civil society and civilian police views in favor of official military and security perspectives (Chomsky 2003: 6–8).

Fourth, articulating differing levels of terrorist threat (especially in the United States) has resulted in a fearful public expressing a willingness to cede some personal liberty in return for an executive promise of security. The re-election victory of President George W. Bush is testimony to the power of the politics of fear.

This stress on state security has been bolstered and reinforced by a compliant media, extensive and well-targeted governmental information campaigns, and the specific privileging of "official" intelligence, executive, and administrative perspectives. When the full power of the state is harnessed behind the promotion of military and coercive orientations to security, it is extremely difficult for more pacific, nonstate citizens' voices to be heard. This inevitably has had a slightly chilling effect on proposals and activities that involve civil-society and nonmilitary political actors. It has certainly resulted in a marginalization of the concept of human security, which addresses both the presenting and underlying problems of terrorist threat with its twin emphases on "freedom from fear" and "freedom from want." The monopolization of security discourse by security specialists and the executive branches of government has also made it difficult for proponents of a "culture of peace" to make much headway against those whose professions have a vested interest in cultures of violence.

Fifth, there have been numerous incidents in recent years where civil-society actors—promoting human rights or unpopular peace initiatives—have been categorized as "oppositional" or worse, "proterrorist." This has led to the arrest and detention of human rights advocates in Liberia, Macedonia, Zimbabwe, Kazakhstan, and elsewhere. It has also resulted in secret arrest warrants in the West, prolonged and clandestine detentions, the illegitimate freezing of bank accounts, the closure of radio stations and newspapers, and widespread intrusions on individual privacy all around the world. In part, such negative activity has resulted from considerable fuzziness about how to define a terrorist, but it also flows from the division of the world into a so-called axis of evil and an axis of the virtuous, with the latter able to do whatever it wishes because of its military superiority and more complex notions of manifest destiny and global political leadership (now somewhat under attack because of an inability to deliver peace, stability, and development to the violent conflict zones of the world).

A Future for Conflict Prevention?

There are some very specific difficulties facing conflict prevention organizations with the advent of the war on terror. Humanitarian groups such as the Quakers, for example, who have delivered both humanitarian assistance, trauma counseling, and nonviolent dialogical processes to Chechens and Russians in Chechnya, have been banned from doing so under draconian antiterror legislation. Russian authorities fear that Quaker efforts to analyze and contextualize the conflict would provide solace to their enemies. Similarly in Indonesia, antiterrorist legislation makes it difficult if not impossible to develop dialogical processes between Jemaah Islamiya and government actors. When the United States or the United Kingdom places specific groups such as the LTTE (Tamil Tigers), Hezbollah, or Hamas on their list of proscribed terror organizations, this effectively prevents conflict prevention groups within these countries from communicating with or engaging these movements in problem-solving processes as well. In the United States, also there is considerable self-censorship on the part of academics and conflict resolution practitioners about what they say and do regarding terrorism and counterterrorism for fear of triggering prosecution under the Patriot Act.

Conflict prevention and peacebuilding organizations, therefore, have to work out ways in which they can continue doing their work without falling afoul of specific pieces of antiterror legislation. If civil-society groups cannot communicate with warring parties, provide safe spaces for difficult discussions, and help individuals and groups frame and reframe their problems in creative ways, the international community loses enormously important insights into ways in which the needs and interests of terrorists or potential terrorists might be satisfied nonviolently.

An East African Perspective

Kenya and Tanzania suffered simultaneous terrorist attacks in August 1998, and Kenya a repeat attack in November 2002. Following the 1998 attacks, the United States attacked Sudan, Kenya's neighbor to the north, accusing it of harboring terrorists. Severally, the "collapsed" state of Somalia has been described as a haven for terrorists. Terrorism, then, in the sense of the indiscriminate use of violence to intimidate or coerce others into a cause, is not far-fetched as far as East Africa is concerned. Nevertheless, the war on terrorism does not excite as much passion in this region as would be expected in countries that have been attacked. If anything, in the case of Kenya, the excitement has been about the way the government was being pushed around to implement "an American agenda," and in particular a proposed antiterrorist legislation.

There is a widespread view that the U.S.-led war on terrorism has largely missed the point on the causes and motivations of terrorism. The few voices that were raised soon after 9/11, to the effect that the world needed to look more closely to the root causes of terrorist acts, were soon silenced. The thesis of this minority voice seems to be that seeking a solution to the Middle East conflict would nip terrorism in the bud. The dominant voice became the one that said that one should never negotiate with terrorists, that they should instead be eliminated. This dominant voice does not accept the view that there may be a connection between terrorism, on the one hand, and the disenchantment of most of the Arab world with how the Palestinian question has been handled, on the other.

It is also noteworthy that terrorism as we know it today did not become real and immediate until after the 9/11 attacks in the United States, three years after the devastating attacks in East Africa.

Another concern has to do with the purposes to which a misplaced war on terrorism could be put. Labels are not innocent. They assign meaning and propose or determine actions and practice. If, for example, the government of Uganda insists that the Lord's Resistance Army (LRA) is a terrorist organization, this then suggests that the only way of dealing with the LRA is to "crush" them. This makes nonsense of the ongoing attempts to resolve the conflict in northern Uganda through dialogue, following the failure of military solutions for the last eighteen years. Second, most of the independent African states were born out of "liberation struggles" led by parties and movements that at one time or another were labeled "terrorist organizations." This is certainly the case in Kenya. For a region with such a history, it is possible that citizens empathize with those accused of terrorism, especially if there appears to be a history of injustices against them.

Note: By George Wachira, director, Nairobi Peace Initiative, Nairobi, Kenya.

Nonterrorist Violence

While the threat may be real, it may also be imagined. For the purposes of terrorist discourse, however, this is immaterial. To challenge such stories, it is important to remind ourselves of other equally compelling narratives. The UN Development Program (UNDP), for example, has some very sobering statistics

A Southeast Asian Perspective

The region of Southeast Asia is as varied as its peoples and cultures. There are numerous ethnic groups in the region, and at least four major religions and beliefs. Its components are Brunei, Indonesia, Malaysia, the Philippines, Singapore, Thailand, Cambodia, Laos, Burma/Myanmar, and Vietnam. With the new nation East Timor being grouped in the region, the SEA region has eleven countries. Yet Southeast Asia is also host to various kinds of conflicts, many of them brutal and longstanding, sometimes still an expression of the colonial past of the countries of the region.

The war on terror, started by the Western governments, has potentially put Southeast Asian countries in the midst of the antiterror fight. The southern Philippines, for example, was mentioned as the second front of the global war on terrorism. This presents a very real source of future conflicts. On the one hand, one of the results has been the targeting of Muslim populations as havens or bases for terrorist cells and trainings. On the other, the war on terror may also be creating cleavage among the neighboring countries, especially between the dominant Muslim states like Indonesia and Malaysia and states where Muslims are the minority like the Philippines.

The United States and Australia want Southeast Asian countries on the side of the coalition of the willing and have an ally in the Philippines. The 12 October 2002 bombings in Bali which killed 202 people and injured 209, most of whom were foreign tourists, is considered the deadliest act of terrorism in Indonesian history and swung Indonesia in favor of stronger anti-terror cooperation. Yet Malaysia is a critic of the war on terror and wants it redefined.

Lastly, the attacks on Muslims encouraged by the Western-led war on terror is also resulting in the rise in the region of Islamic extremist groups and their use of terror tactics. Terror groups, including the Jemaah Islamiyah will find fertile ground among the young Muslims enraged with the Western wars in Afghanistan and Iraq.

Note: By Initiatives for International Dialogue (IDD), Phillipines. For more information, see http://www.idd.org.

on violence, most of which have nothing to do with terrorism. Every day, for example, more than thirty thousand children around the world die of preventable diseases; 2.8 billion of the world's population live on less than US$2 per day, with 1.2 billion of them subsisting on less than $1. An estimated 815 million people are undernourished. Every year there are 300 million cases of malaria. More than five hundred thousand women die each year as a result of pregnancy and childbirth (UNDP 2003). This is the daily existential terror faced by the vast majority of mankind. Against these kinds of statistics, the number of those killed in terrorist activity is relatively modest. In the United States, those killed by gun violence each year far exceeds those killed by terrorists.

It is important, therefore, that civil-society groups working for conflict-sensitive development assistance, humanitarian relief, and long-term conflict prevention join forces with regional and global organizations in reminding everyone of some of the basic conditions that might generate terrorism. For example, why did so many social scientists not spend more time explaining and understanding the unanticipated resurgence of evangelical religiosity in all of the Abrahamic religions? What role do grinding poverty, corrupt and arbitrary governance, and the marginalization and exclusion of different peoples play in terrorist activity? How do state systems generate terror for their citizens by politicians and bureaucrats corruptly expropriating public funds or by utilizing state machinery to generate insecurity rather than security for citizens? How do global economic and political dynamics generate higher levels of impoverishment and inequality for the vast majority of the world's population and what role do these play in the determination of global terror?

These matters are as, if not more, important than dealing with shadowy terrorist networks whose raison d'être is to generate bottom-up fear instead of workable solutions to specific social, economic, and political problems. To do this effectively requires a robust well-funded United Nations that is capable of spearheading regional and global responses to some of these problems. This is not optional. It requires the UN to work out ways in which it can combine the activities of the Security Council, its Counter-Terrorism Committee, as well as the Committee on Human Rights and the Human Rights Commission alongside all the diverse development agencies of the UN who are seeking to drain the economic and political swamps within which terrorists and terrorist grievances thrive.

Critical Years Ahead

For those groups concerned with conflict prevention, justice, and long-term peacebuilding, it is vital that we do not succumb to a struggle with wildness in the name of order. On the contrary, it is important that the field of conflict prevention and peacebuilding maintain its commitment to a radical humanism in which no individual or group is dehumanized and demonized. Also, it is important to underline that no one or no group is assumed to be unreachable or incapable of conversation, and where—given the right conditions—everyone is capable of engaging in positive transactions. In particular, it is important that the world is not divided into good and evil, the saved and unsaved, the blessed and the cursed. The next five to ten years are going to be critical for this humanist enterprise.

It is imperative that those of us concerned with generating realistic responses to deal with ruthless enemies work out ways of identifying and separating the really ruthless from those who have political agendas that are capable of being satisfied with enlightened and well-resourced social and economic development policies. For those who are caught in an orgy of violence, the onus on civil-society actors is not to capitulate all responsibility for dealing with such people to the security actors alone. Strong and robust CSOs require heroic individuals, who are willing to cross boundaries of violence and open up difficult dialogues in an effort to confer respect and humanity on those who are unwilling to do this to others. This is not a task for sissies, but equally it is not a task for the marines either. It is a task for enlightened civil-society actors working in concert with politicians and others in conjunction with regional and global organizations. If this does not happen, the prospects for dealing effectively with terrorist violence using existing methods are close to zero.

Professor Kevin P. Clements is the foundation director of the Australian Centre for Peace and Conflict Studies at the University of Queensland, Brisbane, Australia. This is a postgraduate theory, research, and practice center working to prevent and transform violent conflict in the Asia Pacific region.

Selected Bibliography

Barnaby, Frank. 2001. "The New Terrorism: A 21st Century Biological, Chemical and Nuclear Threat," Oxford Research Group Occasional Paper (Oxford: Oxford Research Group).

Benjamin, D., et al. 2004. *The Transatlantic Dialogue on Terrorism* (Washington, DC: CSIS).

Chomsky, Noam. 2003. *Hegemony or Survival: America's Quest for Global Dominance* (Sydney: Allen and Unwin).

Luck, Edward C. 2003. "The U.S., Counter Terrorism, and the Prospects for a Multilateral Alternative," in Jane Boulden and Thomas Weiss, eds., *Terrorism and the UN: Before and After September 11th* (Bloomington: Indiana University Press).

Human Rights Watch. 2004. "Hear No Evil, See no Evil: The UN Security Council's Approach to Human Rights Violations in the Global Counter-Terrorism Effort." Briefing Paper, 10 August (New York: Human Rights Watch).

Nye, Joseph. 2004. "The Role of Soft Power in the War of Ideas." *Futures Direction International* (July).

Stationery Office. 2000. "Terrorism Act 2001" (London: The Stationery Office).

United Nations Development Program (UNDP). 2003. *Human Development Report 2002* (New York: Oxford University Press).

United Nations General Assembly. 2004. "A More Secure World: Our Shared Responsibility." Report of the High-Level Panel on Threats, Challenges, and Change (A/59/565). Online at: http://www.un.org/secureworld/report.pdf.

Wilkinson, Paul, 1986. *Terrorism and the Liberal State* (London: Macmillan).

Wilcox, Philip C. 2002. "Defining Terrorism: Is One Man's Terrorist Really Another Man's Freedom Fighter?" Paper presented to Conflict Resolution and Prevention Forum, 12 February (Washington, DC: Search for Common Ground).

6

People Building Peace: Key Messages and Essential Findings

Paul van Tongeren, Juliette Verhoeven & Jim Wake

People Building Peace is an optimistic book. It is full of stories of courage, ingenuity, faith, commitment, persistence, and stubbornness of the best sort. The title has not been gratuitously chosen. These stories are indeed about people who are making a difference. That is one of the most important messages to emerge from this book. It may be true that governments, multinational corporations, and financial institutions wield enormous power and take decisions profoundly effecting the lives of ordinary peoples—including decisions about war and peace—but it is nonetheless true that individuals have much to offer to peacebuilding, and individuals working together can often be a powerful force for positive change.

Such individuals, and groups of individuals, can call attention to simmering crises, alert the public and the world to injustice, sway public opinion, and even persuade legislators and policymakers to pursue peace and justice. They can bring together adversaries and bridge chasms thought to be unbridgeable. They can build understanding and help to correct misunderstanding, teach children to celebrate diversity rather than to embrace hatred, and help those children who have been sucked into conflict as victims or as soldiers to build a future colored by hope rather than despair. They can win over hearts and minds to the cause of peace.

That is the optimistic message, but it would be a mistake to presume that just because it can happen, it will. Building peace is very hard work, and it requires more than just courage, commitment, ingenuity, and good intentions. It also requires, just to mention a few considerations, strategies, methodologies, organizational skills, a good message and a capacity for communicating it, and adequate funding to apply to the task at hand. Fortunately, just as the wheel does not need to be reinvented every time a new automobile rolls off the assembly line, conflict resolution does not need to be reinvented with every new initiative. There is much to be learned from the many successes, and even the failures, of those who have taken on the challenge of peacebuilding over the years, around the globe. Peacebuilding is, furthermore, a learning process that is ongoing. In fact, as civil society continues to expand, and more and more people are discovering the possibilities they have to engage in work for positive change, one of the challenges is, increasingly, to keep track of all the good things that are happening so that the knowledge is not lost to future peacebuilders.

Peacebuilding also requires individuals to take the first step. It does not happen on its own. It is easy—and tempting—for individuals who are repulsed by depressing images of war and suffering to presume that someone else will take care of the problem. However, if everyone presumes someone else will do the job, no one does the job. Peace is everyone's responsibility. There are opportunities at every level and in every sector of society for individuals to take the initiative. Every individual has the capacity to make a personal contribution to the building of a nonviolent society. Indeed, where violent conflict is present, resilient and sustainable peace can only be achieved when actors are operating at all levels—multitrack peacebuilding involving governments and principals to the conflict, nongovernmental organizations (NGOs) and intergovernmental organizations and agencies, sometimes engaged with the principals and sometimes engaged in work to address the underlying causes of a conflict, and individuals and organizations within civil society focusing on issues, special interests, and key constituencies. In societies at peace, one of the best guarantees that a society will remain at peace is an active civil society where individuals and organizations address—both explicitly and implicitly—the social conditions that can lead to conflict.

As civil society continues to expand, the opportunities for engagement expand as well. Civil-society organizations (CSOs) committed to peace have possibilities—in some cases for the first time—to create safe spaces where people can come together to work for peace and to build societies based on justice and the rule of law. Civil society now affords opportunities not just for the more "traditional" political activists, but also for people from all sectors of society: artists, teachers, students, young people, businessmen and businesswomen, labor union members, academics, environmentalists, journalists, religious leaders and religious lay people; and, at every level—local, national, regional, and international.

Just as peacebuilding will not take place if individuals do not take action, it will not succeed without the support and encouragement of others in the world community not directly engaged in conflict resolution work. Individuals, local and national governments, religious institutions—from the local to the global—the business community, NGOs, and international organizations, including all of those associated with the United Nations have much to contribute, in assets, knowledge and skills, facilities, equipment, experience, publicity, analysis—and even criticism—and far-reaching networks, to make the work of those trying to build a peaceful future ever more effective. The Global Partnership for the Prevention of Armed Conflict (GPPAC) has recently been launched precisely to enhance the role of civil society in conflict prevention and peacebuilding by strengthening civil-society networks, promoting an agenda based on a culture of prevention, and bringing this agenda to the attention of governments, the international community, and individuals at all levels of civil society.

This chapter highlights some of the most compelling findings that emerged from a review of the more than sixty-five cases profiled in these pages. Some of them are "hard" findings—considerations of tactics, organizational requirements, and skills needed for successful peacebuilding work—while others are "soft"—considerations, for example, of how to nurture an environment where conflict resolution can succeed, how to humanize the "other," and how to build trust between adversaries. These findings are just a selected few among many, a suggestion of the richness of the experiences described in detail in the remainder of the book. Beyond these findings, the stories, taken as a whole, communicate several key messages, which are summarized below.

An Inventory of "Good Guidance"

The findings discussed below cover a broad cross-section of peacebuilding concerns. Some of them are general observations about effective approaches and important considerations to keep in mind during both planning and implementation of conflict resolution activities. Others are more specific tips, notes about strategies and tactics, and observations that will help peacebuilders avoid pitfalls that can undermine a valuable initiative and to enhance their impact. There is no blueprint that guarantees success in this challenging work, but good guidance can certainly help to make the work a little bit easier.

Individuals Can Make a Big Difference

Many of the most impressive interventions described in this book began as the idea of a single individual, moved by the pain caused by conflict, by an urge to see justice done, by personal experience, or just consumed by a powerful idea. Many of the most successful actions are those of individuals unaffiliated with organizations. The influence of individuals, acting alone or in concert, is frequently underestimated. Whether individuals are writing letters to decision-makers, or manifesting themselves collectively in a show of "people power," the impacts have been shown, on many occasions, to be far-reaching.

One man who has shown what is possible through individual initiative is Datu Paglas, a businessman on the island of Mindanao in the Philippines. Born into a prosperous family, Paglas set aside a portion of his own family's land for a banana plantation, persuaded other landowners to contribute their land as well, and spurred outside investments that have created thousands of jobs and helped to bring the Muslim, Christian, and indigenous communities closer together. (See Chapter 13.3.)

Multitrack Approaches to Conflict Resolution
Often Improve the Chances of Success

Conflicts are almost always decided among officials, but frequently conflict resolution can be facilitated through unofficial contacts via unofficial channels. Furthermore, governments acting to end conflict without the support of their

Key Messages from the Book

Peacebuilding from below works. It is not only governments and international organizations that can effectively engage in peacebuilding. This book is testimony to the fact that "peacebuilding from below" can be effective, but this fact is not yet fully recognized or adequately appreciated. It is, therefore, incumbent upon those committed to peacebuilding to convey this message to a wider audience.

Peacebuilding is a learning process. Although, because every conflict situation is different, there is no blueprint to follow, there is much to learn from the broad range of experiences accumulated in conflict prevention and peacebuilding work. Evaluation and documentation of peacebuilding experiences, and communication among peacebuilders, are, accordingly, essential to make certain that the lessons learned are widely available.

Peace is everyone's responsibility. Everyone is capable of building peace. Preventing armed conflict requires a multitrack, inclusive, participatory approach that includes contributions from all sectors of society. Educators, artists, the business community, the religious community, public figures who serve as role models, and private individuals with deep-felt concerns all have both the possibility and the responsibility to act.

Civil-society organizations are creating safe spaces where people from all sectors of society can come together and work in meaningful ways toward a better future. The potential for positive change is enormous, but the opportunities are, to date, underexploited. Civil-society organizations, then, should work to continuously expand this space even further and to mobilize individuals and organizations at all levels of society to engage in the effort to build a global culture of peace.

Those who are engaged in peacebuilding and conflict prevention work should be empowered, encouraged, and supported in their work. Peacebuilding requires resources; those engaged in the work need to master a range of skills, and both policymakers and the general public need to be informed about the range of initiatives and activities focusing on conflict prevention. The Global Partnership for the Prevention of Armed Conflict is providing such support at all levels, with initiatives at the local and regional levels to share knowledge, collect lessons learned, and develop regional action agendas; at the international level, the development and promotion of an global action agenda is focusing on conflict prevention and peacebuilding.

people risk failure. However strong the cry may be from the grassroots for an end to conflict, it is almost always up to governments to take the decision that formally ends conflict. It is clear, then, that peacebuilding stands a better chance when, consciously or by accident, multitrack approaches are used, involving official diplomacy at the state level, as well as unofficial interventions at various levels, and a cross-section of civil-society actors.

Outsiders Can Contribute Significantly to Conflict Resolution, but They Should Be Sensitive to Their Impact on Local Efforts

In general, outsiders can best help local and regional conflict prevention activities by creating spaces for local initiatives, providing financial and material support, and otherwise enabling local players and enhancing their capacities. Their presence can also help to increase the safety of local actors. Outsiders need to be sensitive to the fact that, even with the best of intentions, they can sometimes undermine the efforts of local organizations and actors, and that because they generally have greater resources available to them, they can easily displace even an established local effort. Outsiders should also respect the judgments of local players regarding the social and political dynamics at play. The long-term objective of increased peace and security should never be secondary to any short-term objectives.

In Urabá, a contested area in northwest Colombia, Peace Brigades International (PBI) maintains a small team of "outsiders"—non-Colombian volunteers who serve as unarmed "bodyguards" to local human rights and community workers. Though not without risk, their presence serves as a deterrent to violence on the part of the combatants. Furthermore, by offering a modicum of protection in a conflict zone, PBI also helps to create space for human rights workers and community activists. (See Chapter 15.2.)

Bridging the Divide

Conflict often involves a breakdown in communication, and where adversaries are unable to talk to each other, it is unlikely that they can resolve their differences. Without communication, the "other" is frequently dehumanized, and mistrust and fear prevail. Conflict resolution, then, frequently involves finding ways to restore communication and encourage dialogue. This can occur at all levels from the grassroots on up to heads of state. Sometimes the dialogue simply begins when adversaries are in the same room together, and sometimes there are very explicit efforts to get people from opposite sides to address the substantive issues that divide them. Among the activities described in this book are numerous examples of CSOs taking an active role in these efforts to work across the divide and encourage communication.

For example, in strife-torn Kashmir, a project called Athwaas (meaning "a warm handshake") is breaking through the barriers of mistrust and suspicion by first talking to Muslim, Hindu, and Sikh women about their experiences, and then creating safe spaces called Samanbals where meetings, dialogue, and joint activities can take place that bridge the divide and facilitate reconciliation. (See Chapter 7.1.)

There Is a Need for Those Engaged in Development Work to Adequately Consider the Impact That Their Engagement May Have on the Conflict Situations Within the Societies in Which They Are Active

Development may bring improvements in the lives of some citizens within a society, but the benefits of development are not equally distributed. The result is that new resentments may arise when the social dynamic is altered by the process of development, and that already existing conflicts may be aggravated by the perceptions of favoritism toward one or another party to a conflict. Those involved in development work need to be aware of the conflict-sensitive nature of their engagement, and keep the "do no harm" maxim in mind. Furthermore, development projects are an important forum for building peace, not just improving lives.

The Norwegian Church Aid (NCA) experience in northern Mali represents an interesting example of a development organization that decided, when faced with a level of conflict that made its original mandate of development work impossible, to shift its focus to conflict resolution/management. NCA interpreted its mandate for humanitarian assistance broadly, and subsequently embraced an approach facilitating dialogue and making available venues and safe structures for interactions between conflicting parties. (See Chapter 16.1.)

Training Programs and Workshops Can Provide Opportunities for Participants to Learn Conflict Prevention Skills, Informally Explore Conflict Resolution Theory, and Even, on Occasion, to Develop Concrete Proposals for Resolving Disputes

Conflict prevention is complex, and decidedly not always obvious. Organizing skills, communications skills, fund-raising skills, and networking skills are just some of the many skills required. An understanding of the conflict dynamics and insight into effective conflict resolution strategies are also essential, as are the development of leadership skills and, in many cases, a knowledge and understanding of the principles of nonviolent action. Several of the cases described in this book involve explicit programs to facilitate skills acquisition, making use of workshops and other training programs.

In one case, involving members of civil society from Ecuador and Peru, very real contributions to a conflict resolution process already under way resulted from a series of workshops organized in parallel to the official diplomatic efforts to resolve longstanding border disputes between Ecuador and Peru. These efforts began in 1997 around the theme "Ecuador and Peru: Towards a Democratic and Cooperative Conflict Resolution Initiative." The so-called Grupo Maryland provided indispensable input to the officials who managed in 1998 to negotiate an end to the conflict. (See Chapter 21.5.)

Networking Gives Local Organizations Leverage, Distributes Work Among Like-Minded Groups, and Brings Diversity to Peacebuilding Efforts

Networking brings like-minded individuals and organizations together to pursue a common set of objectives. Because the human and material resources available to those engaged in conflict prevention are inevitably limited, the sum of the parts working together will likely exceed the capabilities of the separate organizations working independently. There are other benefits as well— greater diversity within the network means a range of perspectives and experiences to bring to both the analysis of the tasks at hand and the actions taken, greater credibility by virtue of a broader base of support, and the engagement of players at different levels of society, with expanded access to government, international organizations, and across the various layers of civil society.

A noteworthy example of a successful networking initiative is the Nansen Dialogue Network, which is composed of nine multiethnic dialogue centers spread across Bosnia-Herzegovina, Croatia, Serbia, Montenegro, Kosovo, and Macedonia. The network is working to encourage multiethnic dialogue and to provide "space" where it is possible to establish contact and build relationships across ethnic divides among political leaders, young politicians, journalists, academics, educators, government officials, and activists within the NGO community. (See Chapter 19.1.)

A Declaration of Commitment Issued by Respected Leaders Can Be a Powerful Instrument

When leaders unite behind a cause, the people will often follow. Furthermore, when leaders from across a divide declare their commitment to put their differences behind them or to seek peaceful ways to resolve them, and when they clearly and unequivocally condemn violence, their statements can have a profound influence on the dynamics of a conflict.

In northern Nigeria, where violence between Christians and Muslims has claimed thousands of lives, twenty senior leaders from the Muslim and Christian communities have tried to promote a more peaceful climate by issuing the "Kaduna Peace Declaration." Speaking with the moral authority of their positions as religious leaders, they condemned violence, encouraged mutual respect and trust, and pledged themselves to work for peace. (See Chapter 10.2.)

Creating Safe Spaces for Self-Expression and Reconciliation Enhance the Possibilities for Dialogue and the Building of Trust in Situations Where Fear and Mistrust Prevail

Where there is no contact between members of opposing communities, there is no possibility of reconciliation. Initiatives that carve out a space where people can meet each other and talk about their lives, their needs, their expectations, and their experiences help to break down the barriers of fear and mistrust.

In 2000, Christians and Muslims who were engaged in murderous communal violence in Maluku, Indonesia, showed no desire to end the fighting, but peace activist Ichsan Malik remained convinced that he could get the two sides to talk to each other. Baku Bae, the grassroots movement that Malik founded, initially organized meetings away from the scene of the fighting, where it felt safer to engage in dialogue, and later in "neutral zones" between the Muslim and Christian communities. (See Chapter 23.4.)

Early Warning Systems Allow for Timely Intervention

Most conflicts are preceded by all manner of developments that serve as warning signs of future trouble. Since conflict prevention is invariably preferable to conflict resolution, early warning systems to monitor potential conflict situations can be established. Such systems trigger alerts when events threaten to spin out of control.

Among several examples described in this book is one involving the National Council of Churches of Kenya (NCCK), which has established an early warning system to sound the alarm when information comes to the attention of NCCK personnel about the threat of a cattle raid—an occurrence that can frequently escalate into intercommunal violence. With a system in place, it has been possible to detect impending raids and other threats to peace and to defuse potentially dangerous situations. (See Chapter 17.2.)

Positive Visions and Positive Messages Are Crucial

Where there is violence and conflict, there is often much to criticize, but a steady stream of negative messages quickly loses its impact. Especially in grassroots organizing, where contact with people is essential, it is important to communicate the good as well as the bad, to emphasize positive results, to encourage optimism and enthusiasm, and to embrace positive organizing approaches. Even though the aims of an action may be serious, it is not necessary to always *be* serious. With a positive attitude, it is far easier "to keep hope alive," to quote the Reverend Jesse Jackson. Affirming the value of each individual's contributions to a collective effort is also important.

One woman who embodies this positive approach is Emma Kamara, who established the Children's Learning Services (CLS) in Sierra Leone. CLS is a program to nurture both the bodies and the minds of Sierra Leone's children. The philosophy of CLS is not to look back at the dark days of Sierra Leone's conflict, but instead to take positive action to bring hope and restore the dignity of the nation's children. (See Chapter 11.1.)

Some of the Most Effective Actions Are Also the Simplest

Simple actions often highlight one of the most powerful arguments for peace and justice—the essential dignity of all human beings. Often, these simple actions are also cost-effective. Furthermore, simple actions often demonstrate the importance of individuals to the process of conflict prevention and conflict resolution.

After the traumatic war experiences in Croatia following the breakup of Yugoslavia, the Center for Peace, Non-Violence and Human Rights-Osijek launched the Listening Project in 1999, in order to open a space in the local community for dialogue and communication among its residents. Through "active listening," the Listening Project helped the people of Osijek to better articulate their needs and problems and opened ways for better understanding and reconciliation. (See Chapter 23.2.)

Creativity Is One of the Most Valuable Resources
Available to Those Engaged in Conflict Resolution

New isn't always better, but new and different often attracts attention and invites participation. Especially at the grassroots level, there are many examples of how activists use creativity to reach constituencies that are difficult to reach, to engage children in all sorts of activities that impact on violence, tolerance, and conflict, and in some cases to bring conflicting parties together for meaningful peacebuilding work.

Among the stories told in this volume is the story of Peacelinks, launched by two Sierra Leonean teenagers who returned from an international children's peace conference in the United States with the idea of looking for productive ways of engaging the skills of other young people. Weekly meetings and singing sessions evolved into a youth organization whose members use the arts to help other young people overcome war trauma, learn new skills, and lead productive lives. (See Chapter 12.1.)

Victim Empowerment Plays an Important Role in Transformation

Victims can be powerful messengers. However, the main source of that power derives from their capacity to transcend the emotions of victimhood, to forgive and reconcile, and in so doing, to demonstrate to others that there is a way to the future that is not shrouded in hatred but rather illuminated with hope. Cases that demonstrate how victims have been empowered and transformed into advocates of reconciliation are among the most inspiring in this volume.

In Burundi, for example, an organization called Jamaa—"friends" in Swahili—has been working to persuade young people who have themselves been involved in Burundi's communal violence to sit down together and talk of reconciliation. In Jamaa, youth leaders have been told that society will forgive them for what they have done in the past if they take positive actions to build a peaceful society. By reintegrating youths—many of whom have killed in the past—back into society, Jamaa has helped to promote justice and reconciliation within and between their war-torn communities. (See Chapter 8.1.)

Part of the Process of Conflict Resolution Is to Transform the Perception of the "Other" from That of an Enemy into That of Another Human with Similar Needs, Desires, and Priorities in Life

The enemy we do not know is a specter without any human qualities. The more that we know about the "others," the more they seem to be like us, and the less acceptable it is to resort to violence against them. Part of the conflict prevention arsenal, then, includes programs that dispel myths and stereotypes, that humanize the enemy, and show the "other" to be someone who just happens to come from the other side of the divide.

Hello Peace does just that, by allowing Israelis and Palestinians to talk to each other by telephone. The program began when an Israeli woman reached a Palestinian man by dialing a wrong number (he traced her number on his mobile and called her back the next day), but has since resulted in close to 500,000 telephone conversations between Israelis and Palestinians. By establishing personal but also safe contact, Hello Peace has helped to put a human face on the "other." (See Chapter 19.2.)

Reconciliation

Reconciliation is not only an effective approach for dealing with postconflict situations but is also a powerful crisis prevention mechanism. While bitter protagonists may understand, on an intellectual level, the need for reconciliation, it is often more difficult for them to act on that understanding and come to terms with the conflict emotionally. Successful reconciliation requires both justice and forgiveness. Reconciliation must address the past so that victims are able to overcome their fears and bitterness, and also look to the future, so as to give protagonists the opportunity to explore the possibilities of more mutually rewarding relationships. In circumstances where reconciliation is not taking place at the higher echelons of leadership, civil-society actors can create momentum for societal reconciliation by starting to work at the grassroots.

In Australia, where thousands of Aboriginal children were forcibly separated from their families, a government-sponsored report recommended that the nation hold a national "Sorry Day" to acknowledge the wrongs done to the indigenous population. The government ignored the recommendation, but the retired judge who had led the inquiry and several CSOs pushed for its observance nonetheless. On 26 May 1998, the day was commemorated with thousands of events. Many Aboriginals were deeply moved. For the first time, they felt that the Australian community understood what they had gone through, and so, a way was opened toward healing and further acts of reconciliation from both sides. (See Chapter 23.1.)

Paul van Tongeren and Juliette Verhoeven are two of the editors of this book. Jim Wake is a free-lance journalist based in the Netherlands.

Selected Bibliography

Anderson, Mary B., and Lara Olson, eds. 2003. *Confronting War: Critical Lessons for Peace Practitioners. Reflecting on Peace Project* (Cambridge: Collaborative for Development Action).

Austin, Alex, Martina Fischer, and Norbert Ropers, eds. 2004. *Transforming Ethnopolitical Conflict: The Berghof Handbook* (Wiesbaden, Germany: Berghof Research Center for Constructive Confict Management and VS Verlag).

Barnes, Catherine, ed. 2002. *Owning the Process: Public Participation in Peacemaking*. Accord: An International Review of Peace Initiatives (London: Conciliation Resources).

Clements, Kevin. "Civil Society and Conflict Prevention." Unpublished presentation at the "Facing Ethnic Conflicts" conference at the Center for Development Research, pp. 14–16.

Crocker, Chester A., Fen Osler Hampson, and Pamela Aall, eds. 2001. *Turbulent Peace: The Challenges of Managing International Conflict* (Washington, DC: United States Institute of Peace Press).

Davies, John, and Edy Kaufman. 2002. *Second Track/Citizens' Diplomacy: Concepts and Techniques for Conflict Transformation* (Lanham, MD: Rowman & Littlefield Publishers).

European Centre for Conflict Prevention (ECCP). 1999. *People Building Peace: 35 Inspiring Stories from Around the World* (Utrecht, Netherlands: ECCP).

Fisher, Simon, et al. *Working with Conflict: Skills and Strategies for Action* (London-Birmingham: Zed Books, Responding to Conflict).

Fitzduff, Mari, and Cheyanne Church, eds. 2004. *NGOs at the Table: Strategies for Influencing Policies in Areas of Conflict* (Lanham, MD: Rowman & Littlefield Publishers).

Galama, Anneke, and Paul van Tongeren. 2002. *Towards Better Peacebuilding Practice: On Lessons Learned, Evaluation Practices, and Aid and Conflict* (Utrecht, Netherlands: European Centre for Conflict Prevention).

Galtung, Johan. 1996. *Peace by Peaceful Means: Peace and Conflict, Development and Civilization* (Oslo: International Peace Research Institute).

Lederach, John Paul. 1997. *Building Peace: Sustainable Reconciliation in Divided Societies* (Washington, DC: United States Institute of Peace Press).

Lederach, John Paul, and Janice Moomaw Jenner, eds. 2002. *Into the Eye of the Storm: A Handbook of International Peacebuilding* (San Fransico: Jossey-Bass).

"Lessons Learned from Peacebuilding Efforts in South East Asia and the Pacific." 2003. Report of a workshop organized by ECCP and the Centre for Security and Peace Studies at UGM, Bali, Indonesia, 5–7 May.

Lund, Michael. 1996. *Preventing Violent Conflicts: A Strategy for Preventive Diplomacy* (Washington, DC: United States Institute of Peace Press).

Mathews, Dylan, ed. 2001. *War Prevention Works: 50 Stories of People Resolving Conflict* (Oxford: Oxford Research Group).

Miall, Hugh, Oliver Ramsbotham, and Tom Woodhouse. 2000. *Contemporary Conflict Resolution: The Prevention, Management, and Transformation of Deadly Conflicts* (Cambridge: Polity Press).

"Peacebuilding in Africa: Lessons, Challenges and Aspirations." 2001. Report from the NPI–Africa Seminar for Practitioners held in Nairobi, Kenya, 26 April.

Peace Direct. 2004. *Unarmed Heroes* (London: Clairview).

Reychler, Luc, and Thania Paffenholz, eds. 2001. *Peacebuilding: A Field Guide* (Boulder, CO: Lynne Rienner Publishers).

Sampson, Cynthia, Mohammed Abu Nimer, et al. 2003. *Positive Approaches to Peacebuilding: A Resource for Innovators* (Washington, DC: Pact Publications).

Schirch, Lisa. 2004. *The Little Book of Strategic Peacebuilding* (Intercourse, PA: Good Books, Little Books Series).

PART 2

Themes and Cases

7

Women:
Using the Gender Lens

Lisa Schirch and Manjrika Sewak

Armed conflicts are never gender-neutral. Whether it is economic deprivation, displacement, poverty or gender-based violence, the costs of conflict are borne disproportionately by women and their children. However, women's identity as victims often obscures the important roles they play in peacebuilding processes. This chapter highlights the contributions of women to peacebuilding and describes why using a gender lens is essential for sustainable peace and security.

It would be incorrect to assert that all women are "natural peacebuilders." Experiences from regions of protracted conflict such as Sri Lanka, the Middle East, and Kashmir reveal that women have also been active agents in perpetuating violent conflict.

However, the contributions of women's groups to peacebuilding have been highly significant. In the case studies that follow this chapter, readers will learn how the Women in Peacebuilding Network in West Africa brought international attention to the lack of women and other civil-society actors in the Liberian national peace talks; how the women of Bougainville initiated a peace settlement between secessionists and the Papua New Guinean government; how women in Argentina protested the disappearance of their grandchildren during the civil strife under a severely repressive government; and how Muslim, Hindu, and Sikh women crossing "enemy lines" in Kashmir, India, continue to initiate joint projects on development, trauma healing, and reconciliation.

In times of violent conflict, men and women face new roles and changing gender expectations. Violent conflict offers opportunities for reshaping both public and private relationships between men and women and taking positive steps toward gender equality. This chapter examines women's roles in peacebuilding, recent developments aimed to support these roles, current debates and challenges facing women's roles in peacebuilding, and some lessons learned and recommendations for the future.

Women's Contributions

Peacebuilding seeks to prevent, reduce, transform, and help people recover from violence in all forms, even structural violence that has not yet led to massive civil unrest. There are four categories of peacebuilding including efforts to (1) wage conflict nonviolently through activism and advocacy; (2) reduce direct violence through peacekeeping, relief aid, and legal systems; (3) transform relationships through dialogue, mediation, negotiation, and trauma healing; and (4) build capacity through training and education, development, military conversion, and research. Women play important roles in each of the four categories of peacebuilding.

Wage Conflict Nonviolently

As activists and advocates for peace, women "wage conflict nonviolently" by pursuing democracy and human rights through strategies that raise awareness of conflict issues and pressure others to bring about change. In the case study from Argentina, for example, women mobilized themselves as mothers and grandmothers and sustained a weekly public protest at a time when other activists had gone into hiding due to severe governmental repression (See Chapter 7.4). In so doing, they emerged as one of the most profound examples of women waging conflict through advocacy and nonviolent action to achieve truth and justice. In the case study from Liberia, the Women's Mass Action for Peace demonstrates that the sustained presence of women demonstrating outside the Liberian peace talks helped create the needed pressure to keep rebel and government leaders at the negotiating table until they reached agreement (See Chapter 7.5). In Bougainville, the Leitana Nehan Women's Development Agency raised awareness of the connections between private and social violence. They brought the issues of rape as a tool of war, domestic violence, and substance abuse to national attention through the use of large-scale protests (See Chapter 7.3).

Reduce Direct Violence

As peacekeepers and relief aid workers, women contribute to "reducing direct violence." In countries around the world, women's groups provide relief and charity work to people in need in their communities, often through their churches, mosques, or temples. They run soup kitchens to provide food to the hungry, offer clothing to those in need, and set up orphanages and shelters for those with no place to go. Women's groups in Bougainville built secret networks for humanitarian assistance when no other groups were able to provide relief to victims of the civil violence. In the war-torn region of Jammu and Kashmir in India, the Athwaas women's initiative works to identify and meet the needs of women whose husbands have been killed or "disappeared" in the fighting (See Chapter 7.1).

Transform Relationships

As mediators, trauma-healing counselors, and policymakers, women also work to "transform relationships" and address the roots of violence. In times of intense conflict, women's dialogue initiatives are often the only channel of communication between hostile communities/nations. In the context of the Israeli-Palestinian conflict, the Jerusalem Link and Women in Black serve as two important examples of women building bridges across the lines of conflict. In the context of the conflict between Pakistan and India, groups such as Women in Security, Conflict Management and Peace (WISCOMP) and Women's Initiative for Peace in South Asia (WIPSA) facilitate sustained dialogue between women's groups in the two countries, even when official diplomatic communication has been caught in war rhetoric and political jingoism and civil-society engagement has been irregular and limited. By providing opportunities for face-to-face interaction and dialogue in settings of hostility, they have facilitated a much-needed humanization of perceived "others." These women's groups have fostered a multitrack approach to peacebuilding with a broad cross-section of civil society, including nongovernmental organizations (NGOs), media, the business community, educators, and community leaders in the two countries. Such multitrack peacebuilding plays a vital role in sustaining negotiated political agreements brokered at the highest levels of government.

Build Capacity

As educators and participants in the development process, women also "build the capacity" of their communities and nations to prevent violent conflict. Mothers can nurture the values of peace, respect, and empathy for others with their children. The West African Network for Women in Peacebuilding (WIPNET) trains women in the skills of peacebuilding to increase their capacity for ongoing peace work in their organizations, communities, and nations. Through grassroots initiatives in peace education and socioeconomic empowerment, Athwaas has emerged as one of the few groups in Kashmir that has transcended the fault lines of faith, ethnicity, class, gender, and political persuasion to facilitate an inclusive, gender-sensitive, and sustained dialogue among diverse stakeholders in the conflict.

The Need to Involve Women

Despite growing awareness of the roles women play in conflict prevention and peacebuilding, resistance to the intentional inclusion of women is still widespread. Many activists on behalf of women's inclusion spend a great deal of their time simply explaining to others why it is important for women to be involved in these processes.

There are multiple ways of asserting the importance of women's involvement in peacebuilding. First, women make up more or less half of every community. Their skills and resources are necessary for the complex tasks of peacebuilding. Second, as central caretakers of their families, everyone suffers when women are oppressed, victimized, and excluded from conflict prevention and peacebuilding. Their centrality to communal life makes their inclusion in these activities essential. Third, women have the capacity for both violence and peace and in many areas of the world are, in fact, actively supporting violent solutions to conflicts. Women must be encouraged to use their special qualities in building peace rather than violence. Women can bring unique insights and values to the process of peacebuilding. Socialization processes in many cultures teach women to foster relationships and avoid violence. In addition, the historical experience of marginalization and unequal relations allows many women to empathize with those oppressed in violent contexts.

Fourth, since women and men have different experiences of violence and peace, women must be allowed and encouraged to bring their unique insights and qualities to the process of peacebuilding. Fifth, women's empowerment should be seen as inherent to the process of building peace because sexism, racism, classism, and ethnic and religious discrimination originate from the same set of beliefs that some people are inherently "better" than others. Like other social structures that set up some people as superior to others, the sexist belief that women's lives are less valuable than men's lives leads to violence against women. When women engage in peacebuilding, they challenge these sexist beliefs along with other structures that discriminate against people. Finally, women have proven themselves to be successful peacebuilders. Basing their strategies on the principles of inclusivity and collaboration, and on the methodology of multitrack peacebuilding, the case studies show how women's groups conceptualize strategies and produce peacebuilding outcomes that are broad-based and sustainable.

Recent Developments

During the 1990s, a broad coalition of women began to discuss how to engage the United Nations Security Council on the impact of armed conflict on women and women's contributions to peace. This diverse coalition of women from war zones, representatives of women's national and international NGOs, eventually formed a working group on women, peace, and security. This civil-society campaign led to the October 2000 signing of UN Security Council Resolution 1325 on "Women, Peace, and Security."

UN Security Council Resolution 1325, hereafter referred to simply as "1325," like other council resolutions, is binding international law that for the first time recognizes that women and children are the vast majority of those negatively affected by conflict and endorses the participation of women as significant contributors to peace and security. 1325 includes calls for women's participation in conflict prevention and resolution initiatives; mainstreaming gender perspectives in peacebuilding and peacekeeping missions; and protection of women in regions of armed conflict. It sends an important gender-sensitizing message to the UN system. It also speaks to civil-society actors engaged in preventing armed conflict. While many international NGOs are including women's concerns and women actors in their peacebuilding programs, many are not. There still remains a conceptual separation between traditional "women's" concerns and the issues embraced by civil-society actors involved in conflict prevention or peacebuilding activities. The U.K.-based organization International Alert launched a Women Building Peace global campaign with the support of a hundred civil-society organizations (CSOs) around the world to lobby for a council resolution and later to urge the implementation of 1325 recommendations both within the UN and across civil-society actors. The campaign aims to address women's exclusion from decision-making processes that address peace, security, and development.

Current Debate

Women are challenging the United Nations (UN), regional, governmental, and other civil-society actors in a variety of ways. Many groups focus on preventing or recovering from civil and international wars. This emphasis on overt direct violence between large groups of people is important, yet it often fails to fully challenge the structural origins of public violence and the private violence (often against women and children) that accompanies public violence. One key debate centers on women civil-society actors' insistence on examining the web of violence that accompanies public violence, pointing to the growing incidence of domestic violence in regions of armed conflict.

The examples of Bougainville, South Africa, and the former Yugoslavia, where instances of domestic violence rose sharply during and after the armed conflict, lie at the heart of the current debate on developing holistic responses to the challenges that the complex relationship between militarization, misogyny, and domestic violence presents. Rita Manchanda, a women's peace activist from India, notes that "women are more likely to see a continuum of violence because they experience the connected forms of domestic and political violence that stretches from the home, to the street, and to the battlefield" (Manchanda 2001: 1959).

Women are also challenging how governments and other civil-society actors are defining peace and security. Women's groups assert that the values of empathy and building community can contribute significantly to a discourse on peace and security that is based on coexistence and cooperation. They advocate for a broadening of the definition of security from one confined to territorial and military security to one that considers issues of individual dignity, water security, food security, humane governance, and environmental security as central to the shaping of what is considered essential to the field of international security—concerns that were earlier considered "soft issues". Further, making a distinction between negative and positive peace, they associate the former with the absence of widespread overt violent conflict where other forms of violence—cultural and structural—continue long after the guns have gone silent. In this context, the notion of positive peace might be introduced as one that includes processes that facilitate social justice, gender equity, active coexistence, economic equality, and ecological security.

For instance, several women's groups working in the context of the peace process between Pakistan and India assert the need to move beyond a peace that involves a mere absence of military conflict and arms races. They advocate for a paradigm that privileges inclusive and mutually beneficial processes for transforming the conflict. A genuine peace requires not only the absence of war but also the elimination of unjust social and economic relations, including unequal gender relations. Women's groups have introduced these new ideas of peace and security into the political diplomacy in the region.

Finally, women challenge other civil-society actors to walk boldly toward greater gender equality. An issue around which there has been considerable debate is the widely held belief that once there is a "critical mass" of women in positions of decisionmaking, the discourse on peace and security will undergo significant change. Many insist that it is important that a discussion on women and peacebuilding not be limited to a preoccupation with numbers or what has been termed as "add women and stir." In other words, while the goal of getting a critical mass of women into decisionmaking positions in peacebuilding organizations is vital, this can only be a starting point. Simply adding women to existing programs or structures is unlikely to bring about lasting change. The challenge lies in building a discourse on peace and security that includes the perspectives of both women and men and holds as central the values of coexistence, nonviolence, and inclusivity. Real structural, economic, political, and social change in the ways all people relate to each other must be the ultimate goal.

Main Challenges

The term "mainstreaming gender" captures the idea that women want more than simply joining in existing peacebuilding approaches. Mainstreaming gender means challenging the way governments, intergovernmental and regional peace and security organizations, and other civil-society actors go about their work so that everyone at every level in every peacebuilding project uses a gender lens in planning, implementing, and evaluating their work.

Gender mainstreaming, represented in Figure 7.1, requires ongoing gender analysis, the goal of gender equality, and including women who represent the concerns of other women in all peacebuilding planning, implementation, and evaluation (Schirch [forthcoming]).

The first challenge is to include gender analysis in all planning, implementation, and evaluation of conflict prevention and peacebuilding programs. Conflict and violence analysis tools are important guides to all peacebuilding planning, yet they often leave out the significant differences between male and female experiences and roles. Gender analysis requires data about how war and violence affect men and women differently; the gender roles of men and women in local cultures including the division of labor and resources; the needs of women from different economic classes, religions, ethnic groups, and ages; and how women are included in all peacebuilding processes from relief aid distribution, peacekeeping programs, and grassroots dialogue, to formal peace talks. Infusing a gender analysis into peacebuilding requires concrete action. Some experts call for a truth commission on violence against women (UNIFEM 2002: 6). Specifically, such a commission could analyze the causes of, and connections between, violence against women in times of war, domestic violence, and trafficking of women.

Figure 7.1 Three Key Steps to Mainstream Gender in Peacebuilding

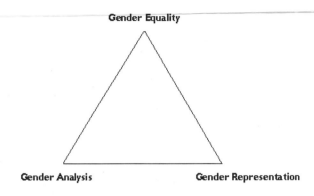

   The second challenge is to embrace the goal of gender equality as a central value for all peacebuilding actors. Gender equality refers to the goal of equal opportunities, resources, and respect for men and women. It does not mean that men and women become the same, but that their lives and work hold equal value. Peacebuilding programs contribute to gender equality when this goal becomes integral to every aspect of peacebuilding and not relegated to one or two programs for women. Since women and men do not have equal access to opportunities, resources, and respect in most communities, peacebuilding programs need to take affirmative action to ensure equal treatment and equal opportunity.

   The third aspect of gender mainstreaming is including women and women's organizations in every stage and activity of peacebuilding alongside men and male-led organizations. Women leaders and organizations need to have access to and active relationships with all peacebuilding actors so that they can communicate their analysis and ideas and can coordinate their energies with other peacebuilding activities. Women-only spaces are important fora to build bridges between women from different identity groups, collect information about the types and effectiveness of current programs to address violence against women, and set priorities and strategies for addressing violence against women. Funders can urge recipient organizations to include women at every level of their staff and board and ensure that these women have the support of other women and women's organizations and are not just token representatives.

Lessons Learned and Best Practices

Research has already proven that women make a difference when they join in the tasks of peacebuilding. Women's experiences in conflict prevention and peacebuilding offer the following lessons learned and best practices.

Women and men experience conflict and violence differently. A redefinition of peace and security that incorporates both male and female concerns is essential to designing peacebuilding programs that bring a just peace to both women and men.

Women play important roles in peacebuilding and are essential to creating long-term, sustainable peace. Their emphasis on building civil-society alliances and engaging in multitrack processes across the lines of conflict enables them to develop holistic understandings of peace and security. Women's peace groups, such as the Athwaas initiative of Muslim, Hindu, and Sikh women in Kashmir, have transcended the boundaries of religion, ethnicity, class, political persuasion, and socioeconomic background to facilitate cross-community and multitrack interaction in their work for peace, at times representing the only group of civil society doing so. Women's peace initiatives have a track record of producing turnarounds in conflict negotiations by conceptualizing agreements that are more inclusive, community-based, and more likely to be successful in the long run.

Women's networks allow women to coordinate their action and multiply their power to bring about change. The case studies that follow detail the importance of strengthening and supporting partnerships among women working in specific regions and across all areas of peacebuilding practice. Women's networks, such as the Argentinean Grandmothers of the Plaza de Mayo, the Liberian Women's Mass Action for Peace, and the Save Somali Women and Children group, have proven that women's cooperative efforts can make a tremendous impact on preventing violence. The collaborative approach gives evidence of women's ability to work nonhierarchically with each other.

Addressing trauma is central to peacebuilding. Many women's groups have taken the lead in addressing one of the most significant yet rarely acknowledged consequences of violent conflict—namely, deep-rooted trauma. In addition to providing psychosocial services, many of these groups are engaged in training and research in order to foreground the role that trauma plays in sustaining social conflict.

Times of social transition and conflict bring challenges to the traditional gender roles of men and women and new opportunities. The case study of women's peacebuilding in Bougainville gives an example of women taking on new leadership roles and emerging in the public sphere as powerful actors during times of violent conflict.

Gender training programs for entire organizations empower everyone to be involved in gender mainstreaming. The presence of trained gender advisors for all peacebuilding organizations and staff, in addition to training in and opportunities for gender analysis by other staff, can help institutionalize a shared responsibility for ongoing gender analysis of all programs. There is evidence that gender awareness training leads to changes in programming. Gender training programs among police in Cambodia, for example, resulted in new police initiatives to address domestic violence and sex trafficking.

Recommendations

The following four recommendations can strengthen women's ability to contribute to peacebuilding.

Support Women's Networks

Women's networks facilitate a cross-fertilization of ideas, best practices, and lessons learned from different regions of conflict. They also enhance knowledge about different approaches to conflict prevention and peacebuilding. Perhaps most significantly, networks provide a context for the generation of financial and human resources that women's groups need to prevent and transform violent conflict. The UN, regional, governmental and civil-society organizations should support women's networks so that women can coordinate and consolidate their power and their ability to act with a united voice. Although women's groups in Bougainville, Liberia, and Kashmir have identified trauma healing and reconciliation as important needs, those with political and economic power have failed to respond adequately to their demand for training and funds for psychosocial counseling centers.

Mainstream Gender

Women's contributions to peacebuilding and their unique experiences of violence signal the need for mainstreaming gender in all conflict prevention and peacebuilding efforts. Gender mainstreaming requires moving beyond an approach that simply includes women in existing peacebuilding programs or creates special women's projects set apart from other programming. The UN, regional, governmental, and CSOs can ensure that all their employees are trained in gender awareness, understand the relevance of gender equality to peacebuilding, and value the inclusion of women in planning, implementing, and evaluating peacebuilding programs.

Empower Women

Many women are already empowered and are playing important roles as decisionmakers at the UN, regional, national, and local structures. Still, many women are not yet able to contribute because they are refused the opportunity to participate and/or do not see themselves as able to participate in peacebuilding. Women's empowerment comes through training, networking, and opportunities where women can participate fully in planning, implementing, and evaluating peacebuilding programs. The UN, regional, governmental, and CSOs can continue and expand training programs specifically for women to increase their sense of empowerment in and knowledge of peacebuilding processes.

Promote Resolution 1325

UN Security Council Resolution 1325 asserts the integration of women and women's groups into conflict prevention and peacebuilding programs. The tools provided in Resolution 1325 advocate for the collection of gender-disaggregated data and testimonies to provide greater accuracy and understanding of women's needs in conflict zones. The UN, regional, governmental, and CSOs can monitor and promote the national and international implementation of Resolution 1325 (Poehlman-Doumbouya and Hill 2001). An important measure in this respect could be the ratification of the Convention on the Elimination of All Forms of Discrimination Against Women (CEDAW). States could bring in new legislation and policy to ensure the effective implementation of CEDAW. The low representation of women in decisionmaking positions and the absence of their perspectives in policy and legislation remains one of the key failures of efforts to implement Resolution 1325. Even though women played a significant role in laying the groundwork for the peace settlement in Bougainville, they are underrepresented in the political structures established after the agreement. Of the 106 members appointed to the Bougainville Peoples' Congress, only 6 are women.

Taking the above recommendations seriously will further strengthen women's ability to contribute to peacebuilding in the nearby future.

Lisa Schirch is an associate professor of peacebuilding at Eastern Mennonite University's Masters in Conflict Transformation Program. A former Fulbright fellow, Schirch teaches graduate courses and consults with a network of strategic partner organizations around the world. Her peacebuilding experience includes facilitating interethnic dialogues, training programs for women in peacebuilding, and the use of the arts and rituals in peacebuilding.

Manjrika Sewak is program officer at WISCOMP, a project of the Foundation for Universal Responsibility of His Holiness the Dalai Lama, New Delhi, India. WISCOMP is a South Asian research and training initiative that facilitates the leadership of women in the areas of security studies, conflict transformation, and peacebuilding.

Selected Bibliography

Manchanda, Rita. 2001. "Redefining and Feminizing Security." *Economic and Political Weekly* 36, no. 22 (Mumbai: 2 June).

Poehlman-Doumbouya, Sara, and Felicity Hill. 2001. "Women and Peace in the United Nations." *New Routes: A Journal of Peace Research and Action* 6, no. 3.

Schirch, Lisa. forthcoming. "Frameworks for Understanding Women as Victims and Peacebuilders," in *Women and Post-Conflict* (Tokyo: United Nations University).

UNIFEM. 2002. *Women, War, and Peace: Executive Summary.* The Independent Experts' Assessment on the Effect of Armed Conflict on Women and the Role of Women in Peacebuilding. Progress of the World's Women, vol. 2.

Resources

Lead Organizations

African Women Solidarity (Femmes Africa Solidarité)—Switzerland and Senegal
E-mail: info@fasngo.org
Website: http://www.fasngo.org

International Alert—United Kingdom
Women Building Peace Campaign
E-mail: general@international-alert.org
Website: http://www.international-alert.org/women/default.html

International Fellowship of Reconciliation—The Netherlands
Women Peacemaker Program
E-mail: WPP@ifor.org
Website: http://www.ifor.org/WPP/

UNIFEM—United States
For contact, please visit website: http://www.unifem.org.

Women's International League for Peace and Freedom—United States
Peace Women Project
E-mail: info@peacewomen.org
Website: http://www.peacewomen.org

Women in Security, Conflict Management and Peace—India
E-mail:wiscomp@vsnl.com
Website: http://www.furhhdl.org/ wiscompindex.htm

Women Waging Peace Global Network— United States
E-mail: info@womenwagingpeace.net
Website:
http://www.womenwagingpeace. net

Websites
The UN's portal on women, peace and security: http://www.womenwar peace.org
The UN's portal on the advancement and empowerment of women: http://www.un.org/womenwatch/ index.html

Publications

Anderlini, Sanam, Rita Machanda, and Shereen Karmali. *Women, Violent Conflict, and Peacebuilding: Global Perspectives.* International Alert, 1999.

Cockburn, Cynthia. *The Space Between Us: Negotiating Gender and National Identities in Conflict.* New York: Zed Books, 1998.

El-Bushra, Judy. "Women Building Peace. Sharing Know-How." Report by International Alert's Gender and Peacebuilding Programme, 2003. Online at: http:// www.international-alert.org/women/publications/KnowHowPaper.pdf.

Juma, Monica Kathina. *Unveiling Women as Pillars of Peace: Peace Building in Communities Fractured by Conflict in Kenya.* An Interim Report. New York: UNDP, 2000.

Manchanda, Rita, ed. *Women, War and Peace in South Asia: Beyond Victimhood to Agency.* New Delhi: Sage Publications, 2001.

McAllister, Pam. *This River of Courage: Generations of Women's Resistance and Action.* Philadelphia: New Society Publishers, 1991.

Meintjes, Sheila, Anu Pillay, and Meredith Tuschen, eds. *The Aftermath: Women in Post-Conflict Transformation.* London: Zed Books, 2002.

Moser, Caroline, and Fiona Clark, eds. *Victims, Perpetrators or Actors? Gender, Armed Conflict and Political Violence.* London: Zed Books, 2001.

Pankhurst, Donna, and Sanam Anderlini. *Mainstreaming Gender in Peacebuilding. A Framework for Action.* England: Women Building Peace Campaign, 2000.

Schmeidl, Susanne, and Eugenia Piza-Lopez. *Gender and Conflict Early Warning: A Framework for Action.* London: Save the Children, 2002.

United Nations. *Women, Peace and Security: The Report of the Secretary-General.* New York: UN, 2002.

Woodward, A. E. *Women at the Peace Tables: Making a Difference.* New York: UNIFEM, 2000.

Personal Story:
"Civil Society Cannot Be Destroyed"—
Queen Noor

My husband once said that "Peace is essential to us in leading a normal life, which is the legitimate right of every individual, in order to dream, plan for oneself, and for the future of one's family, to raise one's standard of living away from fear, worry and confusion."

The desire to have a "normal life" and live in peace—for ourselves and our families—is one of the most intrinsic values we aspire to as human beings. It cuts across the racial, ethnic, gender, geographic, cultural, and religious differences that seem to divide us and fuel the devastating conflicts, wars, and humanitarian crises that destroy countless lives and tear nations apart.

For the better part of the last three decades, I have had the privilege to work beside and witness women, men, and children who are giving up everything they have: creativity, time, resources, and all too often their own safety, to achieve peace and some semblance of normalcy amidst the most daunting challenges and conditions. Seemingly ordinary people under the most horrific circumstances exhibit extraordinary courage and strength as they reach out to others—to recover, to reconcile, to understand, to believe in the basic humanity of others, even of those some would call enemies.

Civil society, I have discovered, cannot be destroyed. It springs up, again and again, like a strong and beautiful flower from the ashes and rubble of conflict and deprivation. It endures because of everyday people—men, women, the young and old, survivors of chaos and conflict—who act and react to build a better life for themselves and future generations.

Breaking Down the Barriers

The most frequent victims of war and conflict are often innocent women and children. Yet, more often than not, these same individuals nurture the flowers of reconciliation, stability and peace.

For years I have worked with Seeds of Peace, an organization that brings together young people from conflict-torn regions to live and work together to begin to break down the barriers of ignorance and prejudice that generate confrontation over communication. Children face old animosities that have been passed down like legacies from their elders. When they go home, they continue to hold out their hands and hearts to each other.

Even now—especially now—Arab and Israeli Seeds graduates phone or e-mail across conflict lines to comfort their friends in the midst of the worst violence their region has seen. They risk the scorn of angry neighbors for the chance to meet and talk and grieve together. Sometimes, they risk their lives, but by those risks, they also inspire their families and neighbors to take a chance on hope and humanity. They have stared hatred in the face and refused to succumb.

In Colombia where two people are being killed every day from landmines and half of all civilian mine victims are children, I met two young cousins, Jose and Jonathon, no more than eleven years old who encountered terror when they picked up what they thought was a toy rocket. They each lost a leg, their cousin Monica lost a leg, and Jose's younger brother perished. They are but a few of the thousands of victims of guerilla warfare, who have lost their innocence.

Now they are also survivors and teachers. Their new mission is to prevent future mine accidents and deaths. In a region where limited government resources exist and narco-guerilla warfare has festered for decades displacing millions of people, two hopeful souls educate local villagers and students about the dangers of landmines. One person at a time, they spread a message of prevention and awareness to thwart future deaths and disability.

I have also witnessed networks of courageous women raising their voices—and sometimes risking their lives—in conflict areas around the world from Africa and the Middle East to the Balkans. They nurture peace in different ways by working for what is best for their families, cutting across ethnic, religious and tribal barriers, and breaking through seemingly insurmountable obstacles to reconciliation and reconstruction.

After the war in Rwanda, fifty women, both Hutu and Tutsi, banded together in the Association of Widows to support each other and the war's orphans. The Mano River Union Women's Network for Peace brings women together to end conflict in Guinea, Liberia and Sierra Leone (see Chapter 7.5). Israeli and Palestinian women have worked with each other—electronically, if violence prevents it physically—in organizations like Jerusalem Link and the Jerusalem Center for Women to further Middle East peace efforts. Senator George Mitchell said women's weariness of conflict was a significant political force in achieving the Good Friday Agreement in Northern Ireland. War widows in Tajikistan who suffered through years of devastating civil war are now working together to understand their legal, social and economic constitutional and Islamic rights. Rural women whose main survival strategy has been to cultivate land are now working together to secure rights to access, manage and inherit land to provide for their families.

For me, the most wrenching and ultimately one of the most inspiring examples of collective action is in Bosnia, where thousands of women lost their families and their homes to ethnic cleansing. I first traveled to Bosnia to reach out to the widows of Srebrenica in 1996, a year after eight thousand men and boys were marched away and never seen again. Several years later I returned as a member of the International Commission on Missing Persons. On two trips in 2001 I met with many of the same women still searching for news of their loved ones—unable to rest or to rebuild their lives without this knowledge, without assurances that the massacre would be memorialized officially and that those responsible would be held accountable. It is largely through their persistence that, eight years after the massacre, the prime minister of the Bosnian Serb Republic acknowledged the tragedy and paid tribute to the victims, and it was they who invited President Clinton to open the Srebrenica Memorial Center in September 2003.

All of these efforts have begun to bring some closure, at least as much as is possible, until those responsible are brought to justice. Still nothing can ever dull the emotional pain these women, and other victims of war, have suffered.

Yet, as I have sat and wept with these women, as they struggled to come to terms with the deaths of their husbands, sons and fathers, I have marveled at their strength. I have seen them reach out to other women, some of whom may well be the wives or mothers of those who perpetrated the massacre. They have chosen to search for threads of humanity amidst the chaos and destruction of civil war. Every one of these women, as they pick up the pieces of their shattered lives, is building a civil society that benefits not only them, but everyone in their region.

King Hussein frequently said, "It should never be forgotten that peace resides ultimately not in the hands of the governments, but in the hands of the people." These extraordinary people that I have met throughout the world, with all their diversity, experiences, and circumstances, provide the seeds of hope for a better future for us all. That, ultimately, is what makes civil society—people voluntarily joined together for a common goal, for the common good. It is truly the most effective agent for peace we have.

Her Majesty Queen Noor of Jordan is an international humanitarian activist and an outspoken voice on issues of world peace and justice. Queen Noor is actively involved in a number of international organizations dealing with global peace-building and conflict recovery and currently serves as an Expert Advisor to the United Nations on these issues. Her autobiography, Leap of Faith: Memoirs of an Unexpected Life *(Miramax Books, 2003) was a New York Times bestseller.*

7.1

Women Breaking the Silence:
The Athwaas Initiative in Kashmir

Sumona DasGupta and Meenakshi Gopinath

In Jammu and Kashmir, a women's peace organization has been engaged in a bold experiment to break through the barriers of pain, mistrust, and fear that prevail in a region that has been plagued by a tragic conflict for many years. It comprises a group of Muslim, Hindu and Sikh women who work to expand constituencies of peace through a range of activities that include active listening, counseling, articulation of the concerns of women to policy makers and government interlocutors, and initiation of programs that facilitate democratic participation and just peace.

The group Women in Security, Conflict Management, and Peace (WISCOMP) is itself a project of the Foundation for Universal Responsibility of His Holiness the Dalai Lama, and their initiative is called Athwaas, a Kashmiri word implying a warm handshake. The members of the Athwaas group accept that they have different political convictions—yet as women they continue to "search for common ground." In an atmosphere marked by mistrust and suspicion, Athwaas strives to create safe spaces for self-expression and reconciliation through sustained dialogue.

Once fabled for its beauty and tranquility, life in the Indian-administered valley of Kashmir was shattered by the outbreak of armed conflict in 1989. Since then, thousands of lives have been lost in this "paradise on earth." Caught between the bullets of the militants and the Indian security forces, innocent people have been the victims of a mindless saga of violence. The vocabulary that now permeates the valley includes terms such as "crackdowns," "cordon and search operations," "area sanitation," "road-opening patrols," and "soft targets," and in normal life citizens are confronted with the daily horrors of ambushes, grenade attacks, bomb blasts, and landmines.

Satellite television has over the years captured the language and the images of violence emanating from the valley—lingering images of armed militants and security forces, bombs, and bullets. The voices of the women of Kashmir have been conspicuously absent.

Transforming the Nature of the Conflict

Deeply cognizant of the fact that the women of Kashmir must find a context in which their voices could be heard, WISCOMP organized a roundtable in December 2000 titled "Breaking the Silence: Women and Kashmir." This was the first substantive step taken by WISCOMP to explore the idea of an inclusive effort to transform the nature of the conflict in the Kashmir Valley. The roundtable provided a platform for Kashmiri women—and men as well—belonging to different faiths, age groups, social backgrounds, professions, and ideologies to express their viewpoints. It was apparent that the violent conflict in Kashmir had brought in its wake not only the loss of loved ones and disintegration of social structures and support systems, but also an increasing emotional distance between communities that had earlier coexisted (Basu 2004).[1]

The events that followed the roundtable were unanticipated. A group of women from Kashmir expressed their desire to carry forward the process of dialogue and to explore possibilities of working across the political and ethnic divide to understand each other's realities, acknowledge each other's pain, and work together to build constituencies of peace. The group, consisting of Muslims, Hindus, and Sikhs, expressed an interest in identifying and strengthening values of coexistence and trust that had historically been a part of Kashmiri society. Following a brainstorming meeting in Srinagar, they decided to visit each other's realities, record women's voices, and build bridges of trust. WISCOMP was asked to facilitate this process.[2]

In November 2001, in the course of the first field trip, Athwaas traveled to remote villages in North and South Kashmir to meet women (of whom the overwhelming majority were from the Muslim community) who had learned how to negotiate violence in everyday life even as they had lost their menfolk to the bullets of either the militants or the Indian security forces. Then in March 2002, Athwaas visited the migrant camps in Jammu, home to the displaced Hindu community of the valley, where the residents lived in the exiled seclusion of one-room tenements.

The women of Kashmir—Muslims, Hindus, and Sikhs—shared with Athwaas their testimonies of horror, custodial deaths, torture, flight, escape, exile, and exploitation. The fractured reality and complex layers of the conflict began to emerge in their starkest forms. Each member of the Athwaas delegation maintained a diary and recorded her observations. One excerpt is revealing of the intensity of the experience: "Women feel oppressed from both the militants and the security forces who have guns. Fear lurks everywhere." Another diary entry captured the sense of fear felt by women in a remote village in North Kashmir: "It is almost as if the women keep looking over their shoulders to ask: Who is he? Where is he? Who is with him? Whose side is he on? Can I trust the person I am talking to? My father is dead. Who killed him? Who is on my side?"[3]

The Athwaas group also visited Dardpora, the "village of widows," nestled in the foothills of the mountains that separate India and Pakistan, about 125 kilometers from Srinagar. Approaching Dardpora, the Athwaas members had to travel under security cover and were stopped by the Indian security forces at several points. The village is home to about 100 to 150 widows and "half widows." Their husbands have been killed either in fratricidal wars by the different militant groups or in encounters with the Indian security forces, or have simply "disappeared" in the course of the conflict. Eight years after the deaths or disappearances of their husbands, these women had reentered the public space. They would go to the relief office, negotiate for assistance, interact with local authorities, collect wood in the jungle, grow maize, and work as laborers. Though they were no longer grieving wives and mothers, the aftermath of the grieving period was perhaps more painful for them than the period of grief itself. They feared for their future, and the society would not permit them any identity other than that of "widow."

The Athwaas members were taken aback by the anger and bitterness of these women, and their deep suspicions about the intentions of Athwaas. It took a Sikh member of Athwaas who knew the local dialect to convince the women that Athwaas was not out to exploit them but had a different mission— to share their grief, listen to their hopes, and possibly communicate their problems to concerned authorities.

Once the walls of mistrust and skepticism were breached, the women shared their life experiences with the group. In Dardpora and in other villages to which the group traveled, they met with several women who had lost their husbands as a result of deception, or in police custody. They shared stories of their struggles to bring up their children alone. They also told of being forced to marry militants, who then abandoned them. They now lived in terror of both the security forces and militants. One poignant narrative was that of a woman in Chandoosa village, in a desolate part of the Baramulla district. In 2001, "unidentified gunmen" killed her husband, a militant who had surrendered to the authorities. She was living in an isolated house on a hillock surrounded by Indian security personnel. Sharing her anguish about being "caged inside her own home," this young widow was struggling to educate her two children.[4]

In March 2003 the Athwaas team visited two camps in Jammu where they listened to the narratives of displaced women who had lost their homes. They heard of the agony of exile, the longing to return to their homes in the valley, the anguish of living in shrunken spaces in unfamiliar terrain, and of trying to hold on to a distinct identity in the midst of a different cultural ethos.

In the course of these visits, Athwaas members listened to the stories and recorded their personal reactions. Where possible they showed the women how to get in touch with the authorities, who to contact, and how to register a self-help group. The idea was to enable the women to make the mental shift from thinking of themselves as victims to that of survivors.

Not One Truth

The physical and emotional journey of Athwaas along a road less traveled was difficult, even traumatic. The group itself was reflective of the diversity of the valley, with members from different communities whose experiences of conflict, ideological convictions, and perceptions on the causes of the conflict differed. The realities they encountered and the firsthand testimonies they heard shook some of these beliefs and perceptions to the core. The roundtable in December 2000 had provided an early indication that there was no "one truth" that superseded other truths in Kashmir. Yet it was not until this composite group traveled across the valley and the camps of Jammu that they could appreciate the extent of this fractured reality. Pain, loss, and suffering interspersed with profiles of courage and determination in the face of adversity were the common thread that united women across diverse communities. The Athwaas members were able to understand firsthand how women negotiate the space between victimhood and agency and how in many cases the boundaries between the two categories get blurred.

The Athwaas members needed time to come to terms with what they were seeing and experiencing and to strategize on the nature of the interventions they wanted to initiate. The WISCOMP team in New Delhi worked closely with Athwaas at every stage along the way, organizing workshops to reflect on their experiences, reviewing the lessons learned from the trips, and strategizing on how to move ahead. WISCOMP facilitated training modules to create a repertoire of tools that could be used in the field, including observation, active listening, interviewing, and basic counseling skills for dealing with individuals under stress. In the field, they used role-playing activities to assess people's needs, or organized simple exercises such as map drawing, which they discovered could reveal volumes about the residents' fears, insecurities, and priorities. Creative ways of eliciting responses became an integral part of the methodology used by the group.[5]

At an intensely personal level, a process of both turmoil and transformation was taking place in the hearts and minds of the Athwaas group. The people of Kashmir had experienced more than a decade of violence. The members of Athwaas were (and are) spatially located in this theater of violent conflict. At the beginning of the journey, the attitude of the Athwaas group to acts of violence had been ambivalent and such acts had been selectively criticized depending on the identity of the perpetrator. A process of inner transformation set in when they actually met those women who had been victimized by violence. Gradually there emerged a consensus among Athwaas members rejecting violence irrespective of whether the horrors had been perpetrated by militants fighting for the "cause" or by members of the Indian security forces.

Another process of emotional turmoil and transformation occurred when the Athwaas group visited the camps of Jammu after their travels in North and South Kashmir. The realization that the pain of one community does not cancel out the pain of the other—that Kashmiri Muslims, Hindus, and Sikhs had all suffered, though in qualitatively different ways, was poignantly driven home when they actually transcended the emotional and geographical divide to visit each other's realities.

An Inclusive Network of Kashmiri Women

In recent months the Athwaas journey has taken a new turn with the setting up of Samanbal Centres in North and South Kashmir and in a migrant camp in

Jammu. "Samanbal" is a Kashmiri term used to describe a place where women can meet to share their hopes, joys, and sorrows. This milestone in the journey of Athwaas came about when individual members volunteered to take responsibility for local initiatives that would provide a physical space and a tangible context for women to come together to rebuild trust and reopen spaces for reconciliation. Each center does have a primary activity such as computer training, embroidering and tailoring, or sharing of counseling skills—but this merely provides the context for women to come together to share their joys and pain and to think in terms of collective action.

It has not always been an easy process, but slowly and surely mutual trust and greater understanding have grown among the Athwaas participants—and ultimately, bonds have been forged that would not have been possible previously. Those touched are reaching out to others, so that the "space" is constantly expanding. As WISCOMP and Athwaas forge ahead to identify and create more constituencies of peace, there is a firm belief that the processes set in place will be able be sustained. This is because the initiative in Kashmir was shaped by the notion that no outside agency can impose a solution—the solution would have to come from within and the women of Kashmir must have a voice in deciding the nature and the pace of movement along the road whose destination is transformation of the conflict. Because of this Athwaas was formed as an inclusive network of Kashmiri women, its composition representing the rich cultural diversity that is so much a part of its historical legacy.

Since one of the objectives of Athwaas is for women to transcend the cultural, experiential, and spiritual differences that have long served as barriers, it is difficult to point to tangible evidence of its impact. Attitudes have softened, women have reached across the divide, they are prepared, sometimes for the first time, to listen to the "other," and a thirst for vengeance has been supplanted by an urge to reconcile.

Perhaps the most unique aspect of the initiative has been its exploratory nature. There were no rigid notions about which strategies would or would not work. For WISCOMP, working with political uncertainties and an ever-changing environment of violence has meant continuous assessment of the possibilities, and adapting to changing circumstances. WISCOMP has continued to encourage the Athwaas initiative to strive toward the ideal that women must ultimately rely on their own strength and reserves to rebuild their lives in a zone of conflict. The personal transformation of many members, the establishment of the Samanbals, and the opportunity it has presented WISCOMP to build on this unique exercise are testimonies to the realization of the vision called Athwaas (Basu 2004).

Meenakshi Gopinath initiated WISCOMP in 1999 and currently serves as honorary director. She is involved in various multitrack peace initiatives in the South Asian region and writes frequently on issues relating to gender, security, and peacebuilding.

Sumona DasGupta is senior program officer at WISCOMP. She holds a doctoral degree in social science and recently concluded a collaborative research study entitled Crossing Lines with the Gender Lens: Interrogating the Dominant Narratives on the Causes of Conflict in Kashmir.

Contact

Women in Security, Conflict management and Peace (WISCOMP)
Foundation for Universal Responsibility of His Holiness the Dalai Lama
Core 4A, Upper Ground Floor, India Habitat Centre
Lodi Road, New Delhi 110003
India
Tel: +91 11 2464 8450
Fax: +91 11 2462 8451
E-mail: wiscomp@vsnl.com
Website: http://www.furhhdl.org/wiscompindex.htm

Notes
1. For an account of the proceedings of this Roundtable see DasGupta, *Breaking the Silence.*
2. For an account on the birth of Athwaas and its guiding principles, see Bhatia (2001).
3. Ashima Kaul Bhatia, Personal Diary, unpublished, 2001.
4. Personal observations of the Athwaas group.
5. The WISCOMP team has documented the proceedings of each of the workshops in a series titled *Stakeholders in Dialogue* (WISCOMP 2004).

Selected Bibliography

Bhatia, Ashima Kaul. n.d. *Recreating Spaces.* Unpublished paper.
———. 2001. *Transcending Faultlines: The Quest for a Culture of Peace* (New Delhi: WISCOMP, Foundation for Universal Responsibility).
Basu, Soumita. 2004. *Building Constituencies of Peace: A Women's Initiative in Kashmir: Documenting the Process* (New Delhi: WISCOMP, Foundation for Universal Responsibility).
DasGupta, Sumona. 2001. *Breaking the Silence: Women and Kashmir* (New Delhi: WISCOMP, Foundation for Universal Responsibility).
WISCOMP. 2004. *Stakeholders in Dialogue* (New Dehli: Foundation for Universal Responsibility of His Holiness the Dalai Lama).
WISCOMP. 2003. *Newsletter Update.* 4, no. 1, August.

7.2

The Other Clan:
Save Somali Women and Children

Somali women are the main victims of the interclan violence that has torn their country apart for nearly fifteen years. Yet they were excluded from both war councils and peace talks—until a group of activists boldly crossed ethnic and gender barriers.

The atmosphere was tense, the mood expectant. As the powerful warlords listened patiently, the president departed from his prepared text and made a somber appeal. President Kibaki said, "You have been wishing and wishing for these fourteen years you have been fighting. Now that peace has been found . . . do not look back to the dark days" (*Daily Nation* 2004).

The scene was State House, Nairobi, Kenya. The date: 29 January 2004. The warlords addressed by the Kenyan leader were responsible for one of Africa's longest-running civil conflicts. They had bargained hard and long. No one was under the illusion the power-sharing deal they were there to sign would end the conflict immediately. Still, hopes were raised by the involvement of all the main combatants.

There was another reason why the function was noteworthy. For the first time, a woman—Asha Hagi Elmi—was signatory to a Somali peace agreement. As chair of Save Somali Women and Children, a body that promotes women's human rights and programs to empower women, Elmi was at the forefront of sustained efforts over many years to break down clan barriers and overcome deep-rooted gender bias. The Nairobi signing ceremony marked a new high point for those efforts.

Create a New Beginning

Two years earlier, in a major breakthrough at the Somali Peace and Reconciliation Conference in Arta, Djibouti, women were represented at the negotiating table for the first time. Save Somali Women and Children got the four clans and coalition of smaller ones—the main combatants—in Arta to accept women as equal partners.

A State Without a Government

Somalia is a coastal state in the Horn of Africa, bordered by Djibouti, Ethiopia, and Kenya. Since the fall of the Siad Barre regime in 1991, it has had no central government. Clans and subclans carved out their own fiefdoms. Their constant battles for control left human suffering and a scarred urban landscape. International intervention, in the form of UN peacekeepers, lasted for three years (1992–1995) before ending in failure. Since then, divided and poverty-stricken, Somalia has alternated between all-out conflict and broken peace deals. The conflict has killed and injured many, and displaced hundreds of thousands. A UN Security Council report in June 2003 said approximately four hundred thousand Somalis were refugees in neighboring countries. Up to 370,000 others were internally displaced. They had no basic services such as water, health facilities, or schools.

Operating as a "Sixth Clan" at those peace talks—held from May to October 2000—they got participants to consider unfamiliar issues such as affirmative action, women's access and control over resources, and the impact of war on women and children. This involvement redefined the whole process.

Like any country whose social fabric is torn apart by war, the peace negotiations in Somalia offered a chance to create a new beginning. The womens' groups were able to convince the clans whose rivalry fuelled the conflict to accept a new and enhanced role for them—around the negotiating table, and in the political structures considered during the talks. They achieved this through advocacy, lobbying, and awareness-raising.

The formation of this Sixth Clan was significant because traditionally in Somalia, women were not allowed full membership in the tightly woven clan and subclan structures. This is where the power has rested, especially since the collapse of the central government in 1991. So that although they were the main victims of the conflict, women had no say in either war decisions or peace efforts. In addition, the clan system also formed a protective shield around combatants, impeding attempts to end indiscriminate acts of violence against women.

Even getting a seat around the table involved a major struggle. The women had to convince skeptical clan leaders and militia figures—and women from within their own ranks—of the need for the peace process to be more gender-sensitive. Their progress, says Elmi,

> did not come by accident, but through well-directed, daring struggles, carried out in phases, spearheaded by conscious women leaders in cooperation with the enlightened segments of civil society and the international community.
>
> Our main agenda was to vote for participatory peace and change as the basis of a new Somalia. We wanted to facilitate the creation of a stable,

democratic, and competitive state in which respect for human rights was preserved.

Because they shared a common gender spirit, and had similar national aspirations and vision for a peaceful and modern Somalia, the Sixth Clan became a distinctive presence in Arta. Their approach and the demands they made for inclusive, fair, and nonbiased participation, were different—and new.

As the negotiations progressed, and participants cemented mutual trust, their role evolved. They were no longer viewed as a special-interest group but respected participants. On occasion, the women were even called on to resolve disputes between the traditional clans. Eventually the atmosphere became "very friendly," says Elmi.

The final "National Document" agreed on in Arta included gender rights–responsive clauses and an affirmative-action quota for women's representation in the transitional House of Representatives.

The women's groups also secured favorable changes to clauses for the preservation of human rights of women, children, and minorities and got agreement on other sound democratic principles that, at least on paper, ranked among the best in the Greater Horn area. Strategic alliances and close working relationships established with other stakeholders gave the group considerable leverage outside of the peace negotiations. "Our lobbying measures paid off and superseded the counterefforts," says Elmi.

Critical Role

Faiza Jama Mohamed of Equality Now—an organization that works for protection and promotion of women's human rights around the world—credits Somali women with playing a critical role in steering the country in the direction of peace. In a speech to the UN Security Council in 2000, she noted that over the years—from the early period of the crisis—groups of Somali women worked to transcend artificial boundaries created by the political and social systems. Their "strong and sustained" efforts included community action to improve security, rehabilitation programs aimed at reintegrating ex-members of militias into normal society, and human rights programs (Mohamed 2000).

Save Somali Women and Children was set up in 1992 as crisis deepened in the wake of the overthrow of Siad Barre. It was formed by a group of activists and intellectuals to offer practical services to women in areas such as human rights and microcredit, and facilitate reconciliation between factions by mobilizing women from different clans and subclans to diffuse tensions.

The Arta peace conference laid such a strong basis for involvement of women in the peace process that when the Somalia Reconciliation Conference—staged under auspices of the Inter-Governmental Authority for Development (IGAD)—began at Eldoret, Kenya, in October 2002, the presence of Save Somali Women and Children was no surprise.

After Arta, women's organizations held a workshop on post-Arta Role and Responsibility of Women in the Promotion of Somalia Peace and Reconciliation

Process, to strengthen grassroots organizations through managerial and logistical support. Training in leadership was provided at a course held in Mogadishu, the Somali capital, in September 2002. Thirty-five women leaders, activists, politicians, and professionals attended this workshop, sponsored by woman worldwide. Its aim was to improve capacity and skills to enhance the role of women in the peace process as equal partners in decisionmaking.

The workshop recommended that women unite under the banner of the Sixth Clan, adhere to its principles, and work to realize its vision.

> The role that women could play in peace building is absolutely crucial—as mothers who educate their children, wives who advise their husbands, and the vital link between families and the communities . . . As citizens in their own right, women should be treated as focal points, who are capable of breaking down barriers in the quest for peace, reconciliation, and national cohesion (Save Somali Women and Children, 2002).

By the time the Kenya peace conference began, a wide cross section of women were well aware of the issues at stake and the significance of getting gender demands accepted. They lobbied hard on the outside to support the gender issues raised inside—especially the demand for 25 percent women participation in all institutions created through the IGAD negotiations.

After the peace deal was signed at State House in Nairobi, the factional leaders walked in triumph toward tents spaced out on the grounds. They were greeted by the ululations of joyful supporters. They hugged each other—remarkable, considering that they hardly addressed each other at the start of the negotiations.

Reason to Be Proud
Elmi noted that, despite these happy scenes, Somali women still faced pervasive violence and harmful traditional practices. They still lived, after all, in a culture based on male preference. "We are confronted by new civil wars," she said, "wars that have created internally displaced persons, the majority of them women." Especially in Mogadishu, the capital, the security situation remained volatile. It would take time for the structures agreed on to be put in place.

Even so, Somali women had reason to feel proud of the distance traveled by the Sixth Clan. Two years after their historic intervention at Arta, the Federal Charter of Somali was signed in Nairobi, stipulating that at least 12 percent of the new 275-member parliament must be women. The deal called for setting up a transitional government to run Somalia as a federal system for five years while a constitution was being completed.

As Nyaradzai Gumbonzvanda, regional director of the United Nations Fund for Women noted: "We can learn a lot from Somali women. They came together and organized themselves and now the Charter recognizes them" (Okello 2004).

Contact

Save Somali Women and Children
P.O. Box 38887–00623
Parklands, Nairobi, Kenya
Tel: +254 20 3744083
Fax: +254 20 3752199
E-mail: shirdon@iconnect.co.ke

Selected Bibliography

African Women's Development Fund. Online at: http://www.awdl.org/runnerapp/ Grantmaking/Grantee_Profiles/index.html.
Daily Nation. 2004. "Breakthrough in Somali Peace Talks." 30 January. Online at: http://www.banadir.com/feb04.shtml.
Mohamed, Faiza Jama. 2000. Statement Made at the UN Security Council. 23 October. Online at: http://www.peacewomen.org/un.sc.aria/faiza.pdf.
Okello, Rosamary. 2004. *The Sixth Clan at the Somalia Negotiating Table.* May. Online at: http://www.awcfs.org/features/womenempowerment0504.html
Save Somali Women and Children. 2002. *Report on the Training in Leadership and Peace Process.* Mogadishu: Save Somali Women and Children.
UNIFEM. Online at: http://www.womenwarpeace.org/somalia/somalia.htm.
Women's International League for Peace and Freedom. Online at: http://www.peace women.org/WPS/Somalia.html.

7.3

Women Weaving Bougainville Together: Leitana Nehan Women's Development Agency in Papua New Guinea

On the Pacific island of Bougainville, there is compelling evidence that it was the persistence of women's grassroots efforts that led to the ending of ten years of war. A weeklong search of some seven hundred women on how to bring about peace worked as a catalyst.

The stereotype of the Pacific island as lushly landscaped and socially tranquil was tainted in the late 1980s when separatist rebels on Bougainville took up arms against the central government in Papua New Guinea. The ensuing civil war was bloody and intense. At its height, government troops blockaded the island. Medicines, clothing, and food supplies were restricted. Guerrillas targeted anyone suspected of being opposed to independence.

The blockade led to the closure of schools. Hospitals and health centers had no medicines. People lived off the land, generating electricity from hydropower and solar panels. They resorted to using coconut oil to operate chainsaws and run vehicles and bush remedies in place of normal medication.

Clandestine Networks

It was in response to this crisis—and a beleaguered population's cry for humanitarian aid—that Leitana Nehan Women's Development Agency was established in 1992. Its motto—"Women Weaving Bougainville Together"—reflected its approach. The organization was part of a humanitarian network of like-minded bodies that found self-reliant and sustainable solutions as a way out of the crisis. These included the Catholic Women's Association and Bougainville Community Integrated Development Agency.

These organizations distributed food, clothing, and medicines to a deprived population in both government zones and areas controlled by the Bougainville Revolutionary Army (BRA). The clandestine networks they set up became the only sources of emergency assistance.

"We were very resourceful," says Helen Hakena, executive director of the Leitana Nehan Women's Development Agency and one of the organization's founders. "We learnt how to look after ourselves."

A Long History of Foreign Influence

Bougainville is one of a cluster of some forty islands comprising Papua New Guinea (PNG), a country located north of Australia in the South Pacific. PNG became independent from Australia in 1975. Bougainville was named after French explorer Louis-Antoine de Bougainville, who landed there in 1768. The island has a long history of foreign influence—indigenous feelings run high.

In 1989, separatists in the Bougainville Revolutionary Army (BRA) declared a "republic of Bougainville" and took up arms. Their campaign raised questions about environmental destruction and other aspects of the operations of Australian copper-mining companies. The Panguna copper mine—then the biggest in the world—was forced to close.

Fighting between the BRA and the Papua New Guinea armed forces continued almost unabated for nine years. The blockade imposed on Bougainville during this time imposed grave economic and other hardships on top of the constant threat of violence from the armed conflict.

The island was divided into pockets of rebel-controlled zones and government zones. In the army-controlled areas, nightly curfews and restrictions were imposed. This limited freedom of movement. Education and health services were disrupted. More than half the population of Bougainville was displaced. Thousands of women and children housed in care centers had no access to basic services. Malnutrition and poverty were widespread. Thousands died from the fighting, and from shortages of medicine and food.

In 1998, a fragile peace treaty was signed between the rebels and the PNG government. That was followed, in August 2001, by the signing of the Bougainville peace agreement in Arawa providing for a referendum in ten to fifteen years on the future political status of the island.

Through prayer meetings, reconciliation ceremonies, peace marches, and petitions, they took a political stand against violence. One silent march against the use of rape as a weapon drew a thousand women. Hakena explains:

> We just couldn't stay and watch while our sisters died in childbirth, were raped, sexually harassed, and emotionally abused. After watching women suffer the most tragic deaths, I was determined to do all I could to end the violence and deprivation. Nobody ever thought there would be a civil war. Nobody ever thought that we would die at the hands of our own people.

Hakena was herself a victim. In 1990 she was seven months pregnant when armed men stormed her house. "I was a teacher before the crisis. Our home was the first to burn. My village was burnt down the next day." She escaped. While on the run, she gave birth, prematurely, to her son, Max, on the floor of an abandoned bank building.

Such experiences were commonplace. Women were most at risk of physical violence and sexual exploitation. They suffered most from personal hardships caused by the blockade. More than 90 percent of refugees in care centers were women and children. It was the women, too, who were in the forefront of the civilian response.

Public Protest

In 1990, on the island of Buka, a group of women staged a public protest when a BRA blockade prevented soldiers from the Papua New Guinea Defence Force from distributing emergency medical supplies. The woman who led the march, Anastasia La Pointe, confronted the BRA commanders. "I told them that it was a women's initiative. If we had involved men, there would have been trouble," she said.

The following month, women from Selau in northern Bougainville, staged a march and appealed to both the Papua New Guinea Defence Force and BRA to put down arms and start peace negotiations. That was followed by an all-night vigil for peace. Five thousand people attended, including children and some BRA members. Selau was declared a "Peace Area" in August 1991. Steps were taken there to disarm local BRA forces.

Traditional Bougainville society is matrilineal: the women's line determines kinship and the inheritance and use of land rights. "Women," goes a local saying, "are mothers of the land." Their authority is respected; the word of the women carries weight.

As the conflict intensified, some women used this status to negotiate peace in their communities, acting as intermediaries to maintain dialogue. In July 1996, after seven years of war and many formal negotiations for peace failed, about seven hundred Bougainville women met in Arawa for a week-long search of how to bring about peace. The meeting became a major catalyst for peace. As a result of that meeting, women began working more actively for peace within their communities. Some mothers went into the bush and tried to convince their sons to return home, helping them to resettle into village life. In some areas, they entered the jungle and negotiated with BRA leaders.

The influence of women was also evident during the crisis over the employment of mercenaries from Sandline International by the Papua New Guinea government. A delegation of women traveled to Port Moresby, the capital, to present a written petition opposing the move to the prime minister's office.

Fifty women from Bougainville traveled to Lincoln, New Zealand, for meetings that led, eventually, to the signing of the Lincoln Peace Agreement in January 1998, which laid the groundwork for the eventual cease-fire in the territory. They drafted their own parallel statement outlining their role in the process. "We, the women, hold custodial rights over our land by clan inheritance. We insist that women leaders must be party to all stages of the political process in determining the future of Bougainville."

The impact of these activities—a mix of outspoken criticism and quiet, behind-the-scenes initiatives—is hard to measure. However, most observers say the role played by grassroots women's organizations like the Leitana Nehan Women's Development Agency helped ease the suffering of civilians, and alerted the international community.

Putting Women in Positions of Power

When the blockade eased, they shifted attention to reconstruction. Programs were developed to address trauma and dislocation caused by the civil war and help restore damaged civil structures.

The Leitana Nehan Women's Development Agency, which was a winner of the First Millennium Peace Prize for Women in 2001, initiated a two-year peace-building project in which trained volunteers—including ex-combatants—taught women and children about HIV/AIDS and the threats of substance abuse, and women's human rights.

The organization also confronted a new scourge: domestic violence. A culture of abuse on the island made life hellish for many women. Rape, incest, child abuse, and domestic violence were rampant. Of particular concern was so-called home brew abuse—violence fueled by a potent locally made alcoholic beverage that became popular on the island after the conflict. Its widespread use by young men is linked to the soaring rates of domestic violence.

The Leitana Nehan Women's Development Agency offered counseling services to help women and young people deal with the emotional trauma of violence. Between 2000 and 2003, it assisted more than 1,400 victims. "Wife-beating is an everyday thing," one of the women assisted with counseling said. "But women don't report it because they know the police will say it's just a domestic thing."

The organization also assisted in the rehabilitation of ex-combatants. It used ex-guerrillas as role models at antiviolence workshops. Says Hakena: "Peace will be just a dream if people's minds are not healed. It will take years to rehabilitate a people who have been severely affected by an uprising such as the Bougainville crisis." She believes that, ultimately, putting women in positions of power can break the cycle of violence:

> The crisis here started about land rights—the Panguna mine, its destruction of the environment, and the lack of compensation it gave to communities around the mine. Up until the crisis, decisions about who could use land may have been made by women at the back, but it was the men at the front doing the talking.

Women's groups have called for the setting up of a women's body supplementary to the Bougainville autonomous government. So far, lobbying efforts have secured four places for women in the provincial government.

Whether they will play key roles in the structures of the new autonomous government remains an open question. Women were underrepresented in the new political organs established under the peace accords. There were only six women of the 106 members of the appointed Bougainville People's Congress. Only two were included in the 52-strong Bougainvillean delegation at the September 2001 talks on autonomy, referendum, and arms disposal.

Nonetheless, as Helen Hakena points out, "Women are not passive victims. We are contributing actively . . . our courage and contributions have made the world a better place to live and work."

Contact

Leitana Nehan Women's Development Agency
P.O. Box 22 Buka
Port Moresby, Bougainville
Papua New Guinea
Tel: +675 973 9062
Fax: +675 973 9062
E-mail: leitananehan@daltron.com.pg

Selected Bibliography

Bougainville peace process. Online at: http://www.c-r.org/accord/boug/accord12/index.
    shtml.
UNIFEM. Online at: http://www.womenwarpeace.org/bougainville.

7.4

The Fate of the Disappeared Children: The Grandmothers of the Plaza de Mayo in Argentina

It was one of the darkest episodes in Argentine history: the disappearances of thousands of opponents of military rule. Many detainees had young children; they also "disappeared." For nearly thirty years, a group of women have fought to discover their fate. What began as essentially a personal struggle, involving their own flesh and blood, has transformed lives, changed laws, and inspired a whole country in the pursuit of truth.

On 30 April 1977, a small group of women gathered at Plaza de Mayo, the airy main square of Buenos Aires, and in the shadows of the cluster of government buildings located there—including the presidential palace and Ministry of Interior—they staged a poignant protest. Marching in circles, and holding aloft placards and photos of loved ones, they demanded answers to a painful question.

The women, soon christened after their regular, almost ritualistic vigils in the square, as Abuelas de La Plaza de Mayo (Grandmothers of the Plaza de Mayo), were protesting the detention of sons and daughters accused of subversion by the military dictatorship, and demanding the return of babies snatched from these "disappeared."

Human rights groups estimate eighty percent of those detained—anywhere between 10,000 and 30,000 people—were aged between sixteen and thirty-five years. Thirty percent were women. Ten percent were pregnant when taken into custody and gave birth in detention centers. Their babies were taken away.

Other "missing" children were kept by authorities in the same detention camps as their parents or other relatives. Eventually, they were given new identities and placed in special homes, or adopted by military officers and their friends. An estimated five hundred children vanished in this way during the period of military rule (1976–1983).

Emotional Strain
Formally constituted as an organization in 1983, Abuelas de La Plaza de Mayo enlisted help from volunteers to force the government into disclosing the

identities of these children. The effort had both political and personal dimensions, for there was no doubting the emotional strain of coping with discovering one's lost identity and connecting with newly discovered blood relatives.

Initially, the Grandmothers' search centered on hospitals and detention centers. They petitioned juvenile courts, scoured orphanages and baby-care centers. Medical and birth certificates and adoption papers were checked and double-checked; they combed archives. They were turned away from many doors. "We can do nothing; go away," people told them. "They paid 5 million for the babies, so they are in good hands." "Do not be concerned."

Their direct appeals to churches got encouragement from some bishops and priests, but not much concrete assistance. Undaunted, the women published announcements in the most important newspapers, appealing for information. They printed posters and leaflets and solicited successive military governments, the supreme court, United Nations, and the Organization of American States.

Thousands of petitions were filed on behalf of family members, relatives of families, and children who had doubts about their identity. Investigations were launched whenever a potential "disappeared" child was found. In such instances, both judicial and psychological factors were examined before the case was handed over to the appropriate authorities.

The Grandmothers argued that the children had an inalienable right to have their own identity and live with their natural families. In other words, they too were entitled to national and internationally recognized rights. Also, they insisted the victims were kidnapped as part of political repression, and that therefore the cloak of impunity should be removed from the military men involved.

Further, they demanded legislation to preserve the right to identify and bring those responsible for kidnapping children to justice while ensuring such atrocities never happened again. In this regard, they published announcements in local newspapers calling on people with information about atrocities to come forward. Posters and leaflets were distributed with photographs and relevant details of the disappeared children.

The focus of the Grandmothers was as much on raising public awareness about human rights in general as on the rights of children. In one landmark case, in 1994 the organization obtained a favorable declaration from the Argentine supreme court supporting its position that adoption of minors who had disappeared was null and void and in violation of the law. That ruling paved the way for obtaining court orders to prosecute ex-military leaders responsible for kidnapping and other atrocities.

International Attention

These activities drew international attention to the human rights situation in Argentina. Over time, a network of national and international solidarity was built up: links were established with like-minded and relevant groups and organizations and teams of professionals.

This enabled a collaborative approach, combining activists and professionals. This was key, given the limited experience and lack of expertise of these devoted women in areas such as law, genetics, and psychology. Through a successful lobbying effort, Articles 7, 8, and 11—on the rights of children to preserve their identities, including nationality, name, and family relations—were inserted into the Convention on the Rights of the Child adopted by the UN General Assembly in 1989. Eventually, Article 8 of that convention was incorporated into new adoption legislation in Argentina.

In the search for missing children, the organization found the easiest approach was to find records related to those who were confiscated immediately after birth. With regard to children born in detention, the real identity of the parents had to be determined. That meant widening the net.

The trail took the Grandmothers and their volunteers to researchers and experts in the field of genetics. Traveling to Sweden, France, and the United States, they found out that it was possible to prove with 99.95 percent accuracy, that a child belonged to a given family through specific blood analysis on the grandparents, the brothers or sisters, and the aunts and uncles of the victims.

With international support, the women were able to lobby for the creation of a National Bank of Genetic Data to preserve the genetic data of relatives of disappeared children. Located in Buenos Aires, this is the only bank of its kind in the world. It has become a model for other countries.

Genetic Data

Over thirty children have had their identities established in this way, using blood sample information. In March 1987, the Argentine Congress unanimously approved a law requiring any child with suspicious adoption records to have their DNA checked against that of relatives of the disappeared stored in the data bank. In 1997, legislation was passed giving full access to adoption records at the age of eighteen. The same legislation invalidated adoptions of kidnapped children.

A total of seventy-seven missing children have been reunited with their natural families as a result of the efforts of the Grandmothers. Some decided to live with their legitimate families. Others remained with the family that raised them and kept in contact with blood relatives.

The deeply emotional nature of discovering one's real identity after so long is exemplified by Horacio Pietragalla Corti, one of the babies snatched and handed over for adoption. He discovered his true origins—he was born to two "disappeared" persons—only in 2003, after taking a DNA test. His real name was Cesar Sebastian Castillo, and his real birthday, 11 March 1976—not 22 May 1977 as he grew up thinking. Horacio recalls the first meeting with his biological family as "very tough": "I was really hoping to meet my grandparents. Unfortunately, by then, all of them had died. And this is one of the things that hurts and upsets me the most. I have more photos than living people to enjoy" (Gotkine 2004).

The Grandmothers have devoted considerable attention to this aspect of their work—dealing with trauma associated with restored identity. With support from the European Union, a rehabilitation center was set up to extend and improve the quality of work being done in this area. Professional volunteers have been drafted into a team to support and help with reintegration.

With help from specialists and professionals from diverse areas, an Inter-Disciplinary Dialogue for Identity was launched—a sort of forum for sharing knowledge. Such efforts have been combined with other psycho-rehabilitative tools including theater, music, cinema, the plastic arts, and literature. Over time, with experience gathered by closely following the process of child restitution, they have learned to determine what the child perceives and thinks, what affects him/her, what he/she considers of value.

In the Pursuit of Truth

In 1997, when the organization celebrated its twentieth anniversary, its members and supporters realized they were no longer dealing with young girls and boys but grown-ups. They also became aware that the question of identity involved social as well as individual meditation.

So now the Grandmothers—who received the 1999 World Methodist Peace Award—struggle for core objectives of restoring the identity of the missing, while adapting to new methods and broadening the range of their work. For example, they have secured the support of Argentine sports stars to make appeals on their behalf. The organization's ideas on the right to identity have been popularized by music and television stars and in the successful theatrical work *A Propósito de la Duda* (*With Regards to the Doubt*) in 2000, which was seen by more than twenty thousand young people. In April 2000, the film *Botín de Guerra* (*War Booty*), which summarizes the history of the Grandmothers and told the story of the children, won several awards at the film festival in Valladolid, Spain, and the Ecumenical Prize at the Berlin Film Festival.

The women, who now gather in front of the Plaza de Mayo only on commemorative days, can look back on nearly thirty years of struggle that has gradually removed the walls of silence that existed about that dark period in Argentine history. Their experience underlines the value of networking, persistence, creativity, and willingness to learn from the experiences of others and incorporate this knowledge into their own work.

Their activities kept the issue of "disappeared" children in the forefront of the Argentine conscience for thirty years. Their actions have restored lost identities, led to the creation of a National Bank of Genetic Data, and drawn the international spotlight onto the general human rights situation in Argentina, at a time when many people were too scared to speak out. With their distinctive trademark white scarves and protest method—the women march in circles to circumvent a law against group assembly—they have become one of the most widely known protest groups in the world.

What began as essentially a personal struggle, involving their own flesh and blood, has transformed lives, changed laws, and inspired a whole country toward the pursuit of truth. Their watchwords—"truth" and "justice"—brought

Cuban Ladies in White

Every Sunday morning, dozens of women dressed in white with only a few details in black on their clothing solemnly wait to receive the communion in the churches of Santa Rita of Cassis in Miramar, the capital district of Havana. The rest of the parishioners watch the women—who invoke with their prayers of faith, hope, and love the freedom of their loved ones—with respect and admiration.

They are Las Damas de Blanco (Ladies in White), a group consisting of the wives of some seventy-five political prisoners in Cuba—sentenced to long prison terms for having committed the "crime of opinion"—who have formed a new movement of pacifist protest in Havana. They try to obtain the release of their husbands and fight, in a notorious but silent way, for the respect for human rights on the island.

Some with small children, others with their grandchildren, the courage of these women has left the world's public opinion in awe, seeing them defending their families with such strength and bravery.

Together, the Ladies in White respectfully attend different masses and ceremonies that are celebrated in Catholic churches in honor of the Virgin Mercedes, whom they, by doing so, consequently have transformed into their patron saint and protector.

Once a month they get together to hold literature meetings, where they share cups of tea and recite poems of Raul Rivero, probably the best-known Cuban political prisoner. Their methods are simple. They hold fasts, days of abstinence, and long silent walks on the Avenida de Miramar as a signal of their peaceful protest, asking for the freedom of those that have been imprisoned unjustly.

The Ladies in White let their claims be heard, while at the same time expressing a clear message of solidarity: "We are living here in Cuba, our husbands are political prisoners here in Cuba and we demand our human rights from the Cuban government. We, the wives of the political prisoners—who are not seventy-five, but closer to three hundred—claim the help of the international community to support us in our search for the freedom of our husbands and family members. We hope to have the support of intellectuals from all over the world."

home to Argentines the lesson that the main way to avoid conflict was not to conceal the past but to discuss it openly.

Contact

Abuelas de La Plaza de Mayo
Av. Corrientes 3284, 4°H
1193 Ciudad Autónoma de Buenos Aires
Argentina
Tel: +54 11 4864 3475
E-mail: abuelas@abuelas.org.ar
Website: http://www.abuelas.org.ar

Selected Bibliography

Arditti, Rita. 1999. *Searching for Life: the Grandmothers of the Plaza de Mayo and the Disappeared Children of Argentina* (Berkeley: University of California Press). Online at: http://www.usfca.edu/fac-staff/webberm/plaza.htm.

Gotkine, Elliott. 2004. "I Was One of Argentina's Stolen Babies." BBC World News, 31 March. Online at: http://news.bbc.co.uk/1/hi/world/americas/3585031.stm.

7.5

Women's Peace Activism in West Africa: The WIPNET Experience

Thelma Aremiebi Ekiyor and Leymah Roberta Gbowee

The Mass Action for Peace and women's participation in the Liberian peace process exemplifies how women can contribute significantly both during peace processes and in the building of postconflict societies. The rebuilding of the new Liberia continues and at each stage women are included and invited to participate. There is no doubt that the invaluable contribution of the Women in Peacebuilding Network, the Mano River Women's Peace Network, and other women's groups is responsible for this development.

In October 1929, the women of Aba in Eastern Nigeria rose up in protest against tax policies, low prices for locally produced goods, the artificially high prices of imported goods, and their hatred of the British appointed warrant chiefs and the native courts. Ten thousand women attacked key targets such as the native courts, European-owned factories, and warrant chiefs presiding over the courts. The women's uprising effectively ended the warrant chief system. Though they were second-class citizens with no formal influence over governance, security, or economics, the Aba women forced a change in African society by using their numbers, their ability to mobilize, and their role in traditional society.

To some extent, the legacy and spirit of the Aba women has remained alive in West Africa, as women's groups have continued to use their numerical strength, sisterhood, and shared experiences to bring about change. Unfortunately, since the mid-1980s social changes have been overshadowed by the plague of armed conflict, and especially the fourteen years of war in Liberia, which has spilled over the country's borders causing horrible suffering throughout the region. Under the circumstances, development has come to a virtual halt.

Starting in 2001, though, women once again played an important role in shaping events with the Women in Peacebuilding Network (WIPNET), helping to push the reluctant warring factions to reach an agreement to end the war in Liberia.

Chaos in Liberia

Although Liberia's warring parties reached a settlement in 1997, and Charles Taylor assumed the presidency, the violence soon started again. By early 1999, hundreds of thousands of Liberians were forced to flee their homes. An estimated twenty thousand child soldiers were fighting for both the rebels and the government. Unaccompanied girls were often captured by combatants and civilian men and used either as forced laborers or as "wives." Women also suffered enormously; many as victims of sexual assaults and rape. When they managed to avoid the fighting, they still had the task of raising and fending for children and the elderly under extremely difficult conditions.

Women served in many other roles as well: as combatants, peacemakers at all levels of society, providers of sanctuary, and as informal mediators. Yet women were largely absent from formal peace processes and peacebuilding initiatives implemented by nongovernmental organizations (NGOs).

Reacting to this marginalization, the West African Network for Peacebuilding (WANEP) decided to establish a women in peacebuilding program in 2001. WANEP was convinced that a better understanding of women's experiences and their contributions to peace was important for developing informed and sustainable peacebuilding strategies.

After thorough consultations with women's groups across West Africa, WANEP launched a regional network called Women in Peacebuilding Network (WIPNET). The goal was to use "women's peace activism" to promote social justice. Women's peace activism was defined not just as antiwar activism, but as the deconstruction of structural forms of violence existing in everyday society. This activism was built on a particular ideology: that systematic violence against women such as rape, forced prostitution, mutilation, etc., was an expression of a deeper systemic disregard for women existing in West African societies. By using women's numerical strength and their ability to mobilize around key issues, it would be possible to ensure that they could play a central role in formal peace processes and decisionmaking in the region.

Following its launch in 2001, WIPNET developed a training manual on peacebuilding; helped to organize numerous regional women's peace networks; organized training workshops, conferences, and other meetings; conducted research; published stories on women's peacebuilding activities; engaged in peacebuilding and democracy-building activities in Nigeria, Guinea-Bissau, Senegal, Gambia, and Mali; and undertook a range of other activities to build regional peace and mobilize women.

Mass Action for Peace

The role WIPNET played in the Liberian peace process is almost certainly its most significant success. By early 2003, WIPNET-Liberia had a substantial network of community-based women's groups. In May 2003, rebel forces controlled most of the Liberian countryside, and began to close in on the capital, Monrovia. Women under the auspices of WIPNET, recalling the example of an advocacy campaign pursued by the Liberian Women's Initiative (LWI) between 1994 and 1996, decided that they would not sit on the sidelines. The experiences of LWI, whose members had engaged in weapons collection activities and, more significantly, attendance at the peace talks, guided WIPNET.

Etweda Cooper of LWI served as WIPNET-Liberia's national adviser throughout this process. WIPNET tagged the campaign Mass Action for Peace. Women from all levels of Liberian society were recruited from displaced camps, churches, markets, schools, ordinary jobs, and NGOs. The campaign chose a simple and effective message: "We Want Peace; No More War." This message soon became a universal mantra and song.

Though all women were committed to the campaign, the greatest sacrifice came from women who had lost loved ones, or had been displaced or separated from their families. They said: "We have nothing to lose; we are ready to do what it takes to end this war."

At first no one took the Mass Action seriously, but the women became a constant presence on the streets of Monrovia. Women carried placards and posters in Monrovia and Totota, and every day, rain or shine, Muslim and Christian women dressed in white came together to pray at the airfield. Bishops and imams came to the airfield to show their solidarity. Slowly people started to take the women more seriously. The protest quickly spread to key sites in Monrovia, support grew, and the women learned how to effectively use the media to reach the international community. They even succeeded in pressuring President Charles Taylor into meeting with them, where they spelled out a clear program calling for an immediate unconditional cease-fire, dialogue for a negotiated settlement, and an intervention force.

When a peace conference was organized in Accra, Ghana, the Mass Action for Peace opened a new front. Maintaining a presence in Accra created new difficulties, especially because of the expenses involved. Previously,

The women of WIPNET protesting for peace near the peace-talks venue

WIPNET had succeeded in securing funds for the Mass Action, but contributions for the presence in Accra were harder to come by. Fortunately, they did secure funding and a delegation of seven women left for Accra on 26 May. Once in Accra, they mobilized Liberian women living in Accra, including residents of the Buduburam refugee camp, to join the campaign.

WIPNET used the media in both Accra and Liberia to excellent effect, and recruited WIPNET members from northern Ghana to join them for a demonstration at the Akosombo conference center where the peace talks were to begin. Heads of state and other dignitaries were greeted by the sight of women sitting on the lawn holding placards demanding peace. Other women's groups such as the Mano River Women's Peace Network (MARWOPNET) and Liberian Women in the Diaspora were delegates at the talks. WIPNET, in collaboration with other women's organizations, issued strongly worded statements expressing concern about civilian casualties in Liberia and appealing to the UN Security Council to deploy an intervention force. The spirit of collaboration would continue among the women's groups for the duration of the peace talks.

WIPNET was also meeting with all parties to the conflict, and with the mediators, including the chief mediator, Abdusalami Abubakar. Since the women were seen as speaking for "ordinary Liberians," all sides, including the rebels, sought to forge alliances with them, which meant that they had extraordinary access.

During the talks, WIPNET also organized a Liberian Women's Forum alongside the peace talks, where women could reflect on progress at the talks, while stressing the importance of continuing with the campaign and not being sidetracked by the politics that surrounded the talks. As the talks dragged on, there were further funding problems and tensions as some of the delegates worried about their relatives back in Liberia. Eventually, four of the seven women returned home, but they were replaced by Liberian women from the refugee camp.

The talks moved several times between Akosombo and Accra, and upon return to Accra the women decided they needed to adopt harsher nonviolent strategies. When the talks reached a stalemate, they barricaded the entrance of the talks preventing the mediators, the warring parties, and other delegates from exiting the venue. The women insisted that the men would not leave until they took the process seriously and committed themselves to reaching an agreement. The new approach was effective, and the women were invited to participate in several meetings exploring strategies for peace with both the rebels and the mediators. Two members of WIPNET represented the women at the political and security committee meeting, to the surprise and consternation of military officials. For WIPNET, attendance at these meetings, where the basic issues concerning the future of Liberia were discussed represented one of the great successes of the Mass Action for Peace campaign. It had shown that the women were stakeholders in the conflict and had a role to play in the peace process.

On 17 June, a cease-fire agreement was signed, but fighting still raged as the parties worked to reach a comprehensive agreement. The talks stalled several times. It seemed as if the Liberians were being held hostage by the delegates, so the women decided to turn the tables on them. WIPNET mobilized women and barricaded the entrance to the room where the negotiations were going on. The chief mediator pleaded with the women to move but they refused. They held up placards that said, "Killers of our people—no impunity this time," "Butchers and murderers of the Liberian people stop!" and "How many babies do you intend to slaughter?" The furor attracted the attention of the press and the standoff was televised. Partly in response to the publicity, the talks resumed. On 11 August, to the surprise of many, President Taylor agreed to resign. A week later, a comprehensive peace agreement was finally reached. Seventy-eight days of tumultuous peace talks ended and Gyude Bryant, a businessman, was selected as the interim chairman. It seemed like normalcy might return to Liberia. The WIPNET delegation returned to Liberia.

Continuing the Work

Following the peace talks, WIPNET remained active, organizing sensitization forums for women, raising their awareness of the content of the peace accord and the responsibilities of the parties to abide by it. WIPNET also marched to the headquarters of the peacekeeping force, both to thank them for bringing calm to Monrovia and to ask for a larger force. They then continued on to the U.S. embassy to ask the United States to provide more logistical support for the peacekeepers.

Through its actions, WIPNET earned the appreciation of the Liberian people. Recognizing the contributions of the women, the transitional government appointed WIPNET members to posts with governmental agencies, the National Human Rights Commission of Liberia, and the Truth and Reconciliation Commission. One member was named deputy minister for foreign affairs.

By accepting these appointments, WIPNET is ensuring that women remain involved in decisionmaking. WIPNET has continued its Mass Action for Peace with a daily presence at the airfield—serving as a reminder that the women were "watching the peace"—and with a march through Monrovia to demand disarmament.

The Mass Action also continues in four other regions focusing on monitoring the implementation of the peace agreement. WIPNET is one of the institutions partnering with the UN Mission in Liberia to promote disarmament, demobilization, reintegration, and repatriation activities, and continues to consult with the transitional leadership about Liberia's future. The WIPNET T-shirt is a major tool for accessing inaccessible areas. As WIPNET women enter communities, they are greeted by children singing "We want peace, No more war."

Successes

Through the Mass Action, WIPNET booked several very important successes.

Created awareness. The advocacy campaign raised awareness of the Liberian conflict among the citizens of the country. It uniquely targeted women in the rural communities and sensitized them on the important roles they could play in bringing peace to Liberia. For many women, the Mass Action was a training camp; it proved what women could do with their numbers, voices, and strength and catapulted women from behind-the-scenes victims to frontline soldiers for peace.

Gave a human face to the conflict. Peace processes are normally attended by the parties in conflict: government representatives and rebel groups. The presence of the women demonstrating at the talks removed the focus from the warring factions to the real people affected by the conflict. The Mass Action reminded everyone at the talks, and the world at large, that an entire population was waiting for the outcome and would not settle for anything less than peace.

Exerted pressure on all sides at the peace table. The Mass Action was not a "respecter of persons." The women targeted all sides in the conflict, meeting with rebels, government representatives, mediators, and the media and ensuring that the right amount of pressure was placed on each target to guarantee a comprehensive and truthful peace agreement.

Sustained action over an extended period of time. Women's nonviolent initiatives often lose steam due to lack of funding, poor morale among members, and frustration that the desired impact is not being achieved. This did not happen in the WIPNET Mass Action for Peace. Though there were daily challenges of poor morale, dwindling funds, and frustration, the women on this campaign were determined not to return to Liberia without a signed peace agreement. They kept referring to "their constituency" in Liberia who were suffering the ongoing bombardments between the rebels and government forces. This commitment sustained the campaign until the peace accord was signed.

Challenges
Certain challenges WIPNET faced and overcame are especially worth noting.

Organizing a campaign in a virtual police state where public gatherings, political activities, and marches were prohibited, and fear of imprisonment and beatings prevailed. The entire Mass Action for Peace was organized in a tense environment. The women in the campaign were regularly threatened by security forces with flogging, arrests, etc.

Bridging a divide between the more educated "elite" and women from grassroots communities. Initially, the elite women in Monrovia did not want to be part of the Mass Action. It was viewed as a rural movement that would be a "flash in the pan." This was frustrating for the leaders of the action who wanted all Liberian women to join forces in the campaign. Once the Mass Action gained recognition and began making impact locally and internationally, more elite women joined.

Meeting the costs, especially when the campaign moved to Accra. Funding the campaign was a major challenge; the violence erupted and people had to respond to it. Women in the Mass Action donated their market sales and savings to the campaign. Once the campaign moved to Accra this was very difficult; WANEP provided some funds but as this was not a budgeted activity, the longer the talks went on the harder the strain was on one organization to foot the bill. Supporters of WIPNET like the African Women Development Fund and Urgent Action Fund met this challenge.

Conclusion
WIPNET was green and perhaps naïve at the start of the campaign, but learned some key lessons during the Liberian peace process.

The peace table reflects a myriad of peace, security, political, and economic interests. Though the peace process belonged to Liberians, the process was influenced by external governments and at times the real objectives could have been subsumed by other interests. In retrospect, it was probably a good thing that WIPNET was new to this process, as the women's intentions were pure and selfless.

The peace table is structured to be an entirely male domain. Men at the peace talks were comfortable with the women demonstrating and crying, but uncomfortable when women insisted on playing a substantive role. WIPNET came to understand that it should insist that the peace table become the domain of all the people, and the peace process should be open to participants in the process regardless of their gender.

By their presence, WIPNET and other women's groups assured that women's issues would be addressed in shaping the new Liberia. Though women's issues might have been addressed in any case, a possibility became a certainty.

Adequate funding is essential. At various points, the shortage of funds threatened the sustainability of the campaign.

Building alliances is extremely important. WIPNET was strengthened in its resolve by the alliances it forged with women's groups across Africa and across the globe, bolstered by local alliances with religious leaders, politicians, professors, and ordinary citizens.

Preserving the psychosocial well-being of women in the campaign was as important as the goal itself. The women who left their families behind were under enormous stress. Many times, they questioned if anyone was listening. They kept themselves going through anecdotes and songs, and were particularly inspired by the words of African-American slave/freedom fighter Harriet Tubman: "If you are tired keep going, if you are hungry keep going, if you are scared keep going, if you want a taste of freedom, keep going" (Clinton 2003: 462–463).

Documentation is important. By recording the daily activities of the action, WIPNET made it possible for generations of women from Liberia and across the world to share in and learn from their experiences.

Like the Aba women's riot in the twentieth century, WIPNET's Mass Action for Peace captured the imagination of West African women and has shown that women can influence change, foster peace, and contribute to building equitable societies.

Thelma Arimiebi Ekiyor is director of programs of WANEP, and was founder and first regional coordinator of WIPNET.

Leymah Gbowee is the coordinator of WIPNET-Liberia and has been appointed to serve on Liberia's Truth and Reconciliation Commission.

Contact

West Africa Network for Peacebuilding (WANEP)
Ampomah House, 3rd Floor, 37 Dzorwulu Highway,
P.O. Box CT 4434, Cantonment-Accra,
Ghana
Tel.: +233 (0) 21 221 318 / 88 / 256439/8299
Fax: +233 (0) 21 221 735
E-mail: wanep@wanep.org
Website: http://www.wanep.org

Selected Bibliography

"Aba Women's Riots of October 1929," online at: http://www.ngex.com/nigeria/history/aba_womens_riot.htm.
Clinton, Hillary. 2003. *Living History* (New York; Simon & Schuster).
Ekiyor, Thelma. *The Female Combatant.* WANEP "From the Field" publication.
WANEP Women in Peacebuilding program reports, online at: http://www.wanep.org.

7.6

Leaving Lebanon: Four Mothers Movement in Israel

Three years of advocacy work helped an Israeli grassroots organization to achieve what it was aiming at: the withdrawal of the Israeli army from Lebanon, ending a long-lasting military operation the campaigners believed was senseless while costing the lives of dozens of Israeli and Lebanese sons.

On the night of 4 February 1997, two Israeli helicopters transporting troops to Lebanon collided over She'ar Yashuv in the region of Galilee. All seventy-three servicemen on board were killed. The troops were en route to the self-declared security zone just north of the Israeli border on Lebanese territory, where Israeli forces were patrolling in an effort to protect towns and villages in northern Israel against attacks staged from Palestinian and Hezbollah militants. Each year between ten and thirty Israeli soldiers were killed while on duty in the security zone, and the number of troops killed in the helicopter crash, although not on Lebanese territory, was the highest since the zone had been established in the early 1980s.

It turned out to be a catalyst for grassroots activity. The incident in Galilee was reason for a group of Israeli mothers to transform their gradually growing but simmering unease about the Israeli military presence in Lebanon. They knew the lives of hundreds of Israeli sons were put at risk as a result of the military operation. Some mothers started to doubt whether the risk was worth taking in this particular case. Four women—Rachel Ben-Dor, Miri Sela, Ronit Nahmias, and Zahara Antavi—who had sons serving in Lebanon and who lived in *kibbutzim* and towns in northern Israel, gathered at a street corner during the days immediately after the incident and protested the Israeli military presence in southern Lebanon. It would be the beginning of a grassroots campaign that was to gain huge support in a matter of months.

The women called for the unconditional, unilateral withdrawal of Israeli troops from Lebanon. Their quest was not easy—many people in the political establishment tried to stop or discourage them—but they finally got what they wanted. Israel pulled out its troops in May 2000, a little more than three years after the Four Mothers Movement was established. The movement has been described as "one of the most successful grassroots movements in Israeli history."

An Unsafe Security Zone

The activities of the Four Mothers Movement unfolded in the context of two decades of Israeli policy regarding Lebanon, which was closely linked to security issues and had both political and military dimensions. On 6 June 1982, under the direction of then defense minister Ariel Sharon, Israel invaded Lebanon with a massive force after it had been faced with attacks from Palestinian militants operating for some years from Lebanese territory. The massive Israeli invasion eventually drove the Palestinian forces out of Lebanon. It did not end Israeli operations in the country, however. After the first stage, Israeli troops partially withdrew from Lebanon, but did not retreat from a zone of about 15 kilometers immediately north of the Israeli-Lebanon border. Israeli authorities decided this stretch of land was to be a security zone aimed to keep at bay militants wishing to attack Israel.

The security zone would remain in place until the Israeli retreat in 2000. Despite the initial apparent defeat of Palestinian forces, tension along the Israel-Lebanon border did not cease to exist. Frequent clashes occurred between Israeli forces and fighters of Hezbollah, the militant organization reportedly supported by Iran and Syria. As a result, Israel's security, and that of inhabitants of the northern towns, villages, and *kibbutzim* in particular, remained under threat, thus legitimizing the perpetuation of a security policy based on Israeli military presence in Lebanon.

Since the invasion of Lebanon in 1982 until the Israeli withdrawal in 2000, thousands of Israeli sons were called for duty in Lebanon to protect Israel's northern border. In the mid-1990s, it became increasingly apparent to some Israelis that the security zone did not bring the safety the policymakers had hoped for. Hezbollah fighters were increasingly able to enter the zone, sometimes up to 150 meters from the Israeli border. The militants were able to stage attacks on Israeli forces that were increasingly effective from a military point of view. Gradually, the military situation changed, and not to Israel's advantage. Until 1996, thirteen Israeli soldiers died, on average, in Lebanon per year. After 1996, the annual average rose to more than twenty.

While the government defended its continued military presence in Lebanon, doubts about the legitimacy and effectiveness of Israel's continuous operation in southern Lebanon seemed to be brewing, not only among the general population but among politicians as well. Yet hardly any protests or even debates were openly staged. It would be the Four Mothers Movement that would bring the issue out into the open and into the limelight. The collision of the two helicopters in February 1997 was the immediate occasion for the mothers to take action.

The First Steps

"We were always full of concern and fear, but we felt there was no choice: we were told that they had to be in Lebanon and that's all there was to it," recalls

Ronit Nahmias, whose son served in the Golani Brigade, referring to the days she and her three friends established the Four Mothers Movement. "But the night of the helicopter disaster was a turning point for us. Families very close to us lost their sons and we realized that if not today, then tomorrow we too could lose ours. And we began to ask, why?"

The government's position that the security zone was necessary to protect residents of northern Israel apparently began to ring hollow for the women as they watched Katyusha rockets rain down on nearby communities. Peter Hirschberg, a journalist, wrote in an article published in the *Jerusalem Post* in 1997: "For years, Israelis have watched the funerals of soldiers killed in Lebanon, winced, and pushed aside their fears over their own children fighting there, convincing themselves there is no better alternative" (Hirschberg 1997).

The rising number of body bags coming home from Lebanon increased public debate. Rachel Ben Dor, who would become chairman of the Four Mothers Movement, recalls that she met her friends shortly after the helicopter crash and spoke about the need "to do something": "We had raised our sons together and had shared various periods in their lives and joys, including the beginning of their army service. We were now facing profound sorrow and despair, and also a great anxiety about their future."

That same week, the women had been reinforced in their feelings about Lebanon by an initiative of politicians who had joined in the Kohav Yair Forum and called for a reconsideration of Israel's policy regarding Lebanon. Ben Dor recalled that "their words carried hope. It was then that I started thinking that there may be someone who wants to suppress the fact about this being a protracted and bloody war." Ben Dor explained she realized that many former commanders of the Lebanese war were now Knesset (Israeli parliament) members and might refuse, out of a feeling of pride, to reconsider the military presence in Lebanon, even if they might see reasons to do so. She also felt that "we must educate how to live for our country, not just to educate how to die for it."

The first step Ben Dor and her friends took was to send a letter of support to Knesset members from various parties who participated in the Kohav Yair Forum. "We were surprised about the prompt replies we received from most of them, in which they expressed willingness to meet us," she recalled. Partly as a result of the mothers' initiative, the subject was put on the agenda of the Foreign Affairs and Defense Committee of the Knesset. Subsequently, the women were invited to tell about their feelings and opinions in the *Hakibutz* newspaper, in an article that appeared under the title "Four Mothers," which is a well-known line from a Jewish Passover song. "We decided to adopt this as our name," Ben Dor said.

Strategic Goals

The women quickly decided on the goal of their efforts. Increasing public awareness about the issue and putting pressure on politicians to change Israel's Lebanon policy were the Four Mothers Movement's strategic goals. The Four

Mothers Movement declared that it favored Israel's unilateral withdrawal from its self-declared security zone in southern Lebanon.

One of the first things the Four Mothers Movement did was to stage roadside protests in northern Israel, and later elsewhere in the country, to protest the Israeli military presence in Lebanon. They started to circulate petitions aimed at removing the Israeli army from Lebanon and collected over twenty-five thousand signatures. Supporters began demonstrating across from the Defense Ministry in Tel Aviv on every day a soldier was killed in the security zone. Four Mothers also deployed activities at the Israeli-Lebanese border. The group planted a peace forest there to symbolize the desire for peaceful borders and a return to normalcy in the area. Large demonstrations were organized in Tel Aviv and Jerusalem, where speakers made pleas for a withdrawal from Lebanon.

Representatives of the Four Mothers continued to meet weekly with public officials and Knesset members. They held intensive debates with President Ezer Weizman and several cabinet ministers, including Benjamin Netanyahu, Israeli prime minister from June 1996 to June 1999, as well as over 80 of the 120 members of the Israeli parliament. At these meetings they tried to convince officials to speak out on the issue of Lebanon and to advocate withdrawal. Members of the group also met ambassadors serving in Israel in order to inform them and seek support. They traveled abroad to raise the issue at the United Nations, the U.S. State Department, and at the French and British foreign ministries.

The Four Mothers Movement was considered unique in Israel. It was a truly grassroots organization, not affiliated with any party, drawing supporters from across the political spectrum. The name of the movement did not stop it from recruiting support among a variety of other groups in society. After a few months, it included women and men, students, as well as ex-soldiers, some of whom had served in Lebanon. The movement swelled to several hundred active members.

Four Mothers made sure it remained nonpartisan. Ben-Dor explained that "we engaged politicians from all parties, which were interested in promoting peace, and to bring this war to an end." The movement also sought to forge ties with people across the border. Through its website, Four Mothers made efforts to contact Lebanese citizens, in particular those most directly involved in the conflict in southern Lebanon. The webmaster of the organization regularly sent e-mails to various sites of Hezbollah, but she never received an answer. She started an English version of the website, which was originally in Hebrew only, in order to "let Lebanese know about us." Some signs of Lebanese interest were made manifest in January 2000, when the *Daily Star* English-language newspaper in Beirut published an interview it had conducted by e-mail with a spokesman for the Four Mothers Movement. Subsequently, the movement received messages of support from some Lebanese. One of the messages read, "It is about time we have a direct dialogue and drop the lunatics of both sides."

The movement met resistance. "People from the security establishment tried to frighten us, saying we were causing damage to our own children," Nahmias recalled. A senior army official said the calls for withdrawal endangered the safety of Israeli military in Lebanon. However, the criticism and accusations did not smother the debate. To the contrary, it incited it and made it more widespread. Meanwhile, the women received signals that many soldiers and army officers behind the scenes agreed with their position but felt they could not publicly express their support.

In August 1998, the movement erected a "tent of protest" in front of Israeli prime minister Benjamin Netanyahu's residence in Jerusalem for ten days, to collect more signatures for a petition and provide passers by with information.

Impact

One of the first signs that the Four Mothers' approach made an impact came on 1 April 1998, when then prime minister Netanyahu cited public pressure as the reason for his government to change its policy and agree to accept UN Resolution 425. This UN resolution called for the withdrawal of Israel from Lebanon, although, according to the Israeli government, this could only happen under certain conditions.

The movement's protests are also believed to have significantly contributed to a shift in public opinion in Israel. In 1997, according to a Tel Aviv University poll, 60 percent of Israeli Jews supported the government's policy to stay in Lebanon; 32 percent favored a unilateral pullout. After the Labour Party of Ehud Barak won elections in 1999, it became clear that 70 percent of the population supported the unilateral withdrawal from Lebanon. Barak had promised before the elections that he would retreat the army from Lebanon within a year. He kept his promise. Between May and July 2000, Israeli troops withdrew from the security zone.

Some observers argued that the Four Mothers Movement merely reflected Israeli's growing unease about the military presence in Lebanon and simply rode that wave of content, suggesting developments would not have been any different without the Four Mothers Movement being established. The women disagree with this analysis. Ben-Zvi says, "When we began, Lebanon was a silent war. No one talked about it. There was very little support for a withdrawal, let alone a unilateral withdrawal. We didn't just reflect public opinion, we shaped it." Others say one of the major contributions of the group was that it pulled public debate about Lebanon out of an atmosphere of taboo. Before the Four Mothers Movement came along, a Israeli university professor said, it was considered unpatriotic to discuss a possible withdrawal from Lebanon. He added he believed the women legitimized public debate about the issue.

Gadi Wolfsfeld, professor of political science and communications at Hebrew University, said the media catapulted the movement into the limelight. "The Four Mothers were very active and deserve credit, but I can't separate their activity from that of the media, which raised their status enormously," he was quoted as saying in the *Jerusalem Post* after Israel's withdrawal from Lebanon. The professor also said it was a victory for democracy. "Their success is an important sign that people can make a difference" (Frucht 2000).

In early 2000, the movement held its last meeting at Kibbutz Gadot, the location where it was conceived a little more than three years earlier, and symbolically dissolved itself. An affiliated website opened by former Four Mothers activists has it that the Four Mothers are on "reserve duty," though implying they might remobilize if developments make that appropriate in their eyes.

Selected Bibliography

Frucht, Leora Eren. 2000. "The Movement That Shaped the Lebanon Pullout." *Jerusalem Post*, 8 June.

Shackar, Eran. 1997. "The Home Front Goes on the Offensive." *HaKibutz,* 3 April.

Hirschberg, Peter. 1997. *Lebanon: Israel's Vietnam? The Jerusalem Report,* 11 December.

Four Mothers website: http://www.4mothers.org.il/mothers.htm.

8

Youth:
Protagonists for Peace

L. Randolph Carter and Michael Shipler

While the most visible role of young people in conflict is violent, youth throughout the world are organizing in their own communities and countries in order to protect their own rights and to try to have a positive impact on their environment.

The setting sun brought yet another gloomy night. Having eaten the meager portion of rice and soup rationed for the day, Randolph contemplated what this night would have in store for him and his family. It was late April 1996 and most of the gun and artillery fire occurred under the cover of night. The family lit kerosene lanterns and retreated indoors to what seemed to be the safest place. As he barricaded the doors, Randolph wondered if he had a future. Five months earlier, he had been an active participant in the West and Central African Regional Study of the *Impact of Armed Conflict on Children* (the Machel Study) (UNICEF 1996). He was a youth leader, having served as a peer mediator for a local program funded by the U.S. Agency for International Development. The concerns, resoluteness, and enthusiasm for peace-related programming that his peers and the participants of the study had expressed reminded this young leader that something was being done to ensure that a future did exist and that thousands of other youth were surviving similar circumstances.[1]

A couple of blocks away, Junior Sawyer (who was known as C.O. Dirty Ways) smoked as he watched his nine-year-old prodigy clean his AK-47. Junior had joined the rebel forces in early 1990 at the age of eleven as a result of the constant harassment his family had suffered at the hands of the rebels. His decision to join had brought the family no benefits as he was immediately transferred to the central part of the country to join the Small Boys Unit. Over the next five years, he had seen every major battle front in the country, including the infamous "Operation Octopus" attack on the outskirts of Monrovia. This was his second battle in the capital area, and this time he entered the city. The major armed factional movement had temporarily stalled and Junior

Sawyer and his colleagues used the time to acquire food supplies as well as gather spoils of war.

The sound of loud gunfire and shattering windows brought Randolph to his feet. His house had been attacked for reasons beyond his comprehension. The howling dogs gave every indication that death was right outside the door. Junior Sawyer and his prodigy were shooting at and chasing the young man's dogs, eventually capturing one and wounding the other. Randolph huddled with his family, crying and praying that God would save them from whatever was going on outside. After the shooting had quieted down, they listened as Junior's voice faded into the distance.

In the morning, as they cleaned up the blood, glass, and bullet shells, one of their dogs came in, dragging itself toward them, having suffered severe injuries. The other was nowhere to be seen.

The same morning, Junior entered their yard, pale and trembling with a fever. He requested the presence of Randolph's mother; he had heard she had some medicine. "I ate some dog last night and it has made me sick. Can you please help me?" he said. Randolph was bewildered; had this guy forgotten that he had stood in this very spot, shot and killed their dog, and destroyed their property the night before? As they faced each other, Randolph wondered which of these two youth was the victim of this tragedy.

These young men were both participants in the long and bloody conflict in Liberia; they both longed to have an impact on the world around them yet found themselves involved in profoundly different forces in society. This chapter discusses the myriad ways that youth participate in conflicts around the world and how adult-led institutions can engage them to help them find positive ways of contributing to their societies and create viable alternatives to violence.

Victims of War

First, it is important to recognize that youthhood is a culture-bound concept, differing from country to country. While in some societies people are "youth" until they pass a certain age, most cultures define the concept by life stage, dependent on the individuals' relationships to vocation, marriage, and parents. In situations of conflict and severe poverty, the opportunities for young people to pass through these stages are limited. War destroys family structures, eliminates access to education, and destabilizes the entire ecology of young people. Therefore, the definition of youthhood expands and includes people well into their thirties and forties who have been unable to build the pillars of their lives. The Women's Commission for Refugee Women and Children reported this phenomenon in Sierra Leone. "Because so many young people in their twenties and thirties missed out on schooling during the war and because there are so few opportunities today, many people in their thirties and forties are unskilled and unemployed, remaining youth in the eyes of society," the report on adolescents stated (2002).

In contrast, a child is internationally defined as anyone under the age of eighteen. However, many teenagers, who are still children, may also be defined as youth. As a result of the broadening of the definition of youthhood, programming tends to focus on either young children or young adults and leaves adolescents to the side. Of course, young people of all ages directly participate in conflict.

Like Junior and Randolph, millions of youth are victims of war. Areas affected by current armed conflicts have given rise to alarming statistics relating to HIV/AIDS, gang-related violence, prostitution, and poverty. Young people are displaced, lose their educational and vocational opportunities, and head households. All these vulnerabilities leave youth open to recruitment into armed groups where they come to participate directly in the conflict around them. It is paramount, therefore, to create opportunities for youth to participate in peacebuilding and reconciliation efforts.

In many societies of conflict, youth are a large and important demographic group. For example, in Sierra Leone, the United Nations Population Division estimates that in 2005, 63.9 percent of all people will be under twenty-five years of age. In Colombia, 49.3 percent of the population is under twenty-five (2004). The world is getting younger and youthful generations are increasingly important to engage and support.

Participation in Conflict

Both Randolph and Junior, like many other young people around them, were actively engaged in the conflict raging in their country. Often, the participation of young people in conflict is negative, primarily through violence. Conservative statistics cite over three hundred thousand children as active soldiers in over thirty ongoing wars today (Child Soldiers 2001). The other combatants are mostly young adults. Very little is said about the thousands of children who do not serve as full combatants but are used as couriers, messengers, and spies. The thousands of young women and girls who become sex slaves and wives of soldiers are also often ignored by disarmament, demobilization, and reintegration programs. In less intense conflicts, youth serve as gang members and ideologues, perpetuating ethnic and political divisions in society. Warlords and political elites have recognized the potential of young people and use this group to carry out their ideologies of war and/or politics. In Uganda, for example, the Lords Resistance Army is almost entirely made up of children. The characteristics of youth, such as a desire to have an impact on their environment, a need to belong to something bigger than themselves, susceptibility, manipulability, creativity, and resiliency, all make them potent actors in conflict.

Numerous publications cite conscription and abduction as major vehicles for youth involvement, but peer pressure and the spoils of war, coupled with belonging and acceptance, also serve as factors that pull youth into armed factions. In addition, as Junior's story shows, the desire for self and family protection prompts many to join such groups.

Protecting Their Own Rights and Promoting Peace

While the most visible role of young people in conflict is violent, youth throughout the world are organizing in their own communities and countries in order to protect their own rights and to try to have a positive impact on their environment. In Cambodia, for example, a group of four young genocide survivors, led by Outh Renne, created an organization called Youth for Peace (YFP). Their work began under a tree and has primarily focused on helping the younger generation take on a leadership role in reconstructing the country and building a lasting peace based on a renewed traditional culture. Through a series of partnerships with adult-led organizations, YFP has built a solid foundation; they now have a youth center in Phnom Penh and are working throughout the country, even in the Khmer Rouge regions in the north.

In zones of conflict all over the world, youth are coming together, seeking to protect their own rights and to promote peace. Most such groups never formalize their organizations or receive funding from international sources. They exist for a brief time and give young people meaning during crises. Others, such as Youth for Peace and the Burundian organization Jamaa (which is portrayed in Chapter 8.1), link with powerful partners in civil society or with international organizations to build their capacity and to help them gain access to resources. These groups are on the front lines; their work results directly from the conflicts that affect their lives and takes place in spaces in society that no adult-led group can access. They are able to build relationships with those young people who are involved in violence and help them find ways of engaging constructively.

Because of his work with the Student Palava Managers, a network of youth mediators, Randolph could open himself up to Junior, and they began to talk as the soldier waited for his medication. Over a three-month period, a profound friendship developed between the two. Randolph learned and listened to episodes of Junior's involvement in the war, his dreams of becoming an ambassador, and his fear of survival without his weapon. Junior listened to Randolph's struggles during the war, his dream of also becoming an ambassador one day, his involvement with peer mediation and counseling, and his interactions with individuals who were genuinely concerned about their plight as young people. Over time, this friendship prompted Junior to cut his long, unkempt hair (to which he attributed his wartime protection). He switched from his alias to his real name, refused to take the daily ration of drugs that he had been given in order to control him, and left his AK-47 permanently under his bed. This informal interaction had led a young man away from violence and opened up possibilities for him that had not seemed to be there. Threatened by the positive fruits of this interaction, leaders of Junior's rebel group warned that there would drastic action against Randolph's entire family if there was further contact between the young men. Junior was forcibly reenlisted and was last seen tied in the back of a military truck en route to another county.

Creating Alternatives to Violence

Youth-led organizations in zones of conflict are often well-placed to facilitate such interactions that help create viable alternatives to violence. Throughout the world, adult-led groups have begun to recognize the importance of including young people in the leadership of projects that target adolescents and young adults. The rise of youth participation as a technical field has produced a series of initiatives that are designed and run with the significant input of young people. United Nations Children's Fund (UNICEF) defines participation as "involving young people as active participants in the design, implementation, monitoring, and evaluation of sustainable, community-based initiatives" (UNICEF 2004). In the field of HIV/AIDS prevention, young people have been at the forefront of programming, helping to design and implement curriculums aimed at educating their peers in the dangers of the illness. Community-development initiatives, youth media, and other program streams have fully incorporated participation into their methodology.

More importantly, young leaders have begun to be included in national and international-level dialogues on issues that involve them. Children who had been directly affected by conflict were featured prominently at the International Conference on War-Affected Children in Winnipeg, Canada, the Special Session on Children at the United Nations, and the U.S. Department of Labor Conference, Children in the Crossfire. These attempts at bringing young people into policy discussions have not only honored their experiences and perspectives but also have shown that their ideas have value in discussions that are often beyond their reach.

Additionally, the Women's Commission on Refugee Women and Children produced a series of reports on the challenges facing adolescents in Kosovo, Sierra Leone, and northern Uganda that were researched by young people and reflected their own perspectives (see Chapter 8.3). The reports, which were widely disseminated, have created a consciousness that youth not only understand their own situations but that they should be consulted when determining appropriate interventions on their behalf.

In addition to the vast and important participation work of the international community, a global youth movement is seeking to create opportunities for young people to take a lead in political arenas. Numerous local, national, and international networks of young leaders have sprung up, forming youth councils and attempting to influence policy decisionmaking on issues that affect them. However there has been very little engagement by the international community with such groups.

Facilitating the Participation of Youth

Because certain sectors of youth play a significant role in conflict, it is important not only to forge space for young people in programming but also to facilitate their participation in society as a whole so that they can directly contribute to the transformation of their country's conflict. Already, youth-led organizations throughout the world are leading this shift in the notion of participation. Jamaa of Burundi, for example, formed as an association of young people who had been manipulated into violence by political elites. In order to protect themselves and their peers, they created a series of comprehensive activities through which they could engage in society in a constructive way, breaking down barriers between Hutus and Tutsis, facilitating dialogue on interethnic relations, and seeking to reintegrate children who had been involved with fighting forces on both sides.

Youth-led organizations have recognized the importance of engaging youth as participants in society and are leading an ad hoc movement that is seeking to generate opportunities for youth groups to participate in processes that build bridges and promote long-term sustainable peace. In some environments, they are addressing the root causes of youth vulnerabilities including unemployment, inadequate or irrelevant education, the disruption of family and social structures, and alienation from mainstream society.

Peacebuilding organizations, such as Search for Common Ground, have recognized that youth are key actors in conflict and need to be engaged as stakeholders who are needed to ensure success in promoting peace on a societal level. Adult-led organizations, by engaging with youth who are directly involved or at risk of being involved in violence, can help to transform young people's impact on conflict so that they are contributing to dialogue and long-term peace.

Lessons Learned

This engagement, whether happening on a community, national, or international level, is not without its challenges. While seeking to address the issues surrounding youth in conflict situations on the ground, there are a number of lessons that might be useful.

Work with youth-led organizations. It is important for international, adult-led institutions to engage youth directly, in the ways that they already organize. Rather than trying to create structures of young people, it is important to work with existing youth-led organizations, including those that are not traditional (i.e., gangs).

Create a five-degree shift. Successful programs seek to cause a "five-degree shift" (rather than a 180-degree turnaround) in young people who are involved in organized violence by directing their existing energies and skills into positive and constructive projects. Gang members who deal drugs, for example, are often entrepreneurial and charismatic, with leadership, management, and marketing skills. All those attributes can be harnessed to promote peace.

Dedicate resources to youth groups. It is important to help youth organizations gain the resources necessary to operate. Financial and technical support should be granted to them so that they can effectively deliver quality programming.

Create adult-youth partnerships. The most successful youth groups have adults, particularly those in civil-society organizations, as partners. This enables people with more experience to mentor and guide young people in developing their institutional structure and programming. A number of initiatives have sought to create such links and partnerships; the Mennonite Central Committee and the

American Friends Service Committee played key roles in supporting the establishment of YFP in Cambodia. The Christian Health Services were instrumental in supporting the Student Palava Managers in Liberia.

Link youth groups together. Youth groups benefit from being linked together both nationally and internationally so that they are able to coordinate efforts, liaise with international policymakers, and learn from one another's creativity.

Considering that it is extremely important to work with youth within their own countries, it is equally key to recognize that young people have perspectives and approaches that can enrich international policy toward themselves. Lessons learned in this arena include:

Ensure quality representation. Rather than simply identifying an "ex-child soldier," organizers should seek to bring youth participants that have connections to their peers. Including young peacebuilders who are involved in the reconstruction process is crucial.

Foster genuine participation. Unlike token participation that has the propensity to involve youth as justifications for grants and collateral for future funding, the inclusion of youth should be genuine. The engagement should be aimed at strengthening dialogue and policies and should result from a series of community-level consultations geared at ensuring that local efforts and challenges are addressed nationally and internationally.

Harness positive energy. Youth involved at this level of participation usually have scores of other young people who anxiously wait to hear about their experience. Seeing their peers meet and interact with prominent figures, who are usually seen as inaccessible, generates a desire to work harder.

Ensure proper follow-up. It is very challenging for young people to go from being conference superstars and the inspiration to many, to not hearing from their "admirers" ever again. Dozens of youth are taken each year from remote villages and war-torn countries and are flown to lavish hotels and conference settings. Going home is not initially difficult as they have scores of their peers eager to hear about their experiences. Participants usually feel that the people there were all so nice and concerned about what they are going through. While this generates an air of positivism, proper follow-up is essential to the long-term welfare of youth and effective policy-level participation.

Monumental Challenges
Direct engagement with youth-led groups allows the international community to develop programming that directly addresses the issues that young people are facing, in addition to helping transform the role of youth within the conflict. By strengthening youth groups' involvement in positive activities, young

people have representatives in society acting as outlets for the frustrations of a generation.

The dramatic increase in youth populations in many countries throughout the world has finally brought attention to the issues faced by young people in situations of conflict. As a significant demographic in most nations, youth have a powerful impact on how a society unfolds; they have economic and educational needs that governments are often ill-equipped to handle. Globally, youth face obstacles to gaining employment and access to relevant education and they are often marginalized from political and economic power. Representatives of the generation organize to create opportunities to be engaged in society, including those that have destructive ends. The international community, including donors, nongovernmental organizations, and multilateral organizations, is seeking ways of grappling with the monumental challenges that face young people. Major initiatives to increase youth employment and to reform education systems are under way throughout the world. However, by themselves, all these efforts cannot bring the participation of youth in violence to an end.

Additional efforts to specifically strengthen the role of youth in conflict situations at a societal level are needed. Young people, if engaged as relevant stakeholders alongside militaries, political elites, women, and governments, can significantly contribute to security and economic development. Those youth who are organizing and mobilizing their generation to play a positive role, building bridges across ethnic and political lines, and seeking to protect their peers need additional support to be propelled into leadership roles. Through their engagement, key young leaders can play a role in promoting peace within their societies and are positioned to create viable alternatives for their peers so that they can avoid involvement in violence.

L. Randolph Carter currently serves as assistant U.S.-resource coordinator for the National Association of Palava Managers (based in Liberia). Having experienced first-hand the devastation of war and civil unrest, Randolph has dedicated fourteen years to the advocacy of children affected by armed conflict.

Michael Shipler is the coordinator of children and youth programs for Search for Common Ground. He has been working with children and youth affected by armed conflict for seven years, developing a range of programs aimed at transforming the role of young people in conflicts.

Note

1. The Randolph referred to here is L. Randolph Carter, the coauthor of this chapter.

Selected Bibliography

Child Soldiers. 2004. *A Global Report from the Coalition to Stop the Use of Child Soldiers*. Online at: http://www.child-soldiers.org.

United Nations Population Division. 2004. Online at: http://esa.un.org/unpp/index. asp?panel=3.

United Nations Children's Fund (UNICEF). 2004. *Adolescent Participation in Programme Activities During Situations of Conflict and Post-Conflict* (New York: UNICEF Office of Emergency Programmes, January).

————. 1996. *Impact of Armed Conflict on Children*. Report of Graça Machel, Expert of the Secretary General of the United Nations, August. Online at: http://www. unicef.org/graca/.

Women's Commission for Refugee Women and Children. 2002. *Precious Resource: Adolescents in the Reconstruction of Sierra Leone* (New York: Women's Commission, September). Online at: http://www.womenscommission.org.

Resources

Lead Organizations

Global Movement for Children—United Kingdom
E-mail: info@gmfc.org
Website: http://www.gmfc.org

Global Youth Action Network—United States
E-mail: gyan@youthlink.org
Website: http://www.youthlink.org

Institute for International Mediation and Conflict Resolution—United States
E-mail: info@iimcr.org
Website: http://www.iimcr.org

International Youth Foundation—United States
E-mail: youth@iyfnet.org
Website: http://www.iyfnet.org

Oxfam International Youth Parliament—Australia
Peacebuilding Action Area
E-mail: info@iyp.oxfam.org
Website: http://www.iyp.oxfam.org

Search for Common Ground—United States
Children and Youth Program
E-mail: search@sfcg.org
Website: http://www.sfcg.org/programmes/children/programmes_children.html

United Nations Children's Fund—United States
Voices of Youth
For contact, please visit website: http://www.unicef.org/voy

United Network of Young Peacebuilders—Netherlands
E-mail: info@unoy.org
Website: http://www.unoy.org

Websites

Council of Europe: peace and intercultural dialogue sector: http://www.coe.int/youth
Portal on children and armed conflict: http://www.essex.ac.uk/armedcon/themes/general/default.htm
Youth for Peace—A global network of youth for peace: http://www.worldpeace.org/youth/

Publications

Brett, Rachel, and Irma Specht. *Young Soldiers. Why They Choose to Fight* (Boulder, CO: Lynne Rienner Publishers and Geneva: International Labour Organization, 2004).

Fischer, Martina, and Astrid Fischer. "Youth Development. A Contribution to the Establishment of a Civil Society and Peacebuilding: Lessons Learned in Bosnia and Herzegovina." Berghof Working Paper No. 2, 2004. Online at: http://www. berghof-center.org.

Fischer, Martina. "Youth Development as a Potential and Challenge for the Peace Process in Bosnia and Herzegovina." Berghof Working Paper No. 1, 2004. Online at: http://www.berghof-center.org.

Golembeek, Silvia. *What Works in Youth Participation: Case Studies from Around the World* (Washington, DC: International Youth Federation, 2000).

Hart, Roger A. *Children's Participation: The Theory and Practice of Involving Young Citizens in Community Development and Environmental Care* (New York: Earthscan Publications and UNICEF, 1997).

Higgins, Jane, and Olivia Martin. "Violence and Young People's Security," in James Arvanitakis, ed., *Highly Affected, Rarely Considered*. The International Youth Parliament Commission's report on the impacts of globalization on youth (Sydney: Oxfam and IYP, 2003).

Kemper, Yvonne. *Youth in War to Peace Transitions: Approaches of International Organizations*. Berghof Report No.10 (Berlin: Berghof Research Center for Constructive Conflict Management, 2004).

McEvoy, Siobhan. "Youth as Social and Political Agents: Issues in Post-Settlement Peacebuilding." Levy Kroc Institute, Occasional Paper 21, no. 2, 2002.

Mokwena, Steve. "Youth Participation and Social Change: Lessons and Perspectives from Around the World. Online at: http://www.unoy.org/downloads/8302.pdf.

"Post-Conflict Situations." 2003. Online at: http://www.unicef.org/emerg/files/Map_of_Programmes.pdf.

Schell-Faucon, Stephanie. "Conflict Transformation Through Educational and Youth Programmes," in *Berghof Handbook for Conflict Transformation* (Berlin: Berghof Research Center for Constructive Conflict Management and VS Verlag, 2003).

———. *Developing Education and Youth-Promotion Measures with Focus on Crisis Prevention and Peace-Building* (Eschborn, Germany: Deutsche Gesellschaft für Technische Zusammenarbeit [GTZ], 2002).

UNICEF. 2002. *Children Affected by Armed Conflict: UNICEF Actions* (New York: UNICEF, May).

Women's Commission for Refugee Women and Children. 2000. *Untapped Potential: Adolescents Affected by Armed Conflict—A Review of Programs and Policies* (New York: Women's Commission for Refugee Women and Children). Online at: http://www.womenscommission.org/pdf/adol2.pdf.

8.1

Picking Up the Pieces:
Jamaa in Burundi

Adrien Tuyaga

"I was in the middle," recalls Adrien Tuyaga. "Each side wanted me to join them and participate in the violence. I thought I would be killing my mother if I joined the Hutus and betraying my father if I joined the Tutsis. This is how I started to think of ways to pull people together."[1] Tuyaga's answer was Jamaa, a Burundian youth organization that promotes peace and reconciliation between Hutu and Tutsi youths.

The story of Tuyaga's and Jamaa's success is an unlikely story. Adrien Tuyaga was born in 1966 to a Tutsi mother and a Hutu father. When he was six, his father was killed during a massacre of Hutus by the Tutsi minority. Later, he was a boxer—and a drug addict. Then, in 1993, Melchior Ndadaye was assassinated, three months after he took office as Burundi's first democratically elected Hutu president. A wave of ethnic killings began that eventually claimed an estimated three hundred thousand lives.

The ethnic fighting led to the sharp division of Burundi into Hutu and Tutsi zones, without any contact between the communities. The youth on both sides often took a leading role in committing acts of violence. It hardly seemed to matter to them that they were fighting their former friends, neighbors, and even relatives. Attempts by the government and initiatives by some local nongovernmental organizations (NGOs) to bring together the warring militias to try to negotiate an end to the violence were futile.

An Alternative to Violence

It was around this time that Adrien Tuyaga began to talk to his close friend and neighbor Abdoul Niyungeko about the violence. Niyungeko was a Hutu, married to a Tutsi. The two men could not understand how former friends and neighbors could be filled with so much hate and driven to such horrific acts of violence. They decided to approach young people, especially youth leaders, and try to convince them to turn away from violence and join a movement for peace and reconciliation. "I targeted the youth leaders because they could start or stop the violence," says Tuyaga.

A Crowded Country with a Legacy of Ethnic Conflict

Burundi, a small country in the Great Lakes region in Central Africa, is often called "the heart of Africa." With 6.8 million inhabitants living on just 27,816 square kilometers, it is the second most densely populated country on the African continent.

Ethnically, Burundi is divided between Hutus, who comprise more than 85 percent of the total population, and Tutsis comprising around 14 percent. From independence in 1962 until 1993, Tutsis controlled the army and the government. On several occasions, the Hutu majority attempted to wrest power from the Tutsis. Since 1993, violence and civil conflict have persisted, and with the violence, political instability has prevailed. In 2000, former South African president Nelson Mandela brokered a cease-fire and a power-sharing agreement, but periodic outbreaks of fighting continue to afflict Burundi. A second South African–brokered power-sharing deal was signed at the end of 2002, but to date, peace has eluded Burundi.

That movement became Jamaa—"friends" in Swahili—which they founded in 1994. Jamaa was established with the understanding that it was necessary to persuade the youth on both sides who had themselves been involved in killings to sit down together and talk about reconciliation. Tuyaga and Niyungeko, who later was tragically killed in a motorcycle accident in 1997, told the youth leaders that society would forgive them for what they had done in the past if they took positive actions to build a peaceful society.

There were enormous risks, but something needed to be done to reintegrate these youth—many of whom had killed during the violence of the previous year—back into society, and to find a way to achieve justice and reconciliation in and between their communities.

The Jamaa Record

The very first activity was a football match organized between Tutsi and Hutu youth in Bujumbura, the capital. Subsequently, Jamaa organized a retreat with more than eighty leaders of youth militias from Bujumbura, as well as the suburbs and rural areas. The participants exchanged views on what was happening, why and how they might stop the violence, and what would be the implications on the leaders of their respective groups if they did take steps to end the violence.

There was no guarantee that the meeting would succeed, or even that it might not end in precisely the sort of violence it was aimed to stop. Many of these youth could not have imagined the possibility of even sitting together, much less discussing a complete change in their attitudes toward each other. The violence was so ingrained that they could look at their own deeds with a remarkable degree of detachment, as if killing and maiming the "other" was a most ordinary activity.

Nonetheless, perhaps surprisingly, the youth broke through an important barrier at that first gathering, and at the end of the retreat they pledged to turn away from violence. After making this pledge, they played a football match with mixed teams whose members included former killers from the two ethnic groups playing together. The match was greeted with great enthusiasm by those who were watching.

The activity helped to break down the fear and suspicion that had grown between the two communities, and slowly confidence and trust was built up and the security situation improved. Encouraged by the agreement among the youth leaders, and the success of the football match, Jamaa organized a whole tournament with mixed teams competing, and organized activities outside the capital.

Following the success with the football matches, the first stage of Jamaa's "real" work began with trauma counseling. That involved talking to the youth about their experiences of violence, accompanied by efforts to reintegrate them back into the community. One former Hutu militia member, for example, admitted his complicity in the killings, explaining that "I reacted from fear, and I was confused. I was made to feel that if I didn't kill the Tutsis they would kill me." Jamaa worked with international NGOs to develop employment opportunities for the youth. They arranged microcredit facilities, with the condition that credit would only be available to applicants whose proposals clearly included a multi-ethnic component (Elworthy 2001).

In 1999, Jamaa made another move to forge relationships between the youth groups as a way to head off threats of violence. This initiative was called Jamaa, Gardons Contact, which means "Friends, let's keep in touch." The idea was that regular contact between youth groups was important, if the previous work of reconciliation was to be kept alive. The organization built up a network of ex-militia leaders and youth-at-risk who could get in touch with each other precisely at the moments when violence appeared likely.

Still another Jamaa initiative proved its value around the time of the signing of the Arusha Accords to put an end to the conflict in August 2000. Violence was increasing in Bujumbura as extremists tried to undermine the talks. Jamaa launched a campaign in the city under the slogan "Yes to Life, No to Violence." They plastered the city with posters, hung banners, and distributed leaflets calling on local people to join them in rejecting violence and asking them to wear a piece of white cloth around their wrists as a symbolic gesture of their choice for peace. A more serious outbreak of violence failed to materialize.

The following year, in collaboration with Search for Common Ground (SFCG), Jamaa published a cartoon book called *Le Meilleur Choix* (The Best Choice). The book used drama and humor to depict the real-life experiences of two young men who had taken part in the ethnic violence and who were attempting to reconcile with the families of their victims. The Ministry of Education in Burundi has now included the book as a formal part of the national curriculum for peace education in schools and colleges throughout the country.

Also in 2001, SFCG called on Jamaa to mobilize thirty-two youth leaders associated with Gardons Contact when it appeared that a new wave of violence might erupt. The youth came together and assisted with emergency food distribution to fifty thousand people displaced by fighting between government troops and rebels. The action was enormously helpful in a practical sense, and also was of great symbolic importance as a demonstration of the commitment of the youth to peace and reconciliation.

Strategies, Priorities, Challenges

Jamaa's strategy is to focus on a variety of issues that must be addressed if peace and stability are to prevail. One of the most important of these is the pressing need to expand educational opportunities that give young people a foundation upon which they can build productive lives. Jamaa is also an advocate for the development of public infrastructure, where the net effect is not only to stimulate economic development and activity, but also to increase interdependency among Burundi's communities. A further strategic focus of Jamaa is to address the difficulties of young Burundians regarding access to land, housing, and employment. Finally, Jamaa actively promotes justice and human rights.

Jamaa's priority today is to work in solidarity with local communities during this sensitive transition period in Burundi. Finding the resources to sustain its programs continues to be a major challenge. Although Jamaa has received local and international recognition for its contributions to peacebuilding within Burundi's still-divided communities, and its *Le Meilleur Choix* was a finalist for the 2003 UNESCO Prize for Children's and Young People's Literature in the Service of Tolerance, its long-term survival can only be assured with support from outside sources.

Looking Back

In ten years of activities, Jamaa has learned a number of valuable lessons. To begin with, the first step to resolving a conflict is to step back from all forms of confrontation, and then to take care not to marginalize any player. Inclusiveness is essential; all actors should be given an opportunity to be involved. The corollary lesson is that there are neither "big" nor "small" actors—each actor must be given his or her due. When engaged in discussion and debate, Jamaa has learned, all arguments must be presented openly and frankly, and respectfully listened to by all the partners. Finally, it is important to be flexible. There is one absolute—respect for the human rights of all, regardless of ethnicity—but many strategies, including ones drawing on local cultures and strategies specific to local contexts, which can be applied to encourage dialogue and reconciliation on the ground.

Jamaa began with a football game, but has grown into a valuable tool for reconciliation. It owes a large part of its success to an understanding that while young people may have participated in ethnic violence, the real perpetrators were politicians who manipulated impressionable youth for their own purposes. As one former Tutsi militia member stated, "I didn't profit from any of the killings. I was poor before and I am poor now. The politicians told us to kill and now we have to pick up the pieces." Thanks to Jamaa, picking up the pieces is a little bit easier.

Adrien Tuyaga is one of the founders and is the permanent coordinator of Jamaa.

Contact

Adrien Tuyaga—coordinator, Jamaa
Avenue des Manguiers no. 1
Bujumbura, Burundi
Tel: +257 22 06 13
Fax: +257 21 63 31
E-mail: adrientuyaga@hotmail.com

Note
1. Quoted by Matthews and McLeod (2002).

Selected Bibliography
"Burundi Civil War." Online at: http://www.globalsecurity.org/military/world/war/burundi.htm.
"Burundi Country Profile." Online at: http://www.news.bbc.co.uk/1/hi/world/africa/country_profiles/1068873.stm.
Christian Aid in Burundi. 2003. "Across the Divide—Reconciliation in Burundi." Online at: http://www.christian-aid.org.uk/world/where/eagl/partners/0301jama.htm.
Elworthy, Scilla. 2001. "Gandhi's Legacy: The Vibrancy of Non-Violent Conflict Resolution in the 21st Century." Paper presented to the Gandhi Memorial Lecture series at the Nehru Centre on 10 October. Online at: http://www.oxfordresearchgroup.org.uk/programmes/conflict/talks/Gandhi101001.htm.
Matthews, Dylan, and Jason McLeod. 2002. "Brave Steps Towards Peace." *New Internationalist Magazine,* no. 352 (December). Online at: http://www.newint.org/issue352/brave.htm.
"The Youth Project." Online at: http://www.sfcg.org/programmes/burundi/burundi_youth.html.

8.2

And a Child Shall Lead:
The Children's Movement for Peace
and Return to Happiness in Colombia

With a bold gesture that captured the national imagination, Colombian children pointed the way toward peaceful resolution of South America's longest-running civil war. Other young people are trying to keep that spirit alive.

Graça Machel, wife of former South African president Nelson Mandela, was visiting towns and villages affected by violence in Colombia when she planted the idea of holding a national exercise in which children would vote on their rights as citizens. The year was 1996. Against the backdrop of a long-running civil war, national elections were approaching in which adults would have their say. The idea of a children's vote quickly took on a life of its own.

Under the auspices of United Nations Children's Fund (UNICEF), sponsors of Machel's visit to Colombia, a children's vote was held successfully in her native country, Mozambique. It was later replicated in Ecuador in 1993. UNICEF organized a workshop to discuss the possibility of holding a national children's referendum in Colombia. Almost thirty young people between ages seven and sixteen from all over the country and all walks of life turned up; it attracted adult organizations as well.

For many of these participants, it was an eye-opening experience. They found themselves sharing common experiences with people from other areas of the country and were able to develop joint approaches. Young people also discovered something important: when children talk about violence, adults tend to listen.

Referendum
This planning workshop became a springboard for a national organization, Movimiento de los Niños por La Paz (Children's Movement for Peace), which made history by organizing a referendum to determine the rights valued most by children. In a country where children were normally helpless victims of violence, the Children's Movement for Peace provided a medium through which many youngsters felt empowered to take their own initiatives.

162

Mayerly Sanchez, a young spokesperson for the Children's Movement for Peace, says that for her the turning point was the stabbing of a young next-door neighbor during a gang fight. This happened a few blocks from home. She pledged to take action against violence and found in the movement an appropriate outlet for her energies.

With help from adult bodies, the Children's Movement for Peace set about organizing the vote.[1] The arrangement of voting was localized, down to neighborhoods, schools, and communities. Over a four-month period, support alliances were set up across the country. As the organization grew, the initial mass-media skepticism gave way to enthusiasm. Important media outlets interviewed the children and offered airtime for commercials.

For the first time, many Colombians saw and heard children—many of them quite articulate—talk with sincerity about their own aspirations for peace. They listened to them recount experiences with violence. The depth of these feelings took many by surprise, and helped foster a favorable national mood. Community organizations, churches, schools, and municipalities signed on to participate in the referendum.

As its reach expanded, the Ministries of Education and Interior provided support. Guerrillas and government troops pledged not to disrupt this unique exercise in democracy. Crucially—given the costs involved—the government accepted its constitutional obligation to facilitate participatory democracy and underwrite the cost of staging the nationwide vote.

The turnout on voting day, 25 October 1996, was overwhelming; the outcome was decisive: 2.7 million children voters rejected violence and chose the right to life and peace. "Peace," said one of the child voters, "is most important because without it you cannot have any other right."

This result, the effort put into organizing the event, and the spirit and mood stimulated across the country by the process, influenced parallel peace movements and initiatives that embraced politicians, civil society, and the public at large. In an important indication of support, the government decreed that henceforth the military draft for youths under the age of eighteen would be voluntary.

Adult Equivalent

One year later, an adult equivalent of the children's vote was organized. In the largest social mobilization ever undertaken in Colombia, 10 million adult voters voted "Yes" for a Citizen's Mandate for Peace, Life, and Freedom. Although this vote was marred by violent incidents and threats of disruptions, and criticized by some as "unworkable," "divisive," and "too dangerous," election day was relatively calm. Voter turnout was 40 percent higher than in normal elections.

The positive outcome of these two voting exercises provided renewed focus for what was, at the time, a largely fragmented and weak peace movement. The idealism and sincerity of the children had made a difference. They had demonstrated to adults that large-scale mobilization was possible around an issue like peace.

This heightened awareness may have influenced representatives of the main guerrilla groups to travel to Germany for exploratory talks with representatives of civil society, religious groups, and government leaders five weeks after the presidential elections of May 1998.

After the heady aftermath of the vote, the Children's Movement for Peace became involved in other activities and became a forum for airing children's opinions on subjects of concern. It set up youth support groups to deal with issues such as street violence and adolescent drug use, mediated in gang wars, and helped children traumatized by violence. The group also hosted a Summit for Children.

Return to Happiness

Mayerly Sanchez says the children's organization defines peace in four words: "love," "acceptance," "forgiveness," and "work"—watchwords that are also present, in one form or another, in the Retorno de la Alegria (Return to Happiness) initiative.

The Return to Happiness program emerged in 1996, during the hopeful period that spawned Children's Movement for Peace. Using a model also tried by UNICEF in Mozambique—an African country that has found peace after a long, intense civil war—Return to Happiness trains adolescent volunteers, supervised by teachers, to give therapeutic support and encourage trust and hope among young children. It uses games, art, puppetry, songs, and storytelling as tools of therapy.

Some five hundred volunteers were initially trained within the space of a month. They were taught how to recognize symptoms of stress in children, and observe and communicate with them. Every available space has been utilized as meeting areas—churches, parks, and kiosks. Using toys and puppets as characters to tell stories that fit the culture of the audience, the volunteers foster personal relationships and create safe environments in which children express feelings and begin to overcome painful conflict experiences.

Volunteers are armed with what was called a "knapsack of dreams"—rag dolls, puppets, wooden toys, and books. Each of these tools served a specific function. The dolls, for example, symbolized characters in the child's life, and could unlock memories and fears. Puppets helped volunteers bring stories to life. The books (*El Miquito Feliz* [The Happy Little Monkey] and *Buenas Noches* [Good Night]) were useful to overcome stress-related problems, sleeplessness, and fears.

All toys, puppets, and learning materials are locally produced to generate income for the community. The program addresses areas such as psychosocial recovery, education for peace, and social mobilization, reconciliation, conflict resolution, health education, and the rebuilding and reconstruction of the community.

"From the start," said UNICEF in a background document on the program, "adolescents proved an ideal role model for the younger children. Adolescents understand very well the child's world—the games, songs, stories, riddles and legends. In the towns and villages of Colombia they feel the same impact of terror and violence. They console and support each other as the volunteers attempted to bring back a sense of normalcy to the lives of younger children."

In the course of teaching others to overcome distress, the adolescent volunteers also learn to cope and the ability to help others builds their own self-esteem. Specialized support and self-help are integrated into the program to help them sort out personal problems.

Community-based participation is encouraged rather than the standard, clinical model of psychological therapy. Individual children, for example, are given attention and enabled to relate to others in a wider group, and in an environment that inspires confidence. Children with symptoms of trauma are helped in afternoon activities. These are conducted in a familiar environment. Where necessary, special treatment and support are provided through appropriate mental health services, including counseling and rehabilitation for the severely traumatized.

Inside schools located in violence-prone regions, volunteers work to improve relationships between teachers and students, and among the children themselves. They also do what they can to strengthen partnerships among NGOs, religious groups, school officials, local government officials, health officials, and young people. This helps raise community awareness of psychosocial issues and strengthens support for mental health services.

In the Panamanian province of Darien—an isolated, sparsely populated, and dangerous place just across the border from Colombia, into which refugees frequently flee—a UNICEF staff member, posted there full time in 1992, started a Return to Happiness therapy program as a focal point for mobilizing the community and establishing links between various groups and organizations.

UNICEF is pleased with the results:

> Although there is continued risk of violence in the refugee communities, the Return to Happiness program has contributed to a sense of security and brought new life to the children. The children have been trained to use the symbol of the human hand to represent the commitment to protect children from harm. Each finger of the hand is raised in protection and identified with a particular quality associated with peace.

UNICEF reports that the real value of Return to Happiness is its overarching impact. The program affects children's health and well-being at home, in school, and in the community; it helps both individuals and the wider community.

Examples to Combatants

These two programs involving Colombian young people certainly have not ended violence and bloodshed; nonetheless, they provide examples to combatants of the existence of a national sentiment in favor of peace. The depth of their reach may well have deprived guerrilla armies and paramilitary groups of potential recruits among the young population.

Children's Movement for Peace has encouraged millions of young Colombians to think and act in the interest of peace, among themselves, and by influencing the adult population in this direction. Return to Happiness, with its combination of psychological support and community-based actions for peace, builds on this foundation to support refugee victims of violence and terror and create a more peaceful environment for children.

Contact

Children's Movement for Peace
Website: http://www.geocities.com/EnchantedForest/Creek/8238/index.htm

Note

1. Support came from World Vision, Colombian Scouts, Colombian Red Cross, Benposta, Children's Defense International, the Public Defenders' Office, Jesuits Program for Peace, Save the Children Fund, Christian Children's Fund, UNESCO, the diplomatic community, local government agencies, schools, community and religious organizations working with children and displaced populations, and UNICEF.

Selected Bibliography

Cameron, Sara. *Out of War: True Stories from the Front Lines of the Children's Movement for Peace in Colombia* (New York: Scholastic Press, 2001).

UNICEF. *Adolescent Participation in Programme Activities During Situations of Conflict and Post-Conflict* (New York: Office of Emergency Programmes, January 2004).

8.3

Young Kosovars Help Themselves: The Kosovar Youth Council

Valon Kurhasani

Rather than feeling sorry for themselves, young people displaced by the war in Kosovo organized themselves to improve their own situation. The group was effective in getting youth issues onto the agendas of the international decisionmakers.

During the late 1990s, the republic of Kosovo stood at the center of a series of upheavals that marked the breakup of the former Yugoslavia. The majority ethnic Albanian population pressed demands for independence; the Serb minority opposed this. With the Kosovo Liberation Army stepping up attacks, the Federal Republic of Yugoslavia government in Belgrade responded with force.

When peace initiatives failed, the North Atlantic Treaty Organization carried out an intense bombing campaign in early 1999 to force Serbian troops out of the territory. The events leading up to this war, the war itself, and its aftermath, demanded an immense human toll.

A week after the bombings began in 1999, more than three hundred thousand ethnic Albanian Kosovars fled into neighboring Albania and Macedonia. Roughly the same number was displaced within the province itself. Overall, some 850,000 people—the vast majority of them of Albanian ethnicity—fled their homes. Thousands died or went missing. Hundreds were imprisoned. Land mines and unexploded ordnance littered the countryside. Many people, traumatized by the conflict, had no clear vision of the future.

The possibilities for reconstruction and reconciliation of the republic in the aftermath of the war was made more complicated by the relatively young age of the Kosovar population, approximately half of whom were under twenty years of age. Reports by the World Bank and European Union, presented at a conference in Brussels in 1999, identified young people between the ages of fifteen and twenty as the greatest potential source of civil unrest in Kosovo.

It was against this background that a youth organization called the Kosovar Youth Council (KYC) stepped up to speak for this huge part of Kosovar society. Its aim was to help young Kosovars overcome the trauma and hardships brought on by this massive expulsion and help them build a new future.

Make a Better Place for a Better Life

The Kosovar Youth Council (KYC) came into being when, in the aftermath of the war, the Albanian Youth Council helped mobilize and organize Kosovar youth, both in refugee camps and in towns. Some twenty thousand of these youth, in six Albanian refugee camps, got together and formed their own youth councils to improve conditions in these camps by organizing sports and music events, improving safety and cleanliness, distributing landmine-awareness information, and providing psychosocial counseling for younger children.

Many continued their community development work when they were repatriated to their home villages and maintained a youth network that promoted local peacebuilding efforts. These efforts sometimes even stretched across ethnic lines, a rare thing in those days. The councils functioned as outlets for youth voices. The young activists were valuable to the reconstruction of Kosovo because they promoted issues such as self-organized education, developed entertainment for other young people, and became actively involved in the creation and development of meaningful youth policies.

With its "Make a Better Place for a Better Life" slogan, KYC set about playing an advisory and leadership coordinating role including, among other things, researching the problems and needs of young people in Kosovo. It broadened its initiatives over time to include more comprehensive efforts aimed at supporting civil society, such as encouraging youth participation by creating youth nongovernmental organizations and coordinating their leadership.

Battle for Peace

The KYC became one of the earliest organizations of young people to push its way onto the radar screens of international bodies and nowadays could be seen as a model of how international agencies can engage with youth groups in postconflict situations. It was effective in getting youth issues onto the agendas of decisionmakers of all levels that were involved in Kosovo, a necessity in a country where youth constitutes almost half of the population.

One reason for its success was that it embraced different ethnic groups, and therefore was viewed as neutral. This helped the group focus on issues concerning young people without regard for their ethnic background.

Children, adolescents, and young adults were particularly exposed to problems caused by the conflict. Many young people in Kosovo lacked confidence and a feeling of self-worth and had very little hope for the future. With social, educational, and economic networks for young people in disarray because of the conflict, young people needed help to find appropriate responses to their situation. Without it, many agreed, the future well-being of the area was in danger.

Reports on the difficulties that young people were facing were plenty, on issues such as girls and young women being kidnapped, youth drug abuse, and

kosovar Youth Council

Students presenting their activities at a local radio station in Gjakova

violence against minorities, and about young people losing their parents and being unable to get proper education opportunities. All these things pointed to the need to know more about the nature and breadth of problems facing youth and what it takes to solve them.

With its multiethnic membership—mainly adolescents, while others were in their twenties—KYC became one of the few organizations serving as an advocacy group on behalf of young Kosovars. Today, KYC has sixty active members operating in several cities, including Pristina, Pejë, and Gjakova, with a main office in Pristina.

One of its most important undertakings was a research project that provided an overview of the problems facing young people and how they could be resolved. The research found that while many young people appeared to be recovering reasonably well from the war, equally as many faced personal crises. In general, according to the research, the situation of all young people required urgent attention to prevent it from getting worse.

Some young people were still carrying weapons, the researchers discovered. Economic and social pressures had led to some terminating their normal education. In some instances, this was because of family pressure—especially in the case of rural girls. There was a lack of motivation and desire. Many young people had no homes. Others suffered in isolation, without a support network. This was especially so in the case of girls who had suffered sexual violence. Most could not speak openly about love relationships, for example. The researchers concluded that the capacity of young people to function as constructive civil-society actors needed to be developed and they should be included in decisionmaking processes affecting Kosovar society.

A Dialogue of Dilemma

"Can we live with Serbs?" an Albanian Kosovar adolescent asked during a discussion at which young Kosovar refugees contemplated their return to Kosovo. "Never!" she answered herself.

Another countered: "But some of them helped us get to safety." A third said, "No, no, you can't trust any of them."

"Never can we live together with Albanians," said a Serbian adolescent girl after she was asked about the possibility of living in a multiethnic society in Kosovo.

Another said, 'Why not? We were friends before. We could be friends again."

In a separate discussion, one Albanian girl commented, "They killed and raped us; how can we live with them?" Another said, "It is difficult now, but perhaps for future generations, yes, if it happens, it will be the youth who will make it possible."

Note: Women's Commission for Refugee Women and Children 1999–2000

Finding Solutions

The KYC research project revealed that international and local actors had failed to adequately consult Kosovo's youth and equally failed to include them in the decisionmaking processes. Young people had also been excluded from reconstruction and development initiatives, and were being left out of mainstream programming interventions aimed at the young. The failure to include the young people—and with that almost half of its population—and to seriously address youth issues meant that the group felt increasingly isolated and almost useless. This resulted not only in human rights violations committed against, but increasingly by, young people who felt left out, and provided a legacy of conflict for future generations.

One of the concrete actions undertaken by KYC was an initiative to work with the Women's Commission for Refugee Women and Children on a project to mobilize adolescents and carry out research into the nature of problems faced by young people, and finding solutions to those problems. It also got young people to speak publicly about their concerns and try to effect change.

KYC joined other actors to offer adolescents and young adults alternatives to violence by promoting respect for the rule of law, and encouraging them to deal with leadership in ways that contribute to their healing and provide a new path to the future for Kosovo as a whole. It was acknowledged that many young people worked hard to care for themselves and their families and engage in activities to support the recovery of their communities.

The participatory nature of the research program led to further youth-initiated and community-based action and confirmed that with support and encouragement, young people could accomplish great things. Significantly, Albanians and Serbs were not required to interact with one another while conducting the research. This was mainly because of security concerns: children and adolescents were at risk if they participated in interethnic activities.

In 2002, KYC conducted a project called "Strengthening Youth Advocacy in Kosova," aimed at providing help to young people to connect with one another and formulate key issues for advocacy and action to address continuing challenges. Such links crossed gender, rural/urban, and ethnic lines. The aim was to help youngsters view issues facing them, and their experiences, as being of relevance not only for their own communities but for society as a whole, and to get them to see the larger picture in which policy, programs, and decisionmaking takes place.

The activities also helped to place young people's concerns at the center of the many challenges facing Kosovo. It was finally accepted that concern and action on the issues young people were facing was important for the future stability of the province, and prevention of further rights abuses.

KYC also provided concrete opportunities for young people to become further involved in youth advocacy in Kosovo. Small teams were established in areas with minority populations and KYC members got directly in touch with youths from minorities wherever they were accessible. When this was not feasible, KYC worked jointly with international organizations to reach minority areas and provided them with the same level of training provided to other teams. They were also invited to participate in seminars. By having young people address the concerns of their peers from all ethnic backgrounds, links were established and young people were exposed to new ways of understanding each other's problems.

During the first two months of the project, KYC brought together young people from several ethnic groups, resulting in young Albanians entering Serb enclaves in Rahavec, without escort, to work with their Serb peers, for the first time. The regions that experienced no clashes during the outbreaks of violence on 17 and 18 March 2004 were those where KYC and other local and international partners worked with all ethnic communities.

More Tolerance

Although the political climate in Kosovo remains very difficult, the interethnic action among youth fostered by conflict resolution and tolerance-building work carried out by KYC laid a solid foundation for continued positive change toward tolerance and nonviolence in the province. This underlines the need to continue in this direction by contributing toward peacebuilding and conflict prevention, and to do this by working together with different ethnic communities as a team to identify and solve our common problems and needs.

Concerns about youth must be seen as essential to all decisionmaking surrounding the reconstruction and development of Kosovo. Efforts are needed to encourage and maximize their participation in all decisions and processes that affect their lives. Their energy, resilience, and optimism may ultimately offer one of the brightest glimmers of hope for a better, more tolerant, and peaceful Kosovo.

The experience of KYC in these activities has shown that young people have a lot to say and can be leading actors to improve their own lives and situations, and that of people in their communities. When given the chance, they have participated with enthusiasm, pointing to the need for these extended activities.

The creation of a nonviolent, peaceful Kosovo, which values the rule of law and the rights and equality of all males and females, is ultimately in the hands of its youth. While the region has received substantial resources to aid its recovery, including resources targeting youth, many young people are falling through the cracks of mainstream programming. Placing their concerns at the center of addressing the multitude of challenges in Kosovo will determine Kosovo's path to stability and the prevention of further rights abuses.

Rather than feeling sorry for themselves because of their misery, the young refugees organized themselves to work together to improve their situation. With such a young population, it becomes critical to understand and deal with the problems of this group; better still if they help themselves as is the case with the Kosovar Youth Council.

Valon Kurhasani is the executive director of the Kosovar Youth Council.

Contact

Kosovar Youth Council
Qamil Hoxha 7/2
Pristina
Kosova-UNMIK
Tel: +381 38 223 184
E-mail: info@kyckosova.org or kyckosova@yahoo.com
Website: http://www.kyckosova.org

Selected Bibliography

Balkan Youth Project. Online at: http://www.balkanyouthproject.net/eng/01/00.html.

Kosovar Youth Council. 2000. "Promoting Kosovar Adolescent/Youth Protection and Capacities: Youth-Identified Problems and Solutions." In cooperation with the Women's Commission for Refugee Women and Children and the International Rescue Committee, May-June. Online at: http://www.war-affected-children.org/kosovo-en.asp.

Organization for Security and Cooperation in Europe (OSCE). Online at: http://www.osce.org/kosovo or http://www.osce-kosovo@omik.org (OSCE has supported Kosovo Youth Assembly).

Pax Christi. Online at: http://www.paxchristi.nl (KYC is a partner organization of Pax Christi).

UNICEF. 2004. *Adolescent Participation in Programme Activities During Situations of Conflict and Post-Conflict* (New York: Office of Emergency Programmes, January).

Women's Commission for Refugee Women and Children. 1999–2000. "Making the Choice for a Better Life, Promoting the Protection and Capacity of Kosovo's Youth." Report of the Women's Commission for Refugee Women and Children's

Mission to Albania and Kosovo. Online at: http://www.womenscommission.org/pdf/yu_adol.pdf.

————. Online at: http://www.womenscommission.org (Women's Commission for Refugee Women and Children, have cooperated with KYC).

Youth Forum. Online at: http://www.youthforum.org/em/index.html.

9

The Media:
Reaching Hearts and Minds

Francis Rolt

Most people immediately make a link between media and conflict, but less often associate the media with peacebuilding. The media—television, radio, and the press—are the channels through which most conflicts around the world are reported, analyzed, and explained. The manner in which this is achieved can encourage and support violent conflict, even when propaganda is not the intention. Conversely, just as the media can have an impact on conflict so conflict can have an impact on the media. What is less commonly recognized is that the media have also long been a power for peace in the world. This chapter is about the ways in which the media can and do promote the peaceful resolution of conflict.

When the great Buddhist emperor Asoka (ca. 304–232 B.C.) commanded a rock pillar to be erected in Afghanistan and for it to be inscribed in two languages describing how his people should live together in peace, he was using a medium of the day (a rock edict) as a peacebuilding tool. Asoka had been so horrified by his own war of conquest against the kingdom of Kalinga, in which a hundred thousand people were killed and a hundred and fifty thousand injured, that he gave up war. In his rock edicts, dotted across India and beyond, Asoka apologizes to his subjects for the Kalinga war, and reassures those beyond the borders of his empire that he has no expansionist intentions toward them. These rock edicts are among the first forms of peacebuilding media we know about.

Another example of historical peacebuilding media might be the "broadcast" of information about a peace treaty by the heralds of ancient Greece, or the town criers of medieval Europe, who were historical newscasters. Heralds were used to announce proposals for a truce or an armistice (although like our modern mass media they would also announce the beginning of hostilities).

Since those times many other forms of peacebuilding media—ways of encouraging people to live in peace, to understand one another—have been developed. They range from posters, public service announcements, street dramas, websites, list servers, car stickers, photo exhibitions, film festivals, leaflets, shirt and dress materials printed with messages, and training classes, to radio and TV documentaries, kids' programs, dramas, soap operas, and news programs. To take one example, the Palestinian nongovernmental organization Middle East Nonviolence and Democracy (MEND) runs a radio soap opera (*Dar Dar Abuna*) that encourages active nonviolence among the Palestinian population. The soap shows by example what can be achieved with active nonviolence, and has a remarkable following among a young audience.

The advent of mass media in the twentieth century—newspapers, radio, TV, and the Internet—meant that war propaganda could be effectively spread among a population. The Nazis were among the first to promote a regime of hatred through the radio (the term "hate media" only came to prominence during the Rwanda genocide when a local radio station promoted and encouraged the killing).

In general, differences of language, religion, history, and ethnicity have frequently been exploited in the mass media by politicians and others to create fear, exclusion, and dominance. From the Balkans to Rwanda to the Middle East and Indonesia, the mass media has been used to demonize the "other" and to legitimize their extermination. Such use of the media is, however, not restricted to violent conflicts or wars; everywhere in the world some parts of the media frequently and consistently perpetuate stereotypes and denigrate the "other"—the British tabloid press, or the American shock-jock radio talk show hosts, are typical. For example, a presenter on a New York–based radio station (WOR-AM) conducted a hate campaign against East Indian immigrants in the New Jersey community of Iselin. Following a particularly vitriolic attack on 12 December 1996, swastikas and ethnic slurs were spray-painted on homes and businesses in Iselin belonging to citizens who came from India. One of these two businesses' windows was also hit with gunfire. Additionally, a home belonging to an African-American family was painted with a slur and a swastika; all these acts took place the following day.[1] In times of crisis or economic difficulty, such prejudice easily leads to violent acts and so to violent conflict.

In contrast to the kinds of hate media described above, the idea of using the modern mass media as tools for peacebuilding was slow to get off the ground. One of the earliest contemporary uses of modern mass media to promote understanding was in 1977, when Walter Cronkite, longtime anchor for the American CBS network, conducted satellite interviews with Egyptian president Anwar Sadat and Israeli prime minister Menachem Begin. Cronkite asked Sadat whether he would be willing to travel to Jerusalem to meet Begin. Sadat agreed, and Cronkite then inquired of Begin whether he would welcome the Egyptian president. By questioning the two presidents directly on the air, Cronkite helped launch the peace process that led to Sadat's historic visit to Jerusalem, the first Camp David negotiations, and the signing of the Israeli-Egyptian peace treaty.

Peacebuilding Through the News Media

On the one hand, reliable news media can have a positive impact on the peaceful resolution of conflicts by reducing the impact and spread of rumors—

which inevitably feed the flames of a conflict. One example of this is a UN–Foundation Hirondelle radio initiative in the Democratic Republic of Congo; Radio Okapi provides reliable news and current affairs for the first time across the vast country in a number of different languages. Okapi quickly has grown into the most popular radio station in the country.

On the other hand, as noted above, news media can have a distinctly negative impact on conflict, and is itself often influenced and changed by the conflict environment. It is important to note that it is not just media organizations that are getting involved; peacebuilding organizations, such as Search for Common Ground (SFCG), have been at the forefront of developing peacebuilding media initiatives for years.

Johan Galtung, founder and director of Transcend, professor of peace studies, and widely regarded as the founder of the academic discipline of peace research, was one of the first people in the West to seriously question the impact of the news media on conflict. At that time few people took his ideas very seriously. Since then, the issue has been taken up and developed by many academics, media professionals, and organizations, including conflictandpeace.org (London), InterNews (Paris), the Institute for Media, Policy, and Civil Society (London), IMPACS (Vancouver), Institute for Media Studies (Copenhagen), and Media for Peace (Bogotá), to name but a few. The main argument has been succinctly expressed by Ross Howard:

> For more than fifty years diplomats, negotiators, and social scientists have studied conflict and developed a sophisticated understanding of it, just like medicine, business, or music. But few journalists have any training in the theory of conflict. Most journalists merely report on the conflict as it happens. By comparison, medical reporters do not just report on a person's illness. They also report on what caused the illness and what may cure it. News reporters can have the same skill when it comes to reporting conflict. (Howard 2003: 6)

The organizations above, which focus almost exclusively on news and current-affairs journalism, conduct training sessions for press, radio, and TV journalists in peace or "conflict sensitive" journalism. They encourage journalists to question closely their roles, their own assumptions, the words they use, and the impact they have on a conflict. Media for Peace (Medios para la Paz), for example, focuses much of its work on approaches to reporting that can have a positive impact on efforts to achieve peace. Its primary goals are to "disarm" the language—exploring and undertaking actions to ensure that the language used to report an event does not contribute to the perpetuation of violence—and to break through the indifference of the mass media with respect to the armed conflict in Colombia (Howard et al. 2003).

Peacebuilding Through the Non-News Media

However, even the organizations mentioned do not take on the full potential range of the modern mass media in building peace, as they deal almost exclusively with news and current-affairs content. This is a shame given that most media content consists of entertainment, education, human interest stories, and advertising—not news. Apart from the twenty-four-hour satellite news channels, news and current affairs rarely fill more than 15 percent of the space available on radio, TV, or in the print media.

What follows is a brief typology of peacebuilding media initiatives that go beyond the usual emphasis on news and current-affairs journalism and training.

Type One. "Edutainment," also known as Entertainment-Education, is a media product or series, packaged as entertainment, that sets out to achieve a specific result in terms of audience perceptions and behavior. Soap operas are popular and successful forms of peacebuilding Edutainment on radio and TV in some countries, but comic books for adolescents and young adults have also been successful, and there are many other possible forms. SFCG, MEND, BBC World Service Trust, and the Panos Institute, among others, all produce such radio soap operas. The Panos Institute West Africa, for example, has been involved in the production of a radio soap opera that focuses on a range of issues related to the conflict in the Casamance region of Senegal. In the words of one scriptwriter,"You could not talk immediately about the conflict because everyone was afraid. We had to make a program of the positive things, of what unites us, and then we could discuss the painful negative things that divide us" (Howard et al. 2003: 159).

Type Two. Cultural productions, such as music programs or comic books that attract a specific audience, have been used to convey specific messages and to bring up subjects for discussion that might be threatening in a more clearly serious program. Some such shows play only songs that emphasize peace. Other examples include productions that demand a joint agreement on "our" history from both sides of a conflict. The project Seeds of Peace, which brings together Palestinian and Israeli kids for a summer camp in the United States, asks the participants to produce jointly a film doing just this, while the magazine *Saudi Aramco World* emphasizes only the cultural ties between peoples.

Type Three. Cross-conflict productions focus on the presenters or hosts of a program, or on the writers of an article. Typically, they may be two well-known ex-combatants from opposite sides who agree to work together in order to help the disarmament and rehabilitation of other ex-combatants. Here the symbolic significance of the two presenters working together and behaving normally with each other is almost the main point of the show. Another example might be two newspaper editors from opposite sides of a conflict who agree to write and sign an article together and publish it on the same day in both publications.

Type Four. Commissioned article and program exchanges in regional conflicts can be extremely effective in terms of normalizing attitudes and relations between different peoples, and in demonstrating that the "other" is facing exactly the same difficulties, problems, joys, and sorrows as the listener/reader. Exchanges can be complicated and expensive to undertake because of the need for cross-translation into each of the participating languages, but often have a significant impact.

Type Five. News agency/distribution, lays a greater emphasis than Type Four on positive viewpoints. In this intervention, an agency commissions, selects, and translates a collection of articles and items that offer constructive perspectives and promote dialogue across a conflict. The articles are disseminated each week (or daily) to all sides/language groups, and to a wide audience (newspapers, magazines, organizations, and individuals) for republication. The intention is to counteract the media's overemphasis on violence and despair, and to stress the positive. The Common Ground News Service does just this.

Current Debate
People working in the field of peacebuilding media question constantly. Some questions are perennial, such as, "Can we prove that what we do really works?" While other questions have to do with sustainability, and the value-added of media as a peacebuilding tool. The main questions are outlined below.

Impact Assessment
If we accept or believe that peacebuilding media works, then how best can we prove it? How are we to measure the impact of what we do on peoples' attitudes, and then on their behavior? After all, it is relatively simple to conduct a survey that demonstrates that a target population's knowledge of peacebuilding techniques has increased, and/or to demonstrate that the number of peacebuilding journalism training sessions and the number of radio/TV stations and magazines or newspapers being published have increased. What is very hard to demonstrate is that all this activity and expenditure has had a significant and positive effect on the attitudes and behavior of that same target audience. This is a major challenge, and one that some agencies and donors are working on together, developing methodologies that can measure these things more accurately.

Sustainability
Can peacebuilding media projects in countries involved in violent conflict ever be self-sustaining? In places where conflict has destroyed and limits all economic activity, media are rarely sustainable without outside funding. The longer the conflict continues, the longer the funding must continue. This is largely true despite some examples that suggest ways in which radio, for example, can be more self-sustaining. In Uganda, for instance, the radio station Mega-FM sells spots to individuals who send messages to friends and loved ones, to announce the loss of a cow, or the imminence of a wedding, and by marketing itself as a mass media tool to humanitarian and aid agencies. Within a short space of time, Mega-FM has managed to become self-supporting.

Added Value

Media can target specific populations and groups (by gender, age, language, etc.) and are relatively cheap to implement. However, what do media add that could not be achieved without them? The broadcast media, in particular, have the ability to build attention over time and across a society. In the short term, no single article or radio or TV program, whether it is a soap opera or a current-affairs program, can turn a war or even low-level conflict into peace. No single article or program can make an individual, a people, a class, or an ethnic group do what they are not already half-convinced to do. In the long term, however, over a number of months and years, targeted media products can reach into the hearts and minds of individuals. In doing so, the media can change the atmosphere within which a conflict occurs, subtly altering the environment and the thinking of a large number of people so that they are less likely to engage in violent acts, more likely to listen to reason, and more likely to trust the "other."

Such media can help their audiences counter the warmongers, help them ignore those politicians and others who would drive them further into violence, or to ever more outrageous acts of hatred and destruction. An example is Search for Common Ground's Studio Ijambo, which, over the past nine years, has been producing radio programs in Burundi. It has been credited with changing the nature of the discourse there, of giving Burundians a language with which to discuss things such as genocide and the role of politicians, conflict, and ethnicity, without resorting to accusation, insult, and violence (see Chapter 9.3).

Challenges

Digital technology, and the changes it has brought, presents peacebuilders and print, radio, and TV journalists, producers, and broadcasters with new challenges. Some of these are negative, but any kind of a challenge can also be taken as a positive opportunity.

Digital technology is relatively cheap, so almost anyone can now create television-quality images. In Nigeria, for example, amateur video dramas sell like hotcakes (at one time seventy per week were hitting the market). This is wonderful in some ways, but it also means that established distribution networks can easily be used to reinforce stereotypes and promote hatred and violence. The opposite is also true, of course: anyone can use the equipment and the distribution systems to promote peace and understanding, but unfortunately drama and violence are inextricably associated in the minds of most program makers. Few amateur program makers would have a clue about what to do if asked to produce a drama without violence.

The same potential for good and bad holds true for news and other information sources provided by individuals and organizations' websites on the Internet, by e-mail list servers, and by bloggers. Much of it is ignorant, prejudiced, and encourages hatred rather than understanding, but the other side also exists.

The airwaves are opening up in many countries, and more and more radio and TV stations are being licensed, meaning that competition for the ears and eyes of the audiences increases. This is as true in the North as in the South. That competition plays out in two areas: ownership and content. In the United States, the National Rifle Association opened a radio station in 2004, which Wayne LaPierre, the organization's executive vice-president, described as a "legitimate packager of news."[2]

In general, media owners, whether governments, businesspeople, or special-interest groups, often have a specific agenda that will benefit other aspects of the power they hold (political/financial/social) or wish to hold. Unfortunately, peacebuilding rarely figures on most owners' agendas. More work needs to be done with the owners and senior-level managers of different media, from the international satellite TV stations, to local newspapers and/or the programmers and manufacturers of computer games. One example of this is the way the Carter Center in Venezuela has been working with both the powerful private media owners and with senior managers within the state-controlled media to lower the tone of the vitriolic debate that splits Venezuelan society—and has threatened to spiral out of control on several occasions—into those in favor of and those against President Chavez.

Collaboration

Media work is rarely enough to effect change; it is also necessary to work with other NGOs, local associations, agencies, and the stakeholders themselves. In order to promote social change at an individual level across society, we must work with farmers, with the military and militias (combatants and officers/leaders), with government officers and politicians, and with the youth and children. The media alone are not very effective over the long term, although they can have a powerful short-term impact. Media are attractive to donors and agencies in violent conflicts (specifically radio, because of its reach and because a radio is small, cheap, and easily transportable—people fleeing conflict often take their radios with them). Real, long-term peacebuilding projects must work with the media, but they also need to be on the ground working with ordinary people facing the difficulties and dangers of the conflict. The media, or radio, by themselves, without reinforcement and support, will have only a temporary effect on a population in real crisis.

Conclusions

The field of media and peacebuilding has expanded enormously over the past twenty years, but it is still a small and relatively unknown field. A Google search for "Media and Peacebuilding" produces only 68,000 pages (September 2004), but a search for "Media and Conflict" produces over 5 million pages. Some of the latter entries may, of course, have more to do with peacebuilding than with conflict, but that is itself indicative of the need for a shift in the way the vocabulary is used.

Social change is a complex and difficult process anywhere in the world, and more so in countries or regions in violent conflict. Media at all levels and of all types can and do play a role in either maintaining or reducing the momentum of those conflicts. Sometimes the same media outlet plays both roles without being aware of it. Much more can be done to raise awareness among such media outlets, to encourage existing broadcasters to incorporate peacebuilding messages or themes, and to use peacebuilding techniques in making and presenting programs—one such initiative is the Radio for Peacebuilding–Africa project.

At the same time, peacebuilders (and donors) must recognize that the media are not a magic bullet that can resolve conflicts with a few well-written soap operas, or with a couple of journalism training sessions. Media products do have an impact, but they work best over time and in conjunction with other practical and down-to-earth activities.

Francis Rolt has been working for Search for Common Ground since 1998, first as director of Studio Ijambo (Burundi), and now as director of Common Ground Radio, based in Brussels. SFCG's mission is to transform how people, individuals, organizations, and governments deal with conflict—away from adversarial approaches and toward cooperative solutions. Rolt has worked in radio since 1986, for the BBC World Service, Radio Netherlands, and Capital Radio (South Africa), among others.

Notes

1. Information from Radio Netherlands website: http://www.rnw.nl/realradio/dossiers/html/hateradioamerica.html (accessed October 2004).

2. BBC World Service website: http://www.bbc.co.uk/worldservice/trust/ (accessed 17 April 2004).

Selected Bibliography

Howard, Ross. 2003. *Conflict Sensitive Journalism Handbook.* IMPACS and IMS.

Howard, Ross, Francis Rolt, Hans van de Veen, and Juliette Verhoeven. 2003. *The Power of the Media: A Handbook for Peacebuilders* (Utrecht, Netherlands: European Centre for Conflict Prevention).

Resources

Lead Organizations

BBC World Service Trust—United Kingdom
E-mail: ws.trust@bbc.co.uk
Website: http://www.bbc.co.uk/worldservice/trust/

Fondation Hirondelle—Switzerland
E-mail: info@hirondelle.org
Website: http://www.hirondelle.org

IMPACS: The Institute for Media, Policy and Civil Society—Canada
E-mail: media@impacs.org
Website: http://www.impacs.org

Institute for Media, Peace and Security—Switzerland
E-mail: imps@upeace.ch
Website: http://www.mediapeace.org

Institute for War and Peace Reporting—United Kingdom
E-mail: info@iwpr.org
Website: http://www.iwpr.net

International Media Support (IMS)—Denmark
Media and Conflict Unit
E-mail: i-m-s@i-m-s.dk
Website: http://www.i-m-s.dk

InterNews Network—United States
Media, War and Peace section
E-mail: info@internews.org
Website: http://www.internews.org

Media Foundation for West Africa—Ghana
E-mail: mfwa@africaonline.com.gh
Website: http://www.mediafoundationwa.org

Media Institute for Southern Africa—Namibia
For contact, please visit website: http://www.misa.org

Panos Institute International—United Kingdom
E-mail: panosinstitute@earthlink.net
Website: http://www.panosinst.org

Reporting the World—United Kingdom
For contact, please visit website: http://www.reportingtheworld.org

Search for Common Ground—United States, Belgium
Common Ground Productions
E-mail: scarch@sfcg.org
Website: http://www.sfcg.org/programmes/cgp/programmes_cgp.html

Websites
African Women's Media Center's directory. Featuring more than 200 media companies,
    NGOs, and programmes in sub-Saharan Africa: http://www.awmc.com/directory
International Freedom of Expression Exchange: http://www.ifex.org
Focuses on media development in Central Asia and the Caucasus: http://www.cimera.org
Articles and publications on peacebuilding and information on peace journalism:
    http://www.trancend.org

Publications
Davis, A., ed. *Regional Media in Conflict: Case Studies in Local War Reporting*. London: Institute for War and Peace Reporting, 2001.
Department for International Development (DFID). *Working with the Media in Conflicts and Other Emergencies*. London: Department for International Development, 2000.
Gardner, E. "The Role of Media in Conflicts," in T. Paffenholz and L. Reychler, eds., *Peacebuilding: A Field Guide*. Boulder, CO: Lynne Rienner Publishers, 2001.
Gowing, N. *Media Coverage: Help or Hindrance in Conflict Prevention?* New York: Carnegie Commission on Preventing Deadly Conflict, 1997.
Hay. R. "The Media and Peacebuilding: A Discussion Paper." Vancouver: IMPACS Draft Operational Framework, 1999.

Hieber, L. *Lifeline Media: Reaching Populations in Crisis. A Guide to Developing Media Projects in Conflict Situations.* Geneva: Media Action International, 2001.

Howard, Ross. *An Operational Framework for Media and Peacebuilding.* Vancouver: Institute for Media, Policy, and Civil Society, 2002.

Lynch, J. *Reporting the World.* Taplow, UK: Conflict and Peace Forums, 2002.

Spurk, C. *Media and Peacebulding: Concepts, Actors, and Challenges.* Bern: KOFF (Swisspeace Centre for Peacebuilding), 2002.

Ukpabi, C., ed. *Handbook on Journalism Ethics: African Case Studies.* Kaapstad: Media Institute Southern Africa (MISA), 2001.

PERSONAL STORY:
"Understand the Differences, Act on the Commonalities"—John Marks

I was 22 years old in 1966 when I joined the U.S. Foreign Service. I anticipated a diplomatic career which, to me, meant a life of negotiating treaties, driving a sports car around Europe, and becoming an ambassador. My first assignment, however, was Vietnam in the midst of war, and I spent 18 months working as a civilian advisor in the *pacification* program. This experience definitely knocked me off my linear career path, as I became convinced that American policy was wrong. In 1970, after the U.S. invasion of Cambodia, I resigned in protest.

I found a job as the principal assistant for foreign policy to a U.S. senator who opposed continuation of the American war. For three years, my main task was to help pass legislation that would end direct U.S. involvement in the war. Next, I coauthored a bestselling book that explored the workings of U.S. intelligence agencies, and then I wrote myself an award-winning book on the secret connections between American intelligence and the behavioral sciences.

I had become an advocate for reform and social change. At the same time, I realised that I was increasingly defined by what I opposed. I came to see another possibility: Namely, that I could live my life and do my work from a place, not of being *against* the old system, but of being *for* a new one. In 1982, I founded Search for Common Ground (SFCG), a nongovernmental organization (NGO) with a lofty vision: To shift the way the world deals with conflict—away from adversarial, *win-lose* approaches, toward nonadversarial solutions.

I saw myself as a social entrepreneur. Unlike a business entrepreneur, my bottom line is not to acquire wealth, but to change the world. SFCG provides the organizational base—the place to stand—from which to do this work.

When I started, I had one coworker, a handful of supporters, and a miniscule budget. With the Cold War raging, we focused on building bridges between the United States and the Soviet Union. In the early 1990s, as global conflict became more diffuse, so did our search for common ground.

We began working closely with governments and multilateral organizations, as we expanded our work into the Middle East, the Balkans, Africa, Indonesia, and the United States. We currently have a staff of about 375 people, operating out of headquarters in Washington and Brussels and field offices in 11 countries. Thousands of people participate directly in our programs, and we reach millions more through media projects.

We try to carry out work on a realistic scale—one step at a time. Indeed, we strive to be incrementally transformational. We appreciate that people and nations will act, as they always have, in their perceived best interest. We believe, however, that everyone's best interest is served by solutions that maximize the gain of those with a stake in the outcome. Current problems—whether ethnic, environmental, or economic—are simply too complex and interconnected to be settled on an adversarial basis. The earth is running out of the space, resources, and recuperative capacity to deal with wasteful conflict.

The methods we use vary as greatly as the places where we work. However, our methodology is based on the one basic operating principle: *Understand the differences; act on the commonalities.* Within this framework, we have developed a diverse *toolbox* for conflict prevention and transformation. It includes such well-known techniques as mediation, facilitation and training, along with less traditional ones like TV production, radio soap opera, back-channel negotiations and mobilising women and youth.

Above all, we do our work because we believe it makes a difference. For example, in Burundi, we apply our *toolbox* across an entire country. In order to promote peace and national reconciliation, we produce 15 hours a week of original radio programming that reaches 90 percent of the population; we work directly with hundreds of women's associations to empower women as peacemakers; we sponsor numerous projects to reintegrate youth who have been involved in violence; and we make wide use of music and culture to try to heal ethnic differences.

Not surprisingly, we have also had our share of setbacks. We have worked for 13 years in the Middle East—where we have held scores of workshops for Arabs, Israelis, and Iranians, produced several TV series and a radio soap opera, operated a weekly news service and sponsored the Middle East Consortium for Infectious Disease Surveillance. Yet, despite our best efforts—and those of many other would-be peacemakers—the conflict has escalated. In Liberia in 2003, looters ransacked and destroyed our radio studio. Still, we remain engaged for the long haul—in Liberia, in the Middle East, and everywhere else we work. We believe that our work represents hope for the future.

Although the world is overly polarized and violent behavior is much too prevalent, we remain essentially optimistic. Our view is that, despite numerous setbacks, history and human consciousness are moving in positive directions. Failures in peacemaking do not cause us to give up. Rather, they convince us that we—and the world—must do much better.

The challenge is extraordinary, and I consider myself immensely privileged to be able to do the work that I do.

John Marks is founder and president of Search for Common Ground in Washington, D.C., and the office in Brussels. He is also a best-selling, award-winning book author, and has produced numerous television series and programs.

9.1

Changing Attitudes Through Children's Television: *Nashe Maalo* in Macedonia

Eran Fraenkel

Growing up in a society that generates fear between the different ethnic communities, Macedonian children have little or no opportunity to get to know children from other ethnic backgrounds. This has hardened existing prejudices and led to the spread of much misinformation. Nashe Maalo (Our Neighborhood) *tries to break this cycle of mistrust by offering children a television program that deals with interethnic issues and conflict resolution, while remaining fun to watch.*

Sometimes, we are told, the walls have ears. In the television series titled *Nashe Maalo,* the walls have eyes, ears, a voice, and a well-developed sense of purpose. The star of *Nashe Maalo* is an animated house named Karmen, whose mission is to harbor peace. Karmen is a bit run-down, but not without hope, despite years of trying to get grown-ups to listen to her pleas for understanding and cooperation. Karmen decides on a new strategy—she will focus on children instead of adults, and so she selects eight children from Macedonian, Roma, Turkish, and Albanian backgrounds, and creates an opportunity for them to meet. The children become friends and together discover the secrets of the building. By leading them on journeys through magical doorways, she provides them with the opportunity to see and learn about the world from each other's perspectives. Along the way, the kids develop a deeper sense of mutual understanding and respect.

A Legacy of Separation

The Republic of Macedonia gained its independence from the Socialist Federal Republic of Yugoslavia in 1991 without going to war. Macedonia is a country of 2.2 million in which the majority of ethnic Macedonians (roughly 65 percent) live alongside ethnic Albanians (roughly 22 percent) and small percentages of ethnic Turks, Roma, Serbs, Vlachs, and others.

Since 1991, the Republic of Macedonia has reformed but not replaced the Yugoslav model defining the positions and privileges of the country's ethnonational communities. Although intended to foster ethno-political pluralism, the result instead has been the deep-seated segregation that is still evident in most domains of Macedonian life.

Children born in the Republic of Macedonia since 1991 have been surrounded by prejudicial images and messages, both private and public, regarding the country's diversity. In many families, children quickly internalize the negative vocabulary and attitudes expressed about the "other." For children attending segregated schools, the notion of "us" and "them" inevitably develops. However, largely due to the influence of a highly polarized mass media, and in particular television, which is pervasive in Macedonia, these attitudes are subtly changed. Except for one state-run radio and TV network, the media are as starkly segregated as society and rigidly defined by language and ethnic group; there is almost no effort by media emanating from one or another of Macedonia's communities to reach beyond their own communities.

Television programming with "positive" social content intended for kids is virtually nonexistent in Macedonia. Children mostly watch cartoons, sports, magazine-style shows, rebroadcast concerts, ubiquitous Spanish-language soap operas, and the news. The inflammatory language and images of TV news reporting only exacerbate this sense of division and hostility among children. Additional television for children consists primarily of films, mostly made in the United States, that typically expound the idea that "might makes right."

Media and Education

Search for Common Ground (SFCG) is an international nongovernmental organization established in 1982 that is dedicated to the transformation and prevention of conflict worldwide. In 1994, the organization established its first field office in the Republic of Macedonia as part of the wider international effort to prevent the spillover of the Yugoslav wars of succession to this newly independent country. From the beginning, Search for Common Ground in Macedonia (SCGM) concentrated on two areas that have remained its primary focus: media and education, which it views as the two crucial vehicles for encouraging and reinforcing the embrace of positive social values in any society. Especially with children, the combination of media and education holds much promise for fundamentally altering the way they view the "other" in their country.

When SCGM first considered the idea of producing an educational children's television program on conflict resolution in 1996, it seemed a very straightforward exercise. "All" that would be required were TV production professionals and people with the requisite knowledge of conflict resolution. However, when production began in 1999, it was clear that even with extensive preparation, moving from concept to realization would be a complex, delicate, and difficult process.

Search for Common Ground produced *Nashe Maalo* during five of Macedonia's most turbulent years, between 1999 and 2004.[1] First, neighboring

Kosovo was engulfed in war in 1999, and then in 2001 Macedonia itself endured several months of intercommunal fighting. Nonetheless, over these seasons *Nashe Maalo* became one of the most widely watched programs in Macedonia, nearly universally known to children and adults alike.

Structure and Premises

Nashe Maalo was intended for children between eight and twelve years of age. Based on a curriculum that set the "educational goals," *Nashe Maalo* was designed to achieve three primary objectives: (1) to model/teach intercultural understanding; (2) to model/teach conflict prevention through increased cultural awareness; and (3) to model/teach specific conflict resolution skills.

Originally conceived of as "conflict resolution television," the program evolved into something more subtle and complex during the two years prior to production—"intended-outcomes television." Conflict resolution television implies that a show's primary objective is to identify and resolve specific conflicts. In preparing the educational curriculum, however, SCGM concluded that conflict is a response to rather than an inherent element of relationships among children, even across ethnic lines. SCGM's long-term "intended outcome" was to affect positive change in the knowledge, attitudes, and behavior of Macedonia's children regarding Macedonia as a multiethnic society and their lives in that society. In other words, it was hoped that children who watched *Nashe Maalo* would no longer view the "other" as strange, threatening, less worthy, or as someone to be viewed with suspicion, but rather that the "other" would be viewed as someone who might be different, but who shared common bonds of citizenship and membership in a common society.

Nashe Maalo was a seamless fusion of entertainment—professionally produced television—and education in the form of continuously researched and monitored messages. To successfully meld the entertainment and educational elements together, SCGM leaned heavily on a model developed by the producer of *Sesame Street*, Children's Television Workshop (now known as Sesame Workshop), consisting of three basic components—research, content, and production.

Before production began in 1999, SCGM had already been working in Macedonia for several years, including projects with elementary-school children. The *Nashe Maalo* team was familiar with the day-to-day life of kids in the show's target age group, with their general social attitudes toward each other, and with their overall behavioral patterns. Nonetheless, the team still needed to conduct baseline research to obtain specific data regarding children's knowledge of "other" children: i.e., their concrete attitudes/beliefs about each other and their own descriptions of how they behave in situations calling for interaction with children from "other" ethnolinguistic groups. This information underlay all subsequent decisions about which issues to present in *Nashe Maalo* and their relative importance. In consultation with experts across a range of relevant disciplines, SCGM decided to focus in particular on intercultural understanding, and conflict prevention flowing forth from this heightened intercultural understanding, with conflict resolution accordingly receiving less emphasis.

The reasoning behind this was that, with so little contact across the ethnic divide, children's perceptions of their own country and its peoples were based on stereotypes, misinformation, or simple ignorance. *Nashe Maalo*'s first premise, therefore, was that through the show the audience should come to a better understanding of Macedonia's diversity and, beyond that, to gain deeper understanding of how those on the other side of the cultural divide actually lived their lives day to day.

A second premise was that by increasing their knowledge, the program could affect children's attitudes about each other. If negative attitudes derive from negative knowledge, positive knowledge should stimulate positive changes in the audience's beliefs and attitudes. Preventing conflict with the "other" was predicated on better understanding the "other," thereby averting the potential escalation of conflict through misunderstanding. The more exposure children had to *Nashe Maalo* the more the series would increase their knowledge and change their attitudes.

The third and most difficult premise was that television could contribute directly to behavioral change—changed attitudes, changed approaches to social interaction, and ultimately (if only theoretically in a distant future) changes in the social dynamic among Macedonia's communities. This was the intended outcome most critical to positive social transformation, since people's actions ultimately determine their society's health and future, even if it would not be possible to predict how long it would take to move from acquiring knowledge to altering attitudes to engaging in new behaviors. For the *Nashe Maalo* team, correlating the program to behavioral change represented an ongoing challenge, because the program's future itself was uncertain. When SCGM first sought funding for *Nashe Maalo*, there was only a pledge of support for one season of eight thirty-minute programs. Further funding was secured in the middle of the first season, and additional funding for the last two seasons of the program was secured, in large part in response to the outbreak of violence in 2001.

Successes and Challenges

Given the three intended outcomes—increasing knowledge, changing attitudes, and modifying behavior—SCGM considered it essential to be vigilant at all stages of the shows' development and production. The producers, directors, and editors strived to create the most engaging visual TV program, while the content team was concerned with both visual and verbal accuracy. At first the content team was not involved with the script once a show went into production. Taking heed from viewer feedback though, in later years, the content team participated in every episode not only during the writing but also during production and postproduction.

Of the three teams—content, research, and production—it was research that was most central to the project and which provided the information that

SCGM used to determine to what extent the program had achieved its objectives. Monitoring, evaluation, and assessment took place in various forms over the five seasons of *Nashe Maalo*. Beyond the initial formative research, SCGM's research team worked with a representative selection of kids between seasons to assess the level of success in attaining its goals. The research examined whether the audience's positive knowledge had increased, and also what, if any, changes could be seen in the attitudes of the viewers.

For example, research following the first season found that kids could not determine the ethnic identity of several main characters. As a result, the scriptwriters and producers had to introduce several identifying markers to help the audience understand who was who. Simultaneously, however, the content team had to ensure that the shows did not rely on stereotypes that would damage its intended outcome of genuine intercultural understanding. In this way, data gleaned from "summative research" after each season became "formative data" used to adjust and improve the next season's episodes.

Nashe Maalo became possibly the most widely recognized TV program in Macedonia. In 2001, between the second and third seasons, an independent audience survey found that among children of all ethnicities, geographic locations, ages, and genders, an average of 76 percent watched *Nashe Maalo* regularly. Although SCGM had created the program for kids aged eight to twelve, the survey found that the show's audience ranged in age from five to seventeen, and nearly half of the children's parents also watched the program, though most kids and parents said they did not discuss *Nashe Maalo* at home. In 2004, following the final season, an audience survey revealed that *Nashe Maalo*'s audience had increased to approximately 95 percent of children and nearly 75 percent of their parents. Most respondents had watched *Nashe Maalo* for at least three years. By 2004, nearly 45 percent of adults reported that they talked about the program with their children. These data clearly indicated that SCGM had successfully reached one of its main objectives: saturation.

One unexpected research finding was that *Nashe Maalo* was not *just* a "kids" TV show, but had become a "family show." However, SCGM did not design the curriculum for adults and was not conducting its summative/formative research with the idea that it could reach adults. When asked to appraise *Nashe Maalo*, adults tended to regard it as "good entertainment" but did not consider that it influenced their own political or social attitudes. It remains an open question whether a television program that expressly intends to affect the lives of children might be designed to also influence adult attitudes. In any case, one important lesson learned is that more frequent and more detailed audience profiling might have revealed opportunities for SCGM to exploit. It might have been possible to take advantage of the family viewing habits in Macedonia to stimulate more interaction between generations regarding the program's messages. SCGM has learned from its other family-based programming that for new ideas and values to take root, not only is exposure necessary but also an array of approaches and tools that families are able to practice in their most familiar environment.

Expanding the Reach

Over the five-year run of *Nashe Maalo,* SFCG learned that if a program is designed and produced well, audiences will watch it even if it addresses controversial topics. The organization also learned that if a program is broadcast long enough to saturate its "market," it can attract a very wide audience and can serve as a catalyst for conversation around topics that might not otherwise be discussed. In other words, good television can be a powerful teaching tool. The challenge for SFCG in producing future intended-outcomes television, however, is to expand the reach of a program beyond teaching from the screen, and to penetrate more fully the daily life of its audience.

Eran Fraenkel was the executive producer of Nashe Maalo *and currently serves as director of Search for Common Ground's Southeast and East Europe Regional Program.*

Contact

Center for Common Ground in Macedonia
Orce Nikolov 63, 91000 Skopje
Republic of Macedonia
Tel: +389 23 118 517 / 572
Fax: +389 23 118 322
E-mail: sfcg@sfcg.org.mk
Website: http://www.sfcg.org/programmes/macedonia/macedonia_television.html

Search for Common Ground (Brussels)
Rue Belliard 205 bte 13
B – 1040 Brussels
Belgium
Tel: +32 2 736 7262
Fax: +32 2 732 3033
E-mail: search@sfcg.be
Website: http://www.sfcg.org

Note

1. Funding was provided by the U.S. Agency for International Development, the Swiss Agency for Development Cooperation, the Dutch Foreign Ministry, the Swedish Agency for International Development, the British Department for International Development, the Mott Foundation, and UNESCO.

Selected Bibliography

Howard, Ross, Francis Rolt, Hans van de Veen, and Juliette Verhoeven. *The Power of the Media: A Handbook for Peacebuilders.* Utrecht, Netherlands: European Centre for Conflict Prevention, 2003.

9.2

Operation Fine Girl Exposes Sexual Violence: WITNESS in Sierra Leone

Sam Gregory

A video produced by human rights activists depicting the horrific impact of sexual violence in conflict situations has instigated discussion in Sierra Leone on the impact of civil war. The film, produced by the international nongovernmental organization WITNESS, shows how media productions integrated into the work of local NGOs can greatly contribute to enhancing postconflict reconciliation processes and, potentially, the prevention of severe human rights violations in the future.

In the early 1990s, the possession and use of video cameras in most industrialized countries had become so widespread that almost any individual who wanted to could get access to this technically sophisticated device. The democratization of home video and filming started to revolutionize the way television producers conceived of their programming, how families documented their lives, and how the news agenda was set. Video and communication technologies were also revolutionizing political advocacy. In 1991, one particular piece of video footage, filmed with a simple handheld camera by a private person, made a group of human rights activists particularly aware of the power of moving pictures. One summer night that year, police confronted a man in Los Angeles after he had reportedly neglected a police stop sign. The man, Rodney King, was subsequently severely kicked and beaten, resulting in serious injury. This could have been an incident destined to be kept out of sight of the larger public. However, a bystander had filmed the beating of the man. This footage was shown on television, with huge consequences. Millions of people saw the beating. Massive protests evolved and a huge wave of violent riots occurred in Los Angeles that lasted for several days.

To the Lawyers' Committee for Human Rights, the Reebok Foundation, and musician Peter Gabriel, the incident proved the emotional and testimonial power of the visual. They decided to establish an organization aimed at putting cameras into the hands of human rights activists all over the world, in order to draw the world's attention to violations and mobilize nonviolent efforts to stop them.

The organization they set up in 1992, called WITNESS, has since distributed cameras to hundreds of local human rights defenders in about fifty countries. It also provides training and guidance in order to enable activists to use visual imagery and powerful testimony from the frontlines. The video production made in Sierra Leone was one in a series of videotaped testimonies and short documentary films.

Supporting Human Rights Groups to Use Video in Advocacy

WITNESS views video as an essential tool in human rights work—one that can be deployed as strategically, purposefully, and effectively as more formal or traditional forms of documentation and advocacy. Human rights groups apply for partnership with WITNESS for project-specific relationships of one to three years. The partners usually receive a digital video camera kit, technical and tactical training, and, crucially, long-term support in producing, editing, and distributing video as part of their advocacy campaigns. With WITNESS's assistance they prepare and use video in ways that will complement, not replace, other more traditional forms of advocacy and dialogue building. They draw on video's unique power to bring individual stories and voices directly to a human rights decisionmaking body, a government policymaker, or a community. Video partnerships are designed to achieve high visibility and/or high impact for these partners' respective advocacy campaigns.

WITNESS works with a core of between twelve to fifteen organizations worldwide, and also provides training on "social justice video advocacy" to broader networks of human rights organizations.

Operation Fine Girl: Rape Used as a Weapon of War in Sierra Leone is a documentary video that traces the devastating impact of a decade-long civil war on Sierra Leone's young women, thousands of whom were abducted, raped, and/or forced into slavery by soldiers on both sides of the conflict. Over the course of forty-seven minutes, viewers learn, from the people themselves, the stories of four young women—Hana, Mabel, Fatmata, and Abie—who became victims of sexual violence during the war. While *Operation Fine Girl* concentrates primarily on the war's impact on women and girls, it also includes testimony by a thirteen-year-old boy, Osman, who was taken from his village, drugged, and forced to fight as a soldier. All five young people speak candidly about their experiences during the civil war and their efforts to put their lives back together in the wake of it. *Operation Fine Girl*, produced by WITNESS, filmmaker Lilibet Foster, and a respected Sierra Leonean gender specialist, Binta Mansaray, brings home the reality of the impact of sexual violence during the war on victims and perpetrators. The film has sparked discussion on the topic in the postwar transition process that Sierra Leone has been experiencing during the past few years.

The first-person accounts of the young women and man are placed in a broader context through the filmmakers' interviews with local health and human rights workers. One nongovernmental organization (NGO) worker, Cooperation International's Marta Bernassola, describes the systematic character of the violence: "First [the women and girls] were abducted, second thing they were terrorized, third thing they were raped. And this was a systematic technique." This and other interviews with health workers underline how individual cases of sexual brutality combine to cause deep and lasting damage to society as a whole. Sexual violence caused widespread trauma and contributed to the spread of HIV/AIDS and other sexually transmitted diseases.

In Sierra Leone, as in many other countries, women who are victims of sexual violence are often blamed for the crime. To present as complete a story as possible, the filmmakers managed—at some risk to their own safety—to interview rebel and government military leaders about their groups' role in the violence. They then left it to the viewers to reach their own judgment about the events.

The people who spoke out in the film did so with the hope that their words would make a difference. When they were asked how they would like the film to be used, two of the people featured replied that the simple fact that people would see what had happened to them would be of tremendous value. "So people will see" seems to be a major drive for participation. One of the young women, Fatmata, said: "I would like you to show the tape to the international audience for them to see what really happened in Sierra Leone. Most of them have only heard about what happened, so this will make them see that we really suffered—but despite that we are strong and if we are given opportunities we will do better things in life."

Osman, the child soldier featured in the film, said he hoped that telling his story would lead to understanding of his position, and eventually forgiveness. He explained, "I want you to show the tape on TV so that people will see that even though we did bad things, we are remorseful."

Ten Years of Civil War
Over fifty thousand people died during the brutal civil war in Sierra Leone that lasted from 1992 to 2002. In addition to clashes between armed rebels and soldiers and large-scale destruction of property, massive human rights abuses took place. After the war, Sierra Leone called on international assistance for reconstruction, rehabilitation of combatants, and refugee resettlement. With help from abroad, Sierra Leoneans started programs to reintegrate former soldiers back into their communities and to resettle thousands of people displaced by the fighting. In August 2000, a Special Court to Sierra Leone was established, based on an agreement between the government of Sierra Leone and the United Nations, and in July 2002 its judges were nominated. Also, a Truth and Reconciliation Commission (TRC) was set up, charged with holding public hearings and gathering evidence to sustain cases brought to the Special Court.

Human rights groups from the outset were convinced that the issue of sexual violence against women and girls needed to be addressed during the period of reconstruction and reconciliation. However, despite the mounting evidence of the scale of the abuse, which had been targeted at all women indiscriminately, regardless of their religious or ethnic background, there was no guarantee that the TRC and the Special Court would focus on the specific nature and dimensions of this type of violence. Rape and sexual slavery had only become the subject of investigation as war crimes as recently as 1998, when special courts were created after wars in Bosnia, Kosovo, and Rwanda. WITNESS, as well as the actors that were to cooperate in the production of the documentary film *Operation Fine Girl,* saw the potential of video to help put the focus on the issue of sexual violence.

Outreach and Screenings

After an initial broadcast on cable television in the United States (WITNESS leveraged funds from Oxygen Television to produce the program), *Operation Fine Girl* was released in Sierra Leone just days after the spectacular burning-of-arms ceremony in January 2002 that formally marked the end of the war. The audience of this first screening consisted of over 160 representatives of NGOs and members of the government.

After *Operation Fine Girl* debuted, requests for copies quickly outstripped supply. More than a hundred copies were distributed to national and some international NGOs in 2002 and 2003. Binta Mansaray, the film's associate producer and WITNESS's local outreach coordinator, advised organizations on when, where, and how to use the tape for maximum impact, in order to draw attention and stimulate advocacy on of the needs of victims and survivors. Many of the public screenings took place outdoors in community settings with large audiences. They were cohosted by a wide variety of organizations, such as women's groups, investigators of the TRC, schools, churches, health clinics, and UN organizations. WITNESS also equipped Binta Mansaray with a television, VCR, and mobile generator to enable her to conduct screenings in rural areas without access to electricity.

In addition to showing the film to the general public, WITNESS was also keen to reach decisionmakers, at both national and community levels. *Operation Fine Girl* was quickly recognized by human rights groups as a valuable advocacy tool in their efforts to petition the international community and the TRC to include the issue of sexual violence in their investigations. Members of the TRC who viewed the film were deeply impressed by the girls' accounts. As a result, they used the film at village-by-village "sensitization" meetings aimed at educating people about the TRC, encouraging them to come forward and testify.

Operation Fine Girl also played an invaluable role in educating judicial officials. After it was shown to four of the commission's investigators of gender-based crimes and violations of child rights in Sierra Leone, the officials decided it should be shown to all prosecutor's teams, as part of their staff sensitization drive on gender issues. The documentary has also helped sensitize traditional leaders responsible for administering customary laws that relate to gender issues. Changing attitudes among local leaders is critical, as customary laws promote community stigma and ostracize women who are raped and suffer sexual violence of any kind.

As reconstruction was getting under way in 2002, the video especially helped spark discussion among professionals in health, education, and social services about the larger psychosocial impacts of the war. It was also shown to audiences of professionals from local and international NGOs, the government, donors, and advocates for programs targeting women and youth. The film helped these officials in fine-tuning their decisions about policies and resource allocation.

Operation Fine Girl has helped sensitize communities to the notion that women and girls did not voluntarily leave their families to join warring factions but were instead abducted and forced into sexual slavery. Seeing the stories of people like themselves gave community members an opportunity to start discussing their own experiences. The film has also spurred former combatants and others to come forward with their own testimony about events during the war. During one particular screening in Eastern Province, an audience of over five hundred people consisting of ex-combatants and civilians, saw the film. This is what WITNESS coordinator Mansaray reported on the event:

> In Segbwema, when the video was screened, some of the ex-combatants shed tears and some of them expressed remorse to the working group team. The overall RUF commander of the Segbwema axis, called Hai Wai—a notorious killer—walked up to the sensitization team and said he didn't realize that what combatants did to women were videotaped. He added that he did not know that this was how women were treated.
>
> Some of the ex-combatant women became very emotional. Some of them cried while listening to the testimony of the girls. It took some time for them to express themselves and when they finally mustered courage to talk, they said they were willing to come forward and explain a lot of what happened to either the Special Court or the TRC. But they added they were concerned about their safety. This information turned out to be very useful because in an NGO meeting with the registrar of the Special Court, I was able to raise the issue of witness protection.

Audiences of up to five and six hundred people have attended similar screenings in communities all over Sierra Leone, as well as at schools. Responses range from shock, to tears of relief, to occasional comments that the events belong to the past and should no longer be discussed. Overwhelmingly though audiences say that the film should be seen by as many people as possible.

Conclusions

The *Operation Fine Girl* video was effective because the interviewees—everyday victims of the civil war—chose to speak out about the truth of their experiences. They told candid personal stories that were representative of the experiences of thousands of people across Sierra Leone. The film opened a window for discussion. In community screenings, audience members were then able to relate it to their own experience, and start talking about how to respond to sexual violence both as individuals and as a society. Many women—and many men—have come forward to tell their stories after seeing *Operation Fine Girl*. Three days of TRC hearings in May 2003 were devoted to the war's impact on women and girls, including testimony by individuals, women's groups, NGOs, and international human rights monitors.

Another reason why the film has been effective is that it reflects the larger process of truth seeking. Viewers see and learn the names of the women; they also see and hear rebel and military officials, who are being confronted with the consequences of violence perpetrated by combatants. The inclusion of both perspectives—victim and perpetrator—strengthens the film's credibility and at the same time sustains a process for uncovering the events of the war, determining responsibility, and preventing similar events from ever happening again.

Operation Fine Girl has also gained an international audience. It has been used for educational and advocacy purposes in other countries in Africa, Europe, and the United States. The film was shown at film festivals, international conferences, and by major international media, including *The Oprah Winfrey Show*, which aired a one-hour program on sexual violence against girls in Africa, featuring footage from *Operation Fine Girl*.

WITNESS's work on the postconflict process in Sierra Leone has not stopped with the film. In 2003–2004 WITNESS partnered with the Truth and Reconciliation Commission (TRC) of Sierra Leone to produce a video version of the commission's final report on the war, making the findings and recommendations more accessible to a far wider audience across Sierra Leone. This video version of the final report will be distributed in English and Krio, and used by a range of locally based organizations to engage local communities in understanding the findings of the TRC, and to mobilize these communities to press their government for action on the recommendations of the TRC.

Sam Gregory is a video producer, advocacy trainer, and human rights activist. Since 2000 he has been the program manager of WITNESS. He has worked as a television researcher/producer in both the United States and the United Kingdom, and for development organizations in Nepal and Vietnam.

Contact

WITNESS
80 Hanson Place, 5th Floor
Brooklyn, New York 11222, USA
Tel: +1 718 783 2000
E-mail: witness@witness.org
Website: www.witness.org.

Selected Bibliography

Excerpts of some WITNESS video productions, are available at the organization's website: http://www.witness.org.

See http://www.witness.org/training for technical and strategic aspects of using video in human rights advocacy, and www.witness.org/partners for information on partnership.

9.3

Unsung Heroes:
Studio Ijambo in Burundi

Lena Slachmuijlder

Radio is by far the most powerful way of spreading information in the Great Lakes region of Africa. Some 85 percent of the people have access to radios. That power has been abused several times. During the horrific killings in Rwanda in 1994, the murders were spurred on by hateful radio broadcasts. Studio Ijambo is attempting to harness the power of radio for constructive purposes.

It is October 1993. Burundi's first democratically elected Hutu president, Melchior Ndadaye, has just been assassinated. Innocent Tutsi civilians are killed by Hutus in revenge for the assassination, seen as having been carried out by the Tutsi-controlled army. This sparks further revenge attacks, with Tutsis killing innocent Hutus to avenge the death of Tutsis. It is a blind cycle of violence.

In Ijenda, in the mountains outside of the capital Bujumbura, a gang of Tutsis arrives, seeking to kill Hutus. Rebecca Hatungimana, a Tutsi woman, immediately takes action, hiding forty-one Hutu neighbors in her house. Along with her husband, a military officer, they defend their compound throughout the night from the attackers armed with spears and machetes. Rebecca fearlessly wards them off. Her husband risks his life to defend the property and livestock of the Hutus. During the days that follow, Rebecca's children escort the Hutus to the fields in search of food, before returning to the compound by nightfall.

Rebecca is one of hundreds of unsung heroes in Burundi. These are ordinary people who demonstrated extraordinary courage to save the lives of people of the other ethnic group during the most difficult moments of Burundi's ethnic violence. For decades, such people were considered traitors for daring to save people who were considered the enemy. Yet Rebecca did not see them as enemies: "I did this because I'm convinced that human life is sacred, and that no one would have benefited from the death of my neighbors. I did not protect them because I am a Tutsi or a Hutu. I did it because morality obliges me to act." Later, when tempers and passions subsided, her Tutsi neighbors thanked her for her bravery. "You prevented us from becoming murderers," they told her, with a mixture of regret and appreciation.

Rebecca Hatungimana was one of approximately two hundred individuals honored in April 2004 at a Heroes Summit, which brought together people featured on a radio program called *Inkingi y'ubuntu,* which means "pillars of humanity" or "heroes" in the Kirundi language. The program, which sought out stories of people like Rebecca who bravely rejected violence during years when Burundi was plagued by ethnic conflict, has been produced by Studio Ijambo every week since September 1999 and broadcast on local radio stations.

Fostering Debate

Studio Ijambo—*ijambo* means "wise words" in Kirundi—is a radio studio set up by Search for Common Ground in 1995 to produce programs aimed at promoting dialogue, peace, and reconciliation. Studio Ijambo's team of twenty Hutu and Tutsi journalists currently produces approximately one hundred radio programs per month, which are broadcast on eight radio stations in Burundi, Tanzania, and the Democratic Republic of Congo (DRC).

The studio endeavors to provide balanced, accurate coverage and information within and outside Burundi, to foster debate and discussion, to advance the peace process, and to maintain links between Burundi and the outside world. Rather than dwelling on differences, Studio Ijambo's productions emphasize the cultural base that all the different communities in Burundi share and, in that way, it strives to keep hope alive during trying times.

In conceptualizing the *Inkingi y'ubuntu* or *Heroes* program, Studio Ijambo aimed to make it known that not everyone had participated in the various killings and massacres over the years. Adrien Sindayigaya, one of the founding journalists of Studio Ijambo and a producer of the *Heroes* program (now deputy director of Studio Ijambo) explains:

> Negative stereotypes of Tutsis and Hutus plagued the society, preventing a climate of trust and collaboration. Each group accused the other of having committed more atrocities than the other; the idea that some individuals had broken away from that negative stereotype and saved human lives was simply unbelievable for many Burundians.

Thus, the idea for the *Heroes* radio program was born, along with many challenges. For each program the producers wanted to include interviews with both the person or persons whose lives had been saved and the "hero" in question, as well as interviews with officials, neighbors, and friends who had witnessed the act of courage. People were often afraid to talk, fearing their testimonies would cause problems with their neighbors and local officials, or even reprisals from neighbors who had committed violent acts.

Slowly, however, people agreed to speak, and the program was produced and broadcast week after week. There was the story of Evariste Ndabaniwe, the cousin of the first democratically elected president, who called for calm

Audience cheering at the Heroes Summit in Burundi

and prevented his neighbors from massacring his Tutsi work colleagues on the morning after the president's assassination. "You cannot tell me your grief is more than mine," he told the attackers. "But this is no reason to lose more human lives." There was the story of Barasukana, a local administrator who defied military officers attempting to round up Hutus to be killed in 1972. Twenty years later, Barasukana was protected by his same Hutu neighbors when the violence turned against Tutsis in his neighborhood.

Promoting Understanding

Inkingi y'ubuntu is just one example of the innovative ways Studio Ijambo uses media to promote understanding and reconciliation. It also produces a wildly successful radio soap opera with a message of reconciliation. *Umbanyi Niwe Umuryango* (Our Neighbors, Our Family) is broadcast every week, and tells the ongoing story of Hutu and Tutsi families who live next door to each other. It focuses on the day-to-day problems of life that they surmount together. One independent survey carried out in the late 1990s reported 90 percent of all listeners had tuned in to at least six out of eight programs broadcast in a one-month period.

Other examples of the sorts of positive programs produced by Studio Ijambo include:

• A repatriation program coproduced by Studio Ijambo and refugee journalists living in the refugee camps in Tanzania

- A program on truth, justice, and reconciliation that includes examples from other countries around the world that have experienced similar transitions
- A program on the implementation of the various peace accords and cease-fire agreements, in which ordinary people, civil-society, political, and government leaders are interviewed
- A children's program that examines the problems they face because of the war, and their dreams and hopes for the future
- A music program featuring musicians around the country who are singing for peace and against AIDS
- A daily youth-driven live phone-in program that tackles issues facing youth and facilitates youth participation by sending journalists into communities with cell phones to enable young people to contribute to the program
- A program that examines women's rights and their participation in the peace process on a grassroots and national level
- Current events magazine programs that examine all issues related to the transitional process, including the road to elections, the demobilization process, and legal and institutional reform
- A human rights program based on real-life cases that seeks to raise awareness of human rights issues and advocate against injustice

Facing Challenges

For the team of journalists at Studio Ijambo, the great challenge is to find ways to use radio to advance the difficult process of transition in Burundi and the Great Lakes region. That means addressing important and vexing issues: the repatriation of hundreds of thousands of refugees; the demobilization of tens of thousands of former rebels and creation of new national armies acceptable to all groups; the search for a way to deal with the crimes and injustices of the past; and the road to democratic elections.

Each of these transitional processes presents its own risks and dangers, with cross-border influences on the conflicts in Burundi, Rwanda, and the DRC. Ethnic groups are still vulnerable to manipulation by political leaders seeking to ignite ethnic sentiments to serve political interests.

Journalists in Burundi inhabit a different reality than most Western journalists. They themselves are intimately involved in the conflict; every single journalist has lost members of his or her immediate family through the decades of violence. They do not always share the same analysis of Burundi's history. Still they do share a vision of the future: a Burundi where conflict is dealt with through dialogue, and not violence.

One strategy that is part of the Studio Ijambo approach is to pair Hutu and Tutsi journalists when doing stories. The original motivation was concern about security—it was thought that it would always be safer to enter a Hutu area if a Hutu was present, and a Tutsi area if a Tutsi was present. It soon became clear that the approach had other advantages. Two reporters from different ethnic groups would have different perspectives, and the listening audience would also perceive the reports as more balanced with both a Hutu and a Tutsi reporter.

Evaluating the Impact

Measuring Studio Ijambo's impact entails an examination of changes in the attitudes, perceptions, and behavior of its listening audience. Unfortunately, in the Great Lakes region that is not always a simple task. In the context of conflict, it is further complicated by the fact that other matters tend to be more than minor distractions; the Studio Ijambo staff is often obliged to respond to destabilizing rumors, erupting crises, and emerging tensions.

Nonetheless, there are key indicators that help to assess the impact of the work, revealed through independent evaluations of Studio Ijambo's programs. For example:

Popularity. Surveys reveal that some of the programs have extremely large and loyal listening audiences.

Credibility. According to an independent evaluation conducted at the end of 2001, 95 percent of respondents answered positively to the question "Do Studio Ijambo programs tell the truth?" In the same evaluation, 89 percent of respondents said that Studio Ijambo programs contribute to the promotion of dialogue, 86 percent said the programs contribute to reconciliation, and 91 percent said they contribute to the return of peace in Burundi.

Acceptance. Studio Ijambo journalists are very rarely refused an interview, or access to a rebel or military-controlled zone of the country. Leaders of all political parties, rebel movements, the military, the government, and civil society collaborate eagerly with Studio Ijambo, confident that their perspectives will not be distorted or manipulated. This is not the case with many other journalists from other media outlets.

Recognition. Studio Ijambo journalists have consistently been recognized for their work both locally and internationally. Recent awards include, locally, the Inform for Peace award and the Fight Against Impunity award, and internationally, recognition as an IFJ Tolerance Prize finalist, the Radio France International Jean-Hélène prize, and runner-up in the OneWorld/UNICEF Children's Lives, Children's Voices Prize.

Promoting dialogue. Studio Ijambo programs aim to bring together diverse viewpoints and to seek solutions to conflict. Statements by Burundians interviewed by the evaluators indicated that those efforts are appreciated. One interviewee commented, "When people fight they do not stop to understand

Talking Drum Studio in Liberia and Sierra Leone

Frances Fortune

The "talking drum," uniquely West African, speaks thorough its sounds and links communities and audiences over generations. The term "talking drum" was appropriated for Search for Common Ground's (SFCG) independent media studios in Liberia and Sierra Leone and has become a powerful tool for peace in two nations beset by violent conflict.

Radio listeners in Liberia have recently become accustomed to the lives of Mama Colbol, who runs a cook shop; Jartu, a young female hustler; and the old storyteller J-West. They are the main characters in the soap opera *Today Is Not Tomorrow,* which is aired three times a week. The events in the drama series generate tremendous discussion and analysis by the audience as they seek to predict what choices the main characters will pursue. Multiple answers and solutions are possible to the various dilemmas and challenges faced by the characters. The ambiguity of the titles is as important as the story that chronicles the day-to-day lives of a diverse group of ordinary people, and provides them with hope. Through these characters, the soap opera intends to educate and create awareness on a wide range of social, political, economic, and conflict issues. *Today Is Not Tomorrow* also provides a source of entertainment and respite from the present hardships of living in Liberia, as well as a source of inspiration to those who relate closely to the characters.

The Liberian soap opera was build on the successful daily soap opera in neighboring Sierra Leone, called *Atunda Ayenda* (Lost and Found). The local Talking Drum Studio (TDS), set up by the international nongovernmental organization SFCG, produces both programs. The organization uses media as a principal tool for peacebuilding and to create opportunities for transforming conflict. TDS are multimedia studios with multiethnic teams of journalists and producers designed to stimulate national dialogue around critical issues. It produces a wide range of radio and audio programming, along with print articles and videos, in a "common ground" approach that factors in all the key stakeholders in the conflicts, while also stimulating the search for solutions.

Both studios' main niche is drama. Drama in the form of radio programming has huge popular appeal across all age groups, including young and old. *Atunda Ayenda* has become a platform for youth issues and concerns. In an impact survey conducted in 2003, youth reported that *Atunda Ayenda* raised important issues that youth were discussing among them. This is compelling in a country where 45 percent of the population consists of young people, and the issues of disenfranchisement that fed the violent cycle of war continue to be present. Every day, following BBC's *Focus on Africa,* Sierra Leoneans all over the country tune to listen to the daily episode that is aired on eighteen stations with almost national coverage.

(continues)

Talking Drum Studio in Liberia and Sierra Leone (continued)

Radio in this region is still in its infancy. There are few if any independent producers on the radio, despite the boundless opportunities to use radio as a tool for peacebuilding and development. Producing programs is costly, and most radio stations do not have the resources to enable them to produce national-level programming. In partnership with local radio stations, radio programs are aired through local FM radio stations around the country. These programs are recorded on cassette tapes and distributed through a variety of networks. The programs are in the lingua franca and TDS is developing its capacity to do more programming in local languages as it appeals to the audience and they have a deeper appreciation of the content. TDS also helps to develop the capacity of the local FM stations to produce good community programming. TDS provides equipment to help them gather community voices, offers training in production processes, and support to their own production capacity.

Note: Talking Drum Studio website: http://www.talkingdrumstudio.org. Frances Fortune is director of the regional office in West Africa of Search for Common Ground.

---

each other's needs. They are busy shooting at each other. Studio Ijambo helps them hear each other's needs and issues; this facilitates negotiations, and puts an end to the fight." Another said, "Many Burundians did not know the conditions in refugee camps. When you do not know these conditions, you do not realize how much they need to come back to their homes. [Studio Ijambo's] work made the link between the refugee camps and the rest of society, which touched many people, including me personally."

Sustainability for the Future

In 2005, Studio Ijambo will celebrate its tenth anniversary. "We are reflecting on how to adapt to the new context," comments Adrien Sindayigaya, who notes that the media environment has changed radically since 1995. Then, there was just one, government-controlled radio station, but now the airwaves are crowded with independent stations. "This is one reason why Studio Ijambo now aims to focus more on training and capacity building in Burundi and the region."

In addition to several national training seminars in recent years, Studio Ijambo organized a nine-day regional peacebuilding media-training seminar in January 2004 with participants from eight countries in the region. This regional seminar is being followed up with other initiatives, including the preparation of a regional peacebuilding radio program in three languages, exchanges of journalists within the region, and the organizing of internships at Studio Ijambo for journalists from the region.

In 2002, journalists from Studio Ijambo created their own local association and launched a private radio station, called Radio Isanganiro, Kirundi for "Crossroads Radio." This radio station has the largest coverage of any private radio station in Burundi, and is also heard in much of Rwanda, in the Burundian refugee camps in western Tanzania and the province of South Kivu in the DRC. Informal surveys have revealed Radio Isanganiro to be one of the two most popular radio stations in Burundi.

Sustaining the positive work of Studio Ijambo will require the diverse team of Studio Ijambo journalists to continue to work together. Just as the heroes of *Inkingi y'ubuntu* took enormous risks when they dared to stand up to pressure and refused to conform to the expectations of their neighbors, Studio Ijambo journalists frequently face pressure and threats from their communities for daring to expose injustice or corruption and for challenging authority. As Adrien Sindayigaya explains: "The strength to resist this pressure and to persevere lies at the heart of the vision that Studio Ijambo journalists share: that we are contributing to building peace. It's our knowledge of this that enables us to work at it step by step, day after day, and not lose hope."

Lena Slachmuijlder is the director of Studio Ijambo.

Contacts

Search for Common Ground Burundi
BP Box 6180 27 Avenue de l'Amitié
Bujumbura, Burundi
Tel: +257 217195 (dir); +257 219696
Fax: +257 216331
E-mail: lenas@lantic.net
Websites: http://www.sfcg.org
http://www.studioijambo.org (in French)

Search for Common Ground in Sierra Leone
Talking Drum Studio–Sierra Leone
44 Bathurst Street
Freetown, Sierra Leone
Tel: +232 22-223-479
Fax: +1 202 232 6718
Website: http://www.talkingdrumstudio.org or www.sfcg.org

Search for Common Ground in Liberia
Talking Drum Studio–Liberia
St. Joseph's Complex, Bushrod Island
Monrovia, Liberia
Tel: +231 226 440
Fax: +231 226 763
Website: http://www.talkingdrumstudio.org or www.sfcg.org

10

Faith-Based Organizations: The Religious Dimensions of Peacebuilding

Douglas Johnston

Religious warfare is a theme running through all of human history, despite the fact that the core of almost all religious traditions is built around a quest for peace. Accepting the fact that religion is both powerful and persuasive, it becomes important to look beyond the secular approaches to conflict prevention or resolution and examine the potential of faith-based interventions.

In the world of diplomacy, particularly in the West, secularism and the rational-actor model of decisionmaking reign supreme. The purposeful exclusion of religious imperatives and other "irrational" considerations that are playing such a significant role in today's disputes has left foreign-policy practitioners with an inadequate frame of reference for dealing with problems of communal identity that typically take the form of ethnic conflict, tribal warfare, and religious hostilities. Clearly, a broader perspective is needed, one that acknowledges that matters of faith can play a central role in conflict, that identity is not determined by lines on a map but by emotional bonds of culture and blood, and that passions of the heart and soul are every bit as important as traditional considerations of political power, resources, and diplomatic protocols when dealing with identity-based conflicts. Here it becomes useful to examine the positive role that religious or spiritual factors can play in actually preventing or resolving conflict.

This chapter explores the potential of faith-based approaches to conflict prevention and conflict resolution. Faith-based approaches represent viable and often very effective alternatives to more traditional approaches. They can take the form of interventions by outside agencies and organizations rooted in religious institutions, or they can involve local religious bodies themselves, acting with the moral authority they possess to cool tempers and promote reconciliation. They can also involve religious leaders in bridging the divide between faiths to engage in dialogue, build relationships, develop trust, and work together in addressing common problems. In fact, there are numerous examples of faith-based interventions by players both large and small, ranging from the Church invoking its temporal power on the one hand to the activities of spiritually motivated laypersons acting on the basis of their personal faith on the other.

Faith-Based Diplomacy

Samuel Huntington noted in his *Clash of Civilizations* (1997) that religion is the defining element of culture; and here a new concept called faith-based diplomacy merits our attention. Simply put, faith-based diplomacy incorporates religious concerns into the practice of international politics. Operationally it involves making religion part of the solution in some of the intractable conflicts that currently plague the international landscape. How this translates in practice varies from one conflict to the next, since every conflict is unique. The approach itself, however, is often built around the role that religious faith plays in the lives of the protagonists, appealing to the moral compass that is presumably inherent in those who are guided by their religious convictions.

Among those who are best equipped to practice this form of diplomacy are religious leaders and institutions and some nongovernmental organizations (NGOs). As the concept of national sovereignty continues to erode under the steady onslaught of economic globalization and technology change, the power of state-centric political bodies is diminishing accordingly, and NGOs are stepping in to fill the vacuum. Nowhere is this more apparent than in the realm of conflict prevention and peacebuilding. With many of today's conflicts exceeding the grasp of traditional diplomacy, religious actors are becoming increasingly engaged in peacemaking around the world. Clearly, religious reconciliation coupled with official or unofficial diplomacy is seen by many to offer greater potential for dealing with identity-based conflicts than do the realpolitik approaches so dominant during the Cold War. As appealing as this sounds, however, there are a number of formidable challenges to using religion as an instrument of peace, not the least of which is the significant role it has played over time in both instigating and exacerbating conflict.

Religion as an Instrument of Peace

As everyone is well aware, religion is a two-edged sword. It can cause conflict or it can abate it. All too often, the religious contribution to social evolution has been characterized by intolerance, divisiveness, and resistance to change. Clearly, the kind of absolutism that sometimes attends religious convictions does not lend itself to negotiating meaningful compromise. Moreover, the key virtues of religious persuasion—neighborly concern, the betterment of humanity, and (in most cases) one's right relation with one's creator (for those religions that include a creator)—are often too weakly rooted to prevent their co-optation by the forces of power politics. Thus it is that religion in far too many instances is used as a badge of identity or a mobilizing vehicle in aiding and abetting conflict for political ends. Sadly, the shelves of the world's libraries are replete with volumes on religion's negative contributions to world history.

Often overlooked in the negative stereotyping of religion's relation to conflict is the positive role it can play in actually preventing or resolving hostilities through the increased trust that it can introduce in certain situations. It was not until the publication about ten years ago of *Religion: The Missing Dimension of Statecraft* (Johnston and Sampson 1984) that this aspect of religious activity was systematically examined. Ever since the Enlightenment, it had been axiomatic that religion was to have a declining influence in the affairs of humankind. Hence, its near-total absence from the policymaker's calculus and the uninformed policy choices that have flowed from that neglect.

With religion's resurgence following the Cold War, it has become clear to many policymakers that religion is now far too important to be marginalized as it has been in the past. Indeed, although there are still many in Western policymaking circles who underappreciate its peacemaking potential, others are beginning to see it as a defining element of national security. Clearly, there is an urgent need to understand the religious dynamics at play in any given conflict situation if one is to deal effectively with their confrontational aspects or, perhaps more importantly, to capitalize effectively on their harmonizing elements.

Faith-Based Intervention
As set forth in *Faith-Based Diplomacy: Trumping Realpolitik* (Johnston 2003), the sequel to *Religion, the Missing Dimension of Statecraft,* there are several situations that particularly lend themselves to faith-based intervention:

- Conflicts in which religion is a significant factor in the identity of one or both parties to the conflict, as is the case in Kashmir
- Third-party mediation in conflicts where there is no particular religious dimension present, as exemplified by the Community of St. Egidio's role in ending the civil war in Mozambique (See Chapter 21.1)
- Conflict situations in which religious leaders on both sides of the dispute can be mobilized to facilitate peace, as has recently taken place through the work of the International Center for Religion and Diplomacy in the civil war between the North and the South of Sudan
- Protracted struggles between two major religious traditions that transcend national borders, as has been the case over time with Islam and Christianity
- Situations in which the forces of realpolitik have led to an extended paralysis of action, as was the case in Cuba prior to the pope's visit to that country in 1998

Included among the attributes that religious leaders and institutions bring to bear in promoting peace and reconciling differences between opposing parties are (1) credibility as a trusted institution; (2) a respected set of values; (3) moral warrants for opposing injustice on the part of governments; (4) unique leverage for promoting reconciliation among conflicting parties, including an ability to rehumanize situations that have become dehumanized over the course of protracted conflict; (5) a capability to mobilize community, national, and international support for a peace process; (6) an ability to follow through locally in the wake of a political settlement; and finally, (7) because religious peacemakers often operate out of a sense of calling, there is an inspired ability to persevere in the face of major, otherwise debilitating obstacles.

Faith-Based NGOs

The range of religious actors spans a continuum, with the temporal power of religious institutions defining one end of the spectrum and the personal initiatives of spiritually motivated laypersons defining the other. Between these extremes lie the initiatives of faith-based NGOs. As contrasted with governments and secular NGOs, faith-based NGOs offer many of the attributes discussed above for religious leaders and institutions, and often operate with two distinct advantages. First, when working through religious institutions as they often do, faith-based NGOs tend to maintain closer linkages with those whom they serve. These institutions provide penetrating access to the local community and are well positioned to reinforce accountability for any agreements that may be reached. The second advantage relates to the moral authority that faith-based NGOs bring to policy debates, which often elicits a greater receptivity to their agendas from the principals to the conflict.

Thus, to the extent that faith-based NGOs can constructively exploit their faith-based identities, relationships of trust, and far-reaching networks, they offer a vital (and too often overlooked) tool for conflict avoidance and mitigation. Beyond their increasingly recognized role in conflict mediation, these NGOs are also well-suited to the tasks of conflict prevention and postconflict peacebuilding, neither of which represents an easy challenge.

As popular as interreligious dialogue has become as a prescribed remedy for reconciling strained relations between disaffected religious factions, its perceived worth is probably overrated if it only amounts to ad hoc meetings and a sterile exchange of views about belief systems. If, however, it includes a mandate for action and a commitment to meet on an ongoing basis, then the relationships that result will likely lead to increased trust, at which point all things become possible. Faith-based NGOs are among the best equipped to facilitate this kind of trust.

Points for Consideration[1]

Every conflict that takes place is inherently unique, driven as much by personalities as circumstances. Not surprisingly, each also has unique lessons to convey. Among the findings gleaned from a range of faith-based interventions by religious leaders and institutions (including faith-based NGOs) are the following.

Credibility and Moral Authority

Credibility is essential for successful mediation. While this is obvious, and as applicable to nonreligious peacemakers as it is to religious peacemakers, the fact that outside religious organizations often have a long-term presence in an area affected by conflict means that their mediators may begin an intervention with credibility that others do not possess at the outset. For example, in northern Mali, Norwegian Church Aid was able to play a constructive role in conflict resolution because of the credibility it had already established in its development work (See Chapter 16.1).

Integrity of practice is equally essential. For example, using faith-based mediation as an entrée for religious proselytization would quickly undermine the intervener's credibility. On the other hand, people will respond to an organization that pursues its work in a manner that is consistent with the task at hand. For example, the Program Pendidikan Damai in Aceh, Indonesia, has focused youth education efforts on traditional Islam and its inherent peacefulness in its efforts to address violence in that region. A similar emphasis has been institutionalized in Cambodia, where Thich Nhat Hanh has organized Dhammayietra peace walks built around the nonviolent nature of Buddhism (See Chapter 10.3).

In third-party mediation/intervention, religious peacemakers should capitalize on religious beliefs and symbols in finding a common religious language of conciliation that can foster a genuine spirit of forgiveness and reconciliation. When sensitively applied, such language and symbolism can aid in getting to the deeper issues, as the International Center for Religion and Diplomacy has experienced in its faith-based work in Kashmir, where enduring reconciliation has been achieved between several Hindu and Muslim communities.

Religious leaders are also uniquely positioned to use their moral authority and influence to encourage mutual understanding within their communities. For example, while the headlines out of Iraq may be portraying Iraq's Sunni and Shiite communities uniting in violent resistance to Coalition forces, the truth is that Iraqi religious networks are working behind the scenes to defuse some of the most explosive confrontations and reign in the most extreme clerics. Whenever possible, serious consideration should be given to including religious leaders in formal peace negotiations. Not only does their presence provide a moral authority that is often otherwise missing and an enhanced capability for dealing with the kinds of religious issues that sometimes arise in such negotiations, but their often unrivaled influence at the grassroots level can be useful in ensuring that any political settlement that emerges will be lasting in nature. In Sri Lanka, both the Congress of Religions and the Inter-Religious Peace Foundation, which are composed of religious leaders from the four main religious groups, have made strides in bringing leaders from the Buddhist and Tamil communities into negotiations with the government. It is clear that in a country such as Sri Lanka, where all religious groups carry a political identity, leaders from each faith must work together to encourage dialogue between their respective community leaders.

Religious communities can also provide social cohesion in the aftermath of violent conflict and spiritual support to help people face the agonizing pain and suffering, with some prospect for the kind of forgiveness that can break the normal cycle of revenge. Illustrative of this dimension is Anglican bishop Desmond Tutu's leadership of the South African Truth and Reconciliation

Commission, which facilitated a peaceful transition to multiracial democracy.

Networks Large and Small

Religious networks are the largest and best-organized civil institutions in the world today. From the smallest village to the largest city, religious communities often provide the largest social infrastructure for human care. Religious communities' mosques, churches, temples, and other social structures are located in virtually every village, district, and city. These organizations range from regularly and frequently convened assemblies designed for worship and reflection to those specifically dedicated to educational, health, humanitarian, or communication missions. Often spanning this remarkable panoply of institutions is a network that includes national, regional, and international religious structures. Taken collectively, religious social structures represent significant channels for communication and action that, when engaged and transformed, enable religious believers to function as powerful agents of change in the transformation of conflict.

Secular institutions are increasingly acknowledging the potential of religious communities to serve as partners in addressing common concerns such as armed conflict, human rights violations, and poverty. International development organizations such as United Nations Children's Fund, for example, are beginning to seek out religious networks for their ability to reach large numbers of people and their formidable capacity to effect change. Whether the structures are part of a network or an association of faith-based organizations, or are less formal, most religious communities are committed to collaborative work for justice and peace, and they generally have dedicated structures that allow for such collaboration.

Connecting with Other Stakeholders

It is important to keep all of the stakeholders closely informed of the proceedings and to effectively coordinate the involvement of Track One and/or Track Two diplomats. Failure to facilitate interreligious dialogue or to work with religious leaders, for example, can sometimes lead to communal schisms and undermine economic development efforts. Such has been the case in Sri Lanka, where several organizations of Buddhist monks have called for the banning of thirty-seven local and international NGOs that they claim support and conduct "unethical conversions" to Christianity. Equally important, it is always preferable to develop indigenous ownership of conflict prevention and peacebuilding initiatives as early in the process as possible.

By contrast, when faith-based organizations work within communities to encourage participatory processes on matters not directly related to conflict prevention—community development activities, for example—those activities can help build trust within the community by bringing together community leaders from different religious and ethnic groups. Where World Vision, the ecumenical Christian relief and development organization, has been engaged with communities in collaborative activities across ethnic and religious divides, it has seen reduced tensions, greater respect for the dignity and rights of other groups, and enhanced capabilities within communities to deal with conflict when it arises.

Some faith-based NGOs have gravitated to peacebuilding as a natural extension of their work in relief and development. A holistic view of development work encompasses peace, justice, and security as integral components, and peacebuilding thus becomes an extension of the traditional emphasis. In the case of Catholic Relief Services (CRS) in Rwanda, for example, this shift in approach evolved naturally from an enhanced understanding of its own role in the community that it was serving, following the genocide of 1994. Where CRS was formerly focused on development and poverty reduction, it is now actively involved around the globe in the promotion of peace and justice, and particularly in addressing the root causes of religious and ethnic conflict.

Conclusion

The challenge of harnessing religion's transcendent qualities in the cause of peace is formidable and not for the faint of heart. Not only is this work of faith-based diplomacy intellectually, psychologically, and emotionally draining, but it involves significant risks as well. There are almost always vested interests in every conflict that want to see that conflict continue, and a number of spiritually inspired peacemakers have paid the ultimate price for their efforts—Mahatma Gandhi, Anwar Sadat, and Martin Luther King, Jr., to name a few of the better known. The need for this kind of spiritual engagement, however, is only growing more urgent with the passage of time. From violence-plagued urban slums to remote villages on the fringes of the Sahara, to the green hills of Mindanao, there is solid proof that it works. The cases described in the following pages are only a few examples of what is possible.

Douglas M. Johnston, Jr., is president and founder of the International Center for Religion and Diplomacy (ICRD), a nongovernmental organization that brings the transcendent aspects of religious faith to bear in preventing or resolving identity-based conflicts that exceed the grasp of traditional diplomacy. The ICRD bridges the political and religious spheres in its practice of faith-based diplomacy in such places as Sudan, Kashmir, Pakistan, and Iran.

Note

1. These points draw on a number of sources, including the United States Institute of Peace (2001) and contributions from William F. Vendley of the World Conference of Religions for Peace.

Selected Bibliography

Huntington, Samuel. 1997. *The Clash of Civilizations and the Remaking of World Order* (New York: Simon & Schuster).

Johnston, Douglas, ed. 2003. *Faith-Based Diplomacy: Trumping Realpolitik* (New York: Oxford University Press).

Johnston, Douglas, and Cynthia Sampson, eds. 1994. *Religion, the Missing Dimension of Statecraft* (New York: Oxford University Press).

United States Institute of Peace. 2001. *Special Report 76: Faith-Based NGOs and International Peacebuilding* (22 October), available online at: http://www.usip.org/pubs/specialreports/sr76.html.

The World Conference of Religions for Peace

Religion sparks violence and impedes efforts to address global problems such as terrorism, according to many. In reality, however, religious networks are also working to eliminate terror, prevent and mediate violent conflicts, and aid the world's most vulnerable populations. Civil society is undergoing a fundamental shift in its attitude toward religion and is beginning to tap the vast social, moral, and spiritual resources of religious communities to tackle the most critical global problems. The World Conference of Religions for Peace, the largest coalition of the world's religions committed to common action, is playing a key role in this transformation.

Throughout history, religion has been associated with violent conflict—Jews and Muslims in Palestine, Muslims and Orthodox Christians in the Balkans, Hindus and Buddhists in Sri Lanka, the Judeo-Christian "West" and Muslim extremists in what Western leaders call the "war on terror." While religious intolerance and extremism are often a source of conflict, religion is more often the convenient scapegoat for underlying political and economic tensions, or bad leadership.

With so many bad examples, it is easy to dismiss religion as a source of conflict without considering the demonstrated capacity of different religious communities to work together to promote peace. In some of the most intractable conflicts around the world, religion is part of the solution, not part of the problem.

The World Conference of Religions for Peace has developed a unique method and builds effective mechanisms specifically designed to help religious communities to cooperate together in the work of transforming conflict.

The method developed by the World Conference of Religions for Peace is unique, practical, and open to continuous creativity. At its simplest, the method involves assisting religious communities to correlate, or work out a connection, between their capacities for action and specific challenges related to stages of conflict. The method, while simple, is powerful. When applied, it reveals large, often hidden or underutilized capacities for action that lie within the reach of religious communities. Importantly, the method also makes clear what kinds of capacity building are needed to better equip religious communities for more effective engagements in conflict transformation.

The mechanisms being built by the World Conference of Religions for Peace are national and regional multireligious councils. These action-oriented councils are not themselves religious organizations, but rather secular or public in character. They are led by religious leaders and designed to provide a platform for cooperative action throughout the different levels of religious communities, from grassroots structures to the senior-most leadership.

The collaborative work of the interreligious councils affiliated with the World Conference of Religions for Peace takes many forms. Interreligious councils can bring adversaries together and work to end conflict or rebuild divided societies. Sierra Leone's religious leaders, Muslims and Christians working together, stopped a bloody civil war and mediated negotiations between the government and the rebels. The Inter-Religious Council of Liberia was instrumental in President Taylor's decision to relinquish power

(continues)

The World Conference of Religions for Peace (continued)

and is now working to achieve reconciliation after years of human rights abuse and violence. Through regional coordinating committees of its affiliated interreligious councils in Côte d'Ivoire, Sierra Leone, Guinea, and Ghana, The World Conference of Religions for Peace is working to mitigate and mediate cross-border conflicts throughout the region.

No form of cooperation has greater potential to improve conditions for more people worldwide than the cooperation of the world's religious communities. Of the world's 6 billion people, 5 billion identify themselves as members of religious communities. The capacity of religious communities to meet the challenges of our time is a vast untapped resource.

Note: By William F. Vendley, secretary-general of the World Conference of Religions for Peace (http://www.religionsforpeace.org).

Resources

Lead Organizations

All Africa Conference of Churches—
Kenya
E-mail: secretariat@aacc-ceta.org
Website: http://www.aacc-ceta.org/

Catholic Relief Services—United States
Peacebuilding Program
E-mail: WebMaster@CatholicRelief.org
Website: http://www.crs.org

Center for World Religions,
Diplomacy and Conflict Resolu-
tion—United States
E-mail: crdc@gmu.edu
Website: http://www.gmu.edu/depts/icar/

Community of St. Egidio—Italy
E-mail: info@santegidio.org
Website: http://www.santegidio.org/en/

Coventry University—United Kingdom
Centre for the Study of Forgiveness and
Reconciliation
E-mail: a.rigby@coventry.ac.uk
Website: http://legacywww.coventry.ac.
uk/legacy/acad/isl/forgive/index.htm

International Center for Religion and
Diplomacy—United States
E-mail: postmaster@icrd.org
Website: http://www.icrd.org

Life and Peace Institute—Sweden
Tools for Peace? The Role of Religion in
Conflicts Programme
E-mail: info@life-peace.org
Website: http://www.life-peace.org/

Mennonite Central Committee—Canada
E-mail: mccwash@mcc.org
Website: http://www.mcc.org/

World Conference of Religions for
Peace—United States
E-mail: info@wcrp.org
Website: http://www.wcrp.org

World Council of Churches—Switzerland
Justice, Peace and Creation Programme
For contact, please visit website:
http://www.wcc-coe.org/

Website

United States Institute of Peace: resource portal on religion and peacemaking: http://
www.usip.org/religionpeace/index.html

Publications

Abu-Nimer, Mohammed. *Nonviolence and Peacebuilding in Islam: Theory And Practice.* Gainesville: University Press of Florida, 2003.

Appleby, R. Scott. *Ambivalence of the Sacred: Religion, Violence and Reconciliation.* Lanham, MD: Rowman & Littlefield Publishers, 2000.

Berger, Peter. *The Desecularisation of the World: Resurgent Religion and World Politics.* Grand Rapids, MI: Eerdmans Publishing Co., 1999.

Coward, Harold, and Gordon S. Smith, eds. *Religion and Peace Building.* New York: SUNY Press, 2004.

Gopin, Marc. *Between Eden and Armageddon: The Future of World Religions, Violence, and Peacemaking.* New York: Oxford University Press, 2002.

——. *Holy War And Holy Peace: How Religion Can Bring Peace to the Middle East.* New York: Oxford University Press, 2002.

Helmick, Raymond G., and Rodney Lawrence Petersen, eds. *Forgiveness and Reconciliation: Religion, Public Policy and Conflict Transformation.* Philadelphia: Templeton Foundation Press, 2001.

Kobia, Samuel. *The Courage to Hope: A Challenge for Churches in Africa.* Nairobi, Kenya: Acton Publishers, 2003.

McSpadden, Lucia Ann, ed. *Reaching Reconciliation: Churches in the Transitions to Democracy in Eastern and Central Europe.* Uppsala, Sweden: Life and Peace Institute, 2000.

Muhammad, Ustaz Nurayn Ashafa, and James Movel Wuye. *The Pastor and the Imam: Responding to Conflict.* Lagos: Ibrash Publications, Ltd., 1999.

Sampson, Cynthia, and John Paul Lederach, eds. *From the Ground Up: Mennonite Contributions to International Peacemaking.* New York: Oxford University Press, 2000.

Smock, David, ed. *Interfaith Dialogue and Peace Building.* Washington, DC: United States Institute of Peace Press, 2002.

United States Institute of Peace, special reports and peace works:

   Can Faith-Based NGOs Advance Interfaith Reconciliation? The Case of Bosnia and Herzegovina. Special Report, March 2003.

   Building Interreligious Trust in a Climate of Fear: An Abrahamic Trialogue. Special Report, February 2003.

   Islamic Perspectives on Peace and Violence. Special Report, October 2001.

   Faith-Based NGOs and International Peacebuilding. Special Report, October 2001.

   Catholic Contributions to International Peace. Special Report, April 2001.

   Healing the Holy Land: Religious Peacebuilding in Israel/Palestine. Special Report, September 2003.

10.1

Struggling for a Just Peace:
Naga Churches in Northeast India

Daniel Buttry

Through a mix of military and political measures and economic incentives, the government of India has tried—and failed—for years to solve the several conflicts in the northeast of the country. From the Naga side, a long and violent insurgency had failed to achieve the goal of political independence. That is why the churches and civil organizations stepped in and did what the government could not: stimulating the participation of insurgent groups in a peace process, developing an active constituency for a peaceful settlement, and bringing hope that a viable and mutually agreeable solution could be found.

In January 2000 a small crowd of Christians gathered in front of the tomb of Mahatma Gandhi, the Hindu activist called "the Father of India." The Christians were all Nagas, an indigenous people of Mongolian origin living in the hills of northeast India and northwest Myanmar. They prayed for peace at Gandhi's tomb, laying a wreath. Then they marched in the streets of Delhi, joined by many Naga students from nearby universities. Gandhi was revered by the Nagas because in 1947 he told a delegation of Naga leaders, "Nagas have every right to be independent." Nagas declared their independence on 14 August 1947, one day before India's independence from British rule. When Gandhi was assassinated, his assurances died with him as the new Indian government refused to recognize Naga aspirations for independence.

Naga protests and resistance to the incorporation of their land into the Indian union began to steadily grow. Then in 1955 the Indian army occupied the Naga areas and martial law was declared. Violence quickly escalated. The Indian army engaged in massive destruction, destroying entire villages and sending families into the jungles where many starved. Naga church and human rights officials estimate that over two hundred thousand Nagas have died in the conflict since 1955, a number that the government to India claims is grossly inflated. However, every Naga can tell a story of personal loss from the war.

India's Longest-Running Insurgency

India's northeast is one of Asia's hottest trouble spots, with as many as thirty armed insurgent organizations operating and pushing demands ranging from autonomy to secession. Four of the seven northeastern Indian states, Assam, Manipur, Nagaland, and Tripura, witness scales of conflict that can be categorized as low-intensity wars. Between 1992 and 2002, there were 12,175 fatalities due to insurgency and other armed conflicts in the region. The fight of the Naga tribal separatists is India's longest-running insurgency. Nagaland is one of the few regions of India that is predominantly Christian.

In the 1960s and 1970s, Baptist Church leaders initiated efforts to halt the violence. Eventually the Shillong Accord was signed in 1975 as a result of these efforts, but the peace agreement was fatally flawed. Key Naga resistance leaders were left out of the process, and the accord agreed to incorporation into the Indian union. The Nagas, who had only one political organization up to that point, the Naga National Council (NNC), split into factions supporting and opposing the Shillong Accord. The new opposition faction was the National Socialist Council of Nagaland (NSCN). The factions began fighting each other. Later, both the NSCN and NNC splintered further, sometimes with horrifying violence, over issues of leadership, distrust, and fears of secret agreements with India. Since 1975 as many Nagas have been killed by other Nagas as have been killed by Indian military forces.

A New Peacemaking Strategy

A new generation of church leaders emerged in the 1990s who were determined to pursue fresh peace initiatives. The vast majority of Nagas, perhaps as many as 80 percent, identify themselves as Baptists, the fruit of over 130 years of U.S. Baptist missionary work. The missionaries had been expelled by the Indian government in the early years of the war, but the Naga Baptists continued to grow and thrive even amid dire circumstances. In November 1996, after some preliminary contacts, Baptist leaders V. K. Nuh and Wati Aier met with leaders of the Baptist Peace Fellowship of North America (BPFNA) at a training conference on conflict transformation in Thailand, sponsored by Asian Baptists. In late-night meetings at the conference they laid the foundation for a new peacemaking strategy.

V. K. Nuh and Wati Aier began contacting the various faction leaders, and in July 1997 three of the four factions (the group that did not attend was NSCN-IM, the IM referring to Isak and Muivah, the leaders of the group) met in Atlanta along with some other political and communal leaders. The BPFNA, led by Ken Sehested and Daniel Buttry, hosted the talks that culminated in a jointly agreed-upon statement calling for a cease-fire, for Naga unity, and the pursuit of peace. The official Naga Baptist bodies did not publicly endorse the Atlanta meetings, but Nuh and Aier were both leaders of stature among the Baptists.

During the Atlanta talks, the government of India and the NSCN-IM agreed to a three-month cease-fire to facilitate political talks at the highest levels in a third neutral country. However, following the Atlanta talks violence increased as the cease-fire did not encompass all parties, especially between the factions. The NSCN-IM condemned the Atlanta talks and the church leaders who had participated in them. However, Aier doggedly continued to communicate through convoluted channels with that faction, asking for a face-to-face meeting with Isak and Muivah. That November they agreed to meet, and Aier and Buttry of the BPFNA met for three days with them. At the end of those talks they secured the first cease-fire in over twenty years of intra-Naga fighting. The cease-fire was informal and it was only for four days, but it was a start.

The four days of the cease-fire were for the celebration of the 125th anniversary of the coming of Christianity to the Nagas, observed in late November 1997. During a powerful prayer service in which over one hundred thousand Nagas were gathered, the fervent desire for peace was expressed. The fervor of those moments turned that informal four-day cease-fire into one that lasted over a year and a half, and still continues to put a damper on small violent flare-ups. The cease-fires with the government of India were periodically renewed and extended to the remaining groups, sometimes with bilateral agreements and sometimes unilaterally declared by India.

Democratization of the Peace Process

The formal cease-fires and commitment to political talks between the insurgents and the government of India and the informal ccase-fires between the Naga factions broadened the social space for the democratization of the peace process. Mass-based organizations and the churches now had a more conducive context in which to raise their voices and act. The next major step in the movement was sparked by the Indian parliamentary elections. Many Naga community leaders were calling for a boycott of the elections, which they saw as a legitimization of the incorporation of the Nagas into the Indian nation-state. However, leading Naga insurgents were threatening to assassinate people who participated in the election. So Aier and the BPFNA leaders convened a meeting outside India with Muivah, who had threatened the violence, and the general-secretary of the Naga Baptist Church Council. An agreement was reached to not engage in any violence related to the election, but that the churches would lead a nonviolent boycott calling for a genuine solution to the Naga situation. The insurgents laid low while the churches held prayer meetings followed by massive boycotts and the display of white flags and banners for peace. The boycott was 85 percent effective, revealing the lack of public support for the Nagas participating in the Indian state government of Nagaland.

Further mediation efforts to build unity among the Nagas, particularly the opposing factions, stalled. Many church and civic-sector groups shuttled between the factional leaders. Later consultative meetings were held between the mass-based organizations and the various resistance groups. Violence was restrained, but nothing the peacemaking groups could do would bring the insurgent leaders to the table. So a different approach was tried: mobilizing the community groups for more assertive action.

In 1999, Buttry twice traveled to India to hold extensive training and strategizing workshops with leaders of the Baptist churches and various peoples organizations such as the Naga People's Movement for Human Rights, the Naga Mothers' Association, and the Naga Student Federation. Besides learning peacebuilding skills, there was a need for building trust between the older church leaders and the critical student activists. As they listened, shared stories, engaged in team-building exercises, and ate together, a sense of unity and common commitment grew. The isolation built up by years of fear and military repression was overcome. By the end of the second workshop the participants engaged in planning that resulted in launching "The Journey of Conscience."

Journey of Conscience

Initially, this was a three-day event in Delhi. A delegation of Naga church leaders, human rights activists, leaders of various civic organizations, and two choirs from a seminary and a Christian college traveled by train from Nagaland to the Indian capital. Once in Delhi, the delegation held a conference with Indian human rights groups, academics, journalists, and retired politicians. The conference presented the Naga plight and provided an opportunity for dialogue between Nagas and the general Indian public about what was happening

Rally in Support of the Naga Cease-fire (2004)

and various hopes for the future. On the second day the delegation visited Gandhi's tomb to lay a wreath and pray, making public statements about Gandhi's support of Naga independence and their desire for a peaceful solution to the conflict. The final day was taken up with a march and rally in downtown Delhi with various Naga activists calling for justice and peace.

The response of many in the Indian activist community was surprise and affirmation. Nagas had been portrayed as savages, and until the Journey of Conscience most of the publicity about the conflict was about the violence of the insurgents. Because of the geographic remoteness of the Naga areas in relation to the rest of India, most of the Indian public had only a dim awareness of the conflict if any at all. Many Indian activists and organizations accepted an invitation from Journey of Conscience leaders to visit Nagaland and see for themselves what was happening. Public events were held during the Nagaland visit, and a joint statement was issued from the Indian and Naga participants calling for a negotiated political settlement. One insurgent leader was delightfully astonished at the statement, as this was the first time major Indian voices had been raised on behalf of a just and peaceful solution. He praised the Naga civil-society groups for what they had accomplished through their nonviolent campaign.

Since the beginning of the Journey of Conscience campaign, Naga activists have been connected to outside organizations and educational institutions such as Training for Change and Eastern Mennonite University to refine their skills in conflict transformation and grassroots education. Leaders in the mass organizations have engaged in widespread training of Naga church members, students, and women's groups in various dimensions of peacebuilding. Occasionally the BPFNA and the Quaker Peace and Social Witness Group from the United Kingdom have helped with further training and consultation, but now the Naga activists have their own skills, experience, and intellectual base for taking strong and creative action. A Naga activist and a BPFNA trainer provided training in negotiation for Naga resistance leaders so they could effectively and appropriately participate in political discussions with the government of India.

The coalition of Naga civil-society groups has also designed programs to give more international visibility to the Nagas and their situation. Cultural programs have been produced and held in various countries. International advocacy campaigns have been launched to urge India to repeal the Armed Forces Special Powers Act, which gives legal license to the human rights abuses of the Indian army in Nagaland and the neighboring state of Manipur. Videos have been produced by both Naga organizations and a sympathetic Indian film producer to give wider publicity to what is going on. As a result, these efforts are breaking through the barriers of silence and isolation of the Nagas that had allowed India to act with impunity in the region.

The negotiation process between the government of India and the Naga insurgent leaders continues to be a faltering but continuing affair. The Naga resistance groups remain at odds with each other, though violence is rare. The public voices for peace, respect of human rights, and a just settlement of the conflict are much stronger and more cogent, both from the Naga side and from within India. This public assertiveness has put more pressure on Indian and Naga political leaders to move forward on the peace agenda and not to fall back on taking military action. The slow progress of political talks could deflate the energy of the civil-society organizations, but the theological ferment related to peacemaking coming out of the churches, the passion of youthful leadership, and the continuing status of concrete targets for activist strategies such as the Special Powers Act have so far helped sustain the activist momentum.

Conclusion

There are some dynamics in the Naga struggle that might be witnessed in other contexts. The institutional church has been generally supportive of peacemaking initiatives, but the institutional leaders have sometimes exhibited caution to the point of not taking the lead at key turning points. Individuals from among the church leadership have acted on their own, such as Aier, taking courageous action when the institutional leadership would formally hold back. The leadership of these key individuals was critical at many points along the way. Most if not all of the secular community organizations were led by Baptists whose values were shaped in the context of the churches; so though they acted from the organizational base of human rights, women, and student groups, much of their personal perspectives and motivations were fed by their faith. At critical points, the churches as religious bodies or through their recognized leadership did join in the actions, which gave a huge boost of social credibility and power to the movement's actions. Baptist churches are not hierarchical, so leadership emerging out of the community of faith rather than mainly from the top of the denominational organization is consistent with Baptist ecclesiology.

Developing the skill base and ability for critical analysis and thinking was a major part of the growth of the movement. Bringing outside trainers into Nagaland and sending key leaders to established educational institutions and organizations helped to build leadership resources for the Naga groups. Outside groups for the most part avoided paternalism in presuming to tell the Nagas what they should do. Instead, they provided catalytic support and tools for the Nagas to do their own work in analyzing their situation and strategizing for how best to address their problems. This led to greater confidence in the emerging Naga leaders and healthy solidarity partnerships with outside groups.

As of early 2005, the conflict is unresolved, but many of the dynamics are moving in a positive direction. The lessons learned along the way by the churches and community organizations have provided a solid foundation for them to make significant contributions to the eventual settlement of the conflict.

Daniel Buttry was involved in the Naga peace process, first as a representative of the Baptist Peace Fellowship of North America, then as the Global Service Missionary for Peace and Justice with International Ministries of the American Baptist Churches. He is also the author of Christian Peacemaking: From Heritage to Hope *(Judson Press, 1994).*

Contacts

Naga Peoples' Movement for Human Rights
Midland—251, Opposite World War II Cemetery
Kohima—797 001, Nagaland, India
E-mail: npmhr1@usa.net
Website: http://www.npmhr.org

Baptist Peace Fellowship of North America
4800 Wedgewood Dr.
Charlotte, North Carolina 28210, USA
Tel: +1 7040521 6051
E-mail: bpfna@bpfna.org
Website: http://www.bpfna.org/

Daniel Buttry, International Ministries
20798 Syracuse Ave.
Warren, Michigan 48091, USA
E-mail: dbuttry@comcast.net

10.2

The Pastor and the Imam:
The Muslim-Christian Dialogue Forum in Nigeria

James Wuye and Muhammed Ashafa

In recent years, Nigeria has been plagued with alarming frequency by violence between its Muslim and Christian communities. One of the worst-hit regions has been Kaduna State. The cofounders and national coordinators of the Muslim-Christian Dialogue Forum of Kaduna in 1995 are two men with deep roots in the opposing communities, both of whom have turned away from violence and militancy action and instead embraced nonviolence, reconciliation, and the advocacy of peaceful relations between their communities.

Once they were bitter rivals, but now they consider themselves brothers. In fact, at one time, they each tried to have the other killed. James Wuye and Muhammed Ashafa are living proof that people can change, and that the urge for revenge can be replaced by an urge to foster reconciliation and peaceful coexistence. Pastor James Wuye readily acknowledges that he was a militant in his youth. For that, he paid a price—he lost his arm during this struggle of communal violence in 1992. Imam Muhammed Nurayn Ashafa was a militant as well. During that same eruption of unrestrained violence in 1992, he lost his teacher and two sons. For both men, coming to terms with terrible loss forced reflection, and reflection brought transformation. "Both began to question the cost of violence and turned to the Bible and the Koran, where they found passages showing commonalities between Islam and Christianity and calling on believers to be peacemakers," writes *Christian Science Monitor* reporter Mike Crawley (2003). Yet, "when the pair first met face to face in 1995, distrust lingered. At the urging of a civil society leader, they agreed to try to work out some sort of understanding, and they say the resulting dialogue helped them to overcome stereotypes and misconceptions and gain respect for each other."

They staged a public debate—no easy task in such a charged atmosphere—and this early effort at dialogue has since become an ongoing exchange through the Muslim-Christian Dialogue Forum. Each of them has made a quantum leap—from violent youth leader to successful nonviolent mediator of Muslim-Christian conflicts. Now, they listen to the each other's sermons. In fact, together they have published a book, *The Pastor and the Imam: Responding to Conflict*, which examines the perceptions of Muslims and Christians about each other, explores the commonalities at the root of the two faiths—and the differences—and then describes the efforts, at first tenuous and later more confident, to forge a common effort to promote understanding between the communities.

Intercommunal Violence

Kaduna State is the seat of Nigeria's northern elite, including senior military, religious, and traditional figures. Its population of approximately 3.5 million is divided more or less equally between Muslims and Christians. Kaduna has also, unfortunately, been at the epicenter of intercommunal conflict—conflict that has only worsened since the Kaduna state government's declaration of its intent to introduce *shariah* law. This declaration sparked an outbreak of violence in late February 1999, and subsequent anti-Muslim reprisals in various southern towns, that left an estimated two thousand people dead, eighty thousand displaced, and many private homes and business premises looted and destroyed.

With its mix of ethnic and religious groups, Kaduna continues to be one of the most conflict-prone states in the country. The various communities compete for a greater share of the limited socioeconomic resources and for political power, each feeling itself politically and economically marginalized. In that environment, religion is, in a sense, "perverted" as it is invoked in the political arena, and youth are exploited by those who seek to gain personally from the conflict.

A Myriad of Contributing Factors

Ethnic and religious differences have been a source of tension throughout Nigeria's turbulent postindependence history, which has been marked by decades of military rule. The third and most recent attempt at instituting democracy in the federal republic has been under way since 1999.

Pastor Wuye stresses that during the long periods of military rule, ethnic and religious tensions have tended to increase. Official appointments to federal posts have often been made on the basis of patronage as opposed to merit, which has favored Muslim northerners who have been quite dominant in the Nigerian military. Thus, Christian clerics have preached against what they perceive to be injustice in the trend of federal government appointments under military regimes.

Another factor that has contributed to Nigeria's ethnic tensions has been the country's poor progress toward economic development. In spite of its abundant petroleum and natural gas reserves, the United Nations Development Program ranked Nigeria as 151st of 174 countries evaluated in terms of human development. Imam Ashafa also notes that when the bubble that was Nigeria's oil economy burst in the 1980s, there was an apparently related increase in ethnic conflict with religious undertones.

In view of such linkages, observes Pastor Wuye, one can reasonably conclude that "most of the problems in Nigeria do not come from religion but economics and social conditions."

Multitrack Approach

Imam Ashafa and Pastor Wuye share a view that civil-society organizations—such as the Interfaith Mediation Centre, which they set up—can do a better job of defusing potentially violent situations in Nigeria than security forces. According to Pastor Wuye, the Interfaith Mediation Centre uses a multitrack approach to address issues of intercommunal violence. "We 'deprogram' people by making them aware of what the other side is thinking."

The project that the two men launched, which consists of both the Muslim-Christian Dialogue Forum and the Inter-Faith Mediation Centre, aims to prevent the recurrence of violent conflict and to contribute to an increase in the level of trust and tolerance between Christians and Muslims in Kaduna State. With trust, tolerance, and an absence of violence, reconciliation can begin through the development over time of collaborative relationships and cohesive peace constituencies in both communities. At the same time, as such reconciliation takes root, the communities' capacity to resolve conflicts will also be enhanced.

Five specific objectives have been identified:

1. To reestablish relationships that have been damaged due to recurring violence over the last five years
2. To minimize the reoccurrence of violence amongst various groups in the community
3. To initiate programs and projects that require and encourage the involvement of Christians and Muslims (including dialogues, workshops, cultural events, and the establishment of a resource center)
4. To enhance interreligious relationships and cooperation within the state
5. To support and build the capacity of local partners who are involved in peacemaking

The center organizes a range of activities to bring together religious leaders, policymakers, technocrats, small-business owners and traders, grassroots participants including women, youth, and religious leaders, and other stakeholders. The inclusion of women is especially important because of the role women play in educating children at home. Engaging youth is vital because it is youth, in fact, who are often the perpetrators of violence (Nigerians, observes Pastor Wuye, tend to be fiercely passionate about their faith. For many Nigerian youth, religion is everything. He draws an important distinction—that one can be "religious" without being "godly"). Because operators of businesses and traders have a vested interest in peace and stability in the community, they are viewed as valuable potential partners in the peace and reconciliation process.

Some of the activities that take place include programs focusing on dialogue among the various constituencies; intensive problem-solving workshops for women and youth groups; annual cultural events; capacity-building training programs for local community leaders and members of civil society; and programs designed to address the trauma that citizens have suffered as a result of the violence.

One of the most significant achievements of the center has been the drafting of the "Kaduna Peace Declaration," which is an articulation of a common vision to put in place effective machinery appropriate for building and sustaining long-term peaceful coexistence between the Christian and Muslim communities. The document was carefully formulated so as to be broadly acceptable and realistic in its goals, and the potential signers were encouraged to review it together with their constituents. In August 2002, some twenty senior religious leaders signed the Kaduna Peace Declaration and declared that each year, 22 August would be observed as Peace Day in Kaduna State.

Impact

Since the signing of the Kaduna Peace Declaration, grassroots efforts to maintain peace have continued, but the challenges have remained as well. Any incident runs the risk of turning into a crisis. In November 2002, for example, protests over a newspaper article connecting the prophet Mohammed to the Miss World beauty pageant caused much tension. Both Pastor James and Imam Ashafa, in union with transformed religious leaders, drove around affected neighborhoods on a bus and arranged to have them appear on television to appeal for calm. The intervention only was made possible because of the commitments made in the Kaduna Peace Declaration, which was an important factor in containing a volatile situation.

Religious leaders who have signed the declaration are also credited with helping to control violence and vote rigging during elections at both the state and federal levels. In addition, they have, on numerous occasions, intervened in conflicts in the schools, when minor arguments threatened to turn into major incidents. Indeed, some instigators are intent on using schools as a breeding ground for religious conflict. To stem this tide, the Interfaith Mediation Centre, in collaboration with signers of the Kaduna Peace Declaration, has embarked on a program to provide conflict resolution training to religious instructors and secondary-school officials.

Other Approaches

The consultative approach of the center stands in stark contrast to the approach of the federal Nigerian government, which has attempted to achieve peace by viewing conflict, especially in Kaduna, as a question of law and order. This has systematically failed and attracted international criticism. On the other hand, at the state level, it can be said that the Kaduna state government has played a somewhat more constructive role. It has tried to transform the conflict in the region through rudimentary arbitration and mediation methods utilizing official Track One approaches—governmental agencies and government-sponsored dialogue. Such efforts have changed the conflict's dynamics but not contributed to resolving it; nonetheless, Kaduna State's efforts have been somewhat promising in view of the fact that the state has attempted to address the fundamental structural causes of the conflicts. This work has been informed by intensive research and consultation with local partners, especially the Kaduna Peace Committee, an organization with extensive knowledge of the conflict dynamics and issues at stake in Kaduna and the greater north, and familiarity with parties to the conflicts.

One other important result of the cooperation between Imam Ashafa and Pastor Wuye has been a successful initiative to bring together two warring communities of Plateau State, the nomadic Fulani cattle rearers and the native Beroms. To settle long-standing disputes, Imam Ashafa and Pastor Wuye arranged to hold talks and actively facilitated a mediation process. In 2003, the two parties made a start on engaging in a healing process and exploring pragmatic solutions to the conflict.

Overall, Imam Ashafa and Pastor Wuye have successfully facilitated dozens of conflict resolution activities. Whereas their efforts were once confined to their hometown of Kaduna, they are increasingly working in other regions as well. Through its perseverance, the Interfaith Mediation Centre has gathered the strength to break free from one-time interventions and extend its reach and influence across Nigeria.

Lessons Learned

For Imam Ashafa and Pastor Wuye, it has been a long and difficult journey, from outright animosity to cautious steps to get to know each other—still holding much suspicion and mistrust—to trust and acceptance, and finally to cooperation. Imam Ashafa and Pastor Wuye have come to see, by engaging in dialogue, that they, as believers in their faith, are more similar than dissimilar. The greatest threat to peaceful coexistence, as they see it, comes not as a result of cultural or religious difference, but from ignorance of the humanity that binds people together. "Erroneous perceptions affecting Christian-Muslim relationships have been a source of commotion and tears," they write in *The Pastor and the Imam*. "They have bred assumptions, stereotypes, and suspicions. As long as we insist on passing judgment on others by the verdict of our perceptions, and refuse them opportunity to explain . . . to us who and what they are, we are creating room for conflict in our inter-personal and inter-religious relationships" (Wuye and Ashafa 1999: 24).

The refreshing, if simple, discovery of the pastor and the imam is that they can draw strength and inspiration from the very faith that is so central to

A Surprising Meeting of Minds

We both, in the past, had been involved in a war of words through various publications . . . In these papers we expressed radical, provocative ideas from the stand points of our religions, on which we would refuse to negotiate for any reason. These uncompromising attitudes, in the past, had resulted in a tense atmosphere that did not allow room for dialogue or for any form of interaction between us. Everyone was trying to outwit the other. To the Pastor, the goal was total evangelization of the country, while for the Imam it was total Islamization. These were our positions before that fateful meeting and introduction.

Then we started talking, each of us carefully selecting his words, We were conscious that here were two "enemies" coming face to face for the first time, on a ground that was not conducive to flexing of muscles. But in our eyes, one could read hatred, anger and resentment, all covered with the cynical smiles that frequently flashed across our faces. Each was highly suspicious of the other.

To our very great surprise, as this discussion progressed, we were both startled by some discoveries. Hidden behind the turbaned Imam was a gentleman, not the violent man that the Pastor had assumed he was. Similarly, the suited Pastor was a bird of the same feather as the Imam. We found that we had a lot of things in common. From this, the idea of collaborative problem solving was initiated. At the end of that meeting we resolved to meet again to further harness this idea of responding to our conflicts.

Note: From: *The Pastor and the Imam* (Wuye and Ashafa 1999: 20).

their lives, by looking to the messages of Jesus Christ and the prophet Mohammed, to eschew conflict and violence and instead pursue justice, love, and peaceful coexistence.

Pastor James Movel Wuye and Imam Mohammed Nurayn Ashafa are the founders and coordinators of the Inter-Faith Mediation Centre/Muslim-Christian Dialogue Forum.

Contact

Inter-Faith Mediation Centre/Muslim-Christian Dialogue Forum
East Wing, 6th Floor NNIL Building
(Waff Road), Kaduna, Nigeria
Tel.: +234 (0) 62 243 816
E-mail: mcdf2002@yahoo.com

Selected Bibliography

Crawley, Mike. 2003. "Two Men Create Bridge over Nigeria's Troubled Waters." *Christian Science Monitor,* 28 February. Online at: http://www.csmonitor.com/2003/0228/p07s01-woaf.html.

Fischer-Thompson, Jim. 2001. "Muslim-Christian Dialogue Forum Works for Change in Nigeria." Public Affairs Section, U.S. Embassy in Nigeria. Online at: http://usembassy.state.gov/nigeria/wwwhp121401a.html.
Wuye, James Movel, and Muhammad Nurayn Ashafa. 1999. *The Pastor and the Imam: Responding to Conflict* (Lagos, Nigeria: Ibrash Publications, Ltd.).

10.3

Step by Step on the Way to Peace: The Dhammayietra Peace Walk in Cambodia

Though a formal peace treaty was signed in 1991, the conflict in Cambodia continued and the Cambodian people continued to suffer. In 1992, a number of local and foreign peace activists initiated the first Dhammayietra peace walk—literally, a "Pilgrimage of Truth." It has taken place around the time of the Cambodian New Year ever since. Villagers along the way see the walk and the gradual return of Buddhism and Buddhist monks as a sign that peace is real, despite the continued hardships that are a result of the war.

"We must find the courage to leave our temples and enter the temples of human experience, temples that are filled with suffering. If we listen to the Buddha, Christ, or Gandhi, we can do nothing else. The refugee camps, the prisons, the ghettoes, and the battlefields will then become our temples."
—Maha Ghosananda

On 22 March 2004, a group of 140 monks, lay people, and volunteers concluded a 6-kilometer hike up a steep rocky trail and climbed the steps of Preah Vihear, a mountaintop temple in northern Cambodia. They had just completed a twenty-one-day 375-kilometer walk through the Cambodian countryside—the fourteenth Dhammayietra for peace and understanding. The youngest walkers were just fourteen. The oldest was a seventy-seven-year-old man named Dom Chem. All were united by the aim of the pilgrimage, "to promote awareness of the five precepts of Buddhism and to promote the ideals of compassion, loving kindness, generosity, honesty, and tolerance."

The Dhammayietra was inspired and originally led by Somdet Phra Maha Ghosananda, one of Cambodia's most respected Buddhist monks, who has continued to serve as its spiritual leader. In a nation devastated by the horrors of the Pol Pot regime and beaten down and discouraged by years and years of war, that first Dhammayietra in 1992 was a spectacular success. Thousands of Cambodians spontaneously joined the pilgrims along the route leading to Phnom Penh, and tens of thousands more gathered to urge the walkers on as

233

they passed through provincial seats along the way. It attracted significant media coverage, with one result being that the world was confronted with Cambodia's suffering. Each year since then, a group of private citizens has walked through the Cambodian countryside on what is considered to be both a physical and a spiritual pilgrimage, traversing war zones and minefields, subject to blistering heat and monsoon rains. Often, the crowds have included soldiers who laid down their weapons, offered prayers for the marchers, and provided the pilgrims with food and water.

These pilgrims come from all religions, nationalities, and backgrounds, united only by a commitment to peace and truth. Although the Dhammayietra is not, strictly speaking, a religious procession, the Dhammayietra walks are a very specific application of Buddhist teachings on the linkage between spiritual awareness and nonviolent conflict resolution. Maha Ghosananda, who is often referred to as the "Gandhi of Cambodia," notes that the Dhammayietra tradition dates back over 2,500 years.

Maha Ghosananda is a firm believer in the power of compassion. Reconciliation, he believes, flows forth from a deep-rooted sense of compassion—not just to wish to leave the struggle behind, so to speak, but to embrace the humanity of the adversary, the victim, the perpetrator, and indeed, of all people. "It is a law of the universe that retaliation, hatred, and revenge only continue the cycle and never stop it," he has said. "Reconciliation does not mean that we surrender rights and conditions, but rather that we use love. Our wisdom and our compassion must walk together. Having one without the other is like walking on one foot; you will fall. Balancing the two, you will walk very well, step by step."

Training Programs

The Dhammayietra is both physically and mentally grueling. Therefore, all participants prepare for the lengthy walk by attending nonviolence training programs at one of several locations in Cambodia. The first sessions at these training programs are taken up with fundamentals: the philosophy of the walk, an introduction on meditation for peace, and an understanding of how basic Buddhist concepts can be applied to the difficulties of everyday life. There are also sessions on peacemaking, the theory and application of nonviolence, strategies for handling fear, and role-playing sessions to familiarize participants with potential situations they might encounter during the walk. Because of the serious risks of injury from unexploded mines, the training also includes sessions on mine awareness, provided by nongovernmental agencies.

Such training not only prepares the walkers for the Dhammayietra itself, but also creates a large network of individuals trained in nonviolent action and theory, capable of passing that knowledge on to other members of their own communities. Over the years, thousands of people have attended nonviolence training sessions. One of the enduring benefits of the Dhammayietra has been the development of this network, which extends not only throughout Cambodia but to neighboring countries as well, and with many international participants around the globe.

Philosophical Underpinnings

The central value that is the key to both the power and the success of the Dhammayietra is the compassion to which Maha Ghosananda eloquently refers, viewed from a Buddhist perspective as both the means and the end of personal and social liberation. Compassion is considered to be the one virtue that enables peacemakers to persist in nonviolent action when confronted with violence and frustration. To quote from a poem by Maha Ghosananda, "Great compassion makes a peaceful heart, a peaceful heart makes a peaceful person, a peaceful person makes a peaceful family, a peaceful family makes a peaceful community, a peaceful community makes a peaceful nation, and a peaceful nation makes a peaceful world." While members of the Dhammayietra movement recognize that the development of compassion is a long-term process, they offer several lessons from Buddhist practice as strategies that can be useful in cultivating it. Compassion serves as a defense against fear, which is seen as a precursor to violence.

As a corollary to the cultivation of compassion, the Dhammayietra philosophy advocates the cultivation of "active mindfulness." By this it is meant that when an individual is confronted with a difficult situation, he or she is capable of either quickly acting—or not acting, if that is more appropriate—with clarity of mind, based on one's own knowledge, experience, and understanding, rather than reacting to and being controlled by that situation.

If these two qualities are aspired to for the individual participants of a Dhammayietra, the quality that is essential to guarantee the integrity and credibility of the group process is nonpartisanship. In Buddhist terminology, the Dhammayietra treads the "Middle Path." The Dhammayietra is making a statement for peace and nonviolence, and against policies, strategies, and actions that lead to violence, but that stance does not imply that it is opposing one side or another in a violent conflict. The position of the Dhammayietra is a clear expression of Gandhi's admonition to "oppose the evil, not the evildoer."

New Issues

The Dhammayietra is an expression of commitment to nonviolence, but it is also a complicated ongoing event, and it thus requires order, discipline, and logistical planning. In the first years of the Cambodian Dhammayietras, the ideal itself was considered strong enough to assure discipline and success, but in response to difficulties encountered along the way, an organizational structure developed.

Overall coordination was placed in the hands of a small committee consisting of Cambodian monks, nuns, and laypersons (in earlier years a smaller committee including expatriates coordinated the walks). The participants were divided into groups of about ten walkers, each with a group leader selected by the members. These leaders participated in meetings with the walk committee to assure a democratic decisionmaking process. Other members of each group were designated to serve as assistants and representatives, with responsibilities for the distribution of essential supplies, food, water, and information.

Perhaps the most important provision introduced after the first few walks was a set of guidelines for participants. These stipulated that walkers would attend the prewalk nonviolence training and refrain from riding in vehicles, using drugs, carrying weapons, wearing uniforms, or carrying flags.

Beginning with the fourth Dhammayietra in 1995, walk organizers incorporated a public-education element. This included the distribution of pamphlets, dissemination of a "Peace Health" message articulating the belief among health workers that war "is the number one health problem in Cambodia," and public talks at villages along the route of the walk. At these talks, Maha Ghosananda would spread his message that Buddhism can serve as a basis for social reconciliation and compassion. Such events also provided opportunities for landmine awareness trainers to make presentations to local residents.

As the threat of civil war has receded somewhat, the Dhammayietras have increasingly focused on a range of other issues besides peace and nonviolence. In 1995, for example, the focus was on the international campaign to ban landmines, and in 1996 attention was directed to the environment, and particularly the need to preserve Cambodia's forests, which are an important symbol of renewal in Buddhism, and vital to the country's environmental health. Unfortunately, Cambodia's rich timber resources have suffered as combatants during the Cambodian civil war exploited them as a source of income. Accordingly, during the 1996 walk, thousands of trees were planted along the route.

The urgent issues of HIV/AIDS and drug addiction have also been important themes over the past several years. Dhammayietra fourteen, for example, focused on the need to nurture tolerance and compassion for people living with HIV/AIDS.

A Risky Endeavor

Although nonviolent action is undertaken in the hope that a principled commitment to nonviolence can provide a degree of protection for participants, nonviolent action in a climate of violence remains a risky endeavor. This was vividly and tragically demonstrated during the Dhammayietras of 1993 and 1994. The first Dhammayietra in 1992 had succeeded beyond its organizers' expectations. Walkers had begun the Dhammayietra in refugee camps on the Thai side of the Thai-Cambodian border, and had walked to Phnom Penh. As a result of the walk, many refugees had been reunited with family members they had not seen since the 1970s, and the walk had succeeded—at least for a time—in breaking through the insidious climate of fear that pervaded the society.

At the beginning of the second Dhammayietra, from Siem Reap in the north of the country to Phnom Penh, several walkers were wounded when they were caught in a crossfire between government forces and Khmer Rouge fighters.

Walkers also braved ongoing shelling that, though not directed at the walk, occurred on a daily basis along the first part of the route. The walk continued nonetheless, and by the time it reached the capital, the total number of participants had swelled to about three thousand.

The following year, with a fragile coalition between former combatants in place in Phnom Penh after UN-supervised elections, the organizers elected to walk from Battambang to Siem Reap—directly through a region of the country where the civil war still raged. Their hope was to maintain "a zone of peace" around the walk. On the seventh day of the Dhammayietra, the walkers were accompanied by unarmed soldiers who were showing them a mine-free route, and as they walked, they encountered other armed soldiers conducting military patrols.

"Suddenly," wrote U.S. participant Liz Bernstein, "the walkers encountered a group of [Khmer Rouge] soldiers and a firefight ensued. Bullets and rockets flew as the walkers lay on the ground." The Dhammayietra had once again been caught in a crossfire, and this time two walkers were killed. Following this incident, there was considerable confusion about whether or not the walk would continue, and some organizers and participants left the walk, while others continued, by an alternate route, to the end.

After the sobering experience of 1994, organizers redoubled their efforts to provide adequate training to participants and to ensure that no soldiers would accompany the Dhammayietra. Since the tragic events of 1994, the Dhammayietra has been completed each year without violence.

Accomplishments

Still, in view of the deaths and injuries that have occurred, and the ever-present risk, it is fair to ask what, if anything, is accomplished by the Dhammayietra. Canadian anthropologist Monique Skidmore observed the Dhammayietra was a "new cultural ritual of remembering," and that "through the creation of new collective memories it will allow some Cambodians to emerge from the culture of violence created by the last twenty years of war." Australian nonviolence trainers Robert Burrowes and George Lakey both believe that the Dhammayietras build "nonviolent solidarity" between the participants who pass through zones of conflict and the local people who must endure the suffering caused by violence. Such solidarity, writes Yeshua Moser-Puangsuwan, of the Southeast Asia office of Non-Violence International, "further generates awareness of, and support for grassroots initiatives to halt the war. It also generates solidarity actions by grassroots activists in other parts of the world" (European Centre for Conflict Prevention 1999: 223). Moser-Puangsuwan believes that in this way the Dhammayietra can serve as a model for nonviolent struggle in other parts of the world.

Since 1999, the prime mover behind the walks has been SyVorn, a forty-four-year-old woman who notes that she has lived through many regimes and many wars. "Many people, especially government officials, ask why do we still have Dhammayietras?" says SyVorn, "Cambodia has peace now, they say."

But I ask them, has the war in our hearts really ended? Everyday we fight over money, food, power, etc. We get angry about this and that. Our hearts are not yet peaceful. We've walked for over ten years now yet our hearts haven't learned to be at peace. Dhammayietra is not waiting for the next war to begin but comes now to spread information everywhere and to call all to a change of heart, a Khmer heart, a soft, kind, gentle heart.

Contact

Dhammayietra Centre for Peace and Nonviolence
Wat Sampeo Meas, P.O. Box 144, Phnom Penh
Cambodia
Tel: +855 129 24 248
Fax: +855 233 64 205

Selected Bibliography

European Centre for Conflict Prevention (ECCP). 1999. *People Building Peace—35 Inspiring Stories from Around the World* (Utrecht, Netherlands: ECCP).
Khemacaro, Yos Hut."Steering the Middle Path: Buddhism, Non-Violence and Political Change in Cambodia." Online at: http://www.c-r.org/accord/cam/accord5/yoshut.shtml.
"Maha Ghosananda to Receive Fifteenth Niwano Peace Prize." Online at: http://www.interfaith-center.org/oxford/press/niwano98.htm.
"One Million Kilometres for Peace: Five Years of Steps Towards Peace in Cambodia." Online at: http://www.uq.net.au/~zzdkeena/NvT/51/6.html.

10.4

Restoring the Power of Speech:
The REHMI Initiative in Guatemala

Even before the formal end of Guatemala's long civil war, a project was launched, at the initiation of the Catholic Church, to document the abuses committed by both sides. Thousands of interviews were conducted and reported to the nation, with the view that it was essential to know what happened in order to avoid repeating history.

From the early 1960s until the last days of 1996, Guatemala was consumed by a civil war of unspeakable cruelty. In its essence, the war pitted left-wing guerrillas against a right-wing elite. Particularly during the early 1980s, Guatemala's security forces engaged in a campaign of terror and intimidation against the agrarian, mostly indigenous Mayan peasants, who were viewed as sympathetic to the leftist insurgency. Starting in the early 1990s, the warring parties began a dialogue that led, ultimately, to the formal end of the war on 29 December 1996. The war had involved untold horrors and left deep scars. Getting to the truth of those horrors has been an essential part of the healing process still under way in Guatemala.

In 1994, during the process that led to the final peace settlement, the two sides agreed to establish a Commission for Historical Clarification (Comisión para el Esclarecimento Histórico [CEH]), which would begin its work after the final peace agreement went into effect. However, the CEH mandate was too weak to serve as a vehicle for meaningful reconciliation. For one thing, CEH was only given six months to investigate the crimes committed during thirty-six years of fighting, with the possibility of one six-month extension. Further-more, CEH had no power to subpoena witnesses and it was not supposed to ascribe individual responsibility or to name names, but only to clarify the disputed history of Guatemala's recent past. Its influence was further undermined by the extension of a general amnesty covering all but the most egregious crimes (genocide, forced disappearance, and torture). Not surprisingly, then, CEH was strongly criticized by elements within civil society.

An Alternative Force

From the 1960s on, Guatemala's Roman Catholic Church had been a strong advocate for social justice and respect for human rights, issuing pastoral letters in which the causes of armed conflict were traced to the extreme poverty of the Guatemalan peasantry and the absence of democracy. In 1995, in response to the widespread criticism of CEH, the Office of Human Rights of the Archbishop of Guatemala launched the Project for the Reconstruction of a Historical Memory in Guatemala (Proyecto de Recuperación de la Memoria Histórica, or REMHI). It was initially seen as a project that would provide information to CEH, but according to REMHI team member Carlos Martín Beristain, "REMHI developed into an alternative force complementing what the official commission was able to do" (Martín Beristain 1998a: 24).

Whereas CEH was interested primarily in objectively documenting the events that had taken place, REMHI had been established "based on the conviction that the political repression had wiped out the population's power of speech." According to Martín Beristain, "survivors and their relatives had been unable to share their experience, come to an understanding about what had happened, or denounce those responsible" (Martín Beristain 1998a: 24). Giving the victims and survivors of the war the opportunity to tell their stories was crucial to the healing process. Perhaps more significantly, clearly documenting Guatemala's painful past could help to insure that the cruelty of the previous thirty-six years would never be repeated.

Four Phases

The REMHI project would consist of four distinct phases. The first phase, which lasted for a little less than a year, familiarized the nation with the project and the need to afford victims the opportunity to tell their stories. The Church took advantage of its unique position in Guatemalan society to sensitize parishioners to the importance of the work, and also publicized the aims of the project in the media.

The second phase was, in a sense, the heart of the project—the taking of testimonies from thousands of citizens. These were primarily victims, but in some cases, perpetrators as well.

Phase three of the project involved compiling and analyzing the testimonies and producing a report.

The final phase, which is ongoing, involves dissemination of the report findings, and extensive follow-up, including activities to address and ameliorate the trauma caused by the human rights abuses committed during the war. Phase four has also involved exhumations of mass graves to allow for both the gathering of forensic evidence and the ceremonial reburial of the victims.

Methodology

The REMHI project recruited eight hundred Church workers from around the country to take testimonies, and organized workshops to provide training in interviewing techniques. Some of the training was technical—the use of tape recorders, for example—but another important aspect of the training involved the preparation of trainers for the intensely emotional impact that a testimony could have on the interviewee. An important criteria for selection was the ability to gain the trust and confidence of the interviewees; where possible, the interviewers were drawn from people within the local communities.

The REMHI team consulted with international human rights organizations, experts on international law, and forensic scientists and devised a methodology based on methods that had been used in the past by human rights organizations researching reports of abuse. REMHI's intention was to document the full range of experiences of the witnesses. Many had themselves been tortured or physically abused, had lost family members to executions or massacres, survived attempted killings, or witnessed abuses. Beyond that, many had been forced from their homes, survived as internal refugees in the mountains, or fled the country.

Since the primary purpose of the exercise was to "recover memory," rather than to tally statistics about the human rights abuses, the team decided that the primary tool in the process would be the tape recorder. "We in the communities said we weren't interested in the dead," one REMHI associate told Paul Jeffrey, the author of *Recovering Memory*, a book that examines—among other Church initiatives in Guatemala—the REMHI experience in detail.

> We didn't want to know that there were a 100,000 people tortured. That didn't interest us. We wanted to know what we needed to know in order to know what to do afterward with the people. . . . On the tape would go the voice, the word of the people, not as we interpreted it but as they themselves expressed it ... in the language of the people, and people will be able to listen to that in the future. The words will remain alive. (Jeffrey 1998: 50–51)

REMHI distilled the many points of inquiry into a list of seven questions. What happened? When? Where? Who were the people responsible? What effect did this event have on people's lives? What did they do to face up to the situation? Why did they think it happened?

REMHI was not universally supported within the country. There were some, especially within the sizable evangelical Christian community, who felt that the project of recovering memory was a mistake and that it would be better to forgive and forget. Of course, many within the security services and many ex-guerrillas opposed the project as well, for fear of retribution or legal ramifications. On some occasions, military officials issued veiled threats to civilians, warning that they might risk a return to violence if they cooperated. Witnesses were also pressured by guerrilla leaders to withhold any information that might implicate them in abuses.

By the middle of 1997, REMHI had succeeded in taking testimony in most dioceses in Guatemala—more than six thousand interviews conducted in Spanish and seventeen Mayan languages. Most—92 percent—were with victims, but approximately five hundred perpetrators also gave testimony.

One More Trauma

REMHI spent much of the following year compiling the testimonies and writing a four-volume report. Then, on 24 April 1998, Bishop Juan Gerardi Conedera, the driving force behind REMHI, presented *Guatemala: Nunca Más* (*Guatemala: Never Again*) to the public.

The most important findings presented in the report described the full horrifying range of crimes: information on over thirty thousand murders, the identification of three hundred mass graves, documentation of 422 massacres, frequent descriptions of sexual violations, and shocking testimony about the murder of children. The report also made clear that the human toll was compounded by the harsh conditions that those who fled their homes confronted: 11 percent of the deaths attributed to the conflict resulted from hunger and exposure—mostly among children—suffered by internal refugees.

Although, as noted above, the goal of REMHI was not to quantify the violence, a few further findings reveal how devastating the conflict in Guatemala was: out of a total population of around 12.5 million (2000 estimate) approximately one hundred and fifty thousand were killed during the war, fifty thousand "disappeared," 1 million fled their homes, two hundred thousand children were orphaned, and forty thousand women were widowed. Ninety percent of the victims were men, and nearly 75 percent were indigenous adults. Guatemalan security forces were responsible for the overwhelming majority of the abuses, but guerrillas were not exempt from culpability: Insurgents committed 3.7 percent of the massacres.

Bishop Gerardi clearly viewed the REMHI project through the prism of his pastoral calling, as he spoke at the presentation:

> When we began this project, we were interested in discovering the truth in order to share it. We were interested in reconstructing the history of pain and death, seeing the reasons for it, understanding the why and the how. We wanted to show the human drama and to share with others the sorrow and the anguish of the thousands of dead, disappeared, and tortured. We wanted to look at the roots of injustice and the absence of values . . . Christ's mission is a reconciling one. His presence calls us to be reconcilers in this broken society and to try to place the victims and the perpetrators within the framework of justice. There are people who have died for their beliefs. There are executioners who were often used as instruments. Conversion is necessary, and it's up to us to open spaces to bring about that conversion. It's not enough to just accept facts. It is necessary to reflect on them and to recover the values lost. We are gathering the memories of the people because we want to contribute to the construction of a different country. (Lindstrom n.d.)

Two days after presenting the REMHI report, Bishop Gerardi was brutally murdered. Eventually, after attempts were made to blame the murder on others, three military officers were convicted of the crime.

Impact

The aims of the REMHI project were mostly therapeutic. In some ways, then, it is far too early to judge its long-term impact. Certainly, those who suffered terrible losses or were the victims of torture and abuse cannot purge their pain simply by providing testimony. Their own comments on what importance they ascribed to the project and to their testimony suggest something of the potential impact. Witnesses told interviewers that they thought their testimony was important because it would contribute to the discovery and understanding of the truth, that it would dignify the dead, that it would restore the "power of speech" to those who had been effectively silenced, and that the testimony would stand as clear evidence for future generations that it is not possible to erase the collective memory of a people.

Learning the truth about relatives who were murdered has, in some cases, helped to bring a grieving process to closure. Where reburials have occurred, this too, has been important, particularly within Mayan society, where there is a belief that the dead do not leave the community, and so, as Martín Beristain observes, the reinternments "constituted for many people a possible way of reestablishing links which had been destroyed by the violence."

There was also the hope that giving testimony would lead to justice, but in general, this has not been the case. So has REMHI in any way helped to rebuild Guatemalan society or even solidified the footing upon which a new society can be built? Eight years after the end of the conflict, and six and a half years after *Nunca Más* was published, Guatemala is still at peace, and it is at least superficially a functioning democracy. Yet observers ranging from the U.S. State Department to Amnesty International to Human Rights Watch decry a discouraging lack of progress toward securing the protection of human rights and the rule of law.

Uruguayan essayist Eduardo Galeano writes in *La Memoria Subversiva* in *Tiempos: Reencuentro y Esperanza* (quoted in Martín Beristain [1998a: 24]), "Experience demonstrates that it is amnesia which makes history repeat itself over and over like a bad dream. A good memory allows us to learn from the past, because the only reason for recovering the past is to help us transform our present way of life."

REMHI has provided the means by which to banish amnesia from Guatemala's collective consciousness and learn from the past in order to prevent any recurrence of its long nightmare. The risks clearly remain, but in the last few years, positive opportunities for transformation have emerged as well.

Contact

Oficina de Derechos Humanos Arzobispado
  de Guatemala (ODHAG)
6a. calle 7-70, zona 1, 01001
Ciudad de Guatemala
Tel : +502 2850 456
Fax: +502) 2328 384
E-mail: ddhh@odhag.org.gt
Website: http://www.odhag.org.gt

Selected Bibliography

Human Rights Watch. 2004. "Overview of Human Rights Issues in Guatemala," January. Online at: http://hrw.org/english/docs/2004/01/21/guatem6985.htm.

A Long Legacy of Conflict

Guatemala's long civil conflict began in the 1950s when Jacobo Arbenz, the left-leaning, democratically elected president, was overthrown in a coup with the covert support of the United States, which saw Arbenz as a potential ally of its Cold War rival the Soviet Union. Arbenz had been attempting to implement reforms, including land reform, to redistribute some of Guatemala's wealth from a tiny elite that controlled about two-thirds of the nation's arable land to the poorly educated, rural poor—mostly indigenous Mayans—who made up the vast majority of the population. The 1954 coup installed a military dictatorship that halted the reforms and clamped down on dissent. When a coup to oust the new military rulers failed in 1960, some of the coup leaders launched an insurgency. Government counterinsurgency efforts often targeted not only guerrilla fighters, but civilians as well. Especially in the 1980s, the brutality of the counterinsurgency campaign led to the destruction of at least 440 villages. Approximately 1 million Guatemalans fled their homes.

In 1986, following elections, Guatemala's military rulers stood down. Following in 1990, with the assistance of the Lutheran World Federation, representatives of the government and the guerrillas began meeting in Oslo, Norway, to explore the possibilities of a negotiated settlement. Early on, they signed a "Basic Agreement on the Search for Peace by Political Means," but progress toward a comprehensive settlement was slow, and it took six more years before the civil war in Guatemala was finally ended. On 29 December 1996, the final agreement was signed by four guerrilla leaders and four Guatemalan government officials at a ceremony witnessed by 1,200 invited guests.

Jeffrey, Paul. 1998. *Recovering Memory: Guatemalan Churches and the Challenge of Peacemaking* (Uppsala, Sweden: Life and Peace Institute).

Lindstrom, Dave. n.d. "Putting the Pieces Back Together." Foundation of Human Rights in Guatemala. Online at: http://www.fhrg.org/remhi/pieces.htm.

Martín Beristain, Carlos. 1998a. "The Value of Memory." *Forced Migration Review* (August). Online at: http://www.fmreview.org/FMRpdfs/FMR02/fmr207.pdf.

———. 1998b. "Guatemala: Nunca Más." *Forced Migration Review* (December). Online at: www.fmreview.org/FMRpdfs/FMR03/fmr306.pdf.

Mathews, Dylan. 2001. *War Prevention Works: 50 Stories of People Resolving Conflict* (Oxford: Oxford Research Group).

U.S. Department of State. 2003. "Country Reports on Human Rights Practices—2003." Bureau of Democracy, Human Rights, and Labor. Online at: http://www.state.gov/g/drl/rls/hrrpt/2003/27900.htm.

11

Education That Makes a Difference

Tricia S. Jones

Perhaps more than ever, there is a need for innovative and successful approaches to developing the defenses of peace in the minds of all humanity. We have witnessed the consequences of not attending to these needs in the many and varied international, interethnic, and intergroup conflicts around the globe. Fortunately, there are wonderful programs and practices in the area of conflict resolution education and peace education that have proven effective in building peaceful behavior and peaceful orientations. We know these kinds of education can make a difference. By allowing others to know of the possibilities, we can help sow the seeds of peace.

"Since wars begin in the minds of men, it is in the minds of men that the defenses of peace must be constructed."
—Preamble of the Constitution of the United Nations,
Educational, Scientific, and Cultural Organization (UNESCO)

The cases discussed in this chapter present experiences and successes of conflict and peace educators around the world: in Sierra Leone, India, Lebanon, and the United States. In each of these cases we learn about best practices for conflict resolution and peace education and we come to appreciate the challenges of this work.

We begin by defining conflict resolution and peace education. Then, several challenges are raised that face these efforts and suggest ways that the cases in the following chapters help us overcome these challenges. Finally, this introductory chapter ends with a brief recommendation of additional work needed in this field.

Conflict Resolution Education and Peace Education

Conflict resolution education programs focus on developing critical skills and abilities for a person to deal constructively with conflict. In most cases these programs occur in schools, but they may also be used in after-school programs, community centers, church groups, etc.

What do children learn in conflict resolution education? These programs give children an understanding of the nature of conflict—what conflict is and how it develops as well as what one can do to manage it. Children learn to appreciate that conflict exists whenever there is a disagreement about goals and/or methods to achieve those goals; and as a result, conflict is natural, necessary, and important. Children learn to understand the dynamics of power and influence that operate in all conflict situations. Furthermore, they become aware of the role of culture in how we see and respond to conflict.

An awareness of the nature of conflict helps children appreciate the variety of ways that people can manage or respond to conflict—another common program component. By learning a range of conflict styles (such as competing, collaborating, accommodating, avoiding, and compromising), children can consider the advantages and disadvantages of each. As effective conflict managers know, no approach to conflict management works all the time; the key is to know which approach is best for the situation at hand. However, conflict resolution education emphasizes that a violent response to conflict is almost never an appropriate response.

An extremely important program component involves providing children with social and emotional skills to prevent conflict and reinforce their use of prosocial strategies in conflict. Some of the skills that conflict resolution education helps develop include effective listening, perspective taking, emotional awareness, and emotional control. Of these, perhaps the most important is perspective taking. When children learn to take the perspective of another, they are increasing their ability to empathize with the other person. The more we empathize with someone, the less we are likely to want to hurt them.

The Peace Education Working Group at United Nations Children's Fund (UNICEF) defines peace education as "the process of promoting the knowledge, skills, attitudes, and values needed to bring about behavior changes that will enable children, youth, and adults to prevent conflict and violence, both overt and structural; to resolve conflict peacefully; and to create the conditions conducive to peace, whether at an intrapersonal, interpersonal, inter-group, national, or international level" (UNICEF 2004). Gavriel Salomon states that peace education usually includes such topics as "antiracism, conflict resolution, multiculturalism, cross-cultural training, and the cultivation of a generally peaceful outlook" (Salomon 2002: 7). Using the UNICEF definition and Salomon's conclusion, we may consider peace education the larger effort and conflict resolution education as one of the key areas within peace education.

Marc Sommers (2003) suggests that peace education is best understood in terms of the specific skills, attitudes, and knowledge imparted. Peace education programs help people develop communication skills of active listening and assertive speech; problem-solving skills of brainstorming or consensus building; and orientation skills of cultural awareness and empathy. Furthermore, peace education builds positive attitudes about justice, respect, and democracy, though respect for democracy may be expressed indirectly through respect for individual choice. Peace education emphasizes understanding the dynamics of social conflict, warfare, and conflict resolution and the dynamics of peace. In particular, participants in peace education are introduced to the distinctions of negative and positive peace. Participants may learn about different ways of handling conflict, such as negotiation, mediation, or facilitation.

A quick perusal of the definition, characteristics, and content of conflict resolution education and peace education programs suggests that both areas overlap considerably. The basic motivations are similar, the goals for programs are similar, and the key skills and content are similar. Sommers (2001) notes that similarities are also shared between peace education and many kinds of "values education programs," such as human rights education, antibias training, and tolerance education. These all share a commitment to enhancing the quality of life by emphasizing the dignity of life. In all three examples, violence is rejected and participants are encouraged to find alternative ways of handling problems.

Challenges

Building Community

What does it take to make a constructive, caring community? How can conflict resolution education and peace education help in that quest? These may be the essential questions of our work.

Most peace educators realize that they have the potential to make a "home" for children by building a caring community. Furthermore, realistically that means that before anything else can be accomplished, basic physical needs for food, water, and shelter must be met, as Emma Kamara and Keith Neal explain in their discussion of the Children's Learning Services in Sierra Leone (See Chapter 11.1). Once physical needs have been met, the children and the community understand the commitment to them and are more receptive to learning peace skills.

Building a community also means emphasizing inclusion in the community and counteracting sources of discrimination. For example, in the *Sawa* children's magazine developed in Lebanon, there was an emphasis on encouraging inclusion and discouraging bias and discrimination based on ethnic and religious difference (See Chapter 11.3).

Susan Fountain has worked with many schools to help them develop more positive communities. After working with UNICEF, Creative Response to Conflict, and Educators for Social Responsibility, she has considerable experience. She remembers working with one school in particular:

> In [one] class they had a student come in the middle of the year when it's very tough to be accepted. The boy who joined was overweight and was fairly young in terms of his social skills. He had extreme learning problems. Kids started to tease and scapegoat him. The parents actually got involved in this as well, even tried to get the kid kicked out of the school. They called him a monster. This developed into a very bad situation. [I] worked with the class, did a lot of group building, cooperative games then moved to exercises

on inclusion and exclusion. This provoked some very deep and honest discussion for the kids. They got the kids working in groups together to build acceptance. I used the game where you have kids close their eyes and put a different color sticker on their heads and get into a group with the same color. Knowing who the kids were who were at the forefront of the exclusion [I] allowed these kids to have the experience of having a "different" dot, so they could feel what it's like. This also got some very profound discussions going. Then they moved to doing some role plays about the reasons that kids get excluded in this school—gender, wearing glasses, different preferences, lik[ing] sports or not. They talked about what the kids could do if they were excluded or as a bystander seeing someone else is excluded. (Jones and Compton 2203: 293)

After a great deal of work, this school was able to develop a positive and nurturing community. However, first the students needed to understand their own dynamics of disrespect and agree to disallow that behavior.

In Ohio, the Students Offering Acceptance and Respect (SOAR) program is a wonderful example of students building a caring and respectful community through antibullying programs. When individual students refuse to treat others with respect, it is the responsibility of other members of that community to stand up for them. (See Chapter 11.4.)

Having acknowledged the importance of community and the role of conflict resolution education in creating positive community, what are some of the things that may prevent conflict resolution education and peace education from achieving maximum benefit in terms of developing constructive and caring communities?

If students, teachers, parents, and community members are not given the necessary skills, they will not be able to build community. Providing those tools forces us to face difficult resource issues. Skill development does not happen overnight. There is always a learning curve needed for children and adults to acquire new skills. Knowledge is only the first step. Without practice, application, and review, the new skill will not really be learned.

It seems appropriate to remember that conflict resolution education and peace education programs are most successful when adults model constructive conflict management and caring community for children. We do not want to give the impression that community-building efforts are only something that adults should "help children do." It is as important for the adult members of schools and external communities to learn and enact these constructive behaviors for themselves.

However, the challenge of conflict resolution education and peace education programs in terms of building community is different in societies that are experiencing or have recently experienced serious conflict. Conflict-ridden societies, especially in cases of interethnic conflicts, are more damaged and require more reparation of emotional issues before skills development can be the focus. In conflict-ridden societies the need to provide for the basic safety and security needs of all clearly comes first. Furthermore, once those are secured, educators may find that normal outlets for education—such as schools or community centers—no longer exist as places to conduct this important learning.

However, the most important realization is that there is a lot of healing that must be done. Children who have experienced serious conflict or war are traumatized and emotionally scarred by that experience. They, and the adults who live with them, need help in managing these emotional wounds. Such work is often an initial focus of peace educators, and it may take many months or even years to overcome the trauma and help the child be ready to move forward in learning peace.

Connections that Empower

If one tool is good, several tools may be better—especially for complex issues and complex goals. All of the cases presented in the following chapters reinforce this wisdom. Perhaps most striking is the example of the Ohio Commission for Dispute Resolution's support of truly comprehensive, school-wide, conflict resolution education efforts. The commission and their model, the Winning Against Violent Environments program (WAVE) and SOAR programs give us insights about how to combine conflict resolution and peace education efforts for optimum sensitivity to the needs of the community or school.

A critical part of any effort is social and emotional learning. When children develop emotional competence, it is integrally intertwined with the development of conflict competence and social competence. If we want our children to be able to manage conflict effectively, we need to appreciate that conflict is an inherently emotional experience. An emotionally traumatized student cannot be an effective manager of their own conflicts and cannot reasonably help others manage their conflicts—as the experience in Sierra Leone so convincingly suggests.

In addition to the various techniques and materials educators can use to promote social and emotional development, there is a need to value the expressive arts as a means of conflict discovery. Through the arts children of all ages can come to a much deeper awareness of their emotional selves, their emotional reactions to conflict, and their emotional growth through conflict. Furthermore, expressive arts are particularly effective in helping children overcome trauma by first representing the trauma in music, dance, drama, or visual art.

Peer mediation is the most prevalent, best-known, and best-understood form of conflict resolution education. Peer mediation is powerful on its own, but it can be more powerful if it is partnered with other conflict resolution education and peace education efforts. Having peer mediators involved with bias awareness initiatives, restorative justice, and antibullying efforts are powerful possibilities. With appropriate guidance, the peer mediators can help manage lower-level conflict involving bias and power abuse. Mediators can become mentors who educate younger children, as the WAVE program in Ohio demonstrates.

Peace Boat's International Student Program

Since its foundation in 1983, Peace Boat has been active in the field of education for peace and sustainability through the organization of educational voyages, based on lectures, workshops, and study-exchange programs both onboard the ship and in ports of call. Its International Student (IS) programs in particular provide innovative approaches to peace and sustainability-related studies through intensive learning onboard and direct exposure to issues in various countries.

Peace Boat aims to increase access to peace education and conflict resolution training to young people from regions in military or political conflict through the IS program. A selected number of young people from opposing sides of conflicts are invited to participate in an advanced conflict analysis and peaceful conflict resolution training program, on a scholarship basis. As well as peace training, the international students help other participants onboard Peace Boat's educational voyages understand their lives and challenges, thus contributing greatly to the participants' overall understanding of the nature of conflict.

The aim of the IS program is for students to learn about peaceful conflict resolution and develop the knowledge, skills, experience, and motivation that will equip them with the means to work for peace when they return to their homes.

To date, there have been six IS programs, involving thirty-seven students from Palestine, Israel, Serbia, Croatia, Cyprus, India, Pakistan, Northern Ireland, Colombia, the United States, Korea, China, and Taiwan.

For more information see http://www.peaceboat.org.

Contextually and Culturally Sensitive Programs and Practices

All of the successful cases in the following chapters have something in common—none of them used a "canned" program to accomplish their conflict resolution education or peace education goals. Is this merely a coincidence? No, it is not. It was a conscious and intentional move on their part to not use a lockstep program because it simply would not meet the needs of the children or the community.

While programs and curricula are valuable tools in a larger effort, they are not sufficient in and of themselves and may do harm if applied inflexibly. Most successful conflict resolution education and peace education efforts are the result of careful consideration of the underlying principles and philosophy the school or community is trying to achieve.

This requires the community leaders, parents, school administrators, teachers, staff, and other stakeholders to identify their goals and principles. Once stakeholders can agree to a core set of principles, they can develop an array of techniques and use them as needed and in concert in order to determine the approach that best maximizes the principle at that time. The experience of the

City Montessori School in Lucknow, Uttar Pradesh, India, is an excellent example. Their establishment of a peace education curriculum and culture resulted in their ability to discourage violence in their broader community (See Chapter 11.2).

Best Practices

Several authors of the cases in the following chapters commented on the challenges of institutionalization. What are some guidelines or best practices for making these efforts last? The following suggest some of the proven best practices in our field.

Involving key people in planning. Most change agents know that strategic planning is a key to the success of a new initiative. The schools and communities that succeed in conflict resolution education and peace education make sure that critical stakeholders are involved in making decisions and share responsibility for their implementation.

Setting goals and objectives. Successful schools and communities clarify what they want to achieve, how they will get there, and how they will know when it happens. They also realize that goals change over time and what they wanted to accomplish in the past may not be what they want to accomplish now.

Expanding and adapting. One key to institutionalization is adopting a "growth" frame of mind. If you think in terms of growth and incremental achievement, you automatically think in terms of expansion and flexibility. Schools and the communities they serve are dynamic. Conflict resolution education and peace education must be dynamic as well. All of the cases presented in the following chapters are excellent examples of this guideline.

Listening to children. We cannot overstate the importance of listening to youth when creating, evaluating, and improving programs. Their feedback is critical. Too often programs are adult-centered and when they become child-centered and even child-driven there is more commitment, authenticity, and freshness.

Proven Benefits

Although it is beyond the scope of this introduction to provide a summary of the proven benefits of peace education and conflict resolution education, it is important to note that these proven benefits have been demonstrated and reported in the research. We know that these efforts can work and do provide important advantages for children. Two general reviews of research, one in peace education and the second in conflict resolution education, are briefly mentioned here.

Baruch Nevo and Iris Brem (2002) gathered the past twenty years of evaluation research on the effectiveness of peace education programs. They note that between 1981 and 2000 approximately one thousand articles, chapters, reports, and symposia proceedings dealing with a broadly defined peace education area were available for review. About a hundred of these focused on peace education interventions and had some report of effectiveness evaluation, but only seventy-nine had sufficient detail for any analysis. Nevo and Brem examined these seventy-nine studies and found that the majority of these programs (fifty-one out of seventy-nine) were found to be partially or highly effective in teaching peace and conflict skills.

In the area of conflict resolution education, Dan Kmitta and I edited a volume (2000) that summarizes the results of a research symposium on conflict resolution education sponsored by the U.S. Department of Education. The purpose of the symposium was to examine the results of current research and evaluation of school-based conflict resolution education programs (kindergarten–twelfth grade). The major findings demonstrate that these programs increase academic achievement, positive attitudes toward school, assertiveness, cooperation, communication skills, healthy interpersonal/intergroup relations, constructive conflict resolution at home and school, and self-control. Research also suggests that conflict resolution education decreases aggressiveness, discipline referrals, dropout rates, social withdrawal, suspension rates, victimized behavior, and violence. There is also substantial evidence that this kind of education positively impacts school climate in terms of reducing disciplinary actions and suspensions, improving school climate (especially for elementary schools), and improving classroom climate.

Conclusion

Hopefully, this introduction has accomplished its goals—to introduce you to peace education and conflict resolution education, to summarize some of the challenges facing educators in these programs, to suggest best practices in implementing these programs, and to summarize the proven benefits of these programs. As you will see in the cases that comprise the following chapters— conflict resolution education and peace education are a critical part of any peacebuilding effort.

Tricia S. Jones is a professor in the Department of Psychological Studies in Education at Temple University in Philadelphia, Pennsylvania. Temple University is a "Research I" status public university of forty thousand students and faculty.

Selected Bibliography

Jones, Tricia S., and Daniel Kmitta, eds. 2000. *Does It Work? The Case for Conflict Education in Our Nation's Schools* (Washington, DC: Conflict Resolution Education Network (renamed: Association for Conflict Resolution).

Nevo, Baruch, and Iris Brem. 2002. "Peace Education Programs and the Evaluation of Their Effectiveness," in Gavriel Salomon and Baruch Nevo, eds., *Peace Education: The Concept, Principles, and Practices Around the World* (London and Mahwah, NJ: Lawrence Erlbaum Associates).

Salomon, Gavriel. 2002. "The Nature of Peace Education: Not All Programs Are Created Equal," in Gavriel Salomon and Baruch Nevo, eds., *Peace Education: The Concept, Principles, and Practices Around the World* (London and Mahwah, NJ: Lawrence Erlbaum Associates).

Sommers, Marc. 2001. "Peace Education and Refugee Youth," in Jeff Crisp, Christopher Talbot, and Daiana B. Cipollone, eds., *Learning for a Future: Refugee Education in Developing Countries* (Geneva: UN High Commissioner for Refugees).

———. 2003. "Peace Education: Opportunities and Challenges." Presentation at the Building Bridges to Peace and Prosperity: Education and Training for Action, sponsored by the U.S. Agency for International Development, Washington, DC, 11–15 August.

UNESCO. 2002. *UNESCO: IBE Education Thesaurus,* 6th ed. (Geneva: UNESCO, International Bureau of Education).

UNICEF website. www.unicef.org/girlseducation/index_focus_peace_education, accessed 2/8/04.

Resources

Lead Organizations

Association for Conflict Resolution— United States
E-mail: acr@ACRnet.org
Website: http://www.acresolution.org

Association for the Development of Education in Africa—France
E-mail: adea@iiep.unesco.org
Website: http://www.adeanet.org

Centre for Conflict Resolution— South Africa
Towards Peaceable School Communities Programme
E-mail: mailbox@ccr.uct.ac.za
Website: http://ccrweb.ccr.uct.ac.za

Educators for Social Responsibility— United States
E-mail: educators@esrnational.org
Website: http://www.esrnational.org

Hague Appeal for Peace—United States
E-mail: hap@haguepeace.org
Website: http://www.haguepeace.org

International Peace Bureau— Switzerland
Peace Education Programme
E-mail: mailbox@ipb.org
Website: http://www.ipb.org

Living Values Education—United States
Office for the United Nations
E-mail: lv@livingvalues.net
Website: http://www.livingvalues.net

Ohio Commission in Dispute Resolution and Conflict Management—United States
E-mail: website@cdr.state.oh.us
Website: http://disputeresolution.ohio.gov/schools.htm

United Nations Educational, Scientific and Cultural Organization (UNESCO)—France
Culture of Peace Program
For contact, please visit website: http://www.unesco.org/education/ccp/index.htm

West Africa Network for Peacebuilding— Ghana (WANEP)
Active Nonviolence and Peace Education programme
E-mail: wanep@wanep.org
Website: http://www.wanep.org/programmes/peace_education.htm

Websites

Peace & Non-Violence, Canadian Centers for Teaching Peace: http://www.peace.ca/

This site includes a selected bibliography on conflict resolution and peacebuilding: http://www.peacemakers.ca

Education resources database: http://searcheric.org

Eliminating violence through school, parent, and community education: http://www.teachingpeace.org

Conflict Resolution and Peer Mediation research project: http://www.coe.ufl.edu/CRPM/CRPMhome.html

UNICEF website: http://www.unicef.org/girlseducation/index_focus_peace_education
United Nations Cyberschoolbus: http://www.un.org/pubs/cyberschoolbus/peace

Publications

Bodine, Richard J., Donna K. Crawford, and Fred Schrumpf. *Creating the Peaceable School: A Comprehensive Program for Teaching Conflict Resolution*. National Center for Conflict Resolution Education, 2002.

Cabezudo, Alicia, and Betty A. Reardon. *Learning to Abolish War: Teaching Toward a Culture of Peace*. New York: Hague Appeal for Peace, 2002.

Cohen, Richard. *Students Resolving Conflict: Peer Mediation in Schools*. Glenview: Good Year Books, 1995.

Compton, Randy, and Tricia S. Jones. *Kids Working It Out: Stories and Strategies for Making Peace in Schools*. San Francisco: Jossey-Bass, 2003.

Debardieux, Eric, and Catherine Blaya, eds. *Violence in Schools: Ten Approaches in Europe*. Issy-les-Moulinaux, France: ESF éditeur, 2001.

Harris, Ian M., and M. L. Morrison. *Peace Education*. Jefferson, NC: McFarland & Company Publishers, 2003.

Hendrick, Diane, Ursula Schwendenwein, and Rüdiger Teutsch. *Peace Education and Conflict Resolution: Handbook for School-Based Projects*. Vienna: Bundesministerium für Bildung, Wisenschaft und Kultur, 2002.

International Center for Conflict Resolution and Mediation. *Conflict Resolution in Elementary Schools*. Montreal: International Center for Conflict Resolution and Mediation, 2002.

Liebmann, Marian, ed. *Mediation Works! Conflict Resolution and Peer Mediation Manual for Secondary Schools and Colleges*. Bristol: Mediation UK, 1998.

UNESCO. *Best Practices of Non-Violent Conflict Resolution in and out of School: Some Examples*. Paris: UNESCO Division for the Promotion of Quality Education, 2002.

Van Tongeren, Paul, and Emmy Toonen, eds. *Conflict Resolution in Schools: Learning to Live Together*. An International Conference, Urbana, IL, Final Report. Utrecht, Netherlands: European Centre for Conflict Prevention, 2003.

Personal Story:
"Institutions of Civil Society—The Role of the Scientific Community in Preventing War" —David Hamburg

How can nongovernmental organizations, religious leaders and institutions, educational and scientific communities, business firms, and the mass media usefully contribute to the prevention of deadly conflict? How can their capacities be mobilized in societies where violence threatens? It is crucial to identify and support those elements of civil society that can reduce intergroup antagonisms, enhance attitudes of concern, social responsibility, and mutual aid within and between groups—and to provide the technical and financial resources they need to operate effectively.

The scientific community provides understanding, insight, and stimulating ways of viewing important problems—none more important than deadly conflict. It can generate new knowledge and explore the application of such knowledge to urgent problems in contemporary society. Human conflict and its ongoing resolution—thereby averting mass violence—is a subject that deserves major research efforts. High standards of inquiry must be applied to this field, involving many sciences functioning in collaborative ways.

Several interesting and potentially useful approaches have emerged. Among these is the neurobiology of aggressive behavior that gives insight into how cells, circuits, and chemistry mediate such activity. Related to this is research into the biomedical aspects of individual violence. Research into child abuse and its effect on subsequent development also has relevance in understanding aggression, as do other factors influencing pro-social and anti-social child and adolescent development.

Behavioral scientists do experimental research on simulated conflicts, including negotiations not only in simulated circumstances, but in real-life situations as well. The Cold War stimulated systematic inquiry into the origin and resolution of past conflicts and ongoing efforts in relation to contemporary ones, including the study of intergroup and international institutions and processes pertinent to large-scale conflict. All of this facilitates research specifically focusing on war and peace, including ways to diminish the likelihood of nuclear war by arms control, crisis prevention, reducing the risk of accidental or inadvertent nuclear confrontation, and improvement of relations among the nuclear nations.

The scientific community has contributed much to coping with the nuclear danger. During the decades of the Cold War, this community sought ways to reduce the number of weapons greatly, and especially their capacity for a first strike; to decrease the chance of accidental or inadvertent nuclear war; to find safeguards against unauthorized launch and against serious miscalculation; and to improve the relations between the superpowers, partly through international cooperative efforts in key fields bearing on the health and safety of humanity.

A prominent example of international scientific cooperation during the Cold War was the Pugwash Conference on Science and World Affairs, recognized in 1995 by the Nobel Peace Prize.

In the world of the twenty-first century, it is crucial to understand incentives for cooperation, obstacles to cooperation, factors that favor cooperation, and strategies that tend to make cooperation useful and effective. Such cooperative agreements in security matters are means to a variety of peaceful ends, but centrally involve reducing the risk of catastrophic war.

To some extent, the scientific community can provide a model for human relations that might transcend some of the biases and dogmas that have torn the species apart throughout history, and have recently become so much more dangerous than ever before. Science can contribute to a better future by its ideals and its processes, as well as by the specific content of its research, and all these must be brought to bear on the problem of human conflict.

Dr. David A. Hamburg is president emeritus at the Carnegie Corporation of New York, where he served as president from 1982 till 1997. He is a DeWitt Wallace Distinguished Scholar at Cornell University, and Distinguished Presidential Fellow for International Affairs at the National Academy of Sciences.

11.1

Food, Education, and Peacebuilding: Children's Learning Services in Sierra Leone

Emma Kamara and Keith Neal

After more than a decade of civil war, Sierra Leone is attempting to put back the pieces of a shattered society. Perhaps nothing is more crucial to those efforts than to invest in the nation's children, who suffered so terribly during the war. That is precisely what is happening with Children's Learning Services, an initiative of a former university lecturer and the mother of five children, who was herself driven from her home during the war. After addressing the children's basic needs, talking about peace is on the menu.

Children's Learning Services (CLS) has been involved in equipping schoolchildren, young adults, and teachers with conflict resolution skills. A basic premise of CLS is that while peacebuilding skills may not be inherent, they can be learned. An equally important premise of CLS is that both the body and the mind must be nurtured to secure the future of Sierra Leone's children. As Emma Kamara, the founder and coordinator of CLS, says: "First we address some basic needs. When the child has had something to eat and has been able to learn something, then he or she knows that you are concerned about him or her. Only then can you begin to talk about peace. So first we look for ways to feed the children by trying to link community food production and schools."

Virtually all of Sierra Leone's citizens—and particularly its children—were subjected to violence during the civil war that officially ended in January 2002, and many encountered unspeakably traumatic experiences. In 1999, after rebels attacked and killed many residents of the capital, Freetown, Kamara decided that positive action had to be taken to bring hope and restore dignity to children. Drawing on her own spiritual faith, she started out with one hundred children between the ages of four and ten who attended her church. She taught them academic skills, introduced faith-building songs, and encouraged them to become peacebuilders.

Encouraged by the response of the children, the church, and the local community to this program, Emma's vision began to grow. Her professional experience in education was invaluable. She was already thinking about how to restore the huge losses in educational opportunity caused by the war. So she committed herself to working to involve all the children of Sierra Leone in peacebuilding.

It was a huge challenge to develop this vision with almost no resources. However, in 2001, with the support and encouragement of a few friends and churches in Sierra Leone and the United Kingdom, Kamara founded Children's Learning Services as a Christian community-based organization focusing on child development. The aim was to give support in three key areas: quality basic education, peacebuilding, and nutrition security. CLS started a pilot peace education project at the Freetown Modern Preparatory School. Video and computer classes were organized to enrich children's learning experiences. CLS also conducted in-service teacher-training sessions in peace education. Numeracy and literacy were promoted using basic learning materials donated by the community. Parents and teachers were included in this endeavor. From this early experience, CLS showed that peace education can be integrated into the curriculum and provide life skills necessary for resolving day-to-day conflicts at home and in school.

As program coordinator, Kamara soon found that the work demanded a full-time commitment, so she resigned her university post. The sheer magnitude of the task ahead became apparent once it was possible to travel more freely and evaluate the needs of children outside Freetown.

CLS identified with several other organizations in recognizing the fact that many children were forced to participate in the armed conflict and many more were helpless victims. After the war it became commonplace to find many ex-combatants among the nation's students. Once they had gone through the processes of demobilization, disarmament, and reintegration, it was official policy to return them to school or some other training institution. Administrators are now facing the huge challenge of insuring that schools attended by ex-soldiers remain peaceful. Not only must they maintain the desired discipline of coexistence and tolerance, but also they need to learn conflict resolution skills to resolve day-to-day conflicts.

"The worst problem is that the children are deeply traumatized," says Kamara. "In a way they have lost their hope for a better future. And most of them have lost their positive self-image. If someone threatens to kill you, it feels as if you are worth nothing. And then there are children who have killed." Accordingly, the program begins not by directly addressing peacebuilding, but with stress management and trauma healing. "Before being able to talk about peace, we give them skills to be able to handle their emotions, their fears and doubts."

Significantly, nearly all the trauma-healing and peacebuilding programs set up at the end of the war were targeted at adults, and most operated at the community level. Schools did not consider peacebuilding to be a responsibility they should assume. However, the CLS perspective is that, since young people, particularly schoolchildren, form a crucial part of every community, it is essential that they be given the means to help equip their local communities with conflict resolution skills and to bring their peacebuilding initiatives to fruition.

Since 2001 CLS has mobilized a number of volunteers and practitioners in peacebuilding, quality basic education, and nutrition security in and out of school. The work is done through the implementation of a variety of projects in collaboration with local communities, government ministries, and other community-based organizations (CBOs) and nongovernmental organizations. Among the organizations with which CLS is working is the National Collaborative Network for Peace Building in Sierra Leone (NCP-SL), the local affiliate of the West African Network for Peacebuilding (WANEP). WANEP has been involved in implementing active nonviolence and peace education programs in various West African countries, and has supported this program to complement the efforts of various peace education initiatives by national governments and civil-society groups. CLS was invited through NCP-SL to introduce a newly developed curriculum on active nonviolence and peace education in schools. Both WANEP and CLS initiatives were particularly timely, as they complemented the peacebuilding initiatives and projects of the government of Sierra Leone for teacher training, funded by the World Bank, to develop peace education materials.

Grassroots Level

The CLS staff, after being trained to use the WANEP curriculum, embarked on the second phase of a highly regarded community reintegration program in the town of Port Loko, with support from the British Department for International Development. The intervention in Port Loko followed an outbreak of violence between students attending two secondary schools in Port Loko District after a football match in December 2002.

The community reintegration program organized a one-day workshop in January 2003 on the Promotion of Peace and Unity among Port Loko students and youth. In April 2003, CLS approached the organization with a proposal to promote conflict resolution and peacebuilding skills in the schools. This proved to be the first conflict resolution and peacebuilding program in the district targeting student communities. It was also one of the very few early interventions to ensure peaceful coexistence between victims and perpetrators of violence in the school setting. According to the principal of Schelenker Secondary School, this program was particularly important in creating linkages between the ongoing efforts to bring about reintegration, on the one hand, and the separate efforts within the school to promote peaceful coexistence between ex-combatants and victims of the atrocities of war on the other.

Students, teachers, and administrators in the so-called Peace Clubs were given training in active nonviolence and peer mediation. Peer mediation is regarded as a form of conflict resolution in which trained student leaders help their peers to work together to resolve everyday disputes. Participation in peer mediation is voluntary and all matters discussed in mediation sessions remain confidential.

CLS and partners such as the Ministry of Education, Science, and Technology Inspectorate in Port Loko also worked together to develop a students' peace accord. This formed the main agenda item at a ceremony to launch school Peace Clubs in July 2003. Here, for the first time, six schools that had been in conflict with each other for several years came together. School-based peer mediation has now been accepted and is popular in these schools as an effective approach to conflict resolution and peacebuilding. The schools look forward to the continued support of CLS to keep their schools peaceful.

CLS and education officials alike are now determined to give every school the opportunity to set up a Peace Club and sign a students' peace accord. If successful, this will make a significant contribution toward facilitating personal, community, and national peacebuilding after a decade of brutal civil war. It is reported that their "policing" influence is also valued and is being extended into community sports and recreation programs.

Added Value

One of the unique strengths of the CLS approach is its holistic view of education. So CLS strives to meet basic needs of children within the peacebuilding process. Furthermore, food shortages can themselves be a source of conflict. CLS has accordingly shaped its program so that in schools where communities cannot afford a meal for a schoolchild, CLS advocates, and now works toward, linking community food production and school feeding programs.

CLS has modified the WANEP curriculum in ways that have strengthened both the peace education elements of the program as well as the educational process in general. For example, CLS has separated the stress management and trauma-healing training modules from other modules, giving these subjects greater emphasis. Significantly, the peacebuilding activities have been implemented within the framework of general educational objectives. Video and computer classes have been included to facilitate the reinforcement of literacy, numeracy, and other skills. Furthermore, since well-resourced school libraries are not common in Sierra Leone, CLS has worked to establish long-term partnerships with schools to help them build up their libraries.

Impact

For both students and teachers, Peace Clubs and peer mediation are new concepts that have been well received. At the schools involved in these activities, a real effort has been made to foster school and community healing. Sometimes healing at a personal level takes place as well. There is a clear recognition that the ultimate goal is successful peacebuilding on a national scale. The value of these school-based mediation schemes is now widely recognized. Schools assume the responsibility for promoting active nonviolence and providing security among students, particularly during and after games and other recreational events.

One school official, the principal of Murialdo Secondary School, says of the

David Baughan

A student from a secondary school in Lunsar, Northern Province, speaking after a peace pole planting ceremony

program at his school that the authorities sense that they are beginning to make progress. The burden of dealing with so many student conflicts and disputes is slowly easing. In addition, the authorities are committed to actions to ensure the establishment of a Peace Club with the aim of fostering an educational environment conducive to learning without the fear of sporadic outbreaks of violence. Another school official, the principal of the only girls' school in this program, also reported favorably on the initiative. "This active nonviolence and peer mediation work," she said, "is a valuable service to both the school and to the community. The students and teachers have my full support in making the operations of the Peace Clubs successful."

The deputy director of the Ministry of Education in Port Loko has remarked that the mere fact that children and young people are involved in peacemaking ventures of this nature is impressive. "This is going to bring and promote an awareness of peaceful coexistence as an essential part of school and community life. It is true that schools in Port Loko have had a long struggle with conflicts. This program provides a framework for students to practice the art of learning to live at peace with each other."

To date, only limited internal evaluation of the CLS program has been carried out, but CLS hopes to begin a more detailed evaluation of the active nonviolence and peer mediation program in the near future, to run in parallel with a psychosocial needs assessment that it also plans to carry out. It is certainly encouraging that students themselves clearly express their gratitude for the significant role Peace Clubs have played in ensuring peaceful interactions between schools, especially during games and sports competitions. In those situations, clearly visible peer mediators wearing identifiable T-shirts have almost certainly played a constructive role in insuring that these events conclude without violence.

Challenges

As with most activities of this sort, the primary challenges CLS faces involve funding and personnel. The best hope for raising adequate funds and finding the trained personnel who will be ready to implement the programs on a long-term basis rests with the forging of fruitful partnerships between government and civil-society organizations.

Responding to cultural differences is another challenge CLS faces. It is vitally important that the training modules are implemented with adequate sensitivity for local cultural norms and, where necessary, that appropriate modifications to the curriculum be made in response to those prevailing cultural norms.

Peace Clubs have now been launched in a number of schools and their existence and operations are long-term in scope and nature. CLS, the Ministry of Education, Science, and Technology, and the Schools Administration have a long-term partnership that provides a supportive framework. Students are asking for further training and supervision that will build their capacity and empower them to continue operating the Peace Clubs on a sustainable basis.

The government recognizes that the war was fueled by rampant violent conflict on the campuses of secondary schools and colleges, and that a peace-building curriculum can help prevent a repeat of this tragedy. It also understands that students need to learn and practice tolerance and coexistence to ensure that schools are the peaceful places they are meant to be. This can only be accomplished by consciously setting aside time for reflection on how to heal the wounds resulting from war, abuse, violence, and deprivation. Only when students can consider these matters at length will they have the capability to build peace and transform their schools and communities.

What has worked well in a few schools must be extended to the whole country in the shortest possible time. All students, youth, and young adults are, potentially, key actors in the national peacebuilding process. That the potential is beginning to be realized is evident from the reactions of the parents of children already participating in CLS programs. According to Emma Kamara, they often ask her: "What did you do with the children that made them so positive?"

Emma Kamara is the founder and coordinator of CLS.

Keith Neal, now retired, spent thirty-eight years teaching at the secondary-school level in the United Kingdom. Since his student days, he has been associated with the global work of Initiatives of Change. In recent years he has been particularly involved in building bridges with people in India, China, East Africa, and Sierra Leone.

Contacts

National CLS Office
34 Trelawney Street
Off High Broad Street
Murray Town, Freetown
Sierra Leone
E-mail: childrensl@yahoo.co.uk

Contact desk in the UK:
3 Carlton Road, Hale
Altrincham
Cheshire WA15 8RH
United Kingdom

Brochures and further information can be obtained by contacting either of the above addresses.

Selected Bibliography

Neal, Keith, and Ruth Neal. 2003. "Sierra Leone's Grassroots Peace-Builders." *For a Change: Healing History/Transforming Relationships/Building Community* (April-May). Online at: http://www.forachange.co.uk/index.php?se=reconciliation&stoid=307.

IJssel, Suzette van . 2004. "Food First, Then Peace." *SIMS Share International Media Service* (March). Online at: http://www.simedia.org/new/soc-econ-pol/food-first.html.

11.2

Committed to Building Peace:
City Montessori School in India

Priti Barman

It was 23 September 2002. History was being written in the glittering hall of the United Nations Educational, Scientific and Cultural Organization (UNESCO) headquarters in Paris. For the first time in the award's long history, a school was being awarded the UNESCO Prize for Peace Education. The recipient was India's City Montessori School, the world's largest private school.

Located in Lucknow, the capital of Uttar Pradesh, India's most populous state, City Montessori School (CMS), has been making pioneering efforts in the field of education ever since its founding over four decades ago. The school provides education from the preschool level through secondary school. Not only does CMS embrace as its ambitious primary objective the task of "equipping children with spiritual, moral, and material knowledge," but also developing "the capacities latent in human nature and [coordinating] their expression for the enrichment and progress of society." It does that by integrating countless outward-looking activities into its program. Perhaps unique in the world, CMS has a full-fledged World Unity and Peace Education Department. The CMS philosophy revolves around the "twin poles" of globalism and godliness, and the school's mission is to promote world unity and peace by shaping future generations as "world citizens" whose minds have the virtues of unity and peace impressed upon them from day one. CMS seeks to send students into the world with a commitment to make it a better place for all, and with the moral and spiritual strength necessary to realize that commitment.

CMS is unique in another way—with over 29,000 students, it can boast of the largest enrollment of any city-based private school in the world, a fact duly noted in the *Guinness Book of World Records*. The beginnings, of course, were considerably more humble. Established in 1959 on a borrowed capital of 300 rupees (about US$10 at the time) by Jagdish Gandhi and his wife Bharti Gandhi, CMS started off with just five students. Staunch followers of Mahatma Gandhi, the couple was deeply committed to the ideals of world unity and peace and firmly believed education was key. The institution thus took on the charge of educating young, impressionable minds and producing a new generation of "world citizens." Indeed, for its motto, CMS adopted the words of Mahatma Gandhi, *Jai Jagat* ("Glory be to the world"), which has served for many years as the greeting call of all staff members and students.

"A school must act as a lighthouse to society; providing direction, guidance and leadership to students, parents, and society and also concern itself with the affairs of the age" is one of the core beliefs of CMS. The school also believes that true education releases capacities; develops analytical abilities, self-confidence, will power, and goal-setting competencies; and instills the vision that enables one to become a self-motivated agent of social change serving the interests of the community. So CMS strives to provide its students with a spiritual outlook and a global vision. CMS students are prepared not just for exams but for life itself—to become conscious and contributing members of society, proactive agents of change, promoters of peace, and upholders of high moral values.

Defusing a Tense Situation

In 1992, CMS was credited with playing a crucial role in staving off religious violence in Lucknow after Hindu extremists destroyed the nearly five-hundred-year-old mosque in nearby Ayodhya, sparking ethnic fighting that claimed an estimated two thousand lives. With 40 percent of the population being Muslim, Lucknow braced itself for violence. The risk of Hindu-Muslim fighting was heightened by the fact that only a skeletal police presence remained in the city, with most of the police force being sent to Ayodhya to deal with the violence there. The students of CMS tried to prevent further violence. They rode through the streets of Lucknow on a Jeep equipped with loudspeakers, playing unity songs and leading a procession of thousands of children and parents carrying banners with slogans such as: "We Should Live in Unity"; "The Name of God Is Both Muslim and Hindu"; "God Is One, Mankind Is One"; "All Religions Are One."

The governor saw this as an opportunity to control the violence and animosity. He asked the City Montessori School to provide a meeting place for the heads of all the city's religions. CMS organized daily meetings that were attended by the religious leaders, who regularly called and prayed together for communal harmony. Each evening, these leaders returned to their own communities and worked to maintain calm. While violence flared nearby, Lucknow remained peaceful.

It has been speculated that the success in avoiding violence could, at least in part, be attributed to "the structural change" within the city that CMS has brought about over the past forty-plus years (European Centre for Conflict Prevention 1999).

Over 250,000 children have passed through CMS since it first opened its doors in 1959, the vast majority of which have come from Lucknow. Given that CMS encourages the family to participate in their children's development at the school (from helping shape the curriculum to a myriad of other pioneering activities) there can be little doubt that a great many families in Lucknow actively participated in the CMS peace initiative. (Mathews 2001: 25)

A Program of Peace Education

Fortunately, CMS has not been called upon to intervene in a similar crisis since 1992, but it continues to stamp its influence on the community with its educational program, based on the four building blocks of its curriculum: universal values, global understanding, excellence in all things, and service to humanity. Furthermore it organizes or participates in literally dozens of peace-focused or peace-related events for its students, the surrounding community, and young people much further afield.

Just a few examples exemplifying CMS's involvement in peacebuilding follow.

CMS is a member of the U.K.-based Children's International Summer Village (CISV) Society. CISV organizes four-week-long camps where children from participating countries live together and learn valuable lessons in coexistence by personally experiencing cross-cultural interaction. Since 1993, CMS has been hosting a CISV camp in Lucknow every year; on average, delegations from about a dozen countries participate at the camp. Likewise, CMS delegations participate at CISV camps held abroad every year.

CMS is also a member of the International School-to-School Experience (ISSE). CMS facilitates exchange visits between schools from different cultures via ISSE, a sister concern of CISV. The ISSE exchange also enables the children to learn about each other's culture as well as the learning-teaching methods practiced in different schools. CMS has ISSE exchanges with schools in Mexico, Australia, Malaysia, Japan, and Iceland.

CMS organizes simulated "world parliament" sessions. Children posing as leaders of various countries of the world form a "world government" and discuss serious issues threatening the very survival of life on our planet. Issues discussed include the growing threat posed by ever greater quantities of armaments, environmental issues, and increasing violence and social tensions. Participants deliberate on ways and means to ameliorate these problems. The central theme of all discussions is again to find ways to ensure lasting world peace. Growing out of these sessions, and the realization that issues such as the increasing nuclear stockpile, terrorism, and the breakdown of social, economic, and political order cannot be tackled by any one country or group of like-minded countries, CMS is committed to work for the establishment of a world government.

CMS launched the Indo-Pak Children's Penfriends' Club. Aao Dosti Karein ("Come, let's be friends") was launched by CMS in 2002. With this program,

CMS has arranged for the exchange of thousands of letters between Indian and Pakistani schoolchildren with the aim of eliminating mutual misunderstanding by facilitating one-to-one contact between schoolchildren that eventually percolates down to the masses of both countries. The premise of this program is that the seeds of peace sown today will grow into a tree bearing the fruits of unity tomorrow. The ultimate objective of the exercise is to mobilize public opinion in both countries and compel their respective governments to adopt conciliatory rather than aggressive approaches to their mutual relations.

Chief Justices of the World

In December 2004, City Montessori School hosted the Fifth International Conference of Chief Justices of the World under Article 51 of the constitution of India. This provision of the constitution specifically pledges the Indian state to pursue peace, encourage the peaceful resolution of international disputes, and to foster respect for international law. The primary focus of the conference was on the need to establish a world parliament with sufficient authority to enact a body of international law that can be equally applicable on all the peoples and countries of the world.

World Citizenship

CMS views the world as a village—the home to many nations and peoples. In this village, it is no longer possible for the diverse peoples to live in isolation. So, in a sense, its advocacy of "globalism" is simply a response to today's reality. The CMS approach aims to break down the barriers between peoples and to open up possibilities for global cooperation. When it proclaims Jai Jagat, it is encouraging its students to embrace a global perspective and the concept of world citizenship—a concept that is symbolized in the World Citizenship Dress that is worn at the World Peace Prayer ceremony incorporated into all CMS functions, and which depicts symbols of all the major world religions and the flags of every member of the United Nations. That concept of world citizenship is not unique to CMS, of course. As John Lennon so effectively articulated it in a popular anthem oft-repeated since he first sang it more than thirty years ago: "You may say I'm a dreamer, but I'm not the only one. I hope someday you will join us, and the world will be as one."

Priti Barman recently joined the staff of CMS's Department of World Unity and Peace Education. Previously, she worked as a journalist for the Times of India *and ETV, a national television channel.*

Contact

Raj Shekhar Chandola
City Montessori School Jai Jagat House
12 Station Road

Lucknow, India
Tel: +91 522 638606
Fax: +91 522 638 008
E-mail: rajchandola@cmseducation.org or pritibarman@yahoo.com
Website: http://www.cmseducation.org

Selected Bibliography

European Centre for Conflict Prevention (ECCP). 1999. *People Building Peace: 35 Inspiring Stories from Around the World* (Utrecht, Netherlands: ECCP).
Mathews, Dylan. 2001. *War Prevention Works: 50 Stories of People Resolving Conflict* (Oxford: Oxford Research Group).

11.3

Uniting Children During War: *Sawa*-UNICEF in Lebanon

Amal Dibo

Toward the end of Lebanon's long civil war, UN Children's Fund (UNICEF) reacted to a new crisis with a simple but effective way to reach the children, in spite of the fighting—a magazine, called Sawa *(meaning "together" in Arabic). It bridged the front lines and the ethnic divides with useful educational tools and a message of peace, understanding, reconciliation, and hope. Building on the success of* Sawa, *UNICEF also organized a successful summer peace camp program in Lebanon.*

As if fourteen years of civil war had not been traumatic enough, in March 1989 the most densely populated areas of Beirut were subjected to an onslaught of rocket and artillery fire that was to continue intermittently, for more than a year. Beirut's war-weary citizens retreated with regularity to the cellars and bomb shelters, sometimes for weeks at a time. What little semblance of normality remained was shattered. Businesses shut their doors and 60 percent of Lebanon's schools were closed.

During the war years, United Nations Children's Fund (UNICEF) offered emergency relief assistance, health care and medicine, and educational programs in Lebanon. With its active, high-profile presence, UNICEF had become an experienced, trusted, and well-known organization, capable of acting quickly and effectively in a crisis, and even able to extend its programs to all regions of Lebanon despite the country's fragmentation along territorial lines. With the renewed outbreak of violence in 1989, traditional educational assistance was rendered impossible. The UNICEF staff was increasingly frustrated by the appalling conditions facing children and their own inability to do something for them in the shelters.

Most of the UNICEF programs in the areas of health care brought UNICEF into contact with the parents, rather than the children. The challenge was to find a way to reach children in spite of the fighting, to give them a chance to learn and play wherever they were—to make up for the lack of schooling, to help young people to deal with their day-to-day hardships and fill the long, tedious hours in the dim lights of the bomb shelters. What UNICEF wanted was to find some way to bring them together when forces beyond their control were driving them further and further apart.

One day, literally as the shells were raining down on the city, UNICEF's representative in Lebanon, André Roberfroid, his wife, and UNICEF staff members Anna Mansour and the author started throwing around ideas during a brainstorming session in the UNICEF cellar where they had gathered to wait out the artillery battle. It was during that brainstorming session that the idea emerged to publish a children's magazine and use it as an educational tool.

A Complex Country

Once Lebanon was known as one of the most liberal and modern societies in the Middle East. Now it is predominantly known as one of the complex countries in the heart of the region, with a mix of Christians, Sunni Muslims, Shia Muslims, Druze, Palestinians, and others among its 3.7 million inhabitants. During the first half of the 1970s, the social fiber of Lebanon began to unravel and it became increasingly unstable. Thousands of Palestine Liberation Organization (PLO) fighters had set up bases in Lebanon after they had been evicted from Jordan, and their presence contributed greatly to the increasing instability. PLO fighters launched attacks against Israel from their Lebanese bases, the Israeli military retaliated with attacks against PLO interests in Lebanon, and efforts by the Lebanese government and Lebanese army to reassert control led only to greater tension among the various Lebanese communities. With the increasing instability, numerous militias were established, not only within the various communities but also by political parties and other elements of Lebanese society. By 1975, the PLO had established a virtual "state within a state." In April 1975, factional fighting broke out, at first between Palestinian fighters and the Lebanese army, but subsequently, more generally, involving the militias of most of the other communities as well. In subsequent years, the civil war drew Israel, Syria, the United States, and France into a conflict that defied resolution. Finally, in 1989, with the Arab League playing a crucial role, a agreement was signed at Taif, Saudi Arabia, leading to a tenuous peace and the beginning of a reconciliation process. While some shelling and acts of terror did take place between 1989 and 1991, the Taif agreement formed the basis for the restoration of calm, with a new parliament installed in 1990, and the dissolution of most militias by May 1991. By then, more than one hundred thousand people had died in the war and nine hundred thousand people had been displaced.

Overwhelming Response

UNICEF saw the project as a gift to Lebanon's children. *Sawa* would include not only school exercises, but also stories, arts and crafts activities, arithmetic, and so on. Yet in war-torn Lebanon, distribution would be complicated. For that, UNICEF made use of the network of dispensaries it had managed to maintain in spite of the fighting. To publicize the new magazine, UNICEF produced public service announcements and rushed them to local radio stations. The message was simple: "Kids, tell your parents to go to the dispensary when it's safe. UNICEF has something fun for you and your friends there." In the following weeks, three newsletters were produced and distributed free of charge. The response was overwhelming and the newsletters disappeared from the dispensaries as quickly as they could be delivered.

The decision was quickly made to formalize the project and to provide the magazine to Lebanese children for free on a regular basis. *Sawa* would provide children with an opportunity to learn and play wherever they were, and it would prepare a new generation for life in a society at peace. Funding was initially made available for fifty thousand copies (later increased to seventy thousand) of a thirty-page magazine every six weeks.

Each issue of *Sawa* focused on a central theme, carefully chosen in the context of the war environment, to take children beyond the confines of the shelters, stimulate their imagination, encourage them to think, provide entertainment, and impart lessons in an interactive and approachable way. The first page of each issue was devoted to a letter addressed to the young reader. Each issue consisted of a range of regular features that not only entertained the young readers but also advanced an inclusive view of the world:

• "Know Your Country" took readers on imaginary tours to different areas of Lebanon—to Baalbeck, the Cedars, or simply across the "Green Line" of Beirut; or it described to them, making use of a map of Lebanon, the different foods or crafts from each region. For the children of Lebanon who tended to view people in terms of their religion, ethnicity, or clan affiliation, the "Know Your Country" feature offered an alternative, emphasizing a Lebanese identity.
• "From Our Culture" featured Lebanese proverbs and folktales, or told about prominent figures from Lebanese history, often combining educational material on culture with a moral message. The features cut across ethnic and cultural lines to provide young readers with a point of contact with the "other."
• "Living Sawa" was the primary vehicle for promoting a more or less explicit message of peace. This included stories and parables illustrating children's rights, solidarity, unity, and nonviolence.
• "Right or Wrong?" provided a chance for the children to decide appropriate forms of behavior in different situations.

Sawa also included features on health, world cultures, science, arts and crafts, and information about ongoing UNICEF programs.

Impact

Sawa's pedagogical approach was interactive, not pedantic: it sought to involve children on their own terms by seeing the world through their eyes. Those involved with *Sawa* knew that education is most effective when the children enjoy what they are doing. The creative team behind *Sawa* understood that success depended on understanding the reality of the daily lives of children and then finding ways to take them beyond those boundaries imposed upon them by the war. Each colorfully bound issue invited kids to play with word games, puzzles, jokes and riddles, coloring and drawing exercises, and even magic tricks, providing them with hours of entertainment. *Sawa*'s content was thoughtfully designed to send an unthreatening message while helping to fill the gap left by the closure of schools. Stories were written for *Sawa* that presented a problem or an exercise involving looking at the world from various perspectives. Sometimes the readers were challenged to finish a story, or challenged to think about the story's consequences.

With each issue, *Sawa*'s content came to be increasingly determined by the children themselves. Following the distribution of the first issue, UNICEF received 1,500 letters from children thanking the agency for the magazine, as well as stories, drawings, poems, and jokes. From the second issue onwards, *Sawa* devoted two pages to a readers' section called "Have Your Say," and the children were encouraged to bring their contributions to the points where *Sawa* was distributed. The effect was like opening a floodgate: UNICEF was soon receiving an average of 2,500 replies from each issue. These were carefully read and sorted, and the selected responses were published in a new "Return Mail" section of *Sawa* that often included suggestions from readers on what they would like to see next.

The contributions became an integral part of *Sawa*, and it was from this source of feedback that the magazine began to take on a more overtly peace-oriented and activist role. Through *Sawa*, children spontaneously began to give expression to their yearning for a better life. Poems, pictures, stories, and prayers from the children talked about peace and possibilities, not about war and violence. Although the war was always there in the background, very few of the 45,000 responses received actually spoke of the war and its hardships.

Sawa continued to appear regularly until the end of the war late in 1990. As the needs of Lebanon's children changed, the *Sawa* project changed as well. With the implementation in 1991 of the National Reconciliation Charter, relative calm was restored to all of Lebanon except for the southern areas bordering on Israel. UNICEF shifted away from the emergency mode in which it had functioned during the war years, and with the shift, funding of existing projects came under review. Responsibility for *Sawa* was turned over to the Education Program, and the magazine took on a new function in support of an initiative called "Learning for Life." Publication of *Sawa* ceased altogether in 1994.

The UNICEF Peace Camp Program

Prior to the outbreak of war in Lebanon, local organizations and nongovernmental organizations (NGOs) had operated summer camps. Simultaneous with the successful launch of *Sawa*, as UNICEF staff considered ways to build on *Sawa*'s success, they began to entertain the idea of organizing summer camp programs as a way to get children from across ethnic and religious barriers to meet each other. UNICEF program officer for education Anna Mansour approached some fifty NGOs, mostly organizations with a confessional affiliation, and asked them to help recruit children from their communities for a summer camp program. UNICEF would provide funding, logistics, and training for camp staff.

UNICEF articulated three simple principles for the camp program: that the camps would bring together youth of different regions, religions, and social status; that they would give youth and children a better chance to know one another and to know their country through discovery and sharing; and that youth and children would experience "living together" positively, sharing human, social, and relational values through creative and recreational activities.

Despite the obstacles posed by the wartime environment, planning went ahead in the spring of 1989, with the training of staff and arrangements for the complicated logistics. UNICEF representative André Roberfroid played on the credibility of his organization to persuade local leaders to cooperate in moving the children securely around the country. The camps began in earnest in the summer of 1989, and were, from the outset, remarkably successful. Children who had, in many cases, never met anyone from one of the other communities, were often slightly cautious and apprehensive at first, but after a few days, recalls Roberfroid, there was a "sort of explosion of will to live together, as if they had been thirsty for it." Besides the benefits for the young campers who met each other and played together for the first time, the older monitors, some of whom had served as militia members during the war, also underwent a transformation. They had been trained as "youth animators," but the staff was uncertain if they would be able to transcend the mistrust and animosity that had developed. To the surprise of some UNICEF staff, they responded enthusiastically to the camp environment. According to Roberfroid, "The more they had been extremists during the war, the more involved they became in the program. These were the most energetic young people in Lebanon."

In its first year, 29,000 Lebanese children attended thirty-four summer peace camps and seventy-nine day camps, concluding in September with a daylong "Peace Festival" bringing together seven hundred youth animators and nine thousand children. By September 1991, UNICEF peace camps had reached one hundred thousand children and had mobilized 240 NGOs to work on the program.

Looking Back

In practical terms, the *Sawa* team learned as the project progressed about the importance of distribution, and increasingly worked not only with its own network of dispensaries, but also with NGO partners and other institutions, including youth groups, women's organizations, and sports clubs, to achieve widespread coverage. *Sawa* was distributed via children's groups, day-care centers, playgrounds, churches, mosques, shelters, and other public areas, and ten thousand copies of every issue were distributed to Palestinian refugee camps. Responses from children would be picked up and taken back to the dispensaries and from there to the *Sawa* team at UNICEF headquarters in Beirut. Many UNICEF field staff eagerly embraced their new roles in the promotion of *Sawa,* since it enhanced their relationship with the NGOs.

More in the realm of theory, the *Sawa* and peace camp projects demonstrated that when peace activities are focused on youth, even ostensible adversaries may exhibit more tolerant attitudes. This may be because the adult community has a genuine wish for their children to live in peace, or because large segments of the adult community view children as a sort of "zone of peace." Whatever the reasons, the successful implementation of peacebuilding activities focused on children led to opportunities to expand the peacebuilding initiatives into the society at large.

Finally, perhaps one of the most important—and surprising—lessons learned by the *Sawa* and summer camp programs was that it was indeed possible to mobilize for peace even in the midst of a war environment. This should give hope to those in other conflict zones about the potential to organize peacebuilding activities even when a climate of violence poses serious obstacles.

Amal Dibo is a former UNICEF program officer in charge of emergency assistance to the displaced, health programs (namely, vaccination), and education programs on human rights, among others serving as an editor of Sawa. *Presently she is teaching history of civilization at the American University of Beirut and is active in nongovernmental organizations working for art, science, culture, and peace.*

Contact

UNICEF Lebanon
P.O. Box 11-5902
Rjad El-Solh
Beirut, Lebanon
11 07 2200
Tel: +961 1 981 301-311
Fax: +961 1 983 055
E-mail: beirut@unicef.org

Amal Dibo
American University of Beirut
Faculty of Arts and Science
P.O. Box 11 0236
Riad El Sohl
Beirut 11 07 2020
Lebanon
E-mail: ad04@aub.edu.lb

11.4

Managing Conflict at School: Ohio Commission on Dispute Resolution and Conflict Management in the United States

Jennifer Batton

With the number of physical confrontations increasing across Ohio's school districts, serious discipline problems in the classrooms, and escalating violence-related costs, educators are taking it upon themselves to address these issues by creating comprehensive school conflict management programs. As a result, Ohio now leads the United States in creating effective responses.

A fifteen-year-old boy relates: "When my brother and sister were fighting I broke it up. Then I started using my ground rules. I told them to stop and I told them what I knew about mediation. Then they shook hands at the end and worked out the problem." An eight-year-old girl shares this story: "My sister was mad at her boyfriend because she said he went out all the time and did not invite her. Her boyfriend said the same thing, that his girlfriend (the older sister) did things with friends and didn't invite him or make time to spend with him. After I mediated, they agreed to go out once a week."

Like hundreds of others in Ohio, these students learned their peacemaking and mediation skills through a school-based conflict management program. Between 1990 and 2003, the number of the 612 Ohio school districts with some form of conflict management program grew from 30 to more than 400. While in 1993 there were a mere 208 schools actively addressing the problem, by 2004 more than 1,700 schools had established peer mediation and conflict management programs.

Moreover, Ohio's educators are moving beyond traditional peer mediation, which focuses primarily on student-student conflicts, to a more holistic model that provides dispute resolution methods and skills not just within the school building but for the entire school community. Effective institutionalization requires a sustained capacity for program development in each school, and participating schools should be committed to four levels of intervention: school culture, pedagogy, curriculum integration, and student programming.

School culture looks at policies and procedures, shared goals, structures, and systems. Administrators should support the modeling of conflict management skills and utilization of these skills in the schools' daily operations. One example would be in how conflicts are resolved by students, such as through the development of a peer mediation program.

Pedagogy addresses the art of teaching including strategies such as cooperative learning, multicultural teaching methods, positive discipline, and social and emotional learning strategies.

Curriculum integration includes integration of conflict resolution topics across subject areas. English, social studies, and history courses offer numerous opportunities to talk about conflict and positive and negative approaches to disputes. English lessons can integrate discussions of dispute resolution by including biographies and historical novels. Social studies can consider community or civil disputes over land, historical preservation, discrimination, etc. History, of course, offers countless opportunities for discussing disputes and alternatives to violence and war.

Student programming includes implementing programs such as peer mediation, peer mentoring programs, or a student conduct plan using conflict management strategies and philosophies as a premise.

For schools to see significant positive changes, it is vital to train all adults who interact with students, including parents, administrators, classroom educators, bus drivers, playground assistants, school secretaries, and cafeteria workers. This ensures that these skills are modeled and reinforced from the time the student boards the school bus or walks onto school property, to the end of the school day—and continue at home.

A ten-year-old fifth-grade boy illustrates the importance of this transfer of conflict resolution skills from school to home and community: "When I walk, run, or ride my bike I listen for arguments around the neighborhood. Once, I saw my cousin arguing with his neighbor. I ran to see what was happening. They were going to fight so I stopped them."

In the following boxes there are two examples of school districts in the state, one rural and one urban, representing different cultural populations, both of which are experiencing success as they develop their comprehensive school conflict management programs.

The Ohio Commission

The state of Ohio leads the United States in school-based conflict management, in part due to the work in education of the Ohio Commission on Dispute Resolution and Conflict Management. The commission plays a pivotal role by supporting the efforts of the school districts, setting up training programs, and providing program development leadership and expertise. The commission, established in 1989, provides dispute resolution and conflict management resources, training, and direct services to Ohio schools, colleges, universities, courts, communities, and state and local governments. It was the United States' first and currently only government-sponsored commission to promote

Winning Against Violent Environments

Students can do more than learn about techniques of conflict management; they themselves can become agents of change by taking those skills into their communities. Young people are empowered by providing them with skills such as effective decisionmaking, communication, and problem solving, and encouraging them to use them in their daily lives, providing assistance to others.

The Winning Against Violent Environments Program (WAVE) in the Cleveland Municipal School District not only subscribes to this philosophy, but implements it through its conflict management advisors in Cleveland's public schools. The program, run out of Martin Luther King Jr. Law and Municipal Careers High School in Cleveland, is located in Hough, one of the city's toughest neighborhoods. This program began in 1983 and is the oldest school-based conflict resolution program in Ohio, and one of the oldest in the United States.

WAVE students and an adult coordinator train other students and adults as conflict managers and mediators. The two main conflict resolution processes taught by WAVE trainers are a formal mediation model for students and adults in middle school and high school (grades six through twelve), and a less formal process for use on the playground, cafeteria, or in the classroom. Under an additional "student trainer" model, the students teach the lessons and lead the training activities, thus involving urban youth as positive agents of change in their schools and communities.

While in the beginning WAVE focused strictly on peer mediation, it has now adopted a more comprehensive approach where, for example, the program advisors teach lessons across subject areas to all of their students, giving in-service training to their fellow educators on the skills of conflict management. They also conduct school- and community-wide activities such as peace walks in the neighborhood, working with student conflict managers to raise money to provide food baskets for needy families, and holding peace assemblies for parents, students, and staff. WAVE has "trained thousands of students grades K–12, provided professional development to teachers, led parent meetings and training sessions, conducted faculty and staff in-service programs, developed the grades K–12 training model, and facilitated public meetings of young people and adults" (Close and Lechman 1997).

WAVE still includes peer mediation as a component of many of the schools' conflict management programs. During the 2003–2004 school year alone, student mediators in the district conducted more than nine thousand mediations. The benefits were revealed in an evaluation of the WAVE program by Kathy Bickmore, Ph.D., of the Ontario Institute for Studies in Education at the University of Toronto. Her research showed "significant improvements in students understanding and capacity to positively deal with conflicts, improved student attitudes toward attending school, a reduction in suspensions for negative behaviors, and an improvement in academic achievement by those students who were trained in these important life skills" (2000).

The WAVE program has been a school conflict management catalyst for other districts. WAVE training, combined with a state-sponsored grant training program, led to the development of a district-wide school conflict management program in Pioneer, Ohio.

dispute resolution at all levels of society. The commission's evaluations demonstrate that its work leads to significant reductions in interpersonal conflict, particularly in public schools.

In 1989, Richard F. Celeste, governor of Ohio, created the Governor's Peace and Conflict Management Commission to review the status of peace and conflict management programs in the state and to develop new initiatives to help Ohioans better resolve their disputes. The commission focused on four primary areas: primary and secondary education, higher education, the courts, and community and public policy. As part of its final report to Governor Celeste, this commission recommended that the State of Ohio create a permanent Commission on Dispute Resolution and Conflict Management (OCDRCM) to develop practical programs that teach people how to resolve disputes without conflict or resorting to lawsuits.

Under Governor Celeste, former Peace Corps director in the Carter administration, Ohio had the philosophical conditions for mediation and conflict resolution programs to flourish. In 1989 the Ohio General Assembly, with the support of the chief justice of the Supreme Court of Ohio, the Ohio Bar Association, and the Ohio Council of Churches, enacted legislation that created the OCDRCM. The commission is jointly governed by members appointed by the legislative, judicial, and executive branches of government.

Education Programming

The commission, in partnership with the Ohio Department of Education, has promoted conflict resolution education programs in primary and secondary schools, colleges, and universities through grants, training, and resource development with the goal of institutionalizing conflict resolution education into their daily operations.

Five years ago, the commission began a pilot project with the American Association of Health Educators and the Conflict Resolution Education Network to integrate conflict resolution into higher education. Faculty at Ohio's colleges and universities are invited to take part in this annual Conflict Resolution Education Institute. Currently thirty-six Ohio colleges and universities have participated. Participants learn to understand the rationale for the integration of conflict resolution into higher education, to demonstrate the knowledge of core concepts, and to develop an action plan to implement a conflict resolution curriculum in teacher education.

Results

Most educators look for a reduction in disciplinary actions (suspensions, expulsions, truancy) and general disruptions in the classroom when they propose developing a school conflict management program. The commission is interested not only in affecting change in student behavior, but also in creating a safe and supportive learning environment for students, teachers, and parents. This stems from the idea that academics are positively affected if the philosophy and skills of school conflict management are fully integrated into daily

Students Offering Acceptance and Respect

In the mid-1990s, the guidance counselors at the North Central Local School System in Pioneer, Ohio, decided they wanted to make the atmosphere of their school system more inviting and peaceful for everyone. They began by doing research on different conflict management programs across the state. With a grant from the Ohio Commission on Dispute Resolution and Conflict Management, in 1999 they were on their way.

Gandhi once said, "You must be the change you want to see in the world." The counselors knew that in order to embark on a journey toward change, they needed to identify a group of individuals within the school who would "be the change [they] want[ed] to see in the world," so they began with the students. North Central soon had the Students Offering Acceptance and Respect (SOAR) program, which initially began as a peer mediation program, with students (grades 5–12) trained to help their peers find nonviolent solutions to their conflicts.

As more needs and concerns came to the counselors, they and the students developed (over the next five years) a comprehensive conflict management program for students and staff, grades kindergarten (K) through twelve. New peer mediators continue to be trained each year in a six-step mediation process. In addition, high school SOAR members began going into elementary classrooms to teach younger students about conflict management, feelings, peer pressure, bullying, and decisionmaking. Students in the middle grades work one-on-one to mentor younger students on self-esteem issues and friendship skills.

Since the advent of the SOAR program, the number of discipline occurrences at the school have dramatically declined. It is not unusual for older students to ask if they can talk out their differences with one another privately, before it escalates into a major conflict. The school's atmosphere is more positive and inviting. Staff members have been encouraged to attend conferences on infusing conflict management lessons into their classrooms. It is not unusual to see a "Peace Corner" in an elementary classroom, or have "Diversity Days" at the junior high and high school levels. There is also an annual "Peace Week" where elementary students are recognized for being peacemakers throughout the school year. Parents are invited to this celebration to honor those students who are the community's and nation's future peacemakers. Middle-school students design and create peace banners that are proudly hung in the cafeteria, and high-school students take part in activities promoting peace.

North Central has also introduced the program to their community. Parent meetings encourage peaceful communication at home. SOAR members make presentations to local civic groups to explain their program. On 11 September 2003, North Central school unveiled its "Peace Pole," where students and community members are reminded of the importance of peace in six languages. The pole is proudly displayed beside the school marquee, visible to all who pass by.

(continues)

Students Offering Acceptance and Respect (continued)

One of the biggest successes of the program has been an annual Visions of Peace Conference, which SOAR hosts each spring. Schools throughout northwest Ohio are invited to attend. Participants, over three hundred in two years, learn about peer mediation, Peace Week, team building, social justice, and dealing with flash judgments. Every year students from thirteen different schools gather to learn how they can start or enhance a peacemaking program at their own school.

The SOAR program empowers others to commit to peace, in the conviction that the only way the world will change is if we believe we can make a difference, and begin to make that difference in our world, however small that change or that world may be.

SOAR continues to develop each year. Student comments such as "I think it is a great program because it improves student relations," and, "Peer Mediation definitely eases tension among students" encourage SOAR members to continue to make their school a safe and positive environment. Students and staff at North Central are taking Gandhi's words to heart and working toward "be[ing] the change [they] want to see in the world."

---

school life. Evaluations of the Ohio experience show that schools focusing on the whole-school approach see improved academic achievement, reduced truancy, fewer suspensions and expulsions, less time spent on dealing with discipline, financial cost savings to schools, and an improvement in overall school climate.

The annual cost per student to administer the school conflict management grant training program is approximately $12. When compared to the per student cost of suspending a child ($231) or expelling a student ($431), the program is clearly cost-effective. Independent evaluations of the truancy prevention mediation program demonstrate a significant increase in pupil attendance and decrease in tardiness for participating schools resulting in an average cost savings of $1,889 per school. With 171 participating schools (currently funded by the commission), total program cost savings for the 2002–2003 school year was estimated at $323,019.

The Future

To further institutionalize conflict resolution education in Ohio, the commission recently partnered with Temple University, Cleveland State University, and Kent State University to design the Conflict Resolution Education in Teacher Education project, which addresses two crises in urban education across the United States—teacher attrition and unsafe, conflict-ridden learning environments. Through this project the partnership will develop a conflict resolution education/social and emotional learning curriculum and training process for higher-education faculty, and develop a curriculum for the continuing education units all teachers must earn to retain their certification. The impact of curricula and training processes on teacher success in classroom management, establishing positive classroom climates, student learning and academic achievement, and teacher satisfaction and teacher retention will be evaluated. A version of the curriculum suitable for use in traditional and online/distance education formats will be developed, along with a mentoring structure that utilizes university-based teacher educators and school-based educators.

Conclusions

While Ohio's comprehensive model is paving the way for more effective program institutionalization, more work is needed to establish conflict resolution education as a permanent fixture in the nation's education system. Despite statewide education statistics showing that disciplinary incidents in schools in Ohio for fighting far outnumber disciplinary incidents related to alcohol, tobacco, and other drugs (which have attracted substantial prevention funding), funding continues to decrease for conflict resolution education efforts. Yet conflict resolution evaluations show that significant decreases in discipline-related problems such as fighting result in significant cost savings to the school district and the state.

This lack of funding targeted at prevention of interpersonal violence through efforts such as conflict resolution education is not a phenomenon unique to the state of Ohio. It is critical to better inform funders and policymakers of the data that links this kind of education in our schools and universities with a reduction in violent incidents. A recent World Health Organization report on interpersonal violence (excluding the costs related to war) shows this violence costs the United States around $300 billion annually, with violent crime committed by a single minor generally costing the victim approximately $61,000 in expenses. Funders should be made aware that investing in K–12 dispute resolution education is critical to seeing a reduction in societal violence. The billions saved by investing in prevention can then be reallocated from more punitive efforts (court costs, juvenile detention centers, prisons, etc.) and redirected toward critical needs such as health, education, and economic development.

Jennifer Batton is director of education programs for the Ohio Commission on Dispute Resolution and Conflict Management. Assistance in preparing this chapter was provided by Edward M. Krauss, director of community and court programs.

Contact

Ohio Commission on Dispute Resolution and Conflict Management
77 S. High St., 24th Floor
Columbus, Ohio 43215-6108
USA
Tel: +1 614 644 9275
E-mail: Jennifer.Batton@cdr.state.oh.us
Website: http://disputeresolution.ohio.gov

Selected Bibliography

Bickmore, Kathy. 2000. *Evaluation Research Report: Cleveland Municipal School District Center for Conflict Resolution. Elementary School Conflict Resolution Initiative. Peer Mediation Training and Program Implementation, September 1997 to May 1999.* Ontario Institute for Studies in Education. University of Toronto. Toronto, Canada. July.

Close, Carole, and Kathy Lechman. 1997. Fostering Youth Leadership: Students Train Students and Adults in Conflict Resolution. *Theory Into Practice.* Vol. 36, Number 1. Winter.

12

The Arts and Peacebuilding: Using Imagination and Creativity

John Paul Lederach

The importance and potential of arts as a tool for peacebuilding should not be underestimated. To illustrate this, my introduction tells some modern "Pied Piper" tales. The cases following this text elaborate further on how the arts are currently being used in peacebuilding activities in different regions around the world.[1]

As a young child, I remember hearing the fairy tale of the Pied Piper. A town was beset with a great rat infestation and had no hope on the horizon that it would change soon. Experts and advisors came and went but nobody could move the rats. Then a stranger showed up and promised, for a considerable sum of money, to clean the town of this life-destroying problem. The mayor agreed. The following day the stranger turned out to be a piper, a flutist of sorts, and lifting the pipe to his lips he played a melody that floated out across the streets. The rats began to move, drawn to the music. More and more rats gathered following the sounds of the music. He led them out of town and straight into a river where the rats drowned. Back in town celebrations were breaking out everywhere. The Piper, pleased with his work, approached the mayor for his due compensation. With the problem now gone, the mayor hemmed and hawed, feigned financial difficulties, and turned the Piper away without a single coin. Disgruntled, the Piper returned the next day to the streets and lifted his fluted melody again. This time the children came and then followed the Piper out of town leaving the community without the joys of young voices or life for the future. The moral of the story seemed clear: when you give a promise, you had best keep your word.

Four decades later, when I read the story again, this was not the moral that caught my attention. What I saw was the power of a flutist to move a town, address an evil, and bring the powerful to accountability. Without any form of power or even prestige, much less a violent weapon, a flutist transformed a whole community. I was struck with the nonviolent power of music and the creative act itself. The moral of the story now seemed to be: watch out for the flutist and his creative music for like the invisible wind it touches and moves all that it encounters in its path.

Artful Change

In 1996 I found myself sitting in the Killyhevlin Hotel in Fermanagh, Northern Ireland. I was a keynote speaker at a conference titled "Remember and Change," a phrase that had been pulled from a talk I had given in Belfast a year earlier (Lederach 1995). In 1994, at the time of the cease-fire declarations by both Republican and Loyalist paramilitary groups, people engaged in the conflict transformation and peacebuilding work had requested some reflections on what might beset them as they entered a postaccord phase of violent conflict. In that talk, I suggested that reconciliation was not forgive and forget. It was remember and change.

The conference in the Killyhevlin Hotel was attended by delegates from peace and reconciliation partnerships across Northern Ireland representing all sides of the conflict and a wide range of community, economic, and political interests, now trying to move toward a new horizon. The hotel is located on the shore of Lough Erne, near Enniskillen. The venue was not without symbol and purpose. On a number of occasions bombs had all but destroyed it. The conference was for the most part a series of talking heads like myself giving speeches and exchanging insights and ideas that were to translate to programs. The one exception was just following the lunch. The planners had decided to make what was considered a delicate addition. They had commissioned a troupe of dancers made up of young local Catholic and Protestant girls to choreograph an expressive dance to the background of music. The song chosen was Irish folk artist Paul Brady's "The Island." Behind the stage there was a large screen. While the young women performed their dance, slides—pictures everyone knew, capturing the scenes of the thirty-two-year-old "Troubles"—would appear without comment.

The artistic process was not without its risks. When Brady's song had first emerged a decade earlier it came in the heat of the worst cycles of violence in the Irish conflict. "The Island" raised a question about the reasons and logic of the violence and those who justified it on one side or another. A solo voice accompanied by a piano, the lyrics are profound, suggesting that violence was trying to "carve tomorrow from a tombstone" and was wasting our children's future "for the worn-out dreams of yesterday" (Brady 1992).

When first played publicly, the song generated immediate controversy. Perceived as being written by a well-known artist from one community criticizing people engaged in the violence, threats went out from the paramilitaries against the artist and radio stations that would play the music or stores that would sell it. For years "The Island" was not played or circulated publicly.

In the early afternoon I found myself seated between one of the highest-ranking officials of the police force in Northern Ireland and the mayor of the town, both fine and dedicated men, from different sides of the conflict, and both pleasant but also rather formal in demeanor, toughened, you might say, by the years of their experience and the nature of their positions. The song began and the dance troupe's graceful first steps brought hundreds in the audience to complete silence. The color slides of Belfast's troubled murals, children running from fire bombs, funeral processions, parades, riveted the eyes and captured the haunting feel of the music and lyrics juxtaposed against the ballet-like movement of these young women moving together though from different sides of the violent divide. The whole of the Irish conflict was held in a public space, captured in a moment that lasted less than five minutes.

Near the end of the performance, I suddenly noticed that the two men on both my sides were discretely pulling handkerchiefs from pockets and wiping tears. Behind me I could hear and feel the same thing happening. One of the men leaned over and apologized to me, as if, somehow it were a lack of professional etiquette to have displayed such emotion in public. The seminar proceeded. Speeches were given. Program initiatives were proposed and evaluated. It was a day in the process of a long slow transformation. Looking back now, nearly a decade later, it would be interesting to know what people remember of that day. Without locating the specific documents, I know that I cannot remember a single speech, proposal, or formal panel response. I do remember, vividly, the image and feeling of those five minutes of combined music, lyrics, choreography, and photos. It created an echo in the head that has not gone away. It moved me.

A West African Pied Piper

In the larger picture of politics and social change, many would say, "And so what? What difference does something like this artistic five minutes actually make?" I am not sure I can answer that question. On the other side of the coin, I would ask a different but parallel question: How, when, and why did politics and developing responses to needed social change come to be seen as something separate from the whole of human experience? The artistic five minutes, I have found rather consistently, when it is given space and acknowledged as something far beyond entertainment, accomplishes what most of politics has been unable to attain: It helps us return to humanity, a transcendent journey that, like the moral imagination, can build a sense that we *are,* after all, a human community.

Let me illustrate it with another example. In the 1980s, the countries of Burkina Faso and Mali exploded into war over border issues. International mediation efforts failed on numerous occasions to stop the fighting. Then the neighboring president of Guinea, Ahmed Sekou Toure, persuaded his fellow presidents of Burkina Faso and Mali to attend a meeting at his palace. Samuel Doe and Emmanuel Bombande recount the unexpected events that followed:

> In front of the Presidential Palace in Conakry, one of West Africa's celebrated griots (praise singers), Kanja Kouyate, put on a spectacular performance

before the host and visiting presidents. The performance took on the form of entertainment, but Kanja Kouyate was calling on the two presidents at war to make peace. He did this by evoking their ancestors and appealing to their inherent human goodness as leaders to lead their people out of conflict. Through poetry, song, and dance he brought out qualities that were a hallmark of a true African leader and challenged the two presidents to look to their ancestors and bring back dignity instead of shame and suffering to their peoples. So emotional was the performance that the two presidents not only shed tears and embraced publicly, but took a solemn oath before the public and witnessed by their ancestors not to return to war. (Doe and Bombande 2002: 164)

The story does not end there. In the next months, pushed by the presidents, a peace agreement was signed. It has not been violated since. It would seem that the peoples of Burkina Faso and Mali serendipitously received a visit from the Pied Piper.

Paper Flowers

Going back to Northern Ireland, the last major bomb that destroyed buildings and lives in the "Troubles" came several years after the cease-fires had been declared. On 15 August 1998, in the town of Omagh, the warnings about the bomb were misleading. As a result, instead of people being directed away from the threat they were evacuated into the path of the bomb. The hidden device exploded. Twenty-nine people and two unborn children died. Over four hundred were injured. The events in the community of Omagh sent waves of shock across the world. Many feared the Northern Irish peace process would collapse. Return to the cycles of violence seemed imminent.

The public—local and well beyond—responded much as they had to the death of Princess Diana the previous year. Flowers and wreaths arrived by the hundreds, filling the bomb site, the surrounding streets, and the grounds of the local hospital. It was an extraordinary outpouring of grief and solidarity. Some weeks later, still reeling with the devastation, town officials felt a certain quandary that was expressed openly by the mayor in a radio interview. "What are we going to do with all the flowers?" The flowers were now wilting, yet they were like a sacred shrine that could not be removed. Traveling in her car, artist Carole Kane listened to that interview and had an immediate idea: make paper. She called Frank Sweeney, head of the Department of Arts and Tourism of the Omagh District. Thus began the healing journey that came to be known as the Petals of Hope (Kane 1999).

Men, women, and children from all walks of life and both sides of the identity divide in Omagh participated in a series of workshops that saved the flower petals and processed the raw material of the wreaths and arrangements. Over time the organic mush became textured paper of different hues. Common everyday people seeking for a way to respond became the artists that crafted small and large pieces from the paper, incorporating the preserved petals. Carol Kane developed a number of pieces alongside them. As people worked with their hands, they talked about where they had been when the bomb went off, what they remembered and experienced. Touching and making something while talking began the healing.

On 10 March 1999, a private viewing of the paper pieces produced was opened for the families who had lost members in the bombing. Those who had worked and created the art chose one piece to give to each family who had lost someone in the bomb. In a book of condolences sent to Omagh, Nobel prizewinning poet Seamus Heaney had written three stanzas from "The Cure of Troy." He gave permission for these lines to be used as titles of three pieces.

So hope for a great sea-change
On the far side of revenge

Believe that a farther shore
Is reachable from here.

Believe in miracles
And cures and healing wells.

The exhibit was then opened to the public and has since traveled around Ireland and Europe. Kane (1999: 32) recounts her experience watching the families see the pieces for the first time:

On the night of the private viewing there was a quietness about the exhibition space. It felt like a sanctuary . . . families spoke quietly to each other. . . . This wasn't like an ordinary opening, where I'd be concerned about people liking the images and buying the work. None of the normal things mattered . . . I spoke to Stanley McCombe about his picture as the lady who had made this piece had requested it would be given in memory of Stanley's wife. This was the picture of the dove, which was given from a Roman Catholic person to a Protestant person. This summed up what all my work was about and Stanley was touched by this gesture.

Belief in the creative act, as Heaney puts it, is belief in "cures and healing wells."

How do we transcend the patterns that create such great pain and still attend to the difficult bogs where our feet seem mired? I have come to believe that it has something to do with the artistic endeavor more than the feat of engineering. It is a process that must breathe life, put wings on the pepper pod, and paint the canvas of what could be while not forgetting what has been. Omagh, too, found its Pied Piper.

John Paul Lederach is professor of international peacebuilding at the Joan B. Kroc Institute for International Peace Studies at the University of Notre Dame. He was the

Conversation, Collaboration, and Culture: Peace Festivals in Sierra Leone

In 2001, Search for Common Ground in Sierra Leone (SFCG-SL) organized its first Peace Festival in Bo, Sierra Leone's southern capital. The festival focused on social-reintegration issues and on the empowerment of youth in Bo. Helped by the famous Sierra Leonean musician Steady Bongo and many local artists, this first Peace Festival was a resounding success, raising money for local youth organizations and providing a forum for discussing important local and national issues. Following the success of the first festival, SFCG-SL has made Peace Festivals an ongoing tool in its work in Sierra Leone, with annual festivals now in Bo, Makeni, and Kenema.

Philosophy

Through entertainment, cultural expression, and dialogue, the festivals have created a forum for promoting social reintegration. Peace Festivals:

- Strengthen civil society and build trust, by promoting local collaboration between diverse interest groups
- Reach a wide audience with messages about social reintegration and coexistence
- Support local artists and provide a popular forum for cultural expression
- Raise money for local organizations
- Are peacebuilding activities in themselves
- Symbolize the return, and the significance, of indigenous culture
- Inspire hope that the return to normal life is possible

SFCG-SL works with local partners to adapt festival themes to the context of the local community, allowing for local ownership of the process and ensuring that the needs of the host communities are met. Festivals have addressed topics such as organization and collaboration among youth, and maintaining postconflict law and order.

Methodology

Peace festivals are alive with energy. Music floats through the air as people gather from miles around to watch, listen, dance, and taste the joys of the festival. Old friends meet and new partnerships are formed. An intentional methodology has been developed for creating large-scale Peace Festivals in Sierra Leone, with each festival becoming an exercise in collaborative problem solving.

Identifying Stakeholders

Planning begins by identifying and recruiting interested stakeholders. These often include local partnership boards, chiefs, radio stations, youth organizations, and political parties. In Makeni, considerable collaboration took place between the army and the police, who overcame long-held differences to work together.

(continues)

Conversation, Collaboration, and Culture:
Peace Festivals in Sierra Leone (continued)

Forming Committees

After the stakeholders have met for discussions, representatives from local organizations are chosen to head committees charged with the festival planning process. These committees are responsible for finance, grounds, publicity, security, and organization. Youth organizations have a representative on each committee, allowing everyone to have a full stake and voice in the process.

Organizing Musicians and Actors

Local and national artists are selected in advance of the festivals to give them time to develop their programs on the central theme(s). Famous musician Steady Bongo and a team of organizers select the local dramatists and musicians to participate in the festivals. This artistic process has ensured that the festivals are entertaining celebrations as well as focused approaches to social reintegration.

Dialogues and Radio Broadcasts

The festivals are broadcast live throughout the region, and feature discussions with local representatives on important themes of social reintegration. These panel discussions and radio dialogues augment the messages embedded in the cultural activities.

Moving Forward After the Festival

At the conclusion of a festival, finances must be accounted for and dispersed, creating another chance for partnership building. A committee is created to assess the festival, document the successes, and work toward constant improvement. Each organizing committee identifies a future event that benefits from the proceeds of the festival, and reports back to the community on the use of the funds and progress of the new project. This promotes greater transparency and accountability at the local level.

Other SFCG Art and Peacebuilding Initiatives

Angolan Peace Song

Search for Common Ground (SFCG) brought thirty-five Angolan musicians—from both sides of the civil war—to write and record an anthem for reconciliation. "A Paz E Que O Povo Chama" (People Are Calling for Peace) was recorded and launched at a peace concert in Luanda, and subsequently became one of the most frequently played songs on Angolan radio. In a society where music plays a vital role in social and political life, the commitment to peace and reconciliation by Angolan cultural icons sent a powerful message to the entire country.

(continues)

Conversation, Collaboration, and Culture: Peace Festivals in Sierra Leone (continued)

Sangwe Festivals in Burundi

SFCG has held two large-scale Peace Festivals in Burundi's capital of Bujumbura. These four-day festivals for peace brought together hundreds of artists—dancers, drummers, storytellers, bands, and drama troupes—from throughout Burundi and the diaspora. Thousands of Burundians gathered peacefully to rock to the rhythms of dancers and sway to the sounds of music. The festival was broadcast throughout Burundi on radio and television.

Common Ground Film Festival in Jerusalem

More than a thousand people attended the four-day festival in Jerusalem during one of the most tense times in the Middle East. The events were held at the historic YMCA, which is one of the rare places in Israel that still has Arab-Israeli programming, including an Arab-Israeli kindergarten. The films were followed by discussions between the filmmakers and the audience about the topics shown in the films. The conversations were often difficult and emotional, but audience members expressed their gratitude for the opportunity to come together, in a mixed audience, to discuss the difficulties and challenges facing them.

The United Nations will bring the Common Ground Film Festival to UN headquarters in New York, starting in February 2005.

Music Videos

SFCG has found that musicians can reach large segments of a society, particularly youth, in extraordinary ways. Musicians have become their country's cultural icons and are emulated by their young fans. SFCG music projects include:

- Macedonia: A music video with two young singers—a Macedonian and an Albanian—singing the theme song from *Nashe Maalo* (Our Neighborhood), an SFCG-produced children's television series that encourages intercultural understanding in an ethnically polarized society. The two singers appear together and sing in each other's language along with the children from the TV series (See Chapter 9.1).
- Indonesia: An interethnic group of some of the country's biggest stars joined together to record a song calling for peaceful national elections, titled: "As Long as We Choose the Peaceful Way."
- Middle East: Two of the biggest Israeli and Palestinian stars recorded the theme song from the new Middle East SFCG documentary TV series. They poignantly sing about a future where life can be lived with all its possibilities.

Note: Written by Susan Koscis, Search for Common Ground.

founding director of the Conflict Transformation Program at Eastern Mennonite University, where he has been named a distinguished scholar. He works extensively as a practitioner in conciliation processes, active in Latin America, Africa, and Southeast and Central Asia.

Note

1. This chapter is a condensed version of John Paul Lederach's chapter "On Pied Pipers: Imagination and Creativity" in the forthcoming publication by the same author entitled *The Moral Imagination: The Art and Soul of Building Peace,* ©2005 by Oxford University Press, Inc. Used by permission of Oxford University Press, Inc.

The author wants to acknowledge the guiding hand and help of David Bolton and Herm Weaver in the development of this chapter.

Selected Bibliography

Brady, Paul. 1992. "The Island" on *Songs and Crazy Dreams* (CD. London: Fontana).

Doe, Samuel Gbaydee, and Emmanuel Habuka Bombande. 2002. "A View from West Africa," in John Paul Lederach and Janice Moomaw Jenner, eds., *Into the Eye of the Storm* (San Francisco: Jossey Bass).

Kane, Carole. 1999. *Petals of Hope* (Omagh, Northern Ireland: Omagh District Council).

Lederach. John Paul. 1995. "Beyond Violence: Building Sustainable Peace," in Arthur Williamson, ed., *Beyond Violence* (Belfast: Community Relations Council).

Resources

Lead Organizations

CompArt—The Netherlands
For contact, please visit website:
http://www.compart-foundation.org

Peace Troupe—United States
E-mail: peacetroupe@culturalanimator.org
Website: http://peacetroupe.org

Search for Common Ground—United States
E-mail: search@sfcg.org
Website: http://www.sfcg.org

Warchild—United Kingdom
E-mail: info@warchild.org.uk
Website: http://www.warchild.org

Websites

Animating Democracy: Strengthening the role of the arts in civic dialogue: http://www.americansforthearts.org/animatingdemocracy

Creative Exchange—Network of organizations involved in arts, culture, and development: http://www.creativexchange.org

Information and organizations around arts and development, community strengthening and civic dialogue: http://www.communityarts.net/readingroom

Publications

Cohen, C. E. "A Poetics of Reconciliation: The Aesthetic Mediation of Conflict." Unpublished doctoral dissertation, University of New Hampshire, 1997.

Kalmanowitz, D., and B. Lloyd. "Fragments of Art at Work: Art Therapy in the Former Yugoslavia." *The Arts in Psychotherapy* 26, no. 1 (1999): 15–25.

Lederach, John Paul. *The Moral Imagination: The Art and Soul of Building Peace.* Oxford: Oxford University Press, 2005

Liebmann, M., ed. *Arts Approaches to Conflict.* Bristol: Jessica Kingsley Publishers, 1996.

Pipkin, W., and S. Dimenna. "Using Creative Dramatics to Teach Conflict Resolution: Exploiting the Drama/Conflict Dialectic." *Journal of Humanistic Education and Development* 28, no. 2 (1989): 104–112.

Scrampickal, J. *Voice to the Voiceless: The Power of People's Theatre.* New Delhi: Manohar Publishers, 1994.

Senehi, Jessica. "Constructive Storytelling: A Peace Process." *Peace and Conflict Studies* 9, no. 2 (2002): 41–63.

Snir, R. "Palestinian Theatre as a Junction of Cultures: The Case of Samih Alqasim's Qaraqash." *Journal of Theatre and Drama* (University of Haifa) 2 (1996): 101–120.

Yaffe, K. "Teaching Conflict Resolution Using the Arts." *The Fourth R.* 27 (June–July 2000): 1–6.

12.1

Using Creative Arts to Deglamorize War: Peacelinks in Sierra Leone

Vandy Kanyako

In Sierra Leone, there is little chance of stifling a rich tradition of artistic expression. Neither colonial antipathy to Sierra Leone's visual and performing artists, nor the hard economic times of the 1980s, nor the civil war of the 1990s have stilled their creative output. Barely two years after the end of a devastating civil war, the capital of Freetown is once again awash with performing artists, alive with music emanating from recording studios.

The arts have survived because art is integral to the lives of Sierra Leone's people. Music and dance are the driving forces, ever present at work, worship, weddings, and funerals. From the cradle to the grave, singing and dancing are linked to every facet of Sierra Leonean life. They are powerful vehicles that have been used for generations to entertain, educate, and transmit historical events. Most importantly, songs have been used over the years to cement national unity and rouse people to action. For a country that has witnessed its fair share of political unrest and civil strife, the need for the arts to bring together fractured communities and heal the ravages of war cannot be overemphasized.

In response to the ravages of the war in general and its effects on children in particular, grassroots civil-society organizations have emerged, embracing both conventional and unconventional approaches to healing and reconciliation. Among these groups is Peacelinks, a nonprofit, nondenominational organization made up entirely of young people who have utilized the arts to help other young people overcome their war trauma, learn new skills, and lead productive lives.

Peacelinks was born out of the chaos and uncertainties of the 1990s as a direct response to the marginalization of young people and the terrible effect of the war on children. Comprised largely of ex–child combatants, displaced children, amputees, and street children, the group uses visual and performing arts including painting, drawing, music, dance, and drama to not only help traumatized children recover from their spiritually debilitating experiences but

---

A Vicious Civil War

Sierra Leone was plunged into a vicious civil war in 1991. The war quickly spread, drawing mostly young people, who form an estimated 55 percent of the country's population, into a vortex of tragic violence. Politically marginalized and constantly afflicted by grinding poverty and a chronic shortage of work, youth had, prior to the war, constituted an energetic but disgruntled class itching for the opportunity to redress what was perceived as years of gross imbalance and injustice.

With the war came a sort of outlet. Often cajoled and coerced, many teenagers—and some children as young as eight—joined the warring factions. Indeed, these disenchanted youngsters formed the core of the rebellion that disastrously engulfed the country. An estimated seventy thousand people lost their lives and more than 2.6 million of the country's 4.7 million population were displaced. More than nine thousand children were maimed, orphaned, or separated from their parents.

---

also to comment on social issues such as violence, poverty, discrimination, hunger, illiteracy, joblessness, and military recruitment. The group uses creative arts to "deglamorize" warfare and to bridge the gap between the "victim," be that a displaced person or amputee, and "perpetrator," the former child combatant. Through the arts, the organization creates symbols of national consciousness that reinforce patriotism, peace, love, unity, and hope.

Peacelinks was formed with three main aims:

Empowerment. From its inception, Peacelinks aimed to raise awareness about the dangers of youth militarization and hence to empower young people for positive change. By imparting new skills, the organization gave young people a sense of empowerment and inspired others to use their creative talents and energy for constructive rather than destructive purposes. To this effect most of the organization's volunteer projects have been carried out in communities with large concentrations of deprived and at-risk children.

Reconciliation. Peacelinks aimed to bridge the gap between communities and to heal the wounds of war. The group uses art that specifically carries messages of healing and nonviolence aimed at restoring the trust and confidence that are so essential to closely knit societies. The group creates songs and choreographs dances that utilize symbolic gestures, costumes, and other visual devices to communicate the message of peace and reconciliation. By bringing together children from all the warring factions and all socioeconomic backgrounds, Peacelinks vividly demonstrates to the adult community the possibility of reconciliation between former adversaries.

Influencing policy. With local and international partners including United Nations Children's Fund (UNICEF), Amnesty International, United Network of Young Peacebuilders, and others, Peacelinks aims to influence government policy on issues of general concern to youth. The group campaigns against child recruitment, and to end the service of those already in the ranks, by organizing art exhibitions and seminars, writing newspaper articles, participating in radio discussions, and performing on national television.

Passionate Singing

Peacelinks was formed in 1990 by two Sierra Leonean teenagers after returning from an international children's peace conference in Vermont in the United States. The group started with ten children who met once a week for lively discussions on productive ways of engaging the skills of young people, and who followed their meetings with passionate singing. These weekly meetings proved popular and attracted more young people. Soon, the membership had expanded to fifty mainly at-risk children: street kids, students from various socioeconomic backgrounds, and a sprinkling of displaced and ex-child combatants, mainly from the Liberian civil war.

The discussions resulted in two concrete projects: community volunteering and creative arts for peacebuilding. An organization was set up and the group embarked on community outreach activities by which members volunteered once a month to clean up public places such as parks, hospitals, and community centers, and to plant trees in environmentally degraded areas.

Vandy Kanyako Jr.

Peacelinks members performing for their Stop Child Soldiers campaign

The outbreak of the civil war in 1991 fundamentally changed the composition and activities of the organization. The war produced a new class of disadvantaged children (displaced children, amputees, and ex–child combatants), many parentless and traumatized, with unique needs. Many of these children had arrived in the city unaccompanied and settled in communities where Peacelinks was already active. In 1992, ten ex–child combatants who had learned of the existence of Peacelinks joined the organization. By 1994 more than half of the one hundred members were children with direct experience in the war. Their real-life traumatic experiences provided rich material for the songs, dances, paintings, and drawings for which Peacelinks gained national and international recognition. Through the words, songs, and visual images of children who had experienced the war firsthand, Peacelinks was able to dramatize its effects on these children.

The Program
Once it had determined just what it wished to accomplish, Peacelinks drew up a program consisting of four principal components: outreach programs, recordings, art exhibitions, and leadership skills training.

Outreach. Peacelinks used art to communicate messages of peace, reconciliation, and hope to communities that had been hard hit by the war. The group performed free concerts in schools, refugee camps, interim care centers, and other locations around the war-scarred capital. The idea was not only to entertain but also to open channels of communication among various constituencies that had developed in the course of the war. By bringing ex-child combatants to communities they had once terrorized, and where they were now both feared and loathed, the outreach provided a platform for war-affected children to present their side of the story. As musicians, dancers, and visual artists giving something back to these communities, the children could begin traveling the road to recovery and acceptance.

Music production. In order to further spread the message of peace and reconciliation, and to raise funds, Peacelinks made numerous recordings of original songs, beginning in 1996 with a recording entitled *Believe in Peace. Torch of Love* followed in 1999 and *Reconciliation* in 2002. *Children Are the Future* highlighted the potential of young people as agents of positive change. *Disarm* was a direct call to the leaders to disarm child combatants. Songs in both English and native languages were recorded. Each of the albums became a best-seller in Sierra Leone and thus a source of income and publicity for the organization.

Art exhibitions. Peacelinks periodically organizes art exhibitions that reflect the war experiences of the children. The organization offers the opportunity for children to tell their stories through paintings, drawings, and woodcarvings reflecting a wide range of emotions: sadness and happiness, hate and love, war and

Reconciliation. (Key: G-minor)

Chorus: Reconciliation
It requires patience
It requires waiting
It is good for lasting peace

Chorus (x4)

Solo 1: Now my brothers
Let us learn to forgive one another
And bury the hatchet
And then turn to a new page
All Oh-oh-oh-oh (A-new—page)
This is what we need
For peace to prevail in this land
So we can come together and
Rebuild our land

Chorus (x4)

Solo 2: Reconciliation
That is what the children need
So we should try
And make it a reality
All Oh-oh-oh-oh (Re-a-li-ty)
Put aside all hatred
And forget about the past
So we can come together
And rebuild our land

Chorus (x4)

peace, despair and hope. They have been frequently exhibited over the years and also attract the attention of researchers and organizations from around the world.

Community internship program. Peacelinks runs a community internship program for young people from various Freetown institutions interested in the arts for peace project. The beneficiaries are often directly selected by their communities or institutions and are provided with free hands-on training in music, painting, drawing, carving, and other practical skills such as typing. They can then return to their communities with these skills both to empower others and to lead independent lives.

Added Value

Transformation. Peacelinks brought the issue of child soldiers to the fore in a unique way. By transforming ex-child combatants from agents of destruction to messengers of peace, and by nurturing their talents and honing their skills, the organization helps change society's negative perception and morbid fear of war-affected children. Peacelinks also goes beyond reintegration and resettlement by helping these children to become active members of their communities and positive role models.

Peace music. Peacelinks popularized the concept of peace music with songs conceived, created, and performed with the sole aim of easing tension and building friendship. They stress the lyrical message as much as melody and rhythm, touching on crucial issues in ways that steer clear of divisive politics, in several languages, and incorporating images and sounds that the audience identifies with peace and unity.

Art as a multipurpose peacebuilding tool. Peacelinks uses art as the main vehicle to achieve multiple aims. The organization utilized the medium not only to unite fractured communities and empower and heal traumatized children, but also to raise funds and teach life skills to at-risk youth.

Imparting values. Peacelinks training emphasizes respect for individual opinions and group decisions. All programs are planned and implemented as a group with appointed committees fine-tuning the details and reporting back to the general membership for further comments and recommendations. In this way members learn such important societal values as consensus building, cooperation, patience, and respect. Especially for ex–child soldiers, learning these values of give-and-take and group process are vital if they are to successfully adjust to civilian life.

Challenges

In the course of the war, insecurity was a huge problem and severely hindered the organization's operations. Activities were frequently postponed, suspended, or cancelled due to fighting in or around Freetown. For example, in January 1999, during the invasion of the capital, an outreach team of more than twenty members was detained at a progovernment military checkpoint for hours. The same month, the office was vandalized.

When law and order broke down, as happened so very often in the course of the war, some children were easily enticed to rejoin one or another of the fighting forces. More than ten ex–child combatants with whom the organization had worked were reabducted and rearmed.

For the wider society, there is a stigma associated with being a former child combatant. As such, some parents of Peacelinks members were very reluctant in the beginning to allow their children to closely associate with these children. Their stance has softened with time, but the attitude was all too prevalent and still persists in some quarters today.

Conclusions

Benefits of diversity. Joint programs for youth from diverse backgrounds are extremely important in the rehabilitation and reintegration of ex–child combatants. With a large concentration of former child soldiers, the children will tend to adhere to behaviors learned as fighters; but when they are in groups with other children from diverse backgrounds they will be more likely to modify those behaviors.

Overcoming preconceived notions. It became apparent that with the right kind of approach and dialogue with the community, people are willing to let go of their preconceived notions. As people came to understand that these children were as much victims as they were perpetrators, they slowly let go of their misconceptions about war-affected children. The right approach also involves constant dialogue with the community leaders.

Social support networks. Other social support networks such as family and school are extremely important in the process of helping the children regain their dignity. We found out that children who had such support had a less difficult time than peers who did not.

Youth mentorship. Children tend to talk more easily about their traumatic experiences with other young people than with their elders. They stated this frequently. Many cited the long history of distrust that exists between youth and the elderly based on a culture in which children are expected to obey without question.

Next Steps

Peacelinks has grown from a youth group of ten members in 1990 to a full-fledged community-based organization with a staff of ten assisted by twenty volunteers, a board of directors, and a two-story office building in the heart of the city. As the organization has gained recognition, it has attracted financial and technical support from a variety of sources around the world.

The organization is now regularly consulted by UN agencies and international organizations on various peacebuilding issues. In 2000 the organization worked closely with the Civil Affairs Section of the United Nations Mission in Sierra Leone to develop youth radio discussion programs for the UN's Peace FM radio station. In May 2004 Radio Nederland began discussions with the group and other partners about the possibility of establishing community-based FM radio stations in the country. In spite of these major developments, the organization still remains a youth-led venture. All projects are still planned and implemented by the young people, with the supervision of an adult board.

Sierra Leone has stepped back from the brink of a great abyss. Still dangers lurk and much work must be done to cement a secure future. Naturally, Peacelinks is only one small part of the massive project, but it is an important one. What Peacelinks demonstrates is that even in difficult times, one can be optimistic about the resiliency of youth. That is a good thing, for the future success of Sierra Leone is inextricably linked to the success of its youth in rebuilding a country that has been so terribly devastated in the recent past.

Vandy Kanyako is founder and former executive director of Peacelinks.

Contact

Peacelinks
14 A Williams Street
Freetown, Sierra Leone
Tel: +232 (22) 222 552
Fax: +232 (22) 224 439
E-mail: peacelinks@sierratel.sl, or peacelinks2@yahoo.com

12.2

Artistic Responses to the Siege of Sarajevo: The Cellist and the Film Festival in Bosnia-Herzegovina

While the beautiful, historic city of Sarajevo was under siege, the everyday lives of people were torn apart. Some wondered whether it would ever be possible to heal the scars of such suffering. Yet the Sarajevan people proved to be stronger and found ways to pull through. Using their artistic expressions, they responded to the violence they were forced to live with.

When twenty-two of his fellow citizens were killed in the early days of the siege of Sarajevo, cellist Vedran Smailovic responded by taking his cello to the spot of the massacre and playing for the following twenty-two days in their honor. It was a gesture that inspired not only the people of Sarajevo, but the entire caring world.

The first Sarajevo Film Festival also took place during the siege. It has grown into the biggest and most important film festival in southeastern Europe. Organizing the festival in those dark days was a statement—reminiscent of the earlier statement of cellist Vedran Smailovic—that it might be possible to murder Sarajevo's citizens, but not to kill its spirit.

A Hopeful Note in a Time of War

Vedran Smailovic is a cellist. In fact, in 1992, at the age of thirty-six, he was accomplished enough to serve as the principal cellist for the Sarajevo Opera Company. He came from a family of musicians who toured Yugoslavia under the moniker Musica Ad Hominem ("Music for the People") taking their music to small villages, often putting together special programs for children.

Vedran Smailovic would likely have remained just one of many thousands of talented but anonymous cellists in the world but for the accident of his birthplace—Sarajevo—and his response to the slaughter that occurred in his town beginning in the spring of 1992. The siege of Sarajevo had been under way for about a month; already many had died, and the infrastructure of the city had been severely damaged. Rations were in short supply, and basic commodities, including bread, were hard to come by. At four in the afternoon on

27 May, in Vase Miskina Street in central Sarajevo, a few hundred meters from Smailovic's home, several shells lobbed from the hills by Serb gunners exploded as the city's residents waited patiently in a breadline. Twenty-two people were killed and more than a hundred were wounded.

The next day, at four in the afternoon, Vedran Smailovic appeared in Vase Miskina Street, carrying his cello, dressed in the formal evening jacket and white tie he customarily wore when performing for the opera. Despite the carnage of the previous day, there was, once again, a line of people waiting to buy bread. He planted a simple chair in one of the bomb craters and began playing Albinoni's *Adagio,* music which he has described as "the saddest music I know." On each of the following twenty-one days—twenty-two days to honor the memories of the twenty-two Sarajevans who had died—Smailovic returned to the spot of the massacre, even as the shelling continued, to serenade those fellow citizens who braved the snipers and the mortar fire.

When a reporter from CNN asked him whether he was not crazy sitting there playing while the bombardments sustained, Vedran Smailovic replied, "You ask me am I crazy for playing the cello; why do you not ask if they are crazy for shelling Sarajevo?"

It is doubtful whether Vedran Smailovic managed to save a single life, shorten the Bosnian war, or speed the end of the siege of Sarajevo by even one day. Almost certainly, his brave actions made little impression on the Serb gunners who continued their merciless shelling of Sarajevo from the hilltops surrounding the city—if they were aware of his existence at all. He did not see himself as a peacebuilder. Yet his story has been often repeated and his actions have been held up to the world as a symbol of inspiring courage and nonviolent resistance in the face of horrible violence and human suffering.

Smailovic never claimed that he was doing anything extraordinary. In fact, when asked about it by *New York Times* reporter John Burns, he downplayed his action."My mother is a Muslim and my father is a Muslim, but I don't care. I am a Sarajevan, I am a cosmopolitan, I am a pacifist. I am nothing special, I am a musician, I am a part of the town. Like everyone else, I do what I can."

Yet doing what he could made an enormous impression; which, in a sense, begs the question: What should we make of ordinary people who, in extraordinary circumstances, do what would otherwise be ordinary things? What is the value of a gesture of defiance, when it is not going to change the outcome, and it certainly is not going to restore to life and to wholeness those who have been killed and maimed? Where does such an individual act of defiance fit within the traditions of conflict resolution and peacemaking? How should we view such a lonely expression of indignation?

Vedran Smailovic's most immediate impact was on his own neighbors. Sarajevo is a city whose history dates back more than five hundred years, and which had been a symbol of religious and ethnic harmony. It had survived two world wars almost unscathed and served as host to the Winter Olympics in 1984.

However, now it was suffering an indignity that no one who had lived there could have imagined. By refusing to give in to the terror, Smailovic was making a statement, also on behalf of his fellow Sarajevans, that they can kill some of us, but they cannot kill our spirit and they cannot rob us of our dignity or our humanity. This was a very important message, at that early stage, when it was not clear if the city would be able to hold out against the Serbs, or even if it did, whether there would be much of Sarajevo left.

Smailovic made the right gesture at the right moment. The siege continued for more than a thousand days, claiming ten thousand lives and causing enormous physical destruction. Many who could did flee the city, and yet those who remained and survived managed to confront the terror and the fear—to do their jobs; to find ingenious ways to hold their lives and their families together; to publish newspapers and keep radio and television stations on the air throughout the siege; to organize concerts, theater performances, and films; and even to laugh a bit at the absurdity of their existence—returning, as Smailovic said, "to beauty of a life without fear." Not, of course, because of Vedran Smailovic alone, but because of a state of mind that his action embodied, and which was embraced by his fellow Sarajevans over the subsequent forty-four months.

Still, Smailovic also had a wider impact. In fact, it could be said that those unamplified notes played in Sarajevo's devastated center truly were heard around the world. In that sense, the effect was of an absurdly quiet and dignified scream: "Look what they are doing to us. We are civilized, peace-loving people. We just want to go about our business. And they are blowing us to bits."

There is a curious irony in the story of Vedran Smailovic. The notes he played in May and June 1992 quickly faded away. There are no recordings of those twenty-two *Adagios*. Yet the story of the "Cellist of Sarajevo" has been told and retold. The power of the story has been such that an English composer named David Wilde wrote a piece, dedicated to Smailovic, that has been performed and recorded by the celebrated cellist Yo Yo Ma, who described Smailovic as "a real, present-day hero" who showed that "an individual can make a difference in the world." The "Cellist of Sarajevo" has also been cited in sermons and works of fiction.

It has touched many thousands—perhaps millions—of people, evoked many emotions, perhaps been the impetus for reflection and an incremental increase in kindness between neighbors—maybe even between adversaries—and just possibly moved some to work for peace and reconciliation who might never have considered it otherwise. In other words, Smailovic's very personal action has, in ways that he probably never intended, ended up making a global impact.

There can hardly be a more compelling example of how a solitary fighter might embody the power of people's resistance than those adagios rising from the streets of Sarajevo in the spring of 1992.

Stimulating a Sense of Togetherness

While the war in Bosnia is over, and the Sarajevo Film Festival is now primarily a vehicle for advancing the cinematic arts of the region, it has a special role to play in binding the wounds of wars, advancing regional cooperation and reconciliation, and promoting peace and human rights. The festival's year-round Traveling Cinema, which takes film to all corners of Bosnia-Herzegovina, and its Children's Festival, are both viewed as opportunities to promote multiculturalism and reconciliation.

The terror in Sarajevo had already lasted for forty-two months and claimed more than ten thousand lives. A few weeks earlier, a truce had been put in place—not the first time that the two sides had agreed to stop fighting—but truces had been agreed and violated many times in the past. So, when the first Sarajevo Film Festival opened on 25 October 1995, it was more than just another cultural event. Looking back, the organizers recall that that first festival "could have seemed more like a bizarre act of resistance than a real film festival." Though features were shown on big screens, many of the films came from the VHS collections of the organizers. Still, it was a serious effort, running for twelve days and featuring thirty-seven films from fifteen countries. More than fifteen thousand viewers attended the showings; every night was sold out.

The Role of Artistic Processes in Peacebuilding in Bosnia-Herzegovina

How did artists and conflict resolution practitioners use arts during the war and in the postconflict period in Bosnia-Herzegovina? Research suggests that arts can play an important role at all stages of a conflict, including:

- Arts as a barometer: arts-based processes can serve as warnings of the escalation of tensions in society through examining the content of visual, artistic, or theatrical products (latent conflict)
- Arts for resistance and survival: during heightened conflict, arts-based processes can serve as a means of resisting violence and/or provide relief as a means of temporary escape (during manifest or extreme conflict)
- Arts for peacebuilding and healing: arts-based processes can bring together groups in conflict to work collaboratively via creative processes and/or help people release negative feelings (postconflict)

(These categories emerged from the research in part due to an interview with Munir Podumljak, Partnership for Social Development, Croatia.)

Figure 12.1 provides a visual representation of the stage of conflict and area of impact of arts-based activities.

The research focused on both the role of arts-based activities during the war and how various arts-based activities were building peace after the war. During the conflict, the arts had a critical role in keeping the multicultural spirit of Bosnia-Herzegovina alive in the midst of extreme conflict, particularly in Sarajevo. An example is the first Sarajevo International Theater and Film Festival, organized in 1993, that was attended by over twenty thousand people. On a smaller scale, there were countless creative therapy projects to help youth survive the terror of war. Artistic processes provided a basis for people to come together for community building, support, and temporary release from the difficulties of the war.

(continues)

The Role of Artistic Processes in Peacebuilding in
Bosnia-Herzegovina (cont.)

Figure 12.1 Stages of Conflict and Arts

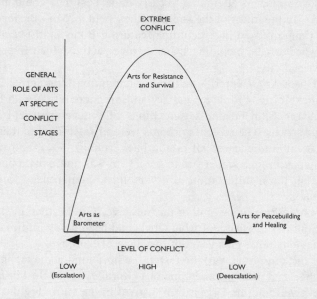

In the postwar period a number of groups have used music, theater, photography, and other arts-based activities as a basis for facilitating interethnic interaction and reconciliation. Examples include the use of theater to bring youth together in Mostar organized by the local youth theater, and Pontanima, an interethnic, interfaith choir started shortly after the end of the war. The choir has used music to build connections among the core participants and also use music as a witness for peace to the larger society.

Impact

It is obvious that arts and peacebuilding projects have significant potential to foster relationship building and greater understanding between groups in a conflicted society. The participants involved in a particular process may experience change in their attitudes, beliefs, and possibly behavior toward others. If an arts-based process involves a formal performance component, there may also be an impact on the audience witnessing the event.

Note: Written by Craig Zelizer, who completed his doctoral degree on the role of artistic processes in peacebuilding in Bosnia-Herzegovina (2004, Institute for Conflict Analysis and Resolution, George Mason University). The author conducted fourteen months of field research between 2000 and 2001 in the area and interviewed sixty-four artists, peacebuilders, and scholars. Zelizer is presently senior partner at Alliance for Conflict Transformation (http://www.conflicttransformation.org; czelizer@conflicttransformation.org).

The War Years

The terrible carnage that began in Sarajevo in April 1992 and raged throughout Bosnia-Herzegovina for four years was all the more horrific because it took place in a country that had always represented an oasis of tolerance and multiculturalism, where many nationalities and cultures had lived peacefully side by side for centuries.

Sarajevo's citizens attempted to carry on as best they could under the circumstances. In the midst of the shelling, they held a "Miss Besieged Sarajevo Pageant" (immortalized in a recording featuring Bono and Luciano Pavarotti) and renowned artists, including U2 and singer-activist Joan Baez, performed in the besieged city.

The Obala Arts Center, a cultural organization long active in Sarajevo, organized exhibitions in its art gallery and, in cooperation with the Locarno and Edinburgh Film Festivals, screenings of independent and art films in improvised spaces. The screening rooms were always filled to their maximum capacity by an audience of all ethnic backgrounds, ages, and religions for whom running through sniper fire to see a film was not really a political act of defiance, but the manifestation of a very basic human need to express and reaffirm life.

The more formal launching of the Sarajevo Film Festival in October 1995 was, then, just an extension of what Obala had been doing informally throughout the previous three-plus years of the siege of Sarajevo.

Since the end of the war, the festival, with a total audience in excess of a hundred thousand, has become a major cultural event in Bosnia-Herzegovina and has evolved into the largest film festival in the entire region, showcasing outstanding films of all sorts, but not to the exclusion of cinematic reflection on Sarajevo's own recent history. During the war, many of Sarajevo's citizens documented their experiences—sometimes with professional equipment, and sometimes with simple camcorders. The festival has provided opportunities to show many of these testimonials to the courage and endurance of the people of Sarajevo, including, for example, a program of shorts at the 1997 festival such as Seadi Hihad Kresevljakovic's *Do You Remember Sarajevo?* (1993–1995), a collection of moments capturing everyday life during the siege, showing the bombings and sniper attacks as well as the more intimate moments of joy among the surviving citizens; Nedzad Begovic's *War Art* (1993), which follows the work of craftsmen who took pieces of twisted debris and transformed them into objects of beauty; and Pjer Zalica's 1995 short *Children Like Any Other*, which records the way in which kids were traumatized by the war. Features addressing the conflict have also been shown, including *The Perfect Circle* by Ademir Kenovic (1997), *Welcome to Sarajevo* (1996) by Michael Winterbottom, and Danis Tanovic's Oscar-winning black comedy, *No Man's Land*.

Bringing Film to the Children

One of the festival's other major efforts is to bring film to the children of Bosnia-Herzegovina. During the year, the festival's crew takes the Traveling

Cinema to all parts of the country, particularly to areas of both the Republic of Srpska and the Federation of Bosnia and Herzegovina, where war damage to the cultural infrastructure has been most severe. Film showings in improvised theaters are offered at a symbolic charge and are available to the entire population—all nationalities and age groups—but with a focus on children and young people. According to the Children's Program director Susanne Prahl, "The program has two equally important goals: to enable children of BiH [Bosnia-Herzegovina] to be informed about the best children's movies produced recently and also to give the children of different ethnic backgrounds an opportunity to meet and thus stimulate the reconciliation in the country."

By showing films reflecting a wide variety of different cultures, the programmers believe they are promoting tolerance and expanding the horizons of those living in relatively closed communities. Where Serbs, Croats, and Bosnian Muslims come together to attend the festival programs, the festival is also promoting the slow process of reintegration and reconciliation. There is also an important educational function; prior to the screening of the main feature film, short films are screened on subjects such as mine-awareness, environmental protection, multiculturalism, and tolerance. Quite apart from any considerations of the war experience, the Traveling Cinema gives kids a chance to move away from the streets and hopefully gives them ideas of other values and possibilities.

Throughout the year, the festival team makes arrangements for children from disadvantaged areas to visit the Children's Festival, which is an integral part of the Sarajevo Film Festival. In addition to film showings, many of which focus especially on the issues that concern kids, such as first love, drug abuse, growing pains, and tolerance for people of different religions and ethnic groups, the Children's Festival features guest appearances by actors appearing in some of the films and additional sport and entertainment programs.

Cultural Nourishment

In 2004, to mark the tenth anniversary of the launch of the Sarajevo Film Festival, it established a new Human Rights Award to pay tribute to artists from the region and the world who celebrate differences and teach the value of peace through the lens of the camera. The award is sponsored by the government of Switzerland. One objective is to generate substantial public and media interest in film makers who focus on ideas such as tolerance, multiculturalism, religious diversity, and peace education. Especially against the backdrop of the experiences of Sarajevo, and within the scope of the powerful medium of film, the award has particular significance.

Perhaps the best assessment of the special role the Sarajevo Film Festival has played and continues to play can be gleaned from the words of Caroline Schmidt Hornstein, head of the Konrad Adenauer Foundation in Bosnia-Herzegovina, who observed,"Culture is nutrition: it nurtures fantasies, innovation, ideas of the possible, and a moral sense for the common good. The Sarajevo Film Festival is feeding it in the best of ways."

Contact

Sarajevo Film Festival
Zelenih Beretki 12-1
71 000 Sarajevo
Bosnia-Herzegovina
Tel: +387 33 209 411, +387 33 221 516
Fax: +387 33 263 380
Contact person: Emina Ganic, International Relations Director, emina.ganic@sff.ba
E-mail: general, info@sff.ba
Website: http://www.sff.ba

Selected Bibliography

"Adagio for Cello and Howitzers." 1992. *New York Times,* 10 June.

Burns, John F. 1992. "People Under Artillery Fire Manage to Retain Humanity." *New York Times,* 8 June.

Burns, John F., and Jon Jones. 1992. "The Dying City of Sarajevo." *New York Times Magazine,* 26 July.

Deats, Richard. 2001. "Adagio in Sarajevo." *The Friendship Ambassador* 30, no. 1: 5. Online at: http://www.faf.org/pdf/Newsletter%20September16.pdf.

"From Tom Clancy to Michael Moore to Documents of Local Tragedy, Sarajevo Fest Addresses Violence in All Its Forms." Online at: http://www.indiewire.com/onthescene/fes_02Sarajevo_020826_wrap.html.

"Lights Sarajevo's Cinematic Fire: Ninth Edition Reaches Peak with Post-War Works." Online at: http://www.indiewire.com/onthescene/onthescene_030828sff.html.

McCreary, Alf. 1994. "A Message of Peace in the Language of Music." *Christian Science Monitor,* 9 March.

Safford, Victoria. n.d. "All That's Past Is Prologue." Online at: http://www.uua.org/ga/ga01/4032,html.

'Sarajevo.' Online at: http://www.kinoeye.org/01/02/pozun02.php.

"The Cellist of Sarajevo." 1995. *Tutti Celli* (Internet Cello Society's bimonthly newsletter) (September-October). Online at: http://www.cwu.edu/~michelj/Newsletter/Articles/sarajevo.html.

13

The Peacebuilding Potential of Local Businesses

Nick Killick and Canan Gündüz

The role of business in conflict areas has often been described in negative terms. There are, however, many ways in which local private companies and international corporations can contribute to the prevention or resolution of conflicts. Indeed, many such attempts have already been made. This chapter explores some of the roles that local business can play in a conflict context.

International attention has turned in recent years toward the critical, some would argue decisive, role that economic factors play in driving and perpetuating contemporary violent conflicts. While the focus has been largely on the economic activities of combatants, especially the financing of rebel groups and economic gain as an incentive for perpetuating violence, the role of private-sector actors in so-called war economies is becoming more and more prominent.

In particular, the focus on the exploitation of natural resources in conflict zones has pointed out the often negative, conflict-feeding role that rich-country companies doing business in or with actors from conflict zones can have. This has been illustrated by the direct impacts of foreign company operations on the ground in Nigeria and Sudan, for instance, but also by the more indirect links of Western companies, through global supply chains for the production of consumer goods, such as with the negative effects of the mining of coltan in the Democratic Republic of Congo (DRC).

Conversely, the role of local business actors has received very little attention so far, both in terms of negative impacts, but equally significantly, in terms of their contribution to conflict prevention and peacebuilding. As definitions of "civil society" continue to evolve, and as some important local business-led peacebuilding initiatives, such as those profiled in this volume, begin to be recognized, deeper exploration of the peacebuilding potential of local businesses is required.

Local Private-Sector Actors

Given that business is often a powerful actor in the political economy of war, and recovery from war, the notion of a peacebuilding role for business is clearly complicated. Some private-sector actors will benefit from conflict, whether directly (by acting as suppliers to the army, for example, or by unfairly winning lucrative government contracts in an environment where transparency and competition are subordinated to the demands of maintaining security and power) or indirectly (by taking advantage of the confusion and chaos to make profits on the black market).

Besides those instances where business activities feed into or profit from violence, they may also sustain structural injustices that can fuel hostilities. Control of the land by big business in Colombia, for example, has been a critical factor in the conflict, as was the support provided by white-owned businesses to the apartheid regime in South Africa; the private sector in both Sri Lanka and Nepal can be seen as promoting or benefiting from a system that has historically excluded or failed large sections of the society.

In addition, businesses or individual business leaders are likely to mirror or reinforce the conflict dynamics by, for example, employing one ethnic or religious group to the exclusion of another, or by competing for access to markets along social-conflict lines.

These negative interactions between the private sector and conflict highlight that any peacebuilding strategy has to address local economic agendas in wars. This has to be based on a good understanding of the makeup of the local private sector, which is diverse and does not have a uniform agenda, neither in peace nor in war. Local businesses range from large, often multinational enterprises, mostly based in national capitals, to regional actors such as chambers of commerce, to grassroots actors spanning small and medium enterprises down to individual market traders. Given the importance in developing countries of the informal sector, both in terms of holding assets and providing jobs and livelihoods for a majority of the population, it has to be included in this actor group.

Almost by definition, then, local private-sector actors are part of the existing conflict context. In a sense, it is this rooted relationship to the conflict that is crucial to local business playing a peacebuilding role—it constitutes a powerful section of society with linkages to different social and political actors and strata, through business relations or other linkages, including political, cultural, ethnic, and religious ones. This highly "networked" position the private sector holds in its own society suggests a new addition to John Paul Lederach's three-tier understanding of the peacebuilding potential of societies.[1] Business people, represented at all levels, are strategically positioned to intervene in a variety of ways (see Figure 13.1).

With this model in mind, it is possible to identify four conditions that can contribute to promoting and sustaining a role for local private sectors, broadly applicable to all sizes and types of business:

Figure 13.1 Local Actors in Conflict Prevention and Resolution

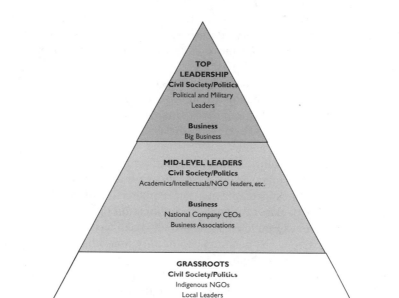

1. Wide recognition of businesses' interest in peace
2. An influential and diverse business sector—influential both in terms of political leverage and active engagement in social issues
3. A (relatively) independent and positively perceived private sector
4. Individual champions prepared to take a lead

These factors point out some of the challenges and questions in promoting a peacebuilding role for the local business community: whether there is a strong argument for involving it; what is needed for creating or strengthening that argument further; in what ways it is best placed to contribute; and what needs to be done to ensure it can maximize its contribution.

Challenges

Business Interests
As discussed above, some businesses actively benefit from conflict contexts. For most legal private-sector activity, however, conflict is bad for business.

This is the fundamental motivation and justification for businesses' involvement in peacebuilding. Destruction of infrastructure, loss of a skilled work force, withdrawal of foreign investment, prohibitive security and insurance costs, loss of markets, regulatory confusion, and diminished support from the government all make doing business in conflict zones a matter of survival rather than growth.

There is much evidence from countries as diverse as South Africa, Northern Ireland, Sri Lanka, and the Philippines to support the view that collective action is central to a successful and sustainable private-sector intervention. Building such a coalition, however, requires broad recognition of the damaging impact of the conflict on individual businesses and the economic environment as a whole. Researching and publicizing the costs of the conflict to business can accelerate the emergence of a business case or interest in peace. Such an advocacy campaign can strengthen a sense of shared suffering and unity of purpose. In both Sri Lanka and Nepal, the publication of documents that outlined the costs of the respective conflicts provided an incentive for joint strategizing and action among the business community that otherwise might have taken much longer to bring about.

A lack of awareness and understanding of their own peacebuilding potential within the business community is partially to blame for the relative scarcity of examples of local business involvement in peace processes. Therefore, raising awareness of successful initiatives from elsewhere (some are mentioned below) is another crucial dimension of making clear how peace is in the interest of business.[2]

An Influential and Diverse Private Sector

The better connected business leaders are to conflict actors, the greater the potential for positively influencing the decisionmaking process but, equally, the greater the risk that influence might be exercised negatively. Nevertheless, the capacity of larger businesses to pressurize governments in particular provides a potential resource that few other sectors can match. Understandably, there is frequently a reluctance to exercise that access and influence given the power that governments in turn exercise over business leaders' ability to carry on doing business. This emphasizes the importance of collective action involving a broad spectrum of businesses. The key is to identify ways in which the influence business leaders have, can be directed toward peaceful ends.

An Independent and Positively Perceived Private Sector

Legitimacy and impartiality are necessary attributes of any peacebuilding actor, including the local private sector. This is crucial for acceptance from conflicting parties as well as affected communities. Undoubtedly, acquiring such acceptance will be a challenge for business, especially where it has played, or is perceived to play, a role in perpetuating economic inequalities, has a history of colluding with corrupt officials, or exerts too much political influence in its own favor. Businesses' own linkages within their societies may additionally feed into perceptions of partiality.

Open dialogue with all relevant stakeholders, together with a clear state-ment of its own agenda and interest in peace, may help to overcome these dif-ficulties. Businesses in Northern Ireland used this strategy to highlight the "peace dividend" (See Chapter 13.2). In South Africa, a number of business leaders were able to build trust over time with both sides on the basis that their agenda was clear and neutral (See Chapter 13.1).

Individual Champions

The success or failure of any peacebuilding initiative critically depends on the strengths and quality of the individuals leading it, including those from the private sector. Obtaining success requires individuals willing and able to gal-vanize others in pursuit of a shared aim. These are people who can articulate the case for a wider private-sector role in peacebuilding and convince doubters to engage, who can exercise their influence without fear of reprisal and are respected both among their peers and the wider society. Identifying and sup-porting such individuals is critical if the private sector is to fulfill its peace-building potential.

Spheres of Engagement

Every conflict context is unique, but by drawing on the lessons and experi-ences from countries where the private sector has played a constructive peace-building role, it is possible to identify different types of roles, which can be a useful guide and source of inspiration to others. They can be broken down into three categories:

1. Core business—meaning the management of a company's operations
2. Social investment—contribution to development, social issues, etc.
3. Policy dialogue—influence at the policy level, institution building, etc.

The most publicized experiences to date are those of big business, discussed in more detail below; less research has been undertaken into the role of provin-cial/regional businesses and grassroots/informal actors.[3] When looking at a peacebuilding role for businesses, it is crucial, however, to move beyond cap-ital-based big businesses, which are often far removed from the actual loca-tions where conflict is taking place.

National Business

Core Business

This covers a range of issues, including corporate governance, ethical business practices, and internal policies and standards. It also includes relations with sup-pliers, job creation and investment, human resources, and infrastructure devel-opment. In different ways, all these can be significant peacebuilding opportuni-ties if approached in a way that considers the potential relevance to and impact on the conflict. Equally, if neglected or pursued in a way that is insensitive to the conflict dynamics, each of these can generate mistrust and resentment.

The core concern of any business is generating wealth. Therefore, shared economic activity across real or potential conflict lines is a crucial contribution the private sector can make. It serves to promote reconciliation and creates a sense of mutual dependency and, crucially, much-needed jobs. The U.S. corporation Peaceworks, for example, has worked since 1994 to establish joint business ventures across the conflict line between Arabs and Israelis, to source gourmet food and other goods for its diverse range of products. This joint business model has since been applied in other conflict contexts, such as Guatemala and Mexico.

On the road to creating wealth, any business should take a good hard look at its own conduct. In recent years, a whole body of literature and practice has evolved around what is known as corporate social responsibility (CSR). While the CSR debate remains a predominantly Northern preoccupation, its importance for countries experiencing violent conflict may be significant. Sound internal policies and standards are key for a sustainable peacebuilding role for businesses. The reasons for this are threefold. First, it is problematic to try to engage business in something as sensitive as peacebuilding if some of the fundamentals of socially responsible business are neglected; second, many of the tenets of responsible business can in themselves support peacebuilding, for example, through addressing corruption or embedding fair employment practices in countries where nepotism and discrimination may be factors in the conflict; and third, commitment to CSR principles may help to change negative perceptions of business as part of the problem. This is a crucial element if other stakeholders are to trust businesses' peacebuilding efforts.

A critical aspect of a company's CSR is its employment policies: a business that deliberately or unintentionally discriminates against one group or another is feeding and perpetuating hostilities. Conversely, an active policy of recruiting from disadvantaged groups and providing the requisite training may, in a small but significant way, contribute to peace. In some contexts, the workplace is the only sphere where divided communities actually meet. This offers tremendous opportunities for reconciliation: in Northern Ireland, for instance, the nongovernmental organization Counteract provides training, advisory, and research services to develop practical ways to develop more neutral and diverse cultures in the workplace.

The key point here is to highlight that peacebuilding need not be purely "political" but can fall directly within the mandate and core competencies of the private sector. All of the examples above illustrate that companies have the capacity to contribute while remaining firmly within their own sphere of control.

Social Investment

Beyond core business activities, many companies are in a position to provide funds to address deep-rooted socioeconomic challenges such as poverty and lack of education. Although this should not be seen as the sum of the private sector's role, it can be important. While the private sector may make useful contributions to some development issues, from a peacebuilding perspective, it has to be assessed whether such interventions address rather than exacerbate root conflict causes. There is much that the private sector can do to support education and health programs, local enterprise development, etc., but these should be targeted in ways that focus on groups or issues particularly pertinent to the conflict itself and utilize the added value of the private sector. In the Philippines, the Philippine Business for Social Progress works to address structural conflict causes such as underdevelopment and lack of employment. In South Africa, the National Business Initiative's Business Trust, managed jointly by business and government representatives, channels funds toward pressing social needs that still divide South African society—for example, job creation and schooling.

Beyond financial resources, the private sector is a repository of skills and experience that lend themselves directly to addressing some of the structural deficiencies within society. In other words, companies have tremendous human resources that can support the capacity building and professionalization of nongovernmental organizations (NGOs) and public institutions.

Policy Dialogue

Policy dialogue and peace advocacy are other areas of possible engagement. This builds on the capacity of the private sector to influence others, which may be harnessed for useful ends. Although policy advocacy is an area most businesses would shy away from, there are many opportunities for utilizing this strength of the business community: no other sector has such expertise in publicity and media campaigns, for instance. In Sri Lanka, this potential was used by Sri Lanka First, and directed toward mobilizing society in demanding a peaceful end to the conflict. In 1994, the Confederation of British Industry in Northern Ireland widely publicized a "peace dividend paper" that spelled out the economic costs of conflict, and projected the economic and social benefits of peace, in terms of freeing up public money for the provision of social services. It generated much discussion, and other stakeholders adopted the term "peace dividend."

Some businesses have even engaged as brokers between conflicting sides, similar to traditional conflict resolution: in South Africa, the business community engaged in a lengthy and patient period of relationship building with both sides of the conflict, enabling it to play a key role in providing technical, logistical, and administrative support to the peace process, an often underestimated need that speaks directly to the skills and resources of many companies. Also, the business-sponsored British Angola Forum has played a significant role in bringing together all sides in the Angolan conflict in an informal setting. Today, the forum continues its work in getting all stakeholders in Angola's future to work toward a more equitable distribution of the country's enormous wealth.

Regional and Grassroots Business Actors

Many of the recommendations above are also relevant for regional and grassroots business actors, although these actors are more likely to struggle against the day-to-day challenges of doing business in the midst of a conflict, which provides them with a different set of challenges and opportunities. They are perhaps more committed to restoring peace (and so more inclined to work together), more in touch with the suffering of the wider population (and therefore more aware of their needs), and closer to those actually doing the fighting (more exposed to the dangers but also better placed to make a difference on the ground).

In Sri Lanka, for example, the Business for Peace Alliance is the only body bringing together representatives from regional chambers of commerce of all provinces, both Tamil and Sinhalese. The group fosters island-wide business-to-business relationships and reconciliation, seeks to generate peace dividends at the local level, and advocates for greater regional involvement in the peace process.

Likewise, grassroots actors such as market traders are often in a good position to mediate community-level disputes. Indeed, business leaders in small towns or villages can be de facto community leaders respected by all parties. During violent conflict, continued interaction between grassroots actors in the economic sphere may be the only lines of communication left open between two sides.

Sadakhlo, an unofficial outdoors market in the South Caucasus, situated on Georgian territory bordering both Azerbaijan and Armenia, is one example: Armenians and Azeris have been trading on the market since the early 1990s, despite the official economic blockade between the two countries. The market on third-country territory provides a "safe space" for ethnic Azeris and Armenians to meet and exchange, and where the topic of politics is carefully avoided.[4]

It should also be stressed that the knowledge and experience of business leaders at these levels can be a valuable resource when it comes to designing economic development plans for the country. Misguided ideas imposed from a central government that fail to acknowledge or address real needs can be themselves a source of conflict and certainly a trigger for a return to conflict, highlighting the need for the participation of businesses of all types. It is well understood among development actors that local ownership is key to making development work. Businesses can not only support this but also facilitate it based on the same principle noted earlier, namely, convening power and (potentially) relative impartiality.

Identifying Partners

Although rarely seen as such, the private sector is a part of civil society and needs to act in concert with other sectors, such as local and international NGOs and others, in order to lend its interventions credibility and a wider mandate, and to strengthen both its specific impact and the collective impact of any wider peace movement. For this to happen, the private sector needs to engage in proper consultation and relationship building, to identify its niche, provide support to the initiatives of others, and perhaps most importantly, to develop the trust necessary to making a positive contribution.

The international community represents both a potential partner and a valuable supporter of business and peace initiatives. Bi- and multilateral donors and international NGOs are usually the main source of support to countries in conflict and have peacebuilding agendas of their own. International actors can be instrumental in galvanizing and encouraging a peacebuilding role for the private sector. To date, however, they have been slow to recognize the private sector's potential, focusing almost exclusively on business as an agent of economic development rather than peacebuilding. Moreover, the international community has to be aware of the negative impacts of its own engagement with the local private sector, even though attempts to address conflict have taken place. For example, the international pressure to get Western governments and companies to completely disengage from the coltan trade with the DRC, while seeking to minimize the negative impact of mineral extraction, overlooks the many livelihoods in the DRC that depend on it informally and would be imperiled by a complete truncation of the trade. An approach that is more accommodating to local needs and the local conflict context is required in such cases.

Equally, the view that private-sector development is good for economic growth, poverty reduction, and therefore by implication in the longer-term for peace, has to be assessed critically from a conflict transformation perspective. It needs to be considered who benefits from such economic development assistance, who loses out, and how these impacts can exacerbate tensions. While "conflict sensitivity" is becoming more and more integrated into mainstream development assistance, it has not yet made its way into interventions promoting private-sector development. This is an area that requires more research and awareness-raising.

Conclusion

Over the last fifteen years, the shift in the geopolitical environment that has seen a clear change in the nature of contemporary conflicts, away from interstate wars to almost exclusively internal conflicts (although with regional and international repercussions), has been accompanied by a parallel shift in attitudes and approaches to conflict resolution and peacebuilding. What was once seen as the preserve of states and multilateral bodies such as the United Nations is now seen as a multifaceted process that attempts to draw in a broad range of sectors, groups, and individuals from the grassroots to the highest levels. Surprisingly, however, this process has yet to include in any systematic or consistent way the role of local private sectors, despite the clear examples, some of which are illustrated in this chapter, of the valuable role that the private sector can play.

This gap in peacebuilding theory and practice may partly stem from the traditional reluctance of the private sector itself, partly from the greater focus on multinational companies, partly from the historically troubled relationship between NGOs and the private sector, and partly also from the perceptions of the private sector as being more often a negative rather than positive influence on conflict. This last point is particularly understandable but, as this chapter has tried to show, it is not only a good reason in itself for attempting to define and encourage a greater peacebuilding role for the private sector, but is also a one-dimensional view.

Clearly the negative should not be ignored, but neither should it serve to mask the positive. In drawing together the lessons from past experience, it is possible to identify a set of basic principles that provide a framework for those, whether within or outside of business, who are trying to identify and promote the private sector's engagement in peacebuilding:

- Leadership—identifying individuals willing and able to galvanize others
- Analysis—both from within the private sector itself of its role in the conflict dynamics and from outside to understand the different interests, capacities, and resources
- Trust/Relationships—as much as possible with all sectors and parties; fundamental to promoting the credibility to intervene and the impartiality to be most effective
- Adaptability/Flexibility—ability to adjust according to changing circumstances
- Added Value—identifying and utilizing the particular skills, expertise, resources, and leverage of the private sector
- Long-Term Commitment—acknowledging the importance of a sustained engagement

---

Canan Gündüz is currently policy project officer for International Alert's Business and Conflict program with particular responsibility for developing research into the role of local business in peacebuilding. Gündüz has a Master of Science in development studies from the London School of Economics and previously worked for the UN Office for the Coordination of Humanitarian Affairs and the UK Department for International Development's Conflict and Humanitarian Affairs Department.

Nick Killick is the manager of International Alert's Business and Conflict program. Killick has been working on business and conflict issues, including both the role of multinational companies and local business, for over five years. He has researched and developed projects focused on promoting a peacebuilding role for the private sector in the South Caucasus, Sri Lanka, Nepal, Burundi, and the Gulf of Guinea.

Notes

1. Adapted from John Paul Lederach, *Building Peace: Sustainable Reconciliation in Divided Societies* (Washington, DC: U.S. Institute of Peace Press, 1997).

2. For more detailed case studies, see " The Role of Local Business in Peacebuilding" in the *Berghof Handbook for Conflict* Online at: http://www.berghof-handbook.net.

3. Building on its fieldwork with local business actors in Sri Lanka and Nepal, International Alert has just begun a large comparative research project seeking to deepen understanding of this important new area of peacebuilding.

4. For more information, see International Alert and Economy and Conflict Research Group of the South Caucasus, *From War Economies to Peace Economies in the South Caucasus* (London: International Alert, 2004).

Resources

Lead Organizations

Center for Business Diplomacy—
  Switzerland
For contact, please visit website:
  http://www.bizdiplomacy.org

Collaborative for Development Agency—
  United States
Corporate Engagement Project
E-mail: cda@cdainc.com
Website: http://www.cdainc.com

Institute for Multi-Track Diplomacy—
  United States
Business and Peacebuilding Initiative
E-mail: imtd@imtd.org
Website: http://www.imtd.org

International Alert—United Kingdom
Business and Conflict Programme
E-mail: general@international-alert.org
Website: http://www.international-
  alert.org/policy/business.htm

Prince of Wales International Business
  Leaders Forum—United Kingdom
Business and Peace Programme
E-mail: info@iblf.org
Website: http://www.iblf.org

Website
The Business and Human Rights Resource Center: http://www.business-humanrights.org

Publications

Amnesty International and Pax Christi International. *Multinational Enterprises and Human Rights.* London: Pax Christi, 1998.

Amnesty International and the Prince of Wales Business Leaders Forum. *Human Rights: Is It Any of Your Business?* London: Prince of Wales Business Leaders Forum, 2000.

Anderson, Mary B., and Luc Zandvliet. "Corporate Options for Breaking Cycles of Conflict." The Collaborative for Development Action, Inc., May 2001. Online at: http://www.cdainc.com/cep/archives/2004/02/CorporateOptions.php.

Bailes, Alyson J. K., and Isabel Frommelt. *Business and Security: Public-Private Sector Relationships in a New Security Environment.* Stockholm International Peace Research Institute. New York: Oxford University Press, 2004.

Banfield, Jessica, Damian Lilly, and Virginia Haufler. *Transnational Corporations in Conflict-Prone Zones: Public Policy Responses and a Framework for Action.* London: International Alert—Business and Conflict Programme, 2003.

Bannon, Ian, and Paul Collier. *Natural Resources and Violent Conflict: Options and Actions.* Washington, DC: World Bank, 2003.

Bennett, J. *The Role of the Private Sector in Zones of Conflict: Conflict Prevention and Revenue-Sharing Regimes.* New York: UN Global Compact, 2002.

Berdal, M., and D. M. Malone, eds. *Greed and Grievance. Economic Agenda's in Civil Wars.* Boulder, CO: Lynne Rienner Publishers, 2000.

De La Rosa, R., M. Stanvovitch, et al. *Breaking the Links Between Economics and Violence in Mindanao.* London: International Alert, 2003.

Haufler, Virginia, ed. *The Role of the Private Sector in Zones Of Conflict: Case Studies of Multi-Stakeholder Partnerships.* New York: UN Global Compact, 2002.

International Alert. "Promoting a Conflict Prevention Approach to OECD Companies and Partnering with Local Business." OECD/DAC Conflict, Peace and Development Co-operation Network Briefing Paper, March 2004.

Killick, Nick, V. S. Srikantha, and C. Gündüz. "Business and Peace: The Role of Local Companies." Berghof Research Center for Constructive Conflict Management, 2005. Online at: http://www.berghof-handbook.net.

Nelson, Jane. *The Business of Peace: The Private Sector as a Partners in Conflict Prevention and Resolution.* London: IA, PWBLF and Council on Economic Priorities, 2000.

Prince of Wales Business Leaders Forum. *Conflict Prevention and Post-Conflict Reconstruction: Observations on the Role of Business.* London: Prince of Wales Business Leaders Forum, 1998.

UN Global Compact. *The Role of Private Sector in Zones of Conflict: A Business Guide to Conflict Impact Assessment and Risk Management.* New York: UN Global Compact, 2002.

Wenger, A., and D. Möckli. *Conflict Prevention: The Untapped Potential of the Business Sector.* Boulder, CO: Lynne Rienner Publishers, 2003.

13.1

Brokering Peace and Building the Nation: The National Business Initiative in South Africa

André Fourie

Ending apartheid and establishing a multiracial democracy in South Africa was a difficult and often violent process. One difficulty throughout the process was to find "honest brokers" to keep the process moving forward and retain the confidence of all major actors. An association of progressive South African business leaders played such a role. Its successor organization focuses on promoting sustainable development.

Tens of thousands of people turned up at the Union Building amphitheater in Pretoria, South Africa, on 27 April 2004 to join visiting African leaders, former president Nelson Mandela, and other dignitaries, for the inauguration of President Thabo Mbeki to a second term in office.

The occasion also marked Freedom Day—ten years since white minority rule ended. President Mbeki captured the mood evoked by the commemoration of this day in a speech highlighting both past achievements and difficulties, and daunting current challenges. He said: "Endemic and widespread poverty continues to disfigure the face of our country. It will always be impossible for us to say that we have fully restored the dignity of all our people as long as this situation persists."

For business leaders who helped foster the climate that made possible a peaceful transition from apartheid to democracy, such words echoed their own concerns. In the 1980s and 1990s, working through the Consultative Business Movement (CBM), progressive businessmen used their neutral status to work as mediators.

Now they have a new body and a different purpose. Through the National Business Initiative (NBI), set up in March 1995, the business community is engaged in programs to create jobs and develop skills to enhance political and economic stability.

An Unlikely Coalition

In the spring of 1991, a year after the African National Conference (ANC) had been "unbanned" by South Africa's white minority government, a mood of pessimism prevailed in South Africa. The government and the ANC had been talking for a year, and had reached some bilateral agreements, but negotiations on substantive issues to end apartheid had stalled. Worse yet, President F. W. de Klerk's failure to consult with the ANC before issuing a call to hold a peace conference had so angered the ANC that it was considering to boycott it. The entire process was threatening to end in a downward spiral of mistrust, chaos, and violence. What saved the process at the time, and helped to restore the trust that was needed to bring a peaceful transition to multiracial government, was a timely intervention by an unlikely coalition between the South African Council of Churches, which had often acted as a peace broker, and CBM, the organization of progressive South African business leaders. This organization had cautiously begun to consult with political leaders on all sides during the 1980s, and in so doing it had developed both the relationships and the credibility to play a vital role in the coming transformation process.

The Business Case for Peace

In South Africa, businesses came first to understand that they themselves could benefit by helping to bring peace and a stable environment, and later on they began to see, in concrete terms, the benefits accruing first from an end to violence and, in the longer term, from democratization and socioeconomic development. In particular, business benefited immediately by avoiding the added costs of conflict, including damage to the corporate reputation, security costs, an unstable environment, a premium required on investment returns, and the opportunity cost of uncertainty, litigation, insurance premiums, and the impact on its employees.

It should be noted that the power of multinationals to influence local groupings and governments is often overestimated by outsiders and the risk of being seen to interfere or to take sides is very real. Few companies are keen to raise their profiles at the risk of being targeted. The South African case demonstrates that it is often more effective for businesses to participate collectively to promote dialogue and institution building. Working in partnership with government institutions and other stakeholders, business coalitions can play a role in addressing some of the structural issues underpinning conflict without raising suspicions that a particular company may be aiming to gain individual advantage.

A South African Case Study

Major corporations in South Africa have a long history of social engagement. The negative domestic impact of the apartheid system on the socioeconomic and business environment and the international isolation of South Africa demanded a unique response from the South African business community. Accordingly, the private sector has undertaken initiatives to address such matters as housing, education, training, the political transition process, the 1994 electoral process, crime prevention, local economic development, and effective local governance. The business sector has played a remarkable role in support of the democratization process; it forged relations with the banned liberation movements in the late 1980s, took the initiative to stimulate debate on democratization and economic growth, confronted violence, helped launch the peace process, facilitated an inclusive democratic election, supported the electoral process, and acted as secretariat to the constitutional negotiation process.

A Focus on Peace

During the violent 1980s, a handful of executives initiated dialogue with South African liberation movement leaders who were, at the time, still "banned." These relationships took on added importance during the early years after the ANC and other organizations were unbanned. This was a particularly violent period, leading eventually to the recognition by nearly all the actors in the conflict of the need for a national peace conference. However, the power dynamics between the National Party (NP) government and ANC threatened to derail such a peace process. When the government did convene a national peace conference and invited all political leaders to participate, the ANC and its partners opposed the plan, on the grounds that the government was an integral part of violence.

That is when CBM and the South African Council of Churches stepped into the breach, facilitating a process that would lead to an inclusive peace conference. Discussions were held at the headquarters of Barlow Rand, Ltd., one of the largest industrial conglomerates in the country, and were cochaired by John Hall, chair of the Chamber of Commerce, and Archbishop Desmond Tutu. This was the start of a long process during which business leaders played an active (but by no means exclusive) part in working with political parties, women's groups, religious groupings, nongovernmental organizations, labor unions, and other interested parties.

In September 1991, the principal peace conference participants signed a national peace accord. The peace process eventually involved hundreds of local peace committees across the country. Most of these structures involved local business players to some extent. The accord was based on three interrelated elements.

The National Peace Committee was set up to monitor the implementation of the accord and compliance by political organizations and parties with the accord's code of conduct. The committee was charged with the responsibility of resolving disputes concerning compliance with the terms of the accord.

The National Peace Secretariat was established to coordinate regional and local dispute resolution committees. The peace committees were representative of local communities they served. Representatives of political parties, churches, trade unions, industry and commerce, as well as local and tribal authorities, served on the committees. Importantly, representatives of the police and defense force also served on the local committees.

The peace structures developed a distinctive blue badge with a white dove, which came to symbolize the entire peace movement. Thousands of ordinary citizens from all walks of life participated in local peace structures as peace monitors. In many cases these structures were better able than were security forces to maintain law and order and prevent violence. To a large extent, this was the result of the broad legitimacy and inclusive nature of the peace structures, at a time when the power and composition of the security forces were still being contested at political levels.

The Commission of Enquiry was established as a high-level judicial instrument to inquire into the phenomenon of public violence, as well as the specific nature and causes of violence. It was chaired by Judge Richard Goldstone and became a very effective instrument for investigating the involvement of state agencies, security forces, and the military wings of political organizations.

From Peace to Constitution Making

During the much acclaimed process of developing a new, inclusive, and democratic South African constitution, the nation's private sector played an important role that was not widely reported outside of South Africa. CBM's involvement at earlier stages in the peace process had given this business-based organization credibility across the political spectrum, and progressive business leaders within CBM had been working together to transform the country's political economy. CBM was asked to use its consultative network and credibility to facilitate multilateral national forums where development actors could meet and discuss the nation's future. This included high-profile national events such as a National Development Workshop, the National Housing Forum, and the National Land Workshop. At the local level, the private sector actively participated and facilitated education and community development trusts, hostel initiatives, peace forums, electrification initiatives, training projects, and rural development initiatives.

Following the signing of the peace accord, with the endorsement of both the NP and ANC, CBM was asked to manage administrative and organizational facets of the multiparty constitutional negotiations. As a credible, professional, nonpartisan organization, CBM had the credibility to take on these responsibilities, in effect depoliticizing the management of discussions that were bound to be politically charged in so many other ways. The CBM thus provided process and facilitation support to the Convention for a Democratic South Africa (CODESA). In mid-1992, during the second round of these negotiations, CODESA 2, political violence led to a deadlock between the major political parties. CBM leadership was instrumental in maintaining contact with all political parties, and facilitated debate at a time when the major political forces had broken off nearly all contacts with each other.

Eventually, the ANC and NP government signed a "Record of Understanding" and a new negotiation process started in March 1993, known as the Multi-Party Negotiation Process. This time, CBM was asked to assume full administrative responsibility for the process. It also convened an international and local expert group on regionalism for a three-week workshop process.

This resulted in a report, *Constitutional Options and Their Implications for Good Governance and a Sound Economy,* which played a major role in guiding discussions and reaching consensus on language in the interim constitution addressing power structures at the regional level.

Business in the New South Africa

Following the country's first democratic election in 1994, after consultations with business, government, community, and labor leaders, and with the encouragement of President Nelson Mandela, CBM was merged into a new organization, the NBI, which also absorbed the Urban Foundation. The NBI was viewed as a way to involve business in the government's Reconstruction and Development Program. The initial focus was on the role of business in growth, development, and democracy, with attention directed, for instance, toward economic growth and development including housing, tourism, and small, micro, and medium enterprise development, education and training, effective governance (including assistance with the local government elections), and building relations between business and the new South African government.

Focus on Sustainable Development

Today, the NBI is a voluntary coalition of 150 leading South African corporations, focused on building prosperity. Major corporations such as Anglo American, Standard Bank, and South African Breweries all play leadership roles in helping to rebuild South Africa's economy and society. The NBI vision is of South Africa as a stable democracy in which a market economy functions for the benefit of all. The organization aims to enhance the private sector's contribution to sustainable growth and development in South Africa. A primary objective is to mobilize business leadership and resources in promoting sustainable development. The NBI believes sustainable development in South Africa is built on the key pillars of economic growth, social development, ecological balance, and democratic consolidation.

To give an idea of its activities, here are some recent NBI contributions. The organization supported more than six thousand schools and more than one million students through its Educational Quality Improvement Partnerships Program, and its school-based Travel and Tourism Program. The Enter-Prize entrepreneurship support program has supported the direct creation of more than one thousand job opportunities and reached more than twenty-five hundred aspiring entrepreneurs through formal training and mentoring programs. The Public-Private Partnership's capacity-building program has reached more than one thousand municipal councilors and officials as well as over two hundred national and provincial officials. The Nkwe microfinance initiative has shown that it is possible to develop relevant responses to the challenging conditions in this sector. The Colleges Collaboration Fund finally played a critical role in restructuring the Further Education and Training college landscape.

Conclusion

In view of the success of the "new" South Africa, it can be safely claimed that the interventions and activities of CBM provide clear evidence that business not only can make important contributions to peacebuilding, but that in spite of the apparent risks, business can itself be an important beneficiary of such interventions. Helping to stabilize unstable communities is, of course, of vital importance in the short term, but it is important to keep in mind that long-term peace is more than the absence of conflict. The private sector needs, therefore, to consider the longer-term development parameters and to engage, as has occurred in South Africa, with stakeholders to determine how large and small corporations can most effectively contribute on an ongoing basis to development, prosperity, and security.

Among the areas where business can have a positive impact on sustainable development are education, community development, environmental protection, energy efficiency, and capacity building. However, it is important to ensure that as business takes on added responsibilities in the social arena, it does not lose sight of primary functions in society, namely producing goods and services, providing employment, and developing human resources.

André Fourie is the chief executive officer of the National Business Initiative in South Africa.

Contact

NBI—National Office
13th Floor, Metal Box Centre
25 Owl Street, Auckland Park 2092
P.O. Box 294, Auckland Park 2006
Johannesburg, South Africa
Tel: +27 (001) 482 5100
Fax: +27 (001) 482 5507/8
E-mail: info@nbi.org.za
Website: http://www.nbi.org.za

Selected Bibliography

European Centre for Conflict Prevention (ECCP). 1999. *People Building Peace: 35 Inspiring Stories from Around the World* (Utrecht, Netherlands: ECCP).
Mathews, Dylan. 2001. *War Prevention Works: 50 Stories of People Resolving Conflict* (Oxford: Oxford Research Group).

13.2

A Profitable Peace:
The Confederation of British Industry
in Northern Ireland

The sectarian conflict that ravaged Northern Ireland for three decades stifled its economic growth. When peace efforts gathered pace in the 1990s, the picture changed—offering vindication for business leaders who stressed the link between political instability and economic stagnation.

Summers in Northern Ireland are normally associated with marches and parades, which turn into flashpoints for sectarian violence. When the "marching season" of 2003 (and later also 2004) passed without major incidents, the sense of relief was palpable. The Northern Ireland branch of the Confederation of British Industry (CBI) was among those welcoming the development. It noted, in a background paper, that elimination of sectarianism was key to achieving a more favorable environment for doing business in Northern Ireland:

> The events which took place every summer since 1996—although largely absent in 2003—in relation to parades and marches, have been extremely damaging to many aspects of the local economy, including an increase in sectarianism and community polarisation, delaying the transition to a stable society which the community wishes to see, and which is essential if Northern Ireland is to achieve the competitiveness essential for success in the global economy (CBI Northern Ireland 2003:2).

These words had a familiar ring—echoing the tone of language used by business leaders in the territory from the moment of their initial involvement in efforts to end the sectarian conflict. In *Peace—A Challenging New Era*, a landmark document published in 1994 that became widely known as *The Peace Dividend Paper*, CBI Northern Ireland argued that loss of life, property destruction, and high security costs were directly related to lack of investment and economic decay.

327

Peace Dividend

The CBI, which has 250,000 members across the United Kingdom (U.K.), was generally seen as a nonpolitical private-sector actor in Northern Ireland. It played the double role of think tank and political lobbying group, building bridges of understanding between rival groups. *The Peace Dividend Paper* became a reference point for the peace process. It thrust a business perspective onto the agenda, articulating the case that an end to violence would burnish the image of the territory and make it more attractive to investors. The document suggested that savings from security costs be reinvested in education and infrastructure to further boost the economy. The choice, starkly placed, was this: Northern Ireland could have "peace, progress and prosperity" or remain an irredeemable trouble spot.

The media and politicians soon picked up the term "peace dividend" and it became a reference to the business point of view on peace, and with that it gave new momentum to the peace process. More so, with the cease-fire later that year and the following economic improvements, the rationale of the CBI gained practical legitimacy. Within a year, tourism arrivals increased by 20 percent. Unemployment fell to the lowest level in fourteen years. Thirty million pounds sterling in new investment ventures flowed in.

In 1996 CBI joined with other trade and business organizations in an association called the G7. As they stood for the collective voice of many Northern Irish economic interests, they gained considerable authority. Among other things, they organized several meetings in Belfast, inviting all nine political parties. It further played an important role on occasion in mediation and media awareness campaigning. In June 1998 CBI assisted in arranging the visit to Northern Ireland of a delegation of business leaders led by U.S. Secretary of Commerce William Daley. The visit symbolized the support for the peace process by facilitating business relations between Northern Ireland and the rest of the world.

In the same year, the CBI, under the auspices of the Community Relations Council, joined with other business organizations to publish a set of antisectarian guidelines for employers and management. Instead of emphasizing the complications, they stressed the positive outcomes of diversity.

Then the Good Friday Agreement (also known as the Belfast Agreement) was signed by unionist and nationalist political parties. This landmark accord was seen as providing a framework for future stability—and almost certainly helped to sustain the economic improvement that continued throughout the 1990s.

During the "Troubles," Northern Ireland had the worst rate of unemployment in the United Kingdom. In 1986, more than 123,000 people—a record 17.2 percent—were out of work. By 2001, as a fragile peace took hold, this level fell dramatically, to 6.2 percent, and stood at 5.2 percent in early 2004.

The decline in unemployment was coupled with other signs of economic growth. During the 1990s, Northern Ireland had one of the best economic performances of any region in the U.K. Official figures showed a rise in inward investment, particularly in the information technology and service sectors.

These investments originated from both the U.K. and North America. They benefited call centers, the financial services sector, and engineering firms. In surveys carried out by the CBI, business confidence was at a high.

The picture was not all rosy. For example, although factory output rose by almost 3 percent in 2003—in contrast to the rest of the U.K., where it was virtually static—traditional big employers in the region's food and textiles industries struggled to compete in international markets.

At Risk

Nonetheless, the improvement in the overall economic picture was clear. Of overriding concern was whether this peace—however fragile—was durable. Lurking in the back of everyone's mind was the danger of renewed conflict, which meant more political uncertainty, and reduced investment flows.

As Geoff McEnroe, director of the IBEC/CBI Joint Business Council, which was set up to run a North-South trade and business development program, noted: "Political uncertainty makes inward investors think twice. They either take Northern Ireland out of their thinking frame or delay investment; or their shareholders say: why should you invest in a country where there is not the stability you would expect?"

Also at risk was the money pumped into Northern Ireland by the European Union (EU) to support groups and organizations involved in peace and reconciliation. With the expansion of the EU, these amounts could be substantially reduced or dry up, as priorities change in Brussels.

Democratic Dialogue, a think tank based in Belfast, said continued EU funding was critical for Northern Ireland to become "a normal civil society, enjoying economic prosperity, social inclusion and—above all—political stability, including in its relationship with the rest of the island. The always over-committed nature of public-expenditure planning, not to mention the expectation that Northern Ireland can expect a colder public spending climate in the years to come, means support from EU structural funds is of critical value to the necessary policy of innovation and learning" (Wilson 2000).

Nigel Smyth, director of CBI Northern Ireland said, "The big issue is uncertainty in terms of the political situation." He said the institutions set up under the Good Friday Agreement were working and were in the best interest of business and the community as a whole. "Our real issue is an image problem. There isn't sufficient appreciation of the peace dividend" (Ryan 2001).

Recent Developments

In recent years, the CBI itself has not undertaken any new initiatives on the peace and reconciliation front. The emphasis of civil society has shifted—toward efforts to ensure peace endures. Under the peace accords, new democratic political structures were erected, and a peace and reconciliation infrastructure was put in place as well. Many of the bodies established for this purpose—such as the Human Rights Commission, the Equality Commission, and the Civic Forum—have membership from a wide cross section of the community.

These institutions have as their primary aim the building of bridges of understanding across sectarian fault lines. The Civic Forum, for example, a body set up under the Good Friday Agreement, maintains contact between civil society and politicians. Counteract, established by the umbrella Irish Congress of Trade Unions, helps eliminate sectarian harassment within the workplace and community. It has set as its task ensuring no one suffers unfair treatment because of religious belief or political opinion. The Community Relations Council uses funds from the EU and the government to help community projects that involve bringing people from different traditions to develop relationships of trust and understanding—and the confidence to address issues of difference between them.

In the background paper issued after the 2003 marching season, the CBI stressed the role of business in finding solutions to the problems of improving community relations and promoting social inclusion. One of the points it

---

The Business of Peace

What is the role of private business in an area of violent conflict? Jane Nelson, author of *The Business of Peace,* argues that because most businesses do not benefit from conflict, they should get involved in prevention:

> Conflict is almost always an impediment rather than a spur to private-sector investment and economic growth. With the exception of the 3–4 percent of world trade generated by the arms industry, certain illegal commercial activities, and situations where business gains directly from being part of war economies, few industries benefit from violent conflict. (Nelson 2000: 20)

In fact, notes Nelson, conflict disrupts business, interferes with normal business affairs, and inhibits open and free markets.

Her book—published in 2000 by the Prince of Wales Business Leaders Forum in London—presents a business case for engagement in conflict prevention. It analyzes the cost and benefit factors involved, and makes a case for private corporate engagement in prevention of violent societal conflict.

More than 70 of the 190 independent states in the world are classified as being of medium or high security risk for businesses operating internationally. The changing nature of conflict, and rapid globalization of the world economy in the last decade, have combined to make the private sector an important actor in many societies affected by conflict. Nelson, and others, argue, that by working with other sectors, business can make an important contribution to structural stability. This means going beyond risk assessment and reputation management.

made would seem self-evident elsewhere; in the context of Northern Ireland's "Troubles," it had a special resonance—and made a clear case for the peace dividend. This was that employers in the region were interested in attracting the widest range of people with the best abilities to work in their businesses. "An increasing number of employers are also recognising the business benefits of having a diverse workforce" (CBI Northern Ireland 2003: 3).

Given the depth of animosity that has always existed between the different factions, it is unlikely that political tension will completely disappear in the short term. There is, though, general consensus that even a fragile peace is better than open conflict—and more likely to foster economic prosperity.

Contacts

CBI Northern Ireland
Scottish Amicable Building
11 Donegal Square South
Belfast, BT1 5JE
Tel: +44 28 9032 6658
Fax: +44 28 9024 5915
Website: http://www.cbi.org.uk/
    northernireland

Community Relations Council
6 Murray Street
Belfast BT1 6DN
Tel: +44 28 90 227 500

Fax: +44 28 90 227 551
E-mail: info@community-relations.org.uk
Website: http://www.community-
    relations.org.uk/community-
    relations

Counteract
123 York Street
Belfast BT15 1AB
Tel: +44 28 9023 7023
Fax: +44 28 9031 3585
E-mail: counteract@btconnect.com
Website: http://www.counteract.org

Selected Bibliography

"CBI Response to 'A Shared Future—A Consultation Paper on Improving Relations in Northern Ireland' " (Belfast, Northern Ireland: CBI Northern Ireland, September 2003. Online at: http://www.asharedfuture.gov.uk/pdf_docuemnts/cbi.pdf.

Nelson, Jane. 2000. *The Business of Peace: The Private Sector as a Partner in Conflict Prevention and Resolution* (London: International Alert, Council on Economic Priorities, and Prince of Wales Business Leaders Forum).

Ryan, Orla. 2001. "Northern Ireland's Economic Fears," (BBC News Online, 22 June). Online at: http://news.bbc.co.uk/1/hi/business/1402261.stm.

"Striking a Balance: The Northern Ireland Peace Process." 1999. Conciliation Resources, *Accord* magazine series. Issue editor: Clem McCartney. Online at: http://www.c-r.org/accord/ireland/accord8/index.shtml.

Wilson, Robin. 2000. "Structurally Unsound: Northern Ireland Bids for Further EU Monies" (Belfast, Northern Ireland: Democratic Dialogue). Online at: http://cain.ulst.ac.uk/dd/papers/unsound.htm

13.3

Planting Peace:
Philippine Business for Social Progress

Ruth G. Honculada

Enlightened self-interest of business and the human quest for peace and stability can go hand in hand, a concrete example from the Philippine island of Mindanao has shown. A local businessman convinced foreign investors to inject capital into a new banana-producing company, which has lured young men out of the ranks of a rebel group.

Upon seeing the bustling lively town of Paglas in Maguindanao, located in the southern region of Mindanao, Philippines, it is hard to imagine that this peaceful community of Christians, Muslims, and Lumads (an indigenous people in the region) was once a virtual "no-man's-land." Rife with bitter interethnic differences, high crime rates, and extreme poverty, it took a maverick leader like Datu Paglas, president and chief executive director of Paglas Corporation, to show the way toward building lasting peace. Because of his inspiring journey, more companies are now realizing that the business of peace pays good dividends.

Datu Paglas, who originates from an old and respected Mindanao family, managed to establish a banana plantation, the first of its scale on the poverty-stricken island. In the years since its inception in 1998, the plantation has changed the lives of many people. It created jobs. It also generated additional economic activities. One of the major characteristics of the new banana business is that it has helped to reduce the gap between Christians and Muslims, the two groups that for decades have been seen as rivals, creating animosity that has been perceived to be one of the factors behind the armed conflict on Mindanao.

Datu Paglas's initiative triggered the interest of the Philippine Business for Social Progress (PBSP), a foundation set up in the early 1970s by Philippine corporations to help poor communities help themselves. PBSP grew out to become the country's largest business-led foundation supporting social development. Its role is unique in Asia. The apparent success of Datu Paglas's company to overcome differences between Christians and Muslims, and to reduce poverty in Mindanao, reportedly was one of the reasons why PBSP

A Hotbed for Rebel Recruitment

Like many of its neighboring towns, Paglas was once a hotbed for the recruitment of rebels. Many, usually unemployed young men, were drawn into the Moro Islamic Liberation Front (MILF). To understand the story of this town, one must see it in the context of the Mindanao conflict in the southern part of the Philippines. Since Spanish and U.S. domination, the Philippines have evolved into a predominantly Catholic country that has its center of gravity in the north and middle of the country. The political and economic strongholds over the past century were traditionally centered in Luzon, the northern region where the capital of Manila is located, and Visayas, the predominantly Christian central region of the country. Mindanao, the huge island in the south, inhabited by Muslims and the indigenous Lumads, is considered to be a neglected area.

Muslim rebels took up arms against the central government in the 1970s. Most rebels operated as MILF fighters. Some analysts attribute the conflict in Mindanao to the nonintegration of Muslims and the Lumads into the national mainstream because of Christian prejudices against Muslims, the government's neglect for their welfare, and the Muslims' firm insistence on self-rule. Others trace it to deep-rooted injustice, as indigenous people over the years found their ancestral land taken over by immigrants.

Fighting between government troops and the MILF, as well as the Abu Sayyaf, another small armed group, escalated in the late 1990s. The government's all-out war against the MILF in the late 1990s, which flared up after a failed peace agreement and a hostage crises that ended in a bloody rescue attempt by the government, slowed the momentum for peace efforts. Beyond the conflict lies the deeper problem of lack of socioeconomic development in the Muslim-dominated provinces. Mindanao has the highest poverty incidence of the Philippines, while the region where Datu Paglas's company is located, is even poorer. The poverty incidence of this autonomous region was 62.9 percent, meaning that more than half of its population was living below the poverty line.

The irony is that, although Mindanao is considered to be a neglected area, harassed by conflict, the island is rich in resources and possesses incomparable natural wealth. Its rich soil makes it the leading producer of agricultural crops in the country. The region leads in the production of fruits and vegetables and is a major producer of livestock. Its rich fishing grounds contributed 42 percent of the country's fish production in 1998. It has an extensive sea and river system, but its potential for maritime transport has yet to be tapped. Mindanao also boasts rich mineral deposits and metallic reserves. Its proximity to neighboring Asian countries and Australia gives it a comparative advantage for trade.

judged the time was ripe to enter the region with programs aimed at promoting peace through business. In 2001, PBSP started the Business and Peace Program, in partnership with the London-based nongovernmental organization Prince of Wales International Business Leaders Forum, International Alert, the British embassy in Manila, and the British Chamber of Commerce of the Philippines.

Through this Business and Peace Program, PBSP enables member companies to develop a business-sector response to the problems related to peace and development in Mindanao. The approach of the program is to encourage local companies to adopt internal management policies that promote peace and stability. Datu Paglas has become one of the major representatives of the PBSP program and Paglas Corporation, a second company he established in addition to the banana plantation, joined the organization in 2002.

Maverick Leadership

Datu Ibrahim Pendatun Paglas III was in second grade of elementary school when he realized for the first time that, in his perception, something was wrong with the way people lived in his hometown in Maguindanao. Coming from a dominant political and economic clan, he saw that while he and other families were living well, other members of the community remained poor. "I did not see any economic development in Muslim areas, where only the leaders seemed to have a good life. I was not comfortable with it," Datu Paglas said, reflecting on the awakening of his social conscience. Thus, when he turned twenty-eight and became the mayor of Paglas town (the town was named after his grandfather), he decided to do something to change the situation. He chose the way of peace.

Datu Paglas's goal was to demonstrate how investments could facilitate peace and development in areas of conflict. His approach departed from the traditional way of thinking, according to which development can only be achieved if there is already peace. On the contrary, he says, "It is the other way around. The logic behind it is simple. A person who has nothing to lose is not afraid to die but he who has a lot in life cannot afford to waste life nor take another's person's life."

Datu Paglas knew that he could use his influence for the good of the community. His family ties to many of the Moro Islamic Liberation Front (MILF) commanders meant that he was able to appeal directly to the leadership of the rebel group. By the mid-1990s, the peace and order situation had significantly improved. After committing a substantial amount of his family's land to the new project he had in mind, he convinced a group of neighboring landowners to do the same. His plan was to set up a banana plantation. After succeeding to obtain a total of 1,300 hectares, Datu Paglas actively began to seek investments. Courting several foreign investors who already had vested interests in various Mindanao plantations, he persuaded them to expand their businesses in Paglas town.

Given the town's reputation of strife and conflict, many were hesitant. Still, considering the dynamism of the leadership, vast tract of fertile land, limitless supplies of fresh water, and the ready supply of local labor, investors believed they should give it a try.

An Economic Issue

The initiative led to one of the biggest investments ever made in the economy of Mindanao. Two companies were involved in this project. One was the banana plantation proper, called La Frutera, Inc., managed by an investment group in Manila, and established with overseas investments from Italy, Saudi Arabia, and the United States, including the Chiquita banana brand. La Frutera's initial investment amounted to $26 million. Datu Paglas then set up Paglas Corporation, the second company, which would provide labor, security, and transport services to the plantation.

The late MILF chair Hashim Salamat was also said to have been instrumental in securing the peace and maintaining it. Understanding that the road to peace and prosperity was largely an economic issue, he had given his personal assurance that MILF soldiers would not enter Paglas town, and that no personnel, equipment, or transport vehicle of La Frutera or Paglas Corporation would be compromised. Investors stress that no protection money has ever been paid, and absolutely no donations have been made by either company to the MILF, nor have there been solicitations made by the MILF itself.

Today, the plantation boasts of its state-of-the-art irrigation technology, provided by an Israeli engineering firm. In six years' time, production grew to close to 10 million tons of Cavendish bananas. The bananas are being exported to Japan, China, Korea, and the Middle East.

Paglas town also started to reap the benefits of the investment. The banana industry infuses at least $400,000 into the local economy of Paglas town every month in the form of payroll and payment to local service contractors. An additional 2,300 hectares of land has been allocated to banana production, enabling

The Banana Plantation in previously war-torn Mindanao

it to expand, which has already led to three thousand employees from Paglas town and its outskirts being hired. Datu Paglas persuaded his investors to infuse an additional $50 million into the economy of Muslim Mindanao to back the expansion. In addition, Datu Paglas himself established yet another company, the Paglas Rural Bank. It has three thousand local customers, many of whom never held a bank account before, and supports more than fifty small business enterprises in the region.

Uniting Business for Peace

Philippine Business for Social Progress (PBSP) is a private nonprofit foundation dedicated to promoting corporate social responsibility. It was organized in December 1970 by fifty of the country's prominent business leaders, and has since grown to become the nation's largest and most influential business-led social development foundation. From its initial membership, it has grown to more than 180 members, worked with some 2,500 partner organizations, provided financial assistance that supported over 5,000 projects, and benefited close to 2.5 million poor households.

PBSP has also conducted and supported research into the relationship between businesses and peace in Mindanao, including identifying "best practices" among companies. In recognition of the need to address socioeconomic disparities and underdevelopment in Mindanao, the PBSP Center for Corporate Citizenship launched a Business and Peace program in October 2001. Scheduled initially to run for three years, the Business and Peace program enables member companies to encourage local companies to adopt internal management policies that promote peace and diversity.

Among the Business and Peace program components are an internship program called Young Muslim Professionals for Business and Peace (YupPeace), which provides internship opportunities for young Muslim professionals to gain practical working experience in Manila-based companies. The concept is to break down the barriers of cultural animosity and enhance skills. Another component of the program consists of efforts to facilitate discussion on diversity in the workplace. Focus-group discussions are being organized at Mindanao-based companies to address the issue of Muslims and Christians working together in business. Yet another part of the project is Business Links, which seeks to incite large companies to help smaller corporations by doing business with them. As a result of this initiative, more and more Philippine businesses are considering the use of business partners in Mindanao as suppliers of raw materials. The BJ Coco Oil Mill, for instance, recently entered a relationship with a Mindanao agricultural company, resulting in the planting of 300 hectares of cassava, benefiting six hundred families. The Mindanao Business and Peace program also provides business training to small and medium-sized Muslim companies. Recently, PBSP has joined a consortium of civil-society organizations that aims to address the various societal divides in the three island provinces of the Autonomous Region in Muslim Mindanao. Under the Business and Peace Program, PBSP anchors business-sector interventions such as workshops and training sessions for local businessmen in these areas.

A Significant Achievement

Beyond the economic benefits lies a major achievement. Now, Christians, Muslims, and Lumads work and live together in peace. Initially, Christian plantation workers were brought in as trainers and supervisors. Datu Paglas gave his personal assurance that they would be under his protection. Christians are no longer viewed as superior to Muslim employees. The company organizes workshops on a regular basis to increase mutual understanding and tolerance. Religious leaders from both sides gave seminars on Islam and Christianity. Christian workers avoid eating pork at lunchtime in front of their Muslim colleagues. Children, regardless of religion, attend a local school together, increasing the elementary school enrollment rate from 50 percent to 70 percent. Referring to the apparent successful cohabitation of Christians and Muslims, Datu Paglas says, "We all worship the same God, we just call him by different names."

A man nicknamed "Spider," an ex–MILF company commander, is now the senior plantation supervisor. Now that his children are in school and are able to eat regular meals, he says he no longer considers rejoining the MILF: "When a man is hungry, he does not fear to kill and he does not fear to die." Spider said he now values greatly the opportunity to live a peaceful and productive life.

There are numerous ex–MILF combatants who have chosen to work in peace on the banana plantations. Still, when the renewed conflict between MILF and government forces broke out in early 2000, many of them offered to go back and resume their posts. MILF chair Hashim Salamat issued an official statement, however, that all plantation workers were to remain on their jobs. He is quoted as saying, "We will not have peace without development. The success of this plantation is critical to the peaceful future of Muslim Mindanao."

Ruth Honculada works at PBSP as manager for the foundation's affairs and handles its public relations and communication requirements. She has been actively involved in promoting corporate social responsibility initiatives for more than nine years.

Contact

Philippine Business for Social Progress
G/F PSDC Building, Magallanes cor. Real Streets
1002 Intramuros, Manila
The Philippines
Tel: +63 (2) 527 7741-51, or 527 3748
Fax: +63 (2) 527 3743
E-mail: pbsp@pbsp.org.ph
Website http://www.pbsp.org.ph

Selected Bibliography

International Alert's Business and Conflict Programme: Breaking the Links Between Economics and Conflict in Mindanao. Online at: http://www.international-alert.org/policy/business/projects/asia_philippines

14

Diasporas:
Untapped Potential for Peacebuilding
in the Homelands

Abdullah A. Mohamoud

The debate on the role of exile communities often focuses dispropor-
tionately on potential threats and negative aspects. However, diaspo-
ras can—and do—make significant contributions to peacebuilding,
conflict transformation, and postconflict reconstruction activities in
their home countries. To maximize this immense potential, it should
be tapped in a more creative and effective manner.

The current globalization process has facilitated the long-distance involvement of various diasporas in events in their respective homelands.
Thanks to inexpensive transportation and rapid communication, diasporas are
exerting an increasing influence on their homeland politics. This advantage
enables diaspora communities to build up vast transnational networks, criss-
crossing countries and continents, linking the process of globalization to local
conditions of their respective countries of origin. Likewise it enables the individuals and groups in the diaspora communities to build up intersecting social,
economic, and political bridges that link their new places of residence with
their original homelands. In this regard, the contemporary diaspora manifests
itself in different ways as being one of the main global forces shaping the
directions and trends of the twenty-first century.

Debates
The existing literature on diasporas focuses disproportionately on potential
threats from the diasporas that overshadow their positive activities. The main
focus is on the political role that diasporas play with regard to homeland conflicts. This proposition generally links the activities of the diasporas with security issues and then concentrates more on global rather than homeland security
concerns. Furthermore, most of the available studies concentrate on the activities of the militant and hard-line groups in the diasporas. The examples most
frequently cited are those informed by the militant activities of the Irish, Sri
Lankan Tamils, Sikhs, and Kurdish diasporas.

Yet the hard-line groups within the diaspora, although their activities are often visible, are neither the majority nor do they represent the whole diaspora of any given country. There are many diaspora groupings with different political and socioeconomic aspirations, and as such the diasporas should be carefully disaggregated. There is no denying that some diaspora groupings sponsor subversive activities in their respective countries of origin. However, adopting creative policy strategies that turn the destructive activities of the diasporas into constructive gains for the people in the homeland can reverse this negative tendency.

This chapter attempts to add value to the current debate on the diasporas and dynamics of conflict in the homeland from a significant and yet a neglected perspective. It concentrates on the critical role that diaspora groupings can, and have, played in promoting peace in their homelands. More specifically, it shows how the involvement of diasporas in the domestic dynamics of their homelands often contributes to fostering conflict transformation, post-conflict reconstruction, and socioeconomic development.

The central argument of this chapter is that diasporas frequently contribute to the peace process in their homelands through political, civil-societal, and developmental means. Furthermore, diasporas, because of their strategic position, have access to financial resources and transnational networks at different levels that, if properly tapped, can make a difference to the situation in their homelands. This strategic potential can be much more fruitfully harnessed when this capacity is better integrated into the foreign and development policy initiatives undertaken in the host countries. This is with the aim of making better use of the immense potential of the diasporas for conflict transformation initiatives and development activities in their countries of origin.

Positive Political Involvement

Contrary to the dominant perception, the "meddling" of the diasporas in the politics of their home countries is not always negative. The simple fact that the diasporas are not monolithic entities means that diverse political views and strategies of engagement are brought to the politics of their homelands. There are therefore cases where the active involvement of diasporas in the struggles in their homelands has resulted in positive changes in their domestic situations.

This involvement takes different forms. One is the tangible support that diasporas provide to the constructive forces on the ground struggling to restore order and political stability in the homeland. Diasporas provide support to local actors in different ways. For example they might sponsor media projects that can be used to educate and raise awareness of the people about the need for peaceful coexistence and social harmony and the promotion of a culture of peace and tolerance. Diasporas frequently use the media as a powerful tool in peacebuilding and democratic development in the homelands. An example of this is the Nuba Mountains radio station in Sudan, sponsored by the Sudanese diaspora, which is now playing an important role in informing the community about the prospects for peace and mobilizing them for the challenges that need to be addressed in postconflict Sudan.

Furthermore, the diasporas channel financial resources and innovative thinking into activities geared to enhancing and upgrading the capacities of subnational and local institutions and organizations at various levels. These include the provision of training to local peace brokers and organizing seminars, workshops, and public debates where information, skills, experience, and new ideas are exchanged and shared. A good example is provided by the activities of the Afghan diaspora living in North America and Europe but currently working in Afghanistan.

Diasporas support the peace forces in their homelands by providing information, new innovative ideas, and creative practices of peacemaking strategies. A significant communication tool for disseminating this valuable information is the emergence of online forums that are able to link various peace forces both in the homeland and in the diaspora into organized discussion and action groups. Diasporas help peace activists at home to make contact with important and powerful networks abroad. These contacts boost the moral and political clout of the positive forces on the ground. It is in this way that diasporas contribute to international efforts that impact positively on their respective homelands in terms of peacebuilding and conflict transformation.

Diasporas can contribute positively to peace initiatives in the homelands through their lobbying activities in the international media, international organizations, and in the host countries where they reside. Diasporas initiate these advocacy activities to galvanize support, persuade, and also pressurize the international community to take punitive measures against rebel groups, factional leaders, and governments in their respective homelands that they regard as oppressive, undemocratic, and dictatorial. In this respect, diasporas serve as positive bridge builders to international political actors and organizations supporting the peace and democratization process in their homelands. It is in this endeavor that some individuals and groups within the diaspora become proactive peace ambassadors for the homeland they have left behind physically but have not abandoned emotionally. Good examples are the Afghan diaspora in North America and Europe and the Congolese diaspora in France, Belgium, and the Netherlands, who act as pressure groups and are now undertaking transnational advocacy activities through expert meetings, seminars, and workshops aimed at influencing policy matters at the European Union level. According to Yesu Kitenga of the Congolese Lisanga organization in the Netherlands,

> our main task is to provide reliable information from the homeland, to raise awareness among the concerned organizations and government decisionmakers about certain politically motivated persecutions and human rights violations of which often little is known outside a country, but also guide the policymakers towards adopting the right policy approach towards our homeland.[1]

The diaspora can contribute positively to the peace dialogue by making their expertise available to the conflicting parties in the homeland in order to help them settle their differences through negotiation. Diasporas have on many occasions shown that they have the expertise to help enhance the articulation and negotiating capacities of the local protagonists. More concretely, the diaspora can undertake to draft negotiation strategies that can sometimes serve as a basis for dialogue between the conflicting factions in the homeland. Furthermore, during the postconflict reconstruction period, the diasporas, due to their generally advanced educational levels, can assist new governments in drafting treaties, agreements, and constitutions; identifying policy priorities for social, economic, and political reconstruction; and formulating strategies for implementation. They can also provide advice to the governments in the homelands on diverse policy issues ranging from rebuilding justice systems to disarming the militias. In this way diasporas contribute to rehabilitation of political institutions and civil administrations badly weakened or devastated by conflict. In fact, the highly visible and increasing involvement of diasporas in conflict transformation efforts and in the postconflict reconstruction and socioeconomic development of their homelands is a new phenomenon that crystallizes emerging forms of local and global connections and networks in many parts of the world today.[2] Concrete examples include the Afghan diaspora's contribution to the peace settlement in the Petersburg reconciliation talks on postwar Afghanistan in 2002; the Sri Lankan diaspora's contribution to the peace negotiations in 2002–2003; and that of the Somali diaspora in the Nairobi peace talks between the political factions in 2003–2004. It is interesting to note here that all these examples challenge the often-cited argument advanced by Paul Collier that the activities of diasporas in their homelands tend to exacerbate conflict rather than contribute to constructive conflict transformation.[3]

Civic-oriented Involvement

Diaspora involvement in the social and political dynamics in the homeland is not always along political lines. There are diaspora groupings that choose to be neutral on political issues with regard to homeland conflicts and opt instead to play active roles in domestic development through civil society. Often this is because these diaspora groupings see themselves as natural allies of the civil society rather than the political society in the homeland. As such, these diasporas help widen the civil society's peace constituency in the homeland. The impact of this form of diaspora involvement in domestic development can be better observed at subnational, local, and village levels rather than national levels. These diaspora groupings hold the view that viable peace in the homeland must be not only from the top down, but also from the bottom up, in a spirit of diligence and complementarity. They therefore argue that peacebuilding can only be effective if the national, subnational, and local processes and initiatives are consciously linked between different strategic sites and actors. It is from this point of view that these diaspora groupings support local human rights organizations, women's associations, and sponsor civic-oriented programs. For

Afghan Diaspora

Afghan diaspora groups have played a significant political role in ensuring that a peaceful power transition took place in Afghanistan in the aftermath of the U.S.-led NATO military intervention in 2001–2002. Diaspora members played a crucial role during the Petersburg peace dialogue and the formation of the postconflict government in Afghanistan at a major conference in Bonn. Influential political figures among the diaspora were directly involved in the talks on the transitional government in Bonn. Examples include the Rome-based delegation of former king Zaher Shah, and the Cyprus-based intellectuals who had been discussing and pondering policy options and strategies for resolving the political crisis in Afghanistan for some years. During the reconciliation talks, members of the Afghan diaspora have played bridge-building roles as strategic agents to the international actors and organizations facilitating the peace process. Moreover, certain Afghan diaspora groups contributed to the peace dialogue by making their expertise available to the conflicting political factions and groupings in Afghanistan to help them settle their differences by diplomatic means. Their expertise helped enhance the articulation and negotiating capacities of the local political factions. More concretely, they undertook to draft negotiation strategies that served as the basis for dialogue between the conflicting factions in Afghanistan. Others gave up well-paid careers in the West and returned home in order to support the consolidation for the peacebuilding process and sound governance in Afghanistan.

Source: M. Ashraf Haidari, "Rebuilding Afghanistan: The Diaspora Role," *The Asian Magazine,* 10 October 2004.

---

example, they channel more resources and innovative thinking into activities geared to enhancing and upgrading the capacities of subnational and local institutions and organizations at various levels, such as providing training to local peace brokers, organizing seminars, workshops, and public debates, where information, skills, experience, and new ideas are exchanged and shared. They also channel more funding and expertise to democratization projects that are geared to promote social emancipation, empowerment, political participation, and good governance in the country at different social levels. Furthermore, they sponsor new development projects (which are sometimes set up in collaboration with local activists) that are geared to capacity enhancement and genuine social emancipation.

The reasoning behind diaspora involvement is that empowered and emancipated people are best positioned to use their maximum potential for self-development to make a break with the past and take their destiny into their own hands. Many diasporas identify these socially oriented projects as priorities in building peace constituencies and good governance culture in their countries of origin. They therefore urge and persuade the mainstream donor development organizations in their host countries to orient their development assistance in the homelands toward these efforts. In this respect, diasporas set the agenda for an alternative approach to postconflict democratic development. In fact, this new alternative approach is very much needed since good governance can only take root in the homelands if it is anchored in solid subnational and local social institutions.

On top of all this, diasporas, because of their position, can play bridge-building roles by helping local organizations and civic associations, such as human rights activists, journalists and others, to connect with organizations and institutions in the host countries. This activity helps local civic associations and peace activists gain access to influential and powerful civil-society networks abroad that it would otherwise have been difficult to access. Furthermore, being a part of global networks enhances the profile of local peace groups and organizations and also helps them to gain access to information, resources, and external partners that could boost their position in domestic power relations.

Another aspect that has received little publicity is the innovative manner in which some diaspora groupings and organizations are addressing the conflict back home. They are attempting to foster the peace process in their homelands by mobilizing and promoting alternative and genuine nonpolitical peacemakers from civil society, both in the homelands and among the diaspora. These "alternative" peacemakers include public personalities such as poets, writers, musicians, prominent scholars, and sports stars such as football players. These notables are selected on the condition that they have a moral authority and command public respect across ethnic, clan, and group lines and, above all, cannot be accused of seeking political office. This innovative initiative is commendable and deserves to be more widely popularized.

Promoting Peace Through Development

Some diasporas hold the view that peace can be effectively promoted in the homeland through development. The logic behind this vision is that in many instances domestic conflicts are caused not only by power struggles at the national level, but are also triggered by unequal distribution of the national resources, extreme social and economic imbalances, marginalization, and grinding poverty at different societal levels. These multiple levels of the conflict need to be separately addressed. Diaspora groupings therefore address some of the economic causes of the conflicts and thereby make a positive contribution to the reduction and stabilization of the social tensions of the economically marginalized groups at the bottom of society. Diasporas undertake this effort by setting up community and welfare projects at local levels. Most of the projects sponsored by the diasporas are geared to rehabilitating health centers and facilities, building schools, supporting rural farmers, and helping create income-generating activities for destitute and marginalized groups. Diasporas undertake these community projects through individual and collective efforts. For example, in some instances, individuals and groups within a diaspora donate cash, materials, and needed equipment to various bodies and institutions in the homeland that help improve community facilities at the village and town levels. These efforts also greatly contribute to poverty alleviation among individuals through job creation, and provide needed services to the communities through the provision of basic public goods and service delivery.

A good example of such an effort is the Tamils Rehabilitation Organisation based in the United Kingdom. The aims of the organization include the provision of short-term relief and long-term rehabilitation to the displaced and war-affected Tamils, channeling expertise and funds to promote economic development, and raising the living conditions of Tamils displaced by war.

Conclusion
The positive activities of diasporas are having a moderating influence on conflict dynamics in their respective homelands. For example, "the moderating influence—and decreased financial support—of the Irish diaspora in the United States played a key role in convincing the IRA to accept the Good Friday Agreement in Northern Ireland in April 1998" (Newland and Patrick 2004: 26). There is enough evidence to state that "the positive potentials of diaspora communities for conflict transformation in their home countries outweigh their negative potential to become spoils" (Zunzer 2004: 4).

The activities of the diaspora should not solely be regarded from the political dimension, as is now generally the case. They should also be seen in terms of the nonpolitical lines in their civil-society and development-related dimensions. This perspective enables us to gain a better knowledge of the activities of the positive forces within the diasporas and the less-publicized roles they play in fostering the transformation of conflicts in their countries of origin. Diasporas often possess vast transnational networks, huge financial resources, and much-needed human capital due to their higher educational levels. All these advantages enable diasporas to make a difference for the better to the situations in their homelands. There is therefore an urgent need to develop better research tools and policy strategies that facilitate the effective harnessing of the vast capacities of the diasporas for the promotion of peace, viable governance, and sustainable development in their respective homelands.

Abdullah A. Mohamoud is a consultant in the areas of development cooperation, conflict and postconflict development, migration, and diasporas and has established SAHAN, a research and advice bureau. He holds a doctoral degree in state collapse and postconflict development in Africa from the University of Amsterdam and has authored numerous publications on peacebuilding processes, postconflict social reconstruction, diasporas, and promotion of peace with regard to Africa.

Notes
1. Interview, Amsterdam, 16 August 2004.

2, For a good analysis of emerging local-global linkages, see Mark Duffield (2001).

3. See Paul Collier (2000). Collier was the director of the Development Research group at the World Bank from April 1998 to April 2003.

Selected Bibliography

Collier, Paul. 2000. "Economic Causes of Civil Conflict and Their Implications for Policy." Policy Research Working Paper (Washington, DC: World Bank).

Collier, Paul, and Anke Hoeffler. 2000. "Greed and Grievance in Civil War." Policy Research Working Paper (Washington, DC: World Bank).

"Diasporas: A World of Exiles." 2003. Special Report. *The Economist* 4 (January).

Duffield, Mark. 2001. *Global Governance and the New Wars: The Merging of Development and Security* (London: Zed Books).

Junne, Gerd, and Abdullah A. Mohamoud. 2004. "Mobilising African Diaspora for the Promotion of Peace in Africa." A Feasibility Study undertaken by SAHAN Research Bureau and the Network University, Amsterdam.

Lyons, Terrance. 2004. "Engaging Diasporas to Promote Conflict Resolution: Transforming Hawks into Doves." Working Paper (Washington, DC: Institute of Conflict Analysis and Resolution, George Mason University).

Nassery, Homira G. 2003. "The Reverse Brain Drain: Afghan-American Diaspora in Postconflict Peacebuilding and Reconstruction." Online at: http://www.aisk.org/reports/diaspora.pdf.

Newland, Kathleen, and Erin Patrick. 2004. *Beyond Remittances: The Role of Diaspora in Poverty Reduction in Their Countries of Origin* (Washington, DC: Migration Policy Institute).

Sheffer, Gabriel. 2004. *Diaspora Politics: At Home Abroad* (Cambridge: Cambridge University Press).

Shain, Yossi. 2002. "The Role of Diasporas in Conflict Perpetuation or Resolution." *SAIS Review* XXII, no. 2 (Summer–Fall).

Van Hear, Nicholas. 2003. "Refugee Diasporas, Remittances, Development, and Conflict." Online at: http://www.migrationinformation.org.

Zunzer, Wolfram. 2004. "Diaspora Communities and Civil Transformation." Occasional Paper No. 26. (Germany: Berghof Research Centre for Constructive Conflict Management).

Resources

Lead Organizations

Institute for Migration and Ethnic Studies—The Netherlands
E-mail: imes@fmg.uva.nl
Website: http://www2.fmg.uva.nl/imes/

Information Centre About Asylum and Refugees in the U.K. (ICAR)— United Kingdom
E-mail: icar@kcl.ac.uk
Website: http://www.icar.org.uk

Centre for Refugee Studies—Canada
Various research programmes on diaspora communities, return, and reconciliation
E-mail: crs@yorku.ca
Website: http://www.yorku.ca/crs/

Berghof Foundation—Sri Lanka Network
E-mail: info@berghof-foundation.lk
Website: http://www.berghof-foundation.lk

Website

Migration Policy Institute: http://www.migrationinformation.org

Publications

Calliess, Joerg, ed. "When It Is a Matter of War and Peace at Home: The Role of Exiled/Diaspora Communities in the Development of Crisis and Civil Conflict Management." Loccumer Protokolle, 2004. Online at: http://www.loccum.de.

Cheran, Rudhramoorthy. "Diaspora Circulation and Transnationalism as Agents for Change in the North-East of Sri Lanka." Research report written for the Berghof Foundation for Conflict Studies. Toronto: York University, 2003. Online at: http://www.berghof-foundation.lk/publications/diaspora.pdf.

Koser, Khalid, and Nicholas Van Hear. "Asylum Migration and Implications for Countries of Origin." Paper presented at WIDER conference on Poverty, International Migration, and Asylum, Helsinki, 2003.

Sheffer, Gabriel. "From Diasporas to Migrants, From Migrants to Diaspora," in Rainer Ohliger, ed., *Diasporas and Ethnic Migrants: Germany, Israel, and Post-Soviet Successor States in Comparative Perspective*. London/Portland: Frank Cass, 2003, pp. 21–37.

14.1

Fear and Hope in Acholiland: Kacoke Madit in Uganda and the United Kingdom

Since the mid-1980s, the Acholi people of northern Uganda have borne the brunt of a debilitating war. In their search for peace, Acholis living abroad invoked a "big meeting" tradition. With external agencies having failed to deliver peace, the onus for a resolution is on Uganda and Ugandans.

A UN official once described the situation in northern Uganda as the world's worst humanitarian crisis. The territory of Acholiland sits at the heart of this protracted conflict; the Acholi people are among its main victims. Killings, abductions, rape, and torture are commonplace. Schools and health centers have been destroyed. Slicing off victims' body parts is a gruesome trademark of the Lord's Resistance Army (LRA), the rebel group that has battled the government of President Yoweri Museveni since the mid-1980s. The national army has also been accused of committing atrocities; critics say neither party is serious about peace.

Human rights bodies say the conflict has displaced hundreds of thousands of people, mainly Acholis, a large number of whom are crammed into refugee camps. For Acholis who form a far-flung diaspora across Europe and North America, the conflict is never far from their thoughts. Since the mid-1990s, they have used a traditional Acholi system of convening big meetings to get the parties to at least talk to each other.

Their efforts have created an organization called Kacoke Madit (KM, "big meeting" or "big conference" in Luo, the language of the Acholi), which has staged a series of conferences to build a consensus for sustainable peace. These open events, to which all groups with an interest in bringing the conflict to a peaceful end are invited, have proven vital given the absence of any major international effort to secure peace in northern Uganda.

With a charter providing for participation by all Acholi people, irrespective of views or religious and political belief, in peace initiatives, KM supports an inclusive dialogue process that combines the search for peace with education within affected communities and other practical efforts.

A Long History of Conflict

The war in northern Uganda is related to the rise to power of Yoweri Museveni's National Resistance Movement/National Resistance Army, which is rooted in a long history of conflicts.

After General Idi Amin seized power from Milton Obote in 1971, he ordered soldiers belonging to the Acholi and Langi ethnic groups, the very backbone of the army, to surrender their arms. Many of those who did so were killed. New soldiers were recruited from other regions of the country.

Many Acholi and Langi soldiers went into exile abroad after this, and in April 1979, with help from the Tanzanian army and Yoweri Museveni's Front for National Salvation, they returned and overthrew Amin. Various power shifts followed, caused, in the main, by ideological and ethnic differences, until elections were held in 1980. These polls were won by Milton Obote's Uganda People's Congress, but the outcome was disputed. Eventually, a conflict between Langi and Acholi soldiers—that shattered a long-standing military alliance between these two groups—led to Obote's overthrow in July 1985.

This coup brought General Tito Okello to power, and he managed to unite the various rebel groups and political parties under his government while negotiating with one that remained on the outside, the National Resistance Army (NRA) headed by Museveni. The NRA eventually seized power in January 1986.

This was a major blow to the Acholi because for the first time socioeconomic, political, and military powers were concentrated in the south. Tension between Acholi soldiers in the defeated army and the NRA escalated after reports that NRA soldiers operating in northern Uganda committed atrocities including rape, abduction, and confiscation of property.

In May 1986, the government ordered all former Uganda National Liberation Army (UNLA) soldiers to report to barracks. Many went into hiding. Others fled to Sudan. Some took up arms. Soon, these ex-soldiers were joined by a stream of youth fleeing NRA operations in the north. Various groups of Acholi refugee combatants were subsequently formed, including the Lord's Resistance Army (LRA).

The war has lasted for almost two decades, partly because it has become an extension of regional and international power struggles. The Sudanese government provided sanctuary and military hardware to the LRA because the Ugandan government supported Sudan People's Liberation Army (SPLA), one of the Sudanese rebel groups. The conflict is also a source and cover for clandestine income for high-ranking military and government officials and other profiteers.

Kidnapping of Children

It was in the districts of Gulu, Kitgum, and Pader in Acholiland that rebels first took up arms in the 1980s, after accusing army elements of carrying out atrocities in the area. The LRA, which eventually emerged as the main rebel force, is led by a self-proclaimed "prophet," Joseph Kony, whose professed aim is to rule Uganda in accordance with the principles of the Biblical Ten Commandments.

For many years, the movement had sanctuary in neighboring Sudan and carried out cross-border raids. In 2002, the government, through an agreement with Sudan, pursued them across the border. Yet the operation—called Iron Fist—failed, and as the rebels increased attacks inside Uganda, the Uganda People's Defense Forces were unable to provide adequate protection for civilians affected by the backlash.

Some observers believe no military solution is likely to succeed and have criticized the Museveni government for its rigid pursuit of a military solution. The government's amnesty offers to the rebels, have largely been ignored.

The human rights picture has largely been defined by the kidnapping of young children during nighttime raids in rural villages. Many of these kidnappings occurred as acts of reprisal during Operation Iron Fist. Human rights groups say there have been more than 22,000 abductions, creating an atmosphere of fear. Many are taken to camps in southern Sudan; such children make up 85 percent of the LRA's forces. They are forced to kill their own kin, and are abused both physically and sexually before getting military training and coming into confrontation with government forces that were originally supposed to have protected them from abduction.

Every evening, large numbers of children who live near urban centers move unaccompanied to seek shelter overnight in churches, hospital compounds, and shop verandas. It is estimated that there are up to twenty thousand such "night commuters."

Baker Ochola, retired bishop of Kitgum, said the kidnappings were actually destroying Acholi society from the roots. "A child who is threatened is supposed to run to its mother. But now, children are running away from home to be safe from abduction. This means we are cultivating a new culture. Children no longer have an identity." The entire civilian population suffers in this conflict: in the two districts where the war is most heavily concentrated, infrastructure has been decimated and no significant economic development is taking place.

A Big Meeting

Against this backdrop, Acholis living in North America felt compelled to raise the issue when they attended a convention of the Uganda North America Association in Chicago in 1996. They were rebuffed. Surprised by the lack of interest, they organized a separate meeting in Toronto, Canada, in 1996, agreed to a nine-point resolution calling for peace, and delivered it to President Yoweri Museveni. He did not respond; they pressed ahead anyway.

The meeting in Canada was followed by a more structured and organized Kacoke Madit in London on 5–6 April 1997. Organized by Acholis in the United Kingdom, this gathering drew more than three hundred delegates from Uganda, the United States, Canada, the United Kingdom, Sweden, Germany, Denmark, and Kenya. It was at this meeting that the organization Kacoke Madit took form.

Organizers were encouraged by the presence of representatives from both the Ugandan government and the rebels: the ministers responsible for foreign affairs and northern Uganda were there; the LRA sent its secretary for external affairs and mobilization and two members of the military high command.

This encouraging start was reinforced by the adoption of an eleven-point resolution calling on the government and LRA to cease hostilities and find ways to peacefully resolve the conflict. Despite the strength of these resolutions, however, and the commitment of everyone attending to implement them, neither the LRA nor the government established a viable negotiating process. To help push things along, a follow-up meeting was held in London, on 17–19 July 1998 under the theme "Removing the Obstacles to Peace."

More than three hundred delegates came, from all sectors of the Acholi communities, non-Ugandan individuals, representatives of governments, and international nongovernmental organizations (NGOs). They tried to identify obstacles to peace and ways of overcoming them. In the end, a resolution was adopted reaffirming the validity of commitments enunciated at the 1997 Kacoke Madit. The conference also brought victims of the war to make their presentation. One of them was a woman whose lips were cut by the rebels. This brought home the message to those who were still sympathetic to the LRA rebels' activities.

Similar international conferences were held annually until 2000, when the last Kacoke Madit took place in Nairobi, Kenya, with delegates from northern Uganda, the Acholi diaspora, the government of Sudan, the LRA, representatives of the international community, and other stakeholders attending.

Reaching Consensus

By then a consensus had emerged that the conflict in northern Uganda "can only be successfully resolved if there is a comprehensive negotiation process resulting in a peaceful settlement, including a resettlement and reintegration program and an environment in which reconciliation can take place."

Kacoke Madit underlined its commitment to "working to develop dialogue and to building trust between parties to the conflict; and between them and the Acholi people into whose midst the ex-combatants must eventually resettle, with the ultimate aim of bringing about direct negotiations between the LRA and the government of Uganda" (Kacoke Madit, n.d.).

These big meetings were organized by a seven-member secretariat based in London that functioned as a coordinating point for not only Kacoke Madit but partner and community groups within and outside Uganda—an entire network of regional co-coordinators based in Uganda, southern Africa, the United States, Canada, Scandinavia, and the rest of Europe.

The role played by this secretariat was not limited to promoting peace. For example, it focused on conflict-sensitive international approaches to the plight of war-affected children, and lobbied for whatever amnesty was offered by the government to be implemented in the context of overall resolution of the conflict—rather than as an end in itself.

Close liaison was established with political, religious, and cultural groups based in Uganda.[1] All these groups were given a voice on the Kacoke Madit Consultative Council, an advisory body designed to help develop and implement policies and resolutions for the secretariat. Some were directly involved in ongoing—if largely unsuccessful—efforts by civil-society groups in northern Uganda to mediate between rebels and government. The Acholi Religious Leaders'

International Conference on Peace in Northern Uganda, organized by the Ugandans in the Diaspora Working for Peace, Kacoke Madit in support of local voices

Peace Initiative, for example, tried to get rebels and government around the negotiating table, though its efforts were frustrated by the intensity of the ongoing conflict.

Through these interlinked efforts and initiatives, different strands of Acholi community, at home and abroad, were able to discuss peace and post-war development plans and strategies, and ways of attending to the socio-economic and development needs of war-ravaged districts.

The worldwide network of community groups and organizations that emerged began working together toward a common purpose that led eventually to Acholis, other Ugandans, and interested groups from the international community reaching consensus to resolve the conflict by peaceful means.

The annual meetings were not just gatherings to share peace ideas. They served as a forum at which various parties, involved in a variety of related actions, had a chance to share a variety of experiences and ideas. They also heightened awareness about what was happening in northern Uganda and explored different positions and approaches. Contacts made during these meetings allowed the different interest groups to be more aware of each other's positions and get exposure to on-the-ground realities.

Quiet Diplomacy

After the last meeting in 2000, attention shifted to promoting dialogue between the Museveni government and Acholi civil society about past experiences and suitable approaches in building better understanding. Kacoke Madit continues to lobby the Ugandan government, the government of Sudan, the rebels, and the international community, to accept dialogue to end the violence. This "quiet diplomacy," says Nyeko Caesar Poblicks, one of Kacoke Madit's leaders, is more "farreaching" than when carried out in the glare of publicity.

Using a variety of methods, including the Internet and a weekly e-mail–based newsletter, the organization also disseminates information about the conflict and peace initiatives. It has started a Diaspora Volunteer Scheme providing opportunities for skilled and experienced people from northern Uganda to return to affected districts and contribute to development, poverty alleviation, education, and health care.

Over the nearly ten years of its existence, Kacoke Madit, serving as a voice of the Acholi people, has raised global awareness about the conflict and its consequences—especially the humanitarian cost. By establishing itself as a group that transcends political, religious, gender, and other boundaries, it has highlighted the existence of many voices appealing for peace in northern Uganda.

Its initiatives have helped stimulate support for peace among governments and NGOs and led to direct contacts between the government and the LRA. With external agencies having failed to "deliver peace," the onus for a resolution is on Uganda and Ugandans, says Nyeko Caesar Poblicks. "KM and its partners will continue to play their part in meeting the challenge."

Contact

Kacoke Madit Secretariat
173 Upperstreet
Islington
London N1 1RG
United Kingdom
Tel: +44 (0)207 288 2768
Fax: +44 (0)207 288 1988
E-mail: km@km-net.org

Selected Bibliography

Kacoke Madit. N.d. "About Kacoke Madit (KM)" Online at: http://www.km-net.org.
Websites:
> http://www.km-net.org
> http://www.irinnews.org/webspecials/uga_crisis/testimonies.asp
> http://news.bbc.co.uk/1/hi/world/africa/3514473.stm
> http://www.acholipeace.org
> http://www.c-r.org/accord/uganda

Note

1. These included the Acholi Parliamentary Group (APG), which was comprised of all members of parliament from the conflict area; the Acholi Religious Leaders Peace Initiatives (ARLPI), a cross-denominational group working for peace and reconciliation; Acholi Development Association (ADA); Kitgum Peace Initiative (KPI); the Catholic Justice and Peace Committee, Peoples' Voice for Peace (PvP), the Council of Acholi Chiefs, and other local stakeholders.

14.2

Contributing to Peace at Home: The Berghof Foundation in Sri Lanka

Wolfram Zunzer

Since their country achieved independence in 1948, many Sri Lankans have migrated to Europe, North America, and Australia as well as to neighboring countries. Reasons vary, but from the mid-1970s ethnic differences and civil war have contributed significantly to this wave of emigration. As a result, large Tamil and some substantial Singhalese diaspora communities have emerged, both of which play a role within the politics of peace and war at home. Realizing this, the Berghof Foundation set up different programs working with these groups.

The signing of a cease-fire agreement in 2002 presaged not only an increase in the social exchange between the separated parts of the country, but also increased interest from the Sri Lankan diaspora, reflected in the large number of visits and of short- and medium-term investments. Given the West's heightened suspicion of immigrants after 9/11, and the near-total absence of serious empirical studies on the subject, many publications in peace and security studies have fostered a negative image of the diaspora's role in peacebuilding. Given this background, the Berghof Foundation has initiated a program of action-oriented research and supported selected pilot-project activities by key partner organizations. These activities are part of the Resource Network for Conflict Studies and Transformation of the Sri Lanka office, which was established with the mandate of enhancing and supporting the capacities for constructive conflict transformation already existing in the country.

Activities

Work with the Sri Lankan diaspora was conducted in three phases. In phase one the communities in Germany and Switzerland were mapped and contacts were established. In phase two, which took place between 2002 and 2003, expert workshops, conferences, and a diaspora dialogue study tour to Sri Lanka were organized. Currently, the activities with cooperating partners, especially with the Friendship Circle Berlin, the Tamil Rehabilitation Organization (TRO), and key individuals in the diaspora are being consolidated.

In October 2003 the Berghof Foundation organized a diaspora dialogue study tour for key community members from Western host countries. The main purpose of the study tour, which was joined by Sri Lankan diaspora members from Great Britain, Switzerland, Germany, and Canada, was to learn, in an ethnically mixed group, about the socioeconomic and political situation in all parts of the country. It was hoped that this would create closer links between strategic groups at home and diaspora groups abroad.

This approach has to be seen in the peace process at large, in which—based on the cease-fire agreement of February 2002—a strategy giving priority to the socioeconomic "normalization" of the war-torn regions of the north and east was pursued. A major and as yet unresolved challenge to the peace process emerged in 2003 when the parties to the conflict were unable to agree on an institutional mechanism for the distribution of internationally pledged development funds. The knowledge, capacities, competencies, contacts, and funds from the diaspora have subsequently attracted far greater attention, particularly that of the Tamil stakeholders.

The study tour program included workshops on the socioeconomic situation and provided opportunities for contributions from the diaspora communities in the South, in Jaffna, in Kilinochi, and in the eastern province, including on-site visits, workshops, and discussions with key representatives and a meeting with the head of the government Peace Secretariat in Colombo. Experts provided input on the current challenges facing the political peace process and on the concept of the circulating diaspora. Many prominent members of local nongovernmental organizations (NGOs) and government institutions met the group in a cordial atmosphere, giving rise to numerous informal contacts and ideas for collaboration. Participants were invited and exchanged concrete projects ideas. Some follow-up activities are currently being organized, such as support activities by the newly founded Transnational and Diaspora Network for Development–Canada.

Another aim of the study tour, namely to learn in an ethnically mixed group about the socioeconomic and political situation in all parts of the country, was fully met. After the frequent and thorough discussions, many participants expressed an increased understanding of the other ethnic groups' socioeconomic living conditions and their challenges. Some Tamil group members also shared a personal experience: having been told by their families in the past not to go further than 50 kilometers south of Colombo, as part of this group they were able to cross this notional border for the first time in their lives.

The last three years have seen a marked increase in the activities of the above-mentioned organizations and many other Tamil and Singhalese organizations in Europe and Canada. Propeace advocacy activities in Switzerland and Germany have also increased, while the TRO in Sri Lanka, as well as representatives from the state bureaucracy and the Sri Lanka office of the UN Development Program, have signaled increasing interest. The same is true

A Unique Opportunity for a Lasting Peace

The conflict in Sri Lanka can best be characterized as ethnopolitical. Underlying the violent conflict, which began in the mid-1970s, lies a struggle between the Tamil and Singhalese. Major outbreaks of violence in the 1990s have reinforced the division of the state into a North, dominated by the Liberation Tigers of Tamil Eelam (LTTE), and a South, dominated by the government of Sri Lanka. The last major attempt to heal this schism was launched in 2002 under the government of the newly inaugurated prime minister, Ranil Wickramasinghe, with the support of Norwegian facilitators. Its outcome was the current cease-fire agreement and an initial series of negotiations between September 2002 and March 2003. In national politics, a new situation has occurred, as the social democrats under President Chandrika Kumaratunga together with the Marxist-nationalist Janatha Vimukht Peramuna (Peoples Liberation Front) won the elections in April 2004 with a very small majority, ousting the sitting prime minister, Ranil Wickramasinghe, and his United National Party, who had signed the cease-fire agreement in February 2002 and relaunched negotiations with the LTTE. Sri Lanka is still in an interim or post–cease-fire phase, in which smaller groups such as the Muslims and upcountry Tamils have also made their voices heard. Having been in place for two years, the cease-fire agreement has lasted much longer than all previous agreements, and it has created a unique opportunity for achieving a lasting peace. Even though the framework conditions have deteriorated since the parliamentary elections on 2 April 2004, which resulted in a hung parliament, the vast majority of people living in Sri Lanka do not want to risk any reescalation of the ethnic conflict. The essence of the conflict resolution process facilitated by Norway so far has found expression in the Oslo Declaration in 2002, aiming at a genuine federal Sri Lankan state. To attain this goal, a fundamental restructuring of the Sri Lankan state and the transformation of the LTTE from a purely military organization into a reliable political player is required.

with state-funded development and peace organizations in Europe, such as the German Technical Service (GTZ) and SwissPeace.

Conflict and Potentials

The Berghof Foundation was motivated to work on the issue of, and to engage with, the Sri Lankan diaspora communities by its research into the role and theoretical potential of the diaspora for conflict transformation activities in Sri Lanka. Four key potentials were identified that make them important stakeholders in the political arena:

1. A large number of Tamil organizations and individuals support the population in need in the Northeast, as well as the organizations affiliated with the Liberation Tigers of Tamil Eelam (LTTE), through substantial money transfers.

2. Many Western-based Tamils as well as the smaller group of Singhalese are highly qualified and some have accumulated large private assets. Since the cease-fire, some activities of this group in Sri Lanka, such as the acquisition of property, have increased.

3. Remittances are a major part of the gross domestic product of Sri Lanka. It is estimated that more than 25 percent of the gross domestic product (GDP) is due to the influx of small sums of private capital and goods.

4. A comparatively high number of diaspora members are well-informed and politically proactive, and due to the Internet, are continually updated on the situation in Sri Lanka.

Through interaction with diaspora members, Berghof developed two propositions that underpin its specific perspective on the role of diasporas in conflict transformation in Sri Lanka. First, as a "peace connector," the Sri Lankan diaspora has a general potential for building peace and transforming the violent conflicts at home. Second, through fostering transnational relationship networks (temporary return of qualified experts/elites) and dialogue spaces (workshops, study tours, etc.), the human capital (knowledge, capacities, competencies) and the sociopolitical capital (contacts and connections) in Sri Lanka can be increased.

That the abstractly identified potentials have already had some practical impact is illustrated by the activities of key and influential figures of the Sri Lankan diaspora in the framework of the official peace negotiations. The character of the peace negotiations between the LTTE and the government of Sri Lanka in 2002–2003 differed substantially from the 1995 and 2000 peace talks.

This time the international community had a strong interest in a constructive and peaceful settlement of the conflict, and was very willing to engage in its practice. Norway as the official facilitator of the peace talks, supported by the co-chairs Japan, the United States, and India, as well as many activities by the U.K., Switzerland, Germany, and the Netherlands, have internationalized the conflict. Functional elites served as bridges between the Sri Lankan political actors and the international political and socioeconomic support structure. Below the macropolitical level of the peace negotiations, NGOs in Sri Lanka initiated many peacebuilding and related socioeconomic rehabilitation activities. Existing NGOs expanded their portfolio and new organizations were founded. Here, too, the diaspora has been influential.

To assess whether and how the diaspora communities at large can become more involved in peacebuilding, their sociopolitical setup needs to be better understood. The majority of diaspora groups are Tamils and, in fewer numbers, Singhalese, while, with some exceptions in the U.K., Muslims are largely absent in the West. Both diaspora communities not only react to input from the larger political actors; they also exert influence themselves—at least on the level of formal and many informal networks and in providing economic support. There is a dialectical relationship between diaspora communities in the host countries, the home country, the LTTE, and the government of Sri Lanka. While the first generation of refugees and economic migrants still hopes to return to Sri Lanka, the second and third generations want to return only for limited periods. The younger and often better-educated second-generation Tamils have the greatest potential for supporting the development of the still devastated North and East, as well as for supporting the transformation of the LTTE from a purely military organization into an important political player. The same holds true with respect to modernizing political institutions and development administration in the South.

Preliminary investigations such as mapping and building up a network of key persons and experts on diaspora issues resulted in the identification of three organizations, among others, with which the Berghof Foundation now cooperates. There are two important smaller associations of Sri Lankans in Germany, which have a politically engaged, multiethnic membership: the Sri Lanka Friendship Circle in Munich and the Sri Lanka Circle in Berlin. Both associations are working for peace among the different ethnic communities in Sri Lanka and both have shown that a peaceful coexistence—at least as migrants in host countries—is possible. In order to achieve their objectives, political discussions and cultural events are organized and projects on peace education in Sri Lanka supported. A follow-through of both associations is a new NGO called the Society for Conflict Prevention, Democracy and Minority Rights, which initiates projects in Sri Lanka for strengthening the knowledge about and acceptance of federal democracy.

A major actor in the generally very well-organized worldwide Tamil diaspora is the TRO and other closely affiliated organizations. The humanitarian and socioeconomic engagement of the Tamil diaspora for the Northeast has largely been organized through the TRO. Their strength lies not only in organizing Tamils in the diaspora, but also in its leading role in the implementation of socioeconomic development measures in the Northeast. Both external diaspora experts and the Berghof Foundation try to facilitate the organizational development processes of these groups, as demand is articulated and financial resources become available.

Explorations

In 2001 and 2002, explorations of the Sri Lankan diaspora in Germany and Switzerland through mapping and networking were central activities. At the end of 2002 a diaspora expert workshop with experts mostly from European countries was initiated to discuss the way forward for propeace diaspora work. It was a trust-building and dialogue exercise, as different perceptions, hopes, and fears of the Tamil, Singhalese, Muslim participants, as well as non–Sri Lankan participants, vis-à-vis the peace process, were exchanged. The changing relationships between the political constituencies of diverse Sri Lankan diaspora communities and the political (peace) processes in Sri Lanka were also discussed in depth. Possible steps for actively involving the diaspora in the interim phase of the peace process were debated.

Another activity in May 2003 was the conference "Peace Talks and Federalism as the Solution for the Conflict in Sri Lanka" in Munich, organized by the Sri Lanka Friendship circles. The 120 participants from all major European countries, Canada, and Sri Lanka adopted a declaration in which the dialogue between the government of Sri Lanka and the LTTE was welcomed and federalism was called "the only possible way of permanently resolving the ethnic conflict in Sri Lanka." It was acknowledged that a federal system for Sri Lanka would remold the political and power structures of the island, taking into consideration the injustices suffered by all the people, especially by the minorities, and their fears for the future. The participants called for a democratic way of changing the people's attitudes through media campaigns and public-education programs.

The main purpose of the International Diaspora Workshop in Loccum in November 2003 was to provide a forum for in-depth discussions on the role of diasporas in conflict dynamics and to identify existing opportunities to improve the integration of diaspora communities into processes of postwar reconstruction, reconciliation, and peacebuilding. Three influential persons from different ethnic groups presented their interpretation of the current conflict situation in Sri Lanka, which started an in-depth discussion. Other specialists provided their input, for example, on existing initiatives of diaspora communities in Switzerland, Norway, and Canada. Innovative ideas for expanding and deepening propeace and development activities were brainstormed.

Challenges

In comparison to the many Sri Lankan diaspora organizations that exist throughout the world, the Berghof Foundation could only foster a very limited number of pilot activities in the diaspora in support of the peace process. The foundation will continue to support activities of key persons from the Sri Lankan diaspora, such as support for organizing dialogue events such as a "Round Table Sri Lanka," diaspora expert conferences and workshops, action-oriented research on political attitudes, and entry points for propeace activities in Western host countries, and facilitate the development and transformation of organizations such as TRO, the Transnational and Diaspora Network for Development–Canada, and the Society for Conflict Prevention, Democracy and Minority Rights.

Over the last two years, through mapping, workshops, study tours, and by jointly reviewing activities with the partner organizations, the Berghof Foundation experienced the great preparedness of organizations and individuals from the Sri Lankan diaspora to become more influential in the peace process at home. This is reflected in the large number of Sri Lankan diaspora organizations and individuals in all major Western countries that already support humanitarian, development, and politically transformative initiatives in their home countries. One major challenge is the obvious scarcity of funds available to NGOs for specific bridge-building activities such as dialogue workshops, second-generation student exchanges, country-specific round table workshops, or programs for supporting the time-limited engagement of experts in their home countries. Even though information and communication technologies make transnational communication relatively cheap for personal trust-building, dialogue processes and organizational capacity building, dialogue spaces based on personal encounters have to be regularly created, which demands adequate personal capacities and funding.

Another challenge is to determine how the impact of often rather broadly designed advocacy, development, or dialogue initiatives from diaspora groups can become more focused, so as to have a more direct impact on the level of the macropolitical peace process. One way might be to emphasize mono-communal capacity building to increase the political impact on one party to the conflict. Still, the question remains as to whether and for how long such mono-ethnic capacity building should be pursued given the often inverse power structures throughout the worldwide diaspora and the need for improving communication between representatives of the different ethnic groups for achieving sustainable peace. Another way forward for many diaspora organizations and NGOs would be to develop more focused and tailor-made strategies.

From a conceptual point of view, a more comprehensive approach for strengthening the diaspora's potential for peacebuilding and development should still be considered. One way would be to apply John Paul Lederach's famous insight that one needs to support activities from the diplomatic down to the grassroots level in an interlocking way to the transnational level in the case of Sri Lanka. Such a comprehensive strategy for fostering diaspora involvement in peacebuilding would need substantially more personal and financial resources, which will only become available if the donor agencies' change of perception vis-à-vis the peacebuilding and development potential of diaspora groups can be turned into sustainable program policies.

At the same time, action-oriented empirical research on entry points for peacebuilding and development through diaspora engagement need to be intensified. In this respect it would be helpful if fewer normative assumptions would be taken for granted, such as those regarding the political orientation of diaspora communities in exile per se, and much more empirical research on political attitudes, remittances, circulation with the country of origin, and political preference structures would become the focus of scholarly attention. This in turn would make a major contribution to facilitating the development of more numerous and more strategically focused peacebuilding initiatives by diaspora groups and NGOs.

Wolfram Zunzer is a researcher and liaison person for the Resource Network for Conflict Studies and Transformation–Sri Lanka at Berghof Center, Berlin. He has firsthand experience of coordinating state and nonstate actors in conflict management, including two years of experience of in bridge-building among Sri Lankan diasporas.

Contacts

Berghof Center for Constructive Conflict Management
Altentensteinstraße 48a
D-14195 Berlin, Germany
Tel: +49 (0)30 844 154-0
Fax +49 (0)30 844 154-99
E-mail: wolfram.zunzer@berghof-center.org
Website: http://www.berghof-center.org

Berghof Foundation for Conflict Studies—Sri Lanka Office
Sri Lanka Office, 1 Gower Street
Colombo 5, Sri Lanka
Tel: +94 (0)11 259 3301/259 3201
Fax: +94 (0)11 259 3865
E-mail: info@berghof-foundation.lk
Website: http://www.berghof-foundation.lk

Selected Bibliography

Calliess, Joerg, ed. 2004. "When It Is a Matter of War and Peace at Home: The Role of Exiled/Diaspora Communities in the Development of Crisis and Civil Conflict Management." Loccumer Protokolle, 2004. Online at: http://www.loccum.de.

Centre for Refugee Studies. Online at: http://www.yorku.ca/crs (Centre for Refugees).

Cheran, Rudhramoorthy. 2003. "Diaspora Circulation and Transnationalism as Agents for Change in the North-East of Sri Lanka, Colombo." Research report written for the Berghof Foundation for Conflict Studies Colombo Office. Online: http://www.berghof-foundation.lk/publications.htm.

Ferdinands, Tyrol, Kumar Rupesinghe, Paikiasothy Saravanamutthu, Jayadeva Uyangoda, and Norbert Ropers. 2004. "The Sri Lanka Peace Process at a Crossroads: Lessons, Opportunities and Ideas for Principled Negotiations and Conflict Transformation." Colombo. Online at: http://www.berghof-foundation.lk/publications/prg.pdf.

Koser, Khalid, and Nicholas Van Hear. 2003. "Asylum, Migration and Implications for Countries of Origin." In United Nations University / WIDER Discussion Paper No. 2003/20, Helsinki.

Lederach, John Paul. 1997. *Building Peace—Sustainable Reconciliation in Divided Societies.* (Washington, DC: U.S. Institute of Peace).

McDowell, Christopher. 1996. *A Tamil Asylum Diaspora: Sri Lankan Migration, Settlement, and Politics in Switzerland* (Oxford: Berghahn Books).

Sriskandarajah, Dhananjayan. 2004. "Tamil Diaspora Politics," in *Encyclopedia of Diasporas* (New Haven, CT: Yale University Press/Kluwer).

Tamil Rehabilitation Organization. Online at: http://www.troonline.org.

Zunzer, Wolfram. 2004. "Diaspora Communities and Civil Conflict Transformation." Berghof Occasional Paper No. 26, Berlin. Online at: http://www.berghof-center.org/publications/occasional/boc26e.pdf.

15

Civilian Peacekeepers:
Creating a Safe Environment for Peacebuilding

Tim Wallis and Claudia Samayoa

Most people think of peacekeeping as a military activity, involving troops sent into a conflict area by the United Nations or some other official body to stop the fighting and restore order. In its broader sense, however, peacekeeping can include any activity that seeks to reduce violence and create a safe environment for other peacebuilding activities to take place. Many peacekeeping activities can be carried out just as effectively by unarmed civilians. This chapter looks at some examples of civilian peacekeeping as well as some of the issues involved.

People cannot create or reestablish peaceful communities while they are being threatened, intimidated, or attacked. A certain degree of personal security is needed in order to use any of the peacebuilding tools described in the other chapters of this book. The aim of civilian peacekeeping is to establish and maintain that minimum level of security that enables people to feel safe enough to move around, organize, and take effective action to defend human rights and promote peace. Civilian peacekeeping cannot resolve a conflict or build peace, but it can enable other peacemaking and peacebuilding activities to take place.

Civilian peacekeeping involves a set of tools that have proven to be effective in deterring violent attacks and opening up the political space within which local people can engage in peacebuilding activities. The organizations that have developed and continue to use these tools do not necessarily see themselves as "peacekeepers." Some describe themselves as "unarmed bodyguards" or "human shields." Others talk about being "witnesses," "monitors," or providing a "presence." All the activities included in this chapter, however, involve attempts to stop or deter violence and therefore we feel justified in using the generic "peacekeeping" term to describe them.

Deterring Violence, Changing Behavior
All peacekeeping, whether civilian or military, has as its foundation the concept of a "presence which can deter violence and change behavior." During

the Contra war in Nicaragua, attacks on border villages would cease whenever a delegation from Witness for Peace was in the area (See Chapter 1.3). At Israeli checkpoints on the West Bank, treatment of Palestinians has been markedly more civilized when journalists or foreign peace activists have been present. Such responses cannot, of course, be guaranteed, but establishing a "presence" has become an effective tool for averting violence in many parts of the world.

Monitoring of cease-fire agreements and of military or police activities is something that civilians have been doing alongside military peacekeepers for some time. In 1998–1999, the entirely unarmed Organization for Security and Cooperation in Europe (OSCE) Kosovo Verification Mission was responsible for monitoring the withdrawal of Serbian troops and return of Kosovar refugees to their homes. Since 2000, civilian monitors with the OSCE have been monitoring the border between Georgia and Chechnya. Civil-society organizations (CSOs) have tended to focus on more specialist monitoring activities such as monitoring of election violence and policing of peaceful demonstrations.

Protective accompaniment is a more specific peacekeeping tool developed by Peace Brigades International (PBI) and now used by a number of other organizations working in Latin America and other parts of the world. This involves being with individuals (human rights activists, for example) or groups for up to twenty-four hours a day who are under threat of violent attack. It relies upon various forms of political pressure to dissuade the attackers from carrying out their threat. This has proven highly effective in certain situations, although it is dangerous to assume it will work in situations where the perpetrators of violence are not so susceptible to outside pressures.

Many people assume that peacekeeping is essentially about getting between opposing armies and preventing them from fighting. Unless the aim of a military intervention is to fight and defeat one or other party militarily, however, the only way a peacekeeping force can effectively "keep the peace" is if all sides consent to their presence and have already agreed to a cease-fire. Civilians are even less able to stand between opposing armies and make them stop fighting, although there have been valiant attempts to do just this. On a smaller scale, however, civilians have certainly "interposed" themselves between attacker and victim and in many individual cases this has prevented an attack from taking place.

Brief Survey

Civilian peacekeeping techniques have evolved in part from their military equivalents. However, many techniques also have their own history that can be traced back to Gandhi and other visionaries who proposed purely nonviolent methods of preventing or stopping violence. In 1922, Gandhi proposed the establishment of a *Shanti Sena* or "peace army" made up of trained volunteers who would intervene nonviolently to prevent communal bloodshed throughout India. This *Shanti Sena* was later set up after his death and spread from India to other parts of Asia, where they continue to this day, although focused more on rural development than on civilian peacekeeping as such.

The civilian component of official United Nations (UN) peacekeeping missions has risen dramatically, now accounting for over one-quarter of all UN peacekeeping staff. Purely civilian missions, such as those of the OSCE and the European Union, have also grown in recent years. The OSCE alone currently has over one thousand international field staff and two thousand local staff on eighteen missions throughout Eastern Europe and Central Asia. These are engaged in monitoring and promoting human rights, elections, democratization, and the rule of law, as well as basic monitoring of violence and military activity. Other civilian missions have been established on an ad hoc basis; for instance, the Bougainville Peace Monitoring Group, the Temporary International Presence in Hebron, and the Sri Lanka Monitoring Mission are all official civilian missions but not directly under the auspices of the UN.

There has been a proliferation of CSOs engaged in peacekeeping activities since the launch of PBI in 1981. Growing itself out of earlier projects, it was the pioneering work of this organization in Guatemala during the early 1980s that demonstrated how effective this work could be and set the scene for other organizations to follow. During the 1980s and 1990s, Witness for Peace, Christian Peacemaker Teams, Balkan Peace Team, Cry for Justice (Haiti), and the International Service for Peace in Chiapas brought larger and larger numbers of Europeans and North Americans face to face with the realities of conflict and began to make a significant impact on the ability of local groups to function and organize in those regions.

In 1994, the Ecumenical Monitoring Programme for South Africa brought over four hundred people to South Africa to help monitor and prevent violence before, during, and after the first postapartheid elections in that country.

Since the second Palestinian intifada began in 2001, many hundreds of people have gone to be part of the international presence there, through organizations such as the International Solidarity Movement, Grassroots Initiative for the Protection of the Palestinians, United Civilians for Peace, the Women's International Peace Service for Palestine, and the Ecumenical Accompaniment Program in Palestine and Israel.

Challenges

The changing nature of civilian peacekeeping is illustrated by the Bantay Ceasefire case, where an intervention in the South is done by groups also from the South (See Chapter 15.4). With the emergence of the South as an actor in this field and not only as a passive recipient of interventions from the North, other issues about the nature of civilian peacekeeping have arisen. For Northerners, civilian peacekeeping has been largely seen as an activity for external third parties, but there are conflict situations where local groups can play the role of peacekeeping more effectively than outsiders. In Colombia, Guatemala, Sri Lanka, India, the Philippines, and elsewhere, the tools and techniques are being used more and more by local actors to prevent violence in their own communities. In this context, the role of outsiders has become one of capacity building with local organizations as a way of recognizing and strengthening their own peacekeeping potential.

As new patterns of violence emerge in the South that involve not only state-sponsored violence, but also organized crime and transnational corporations, new and more creative solutions to the problem of tackling violence and intimidation are required, but protection by respected outsiders in many cases is still the only resort there is to create space for local groups to operate.

There is a continuing tension between the voluntary nature of many organizations engaged in this work versus the need for professionalism and specialist skills. When PBI began working in Guatemala, for instance, young volunteers with no training or experience would join the teams for as few as three weeks. Other projects in the Balkans and elsewhere have relied on young conscientious objectors doing their alternative to military service. These experiences have led many organizations to set higher standards for the level of maturity and specific skills required for the very sensitive situations faced by civilian peacekeepers. For example, PBI now requires that volunteers are at least twenty-five years old, undertake an intensive period of training and long-distance learning, and commit to volunteering in the field for at least one year.

Another challenge facing civilian peacekeepers is their relation to governments and official (military) peacekeeping missions. Unarmed civilians may be able to influence the behavior of armed actors precisely because of their independence from governments. However, they may also need political and financial support from governments in order to be there at all. Finding the right balance between these two positions can be very difficult, particularly on the ground where complete separation from official missions operating in the same area may be impossible.

Many of the organizations involved in this work have grown out of a strong religious or ideological commitment to nonviolence. This has affected both the ways in which this work has been described as well as the constituencies to whom it appeals. As the field becomes more professionalized, there is a growing tendency to describe it more pragmatically in language understood by more mainstream audiences. The tension between the ideological and pragmatic approaches to this work continues to manifest itself over issues such as nonpartisanship versus solidarity with local partner organizations.

Another tricky area facing civilian peacekeepers is their relationship to international media. Peacekeepers want to encourage media interest in the conflict and on the peace work that is being done locally. When these are not in themselves of mainstream interest, however, the media tend to focus on the personal stories of outside peacekeepers. This is sometimes helpful but can also be extremely counterproductive and therefore requires careful consideration by the organizations engaged in this work.

Building Global Capacity

Some of the lessons learned over the last half century of civilian peacekeeping are that neither military nor civilian peacekeepers can "stop wars" just by standing in the middle of the battlefield. There is a need for long-term commitment and for many different types of complementary activities to effectively stop wars or build a sustainable peace. The local conditions must be right for civilian peacekeeping to have any chance of success. Furthermore, it has proven to be crucially important that outsiders work with and through local partners on the ground and that they are backed up with political and other pressures from outside. Civilian peacekeepers, like their military counterparts, need proper training and preparation. They need adequate backup support and an effective infrastructure to maintain the sustainability of the work over time.

The most comprehensive attempt to evaluate best practices and lessons learned in civilian peacekeeping to date was commissioned by Peaceworkers (United States) in 1999. This two-year research project looked at mandates, strategies, infrastructure, field relationships, personnel issues, training, recruitment, funding, and political support behind the civilian peacekeeping efforts of fifty-seven civil-society initiatives between 1914 and 2001. It also looked at a number of larger-scale civilian or predominantly civilian missions of the UN, OSCE, and other official bodies.

Out of this research effort has come a global initiative of over ninety organizations from forty-seven countries to build the capacity for larger-scale civilian peacekeeping interventions by civil society. The Nonviolent Peaceforce was officially launched in India in 2002 and is currently running its first pilot project in Sri Lanka.

Although the Sri Lanka project is still on a comparatively small scale, the Nonviolent Peaceforce is building a pool of people with appropriate skills and experience for much larger missions if and when these are needed. It is also collaborating with other CSOs engaged in this work to ensure that best practices and lessons learned are shared and used to strengthen and improve future efforts in civilian peacekeeping.

As the Nonviolent Peaceforce experiments with the possibilities of civilian peacekeeping on a larger scale, other organizations in this field are continuing to develop and refine the techniques required to meet the challenges of violence in the twenty-first century. Still a largely untapped resource, civilian peacekeeping is rapidly becoming an essential element of the peacebuilder's toolbox.

Tim Wallis and Claudia Samayoa are co-chairs of the Nonviolent Peaceforce. Wallis is a former international secretary of PBI and currently director of Peaceworkers UK in London. Samayoa is a Guatemalan human rights defender and acting secretary to the Coalition of Human Rights Against Clandestine Structures.

Selected Bibliography

Mahoney, Liam, and Luis Enrique Eguren. 1997. *Unarmed Bodyguards. International Accompaniment for the Protection of Human Rights.* (Hartford, CT: Kumarian Press).

Schirch, Lisa. 1995. *Keeping the Peace: Exploring Civilian Alternatives to Violence Prevention.* (Uppsala, Sweden: Life and Peace Institute).

Schweitzer, Christine, et al. 2001. *Nonviolent Peaceforce: Feasibility Study.* (St. Paul, MN: Nonviolent Peaceforce).

Weber, Thomas, and Jeshua Moser-Puangsuwan. 2000. *Nonviolent Intervention Across Borders: A Recurring Vision.* (Honolulu: University of Hawaii Press).

Resources

Lead Organizations

Christian Peacemaker Teams—
*   United States*
E-mail: peacemakers@cpt.org
Website: http://www.cpt.org

International Service for Peace
*   (SIPAZ)—Mexico*
E-mail: Chiapas@sipaz.org
Website: http://www.sipaz.org

Nonviolent Peace Force—United States
E-mail: info@nonviolentpeaceforce.org
Website: http://www.
    nonviolentpeaceforce.org

Peace Brigades International—
*   United Kingdom*
E-mail: info@peacebrigades.org
Website: http://www.peacebrigades.org

Witness for Peace—United States
For contact, please visit website:
    http://www.witnessforpeace.org

Peaceworkers—United Kingdom
E-mail: info@peaceworkers.org.uk
Website: http://www.peaceworkers.
    org.uk

United Nations Volunteers—Germany
E-mail: information@unv.org
Website: http://www.unv.org

Publications

Ackerman, Peter, and Jack DuVall. *A Force More Powerful: A Century of Nonviolent Conflict.* New York: Palgrave, 2000.

Centre for Peace, Non-violence and Human Rights Osijek, ed., "I Choose Life: Postwar Peace Building in Eastern Croatia," *Building a Democratic Society Based on the Culture of Non-violence.* Report on the first project phase, (1998–2000). Centre for Peace, Non-violence and Human Rights Osijek, 2001.

Coy, Patrick G. "Protecting Human Rights: The Dynamics of International Nonviolent Accompaniment by Peace Brigades International in Sri Lanka," UMI Dissertation Services, 1997.

Eguren, Luis Enrique. "Expanding the Role of International Civilian Observers." *Peace News* (November 2000).

Francis, D. *People, Peace and Power: Conflict Transformation in Action.* New York: Palgrave, 2000.

Nagler, M. N. *Is There No Other Way? The Search for a Nonviolent Future.* Berkeley: Berkeley Hills Books, 2001.

Peace Direct, ed. *Unarmed Heroes. The Courage to Go Beyond Violence: Personal Testimonies and Essays on the Peaceful Resolution of Conflict.* Forest Row, U.K.: Clairview Press, 2004.

15.1

An Experiment at Mixing Roles: The Balkan Peace Team in Croatia and Serbia/Kosovo

Christine Schweitzer

Small groups of international volunteers tried to make a difference in Croatia and the Former Republic of Yugoslavia (FRY) during the conflicts of the 1990s, simply by observing and making their presence known. They supported local activists in their work, finding a niche where internationals could fulfill a unique role.

In May 1995, after the reoccupation of western Slavonia by the Croatian army, the volunteers belonging to Otvorene Oci decided that they wanted to establish a continuous presence of observers in the area, together with the volunteers from other international projects. They also decided to take care of the small circle of well-known, moderate Serbian leaders who, under Croatian domination, could become the targets of Croatian extremists and have to fear for their lives. One of them was the deputy-mayor of G., a Serb who had already experienced interrogation by Croatian authorities but was allowed to return home. Personal protection from UN soldiers was offered to him, but these military personnel went off duty at 7 P.M. The Croatian police, who were supposed to protect the house of the deputy-mayor, said that they could not effectively hinder anyone from entering. Because of this, a volunteer spent some nights in the politician's house, to witness what might happen. Only after the U.S. ambassador and other politicians from Zagreb visited the local politician did he gain enough confidence in the promise that the UN surveillance would safeguard him and his property.[1]

Preventative Presence

Between 1994 and 2001, in Croatia and the FRY, volunteer civilians of the Balkan Peace Team[2] (BPT) were involved in countless such actions. With eyes and ears, cameras and notebooks, they observed what was going on, and let others see what they were doing. The volunteer groups (usually numbering three people) accompanied peace and human rights activists, forming a preventive presence at evictions and court trials. They pursued official contacts,

369

visited refugee camps, networked with local people, and, in general, tried to stimulate civil society by using their status as outsiders. They did more than just observe. The volunteers encouraged dialogue and functioned as a bridge between like-minded peacebuilders on opposing sides. They also helped to promote an information flow within and outside the region.

The BPT started in the third year of the conflicts in the former Yugoslavia. Officially, the war in Croatia had ended. A not-too-stable cease-fire was being monitored by a UN peacekeeping force (UNPROFOR). About one-third of Croatia had become a self-proclaimed (Serbian) Republic of Krajina and was no longer under government control. In Bosnia, a more severe war had been raging since April 1992.

The international community presented one peace plan after another and offered humanitarian aid under UNPROFOR protection. In Kosovo, the Serbian province inhabited by around 90 percent ethnic Albanians, the Serbian police had established a system of intimidation and systematic human rights violations in reaction to Albanian protests aiming at self-determination and separation from Serbia/Yugoslavia. Many people predicted the war would spread next to Kosovo.

The BPT was founded to contribute to the "peaceful resolution of the conflicts, demonstrating an international commitment to peace, and working to increase that commitment." The founding organizations were almost all pacifist organizations. They sought an alternative to military intervention. The BPT was conceived as a combination of dialogue-promotion, civil-society development, human rights advocacy, and, where necessary, direct protective work.

Unlike most other international nongovernmental organizations (NGOs) active in the area, up to 1999 the BPT did not set up independent projects. Rather, it supported local activists in their work by identifying ways in which its status as an international project could be useful to them. The BPT consciously tried to avoid replacing, or duplicating, the activities of local activists; instead, it tried to find a niche where internationals could fulfill a unique role.

Protection, Dialogue, and Civil-Society Building

The BPT volunteers were drawn from different countries. Most were Europeans and North Americans. Ranging in age from twenty-three to sixty, they operated from local offices, usually in groups of two or three, living and working together.

In Croatia, the BPT operated two such bases. One was in Zagreb (Karlovac, for a time), the other in Split. Their work there focused on providing support for human rights and peace groups. One of its focus points in the early years was on the so-called house evictions. This particular issue would not normally have been on the top of the BPT's agenda, but since it was a major concern in Croatia, and particularly of human rights groups, the organization took it on.

Croatian authorities confiscated flats previously owned by the Yugoslav Peoples' Army, evicted the occupants—who were often Croats of ethnic Serbian identity—and turned over the flats to soldiers, or former soldiers, of the new

Croatian army. In many cases, the manner in which this was carried out violated Croatian law. The occupants were normally told beforehand and were thus able to alert local human rights groups that, in turn, alerted the BPT and other international observers (including OSCE and the media). In some cases the presence of human rights activists succeeded in helping the occupants.

In the summer of 1995, after the Croatian army reoccupied Krajina, BPT groups were among the first internationals to reenter the area. They provided humanitarian support and protection to those Serbs who had decided to stay or were incapable of joining the exodus. Those left behind were mostly elderly. They were vulnerable to attacks by marauding paramilitaries who set houses on fire and killed Serbians.

This international presence served as a deterrent, although the small number of volunteers mustered by the BPT was unable to provide the permanent presence that would have been necessary in hundreds of villages to stop the arson, killings, and evictions that went on for some time after the reoccupation. Croatian security forces took no action to stop it. The BPT's work in Croatia ended in 1998–1999, when the situation was sufficiently calm and local groups no longer felt the need for the kind of presence the BPT was there to offer.

In the FRY, the BPT maintained a group that spent part of its time in Belgrade and the rest in Kosovo. (The attempt to set up full-time residence in Kosovo failed because of pressure from Serbian authorities, which did not encourage foreign presence there.)

The BPT group functioned differently in FRY than it did in Croatia. For one thing, the link to local partners was weaker. Especially in 1996–1997, the focus was on using multiple contacts and partnerships to groups and students in both Belgrade and Pristina to promote meetings between ethnic Serbs and Albanians in Pristina. This was mainly dialogue support, or what in the world of diplomacy would be called "good offices."

The volunteers themselves did not participate in these meetings. They helped set them up, prepared the groups for the meeting (including, in one case, providing training in prejudice reduction), and accompanied Serbian activists from Belgrade and Vis to Pristina to mitigate their safety concerns about traveling to "enemy country." Their work in the FRY was disrupted by the Kosovo/Yugoslavia wars of 1998 and 1999 when the North Atlantic Treaty Organization (NATO) intervened militarily.

Afterward, the BPT was unable to resume its dialogue-based activities. Instead, the organization concentrated on trying to establish a youth center in a biethnic community in southeast Kosovo. At the beginning of 2001, unable to cope with the changed situation, and the huge influx of internationals in Kosovo after the war, this center was eventually closed down.

On the ground, BPT volunteers not only worked with local groups; they were also careful to make contact with international agencies involved in Croatia at that time, especially those dealing with refugees and internally displaced persons, and human rights in general. Its reports on the human rights situation in Croatia, in particular, were used more than once as reference sources by international NGOs and governmental organizations.

The BPT clearly defined the limits of its cooperation. There were tactical and principled aspects to this. The tactical aspect emphasized nonpartisanship. This was an important consideration, given the image of other international actors at the time, including European Community Monitor Mission observers and UNPROFOR, which were considered partisan and not particularly well-liked in either Croatia or Serbia. Not riding with UN-provided cars, and not being seen to cooperate with them more than necessary, were distinct advantages for the BPT in these countries.

The "principled" element had to do with avoiding, where possible, being too closely associated with the military—eschewing military protection, for example, and distancing oneself from human rights violators in general.

Impact

The Balkan Peace Team has been one of quite a large number of peace team and civil peace service projects that have been founded in the last twenty years, and thus cannot claim to be singular. Nevertheless, it has been a very important example of what internationals can do in situations of crisis and war.

The BPT was an experiment in combining several roles that other projects tended to keep apart. Unlike many peacebuilding projects, it focused on human security/protection (civil peacekeeping) without rigidly limiting its role to this one aspect. Furthermore, unlike Peace Brigades International or some peace teams in the realm of civilian protection, it allowed itself to get involved in a large variety of peacebuilding activities without feeling that by doing so it would lose its character or endanger its nonpartisanship.

The ways in which the BPT made a difference include:

Serving a preventive function in regard to potential human rights violations. It was the presence of international BPT volunteers that helped local NGOs in their work against house evictions in Croatia in 1994–1995. They also provided a protective presence in Krajina. The BPT has been one of very few, and for some time the only, international NGO present in certain areas. Its reports have been read and used by a number of large—including governmental—human rights monitoring organizations.

Fulfilling a mediating role between local NGOs and international organizations or international NGOs. In Croatia, BPT groups were often called upon because, as an international NGO, it had easier access to other "internationals" than local activists. Unfortunately, this was not only a question of language, but also whether internationals were prepared to take local groups seriously. This is actually a very important role for international NGOs because it is an essential element of empowering civil society.

Serving as a bridge between local NGOs or private citizens and local authorities. Here again, they found it easier to use their international status to get access and respect. This proved important in helping Serbs who chose to remain in Croatia after the 1995 struggle to gain/maintain legal status.

Mediating between NGOs from "different sides." As internationals, the BPT had more freedom of movement between the conflict areas than local NGOs— between Croatia and Kraijna, between Serbia and Kosovo, between Croatia and the FRY. This placed the organization in the position to support dialogue between organizations, and eventually to arrange meetings. The meetings between Serbian and Kosovar students and activists that the BPT mediated have had a very different character from other dialogue meetings because they did not happen abroad (as most dialogue projects prefer), but they accompanied people visiting each other in their towns, which gave the participants a much greater feeling of ownership over the meetings than any international workshop can do.

Carrying out an active advocacy role. The BPT alerted other international organizations about, for example, the policy of Croatia regarding refugees from Bosnia (especially Bihac); the sometimes less-than-helpful role UNPROFOR played in Croatia; the situation in the Krajina and eastern Slavonia; and the situation in Kosovo after the war of 1999 when local experts were snapped up by international organizations that were able to pay them much better.

After being forced to leave, during the 1999 war, BPT volunteers traveled across Europe to inform people about what was going on, regroup as a team, and plan what to do when they could enter the countries again. As soon as the worst violence was over, they returned.

Its grassroots approach and its focus on supporting local groups rather than setting up "projects" as virtually hundreds of other NGOs have been doing in the region singles the BPT out. At least until 1999 it did not fall into the trap of coming into the countries with its own agenda and finding so-called implementing partners to carry this agenda out, but rather followed the lead and heeded the needs of the local groups.

The End of the Project

In 2001 the BPT, after conducting one of their standard evaluations, concluded that considering their resources and organization, they were not able to continue a good standard of work. The last BPT volunteer left the field in March 2001. The international office, which was located in Germany, was eventually closed.

The organization can look back on its work with a degree of satisfaction. One of its main achievements was the degree of cooperation reached with local groups. Except for the last phase of the Kosovo war in 1999, the BPT did not seek to do projects on its own. It tried to avoid the trap of "peace colonialism" by focusing on strengthening self-reliance. It acted only on invitation and tried not to duplicate the work of others. It did not want to supplant what it considered to be the task of local groups, or make them its implementing partner for an agenda developed elsewhere. Rather, it saw itself as a civilian peacekeeping body, motivated by the goal of preventing violence and human rights violations.

The BPT managed to set up a system with a general assembly, a co-ordinating committee, subgroups, an international office, and the volunteer groups in the field that made it possible for the coalition to work together successfully, therefore offering an example for future cooperation between different groups. A singular achievement of this body was the example it provided of practical international cooperation between peace groups and peace services—as against conferences/advocacy or gathering at major international events.[3]

The work of the BPT has been documented fairly well, enabling a thorough account of what happened, the evaluation, and the lessons learned. In general, the BPT has been deemed as a valuable asset to the attempt of reconciliation on the Balkans.

Christine Schweitzer is a researcher with the Institute for Peace Work and Nonviolent Conflict Transformation (http://www.ifgk.de) and research and planning director of Nonviolent Peaceforce. She has been one of the cofounders and members of the Coordinating Committee of the BPT.

Contact

Balkan Peace Team was dissolved in 2001–2002. Questions on the project should be addressed to the author. The archives of the BPT are in the Dutch International Intitute of Social History (Amsterdam).

E-mail: CSchweitzerIFGK@aol.com

Website: http://www.balkanpeaceteam.org

Notes

1. This story was adapted, with kind permission, from Barbara Müller's (2004) study on the Balkan Peace Team.

2. The Balkan Peace Team was founded and run by a group of mainly European-based peace organizations from Austria, France, Germany, the Netherlands, Switzerland, and the United Kingdom. They included Austrian Peace Service, International Fellowship of Reconciliation, War Resisters International, Federation for Social Defence (Germany), Brethren Service (United States), Peace Brigades International, and Mouvement pour une Alternative Nonviolente (France). Its tightly run coordinating office was based in Germany.

3. Barbara Müller (2004) focuses a lot on this aspect.

Selected Bibliography

Bekkering, Dave. 2000. "Balkan Peace Team International in Croatia: Otvorene Oci (Open Eyes)," in Yeshua Moser-Puangsuwan and Thomas Weber, eds., *Nonviolent Intervention Across Borders: A Recurrent Vision* (Honolulu: Spark M. Matsunaga Institute for Peace).

Committee for Conflict Transformation Support. http://www.c-r.org/ccts/ccts7/clark7.htm

Müller, Barbara. 2004. Balkan Peace Team 1994–2001. *Mit Freiwilligenteams im gewaltfreien Einsatz in Krisenregionen* (Braunschweig, Germany: Bildungsvereiniging Arbeit und Leben Niedersachsen e.V., Arbeitsstelle "Rechtsextremismus und Gewalt"). http://www.svenskafred.se/konflicthantering/ickevald/Muller.pdf

Peace Brigades International. http://www.peacebrigades.org.bpt.html

Schweitzer, Christine, and Howard Clarck. 2002. "Nonviolent Intervention in the Conflicts of Former Yugoslavia: Sending Teams of International Volunteers, A Final Internal Assessment of Its Functioning and Activities" Hintergrund—und Diskussionspapier Nr. 11 des Bund für Soziale Verteidigung (Minden, Germany; Balkan Peace Team—International e.V. and the Federation for Social Defense) Online at: http://www.wri-irg.org/news/2002/bpt-11-en.html

War Resisters' International. http://www.wri-irg.org/archive/xyu/en/bptfry1.html

15.2

Protecting the Protectors: Peace Brigades International in Colombia

Helen Yuill

In conflict zones across the globe, volunteers risk their lives by functioning as unarmed bodyguards for local human rights organizations and communities—in effect using their status as foreigners to deter potential killers.

Violence is widespread—and, in some places, totally random—in Colombia. Four decades of armed conflict involving left-wing guerrillas, paramilitary forces, and the national army show no signs of ending. Caught in the middle is a civilian population exposed to the military, political, and psychological violence of all sides. Colombian nongovernmental organizations (NGOs) estimate that, since 1995, internal displacement has affected 3 million people. Successive reports from UN agencies highlight the number of peacemakers, human rights advocates, trade union leaders, peasants, members of indigenous and Afro-Colombian communities, and other civilians caught in the crossfire.

This situation attracted Peace Brigades International (PBI) to Colombia in 1994. Responding to an invitation from local human rights groups, the organization began its Colombia project. By 2004 forty volunteers were based in Urabá, Magdalena Medio, Medellín, and Bogotá, supported by personnel in London and at regional offices in Europe and North America.

The Colombia Project follows the protective accompaniment model developed by PBI in other areas of conflict since it was set up in 1981. This involves protecting human rights defenders and displaced communities from threats of violence and creating space to address injustice through nonviolent means.

In 2003 PBI volunteers came from twenty-five countries, but the majority were from Europe and North America. They accompany individuals and communities threatened by violence—in their workplaces, to meetings, and in their communities. The hope is that the presence of foreigners at the side of

376

the intended victims will dissuade potential killers.

Deterring Attacks

The whole approach may appear dangerous and foolhardy to some. However, there is a clear multilayered method at local, national, and international levels to deter attacks by making it known that there will be an international response to whatever violence a PBI volunteer witnesses. "Accompaniment extends the boundaries of the international community beyond governments and the UN. International volunteers are a bridge between the threatened activists and the outside world. They embody international concern for the protection of human rights" (Mahoney and Eguren 1997: 256).

The teams share information and raise concerns about the situation of the organizations they accompany with civilian and military authorities as well as state entities, NGOs, the Catholic church, the diplomatic corps, and international organizations (the organization has associate status with the UN Department of Public Information).

PBI, and others involved in protective accompaniment, must ensure that a number of factors are in place to maximize effectiveness. They must know who the aggressor is. The aggressor must be clearly informed that PBI intends to begin accompaniment in a given area and that repercussions will follow if there is an attack. Further, PBI must be able to communicate to the aggressor what types of action are unacceptable (physical intimidation, telephone threats, etc.) and must convince the aggressor that it has international credibility.

By maintaining close ties with military and government officials, the diplomatic corps, international governmental organizations, and UN representatives, PBI provides assurance to local activists that actions against them will attract immediate international response. The volunteer teams are supported by an international structure of project offices. Eighteen country groups are responsible for recruiting and training volunteers, fund raising, publications, outreach, and maintaining and activating a support network of members of parliaments and congresses, international NGOs, prominent church leaders, members of government, and the diplomatic corps.

These networks are activated to apply pressure on the government and country concerned in cases of high levels of threat or to prevent the escalation of violence. The country or government involved is reminded of their obligations to protect human rights defenders and displaced communities under international humanitarian law and the UN declaration on the protection of human rights defenders.

Creating Neutral Zones

The influence of this network was demonstrated in Colombia when Gabriel Torres, a worker for Credhos, the Regional Committee for the Defense of Human Rights, was detained by the army and accused of possessing guerrilla leaflets. PBI immediately set its lobbying machinery into motion. The Dutch and Spanish ambassadors were called. They in turn called Colombia's deputy

Jon Spaull

PBI Volunteers from Brazil and Spain with members of the Peace Community at the entrance board, which says; "The Community freely participates in community work, says no to injustice and impunity, does not participate directly or indirectly in the war, nor carry arms, does not manipulate or pass on information to any of the parties to the conflict"

defense minister. A few hours later, Torres was released. As one soldier put it: "Let him go, or else we'll have those people calling us all day."

Inside Colombia, PBI works with eleven NGOs and two internally displaced communities. These local organizations provide support for families of the "disappeared," give legal advice, protect the human rights of displaced communities, research and document human rights abuses, and defend civil, political, economic, and social rights.

It has a particularly strong presence in Urabá, an area of great economic and military importance in northwest Colombia. The region is rich in timber resources and regarded as a possible site for an interoceanic canal and an extension of the Pan American Highway. It is also associated with contraband and arms and drug trafficking. For these reasons, it is one of the regions most seriously affected by armed conflict involving paramilitary organizations, the Colombian army, and guerrilla forces, principally the Revolutionary Armed Forces of Colombia (FARC). Since 1998 the FARC has intensified military action in an attempt to reclaim territory lost five years earlier.

Not everyone in Urabá wants conflict. In San José de Apartadó, a settlement consisting of a village and several outlying hamlets, local people were forced to flee their homes because of attacks by paramilitary forces in 1996 and 1997. Some sixteen thousand people were displaced, whole villages emptied, and two community leaders killed. In response to the crisis, local

A Day in the Life of a PBI Volunteer

"Waking up in Turbo means gradually becoming aware of the whir of the ceiling fan and the tapping of the computer keyboard. I crawl out from under my mosquito net and stumble out of my bedroom. Evelyn is at the computer. She has been up for some time. Tomás is going to bed after a long night's work on one of the bi-weekly news bulletins we produce. Breakfast is coffee and a mango—one of the principal luxuries of life in the tropics. I sit picking mango fibres from my teeth and reading the papers, scouring each page for any report on the Urabá region. Soon Marta and Juan arrive, sunburnt and filthy after several hours in a small motorboat on the Atrato River. Juan and Marta talk of their trip, of the heartbreaking contrast between the beauty of the subtropical rainforest and the hideous reality of a war in which these Afro-Colombian and indigenous people are seen as obstacles in a military campaign to gain control over territory, natural resources and arms and drug trafficking routes. After lunch, Evelyn and I drive from Turbo, through the banana plantations, to the nearby town of Apartadó. The road between Turbo and Apartadó is one of the best in the country. Its smooth, tarmacked surface is testament to the importance of the banana trade to Colombia's economy.

Some leaders of the Peace Community of San José de Apartadó have asked us to accompany them to a meeting with the commander of the local army brigade to insist on their rights to return to their land. The community leaders are silent as we walk past the garrison parade ground, uncomfortable, nervous and frustrated at the lack of progress.

Evelyn and I greet the commander as we enter his office. We have spoken with him several times before in our own meetings. We explain that we are here accompanying the representatives of the Peace Community and then we leave and wait outside—it is not our job to intervene in these meetings. Two hours later we walk out of the garrison together. The three community members are now confident, proud and relieved. Back in Turbo we sit down for a long meeting to share all the information we are constantly gathering and plan our activities for the next week. Before starting work with PBI, I worried about insomnia. I imagined that the stress of the job would keep me awake at night, but I invariably collapse into bed, physically and emotionally exhausted and I'm quickly lulled to sleep by the whirring of the fans."

Note: Excerpted from the diary of a PBI volunteer in Urabá.

people met the bishop to discuss the possibility of creating a "neutral zone." They called on all armed actors not to involve them in the armed conflict.

In March 1997, they set up a peace community with support from the Inter-Congregational Commission of Justice and Peace, the Centre for Research and Popular Education, the Diocese of Apartadó, and Pax Christi–Netherlands. However, as advocates of nonviolence in such a polarized region, the community has become a target of intimidation from all sides, including military and paramilitary incursions. This has resulted in the killing of 135 members of a community of 1,000 people.

PBI maintains a team of thirteen international volunteers in Urabá. They are particularly active in San José de Apartadó, and in another Peace Community in the Cacarica River basin and have close contact with several other community initiatives in the region. PBI, working with Colombian and other international NGOs, pressures the government to uphold international and national laws relating to the protection of displaced persons and dissuades potential perpetrators of attacks on the community.

Risks Involved

In this highly polarized situation, PBI and other national and international organizations have to counteract suspicions as to their sympathies. However, it has been able to demonstrate the strength and influence of its network—as happened in 2003, after an article in the *Wall Street Journal* raised questions about whether PBI and other organizations were working in support of guerrilla forces.

The contents of the article were distributed widely, including in the town of Turbo where PBI has an office. On 9 December 2003, two PBI volunteers accompanying a member of the Peace Community who had received death threats, were traveling in a vehicle clearly marked as belonging to PBI along a road with regular military checkpoints.

They were stopped and threatened by four armed civilians. The volunteers were ordered to leave the vehicle and hand over the keys. Their mobile phones, checkbooks, identity documents, and a large sum of money belonging to the Peace Community, were stolen. The attackers verbally abused the PBI volunteers, told them they were aware of PBI's work in the region, but that it was of no consequence to them. The organization concluded that this was no isolated act of robbery, but fit into a wider pattern of intimidation aimed at undermining the Peace Community. The local and international PBI network was activated.

Direct appeals were made to high government officials, calling for an investigation into the events. Local NGOs issued statements of solidarity. For the next nine months, no further attacks were carried out against the community while PBI volunteers were present.

Impact

PBI's work in Colombia has won praise. An external evaluation of the Colombia Project, published in August 2004, said it had limited the number of attacks on communities:

> In the midst of barbarity their presence has enabled us . . . to continue accompanying the displaced communities, has prevented the number of killed, disappeared, tortured, and displaced persons from multiplying . . . it has meant protection for us but more importantly the chance for the peace communities to rebuild all that has been destroyed. (Danilo Rueda, quoted in PBI 2004)

PBI has received many prestigious awards for its work, including the 2001 Martin Ennals Award for Human Rights Defenders, granted annually to an individual or an organization who has displayed exceptional courage in combating human rights violations.

The PBI policy of entering an area of conflict after having been invited by at least one party or stakeholder, should be seen as a good code of conduct for other "outsiders" looking to work in conflict areas. By protecting the protectors, PBI not only protects the person or organization it accompanies, but also the people/societies that benefit from the work of that organization. In that way, it effectively opens political space for these groups to work in.

Helen Yuill works in the International Office of Peace Brigades International.

Contact

PBI International Office
The Grayston Centre
28 Charles Square
London N1 6HT, U.K.
Tel: + 44 (0)20 7324 4628
E-mail: info@peacebrigades.org
Website: http://www.peacebrigades.org

PBI Colombia Project Office
The Grayston Centre
28 Charles Square
London N1 6HT, UK
Tel: +44 (0)20 7324 4769
Fax: +44 (0)20 7324 4762
E-mail: pbicolombia@pbicolombia.org
Website: http://www.peacebrigades.org/
    colombia

Selected Bibliography

Mahoney, Liam, and Luis Enrique Eguren. 1997. *Unarmed Bodyguards: International Accompaniment for the Protection of Human Rights* (Hartford, CT: Kumarian Press).

Mathews, Dylan. 2001. "Peace Brigades International–Colombia, 1995–1999," in Dylan Mathews, ed., *War Prevention Works: 50 Stories of People Resolving Conflict* (Oxford: Oxford Research Group).

Peace Brigades International (PBI). 2000.*PBI Newsletter, Quarterly publication of Peace Brigades International European Office,* No. 1, Fourth Quarter (London: PBI) Online:http://www.peacebrigades.org/beo/beonews0004.pdf.

"Peace Brigades International Wins 2001 Martin Ennals Award for Human Rights Defenders," 22 March 2001. Online at: http://www.huridocs.org/presseng.htm.

Schweitzer, C. 2003. *Nonviolent Intervention, CPS Working Paper No. 7* (Tromso, Norway: Centre for Peace Studies, University of Tromso).

15.3

Human Shields to Limit Violence: Witness for Peace in Nicaragua

In the 1980s, Witness for Peace organized visits by delegations of U.S. citizens to Nicaragua to operate as human shields, preventing rebels from attacking villages. On their return to the United States (U.S.), the grassroots delegations incited intense public debate about Washington's Central America policy. The strategy contributed to the decision by the U.S. Congress to cut off military aid to the Contra rebels. It even may have helped to avert an all-out U.S. invasion of Nicaragua.

On 9 April 1983, Gail Phares, a former missionary of the U.S. Maryknoll movement, led a delegation of thirty religious activists from North Carolina into the small Nicaraguan farming community of El Porvenir, a tobacco-growing region close to the border with Honduras. El Porvenir had been under attack by the U.S.-backed Contra rebels. When the U.S. citizens entered the area, a calm set over the village. As they were watching the Contra rebels who were clearly visible in their camp at the other side of the valley, one of the U.S. visitors asked, "Why aren't they shooting now?" "They're not shooting because they can see you," Phares said someone told the group. The experience was an eye-opener to many on the delegation, including Gail Phares.

The mere presence of U.S. citizens in a war/strife zone in Central America, a region long perceived to be part of the U.S. sphere of influence, turned out to have huge impact on the daily life of villagers and townspeople. U.S. citizens of different rank and file could bring peace, simply by traveling south to Central American regions of tension. Many delegation members, most of whom were religious with strong ties to churches, took this as an inspiration to pursue on this road. They helped the movement to develop. Witness for Peace (WfP), as the organization was dubbed, grew to an organization of sixteen thousand people and has helped thousands of citizens to travel abroad and conduct advocacy activities in the U.S. WfP also widened its scope to other countries in the region, as well as in the Caribbean, including Cuba and Haiti.

Seeking an Effective Response

The attacks of Contra rebels on the small town of El Porvenir and other villages in Nicaragua were part of a new phase in Nicaragua's decades-old civil war. The small Central American country, which borders both on the Pacific and the Caribbean, was led by the autocratic regime of the Somoza family and its cronies until the late 1970s. Since 1961, this regime was being fought by the Sandinista National Liberation Front, or Sandinistas. In 1979, the Sandinistas overthrew the Somoza dynasty. Their success was largely due to the popular support they had enjoyed throughout the country. The Sandinistas—a coalition of Marxists, Roman Catholic priests, and liberation theologians—inherited a country riddled with inequality. U.S. president Ronald Reagan and many others considered the Sandinistas a communist threat. Soon after the Sandinistas took power, the U.S. began supporting rebels stationed in Honduras and Costa Rica, known as the Contras, in an attempt to topple the government. The Contras—or "counterrevolutionaries"—waged attacks in the Nicaraguan countryside, burning villages and destroying convents, schools, and hospitals.

Various peace activists, church groups, and students of Latin American liberation theology in the U.S. and Canada had been interested in the struggles of ordinary people throughout Latin America since the 1960s. By 1983, many came to believe that the U.S. government was using the Contras to plan a full-scale invasion and occupation of Nicaragua. Groups traveled to Nicaragua to better understand the situation and seek an effective response.

The initial visit led by Gail Phares to Nicaragua in April 1983 was part of these ongoing activities. Phares represented the Carolina Interfaith Task Force on Central America, a faith-based movement dedicated to changing U.S. policies that it said contributed to "poverty and oppression" in Central America. It had been undertaking advocacy campaigns and organized workshops to put Central America on the agenda. It also sent delegations to the region. However, using these delegations as "human shields" had not been its initial intention. The realization that the presence of foreign citizens could have such an immediate effect on the situation in a region of civil war was relatively new. It was the result of the experience in El Porvenir. One of the members of the delegation said, "If all it takes to stop this killing is to get a bunch of Americans down here, then let's do it." Gail Phares met with Sandinista officials. "What do you think about having a nonviolent presence in the war zone?" she asked. She got clearance to mobilize a citizen-led peace force.

The group set a goal that year of bringing people from all fifty states into Nicaragua by 4 July, the U.S. Independence Day. The plan received instant approval from U.S. peace, religious, and human rights groups. A first follow-up delegation of 157 people arrived at the nearby town of Jalapa three months later to "stand with the Nicaraguan people," again in the hope that their presence would deter Contra attacks. In 1984, Phares lead a two-hundred-person delegation into Nicaragua, representing citizens from all U.S. states. "We became a national movement," Phares said. The group formed a coalition made up of concerned groups in the U.S., including mainstream churches and smaller churches such as the Quakers and Mennonites. Other organizations such as Peace Brigades International also supported the coalition.

As a new coalition, WfP agreed that a long-term team would be supported by short-term visits by delegations, lasting one or two weeks. The long-term team would organize and coordinate the visits of delegations to Nicaragua. Each long-term team member and short-term delegate was intensely trained prior to his or her visit to Nicaragua. Training included role playing involving ambushes and kidnappings, as well as documentation skills in order to be able to report on their experiences in a professional manner.

In addition to living in villages at risk of violence, the witnesses—enjoying the relative protection that their U.S. nationality offered them—soon began following the Contras with notepads and cameras to record everything that they saw. In some places their work took the form of taking testimonials from those who were allegedly brutalized by the Contras. According to human rights organizations, including Amnesty International, human rights abuses were being committed by both the Sandinista government forces and the Contras during the war. The reports by the WfP delegations quickly became one of the most widely used sources of information for the international press reporting on the Contra war.

Upon their return to the U.S., delegations visited local communities all over the country to talk about their experiences and, in most cases, to advocate for ending U.S. assistance to the Contras. In addition, every time the Congress was about to vote on another round of funding for the Contras, the WfP network sprung into action, organizing mass mailings, meetings, and vigils outside every congressional office.

Impact

The approach seemed to work. By 1984 so many members of WfP had returned from Nicaragua and exposed the reality of the war and the consequences of U.S. support to the rebels that Congress, contrary to the will of the Reagan administration, cut off funding for the Contras. According to some observers, the fact that the movement was nonpartisan and appealed to mostly religious people from different ages and socioeconomic backgrounds made its impact in the arena of political advocacy even stronger. "The effect of older church women, business leaders, nuns, and others than the 'usual peace suspects' had a large impact on congressional leaders and many others," according to Michael Westmoreland-White, who joined WfP delegations several times.

Despite the fact that the Reagan government, as became clear a few years later, continued to support the Contras through the so-called Iran-Contra scandal—consisting of illegally selling arms to Iran and funneling the revenues of these transactions to the Contras—the WfP's work has been applauded as being effective. It had had impact in several ways, both on the ground in Nicaragua and in the political arena of Washington.

Thomas Walker, a professor at Ohio University and author of *Nicaragua: Living in the Shadow of the Eagle*, was quoted as saying in the *National Catholic Reporter,* in an article published in August 2003 reflecting on the establishment of WfP twenty years earlier: "Witness for Peace I think prevented war. It made it much more difficult for the United States to pursue an aggressive policy against Nicaragua if Americans of conscience were in the way." In another assessment of WfP's impact on developments in Nicaragua, the Oxford Research Group pointed out that WfP "certainly provided a specific and general deterrent to Contra attacks by accompanying villagers and living in villages at risk of violence."

During the period that WfP delegations were stationed in Jalapa, no Contra attacks occurred against the region. Some analysts, however, pointed to other causes for the absence of attacks, such as the reportedly poor military state of the Contras and the national army at the time. In a book about WfP's Nicaragua experience, Ed Griffin Nolan argues that the presence of U.S. citizens in Nicaragua may actually have helped prevent a U.S. invasion of the country. A significant number of U.S. citizens being located at a port close to where U.S. ships were patrolling in particular could have kept the U.S. from invading Nicaragua, he wrote. This claim has been subject to much debate. According to the Oxford Research Group's report, there is no doubt whatsoever that one of the biggest achievements for WfP was to make U.S. policy in Central America "very public, long before it might have become so in their absence."

"What does Witness for Peace's story teach us?" Michael L. Westmoreland-White rhetorically asked on a more personal note:

> I think it teaches us to dream big and act boldly. A small group of peace activists, most with church connections, with little money and no time to waste, created a thriving citizens' movement, took on an aggressive imperialist military policy of a hugely popular U.S. president during a time of national self-rightcousness and aggression and—at least partially—won. . . . They tapped into the hidden springs of spiritual power in faith groups, especially the Christian churches—even some very conservative Protestant evangelical churches. (Westmoreland-White 2003: 2–3).

The initiative of WfP also met criticism. Proponents of the policy regarding Nicaragua, those who favored U.S. assistance to the Contras, obviously were not happy with WfP's interventions. In a book published in 1986 titled *The Betrayal of the Church,* Edmund W. Robb and Julia Robb, voicing concern among conservative church members, criticized WfP for failing to scrutinize the Sandinista regime, which they said was suppressive of religion and churches. The book also suggests that WfP delegations who went on trips to Nicaragua were not offered an opportunity to assess and judge the situation in Nicaragua independently. They suggested the organizers of the visits had a very clear opinion, as had many citizens volunteering to participate (Robb and Robb 1986).

Extending Activities

Nicaragua's twelve-year civil war formally ended in June 1990 with the demobilization of the Contras. WfP continues to be committed to fight poverty and inequality in Nicaragua and other Central American countries. Over the years, it has expanded its program. Currently it has an office and permanent presence in Mexico, Cuba, Nicaragua, and Colombia. The organization is also very active in Guatemala and Haiti, using the same approach it developed in Nicaragua.

Since 1983, over ten thousand people have traveled to Latin America and the Caribbean with WfP. Delegations, the organization has stated, are the cornerstone of WfP programs, providing "transformative" experiences that contribute to cross-border understanding and lasting bonds of solidarity.

The people gathering under the banner of WfP believe that many aspects of U.S. foreign policy with regard to Latin America and the Caribbean contribute to poverty and injustice. They also believe that many actions and approaches taken by private companies doing business in these regions have a similar detrimental effect on the local populations. The people of WfP seek to change these government and corporate policies. According to a WfP statement: "As U.S. citizens, we feel it is our right and responsibility to demand policies and practices that promote human rights and justice for all peoples throughout the Americas."

Since 1990, it has focused on the effects of economic globalization, many of which are destructive for developing countries, the organization believes. It seeks to change the policies of international financial institutions, such as the International Monetary Fund and the World Bank, that, according to WfP, do not always have the intended outcome in developing countries.

Personal Transformation

A key characteristic of WfP's approach is that to a large extent it hinges on the personal transformation that takes place in people who visit Central America. Testimony after testimony from former delegates relates that WfP changed their lives. The delegates' encounter with local people and a different culture has impact on how they perceive their own reality and that of U.S. society and politics. Although many of them already were highly critical of U.S. foreign policy prior to their WfP experience, the act of actually going to a different region and seeing some of the consequences of U.S. policies on the ground leads to a deeper commitment to seek to change U.S. foreign policy at home. Many delegates are inspired to start working for a cause in their communities in the U.S. or, if they had already been engaged in this type of work, to do so more passionately than before.

Tanya Snyder, a former member of a WfP team in Colombia, said: "In the early days of Witness for Peace, volunteers physically accompanied members of communities at risk. But arguably, the more important work—and what we currently focus is on—is the transformative experience of the delegates themselves and the change they can create back home in their own communities." Snyder, who has been working in Washington to help WfP delegates become "more effective activists," said working toward a radical shift in U.S. policies can feel like a constant swim upstream. "But once you know a country and its people, destructive policies mandated by the Capitol have a profound impact on your life and the lives of those you love. You become part of the struggle, part of the global community of solidarity, part of the solution."

Contact

Witness for Peace
707 8th St., SE Suite 100
Washington DC 20003, U.S.A
Tel: +1 202 547 6112
Fax: +1 202 547 6103
Website: http://www.witnessforpeace.org

Selected Bibliography

Griffin-Nolan, ed. 1991. *Witness for Peace: A Story of Resistance* (Westminster/John Knox Press).

Robb, Edmund W., and Julia Robb. 1986. *The Betrayal of the Church* (Westchester, IL: Crossway Books/Good News Publishers).

Westmoreland-White, Michael L. 2003. *The Story of Witness for Peace: A Random Chapter in the History of Nonviolence*. Column published on the website of Every Church a Peace Church, Akron PA, as chapter 20 in the series "Random Chapters in the History of Nonviolence:" by the same author, 22 June 2003, http://www.ecapc.org/peacemakingarticles.org.

15.4

Grassroots and South-South Cooperation: Bantay Cease-fire in the Philippines

Diomedes Eviota, Jr.

Peace accords in conflict zones usually include a commitment by combatants to cease fire. How to hold them to their word is always a major problem. On the Philippine island of Mindanao, the Bantay Ceasefire team sought wide participation in monitoring.

"We have seen how the Bantay Ceasefire team helped in the common desire of both the government of the Philippines and the Moro Islamic Liberation Front, to preserve peace on the ground . . . I think credit has to be given where credit is due." With these words, Lieutenant General Rodolfo C. Garcia, then vice chief of staff of the armed forces of the Philippines, was addressing a joint meeting of the government's Coordinating Committees for the Cessation of Hostilities (CCCH), which he headed, in February 2004 in Davao City.

At the time, Bantay Ceasefire (BC), a network set up to monitor a cease-fire on Mindanao Island between the Philippine government and Moro Islamic Liberation Front (MILF), was one year old. The fulsome praise heaped on the network by this high official was timely acknowledgement of its contribution in the maintenance of a bilateral cease-fire signed on 18 July 2003. It also reflected the widespread support, recognition, and appreciation for the monitoring mission among most stakeholders in the conflict.

The 2003 accord was the latest in a series of attempts to stop the violence that has afflicted Mindanao for decades (see also the case on the Philippine Business for Social Progress' activities on Mindanao in Chapter 13.3). The island is the only place in the Philippines where Muslim (or Moro) and indigenous Lumad peoples live alongside "majority Filipinos." For more than thirty years, groups asserting rights to traditional lands and demanding self-determination have been in conflict with the government in Manila. Tens of thousands of people have died as a result.

The Final Peace Agreement signed in 1996 between the Moro National Liberation Front (MNLF) and the government was supposed to have ended the conflict. It was anything but "final." In the wake of its signing, some leaders of the MNLF joined the government.

Still, the MILF—which split from MNLF in 1977, and was sidelined in the peace process—continued its armed struggle for a separate independent Islamic state. Various offensives were launched against MILF—in 1997, 2000, and 2003.

The insurgents reciprocated these so-called all-out wars. In between, there were negotiations and peace agreements. Each accord, including a "general cessation of hostilities" agreement on 18 July 1997, was followed by mechanisms to monitor compliance with cease-fires.

Grassroots

The 1997 agreement, for example, provided for setting up the Independent Fact-Finding Committee mandated by both government and MILF to help settle conflicts arising from alleged cease-fire violations. This committee supplanted an earlier body, the Interim Cease-Fire Monitoring Committee, and, eventually, it handed over its monitoring functions to Quick Response Teams. Academics and representatives of civil society largely led these initiatives.

Bantay Ceasefire was distinctly nonofficial and mandated by grassroots people living in conflict areas. In terms of focus, it acted more as a conflict prevention body. It maintained constant vigilance to prevent the outbreak of local conflicts that could spark bigger and more destructive wars. It detected potential conflicts at the *barangay* (village) level, promptly reported them to the network, the joint CCCH, and Local Monitoring Teams. It set up investigative teams, and disseminated reports. Its approach was broad-based: the local Catholic churches and Muslim bodies were engaged to mediate village-level conflicts.

The network was conceived nearing the end of 2002. With the existing cease-fire between the government and the MILF appearing shaky, a core group met to address the situation. Among them were Initiatives for International Dialogue, a Davao-based regional organization; the Immaculate Conception parish in Pikit, Cotabato; and the Mindanao Peoples' Caucus.

This last-named body was a grassroots organization formed from among the three different groups present on Mindanao—Muslims, indigenous peoples, and Christians—after a disastrous "all out" war launched in March 2000. This "all-out" war came after two successive Philippine presidents failed to reach a peace deal with the twenty-thousand-strong MILF. Nearly one million residents in Central Mindanao were displaced by this action.

South-South Cooperation

Bantay Ceasefire's approach was also underpinned by the participation of surrounding countries from the Southern Hemisphere. Its monitoring exercises were undertaken in partnership with not only nongovernmental organizations (NGOs) and humanitarian and evacuee protection groups in Mindanao, but also

Manila-based peace formations and foreign civilians. The thinking behind this was that if groups from the South, especially within the Association of South East Asian Nations (ASEAN) region, shared common problems—insurgent groups, ethnic-based conflicts, or tensions arising from religion—they could share solutions.[1]

This served to further internationalize the Mindanao conflict, which had already seen overseas involvement. Malaysia had facilitated peace talks between the Philippine government and MILF. Indonesia played a role in the 1996 peace agreement. Other Asian member countries of the Organization of Islamic Countries (OIC) used their good offices to help resolve other problems in the south of the Philippines. The United States Institute for Peace was asked by the Bush administration to facilitate negotiations to help create an "equitable and durable peace agreement" to the decades-long conflict.

No Arms

A typical Bantay Ceasefire mission starts out by forming a coordination team to investigate reports of skirmishes. Contact is made with the CCCH to obtain clearance, if needed, from military commanders or the local MILF and village officials.

Once in the field, BC teams try to get the widest range of interviews and documentary evidence about the reported incident. Special attention is paid to the plight of civilians and whether or not human rights have been violated. Where possible, an informal meeting is conducted to educate local people about the existence of a cease-fire agreement that prohibits "hostile" and "provocative" acts, and cease-fire mechanisms.

The mission helps civilians to safety, alerts government agencies to the plight of evacuees, and informs NGO support groups and aid agencies as to the needs of evacuees. In instances where the mission lasts more than a day, nightly assessments are done, and at the end of the mission detailed findings and recommendations are made.

These findings concentrate on whether or not the incident was a cease-fire violation, and ways of protecting the truce. The packaged report is provided to the media, support groups, and top government and armed forces officials, and to the MILF. Sometimes a press conference is arranged, or a meeting is held with relevant officials, to give recommendations or follow up on actions taken. In case of a major war with high civilian displacement, a time-bound campaign such as "Stop the War!" or a humanitarian drive is launched.

Bantay Ceasefire tries to keep the CCCH informed about military activities that might endanger the truce or affect civilians. BC was successful, for example, in stopping the practice bombing runs of an air force plane in Barira, Maguindanao—a area involved in the "all out" war of 2000—that caused panic among civilians on the ground. It did this by informing the CCCH of the effects of the unannounced bombing exercises.

While on missions, the BC monitors do not carry arms. They are careful not to cross firing lines or enter hostile or dangerous areas and do their utmost to ensure the safety and security of members by coordinating movement with officials and local authorities. Because of its high credibility and good networking skills, BC is able to work through the *barangay* power structure, with the armed forces and the MILF, and with the churches and government agencies present in the area. Independence and neutrality are highly valued, so the monitors travel in their own vehicles and use their own resources even while on joint missions. They also carry proper identification.

In general, though, BC's strategy is to work closely with the joint CCCH and Local Monitoring Teams, monitoring mechanisms formed by the peace panels. During 2004, it made joint missions with the CCCH and Local Monitoring Teams, but issued separate reports. When local cease-fire monitoring outposts were established in conflict "hot spot" areas, Bantay Ceasefire monitors were asked to monitor the permanent outposts alongside the government and MILF teams. This represented, in itself, a new monitoring mechanism on the ground.

Major Missions

The main Bantay Ceasefire activities are investigative field missions. Four of these were carried out in 2003. The first—Bantay Ceasefire 1—was conducted in four conflict-affected provinces to probe cease-fire violations and assess the status of provincial-level Local Monitoring Teams. It recommended the formation of a third-party group—preferably international in composition—to take the lead in cease-fire monitoring.

A year later, some seventy Malaysian and Brunei military monitors comprised an International Monitoring Team from the OIC, which supplemented local monitors in Mindanao.

In Bantay Ceasefire 2, a grassroots mission team assessed two communities displaced by the February 2003 war. The team report supported the demand of the returning evacuees that military camps be moved further away as they presented a security risk to civilians.

Bantay Ceasefire 3 in October 2003 centered on the effects of the massive government manhunt for escaped Indonesian terrorist Fathur Rhoman Al-Ghozi in the Lanao provinces (in the areas of the Autonomous Region for Muslim Mindanao). The BC report concluded that the hunt for Al-Ghozi, billed by President Gloria Macapagal-Arroyo as a "terrorism fight in the southern Philippines," instead resulted in human rights violations and displacement in grassroots communities where the military believed the Indonesian fugitive was hiding.

Bantay Ceasefire 4, conducted in December 2003, examined two obstacles to the resumption of formal peace talks between the government and the MILF: (1) the reported links of the MILF to the terror group Jemaah Islamiyah, as alleged by the government; and (2) the pullout of government troops from Buliok complex, which the MILF cited as a "precondition" to the resumption of the talks. Bantay Ceasefire probed this reported link but found no evidence of foreign presence in the area. The government acknowledged the BC report, but made its conclusions subject to future periodic confirmations by the joint CCCH.

With regard to the military pullout from Buliok—something agreed by governmental and MILF panels in exploratory talks held in Kuala Lumpur in October 2003 as a condition for resumption of formal talks—the Bantay Ceasefire team that went to Buliok recommended a "repositioning" of marine units in Buliok as a "confidence building" gesture and to deescalate the existing "eyeball to eyeball" situation between the marines and the remaining MILF units in Buliok. Bantay Ceasefire provided regular updates until the military pullout was completed in mid-2004.

Expansion

The four missions conducted in 2003 popularized the cease-fire agreement in the communities by translating agreements into local dialect. It lobbied for improvement in cease-fire mechanisms and documented the impact of military operations on civilians, especially on abuses and the effects on women and children. A weekly radio program, *MindaLinaw* (Peaceful Mindanao), started in 2004, provided updates on the cease-fire.

During the first nine months of 2004, BC conducted at least five more investigative or field-monitoring missions aimed at smothering threats to the cease-fire. BC members also conducted dialogues in their communities to ensure support for permanent monitoring outposts.

To ensure its efforts are sustained in the future, BC has begun a program to train community monitors in early warning and detection skills. Nearly one hundred volunteer monitors from nine villages in conflict areas of Maguindanao and seven villages in Pikit, Cotabato, were trained in 2004. Village chiefs, who form part of the local government structure, were also involved. These developments indicated the growing acceptability of Bantay Ceasefire and the sense of ownership of people in the conflict areas.

Over the short term, the network plans to expand by recruiting new members, cultivating relationships with organizations, and expanding documentation training for community volunteers. It also plans to continue cease-fire monitoring and lobbying of both the government and the MILF and coordinating with communities to sustain networking, logistics, and trainings.

The Bantay Ceasefire network currently has some twenty organizations and peace networks as members. Some of these are community-based groups linked to peace networks based in Manila and the National Capital Region, and with international solidarity networks. This loose network is sometimes difficult to maintain, but provides volunteer monitors for missions, serves as outlets for BC reports, helps internationalize the Mindanao conflict and current issues, and, generally, serves as a support network for BC initiatives.

Its 2003 mission reports have been compiled into a book, *Bantay Ceasefire 2003,* that is used for lobby and campaigns. For the organizations involved, the network provided lessons in the value of partnerships and synergized efforts. The challenge now is to expand the network to other existing human rights bodies and regional organizations and establish stronger links with international monitoring teams from Malaysia, Brunei, and other OIC countries.

In the meantime, the different sides in the conflict, people on the ground, and observers agree the reason this grassroots-led organization has thus far managed to stave off the outbreak of hostilities is its proactive and participatory approach.

Diomedes Eviota, Jr., is research coordinator of the Davao-based Initiatives for International Dialogue, which has acted as the secretariat of Bantay Ceasefire since its formation in 2003.

Contact

Bantay Ceasefire Secretariat
Initiatives for International Dialogue
27 Galaxy St, Gsis subd, Matina
Davao City, Philippines
Tel: +63 82 299 2574
Fax: +63 82 299 2052
E-mail: maryann@iidnet.org (Mary Ann Arnado);
    or rexall@iidnet.org (Rexall Kaalim)
Websites:
    http://www.iidnet.org
    http://www.mindanews.com

Note

1. This outreach program enabled Bantay Ceasefire field missions to secure participants from such bodies as the Penang-based Southeast Asian Conflict Studies Center; SUARAM (Suara Rakyat–Malaysia), a regional organization; Grupo Feto Foinsae Timor Lorosae (GFTTL) from East Timor; Palaung Women's Organization (Burma); the National Coalition for the Union of Burma; Aceh Institute for Social Political Studies; Suara Rakyat Aceh, and the Center for Security and Peace Studies in Indonesia. It also attracted interns and volunteers from the Mennonite Central Committee in the United States; Philippinenburo of Asienhaus and Arbeiten und Studien Aufenthalte (ASA) in Germany; and the Australian Volunteers International.

Selected Bibliography

Arguillas, Carolyn O. 2003. "Enlarging Spaces and Strengthening Voices for Peace: Civil-Society Initiatives in Mindanao." Conciliation Resources, *Accord* series. Online at: http://www.c-r.org/accord/min/accord6/enlarging.shtml.
SEACSN Bulletin. 2003. (January–March).

16

Development:
No Development Without Peace,
No Peace Without Development

Malin Brenk and Hans van de Veen

Poorly planned and executed aid programs in conflict areas may fail to reduce suffering or may at worst inadvertently exacerbate it. Addressing conflict and supporting sustainable peace is a prerequisite for addressing human need. More and more agencies, as well as governments and intergovernmental organizations, seek to contribute positively to peacebuilding through adopting a conflict-sensitive approach.

Development aid, rehabilitation, relief—aid of whatever character runs the risk of aggravating conflict-prone tendencies within recipient countries and pushing them toward open violence in the following three ways, limiting the examples only to Africa (Jackson 2001: 7).

Political dimensions. Aid can play into a divisive politics of distribution and retribution. It may interact with embedded structural violence (as happened in the case of Rwanda, where successive decades of development assistance laid the foundations for the 1994 genocide). It can be controlled and diverted to political supporters and away from opponents (Moi's Kenya, or the context of aid diversion in the war in Sudan). Or it can be hijacked to support particular political or military agendas (as in the progressive militarization of the refugee camps of eastern Zaire between 1994 and 1996) or to legitimize the power of particular state or nonstate actors.

Economic dimensions. Aid can be co-opted into a corrupt patrimonial politics of graft and redistribution (e.g., Mobutu's Zaire). It can become part of the "economy of war" that develops during a conflict (Somalia in 1992) or a post-conflict environment. Or aid can substitute for the responsibilities of a state, freeing up financial resources that can be devoted to the war effort (as has been argued in the case of Rwanda and Uganda, and their war effort in the Democratic Republic of Congo [DRC], former Zaire).

Sociocultural dimensions. Aid can be misinterpreted as partisan support for a particular political tendency or military faction. It can send out messages of superiority and bias (religious, ethnic, or national) through otherwise reasonable targeting decisions. It can enflame rumors and incite suspicions (e.g., vaccination scares in the DRC).

After the Cold War

Over the last decade of the twentieth century, the mandate of aid has been extended significantly. To understand this, one has to go back to the 1980s, when the end of the Cold War brought about far-reaching political changes that culminated in a great increase in the number of civil wars, especially in Africa and in the former Soviet Union. While traditional diplomacy was unable to cope with this kind of conflicts in remote areas characterized by deep social divisions and weak governance, many nongovernmental relief and development organizations made their entrance. The international community, desperately looking for possibilities to promote democratic and peaceful changes in those same regions, enthusiastically supported the enhanced role of nongovernmental organizations (NGOs). As a result, humanitarian assistance and development aid were confronted with a long extension of their mandate, under increasingly difficult conditions.

Within a few years, a fierce debate emerged on the consequences of the growing importance of humanitarianism and the new role of relief and development NGOs. While working with the best intentions, they were accused of fueling war economies, undermining social contracts, feeding the killers, etc. Humanitarian relief in complex emergencies was called a "fig leaf," covering the disinterest of the international community to seek lasting solutions to political crises in countries that hold little strategic value for Western powers. Within the humanitarian community itself there was much debate regarding such issues as core humanitarian principles (e.g., neutrality, impartiality) and military-humanitarian relations (e.g., protection). All this debate led to a rethinking of the role of NGOs and, more generally, of the role of humanitarian and development assistance in areas affected by chronic political instability.

Donors invested in research and development policies that made a more explicit link between poverty, conflict, and aid. New criteria, policies, and, on occasion, conditionalities were introduced. In 1997, the Organization for Economic Cooperation and Development's (OECD) Development Assistance Committee (DAC) adopted *Guidelines on Conflict, Peace and Development Co-operation.* The DAC guidelines urge the adoption of a "conflict prevention lens" that would integrate the instinct to prevent conflict across all sectors of development activity. The guidelines also contain the crucial statement that "to work effectively towards peace, development agencies need to work alongside partners in developing countries before, during, and after the conflict."

In the wake of the OECD initiative, other donors adapted their own policy. UN Development Program director Gus Speth advised that development assistance should never be stopped during a conflict, whenever possible. "From a development perspective, we must have preventive development before the crisis. We must have ameliorative development during the crisis. And we must have curative development after the crisis."

The European Union also rethought its policy on structural stability in countries going through a process of transition, while the World Bank created a special postconflict unit. In January 2001 the bank adopted its policy entitled "Development Cooperation and Conflict," the strategic framework for its engagement in conflict-affected countries, focusing on conflict prevention, understanding the root causes of conflict, and integrating sensitivity to conflict in the bank's activities. Its Conflict Analysis Framework enhances the bank's capacity to analyze and address conflict as part of poverty reduction and other development strategies. In 2003 the World Bank released a new study, *Breaking the Conflict Trap: Civil War and Development Policy* (see box, World Bank Urges International Action to Prevent Civil Wars).

A number of bilateral donors such as the Canadian International Development Agency (CIDA), the Swedish International Development Cooperation Agency (SIDA), the Directorate General for International Cooperation (DGIS, Netherlands), and the Department for International Development (DFID, U.K.) also developed guidelines for conflict-sensitive aid.

Several humanitarian and development NGOs nowadays are also addressing this linkage by developing new mandates and policies for their projects. In Sri Lanka, for instance, DFID and Oxfam have been working together to design strategies to enable aid and relief to be delivered more effectively in conflict-affected areas, including a preventative capacity.

A general consensus seems to have grown that NGOs working in conflict situations have to choose between to either stick their heads in the sand or confront the issues directly. South African Jacco Cilliers, peacebuilding and justice advisor at Catholic Relief Services is quoted as saying:

> Depending on the nature of the conflict, using a variety of means, NGOs can contribute to the avoidance of violent conflict spiraling into full blown crisis. They can support local communities and civil-society organizations to work for peace and strong ties across social groups. At the international level NGOs can lobby their home governments and international organizations regarding pending violent conflict. There are no easy answers regarding the role of NGOs in preventing deadly conflict, but we can be certain of one thing if conflict prevention is not successful: the inevitable destruction of all that we and the communities we serve have worked to achieve. (van der Veen, 2003: 163)

The Current Debate

If peace is the prerequisite for development, human rights, and justice, then humanitarian and development organizations should devote a much greater share of their resources to the fight for peace, first and foremost, to prevent

World Bank Urges International Action to Prevent Civil Wars

International action to prevent civil wars in poor countries could avert untold suffering, spur poverty reduction, and help to protect people around the world from negative spillover effects, including drug trafficking, disease, and terrorism, according to the World Bank study *Breaking the Conflict Trap: Civil War and Development Policy.*

Contrary to popular opinion, ethnic tensions and ancient political feuds are rarely the primary cause of civil wars, says the study. Instead, economic forces such as entrenched poverty and heavy dependence on natural-resource exports are usually to blame. Because of this, the study concludes that the international community has both compelling reasons and the means to prevent such conflicts. It urges three sets of actions to prevent civil wars: more and better-targeted aid for countries at risk, increased transparency of the revenue derived from natural resources, and better-timed postconflict peacekeeping and aid.

"Every time a civil war breaks out some historian traces its origin to the 14th century and some anthropologist expounds on its ethnic roots," said Paul Collier, the lead author of the report, at its launch. "Some countries are more prone to civil war than others but distant history and ethnic tensions are rarely the best explanations. Instead, look at a nation's recent past and, most important, its economic conditions."

Since 1995 the bank has supported reconstruction in Bosnia-Herzegovina, Rwanda, Kosovo, Sierra Leone, other Balkan states, East Timor, the Democratic Republic of Congo (DRC), and Afghanistan. In response to these and other conflicts, international attention and the bank's own work have focused increasingly on conflict prevention.

The new World Bank study analyzed fifty-two major civil wars that occurred between 1960 and 1999. The typical conflict lasted about seven years and left a legacy of persistent poverty and disease. The study found that the negative effects of these wars extended far beyond the actual fighting, to neighboring countries and even to distant, high-income countries.

Perhaps surprisingly, neither ethnic and religious diversity nor income inequality increased the likelihood that a country would fall into civil war. For the average country in the study, the risk of civil war during any five-year period was about 6 percent. The risk, however, was alarmingly higher if the economy was poor, economically declining, and dependent on natural-resource exports. For a country such as the Democratic Republic of Congo in the late 1990s, with deep poverty, a collapsing economy, and huge mineral exploitation, the risk of civil war was nearly 80 percent.

"Failure to develop greatly increases the chance that a country will be caught in a civil war, and such conflicts in turn destroy the foundations for development," said Collier. "Countries can break this conflict trap by putting in place the policies and institutions necessary for sustained growth. Our new understanding of the causes and consequences of civil wars provides a compelling basis for international action."

(continues)

World Bank Urges International Action (continued)

The study challenges a common assumption that civil war combatants should be left to fight it out among themselves. "This attitude is not just heartless, it is foolish," Collier said. To start with, most of the suffering caused by civil war—death, injury, disease, dislocation, and loss of possessions—is experienced by noncombatants who have little say about whether the war should begin or how long it should last. Moreover, the domestic costs of civil war continue long after the fighting ends. Countries that suffer a civil war often get locked into persistently high levels of military expenditure, capital flight, infectious disease, low growth, and entrenched poverty. A country that has recently emerged from war is at especially high risk of falling into conflict again.

Local Wars, Global Casualties

The negative effects do not stop at the border: neighboring countries suffer immediate and long-term effects, including the costs of providing for refugees, increased infectious disease (such as malaria, HIV/AIDS, and tuberculosis), and higher military expenditure. Throughout the region, investment dries up and economic growth declines, heightening the risk that neighboring countries will themselves fall into civil war.

Globally, three major social evils are in large part the by-product of civil wars: "hard" drugs, HIV/AIDS, and international terrorism. For example, about 95 percent of the global production of illegal narcotics is located in civil-war countries. Epidemiological research suggests that the initial spread of HIV/AIDS was closely associated with the 1979 civil war in Uganda, and the large number of rapes along the border with Tanzania. Finally, international terrorists need areas outside of government control for large-scale training camps, such as those that Al-Qaeda ran in Afghanistan.

"The world is too small and tightly networked for the damages of conflict to be contained within the country at war," said Nicholas Stern, World Bank chief economist and senior vice-president for development economics. "The study shows that even if we are not prepared to act from a sense of common decency, self-interest dictates that the international community must work together to reduce the number and length of these tragic and deeply destructive conflicts."

An Agenda for Action

Fortunately, there is a growing record of successes in such collective action. For example, new international regulations in the diamond trade have cut financing for rebel groups dependent on "blood diamonds," helping to end rebellions in Angola and Sierra Leone. Rich countries' agreement to make bribery of developing country officials a crime has reduced the corruption that is often a contributing factor in the onset of conflict. An international ban on landmines instituted in 1997 has already halved the number of casualties.

(continues)

World Bank Urges International Action (continued)

"There is a growing recognition that there can be no peace without development and no development without peace," says Ian Bannon, head of the bank's Conflict Prevention and Reconstruction Unit. "Developing countries, donors, international organizations, NGOs and private firms have a common interest in ending civil wars and an untapped potential to build peace." The study proposes a three-part agenda for action that incorporates a variety of initiatives already under way:

1. *More and better aid.* Increased aid and changes in allocation and administration could make such assistance more effective in preventing conflict and in supporting countries recently emerged from war. These changes include targeting aid to the poorest countries, which are most at risk of civil war. In extremely poor countries with very weak governance, assistance should focus on a few simple reforms, such as improving elementary education or maternal health, in order to build the constituency for further reforms. The World Bank's most concessionary assistance is already targeted in this manner and a growing number of bilateral aid programs are adopting similar allocation rules.

2. *Improved international governance of natural resources.* Rich endowments of diamonds, timber, oil, gold, and other natural resources are often associated with conflict, poor governance, and economic decline, in part because they provide a tempting source of revenue for would-be rebels. The study proposes a series of measures to address this problem: shutting rebel organizations out of international markets, as is being done with diamonds; reducing poor countries' exposure to commodity price shocks through insurance mechanisms; and increasing the transparency of natural-resource revenues by establishing, for example, a common format for reporting payments and supporting public scrutiny of how these revenues are spent.

3. *Coordinating reductions in military spending and sequencing military interventions with aid and reform.* Civil wars often lead to regional arms races, which undermine development and increase the risk of war. One solution is for regional political organizations to negotiate coordinated cuts in arms spending, and for international financial institutions to monitor compliance. When the international community intervenes militarily to stop a war, the military and aid commitments should last long enough for development to take hold. This typically takes four to five years, but peacekeeping forces and aid are often sharply reduced after just two years, increasing the risk of resumed hostilities.

The study concludes that if these three sets of measures were put into place, then civil wars would be fewer and shorter, and countries emerging from war would be less likely to relapse. As a result, the number of countries in civil war at any given time would fall by half, to about one in twenty, from the current level of about one in ten.

Source: Paul Collier et al. *Breaking the Conflict Trap: Civil War and Development Policy.* Washington, DC: World Bank, 2003.

as well as to put an end to deadly conflict. However, what would that fight look like? The contemporary debate on the role of development aid as a contribution to conflict transformation focuses primarily on the relative strength and weaknesses of three interrelated approaches.

1. The "Do No Harm" approach, developed by Mary Anderson (1999), primarily aims to avoid doing more harm than good, and is vitally concerned with the unintended negative impact of development aid, pointing out that it often tends to aggravate conflict rather than contribute to its resolution.
2. The "Local Capacities for Peace" approach seeks to identify potential entry points for conflict transformation through development aid, and recommends that external donor agencies should focus on supporting local capacities for peace.
3. The discourse on Peace and Conflict Impact Assessment (PCIA) stresses the need for a thorough analysis of the conflict context. From this develops a methodology for the assessment and evaluation of peace and conflict impact that offers a framework for peacebuilding.

See Chapter 2 of this volume for a further elaboration on these three approaches.

Mainstreaming Conflict Prevention

Through the above-mentioned approaches—and several other recent research projects—many lessons have been learned. It is, however, the implications of these lessons that complicate the issue. How should one respond to the realization that aid can do a lot of harm? What does that recognition mean in practical terms for humanitarian aid workers distributing food to refugees in conflict areas? Further, the concept of conflict prevention is not easy to grasp and to translate into explicit activities. For this reason, many development and humanitarian NGOs and workers have, so far, been reluctant to implement the lessons in their daily routine.

Goodhand and Lewer (2001) argue that mainstreaming conflict prevention is easier said than done. How far should this issue be incorporated into the agency's thinking and practice? Furthermore, how far should the mainstreaming be extended? Should development NGOs change into peacebuilding organizations as well? The authors argue that NGOs should indeed try to tackle the roots of the conflict, by working "on" conflict, but also that they should develop a linkage between the conflict and their work, i.e., develop a conflict-sensitive approach, or learn to work "in" conflict.

However, Goodhand and Lewer warn that, when deciding to expand their mandates, NGOs should guard against exceeding their responsibility and engaging themselves in the conflict dynamics as such. This warning is coupled with a second caution: before policymakers decide on the actual agenda of development NGOs, the voices of those actually engaged in the conflict

Teaching in the desert of Mali

should be heard. What are the experiences of and views on the conflict reality they are faced with in their everyday lives?

A number of agencies and programs have been experimenting with new approaches. These include Oxfam Great Britain in Sri Lanka and Norwegian Church Aid (NCA) in Mali. This last case is an illustration of an organization whose involvement in peacebuilding grew "organically" out of its long-term commitment to the development of the areas where it worked. (See Chapter 16.1.) NCA has successfully extended its humanitarian mandate, not by losing its commitment to providing basic support to people affected by war, but by creating ways and means to provide peaceful long-term solutions to the conflict context as well.

At the organizational level, agencies have implemented re-skilling through training workshops, cooperated with research programs, and undergone re-alignments of aims and objectives. It has been shown that introducing peacebuilding elements into daily practice can be achieved in two ways:

1. Top-down efforts: identified by headquarters and then disseminated downward (like Oxfam GB identifying conflict reduction as a regional strategic change objective)
2. Bottom-up efforts: identified by people in the field—pressure from below, based on experience, working with local partners, and consultation with beneficiaries

The most effective way of mainstreaming conflict prevention into aid and relief work involves a combination of top-down and bottom-up efforts, conclude Goodhand and Lewer (2001).

Ongoing NGO experience shows that they have tried to mainstream the issue of peacebuilding by adding it to the management responsibilities of the staff, appointing conflict advisors, forming a special conflict unit, and investing in training and capacity building of staff.

Added Value

On its own, aid cannot promote peace. It should be part of a package of foreign-policy measures—including policy dialogue, preventive diplomacy, cultural, trade and investment policies, and military cooperation—toward a conflict-affected area. To be effective, Leonhardt and Nyheim (1999) argue, policy coherence between these instruments is required, which means that they all should be applied with peace as the ultimate objective in mind. If that condition is met, they say, there are three main areas in which relief, rehabilitation, and development aid can play a positive role in promoting peace.

1. *Long-term conflict prevention.* Aid has the potential to address the structural conditions (or "root causes") that produce violent conflict, such as social exclusion, lack of political participation, unaccountable public institutions, and lack of personal security. It can also support people in creating institutions for the peaceful resolution of social conflict and empower them to become involved in conflict prevention initiatives. Such fundamental social transformations can only be achieved in a long-term perspective. Despite ever-shortening funding cycles, aid does have the capacity to offer such long-term commitment and support to countries at risk of violent conflict.

2. *Supporting peace processes.* During war-peace transitions and in post-conflict situations, aid can help prepare the ground for sustainable peace. Experience has shown that political negotiations (Track One) are unlikely to lead to a lasting peace agreement if a peace process that goes down to the grassroots does not support them. The social groundwork for peace needs to be based on participation, material benefit, and security. In the early stages of the peace process, aid can support citizens in creating social spaces for dialogue, generating public pressure for peace and formulating a people-focused peace agenda. During peace negotiations, their role as facilitators, mediators, and witnesses can be strengthened, while later their participation in the process of reconciliation and building structures to sustain peace is essential. Aid for postconflict rehabilitation and reconstruction can help build trust in the peace process by offering real material improvements to people (e.g., new business or employment opportunities) and making sure that the "peace dividend' is distributed equally among the population. The transformation from a "culture of violence" to a "culture of peace" requires that people can trust in their personal security and the institutions of justice. Prudent support for a reform of the security services can assist in bringing about this change.

3. *Addressing localized violence.* Development aid can support communities in dealing with localized forms of violence and conflict. Such violence can range from cattle rusting in rural Kenya to gang violence in the urban centers of Latin America. These conflicts are often associated with high numbers of unemployed (male) youth, the ready availability of small arms, and a deep

Meeting the Challenges

In a recent publication, International Alert also stresses the need for humanitarian agencies—when aiming for a conflict-sensitive practice—not to work in isolation. Increased consultation by donors with agencies before launching aid efforts and support for conflict-sensitive approaches and critical reflection throughout the intervention are necessary.

Complex emergencies in conflict zones do not develop or recede overnight. Despite short time frames, agencies have an opportunity to influence the planning of aid at an early stage by advocating a higher profile for humanitarian issues in overarching policy frameworks. Rebuilding local capacity to withstand and transform violent conflict is entirely consistent with traditional humanitarian principles. Humanitarian agencies can:

- Strengthen the population's capacity to resist the effects of violent conflict
- Act as witnesses to remind warring parties of their responsibilities, thereby protecting the population
- Adopt a "human security" approach that contributes to creating an environment where people can meet their own basic needs

Source: Maria Lange and Mick Quinn, *Conflict, Humanitarian Assistance and Peacebuilding: Meeting the Challenges.* London: International Alert, Development and Peacebuilding Programme, 2003.

disregard for the value of individual life. In this context, aid can assist people to develop community-based security systems, address the material preconditions of violence, and support local mediation efforts. Traditional ways of conflict resolution can be very effective in these situations and should be explored and strengthened.

Adopting Conflict Sensitivity

In the present debate, there seems to be consensus on the need to ensure that all development actors (donors, national governments, international organizations) and processes are conflict-sensitive, in order to counter negative aspects and seek to contribute positively to peacebuilding. Conflict sensitivity is defined as the ability of an organization to:

- Understand the context in which it operates
- Understand the interaction between the context and its intervention
- Act on this understanding to avoid negative and increase positive impacts on conflict (Lange and Quinn 2003)

To ensure conflict sensitivity, actors should: (1) carry out a conflict analysis and update it regularly; (2) link conflict analysis with the programming cycle;

and (3) plan, implement monitor and evaluate interventions in a conflict-sensitive fashion. In practice, concludes Andrew Sherriff from the Development and Peacebuilding Programme of International Alert at the European Conference on the Role of Civil Society in the Prevention of Armed Conflict, Dublin, 31 March to 2 April 2004, "there is certainly more conflict analysis than before, but linking the conflict analysis to the program/project cycle is still limited. An even bigger challenge is the relative impact of conflict-sensitive interventions

---

Key Recommendations

In its recent publication *Conflict, Humanitarian Assistance and Peacebuilding,* International Alert gives some more key recommendations for how humanitarian agencies can consciously seek to develop and strengthen a conflict-sensitive approach:

- Identify, partner with, and build the capacity of local civil-society organizations that are viewed by their communities as representative and legitimate, and that can play a positive role in more long-term local peacebuilding efforts.
- Integrate conflict-sensitive principles and methods into core programming areas (rather than establishing separate peacebuilding programs), so as to minimize unintended negative consequences, increase accountability, and strengthen positive spillovers on peace.
- Where appropriate, seek to develop new partnerships with other international and local agencies who can assist in meeting the diverse needs created by violent conflict.
- Think through the potential impact of the humanitarian activity on the conflict dynamics and vice versa in the planning stage and incorporate women's and men's perspectives into the design. This includes appreciating the gendered impact of violence and the particular roles of women and men in postconflict peacebuilding.
- Advocate for a higher profile for humanitarian issues and human security realities in overarching (donor) policy frameworks, based on in-depth understanding of realities on the ground.
- Develop and strengthen capacity to understand and analyze the operational context, including the profile, actors, and causes of conflict. Comprehensive and ongoing conflict analysis that extends beyond the immediate local operations to the national and regional levels should be considered an important element of adequate risk assessment, needs assessment, and targeting.
- Invest in evaluations and lessons learned that are based on the perspective of legitimate and representative local partners, who are committed to peaceful change, and their constituencies, and ensure that these lessons are applied in ongoing and future programs.

Source: Maria Lange and Mick Quinn, *Conflict, Humanitarian Assistance and Peacebuilding: Meeting the Challenges.* London: International Alert, Development and Peacebuilding Programme, 2003.

if the wider environment is conflict-insensitive (an island of conflict-sensitivity in a sea of conflict-insensitivity). The role of advocacy in this scenario becomes critical" (Sheriff 2004: 39).

Sheriff is referring here to what has been called the "project trap." Ensuring that a given project does no harm and does some good is an important first step. However, consider the case of the U.K. government in Nepal: while DFID is doing some pathbreaking work on understanding and addressing conflict issues in the country, the Foreign Office is at the same time supplying short-takeoff aircraft to the Royal Nepal Army, a classic case of the left hand needing to know what the right hand is doing. In short, projects that build on better practice can be extremely beneficial within their given contexts, but conflict dynamics are almost never restricted to one particular geographic or political level, so there is a need to think beyond "the project" to the wider picture and links to other levels.

Conclusion

Peace processes can only be sustainable when they are led or at least supported by the peace stakeholders themselves. External intervention is most effective when it provides assistance to ongoing local or national peace processes. When intervening, development and peace practitioners should not work in isolation but draw on each other's competencies (work together, learn form each other, and complement each other in strategy and action).

Malin Brenk is one of the coeditors of this book.
Hans van de Veen is a freelance journalist.

Selected Bibliography

Anderson, Mary B. 2004. *Experiences with Impact Assessment: Can We Know What Good We Do?* (Berlin: Berghof Research Center for Constructive Conflict Management).

Anderson, Mary B. 1999. *Do No Harm: How Aid Can Support Peace—or War* (London and Boulder, CO: Lynne Rienner Publishers).

Austin, Alex, Martina Fischer, and Norbert Ropers, eds. 2004. *Transforming Ethnopolitical Conflict: The Berghof Handbook* (Weisbaden, Germany: Berghof Research Center for Constructive Conflict Management and VS Verlag).

Bigdon, Christine, and Benedikt Korf. 2004. *The Role of Development Aid in Conflict Transformation: Facilitating Empowerment Processes and Community Building* (Berlin: Berghof Research Center for Constructive Conflict Management).

Collier, Paul, et al. 2003. *Breaking the Conflict Trap: Civil War and Development Policy* (Washington, DC: World Bank).

European Centre for Conflict Prevention. 2004. "Dublin Conference Report."

Goodhand, Jonathan, and Nick Lewer. 2001. "Potential and Challenges for NGOs in Mainstreaming Conflict Prevention." Unpublished paper, Bradford University.

Jackson, Stephen. 2001. "Challenges and Contradictions of Development and Conflict." A Background Paper for the INCORE Summer School. Online at: http://www.incore.ulst.ac.uk/cds.themes/SJ_Paper.pdf

Lange, Maria, and Mick Quinn. 2003. *Conflict, Humanitarian Assistance and Peacebuilding: Meeting the Challenges* (London: International Alert, Development and Peacebuilding Programme).

Leonhardt, Manuela, and David Nyheim. 1999. "Promoting Development in Areas of Actual or Potential Violent Conflict: Approaches in Conflict Impact Assessment and Early Warning" (London: International Alert and FEWER Secretariat). Online at: http://payson.tulane.edu/mad/conflict/gdn2.htm.

van de Veen, Hans. 2002. "Feeding Armies and Militias or Supporting a Path to Peace?" in Anneke Galama and Paul van Tongeren, eds., *Towards Better Peacebuilding Practices: On Lessons Learned, Evaluation, Practices, and Aid and Conflict* (Utrecht, Netherlands: European Centre for Conflict Prevention).

Wood, Bernard. 2001. "Development Dimensions of Conflict Prevention and Peacebuilding." An independent study prepared for the Bureau for Crisis Prevention and Recovery, UNDP, Ottawa, Canada.

Resources

Lead Organizations

Catholic Relief Services—United States
Peacebuilding Program
E-mail: webmaster@CatholicRelief.org
Website: http://www.crs.org

Collaborative for Development Action—United States
Do No Harm—Local Capacities for Peace Project
E-mail: cda@cdainc.com
Website: http://www.cdainc.com

International Alert—United Kingdom
Development and Peacebuilding Unit
E-mail: general@international-alert.org
Website: http://www.international-alert.org

International Development Research Centre—Canada
Peacebuilding Programme
E-mail: info@idrc.ca
Website: http://www.idrc.ca/peace/

Saferworld—United Kingdom
Conflict Sensitive Development Approach
E-mail: general@saferworld.org.uk
Website: http://www.saferworld.co.uk/csd.htm

CARE—United Kingdom
Emergency Relief and Post-Conflict Rehabilitation
E-mail: info@ciuk.org
Website: http://www.care.org

World Vision—United States
For contact, please visit website: http://www.worldvision.org

Websites

German Agency for Technical Assistance—Offers a broad array of resources on conflict and development: http://www.gtz.de/english/

The Humanitarian Practice Network—An independent forum for field workers, managers and policymakers in the humanitarian sector http://www.odihpn.org

Publications

Agerbak, Linda. "Breaking the Cycle of Violence: Doing Development in Situations of Conflict," in Deborah Eade, ed., *Development in States of War: A Development In Practice Reader.* Oxford: Oxfam, 1996.

Anderson, Mary B., and Lara Olson, eds. *Confronting War: A Critical Guide for Peace Practitioners.* Cambridge: Collaborative for Development Action, Inc., 2003.

Atmar, Haneef, and Jonathan Goodhand. "Aid, Conflict and Peacebuilding in Afghanistan: What Lessons Can Be Learned?" International Alert, December 2001.

"Conflict-Sensitive Approaches to Development, Humanitarian Assistance and Peace-building: A Resource Pack." Africa Peace Forum, Center for Conflict Resolution, Consortium of Humanitarian Agencies, Forum on Early Warning and Response, International Alert, and Saferworld, 2004.

Goodhand, Jonathan, with Philippa Atkinson. "Conflict and Aid: Enhancing the Peace-building Impact of International Engagement." A synthesis of findings from Afghanistan, Liberia, and Sri Lanka. International Alert, December 2001.

Leonhardt, Manuela, Patricia Ardon, Njeri Karuru, and Andrew Sherriff. "Peace and Conflict Impact Assessment (PCIA) and NGO Peacebuilding: Experiences from Kenya and Guatemala." A briefing paper. International Alert, Centre for Conflict Research, & IEPADES, September 2002.

Lewis, David, and Tina Wallace, eds. New Roles and Relevance: Development NGOs and the Challenge of Change. Bloomfield, CT: Kumarian Press, 2000.

Sherriff, Andrew. "Development/Humanitarian NGOs and Conflict." A bibliography and listing of web sources. International Alert, 2000.

Wallensteen, Peter, et al. "Conflict Prevention Through Development Cooperation: An Inventory of Recent Findings with Implications for International Development Co-Operations." Research report from the Department of Peace and Conflict Research, Uppsala University, Sweden, 2001.

16.1

Peace Aid:
Norwegian Church Aid in Mali

When an external group was needed to help sustain peace in Mali, combatants, government, and local people turned to an intermediary they had come to know and trust. An aid agency became a peacemaker.

A prolonged drought was taking its toll on northern Mali during the great hunger in the Sahel belt when Norwegian Church Aid (NCA) got involved with humanitarian assistance in 1984. First, NCA workers set up a project office in northeastern Gourma to provide immediate help to drought victims. Then, in 1986, in line with its long-standing policy of following up emergency aid with longer-term development assistance, the humanitarian agency expanded this operation into the biggest of its kind in the region: an integrated rural development scheme embracing food production, environmental security, rehabilitation projects, and health services.

By 1990, long-simmering tensions between the vast, isolated northern regions and the south-based government had turned violent. The conflict involved Tuareg and Arab rebel groups, government troops, and various other factions. Northern Mali became virtually lawless. NCA faced pressure to join other development agencies in leaving the area; over a two-year period, the agency lost eight of its Malian workers who were accused of partiality. NCA decided, however, to stay.

Furthermore, the agency representatives used official means to reestablish the humanitarian function of the organization in the area, opening talks with government representatives and setting up informal channels of dialogue with the main actors in the conflict.

The NCA Approach

The peace engagement of NCA had several stages. In the early phase the regional officer responsible at NCA headquarters in Oslo and the resident representative in Mali developed contact with their previous colleagues in the program who now had become actors in this violent conflict. The deputy head and a development coordinator of NCA in Mali became leaders in two rebel movements, while a health coordinator was appointed a minister in the government. Facilitating secret dialogues with the various parties was a high-risk activity. Information and political positions were shifted between the parties and meetings were also held outside the country.

After some time NCA felt a need not only to facilitate dialogues between the two parties, but also to take part in international fora where Mali was on the agenda. By 1994, the fighting in northern Mali had caused the fall of a government—that of Moussa Traore, in 1991—and the installation of demo-cratic rule, but continuing clashes raised fears the country would descend into full-scale civil war. Peace talks initiated by traditional leaders within their own communities—the village chief of Bourem hosted the first in a series of such negotiations in November 1994—were making progress. Nonetheless, a more comprehensive, broad-based approach was considered necessary to make peace sustainable.

The parties sought an influential neutral entity to assist peace moves and called on NCA to play this role. It was one of the few entities trusted by both rebels and government by virtue of its aid work, and NCA had developed good contacts both within the various rebel groups and inside the democratic government. Its staff knew northern Mali well, and was aware of the sense of hopelessness—especially among nomadic Tuaregs and Arabs—that lay at the root of the conflict.

The popular sentiment among people about the Norwegian agency was captured in the published testimony of a northern Malian: "The presence of NCA in Gourma even in the most difficult periods, kept reminding us that peace was possible. Otherwise they would have left." NCA itself was prepared to take on such a role. The organization, founded as a humanitarian body in 1947, had already tested the idea of blending aid work and peacemaking during an operation in Guatemala in the late 1980s. NCA had gone to this Central American nation to provide emergency aid after an earthquake in 1976, but found its work was affected by the civil war. Rather than leaving, the agency used contacts and local knowledge to help mediate between the warring parties. Some have characterized NCA's flexibility and ambitions— "as much as possible, where it is possible, whenever it is possible"—as an NCA approach. In Mali, at least, this had a good effect.

In the second phase, around 1995, of NCA's peace role in Mali, the organization appointed a Norwegian who had been a staffer during the drought to start a more proactive and planned peace engagement. Informal contacts were made with major actors in the conflict and important community leaders in the north. The consultant joined a small group of experienced civil-society leaders who guided local peace initiatives already under way. They set up a facilitation group that agreed to incorporate traditional skills into peacemaking efforts.

At the first community meeting they attended, nomadic chiefs agreed to encourage people in the direction of peace. A second meeting, at Bourem, on

11 January 1995, resulted in a local truce that ended fighting. A number of similar meetings followed, organized and conducted in accordance with traditional conflict resolution methods. These took place at Gao, Menaka, and Asongo. One such meeting, at Aglal—across the river from Timbuktu—ended fighting in Timbuktu province.

The cumulative effect of these gatherings was the creation of a series of localized cease-fires between different movements. Eventually, organized violence stopped in early 1995.

Amid the euphoria that greeted this development, though, many people were aware that more needed to be done to sustain peace. For one thing, the economic and social conditions at the root of the conflict remained largely unchanged. Further, the various communities kept their arms and many refugees were still afraid to return. Such underlying concerns needed to be properly addressed.

Listing Problems

The government tried to keep momentum going by organizing a series of regional meetings involving people from all walks of life to discuss common concerns. Although sometimes unstructured and ad hoc, these meetings demonstrated the existence of a strong desire for peace among local people. The government encouraged civil society to continue along similar lines.

Intercommunity meetings were organized to get people who shared the same land, used the same resources, and shared the same marketplace, but who were divided by the conflict, to discuss their concerns. Because of its neutral profile, NCA's involvement in these meetings encouraged more participation. The agency also provided vital financial support. The meetings blended modern and traditional approaches, tapping knowledge-based experiences spanning generations. No single partner was allowed to dominate the proceedings; participants were encouraged to have an interest in the success of their counterparts.

The facilitation group drew up a list of problems stemming from the war and asked the various communities to develop solutions that would enable economic and social life to function normally. These included ways of verifying information before taking action, common approaches to armed banditry, integration of demobilized fighters and refugees, and processes for collecting and controlling firearms. They were asked to come up with solutions to conflicts over land and water use and encouraged not to discuss issues that they could not control or solve.

The facilitation group established categories of people to play decision-making roles. Rebel leaders and politicians were asked to allow traditional village and nomadic elders and women's and youth groups to make decisions. As Mali is a Muslim country, support and endorsement of Islamic religious leaders were crucial, and sometimes decisive. These leaders were present at all intercommunity gatherings. Decisions were made by consensus. Local politicians and representatives of the government, the armed forces, and development agencies participated only as observers.

The first meeting organized in this way, in Gourma, became a model for others during 1995 and 1996. Subsequent meetings were larger—thousands of people turned up to some—making it necessary to get additional financial help. Other donors became involved, such as Canadian, German, and Swiss development agencies and the Norwegian Ministry of Foreign Affairs. A Fund for Reconciliation and Peace Consolidation in northern Mali was created. The government set up special mobile units to buttress the peace process, help reestablish political administration throughout the country, and promote peace and development.

Just by talking among themselves, the different groups and individuals created an atmosphere of trust that delivered practical results. Combatants became convinced peace was real, and joined in the demobilization process carried out parallel to the peace talks held under the auspices of the UN Development Programme.

Flame of Peace

In March 1996, at a ceremony in Timbuktu, leaders of the various rebel movements and government representatives, including President Konare, reaffirmed support for the Malian constitution and denounced violence. In the presence of many international observers, they set fire to a pyre of thousands of surrendered guns. The symbolism of this was not lost on those who witnessed it. It became known as the "Flame of Peace," a signal that war was over. Demobilization and reintegration have continued since then and the government has taken steps to decentralize authority.

Looking Back

An evaluation of the work done by NCA in Mali, by the International Peace Research Institute, Oslo, concluded that while conditions for peace already existed, the activities of NCA helped to give these concrete form. The foundation laid was built on in later years with further meetings and consultations.

The NCA experience is an interesting example of a development organization deciding to remain on the ground even when conflict makes its functioning almost impossible, and shifting successfully from development work to conflict resolution/management. However, it is acknowledged within the organization itself that "different situations require different strategies." Whereas in Guatemala its approach involved the Norwegian government and a broader network of international supporters to engage in negotiation meetings in Oslo, in Mali NCA started off-the-record interventions among conflicting parties on its own, but became directly involved in intercommunity meetings only in response to local and external requests. Apart from funding, the Norwegian government was not involved in the Mali process.

Its approach centered on dialogue and on promoting peace by providing venues and safe structures for interactions between conflicting parties. NCA staff who worked in such situations say talking helps reduce conflict, produce areas for common action, and promote reconciliation.

Although NCA had been accused by some of siding with the Tuaregs, in general it was perceived as neutral—a crucial element in enabling it to play the role it did. It was known to have profound knowledge of the region and its culture, and people felt confident it did not have a political agenda. Another factor influencing the high degree of trust between NCA staff, local people, and politicians was the organization's record of caring for material welfare. The fact that it was a religious-based agency also gained it respect, even among the Muslim population, says Stein Erik Horjen of NCA. "Churches can play a significant role in organizing negotiations, a role often governments cannot play."

In 1999, NCA institutionalized its work in peacebuilding and human rights/human security by establishing a Department of Policy and Human Rights that reaffirms commitment to peace as part of human rights. Stein Erik Horjen explains:

> There are only a few people in my country working in this field. So we need to be creative and cooperative, government and NGOs. I feel that the NCA has successfully extended its humanitarian mandate. It has done this not by losing its commitment to providing basic support to people affected by war, but by creating ways and means to provide peaceful long-term solutions to the conflict context as well.

Contact

Norwegian Church Aid
P.O. Box 4544, Nydalen
N-0404 Oslo, Norway
Tel: +47 22 09 27 00
Fax: +47 22 09 27 20
E-mail: nca-oslo@nca.no
Website: http://www.nca.no

Selected Bibliography

Anderson, Mary. 2000. "Extending the Humanitarian Mandate: Norwegian Church Aid's Decision to Institutionalise Its Commitment to Peace Work." Collaborative for Development Actions, Inc., and Life and Peace Institute.

Lode, Kare. 2002. "Mali's Peace Process: Context, Analysis, and Evaluation." Conciliation Resources, Accord 13. Online at: http://www.c-r.org/accord/peace/accord13/mapea.shtml. (Also including the traditional CR-techniques process that preceded NCA's involvement.)

Mathews, Dylan. 2001. *War Prevention Works: 50 Stories of People Resolving Conflict* (Oxford Research Group).

16.2

A Journey Toward Peace:
St. Xavier's Social Service Society in India

Father Victor Moses, S.J.

The formation and development of the Jalampuri ni Chali Peace Committee was once a seed sown to strengthen the peace process in Ahmedabad, but a little sapling has emerged from the ground. How it can be nurtured to grow into a tree is the challenge facing all concerned with peace in the city. St. Xavier's Social Service Society has been instrumental in the birth of this sapling as a response to the intense communal riots in Gujarat in the beginning of 2002.

Four Muslim youth are sitting at the Shaher Kotda police station in Ahmedabad city sometime in August 2004. The boys have been rounded up by the police from Jalampuri ni Chali on a complaint from people in a neighboring chali that these boys have killed a dog belonging to them. The boys plead for their innocence, but the police have no basis for believing them.

Then one of the policemen recalls that Jalampuri ni Chali has an active Peace Committee that is well respected in the area. He asks the boys to call any of the Peace Committee members to vouch for their innocence if they want to be set free. One of the boys is allowed to go to the chali and he returns with Abdul-Karim Abdul-Kader Ghanchi, a member of the Jalampuri ni Chali Peace Committee.

The boys are in fact innocent, and Abdul-Karim knows them personally. He explains to the police the sequence of events leading to their roundup and the boys are set free. Such a thing would have been unimaginable in Ahmedabad city two years ago.

St. Xavier's Social Service Society

St. Xavier's Social Service Society (SXSSS) has been involved in grassroots development work in the slums of Ahmedabad and in rural areas of Gujarat State in India since its inception in 1976. Over the years its approach to development has evolved from relief and welfare work to development work to interrelated initiatives that strive to empower people and struggle together toward building an inclusive, participatory, harmonious, and just society.

The vision of SXSSS is "to work for a more humane and just society through the empowerment of the poor and marginalized peoples; very especially women and children, who are most vulnerable people in our society." The approach to this work is through the interrelated dimensions of education, health, environment, and community organization. The major programs of SXSSS are Innovative Education, Community Health Improvement Programme, Community Organisation and Development, Social Forestry Programme, Rural Community Health Workers Training Programme, Disaster Mitigation, Advocacy and Networking, Orientation, and Capacity Building. The Centre for Orientation, Research, and Documentation functions as a resource center to the other programs.

SXSSS is also involved in an ongoing peace initiative called Shanti (which means "peace" in many Indian dialects) to promote peace through a variety of interventions at grassroots and national levels. SXSSS presently works in twenty-five slums of Ahmedabad city and Jalampuri ni Chali is one of them. Over the years the activities initiated under Shanti have included peacebuilding programs at the grassroots; bringing children of diverse faiths and cultures into programs related to peace and harmony; organizing public lectures, symposia, and workshops on issues related to conflict prevention, justice, and peace; public interest litigation and filing lawsuits against communal discord and injustice; bringing together religious leaders of different faiths for dialogues and prayer meetings; building a documentation center on matters related to the topic; and bringing out a dossier of paper clippings titled "Shanti."

The approach of SXSSS to peace efforts has evolved over the years to presently focus strongly on sustainable initiatives grounded in people's participation for peace. The Jalampuri ni Chali Peace Committee is an example of the current focus of their work.

The Context of Jalampuri ni Chali

Jalampuri ni Chali has been an area prone to tensions and skirmishes even when there were no riots or other external forces at play. The mix of Hindu and Muslim populations in the community has made it very vulnerable to fights and squabbles. This chali in the Saraspur area of Ahmedabad is right in the heart of the city and has existed for over fifty years, with the majority of the population being Hindu (some 225 families) and Muslims (125 families). There has been a long history of ongoing interaction and animosity between the two communities in this area, with both sides entrenched in their stereotypes of each other. The communal riots of 2002 in Gujarat saw severe tensions developing between the two communities in many parts of the state and Jalampuri ni Chali was no exception. It was mostly the Muslim community that suffered damage to house and property at the hands of Hindus. Most of the Muslim families left the chali to go and live with relatives in safe places or in relief camps that had been set up for their safety. Yet there were also some Hindu families that went to other camps for refugees.

In the interaction with the residents of the camps for relief work, SXSSS field staff members came in contact with people from Jalampuri ni Chali during March and April 2002. When relief shifted to rehabilitation, people started making efforts to go back to their homes in July and August of the same year, SXSSS also took up rehabilitation work in Jalampuri ni Chali.

The initial interactions with the residents of the area led SXSSS to appoint a two-woman team, one Hindu and one Muslim, to assist them in overseeing the rehabilitation work and reach out to all the affected people of both communities. This team suggested to SXSSS that each of them enlist one member from each lane and each community to facilitate good outreach and representation in the area.

The Jalampuri ni Chali Peace Committee

There are six lanes in the chali and therefore two representatives from each lane and one extra person were identified as the thirteen members of the Peace Committee—seven Muslims and six Hindus. The gender makeup was ten men and three women. SXSSS encouraged the formation of this committee and facilitated the members to become an effective forum. A general meeting of the residents of Jalampuri ni Chali was called in December 2002, when they named the committee members by consensus. Several meetings were held in the area by the functionaries of SXSSS to clarify the role and functions of the Jalampuri ni Chali Peace Committee (JPC). The members formulated rules for themselves regarding holding regular meetings, attendance in meetings, responsibilities of members, etc.

There was consensus among the residents that this was a good thing to happen, but there was also some cynicism and apprehension about the effectiveness of the forum. SXSSS played a facilitator's role by providing input for awareness raising and training to the JPC both in the area and at its office. Members were stimulated to take their responsibilities seriously, to play a neutral role in their interventions with the residents, and to appreciate the importance of peace in the area. They were provided with structured opportunities to interact with resource people from other organizations, from other states, and from other areas in the city.

The JPC became the focal point in the area for all interventions regarding rehabilitation work. The first responsibility was a detailed survey of all the affected households in the area, negotiating the amount of help for each household, seeing the housing intervention to its completion, reinstalling electric meters in all the affected houses, identifying loan recipients for SXSSS livelihood-support intervention, ensuring proper end use of loaned amounts, and assuring their repayment by the recipients. The rehabilitation efforts of SXSSS provided a very good basis for the JPC to gain credibility in the eyes of the residents and also with the field staff and leadership of SXSSS.

Countering the Rumors

The atmosphere of the city was slowly improving, but the slightest rumor was enough to ignite tensions. Muslims were feeling very insecure and would desert their homes in a hurry at any sign of tension. Festivals, elections, and public events were very trying times for the people and the government authorities after the riots. The JPC had to deal with these types of forces to establish its credibility.

Since its formation the JPC has effectively resolved several conflicts in the area, mobilized support from the community for celebrating national holidays and festivals, and has been active in the development initiatives of SXSSS.

Its achievements include resolving a clash between Muslims and Hindus regarding police stopping gambling activities by Muslims but not taking cognizance of similar activities by Hindus, and also during an event when a Hindu boy was beaten by a Muslim boy of another chali; celebrating Ganesh Chaturthi, a Hindu festival, by Hindus and Muslims together; organizing an exhibition against drug addiction; maintaining peace when there was communal tension in the city; celebrating Id, a Muslim festival, by both the communities; organizing Hindu and Muslim youth to offer their services as volunteers to maintain peace during the Rathyatra, a Hindu mass procession involving thousands of people.

Continuing Development

The development interventions of SXSSS in Jalampuri ni Chali have centered around rehabilitation work after the riots, the Innovative Education program for schoolchildren, the Community Health, organizing two self-help groups for savings and credit activities with the women, organizing a sewing class, and observing Children's Day.

JPC members have invested their personal commitment and conviction to peace to achieve what they have been able to. They have initiated dialogue between conflicting parties, learned to play a neutral role, persuaded people to forget the past and learn to relate to each other afresh, spent personal funds, faced criticism from family members and community, and struggled to create unity among the residents. They have persevered, even though some members have become inactive and have dropped out. The JPC now has ten members (five Muslims and five Hindus), out of which seven are men and three are women. Reflecting on their growth and credibility, some of them are quoted below:

> "When we came together in this committee, we had nothing but our faith, our integrity, and our courage. We did not know what we would be able to do, but today we can look back with satisfaction at our contribution to peace in Jalampuri."
>
> "We have overcome many obstacles, faced a lot of criticism from our family members and from the residents of the area, but we persevered. The results have encouraged us to continue this initiative. Now there is no criticism."
>
> "Our worldview has changed. Our understanding of events, of the system, of our own strength, and capability has changed."
>
> "Today the JPC has become known everywhere in our neighborhood, in the police station, in government hospitals, in other organizations. We are recognized and our voice carries some weight."

Outcomes and Challenges

The impact of the JPC has been quite amazing. The residents have faith in them, though everything is not always rosy and tension-free. There is a credible forum and a mechanism in place that can initiate steps to contain, resolve, and prevent conflict.

The JPC has developed into a representative forum of the people, owned and managed by the people themselves. They have links with the nongovernmental organization (NGO)—SXSSS—whose support is acknowledged, but they are increasingly able to act on their own.

They feel the need for formal recognition and means of identification when they are dealing with official systems such as police stations, hospitals, and municipal corporations, because it will enhance their effectiveness as a link for the residents with the outside world.

Dramatic personality changes for the better in some of the individuals on the JPC have taken place. They recognize these changes and credit them to being members of the JPC, coupled with the growing recognition and appreciation from the system for using their leadership potential to help their fellow residents.

The JPC has provided a means to the members to actualize their leadership potential in a positive instead of a negative way. A virtuous spiral is unfolding for peace and development in the area.

They are able to articulate and identify the various types of conflict, the causes for it, and also the solution. They realize that for lasting peace the past will have to be left behind, and stereotypes of religious communities and behavior based on these will have to be shed. They are learning to engage with each other in a positive relationship through community celebration of each other's festivals and national holidays, building a common front when dealing with the outside world.

They are able to articulate leadership qualities and skills in themselves and their peers on the JPC, as well as the lack of these skills. They are able to articulate their own ambition for leadership positions and are willing to work hard toward fulfilling them.

The development interventions of health and education by SXSSS have provided a day-to-day context for work and interaction with the community, the functionaries, and their peers. It has helped to coalesce the JPC as a forum and also tested the quality of their leadership skills. Along with other factors, they have been instrumental in building the credibility of the JPC.

The JPC has reduced in size because members who are not regular in attending meetings have been excluded, including a former president. Although these former members did not feel the need to meet on the basis of rigorous regularity, they remain active and will respond to the demands of the situation as needed.

The Peace Committee is considering the pros and cons of becoming a registered body versus remaining an unregistered forum in their search for identity and recognition vis-à-vis the outside world. The importance of the facilitating role played by an NGO like SXSSS in capacity building of the JPC is understood and appreciated by its members. A sense of gratitude to SXSSS is very strong at present. How this bond will develop, and the role that SXSSS will play in future, have yet to be defined.

Lessons Learned

During the whole process there have been several lessons learned. It has proven to be possible to broker fora for peace even in situations of high mistrust and mutual suspicion between communities—especially if an honest and neutral third party can play this role of brokering peace.

- A representative forum of people, which includes members of all the concerned parties, is necessary to be the vehicle for sustained peace in a given community. Every event that sparks off tension becomes the testing ground for the neutral and genuine functioning of such a newly formed group.
- The credibility of the peace forum has to be painstakingly established, even at the cost of personal criticism by family and community members.
- Mutually negative stereotypes and images of opposing communities can be changed to positive ones by conscious efforts. Building trust through dialogue, stopping rumors, negotiating, reconciling differences, and bringing about change in behavior are possible outcomes.
- Capacity-building efforts for the members of the peace forum have a role to play in sustaining it and improving its effectiveness. The energies of the people can be channeled into positive actions and activities that actualize their leadership potential. The forum created can become a vehicle for fulfilling latent leadership ambitions in a constructive manner.
- Peacebuilding efforts and development interventions with the same set of people can become mutually reinforcing to the benefit of the whole community. The long-term sustenance of both activities has to be planned by design.
- Lastly, grassroots initiatives benefit from networking linkages with other actors and forums. Yet ultimately people have to represent themselves effectively at all levels, from grassroots to national to international.

The experience of the JPC is representative of the symptoms and manifestations of the communal conflicts entrenched in religious intolerance that are experienced by people in many parts of Gujarat and throughout India and the world. It is also suggestive of the actions and processes that can contribute to lasting peace and provide a sustained mechanism for conflict prevention in society at large.

Fr. Victor Moses, S.J. is the present director of St. Xavier's Social Service Society. This article was coauthored by Dr. Usha Jumani and Ms. Paul Agnes Rani, members of Jalampuri ni Chali.

Contact

St. Xavier's Social Service Society
Post Box: 4088
Opp. St. Xavier's Loyola School
Memnagar Road, Navrangpura
Ahmedabad—380 009
Gujarat, India
Tel: +91 79 2791 0654
Fax: +91 79 2791 1181
E-mail: sxsss@sxsss.org
Website: http://www.sxsss.org/pages/1/index.htm

17

Early Warning, Early Response: Preventing Violent Conflicts

Takwa Zebulon Suifon

The process of early warning as a means of preventing violent conflicts is rapidly evolving, although the debate over its relevance, appropriateness, and role still rages. Experience with public health and transport systems has proven that diseases, epidemics, and accidents are all, to an extent, preventable. So too is violent conflict.

It is a noteworthy development that we are no longer debating whether early warning is necessary, but how best to implement early warning systems. Moreover, early warning and conflict prevention are no longer the preserves of governments, nor intergovernmental or international organizations. Small community-based organizations and national nongovernmental organizations (NGOs), and regional as well as international civil-society networks, are now actively involved in early warning to prevent the menace of violence that has stained the beginning of the twenty-first century. Our current preoccupation is with how best to tap and enhance civil society's expertise in early warning and thus conflict prevention.

Issues at Stake

Early warning can be simply defined as the process of reading specific indicators or signals and translating them into some kind of anticipation of the likelihood of the emergence or escalation of violent conflict. It has three goals: prevention, mitigation, and management (which may also imply preparedness for response that can be regarded as mitigation or management). Since the Rwandan genocide of 1994, the debate over early warning has shifted from whether it is important to how to generate an early coordinated and appropriate response. The major shift from the "why" to the "how" of early warning is reshaping the focus of conflict prevention globally.

The reemergence of international terrorism on the international agenda after 11 September 2001 has further strengthened the call for systematic, institutionalized, and coordinated early warning analysis and responses to mitigate violent conflicts. There is now better recognition that effective prevention requires better knowledge of the volatility of a situation and its associated risks (early warning); better knowledge and understanding of the policy measures available to address the issues (a preventive toolbox); and the political will to apply such measures.

It is argued, perhaps rightly, that it is not the basic data or information about conflicts or potential violent conflicts that are lacking, but rather that an informed analysis and the ability to translate data into understandable and practical policy options, along with the will to implement these options, are missing. This, however, is debatable. Inaccurate analyses and diagnoses, and hence faulty predictions, may lead to inappropriate prescriptions and the application of the wrong tools (International Comission on Intervention and State Sovereignty 2001: 21). Nevertheless, the inability to translate problems into sound and practicable policy options and failure to garner the necessary political will seem to be the main problems.

Science and technology have turned weather forecasts and early warning about natural disasters such as typhoons, locust swarms, and famines into an institutionalized practice with enormous predictive success. Early warning about deadly conflicts, in contrast, have essentially been ad hoc and uncoordinated. Disaster early warning is less complicated in terms of outcome and thus information sharing is quite easy. Political or humanitarian early warning, on the other hand, often involves delicate questions, and there is a tendency for information to be hoarded. Increasingly, however, we are moving away from ad hoc initiatives as a wider range of actors is now becoming involved in early warning. These range from government embassies and related intelligence services to civil-society organizations (CSOs) such as national and international human rights organizations, national and international NGOs, academic institutions, think tanks, and the media.

Current Debate

Debate continues to rage around various aspects of early warning with numerous theoretical variations and/or disagreements among academics and early warning actors. Key grounds for debate among actors include issues of coordination; whether to focus on short- or long-term measures; how to communicate early warning; how to translate knowledge into action; how to generate a quick response; and how to give gender a central role in early warning. Rather than reviewing these polemics, debates, and divergences, here we will focus instead on the critical question, "What can, and should be, the role of civil society in national and international preventive action?"

It has often been claimed that civil-society organizations, especially NGOs involved in early warning, lack the coercive powers[1] necessary to provide incentives to local actors and hence are poorly placed to take preventive action. It is also said that they lack the capacity to mobilize resources and provide alternatives to conflict and escalation. This would be true if civil society operated in a world that had absolutely no connection to the state. On the other hand, it is believed that CSOs have a clear comparative advantage of grassroots experience, presence in the field, and personal contacts with the actors. There are many difficulties, vulnerabilities, and risks involved in sounding a warning and of remaining neutral. However, the role of CSOs holds a great potential that is still largely untapped.

Critics of early warning caution its enthusiasts to guard against the possibilities of delusion, perversion, and even diversion, which, they say, are inherent in early warning. First, they argue that the world is deluding itself if it thinks that future events can be foreseen and prevented. There will always be unpredictable factors including the actions of individuals themselves and the acts of nature. There is no satisfactory blueprint for intervening effectively in internal conflicts. Second, the perversion theory argues that early warning can easily exacerbate a crisis and intervening in cases that are not well understood may have unintended consequences and perverse effects. As such, early warning is quite likely to bring about what it hoped to prevent. Third, early warning, while desirable, involves "unacceptable costs" to the system of international preventive cooperation because of the trade-off and inducements involved. Early warning diverts money and energy that could have been spent elsewhere.

Countering this narrowly restricted view of early warning and conflict prevention in general, Susan Schmeidl (2001: 15) points out that too often there have been clear miscalculations in evaluating the cost of conflict. When compared with the actual cost of humanitarian assistance, conflict prevention is relatively cheap (even when the human costs of lives, livelihoods, displacement, trauma, and dehumanization are ignored). Schmeidl suggests that preventive action may also have to go "through the same struggle as preventive medicine in order to convince the world that prevention is not just better, but also cheaper than cure and symptom-oriented treatment" (Schmeidl 2001: 15). She supports her point with this argument from Michael Lund (1996: 397):

> The policy question that government officials need to ask themselves, stated in cost-benefit terms, is whether their government's portion of the shared present costs of launching multilateral preventive responses, plus any undesired side effects, would be far lower than the future costs of doing business as usual. Ideally, these calculations would factor in the human and material costs of possible wars, the consequent price-tag for peacekeeping and other attempted remedies, a nation's economic opportunity cost in lost trade and investment, and the political fallout for leaders who would have to handle a series of such quagmires. This comprehensive accounting is rare.

It is certainly true that there is little consensus on who should be involved, and who should do what, in early warning. This is due in part to the myth of the state and its security monopoly. States have often deliberately excluded civil society from security arrangements both at border and grassroots levels. However, the number of state failures around the world is rising, and many states have become too weak to protect their citizens and are unable to provide basic social amenities such as health care, schools, and even food. Consequently, the state and its security monopoly are becoming increasingly demystified. In some cases, the state itself has become the problem and this has opened up the debate as to what role nonstate actors can play in early warning and conflict prevention in general.

Despite this, scores of early warning organizations and networks have emerged, but their microlevel success stories are often clouded by the very nature of prevention. When early warning successfully averts a conflict, its importance tends to go unrecognized in news media where only conflict makes the headlines. As the violent conflict did not materialize, the world does not realize, or even refuses to acknowledge, that early warning has averted a crisis. Civil society's potential as an agent of conflict prevention is clearly enormous. Indeed, successful breakthroughs by many CSOs at grassroots and community levels have occurred unnoticed. The absence of a culture of publication and lack of coordinated strategies dedicated to highlighting these achievements are serious handicaps facing civil society.

Hitherto the preserve of intergovernmental organizations and a few international organizations, the field of conflict prevention has recently seen the arrival of new actors such as Amnesty International, Human Rights Watch, International Alert, Saferworld, and Oxfam, who have all worked to further advance the early warning agenda.

Challenges

A cursory review of its past successes and shortcomings shows that effective early warning has been frustrated by a series of obstacles. Schmeidl (2001: 10–24) identifies five categories of such obstacles, even though in practice they are sometimes so interlinked and mutually reinforcing that they give the impression of a complex web in which it is difficult to differentiate distinct categories. Drawing heavily on Schmeidl's work (Schmeidl 2001: 10–24), these obstacles can be summarized as follows.

Situational dynamics. The Cold War context has changed and early warning has shifted from the realm of military security to that of preventive mechanisms working for the sake of humanity. The Baltic states were beneficiaries of this situational change. The geopolitical situation of some countries has resulted in them becoming centers of interest. Also, there are certain situations and conflict settings that, because they are more familiar to outside states, tend to encourage preventive action. Whether or not the preventive action occurs by force, without the consent of the actors involved, is also an important factor. Unwanted outside intervention may provoke detrimental outcomes. It is therefore possible to conclude that certain regions of the world provide opportunities, or an enabling environment, for possible incentives that outsiders can offer in order to entice conflicting parties to accede to peaceful negotiation.

Political dynamics. The political dynamic working against early warning is often the most difficult aspect to tackle. "The requirements for successful pre-

Civil-Society Organizations Involved in Early Warning: Some Prominent Examples

SwissPeace, through its FAST program, is perhaps a pacesetter in early warning methodology development. Most early warning structures, especially in the developing countries, were inspired by, or owe allegiance to, SwissPeace, whose tentacles of mentoring and collaboration stretch from Europe to the Americas, Africa, and Asia.

The International Crisis Group (ICG) is also renowned for its in-depth reports and analyses of conflict situations, both potential and actual, for preventive purposes. The credibility of the ICG is reflected in its cooperation with international organizations such as the United Nations and European Union.

CARE International also promotes community-based early warning systems for communities in high-risk areas of El Salvador, Honduras, and Nicaragua in Latin America. The aim is to improve institutional capacities and its target communities' skills to better respond to disasters and conflicts.

The violent conflicts in Africa have earned it an unwelcome reputation as the region hardest hit by conflicts in the twenty-first century. State failure is already a reality in this part of the world and the trend seems to be on the increase. Developing an early warning mechanism to prevent a further descent into chaos and violence is clearly imperative.

In West Africa, the West African Network for Peacebuilding (WANEP) is setting the stage for civil society–based early warning and early response through its West African Early Warning and Response Network (WARN). WARN now operates in twelve of the fifteen member countries of the Economic Community of West African States (ECOWAS) and liaises with the subregional economic grouping to share information and analysis on peace and security matters. In Nigeria, where intercommunal as well as interfaith violence between 1999 and 2004 claimed more than ten thousand lives, civil society is mobilizing to face the challenge of early mitigation and prevention. The Network of Early Warning Monitors has emerged through a national strategy in the six geopolitical zones. Strategically, the stability of West Africa depends largely on the sociopolitical and economic stability of Nigeria as subregional power broker, and Ghana as the gateway to West African stability.

The Institute for Security Studies (ISS) in South Africa is also a key organization in early warning analysis and reporting in Africa. With huge experience and a vast reservoir of expertise, the ISS is creating synergies with African civil society, governments, and intergovernmental organizations such as the Southern African Development Community and the African Union. Based in Pretoria, the ISS is thereby leading a civil-society revolution in Africa with a formidable documentation capacity.

Another example of early warning, described in more detail later in one of the following chapters, is an innovative community-based and technology-propelled project in Northern Ireland, titled the Mobile Phones Network, in which volunteers play an important role in preventing potential conflicts from escalating into outright violence. Mobile phones are used to report rumors, speculation, and minor incidents or skirmishes so to nip them in the bud (See Chapter 17.1).

ventive action—a) warning far in advance, b) ideally eliminating or changing the structures that lead to and/or accelerate conflicts, and c) fostering those structures that lower the chances of conflict escalation—are diametrically opposed to the timeline policy makers work with (political constraints)" (Schmeidl 2001: 13).

"The political dilemma, however, is not simply time, but also the fact that politicians tend to want to please their political electorate which can seriously limit decision making" (Schmeidl, p. 10, in reference to Guilmette 1998). In some cases, political actors have chosen not to take any action at all, thus creating a total impasse. The reward/cost aspect of appropriate early detection can also reduce the policymaker's receptivity to information about emerging threats, for early warning does not necessarily make for easy response. Rather, a warning of an impending crisis often forces policymakers to make difficult decisions.

Human-psychological dynamics. "Psychological dynamics include factors that influence and bias our understanding of the situation" (Schmeidl 2001: 17), as when we hope for best-case scenarios and ignore the likelihood that the reality will be considerably worse. When combined with political considerations, this makes for a situation in which political decisionmaking is blocked or stalled. Though there are important lessons to be learned from the past, decisionmakers still tend to believe that their case is unique and so historical analysis has no connection with their present situation.

Institutional-bureaucratic dynamics. "The concept of early warning and conflict prevention can be perfectly laid out, and even understood, but still fail if there are no proper institutional capacities to implement and follow through with warning (linked to this problem is the issue of red tape, particularly in large bureaucracies)" (Schmeidl 2001: 19). One of the greatest criticisms of the failure of warning in Rwanda was not that there was no warning per se, but of the red tape and bureaucracy within the UN system. Despite the United Nations' laudable intentions to deal with the conflict before it reached a crisis, there were no proper channels to cope with specific warnings in a timely and appropriate manner.

A major area that remains a hurdle is therefore the issue of coordinating early warning information. Information technology has helped to improve information sharing tremendously, but the task of getting the right information into the right hands at the right time has not been fully resolved. Recently there have been calls for the centralization of early warning reports, preferably at UN headquarters. The UN-commissioned Brahimi Report, however, advised against this. "Even though the UN is now trying to establish an early warning system for approximately 20 years, it failed in the past not so much for lacking analytical capacity, but mainly for lacking channels to get any kind of information to the proper departments with the mandate to respond. The very recent Brahimi Report (2000) now recommends a consolidated analytical system in order to improve upon such problems" (Schmeidl 2001: 18–19). Some actors in the field of early warning believe that the UN should not host such an early warning pool of information but should instead tap into it. Consequently, a coordinated information structure that seeks to bridge the wide gap between warning and response is a paramount need.

> Aside from the capacity problem, there is a clear problem of mandate. This means, many institutions are simply not mandated to react to a crisis in progress, or only tasked to deal with certain aspects of it. Response therefore often reflects more the capacities or mandates of organizations/governments, or the areas (both geographic and issue) where they are able (and willing) to act upon, than necessarily an unwillingness to react to warning. (Schmeidl 2001: 19)

Analytical capacity. Apart from the impediments discussed above, there is also the possibility of a lack of analytical capacity and information overload. "The problem here is two-fold. First, warnings may not be fully thought out and analysis may be incomplete or faulty. Secondly, too often too little attention is paid on what to do once warning has been received" (Schmeidl, 2001: 21, in reference to Lund 1998). It is also important to avoid the problem of "underwarning," or of missing developing conflicts while at the same time guarding against "over warning" by inundating policymakers with advice.

Schmeidl cautions that early warning does not always take into account its own impact and should try to balance short-term considerations with long-term goals. Concentrating solely on short-term objectives, for instance, may lead to long-term difficulties, while some long-term strategic considerations can result in short-term hardships. Good early warning demands very specific systems where important elements of the "what," "when," and "how" are addressed. Faulty analysis may lead to misinterpretation and result in a major backlash (Schmeidl 2001: 23).

Many attempts at prevention have been foiled and/or ignored by certain groups or circles, some of whom have direct or indirect incentives or interests in the economies of war. Typically, relief-based organizations are more interested in contingency plans and the resultant effects of crises than their prevention. The same applies to arms-manufacturing firms and brokers. A world without wars threatens their profit base.

So, too, the burgeoning number of NGOs who are engaged in early warning are competing with each other for space, funding, visibility, and influence, and thus reducing the possibilities for effective collaboration and coordination of activities.

Networking, coalition building, and concerted action among civil-society practitioners is highly recommended in early warning information. South-South and North-South collaboration such as the initiatives previously undertaken by the Forum on Early Warning and Early Response (FEWER)[3] and those currently undertaken by the Global Partnership for the Prevention of Armed Conflicts, are an encouraging platform for effective action. The sharing of success stories, experiences, and lessons learned has added strength to civil-society endeavors.

Lessons Learned

Prevention is better than cure. The medical field tells us that prevention is better than cure. Unfortunately, the world seems to be moved by visual images of human calamity rather than reports into the likelihood of conflict. Such was the case in Rwanda, Kosovo, and Sudan. It takes a media offensive (the "CNN factor") to push and pull the international community when humanity faces the risk of conflict or genocide. However, simply "naming and shaming" can be a powerful weapon in the hands of civil society. Journalists should be trained together with the media owners on the virtues of journalism that promotes peace rather than hate.

Early warning must free itself from the academic polemics and begin to learn the lessons of the real world. Like democracy, the process should be allowed to flourish in its various contexts. The complex nature of some conflict situations demands a sophisticated analysis and response. On the other hand, early warning of community-based conflicts requires very little in terms of funding. Use of local monitors and local languages in communicating are valuable and cheap resources that need to be tapped to the maximum.

Strategic partnerships. Early warning must be conceptually, strategically, and operationally backed by early response options. This could be accomplished through strategic partnerships between civil-society and intergovernmental organizations. However, the relationships between CSOs and governments have long been viewed through the prism of the donor and recipient relationship that has resulted in an uneven exchange for both parties. In some cases, antagonism and apparent mistrust has been rife. Increasingly, this conception is changing as better forms of partnership are emerging. In the Horn of Africa, the Intergovernmental Authority on Development (IGAD) built its Conflict Early Warning and Response (CEWARN) Mechanism jointly with civil society, and also included CSOs during the research and analysis stage of its operation. It currently focuses on monitoring and reporting on the pastoral conflicts that have both national and regional ramifications, but plans to develop more general political responses. The West African Network for Peacebuilding (WANEP) has, for its part, entered into a strategic partnership with the Economic Community of West African States (ECOWAS). WANEP now operates a liaison office at the ECOWAS secretariat in an interfacing strategy to bring civil-society perspectives to early warning conflict prevention in a conflict prone subregion where the supranational scope of ECOWAS constitutes an enormous response capacity. Engaging policymakers through analytical early warning policy briefs has added more leverage and visibility as well as credibility for West African civil society through WANEP.

Ultimately, the leverage of civil society arises from collaboration between a diverse group of actors. Women and women's groups in particular should be encouraged to participate in efforts to prevent conflict and build peace as they stand the greatest chance of bringing warring parties to the negotiating table, as was seen recently in Liberia and Somalia (See Chapters 7.5 and 21.3). Developing early warning systems must therefore take into consideration this important, hitherto neglected gender dimension.

Conclusion

Early warning and preventive action are still ongoing processes that need to continue drawing from the pool of lessons learned all over the world, from microlevel community to the national, regional, and international scenes. In addition, early warning must be aligned with early response and this should take into consideration two basic recommendations: (1) early warning must be comprehensive, embracing elements of information, analysis, and response options; and (2) preventive action is not a tool but a strategy that must be ongoing. Preventive action must also provide an opportunity for a comprehensive analysis of the costs of conflicts and the costs of preventive action. By linking structural to operational prevention, it is possible to show that conflict prevention is more meaningful when the structural or root causes of conflicts, such as poverty, political repression, social inequality, the violation of human rights, and neglect of minority rights are addressed.[4]

Speaking to the UN Security Council special session on transborder crime and the proliferation of small arms, light weapons and mercenaries in West Africa in March 2004, the UN secretary-general and West African leaders described small arms as West Africa's weapons of mass destruction. In the same tone, the Brazilian president on the eve of the 2004 UN General Assembly, while lobbying for a seat in the UN Security Council, declared that the greatest weapon of mass destruction is chronic poverty. Whatever one's perspective on weapons of mass destruction, the central message is that conflicts do not just occur. They are nurtured and cultivated. The vast inequality gap between the "haves" and "have nots" has also topped the agenda of the civil society–led world social summit. Poverty-related conflicts, coupled with the monster of youth unemployment and consequent youth disaffection, have been turned into anger. Civil society therefore has a circumscribed but crucial role to play, and cooperation and networking become the greatest sources of strength and visibility. North-South and East-West collaboration is not only crucial in this respect but critical.

Takwa Zebulon Suifon is coordinator of the West Africa Early Warning and Response Network (WARN) of the West Africa Network for Peacebuilding (WANEP). Takwa is also liaison officer to ECOWAS. The author greatly benefited from comments provided by Dr. Susanne Schmeidl, a country representative to SwissPeace-Afghanistan.

Notes

1. I am highlighting Nicolaidis Kalypso's views here. Kalypso is one of the leading critical thinkers in the field of early warning.

2. "In 1971, the total expenditure by refugee, disaster, and humanitarian relief agencies was $200 million; in 1994 it was $8 billion. . . . At one point UNPROFOR [United Nations Protection Force] was costing $1.6 billion per year, accounting for half of the United Nations' total peacekeeping budget. The entire cost of the UNPREDEP Macedonia mission has been less than the per annum budget of the International Criminal Tribunal for the former Yugoslavia (Jentleson 2000: 329)" (Schmeidl 2001: 12).

3. FEWER is undergoing restructuring.

4. For more detail on the points made in this paragraph, please see Schmeidl (2001: 20–28).

Selected Bibliography

Davies, John L., and Ted Robert Gurr. 1998. *Preventive Measures: Building Risk Assessment and Crisis Early Warning Systems* (Lanham, MD: Rowman & Littlefield).

Guilmette, Jean-H. 1998. "The Paradox of Prevention: Successful Prevention Erases the Proof of Its Success: A Case for a New Ethic of Evaluation," in Susanne Schmeidl and Howard Adelman, eds., *Early Warning and Early Response,* Columbia International Affairs Online, Columbia University Press, http://www.ciaonet.org.

International Commission on Intervention and State Sovereignty (ICISS). 2001. *The Responsibility to Protect, Report of the International Commission on Intervention and State Sovereignty* (Ottawa: International Development Research Centre).

Jentleson, Bruce W. 2000. "Preventive Diplomacy: Analytical Conclusions and Policy Lessons," in Jentleson, ed., *Opportunities Missed, Opportunities Seized: Preventive Diplomacy in the Post–Cold War World* (Lanham, MD: Rowman & Littlefield for the Carnegie Commission on Preventing Deadly Conflict).

Lund, Michael S. 1998. "Bridging the Gap Between Warning and Response: Approaches to Analyzing Effective Preventive Intervention," in Susanne Schmeidl and Howard Adelman, eds., *Early Warning and Early Response,* Columbia International Affairs Online, Columbia University Press, http://www.ciaonet.org.

———. 1996. *Preventing Violent Conflicts: A Strategy for Preventive Diplomacy* (Washington, DC: United States Institute for Peace).

Rotberg, Robert O., ed. 1996. *Vigilance and Vengeance: NGOs in Preventing Ethnic Conflict in Divided Societies* (Washington, DC: Brookings Institution Press).

Schmeidl, Susanne. 2002. "Conflict Early Warning and Prevention: Toward a Coherent Terminology," in Ciru Mwaura and Susanne Schmeidl, eds., *Early Warning and Conflict Management in the Horn of Africa* (Lawrenceville, NJ: Red Sea Press).

———. 2001. "Early Warning and Integrated Response Development." *Romanian Journal of Political* Science (Special Issue on Conflict and Reconciliation, sponsored by UNDP Office, Romania).

Schmid, Alex P. 2000. *Thesaurus and Glossary of Early Warning and Conflict Prevention Terms* (FEWER/Erasmus University, Synthesis Foundation).

Resources

Lead Organizations

Amnesty International—United Kingdom
For contact, please visit website: http://www.amnesty.org

Center for the Prevention of Genocide—United States
Tel.: +1 703 528 1002
Fax: +1 703 528 5776
Website: http://genocideprevention.org

Human Rights Watch—United States
E-mail: hrwnyc@hrw.org
Website: http://www.humanrightswatch.org

Institute for Security Studies—South Africa
African Security Analysis Programme
E-mail: iss@iss.org.za
Website: http://www.iss.co.za

Intergovernmental Agency on Development (IGAD)
Conflict Early Warning and Response (CEWARN) Mechanism—Ethiopia
E-mail: cewarn@telecom.net.et
Website: http://www.cewarn.org

International Crisis Group—Belgium
Crisis Watch Database
For contact, please visit website: http://www.crisisweb.org

Network of Ethnological Monitoring and
    Early Warning (EAWARN)—Russia
E-mail: anthpub@iea.msk.su
Website: http://www.eawarn.ru

Stockholm International Peace Research Institute (SIPRI)—Sweden
Early Warning Indicators System for Preventive Policy
E-mail: sipri@sipri.org
Website: http://www.sipri.org

SwissPeace—Switzerland
Early Warning Project FAST
E-mail: FAST@swisspeace.ch
Website: http://www.swisspeace.org/fast/default.htm

UN Office for the Coordination of Humanitarian Affairs (OCHA)—
    United States
For contact, please visit website: http://www.ochaonline.un.org

West Africa Network for Peacebuilding (WANEP)—Ghana
Early Warning Early Response Network (WARN)
E-mail: wanep@wanep.org
Website: http://www.wanep.org/programs/early_warning.htm

Websites
http://www.reliefweb.int/resources/ewarn.html
Reliefweb—portal on resources and information on early warning

http://www.first.sipri.org
Facts on International Relations and Security Trends—
    a collection of databases

http://www.cprnet.net
Conflict Prevention and Post-Conflict Reconstruction Network

http://geds.umd.edu/geds/
Global Event Data System (GEDS project), University of Maryland

http://www.vranet.com
Geo Monitor. Forecasting Foreign Danger Virtual Research Associates, Harvard
   University

Publications

Austin, Alexander. "Early Warning and the Field: A Cargo Cult Science?" in *Transforming Ethnopolitical Conflict. The Berghof Handbook*. Wiesbaden: Berghof Research Center for Constructive Conflict Management and VS Verlag, 2004, pp. 129–150.

Carment, David, and Albrecht Schnabel, eds. *Conflict Prevention: From Rhetoric to Reality*. Vol. 2: *Opportunities and Innovations*. Lanham, MD: Lexington Books, 2004.

Carnegie Commission on Preventing Deadly Conflict. *Preventing Deadly Conflict: Final Report*. New York: Carnegie Corporation, 1997.

Gurr, Ted, and Barbara Harff. *Early Warning of Communal Conflicts and Genocide: Linking Empirical Research to International Responses*. Tokyo: United Nations University Press, 1996.

Hamburg, David. *No More Killing Fields: Preventing Deadly Conflict*. Oxford: Rowman & Littlefield Publishers Inc., 2002.

Hampson, Fen Osler, and David M. Malone, eds. *From Reaction to Conflict Prevention: Opportunities for the UN System*. Boulder, CO: Lynne Rienner Publishers, 2002.

Meier, P. P. "The Role of Civil Society in Early Warning and Crisis Prevention: Policy Recommendations for the Pro-UNCOPAC Initiative." A paper prepared and presented for the Pro-UNCOPAC conference in Berlin on 12–13 February 2004.

Rubin, Barnett. *Blood on the Doorstep: The Politics of Preventive Action*. New York: Century Foundation Press, 2002.

Rupesinghe, Kumar, and Michiko Kuroda, eds. *Early Warning and Conflict Resolution*. Basingstoke, England: Macmillan, 1992.

Schmeidl, Susanne, and Howard Adelman, eds. "Early Warning and Early Response." Columbia International Affairs Online: Columbia University Press, 1998.

SwissPeace. *FAST–Early Recognition of Tension and Fact Finding*. Bern: Institute for Conflict Resolution, 2001.

Woodcock, Ted, and David Davis, eds. *Early and Late Warning by the UN Secretary-General of Threats to the Peace: Article 99 Revisited*. The Cornwallis Group V: Analysis for Crisis Response and Societal Reconstruction, Canadian Peacekeeping Press, 2000.

PERSONAL STORY:
"Early Involvement"—Max van der Stoel

Since the end of World War II there has not been a single moment when arms were silent in all continents. In the second half of the twentieth century there were some large and several smaller armed conflicts between states. Also, armed clashes have occurred increasingly within states between groups with conflicting interests. Moreover, the growing sophistication of modern weapons has resulted in greater numbers of dead and wounded and more widespread devastation.

The lesson we can learn from these wars is that, once a conflict has become violent, it usually proves to be very difficult to put it to an end. On the other hand, experience shows that the best chances of preventing a conflict from escalating into violence present themselves in its early stages. The longer it goes on, the greater the danger of parties becoming ever more rigid in their positions and, as a consequence, less disposed to accepting compromise.

Paradoxically, the chances of the international community intervening at an early stage of an emerging conflict are usually small. Quite often there is a tendency to cling to the hope that parties will find a solution themselves. Moreover, there are usually acute crises diverting attention from emerging ones. This applies to the Security Council which is the main world organ for maintaining peace and security, but equally to more directly interested states. When a conflict arises *within* a state, the Council is usually reluctant to get involved too closely during its early stages. Quite often it restricts itself to discrete diplomatic activities.

A different path has been chosen by the Organisation for Security and Co-operation in Europe, the OSCE. Shocked by the explosion of interethnic violence in Yugoslavia and aware that tensions between majorities and minorities might play a major role in several states of former communist-Europe, its participant states decided in 1992 to create the post of High Commissioner on National Minorities. The Commissioner's task would be to help diffuse interethnic conflicts at an early stage. A step which had to be seen against the background of the 1991 OSCE Moscow Declaration on the human dimension of the OSCE, which stated explicitly that conflicts relating to human rights (of course including minority rights), were not only a matter of concern for the state in which they occurred, but just as much for the community of OSCE states as a whole.

In January 1993 I was appointed as OSCE High Commissioner on National Minorities—a post I occupied for eight-and-a-half years. I was involved in quite a number of emerging conflicts, and my experience very much confirms the view that outside involvement is usually most effective at a very early stage of a dispute. Moreover, I am convinced that certain basic rules have to be respected in order to maximize the chances of success of outside involvement in an internal conflict.

The first is the need for strict objectivity. A mediator will never be accepted as such if he or she is the advocate of one side. Secondly, it is essential that he or she works as much as possible behind the scenes and behaves as "a silent diplomat." During a mission it might not always be possible to avoid publicity. Still, the mediator must be reserved in his comments because public advocacy of the formula he favors usually leads to parties reemphasizing their positions, thus making it more difficult to show flexibility in later negotiations. Thirdly, the mediator must subordinate his personal views to rules and standards in various international instruments to which the state concerned is a party. A compromise formula based on these instruments is more difficult to reject.

Other regional organizations have no organs comparable to the OSCE High Commissioner on National Minorities but they too, in various ways, are showing increasing interest in making conflict prevention one of their most important objectives. It can only be hoped that they will increasingly succeed in doing this. It would greatly help to ensure that conflict prevention will acquire the central place in world politics that is so badly needed.

Yet more has to be done. Governments will have to be constantly reminded that paying lip service to conflict prevention is not enough and that action in this field has to become a priority. Nongovernmental organizations have a vital role to play in this respect, both in dialogue with governments and international organizations and in mobilizing public opinion.

_____

Max van der Stoel is a former Minister of Foreign Affairs of the Netherlands. From 1993 to 2001 he served as OSCE High Commissioner on National Minorities.

17.1

Managing Conflicts by Phone: The Mobile Phones Network in Northern Ireland

Neil Jarman

In Northern Ireland, where intercommunal violence has caused so much pain and suffering, an innovative community-based project enabled volunteers to play an important role in preventing potential conflicts from exploding into outright violence. The project, which was launched during a period of political transition, involved linking activists in a network through the use of mobile telephones to enable them to respond to rumors, speculation, and minor incidents or confrontations, and to intervene before these potential conflicts could spin out of control.

The militarized conflict in Northern Ireland effectively came to an end in August 1994 when the Irish Republican Army, which had been fighting the British state for twenty-five years, declared a cease-fire. However, the cease-fire did not lead to a complete cessation of violence. Hostilities continued between the two main communities, the Protestants, who define themselves as British, and the Catholics, who define themselves as Irish. The focus of the conflict shifted to the many annual parades organized by the Orange Order, a Protestant fraternal organization. These parades, which commemorate the seventeenth victory of the Protestant William of Orange over the Catholic King James II, have taken on great symbolic importance. Protestants view them as an important part of their cultural heritage, but Catholics see them as a symbol of Protestant dominance, and have frequently organized protests against them.

In July 1996 violence broke out when the police stopped members of the Orange Order in Portadown from following their traditional route through a Catholic area of the town. There followed a week of widespread rioting in towns and villages across Northern Ireland. The worst of the violence occurred 60 kilometers away in North Belfast, a highly segregated area, where working-class Protestant and Catholic communities are separated by numerous walls, fences, and barriers, known locally as "peacelines." Following the restrictions on the parade, violence broke out at many locations and, over the next few days, over one hundred households were forced to flee their homes because of intimidation and violence. Although the rioting soon died down, tensions remained high in the area and outbreaks of intercommunal violence continued to occur throughout the autumn and into the winter. Community workers in North Belfast were very concerned that trouble could easily recur the following summer.

The violence in North Belfast in 1996 was underpinned by rumor, mistrust, and suspicion, and was fueled by a breakdown in communication at all levels. During the chaos accompanying the violence, lines of communication within communities, between communities, and between communities and government agencies providing essential public services collapsed. This meant that rumors circulated freely, with the corresponding escalation of suspicion and unrest, facilitating further violence and retaliation. In some situations attempts by the police to restore order only succeeded in provoking further violence. Many people who left their homes had no easy access to the support of statutory agencies. Instead, the community sector was mobilized to move and store their furniture and personal belongings. Subsequent meetings between community organizations and key housing agencies and the social services concluded that there was a need for both an overhaul of contingency planning and a more flexible and imaginative response to major public disorder.

Setting Up the Networks

Staff at the Community Development Centre (CDC) in North Belfast developed a scheme to respond to the problem of the breakdown of communications. They proposed providing mobile telephones to community activists in each of the main interface communities, which would be used to link all the people together in a network. It was hoped that such a network would allow lines of communication to be maintained within communities, between neighboring communities, and with the police, housing, and other agencies. It would also allow activists to remain on the streets to monitor the fluid situations while remaining in contact with people in other areas and government agencies. There were some concerns in official circles at the thought of providing community activists with this relatively new and expensive technology, but after some debate, a government agency agreed to fund the project for two months through the summer of 1997.

Staff at the CDC coordinated the project and formed the hub of the network. They identified key groups and individuals from their existing community networks who were prepared to participate in the mobile phone network. The network members were all volunteers and included people from a wide range of backgrounds, male and female, including a small number with links to paramilitary organizations. All were involved in some form of community activity in their area. In many cases a community group took responsibility for a phone and members of the group took it in shifts to respond to calls.

Each of the phone holders was given the phone numbers of all the other phones in the network, as well as contact numbers of key people in the most important government agencies. The phone holders agreed to keep the phones switched on twenty-four hours a day, seven days a week, from mid-June to the end of August. They also agreed to contact other members of the network in response to rumors or concerns, crowds gathering, or minor incidents, and to respond to all such calls coming to them. The presence of the CDC staff in the network provided an extra line of communication if others failed to work, and also allowed people to pass messages via an intermediary, if they were unwilling to speak to an individual directly. CDC staff also provided support and backup to the activists on the street.

Over the summer many of the phone holders spent long hours on the streets trying to keep children (too often the ones who initiated the trouble), young people, and adults away from peacelines, stopping instances of stone throwing, calming tensions, and refuting rumors. Frequently it would be dawn before people felt that the potential for violence or disorder had passed.

Often a rumor of a crowd gathering would encourage people onto the street, people on the "other side" would then perceive this group as a potential threat, and stone throwing and violence could easily escalate. The phones allowed people on either side to ask questions of their opposite numbers and pass information back to their community. In this way rumors could be discredited and tensions reduced.

In other situations, rumors of trouble might spread across areas of the city and carloads of men might arrive out of the blue to help defend an area from a perceived threat of attack. However, from the perspective of the "other side" the arrival of groups of men in a neighboring area might be seen as the prelude

Neil Jarman

Police line up in anticipation of riots (West-Belfast, 1999)

to an attack on them. The phone network allowed such rumors to be addressed very quickly and to calm the fears of people in nearby estates.

The phones were also used to synchronize attempts to reduce or stop the violence. On occasions when stone throwing began (often the precursor to more serious violence) members of the phone network would coordinate attempts to stop the attacks and move people back away from the peaceline, while explaining to the other side what they were doing. In some situations, the phone network also utilized key local politicians to help reduce tensions by getting them to speak to their counterparts on the "other side."

In other situations, the phones allowed contacts to be maintained with the police so that community workers were given time and space to try to intervene and stop trouble before police in riot uniforms were sent into a developing situation. The riot police were often regarded as an indiscriminate force whose arrival often led to an increase in violence. When local police commanders began to recognize the capacity of the people in the phone network to calm tensions, they increasingly turned to their community contacts as their first point of call.

Sometimes individuals might be no more than a few meters apart, even visible to each other across a street, but while political tensions would prevent direct contact, the phones provided the necessary means of communication to resolve a situation.

Finally, the phone network also enabled community activists to link up with key agencies, such as the Housing Executive, who were responsible for public housing. This meant that people could quickly arrange for repairs to damaged property, such as broken windows, rather than having to wait for several days.

Efficiency and Low Cost

The mobile phone network in North Belfast functioned between 1997 and 2001. It began with mobile phones in ten interface areas in 1997 and expanded to twenty-five areas in 2000. Unfortunately, CDC was forced to end its activities after 2001 because of a lack of funding, so the formally sponsored North Belfast network also ended.

The project, however, has served as a model for similar networks established by other organizations, both in the Belfast area and elsewhere. In Belfast, groups such as Interaction and Belfast Interface Project have established networks in different parts of the city. In the summer of 2000, for example, more than sixty phones were being used by various networks across Belfast. The idea has also been adopted by groups in other towns with tense and problematic interfaces, such as Derry/Londonderry and in Portadown, and the model has furthermore been adapted as part of a wider community safety strategy in a number of other areas.

Acts of violence and disorder have continued to occur in parts of North Belfast, but each year has seen a progressive reduction in the number of serious incidents and clashes between neighboring communities and in the number of households forced to abandon their homes. Although there is a complex range of factors involved in the reduction of violence (and the wider political context is always an important factor), the active participation of local community activists in responding to disorder has been an important component in helping to keep the peace.

An evaluation of the mobile phone networks, funded by the Community Relations Council, indicated that they are highly regarded by a diverse range of governmental agencies as an effective and efficient form of communication that facilitates localized conflict management. In some instances the networks have proved a useful way of consolidating or extending working relationships between different interface communities and building trust between the community and statutory sectors.

The networks have also proved a relatively low-cost option (although the networks undoubtedly do require significant commitments of human resources, especially time commitments from the participating volunteers). The costs are always dependent on the on the number of phones, the length of time they are available for use, and the number of calls made. Still, the costs are small relative to the costs to employ police officers to do similar work. At any rate, the money can be considered well spent if even one carjacking has been prevented or one family is saved from being forced to flee their home.

This is not to say that there have not been problems in maintaining and sustaining the networks. Many of those participating felt drained at the end of the summer because of the time and energy spent responding to calls. A number of phone holders have been challenged (and on occasion assaulted) by people within their own community who question their involvement in the network. There have been numerous complaints that people on the "other side" have not been as responsive as might have been hoped. Also, a number of people have complained that the police have come to expect too much of members of the phone networks and put them under pressure to take a more interventionist role.

Furthermore, a willingness to participate as a phone holder and the ability of people to intervene effectively in emerging conflicts is often dependent on the wider political context. The networks were probably at their most effective in 1998 when the "feel good" factor following the signing of the Belfast Agreement and the Assembly elections was most apparent. In contrast, it proved more difficult to mobilize people to participate in 2001, in large part because, in the face of feuding among Protestant paramilitary groups, individuals and groups within the Protestant community were reluctant to participate.

One of the major difficulties the networks have faced has been financial; the lack of funding commitments has meant that networks have often been set up later than they might have been otherwise, and with less effective preparation. Ironically, the very success and effectiveness of these community-based networks has contributed to the uncertainty over future funding. If the network is successful, and calm prevails in the communities, then this can create a response that "there was very little trouble last year—so why do we need the phones this year?" Of course the phone network is about spending money to try to ensure that nothing does happen.

When the original network was set up in 1997, mobile phones were still something of a novelty, while now they have become much more widely available. That means, fortunately, that the outside support previously required is not so critical. In fact, in some cases people have created their own smaller networks that they run in conjunction with, and thus serve to extend, the established community networks. In other areas people even feel that they can use their existing phone links with relevant people in statutory or community groups without being part of a more formal network.

The original program established by the CDC in North Belfast may no longer exist, but the notion of using low-cost technology to react to potentially dangerous confrontations in divided communities such as those in Northern Ireland has proven its value.

Neil Jarman is the director of the Institute for Conflict Research (ICR), an independent organization specializing in research, evaluation, and training on conflict management and interventions in transitional societies. ICR is based in North Belfast but works across Northern Ireland and internationally. Jarman worked at the Community Development Centre in North Belfast from 1997 to 2001.

Contact

Institute for Conflict Research
North City Business Centre
2 Duncairn Gardens, Belfast
BT15 2GG Northern Ireland
Tel.: +44 (0)28 9074 2682
E-mail: director@conflictresearch.org.uk
Website: http://www.conflictresearch.org.uk

Selected Bibliography

Bryan, Dominic, and Neil Jarman. 1999. *Independent Intervention: Monitoring the Police, Parades and Public Order* (Belfast: Democratic Dialogue).

Jarman, Neil. 1999. *Drawing Back from the Edge: Community-Based Responses to Violence in North Belfast* (Belfast: Community Development Centre).

———. 2002. *Managing Disorder: Responses to Interface Violence in North Belfast and to Public Disorder Related to Disputes over Parade Routes.* Final Project Report for Community Relations Unit, Office of the First Minister/Deputy First Minister.

Jarman, Neil, and Chris O'Halloran. 2000. *Peacelines or Battlefields: Responding to Violence in Interface Areas* (Belfast: Community Development Centre).

Each of these publications is available online at:
http://www.conflictresearch.org.uk/publications/porp.html.

17.2

Working with the Local Wisdom: The National Council of Churches of Kenya Peace Program

Peter Juma Gunja and Selline Otieno Korir

In the thirteen years since the National Council of Churches of Kenya first began its Peace and Reconciliation Project, it has come to understand that there is an enormous reservoir of wisdom at the local level. "We're no longer telling people what's right or wrong; now we're hearing what people are saying is right themselves." Now they have continued this line by using local resources for effective early warning of potential conflicts.

One of the key challenges encountered in the National Council of Churches in Kenya's (NCCK) peace work, particularly in the areas inhabited by pastoralist communities in Kenya's North Rift Valley, were frequent and often devastatingly violent cattle raids. Well-trained and heavily armed young warriors executed these cattle raids with military precision. Not all the raids were surprise attacks. Well before the attacks there were signs of preparation, mobilization, and apprehension by potential victims. NCCK personnel at the community level and members of the peace committees were aware of such rumors of impending raids. The challenge was how to harness these signs into systematic indicators of such looming violence.

The NCCK, and its counterpart, Nairobi Peace Initiative–Africa (NPI-Africa), believed that a properly developed and functioning system could contribute to the reduction of violence if systematic information was sought, processed, disseminated, and responded to appropriately. From the training of five of its staff members in early warning and response mechanisms, the NCCK proceeded to enhance its early warning system, especially in the areas inhabited by pastoralist communities.

In this regard, indicators that are very specific and unique to these communities were developed:

• *Movement to safer grounds.* This indicator refers to the observed movement of would-be victims of attacks away from the perceived targeted area.

In itself this is an indicator that the communities have ways of detecting impending attacks. Mostly women and children are moved to such places, as men and youth remain along the border keeping vigil.

• *Alien footprints.* The communities are able to detect the footprints of outsiders. The communities say that their "enemies" wear different styles of sandals.

• *Preparation rituals and rites of passage.* Traditionally cattle raiding is surrounded by preparatory rituals and taboos. These are carried out to bless the youth going into a raid, and seek divine intervention for their safe return. Given the large number of youths involved in such ceremonies, it is easy to detect these activities.

• *Rumors.* As the saying goes, "where there is smoke, there is fire." Many of the whispers of a planned attack turn out to be true. These are therefore not to be taken lightly. Quite importantly, as per tradition, raiders often send word to their would-be victims, warning them of the forthcoming attack. In these communities, a "sneak" attack is considered cowardly and "ungentlemanly."

• *Women wearing the "prayer belt."* Women put on a special belt when their sons go out on a raid. It is believed that the belt ties the son to the mother when it is put on, thus praying for and ensuring the son's safe return. Nevertheless, in instances when the women do not support the raid, they refuse to tie on the belt.

• *Fires lit at strategic places.* This is done as a means of communication to direct raiders who may have lost their way in the bush. Fires are also lit to provoke the others.

• *Gunshots.* Gunshots are at times fired as a means of communication between raiders, and in most cases it is done at specific times and specific points.

• *Deserted marketplaces.* When people hurriedly disappear from a market place, especially during market days, this is often a sign that a raid is imminent. Maybe some warning about a planned raid is heard, and thus people want to move to safer areas.

• *Presence of firearms and sale of ammunition.* When youth are spotted carrying firearms openly, especially illegally acquired ones, then something ominous is in the offing. At the same time, it is possible to notice the sale of ammunition, usually done discreetly, for example by women. Similarly, signs of heightened alertness on the part of security officers can be seen as an indicator that they have been tipped on a looming raid.

The NCCK has recently been able to use these indicators to set up a program that tries to effectively detect impending raids or other attacks and to facilitate communities to intervene. The program recognizes the vital role of effective early warning for early action mechanisms at the grassroots and national levels.

First introduced in 1997, early warning mechanisms operating at the level of Village Peace Committees and Area Peace and Development Committees have been steadily refined to address shortcomings in dealing with the dynamics of conflict in pastoral communities and urban areas. The NCCK staff has benefited from international training workshops on early warning and peacebuilding organized by NPI-Africa in 2002 and 2003.

In 2003, two workshops were organized to assess the efficiency of the early warning system and to develop proposals that would make it more likely that potential conflicts were recognized early on, allowing for timely intervention. In July 2003 this resulted in the initiation of a new and enhanced Early Warning for Early Action system.

Listening to the Local Voice

Listening to the local voice is the approach that has become the basis for much of the NCCK's success. It is now recognized that cultural traditions, whether that be the slaughter of bulls or reconciliation rituals, are vital and must be respected. In the African context, where Christianity was introduced by missionaries who viewed African rituals as mostly "heathen," the NCCK's acknowledgment of the role of traditional rituals in peacebuilding and reconciliation represents a major recognition of local resources.

NCCK, the umbrella organization for Kenya's Protestant churches, has a long and consistent record of promoting the spiritual, economic, and political development of the country. In 1992, the council launched the Peace and Reconciliation Project in response to ethnic violence in western Kenya that had resulted in many deaths and injuries, massive displacements, and much suffering among innocent Kenyans.

The council originally established the project to provide humanitarian assistance to the victims of the violence. By 1993, the project had recognized the need to move beyond humanitarian assistance to being involved in efforts to help displaced persons to return to the farms they had been forced to leave. Yet this could not be done in the absence of deliberate efforts to bring peace and reconciliation among the communities. The NCCK therefore teamed up with NPI-Africa, an already experienced peacebuilding organization, to begin their peacebuilding and reconciliation work. The council's peace and reconciliation activities targeted aggressors and victims alike, with an emphasis on the need for both repentance and forgiveness to achieve reconciliation, resettlement, and rehabilitation. In a very challenging and difficult environment rife with intimidation, threats, and frustration with the political establishment, the NCCK worked systematically and persistently to build a process that would eventually bring in even the politicians and government officials that were initially opposed to it.

In 1996, a third phase of the Peace and Reconciliation Project was launched with more extensive efforts focusing on community peacebuilding, development, and the reintegration into society of the victims of ethnic violence. The project helped to set up Village Peace and Reconciliation Committees and Area Peace and Rehabilitation Committees, which organized "good neighborliness seminars," open to elders, politicians, community workers, and other peace stakeholders. These seminars provided the participants with the opportunity to discuss the causes and effects of local or regional conflicts and to devise strategies to combat them.

In 2000, the project began a fourth phase, still focusing on community peacebuilding and development, but also engaging in advocacy work. During this phase, the already established community peace structures were utilized, and peace actors at the community level were encouraged to develop appropriate strategies, methodologies, and approaches to conflict prevention and resolution that could be effective within their communities. However, cognizant of the fact that an inherent weakness of this approach was that little effort was made to understand the underlying causes of conflict, NCCK established the National Agenda for Peace (NAP), with the specific mandate of linking community initiatives to higher decisionmaking through lobbying government entities to become more actively involved in conflict-resolution activities.

Learning Process

A key element of the NCCK project is its evolution as a "process of learning." Although the NCCK was effectively engaged in community peacebuilding, the efforts were geographically limited. The NAP, for example, focused on thirteen conflict-prone districts, while the Community Peace Building and Development Project was primarily directed toward interethnic conflict in western Kenya. The need to develop a program with a national perspective became evident, and so, in January 2003, the various conflict resolution activities of NCCK were consolidated under the NCCK Peace Program (NPP) with the unifying theme: "Mobilizing communities for peace advocacy, reconstruction, and reconciliation."

The work undertaken under the NPP addresses both active conflict and the serious issues of inequity and injustice underlying Kenya's conflicts. The program is involved, at both the local and the national levels, in activities as diverse as dealing with interethnic and politically based conflicts, cattle rustling, resource-based conflicts, cross-border conflicts, the influx of illicit arms, increased crime rates in urban and semiurban areas, the plight of the internally displaced people, inadequate government investments in security infrastructure, enactment of a clear land policy, and the creation of a new, enabling constitutional order.

At the local level, the council's peace program continues to build viable partnerships with various stakeholders such as the community elders, politicians, and more community-based and nongovernmental actors to address peace and development issues. On cross-border conflicts and illicit arms, NCCK works closely with the Uganda Joint Christian Council and is in the process of forging a partnership with the New Sudan Council of Churches. In the border regions, the project has developed a framework for facilitating cross-border community peace work to reduce cattle rustling and the influx of guns.

At good neighborliness seminars and *barazas* (public gatherings), the NPP has raised awareness about the need to avoid violence during election campaigns, targeted critical groups involved directly or indirectly in cattle rustling, such as the *ngorokos* (youthful raiders) and *laibons* (elders), and reached other crucial constituencies such as women. The project has established links with communities living along common borders by organizing sporting events, rehabilitating social amenities that bring communities together such as schools and cattle dips, and contributing to capacity building within community peace structures. A number of women's groups have been strengthened through the establishment of income-generating activities and by facilitating seminars and workshops. Finally, the project is engaged in awareness-raising activities, particularly through the distribution of its publication, the *Peace Update.*

Impact

At a general level, the key success of the NCCK is the initiation and sustainability of a peace process with strategic links from the community to the national level. At the local level, NCCK has noted some important successes. These include a decline in reported cases of livestock theft, arson, other property damage, and most significantly, violent attacks and killings; renewed possibilities for school-age children from warring communities to interact with each other as they return to schools serving communities that NCCK has rehabilitated; the establishment of youth peace clubs; and the successful establishment of the Rural Women's Peace Link, which has provided opportunities for women to be actively involved in peacebuilding work. Tangible results have also been recorded in the number of people who have returned to the lands they had earlier been evicted from.

During the 2002 national elections, some NCCK members were elected as civic leaders, placing them in positions to influence decisionmaking at their level. The elections and presidential transition were hailed worldwide as peaceful and exemplary. This contrasted with the previous two elections in 1992 and 1997, which had been marked by widespread violence. NCCK's ten-year work in the volatile Rift Valley and that of other peace organizations throughout Kenya is thought to have played a major role in the peaceful elections and transition.

At the regional and national levels, the decision to integrate peace work into the NCCK structures of member churches throughout the country has yielded important dividends in the extension of its work. This was apparent, for example, during the weeklong global campaign against small arms, which reached Kenyans throughout the country. NCCK's strategy of inclusiveness has brought many new actors and organizations on board to pursue peacebuilding across the country. This, in turn, has prompted the government to draft a policy paper with the aim of better coordinating nationwide peacebuilding activities.

Furthermore, the NCCK has gained important influence in policymaking as the de facto representative of Kenya's religious communities on the government's

National Steering Committee responsible for peacebuilding activities. This committee oversees a wide range of peacebuilding activities, including the campaign against small arms and the development of early warning and response mechanisms.

Challenges

The NCCK has come to a clear understanding that the involvement of community leaders is crucial to the task of resolving local conflicts. Indeed, a key lesson has been the drawing in of elders who themselves may be involved with instigating or supporting violence, and steering them to play more positive roles in their communities. This stems from the observation that the *elderhood* institution in Africa was largely a force for the good of the community, where all wisdom accumulated.

Therefore, mechanisms must be developed for sharing information, drawing on elders who are strategically positioned to monitor and evaluate events on the ground, and continuing efforts that encourage the creation of local and regional peace committees.

A key limitation to this institution is the lack of a legal framework. For example, traditional mechanisms for compensation and reparation are not always recognized by national law. There is therefore a need to confer legal status on traditional compensation mechanisms. Currently, such mechanisms function outside the legal system. As a result, the official criminal justice system may still intervene in cases that have already been resolved by traditional conflict-resolution approaches.

Another key lesson has to do with partnership at different levels. At one level, NCCK was able to forge good relations with funding agencies who supported the work financially over the years. At another level, NCCK forged a working relationship with NPI-Africa that right from the beginning helped to shape the peace interventions of NCCK, based on its experiences working in other settings in Africa. NCCK was also able to build linkages with development-focused organizations at the community level, as a way of linking peace and reconciliation with the livelihood concerns of the communities.

The NCCK has achieved much since it began its peace and reconciliation work in 1992. Still, important challenges remain. Some are social or political, such as the challenge of overcoming deep divisions among religious leaders, or transcending regional and political differences to forge a united front as a church. Others are institutional, such as the lack of peacebuilding skills among various stakeholders, or the lack of sufficient resources to assure the sustainability of programs that contribute to peace and security. Still others are more fundamental: without addressing the root causes of conflict—such as poverty, underdevelopment, and lack of opportunity—peace and security will always be fragile. Addressing all these challenges is exactly what the NCCK sets out to do.

Peter Juma Gunja has worked with NCCK for the last twelve years at various levels. He holds a degree in commerce, with various trainings on peacebuilding and conflict transformation. He is currently NCCK National Peace Programme coordinator.

Selline Otieno Korir has been taking daring risks by working to empower women and children to become active participants in building peace for years. She was responsible for forming the Rural Women's Peace Link, a department of the NCCK that forms a network for women working for peace in their local communities.

The authors would like to acknowledge the additional input from George Wachira, the executive director of NPI-Africa, Kenya, in composing this chapter.

Contact

National Council of Churches of Kenya
Jumuia Place
Lenana Road, Nairobi
P.O. Box 45009, Nairobi 00100
Kenya
Tel.: +254 20 271 1862 / 272 4169
Fax: +254 20 272 4169
E-mail: gsoffice@ncck.org
Website: http://www.ncck.org

Selected Bibliography

European Centre for Conflict Prevention (ECCP). 1999. *People Building Peace—35 Inspiring Stories from Around the World* (Utrecht, Netherlands: ECCP).

"NPI-Africa and NCCK: Responsive and Strategic Evaluation of Peacebuilding: Towards a Learning Model." NPI-Africa and NCCK report, 2002.

"Peacebuilding in Africa: Lessons, Challenges and Aspirations—Reflections from the NPI-Africa Seminar for Practitioners." NPI-Africa and NCCK report, 2001.

18

Traditional and Local Conflict Resolution

Jannie Malan

Ways of preventing and resolving conflict have become widely known in their current form, which has taken shape over the last eighty years. Dealing with conflict is not a new field, however. With regard to the ancient beginnings, we have to rely on imaginative guesswork, but for reconstructing subsequent developments we can build on many traditions that have survived. These traditions are not only of historical significance; they can be of great practical value to all of us who are dealing with conflict and helping others to deal with conflict. What is therefore shared in this chapter is meant to encourage us to learn from traditional ways of dealing with conflict, and to apply the methods, insights, and skills that are indeed relevant in conflict situations of our time.

Contemporary Validity

Some traditions are undoubtedly time-proven and of lasting value, but others have become obsolete and sometimes also ethically objectionable.[1] Debates are therefore continuing between and within groups.[2] Often such discussions are mainly focused on cultural loyalty and current practicality. In many cases, however, racial and political arguments tend to complicate and intensify the debate.

From a Southern postcolonial perspective (Wa Thiango 1986), for instance, the science of Conflict and Peace Studies that has developed in the twentieth century may appear to be a neocolonial import. It is true that this science was to a great extent an outcome of the struggles of disadvantaged people against economic inequity and social injustice. It is also true that in many cases civil campaigning did eventually bring about remarkable results: changed laws, regulations, structures, and some changed attitudes. Still, those who have struggled against the injustices of colonialism may resent the fact that the "new" methods and techniques of negotiation, mediation, arbitration, and conciliation were mainly developed in the cultural settings of the West and the North.

Nevertheless, people in postcolonial situations are frankly acknowledging that important insights and skills have recently been gained by the relevant human sciences all around the world and that certain aspects of traditional methods may today have to be regarded as anachronisms. It has also been admitted that adequate knowledge of the old methods is becoming relatively scarce.[3]

The typical two-fold conclusion of this debate therefore tends to be something similar to the following:

1. There are traditional methods that can still be used in appropriate situations (for instance, the Hozhooji Naat'aanii restorative justice process of the Navajo nation in Arizona and New Mexico, Gacaca traditional courts in Rwanda[4] (See Chapter 18.2), Kacoke Madit meetings in northern Uganda (See Chapter 14.1), and the Ho'o Ponopono process in Hawaii).

2. In the light of contemporary insights and skills that have been developed all over the world, however, it is not merely a matter of reverting to ancient traditions. What may especially be propagated, therefore, is the development of new homegrown methods in which the best current practices and compatible traditions are integrated.

Using Traditional Methods in Appropriate Situations

An appropriate situation for the first of these two options would be one in which the descendants of the people who developed the method are still loyal to the same cultural context. The method may still be respected as a famous tradition, and may still be used, regularly or occasionally. In certain cases some adaptations or amendments may be required to make it acceptable in a contemporary rural or urban setting.

Let us briefly look at one example out of the vast number of traditional methods for conflict management. The Ho'o Ponopono process mentioned above can be summarized as follows (Partners in Conflict in Lesotho Project 2004). First, the community leaders and the parties concerned agree on a person with the needed trust and skills to facilitate the talks. At an appointed time and place, the community gathers in a circle, which includes the perpetrators and the victims. The facilitator ensures that there is agreement on ground rules. He or she emphasizes the objective of reaching a consensus agreement on resolving the conflict. The starting point is to get the facts from each party and from all who want to add a perspective.

The second stage is to go round the circle again, reflecting on why the conflict occurred, how they each share responsibility, and what they might have done to prevent the conflict. Then tasks for the future are considered. All can suggest ideas about compensation or restitution, about community needs, and about preventive and/or punitive measures. At this stage, penitence and forgiveness may be offered. The fourth stage is that of reaching consensus on tasks and the follow-up process. The parties and others in the community commit themselves to actions for reconstituting good community relationships.

In the final stage, closure is achieved by burning all records of facts, closing eyes on the past, and choosing to move forward together. Only the consensus agreement, action commitments, and follow-up arrangements are kept.

Integrating Traditional and Contemporary Methods

An integration of traditional and present-day methods cannot be attempted in a superficial way. The crucially important issue of compatibility has to be discussed until real understanding is reached and appropriately implemented.

The inherently African semantic field of *ubuntu* provides a good example in this regard. It signifies a socially caring and sharing way of thinking and living, which is well captured in the rhyming Xhosa expression, "Umntu ngumntu ngabantu." Literally this means that a human being is a human being through human beings. Or, paraphrased, a human being becomes a true human being through her/his[5] relationships with other human beings. Similar or comparable expressions are found all over Africa[6] and therefore the issue of old and new ways of dealing with conflict cannot properly be talked out if *ubuntu*-minded people are not involved in the planning from the beginning.

One striking example of a well-intentioned but unsuccessful attempt to combine incompatible elements was the UN's way of using the Somali tradition of Shir (gatherings). This tradition is a bottom-up, inclusive process, supported and sponsored by the community. The parties enjoy equal representation. Elders who are experienced mediators and trusted by the community are chosen. Traditional methods of problem solving are used, and the talks proceed according to an open timetable. Agreements are reached through consensus, and are regarded as social treaties (*xeer*). The elders are entrusted with authority and power to ensure the implementation of agreements. The UN version of Shir, however, was a top-down process, held outside the country. There was unequal representation, and lack of confidence in the representatives. Politicians were involved, and not elders. There was a lack of understanding of the problems, and a short timetable was used. No common *xeer* was reached (Murithi 1999: 53–54) (See Chapter 18.1).

There are two options if we want to achieve a valid integration of traditional and contemporary methods. The first is to incorporate a current insight into an old custom. In Burundi there is the tradition of Ubunshingantahe, which is used for resolving conflicts and bringing about harmony in the community. Membership is given to couples, but it is only the husbands who officially sit in the meetings. The wives play an important role by counseling their husbands and by being consulted by them (Murithi 1999: 35). Apparently 80 percent of Burundian men are still in favor of this arrangement, but women activists are campaigning to enable women to become direct and active participants in the meetings.

The second is to concentrate less on the great diversity of traditional methods and more on their inner dynamics. We can do this without trying to generalize, or to construct an "average" method, or to make up a model of eclectically selected details. What we can do is try to imagine ourselves to be in the human contexts where these traditions originated. We may then find that the most important positive influence that traditional methods can have today should not be expected along the way of customs or terms, but rather through the spirit that vitalized those methods and still radiates from them.

Timeless Essentials

The All-Africa Conference on African Principles of Conflict Resolution and Reconciliation, held in Addis Ababa in 1999, was focused on traditional ways of dealing with conflict. Twenty-one African countries were represented (of the 123 participants, 113 were from Africa) and no less than 70 percent of the sixty-four presentations contained descriptions and discussions of traditional methods of particular groups or areas. The objective of the conference was to explore marginalized indigenous approaches to peacemaking in Africa, and possibly develop ways in which general principles and tested practices from the African heritage could complement existing approaches drawn from other sources (Murithi 1999: 97).

What follows is an overview of some core insights and experiences around which traditional methods seem to have developed. Elements such as these have probably enabled traditional methods to be trusted, honored, and utilized throughout extended periods and eras.

Taking Time to Talk Things Out

Talking things out is surely one of the most essential parts of dealing with a conflict. There may be important differences, however, between the talking in current ways of negotiating or mediating and ancient ways of really talking things out. In those days, talks that continued over days or weeks were not uncommon. Participants were usually granted the opportunity to say what they wanted to, without cutting them short. Furthermore, people from an extended family, a neighborhood, or a community were allowed to take part. When talks took place under trees, there were anyway no doors or walls that could keep people out.

While much time was spent in talking, it seems as if usually little time was wasted before the talks began. In cases when the talking started soon after warning signals were noticed, and at the place where this happened, it could even have prevented a conflict from arising. If the social environment were upholding the traditional value that the society is greater than the individual, the people involved would have been strongly oriented toward social harmony. The obvious truth that prevention is better than cure must have been discovered by our early ancestors, and integrated into their methods.[7]

Dealing with Root Causes of Conflicts

Another essential part of dealing with any conflict is penetrating to its root cause or causes. Traditional methods seem to have taken this crucially important but potentially difficult starting point seriously. As the metaphor "root" indicates, the searching for invisible, underlying causes may require "digging" to depths. In some cases the inclusion of the neighborhood or community in traditional talks might have facilitated this process, but in other cases rumors, gossiping, blaming, or partisanship might have complicated everything.

Typical causes of violent conflict were (and in many instances still are) land issues (for instance, trespassing), animal issues (mostly robbery), and personal issues (such as rivalries). Due to the temporary or permanent scarcity of food or other resources, poverty always was, and still is, a major reason for competition and conflict. In modern times, poverty and bad governance are time and again highlighted as root causes. For today's bad governance, deeper roots are also mentioned: ethnocentrism, clanism, and greed for power, prestige, and/or wealth.

Being Oriented Toward Consensus

A process in which conflicts are talked out is usually a comprehensive one that explores the context in which the conflict originated, and works toward a consensus about a fair and satisfactory agreement. Traditionally, the talking probably proceeded without fixed procedures. The elders or chiefs could use their discretion to play certain roles or switch to others. It could be a passive or low-key role, a facilitating or an advisory role, or even a pressurizing or manipulating one. A guilty party could be expected or forced to repent, apologize, ask for forgiveness, and pay compensation. However, through the entire process, the main responsibility of the leading figures was to guide the talks toward an agreement that would reflect as inclusively as possible the consensus of the entire group of relatives, neighbors, friends, and acquaintances.

Promoting Relational Interdependence

The people of those early days must already have discovered that joint solutions reached through consensus tend to be durable. When the parties concerned and the communities involved have accepted ownership of the agreement and coresponsibility for its implementation and monitoring, several advantages may have followed. Behaviors may have changed and relationships may have been restored. Similar conflicts may even have been prevented from occurring.

The concern with relationships was indeed one of the core elements of traditional methods. The calmer relationships before the conflict were reviewed, the tense relations of the conflict were investigated, and a solution was sought that might contribute to improved relationships in the future. This relational orientation was not only revealed in family and neighborhood conflicts but also in political situations. "Reconciliation politics . . . seems to be more consistent with many African traditions, which emphasize community rather than individualism and competition" (Assefa and Wachira 1996: 57–58).

The Mind-Set Challenging Message

When we focus our attention on the main thrust of traditional ways of preventing conflict and building peace, instead of just on interesting details, we can hardly evade the feeling of being challenged to revisit our current methods. For instance, if we evaluate our methods in the light of the essential elements of traditional methods briefly outlined above, we may have to admit

- That we have lost the patience to allow parties the opportunity and time to really talk things out

- That while we do explore root causes of conflicts, we have not yet gathered enough courage to tackle effectively our underlying problems of poverty, inequitable development,[8] and bad governance
- That while we praise the advantages of consensus, we have our convenient excuses for sidelining and trying to silence the "difficult" customers (who may very well have valid objections)
- That our obsession with performance and products has tempted too many of us to label the dimension of human togetherness and relationships as unrealistic idealism

The challenge is not simply to try and traditionalize our current methods by using old terms in our manuals and old designs on their cover pages. Neither are we called upon to try and convince communities that they should once again confirm their agreements by bending spears or drinking bitter herbs.[9]

What we can do, however, is to imagine ourselves into the way of thinking out of which traditional ways of preventing conflict and dealing with conflict developed. Furthermore, if we discover to what extent both those and our methods are based on common sense, we may be reassured that we are not expected to discard our present methods and revert to practices of the past. We may indeed feel empowered to experiment with unhurried talking, deep delving, consensus building, and relationship healing.

Best Practices

Best practices, just as methods in general, should be used with modest realism. It is not necessary, however, to stretch our unpretentiousness too far. There is no need to think that the best methods can only be used in the "milder" areas of interpersonal and intergroup conflict. Nothing prevents them from being applied in the "harsher" areas of interethnic and interstate wars.

We have at our disposal the recent results of a worldwide research project on best practices, under the title of *Confronting War: Critical Lessons for Peace Practitioners* (Anderson and Olson 2003). The findings show how peace practices are indeed working in a variety of violent situations, but also how they might work even better. One of the significant findings was that the efforts to reach "key people" should be linked to ways of involving "more people." It was also found that in both cases two kinds of change should be promoted: changes in attitudes, values, and perceptions; and changes in politics, economics, and justice systems. What often proves to be of the greatest importance is the translating of changed attitudes into changed structures (Alexander and Olson 2003: 54–57, 64–69).

Such findings should stimulate us to reflect on our methods and our mindsets. There are ways of thinking and doing that have come a long way through human history with timeless wisdom and ever-relevant skills. There are also the latest insights, facilities, and capabilities that have made their way into current ways of thinking, acting, and being. So, whenever we are in a position to help prevent or transform a conflict, let us seek clarity on the most appropriate approach and attitude.

Taking Traditional Methods Seriously

We should duly acknowledge the cultural context of a potential or actual conflict situation. The cultural loyalties, affinities, and sensitivities of the parties concerned are always of crucial importance. If only one culture is involved, the interaction may be less complicated, but not necessarily. If the situation is cross-cultural or multicultural, several aspects should be taken into consideration from the very beginning[10]: for instance, the various ways of thinking and behaving, the need for mutual understanding, and the need for a culturally inclusive team of facilitators.

We should commit ourselves to as much preventive problem solving as possible. When it is clear that a particular clue is not an unfounded suspicion but a real warning signal, something should be done as soon as possible, and as close to the problem as possible. If this can be done in the mode of pragmatic problem solving, so that "conflict" need not even be mentioned in the name of the method, so much the better.[11]

We should responsibly and creatively use the best available practices. Although the various groups we belong to have respected traditions from a significant past, we happen to be living in the world of today, where very relevant current practices are at our disposal. These inevitably form our main frame of reference, and from these we can chose the most appropriate approaches for each unique situation. We have to remember, however, that no method should ever be applied as if it were a prescriptive recipe. Open-minded receptivity to the needs and interests of the parties concerned, and innovative flexibility and creativity, are always of crucial importance.

Wherever appropriate, we should integrate meaningful traditions into our work. Applying traditional methods, or incorporating traditional elements that are of lasting value, can have very important advantages. It may provide a sense of ownership, and strengthen our commitment to work toward consensus and coexistence. Moreover, these methods are usually simple and easily understandable. They tend to allow flexibility and creativity. They are not expensive, and the costs involved are often willingly shared by the community. Finally, they may add an ancient, ancestral endorsement to the work we are doing nowadays.

We should internalize the mind-set of fellow-human togetherness and interdependence. If this way of thinking and living has become part of us, conflict-preventing and peacebuilding attitudes, approaches, and actions may follow spontaneously. For instance, groups and individuals can then feel free to be who they happen to be, to belong where they happen to belong, but also to allow others to do the same from their side. Then both "we" and "they" can become befriended in an *ubuntu*-minded "all of us." A particular field in which such interdependence has to be propagated is the relations between governmental authorities and traditional chiefs and elders.

We should encourage and empower as many people as possible to apply their insights and skills. The inspiring stories in this book and its precursor testify to what ordinary people can do. People across the civil-society spectrum, from grassroots level to influential leaders, can indeed initiate processes that may bring about breakthroughs to mutual understanding, conflict resolution, and reconciliation.

We should remain committed to particular and general conflict transformation. If we understand conflict as an everyday social phenomenon, which is always based on some valid or perceived reason, we will not try to escape to a utopian retreat. We will remain willing to listen without being shocked, and to talk out whatever has to be talked out. We will not avoid root causes such as poverty and bad governance. We will promote, according to the circumstances, structural changes and attitudinal changes. In whatever the context, from local to international, we will work toward consensual agreement that will not only resolve the conflict concerned, but also contribute to the most cordial—or otherwise appropriate—relationships for the future.

Traditional ways of dealing with conflict can indeed encourage and inspire us. In spite of the shortcomings they might have had, they have functioned in conflict-preventive, peacebuilding, and reconciliatory ways through the ages. They have enabled our ancestors to address conflict-causing problems, reach consensual solutions, and rebuild relationships. Today there are indeed situations in which we can still use these commonsensical methods, either in their traditional form or with some modifications. There are also many opportunities to multiply the potential effectiveness of contemporary methods by infusing time-proven traditional insights and skills into them.

Jannie Malan is emeritus professor at the University of the Western Cape and senior researcher at the African Centre for the Constructive Resolution of Disputes (ACCORD). Through intervention, training, and research, ACCORD focuses on conflict prevention, management, and resolution in Africa.

Notes

1. The notorious apartheid of the old South Africa was an extreme example of inflicted injustice, but not the only one. In the new South Africa, and Africa in general, gender discrimination is increasingly opposed.

2. It is interesting and encouraging to hear about an ethnocultural group (the Borana Community of East Africa) spending much of their time thinking about their culture and making deliberate attempts to modify their customs (Duba et al. 1997: 16).

3. According to questionnaire responses at a recent international seminar in Zambia (a University for Peace Faculty and Staff Development Seminar on Gender and Peace Building, Kitwe, July 2004), thirty gender and conflict resolution practitioners from eighteen African countries revealed an average familiarity of less than 50 percent with African-specific approaches to gender and peacebuilding.

4. This tradition is indeed being used to fulfill the need for restorative and reparative justice (while the International Criminal Tribunal for Rwanda is just focusing on retributive justice).

5. It is interesting to note that Xhosa does not use separate pronouns (as "her" and "his" in English) for the two genders of humanity. Its basic frame of reference is simply that all of us are human beings. This does not mean, however, that Xhosa-speaking people do not recognize and respect the distinctive roles of women and men in human life.

6. For a good description and discussion of the *ubuntu* concept by various writers from Africa, and for an example of *ubuntu* culture applied (guided by Professor Lovemore Mbigi as an *ubuntu* thinker) to transform a labor conflict, see Coetzee and Roux (2000: 41–50), and Masina (2000).

7. For a contemporary emphasis on conflict prevention, see Adebayo (1999: 22–30).

8. To which may be added the frustration of educated youth, who did not manage to get integrated into the modern sector and are no longer suitable to lead their local communities.

9. As in the Mato Oput tradition in northern Uganda (Murithi 1999: 38–41).

10. In Davies and Kaufman (2003), a section on "Bridging Cultural Divides" is placed within the first eight pages, and a chapter is devoted to "Strategies for Effective Intercultural Conflict Resolution" (pp 149–160), and Avruch (1998).

11. "The desire to solve problems amicably is the main thrust of the African character" (Ngwane 1996: 51).

Selected Bibliography

Adebayo, Adedeji, ed. 1999. *Comprehending and Mastering African Conflicts: The Search for Sustainable Peace and Good Governance* (London: Zed Books).

Anderson, Mary B., and Lara Olson. 2003. *Confronting War: Critical Lessons for Peace Practitioners* (Cambridge, MA: The Collaborative for Development Action).

Assefa, Hizkias, and George Wachira, eds. 1996. *Peacemaking and Democratisation in Africa: Theoretical Perspectives and Church Initiatives* (Nairobi: East African Educational Publishers).

Avruch, Kevin. 1998. *Culture and Conflict Resolution* (Washington, DC: United States Institute for Peace).

Coetzee, Pieter Hendrik, and A.P.J. Roux, eds. 2000. *Philosophy from Africa: A Text with Readings* (Oxford: Oxford University Press).

Davies, John, and Edward Kaufman, eds. 2003. *Second Track/Citizens' Diplomacy: Concepts and Techniques for Conflict Transformation* (Lanham, MD: Rowman & Littlefield).

Duba, Kana Roba, Yara G. Kalacha, John Rigano, Fred Lesekali, Mohamed A. Seikhow, Francis Nikitoria Ole Sakuda, Jonathan Akeno, and Sammi Emweki. 1997. *Honey and Heifer, Grasses, Milk and Water: A Heritage of Diversity in Reconciliation* (Nairobi: Mennonite Central Committee, Kenya).

Masina, Nomonde. 2000. "Xhosa Practices of Ubuntu for South Africa," in William Zartman, ed., *Traditional Cures for Modern Conflicts: African Conflict "Medicine"* (London and Boulder, CO: Lynne Rienner Publishers).

Murithi, Tim, ed. 1999. "Final Report: All-Africa Conference on African Principles of Conflict Resolution and Reconciliation." Paper presented at the United Nations Conference Centre—ECA, Addis Ababa. 8–12 November.

Ngwane, George. 1996. *Settling Disputes in Africa: Traditional Bases for Conflict Resolution* (Yaoundé, Cameroon: Buma Kor).

Partners in Conflict in Lesotho Project. 2004. National University of Lesotho, Moshoeshoe Center for Diplomacy and Conflict Management, and University of Maryland, Center for International Development and Conflict Management. Handout at workshop on Integrative Approaches to Peace-Building and Conflict Transformation in the Region, Maseru, February.

Wa Thiongo, Ngugi. 1986. *Decolonizing the Mind: The Politics of Language in African Literature* (Nairobi: East African Educational Publishers).

Resources

Lead Organizations

African Centre for the Constructive Resolution of Disputes (ACCORD)—South Africa
E-mail: info@accord.org.za
Website: http://www.accord.org.za

Centre for Conflict Resolution (CCR)—South Africa
E-mail: mailbox@ccr.uct.ac.za
Website: http://ccrweb.ccr.uct.ac.za

Centre for Conflict Resolution (CECORE)—Uganda
E-mail: cecore@africaonline.co.ug
Website: http://www.cecore.org

Wajir Peace and Development Committee—Kenya
P.O. Box 444, Wajir
Tel.: + 254 136 21427 /21175/ 21396
Fax: + 254 136 21563
Contact person: Nuria Abdullahi

West Africa Network for Peacebuilding (WANEP)—Ghana
West Africa Peacebuilding Institute (WAPI)
E-mail: wapi@wanep.org
Website: http://www.wanep.org/wapi

Publications

Degefu Koraro, Giday. *Traditional Mechanisms of Conflict Resolution in Ethiopia.* Addis Ababa: Ethiopian International Institute for Peace and Development, 2000.

Irani, George E. "Islamic Mediation Techniques for Middle-East Conflicts." *Middle East Review of International Affairs* 3, no. 2 (1999).

Malan, Jannie. *Conflict Resolution Wisdom from Africa.* South Africa: African Centre for the Constructive Resolution of Disputes, 1997.

Vandeginste, Stef, Filip Reijntjens, and Ahemd Yusuf Farah. "Traditional Approaches to Negotiation and Mediation: Examples from Africa," in Luc Reychler and Thania Paffenholz, eds., *Peacebuilding: A Field Guide*. London and Boulder, CO: Lynne Rienner Publishers, 2001, pp. 128–144.

18.1

Clan Elders as Conflict Mediators: Somaliland

Haroon Yusuf and Robin Le Mare

In Somaliland, traditional conflict resolution methods have been used to successfully resolve conflicts that resulted from a traumatic and destructive civil war. Councils of Elders provided for open discussion with all parties and acted as mediators.

In the last decade, a discouraging concept has gained currency: the "failed state." The term has probably been first applied to Somalia, which disintegrated in the early 1990s after civil war and a rebellion drove longtime dictator Siad Barre from power in 1991. Anarchy and violence soon reigned, as the competing militias of warlords fought for control of resources, territory, and power.

In the northern breakaway region of Somaliland, the new leadership hoped to avoid such devastation, but it was not to be. In January 1992, fighting broke out between politicians and members of the military. Towns were wrecked, economic life came to a standstill, and the optimism that had accompanied Somaliland's bid for nationhood had dissipated.

However, while disorder persisted in Somalia, in Somaliland order was restored. The chief mechanism for doing this was by reverting to some of the oldest strategies for resolving conflict. The mediators of Somaliland's conflicts were its tribal elders.

The Traditional System

The harsh environment from which Somalis extract their pastoral livelihood requires cooperation and the sharing of scant resources, and so a distinctive social structure evolved based on kinship, a system of ethical norms and rules adaptive to the pastoral, subsistence lifestyle of the majority of Somalis.

Two key elements of the kinship are blood ties and a concept known as *xeer* (pronounced "hair"), which is, essentially, an unwritten but loosely accepted code of conduct. *Xeer,* which combines Islamic *sharia* and customary law, emphasizes the values of interdependence and inclusiveness and forms

459

A State Without Status

During colonial times, the British and the Italians each controlled a portion of what became, in 1960, an independent nation called the United Republic of Somalia. The idea was to unite ethnic Somalis, but from early on, rivalries between north and south caused friction and resentment. The situation only worsened after Muhammed Siad Barre seized power in a coup in 1969. Barre favored his own clan to the exclusion of others. In 1988, Barre's opponents formed the Somali National Movement and began a rebellion in the north against Barre's southern-based government. Barre responded with bombings of northern cities and a brutal campaign against the rebels. In 1991, Barre was forced from office. In the wake of the collapse of the Barre regime, the northern provinces—what had been British Somaliland in colonial times—declared their independence on 18 May 1991 and proclaimed the Republic of Somaliland.

Yet Somaliland has failed to win international recognition. The result has been that Somaliland is not a member of the United Nations, unable to pursue normal trade with the status of a sovereign nation or to get assistance from international financial institutions such as the World Bank or the International Monetary Fund. "The most disabling thing is the lack of communication with the international community," said the late Mohammed Ibrahim Egal, who was elected president in May 1993 by a council of elders. "We have no ambassadors. We only have international agencies." Before his death in 2002, President Egal called on the United Nations to grant Somaliland special status, as it had previously done for Kosovo, Palestine, and East Timor.

the basis for social contracts or covenants between lineage groups. It defines obligations, rights, and collective responsibilities (including sanctions) of the group. Within this "contract," members are pledged to support each other.

Xeer lays down rules for cooperative responsibility, and is a source of protection for individual and group rights. It does not eliminate strife but provides accepted and workable ways of dealing with disputes and conflicts. Some of the most important aspects of *xeer* govern entitlements to common resources such as water and pastureland.

The Somali clan system is prone to conflicts, but mechanisms exist to mitigate and resolve them. Dialogue, the mediation of elders, religious sanctions, compensation, and military strength are all traditional means for resolving conflicts.

The Authority of the Elders

The relations among Somali clans are dynamic. When disputes arise over matters such as grazing rights, water, other resources, or political influence, they are arbitrated by what is known as a *shir*—a council of elders. The *shir* deals with relations between groups, in war and peacetime, and lays down the laws and principles by which members act. While all adult males are entitled to participate and be heard in a *shir,* reaching agreement is usually delegated to the elders, who are drawn from all levels of society. An elder (usually a man) may gain prominence and influence through attributes of age, wealth, wisdom, religious knowledge, and powers of oratory. An elder is a clan representative or delegate, rather than a leader with authority.

This pastoral society has no hierarchy of political units or political and administrative offices, but rather emphasizes consensus decisionmaking. Only at the clan level is there a post equivalent to that of a leader or chief—the sultan, *garad,* or *ugaas,* depending on clans. The sultan enjoys respect but not reverence, functions as arbiter and peacemaker in his clan and with other clans, and is said to be able to see "beyond the fight." In a conflict resolution setting, elders undertake the negotiations, while sultans approve the results.

Elders monitor and may influence grassroots opinion. They act as mediators operating in open assembly, not secretly. They work on the basis of enlightened clan interest to produce efficacious results. Through these collective institutions and this rule-bound behavior, social order is maintained and conflict managed. Furthermore, agreed rules of warfare condition the scale of conflict (women and children are not targets), and typically disputes over grazing resources are characterized more by negotiations and the formation of alliances than by warfare.

Turning to the Elders

With the civil war raging between 1988 and 1991, the Somali people turned to their traditional mechanisms to deal with their problems. Confronted with the failure of the state and its system of governance, and with the warlords' ascendant, they sought the guidance and wisdom of the elders to assist in the restoration of stability.

The challenges were enormous. A "crisis of legitimacy" prevailed. The society had fragmented and the established state had collapsed. Clan rivalries had turned to open hostility. Political figures who could legitimately claim to represent national constituencies and who had the requisite authority to broker and enforce peace accords were in short supply. Reconciliation efforts were undermined by powerful groups with vested interests in continued instability, conflict, and anarchy, and who threatened peace constituencies. Armed young men with no faith in any type of "government" roamed the streets of the country, and a massive displacement of the population had occurred.

How the System Works

The traditional system came to be seen as a way out of this conundrum. Honest, willing, and credible elders united and initiated a local council to represent their community interests. Generally one or both parties to a conflict requested an elder or an elders' council to intervene.

Negotiations did not follow fixed procedures and time schedules. They were open in terms of participants (all adults may participate), the setting of the agenda, and the establishment of dynamic processes. Generally, reference to past precedent was made, lengthy oral deliberations held, and an elders' forum created. The negotiations that followed would usually address such issues as access to resources and payments for deaths between clans.

In Somaliland, overall cross-clan peace conferences were frequently preceded by subclan deliberations. Through this process perspectives were gathered, procedural steps negotiated, and the basic parameters set for moving toward a more explicit forum, guided by the elders' council (or *guurti*). Only when these preparations had been completed could the larger peace conference begin. The entire process was a lengthy one; preparing for and holding such a conference commonly took four to six months.

Throughout the process, elders prepared, moderated, listened, and often arbitrated procedural problems. The conference was a public meeting, involving not only lengthy speeches, but even poetry. The elders functioned as a "court" and assumed broad and flexible powers to interpret evidence, manage the process of reconciliation, and help formulate the eventual consensus. While the clan elders authorized peace conference agreements, other community leaders—acceptable politicians and military leaders, religious figures, and poets—also played crucial roles.

Impact

The breakaway Somaliland Republic has been relatively peaceful compared with the chaos that has prevailed in Somalia, where warlords have gained sway and external intervention has yet to show success. Beginning in 1991, Somaliland's elders organized reconciliation conferences at the interclan level, which were followed by meetings at the district and regional levels. The most significant conferences were at Erigavo and Borama towns in early 1993.

The Erigavo conference produced a peace charter, which brought hostilities to an end in several parts of Somaliland and recognized individuals' rights to move, trade, and pursue their aspirations within the clans' boundaries. The charter also stipulated the return of property, land, and other resources occupied, stolen, or looted during the war. Conflict resolution committees were set up at all locations to keep the peace and interpret the charter. With this process in place, peace has been maintained despite significant pressures from less stable neighboring regions.

The Borama conference (January–May 1993) was the watershed for Somaliland's recovery and development. It brought together more than 150 *guurti* members from all of Somaliland's clans, plus hundreds of delegates and observers from inside and outside the country. The significant successes of this conference were:

- The peaceful transfer of power from the liberation movement to an elected president, Mohamed Egal
- A Peace Charter that established a national security framework

- A National Charter that established a bicameral legislature, creating for the first time an Assembly of Elders—or National Guurti—as a non-elected upper house
- An elected lower house

The nascent government was severely tested by conflict between its army and a militia associated with an opposition clan in 1995–1996. A Congress of Somaliland Communities in mid-1997 took three months to resolve the conflict. An important decision taken at this congress was to proceed with a process of demobilization of armed factions, and to consolidate police law enforcement and security authority in three security forces: the army, the police, and a custodial corps. With factional disputes finally resolved, it was possible to condition recruitment into the security forces on the dissolution of local militias, the collection of both small arms and heavy weapons, and mandatory training for recruits.

Much of Somaliland's subsequent peace and stability can be traced to the success of this congress, which also adopted a new constitution and reelected President Egal. The 1997 congress also provided for a five-year transitional period, leading to constitutional rule. In May 2001, Somaliland implemented a new constitution, and mandated that elections be held by February 2002. Still, the government failed to enact the electoral law in time—so the Assembly of Elders asserted itself (as provided for under the constitution), and extended the term of President Egal and his government. President Egal died unexpectedly in May 2002, and was lawfully succeeded by his vice-president.

Somaliland has evolved a hybrid political system with elements of multi-party democracy, including a presidency and a legislative Council of Deputies, but with important elements retained from its traditional clan-based society. As scholar Mohamud A. Jama (2003: 24) observes, "The Council of Elders legitimizes the presidential exercise of power by providing political justification for controversial and difficult actions and decisions by the President." Jama is not without skepticism concerning this hybrid arrangement, however. He sees a number of risks. "The system of clan-based political representation," he writes, "is effective in establishing a basis of stability and peace, but inherently incompatible with holding elected officials accountable for their performance." He is also concerned about the risks of factionalism in a clan-based political system.

Somaliland's future is far from certain. It is a poor land, and without international recognition it has limited access to either development assistance or foreign investment. Much of its infrastructure was destroyed during the civil war from 1988 through 1991. Its government has no money to pay civil servants, teachers, and health care professionals. Young men without jobs but well supplied with arms and ammunition pose a threat to security.

Somaliland has built what Rakiya Omaar (1994), of the London-based human rights organization African Rights, describes as "a broadly-based political framework for resolving disputes in a peaceful manner." The elders succeeded, says Omaar, "because ordinary people gave them the authority to make peace and promote reconciliation. In turn, they made their task a collective endeavor."

The existence of that framework, which draws on traditions that are deeply rooted in Somali society, is not only reason for hope, but also serves as an example that others might look to where the traditional structures of governance and authority retain more influence in the daily lives of a country's citizens than do the structures of the state.

Settling a Water Dispute

In the town of Erigavo, a water supply system was installed in colonial times. During the civil war, the system was destroyed. The international development assistance organization ActionAid was requested to rebuild the system, but before it could begin, it needed to have clarity on a crucial question: To whom did the system belong, since its previous owner—the government—had collapsed?

The town's residents belong to four different clans. If one of those took control of the system, that would not only be in violation of the Peace Charter, but would also be a likely source of conflict. So before ActionAid would commence the system's rehabilitation, a multiclan management committee was established, accountable to the *guurti,* and agreements on the allocation of work (excavation, construction, etc.) were signed. In essence, *xeer* (law) governing the system was agreed in advance, defining roles, rights, and responsibilities of each actor, including ActionAid.

Since completion in 1993, the system has served the people of Erigavo— and many rural people who collect its water by tanker—with no further financial or administrative input from the foreign civil-society organization.

ActionAid observes that other international nongovernmental organizations (NGOs) have failed, with unfortunate consequences, to grasp the importance of the elders, who retain ultimate authority at the local level. There have been occasions, for example, when international NGOs have not understood that they must consult with the NGO Coordinating Committee appointed by the Council of Elders. These organizations found that in the end, they could not continue their involvement in the very projects they had wished to carry out.

Haroon Yusuf is a development resource specialist working with the Togdheer community-based organization and team leader of ActionAid's program in Somaliland. Robin Le Mare represents that program in ActionAid–U.K.

Contact

Action Aid–UK
Hamlyn house
Macdonald Road, Archway
London N19 5PG, United Kingdom
Tel.: +44 (0)20 7561 7561
Fax: +44 (0)20 7272 0899
E-mail: robin.le-mare@actionaid.org
Website: http://www.actionaid.org.uk

Selected Bibliography

Jama, Mohamud A. 2003. *Somalia and Somaliland: Strategies for Dialogue and Consensus on Governance and Democratic Transition.* UNDP Oslo Governance Centre, January. Online at: *http://www.undp.org/oslocentre/docsoslo/conflict%20prevention/OGC%20research%20paper%20on%20Somalia%20and%20Somaliland.pdf.*

Lewis, Ioan Myriddin. 1961. *A Pastoral Democracy* (London: Oxford University Press).

Mamdani, Mahmoud. 1996. *Citizen and Subject: Contemporary Africa and the Legacy of Late Colonialism* (Princeton, NJ: Princeton University Press).

Omaar, Rakiya. 1994. "One Thorn Bush at a Time." *New Internationalist* (June). Online at: http://www.newint.org/issue256/one.htm.

Ostrom, Elinor. 1992. "Crafting Institutions for Self-Governing Irrigation Systems" (San Francisco: Institute of Contemporary Studies).

"Somalia: Ten Years On." BBC World Service. Online at: http://www.bbc.co.uk/worldservice/people/highlights/010430_somaliland.shtml.

18.2

Revitalizing Tradition to Promote Reconciliation: The Gacaca Courts in Rwanda

In an effort to come to terms with some of the consequences of the 1994 genocide, the Rwandan government revitalized a traditional mechanism for seeking justice: the Gacaca system. With its rules adjusted to the twenty-first century's requirements and the specific postgenocidal context, the Gacaca court system seeks to enhance reconciliation and dialogue. It helped survivors and perpetrators of the killings realize that in many ways "both sides have been victims." The system faces challenges though, and has been criticized by human rights organizations.

"The Gacaca jurisdiction has characteristics one cannot find in other judicial systems and which are needed to rehabilitate Rwandan society," the Rwandan government said in a statement issued in 2003, reflecting on its decision to introduce the custom-based court system. Gacaca refers to a traditional Rwandan method of conflict resolution at the village level. In case of conflicts in a community, such as disputes over land, property damage, marital issues, or inheritance rights, meetings were convened between the aggrieved parties, and presided over by community leaders. The meetings not only were meant to sanction violators of the village norms, but also to ensure that those accused, and found guilty, were again fully accepted as members of the community. Reconciliation between violators and their communities was at the core of the traditional Gacaca custom.

The idea of using the Gacaca system in dealing with the aftermath of the genocide had been discussed repeatedly since 1994. After a series of talks between representatives from sectors of government and civil society, the government mandated a commission to study how Gacaca could be applied in Rwanda's efforts to deal with the consequences of the crisis of 1994. This led to the establishment of the Gacaca judicial system by law in early 2001. Implementation of the Gacaca policy began a year later.

The Rwandan government decided to introduce the Gacaca court system partly for pressing pragmatic reasons. With 120,000 people accused of war crimes in prison, experts calculated that it would take 350 years before all defendants would be tried if the official judicial system and procedures would be pursued unaltered. The Gacaca system offered an opportunity to speed up the process in a responsible and effective way, Rwandan authorities thought. Gacaca does not replace, but is additional to, two other judicial mechanisms that are in the process of trying the tens of thousands Rwandan prisoners who stand accused of having committed crimes of genocide.

In addition to practical considerations, interest in the Gacaca courts grew as a result of increased awareness that its traditional ways of dealing with conflict could be a major driver toward reconciliation between the surviving victims and perpetrators of the genocide. Putting an end to a traumatic event and reaching some form of peace and reconciliation is a major goal of probably any judicial or penal system and the Gacaca system was perceived to have particularly suitable characteristics to achieve this in the post-1994 Rwandan context.

The current Gacaca judicial system is not an exact copy of the traditional Gacaca custom, but is loosely based on it. One of the differences is that local elders convened the traditional Gacaca meetings spontaneously, whereas the modern Gacaca system has been initiated by the Rwandan government and is being supervised by officials from the Supreme Court and the Ministry of Justice. Traditional Gacaca dealt with relatively minor interpersonal disputes, while the new version of Gacaca deals with genocide. Yet, similar to the old system, in the Gacaca "modern style" the local population acts as witness, judge, and party to the trials. The government is relying on the population to testify before the courts, to recount the facts, disclose the truth, and participate in the prosecution and trial of the perpetrators.

Categories

According to the plan, the Gacaca trials will be held weekly in ten thousand local jurisdictions, or courts, spread over the country, and will involve more than 250,000 popularly elected "judges" as well as the collective participation of all local community members as witnesses or jurors. The system was first implemented in a pilot project in June 2002. Since then, several hundreds of local Gacaca courts have been established. More than 107,000 judges were elected by the Rwandan population, chosen on the basis of their integrity, conduct, and lack of involvement in the genocide.

Crimes are grouped into four categories—crimes against property (category 4); serious assaults against the person (category 3); criminal acts that place the perpetrators among the perpetrators and accomplices of intentional homicide (category 2); and crimes of the highest level, which include those committed by leaders and planners of the genocide as well as rape and sexual torture (category 1).

Category 2, 3, and 4 crimes will be dealt with by the Gacaca tribunals. The regular courts will process category 1 crimes, which incur the death penalty. The different categories of crimes are assigned to different Gacaca courts. Minor crimes are dealt with by the local Gacaca courts, and more serious crimes by Gacaca courts at the sectoral, district, or provincial levels. The fundamental units of the courts are the weekly meetings of the local (or "cellule") courts that take place weekly within communities. While the Gacaca courts do not have the power to administer the death penalty, they are empowered to impose sentences up to and including life imprisonment. The sentencing system is flexible, however, as all convicted offenders have the option of serving half of their sentences doing community service projects. Convicted offenders who have confessed to their crimes are awarded significantly reduced sentences.

Challenges

The initiative to establish the Gacaca court system was positively welcomed by the majority of the Rwandan people. The international community slowly followed in seeing Gacaca as a positive development. There seemed to be no better alternative and Western methods proved to be too slow to deal with the aftermath of the genocide. However, despite its positive focus on the communal process of reconciliation, the system was criticized as well. Concerns and critiques evolved around logistical, legal, and operational issues and especially around the issue of participation.

Many observers agree that the Gacaca process faces enormous challenges not only in terms of the scale of the endeavor, but also in terms of its practical implementation. Judges have been provided with basic training on the Gacaca laws and the operation of the tribunals, but at the same time are expected to work on a voluntary basis. The lack of compensation for the judges makes it difficult for them to fully exercise their duties and makes them more vulnerable to corruption. Also, neither the defendants nor the victims have a right to legal advice or counsel. Human rights activists raised doubts about the competence of Gacaca judges. They pointed out there could be conflicts of interest for the judges when their own relatives stand accused of crimes, and individuals being nominated as judges who have themselves been accused of having committed genocidal acts is not impossible. There have been documented cases of elected judges being accused of having killed during the genocide, who were then removed from their position as a result of these accusations.

Other serious concerns have been voiced by human rights organizations. For instance, Amnesty International outlined a number of issues, including the unlikely adherence of the Gacaca courts to the principle of the presumption of innocence, reports of confession under torture, and the lack of prohibition against double jeopardy, meaning persons already acquitted under a national court could still be tried under the Gacaca courts. These concerns and critics should seriously be taken into account when judging the Gacaca system. However, one should also recognize that there will not be any easy solution to dealing with the painful and challenging consequences of the genocide that took place.

As already mentioned, another challenge the Gacaca system faces is the issue of participation. As the Gacaca laws do not envisage the provision of compensation, many of the survivors question why they should participate, particularly as the courts will not bring back their families. Testifying before the courts also presents risks for survivors, who fear retaliation from the accused and their families. The Gacaca courts are based on the idea that large sections of the population take part in the process as witness or judge. Some researchers, however, noted hesitancy among the local population to fully participate in the weekly meetings. Of those who do attend meetings, many seem reluctant to speak up out of fear that the accused may retaliate. Human rights activists also said Gacaca might be misused by people to make accusations against community members, and could increase tensions rather than enhance reconciliation. Some note that the system tends to ignore war crimes committed by the Rwandan Patriotic Army, which ended the genocide in 1994, but which is said to have committed crimes as well.

The Rwandan government has countered criticism by saying the Gacaca system should be judged in the context of Rwandan society and against the background of the events of 1994, which it said were unprecedented in world history and required original solutions. As before, in response to the critiques, it again adjusted the system in the summer of 2004.

All of these different issues aside, it must be remembered that the Gacaca process has only just begun. Whether these many issues continue to plague the Gacaca system or whether they are progressively overcome is a question that cannot be answered yet. What can be stated is the significance of this process for Rwanda's future. The way local communities will deal with these issues will be a sign of Rwanda's ability to face the challenges of the postgenocide period.

Jenny Matthews/International Alert

Clothilde Umubyeyi, from International Alert's partner organization ProFemmes Twese Hamwe facilitating an awareness-raising session in Kigali on the Rwandan Gacaca Tribunals.

Impact

Several nongovernmental organizations (NGOs) reported positive results from the Gacaca system. "It is important to recognize that there are no easy solutions to dealing with the aftermath of the genocide, particularly as such a large part of the population was either directly or indirectly implicated," coordinators of a project geared toward women conducted by the Rwandan ProFemmes Twese Hamwe and international NGO International Alert (IA) said in a report. "The efforts of women's organizations testify to the hope that the Gacaca process provides for ordinary people, to overcome the events of the past, and to the possibilities for a peaceful future" (International Alert, 2004: 2).

Within the Gacaca initiative, women have been playing an important role. For the first time, women have been allowed to participate in the Gacaca process—more than 30 percent of the judges are female. The 1994 genocide in Rwanda had a devastating impact on women. Thousands were killed and many more raped or subjected to sexual torture. Women were also among the perpetrators of the genocide and make up 3.5 percent of the prison population.

ProFemmes Twese Hamwe, the main collective of women's organizations in Rwanda and IA, have been working to promote women's roles in the Gacaca process since 2002. "It is vital that women develop the confidence and skills to take part," a report on the project pointed out.

> Ordinary people have been confused over the difference between the traditional Gacaca process, used to address minor, civil disputes, and this new one that deals with crimes of genocides. They need to understand how the process could help them to come to terms with the crimes of the past. If women understand how the Gacaca system can do this they will pass on the message to their husbands, families and relatives. (International Alert, 2004: 2)

The project of IA and ProFemmes Twese Hamwe works to encourage women to participate in the new system of justice and to lobby decisionmakers in order to ensure that women's concerns are taken into account by the legislation around the tribunals. IA and ProFemmes Twese Hamwe assume that the Gacaca system needs to be continually adapted in order to meet new challenges. A major issue has been the treatment of cases of rape and sexual torture. For a case to be categorized, the accusations need to be brought before a public hearing. Although the Gacaca laws allowed for special hearings for these cases, this was not happening in practice. Women were reluctant to come forward and speak about sexual violence. Twese Hamwe lobbied the authorities to bring about changes. In order to encourage more women to come forward, the Gacaca law, which was revised in June 2004, now provides that victims of sexual crimes can submit their complaints to one of the Gacaca judges, rather than bring the complaint before the public hearing in front of the community. In the event that the victim does not have confidence in any of the judges of the Gacaca court, she or he can bring their complaint to the public prosecutor's offices.

At the community level, women have responded very positively to the Gacaca process and play an active role at the Gacaca hearings, Twese Hamwe and IA reported. Women asked community leaders to hold more meetings, which suggests that they really are interested in understanding the process properly. One of the most important things that the project has managed to achieve, according to Twese Hamwe and IA, is to create space for dialogue among the community about what happened in 1994 and the consequences that this has had for the population—both for families of the victims and those of the perpetrators. "In most cases this is the first time that there has been a public discussion on these issues," according to a report on the IA/Twese Hamwe project. "The dialogue meetings have enabled both families of victims and perpetrators to understand that both sides have suffered as a result of this genocide; that both sides have been victims. People have come to understand that many of the perpetrators were manipulated by the political leaders of the time" (International Alert, 2004: 4).

Contact

Collectif ProFemmes Twese Hamwe
Avenue de la Justice, Bâtiment SEFA
Kigali, Rwanda, B.P. 2758
Tel.: +250 511 180
Fax: +250 578 432
E-mail: profemme@rwanda1.com
Website: http://www.profemmes.org

International Alert (IA)
Dolby House, 346 Clapham Road
London SW9 9AP
United Kingdom
Tel.: +44 20 7627 6800
Fax: +44 20 7627 6900
E-mail: general@international-alert.org
Website: http://www.international-alert.org

Selected Bibliography

Amnesty International. 2002. *Rwanda, Gacaca: A Question of Justice* (Amnesty International Report, 17 December) Online at: http://web.amnesty.org/library/index/ENGAFR470072002
———. 2003. *Mise au point au sujet du rapport et différentes correspondances d'Amnesty International* (Kigali, Rwanda: Département des Jurisdiction Gacaca, 7 December).
International Alert. 2004. "How Women Are Promoting Reconciliation in Rwanda After the 1994 Genocide" (London: International Alert, not published).
"Research on the Gacaca—PRI Report V, Penal Reform International." September 2003. Online at: http://www.penalreform.org.
Uvin, Peter, and Charles Mironko. 2003. "Western and Local Approaches to Justice in Rwanda." *Global Governance* 9, no. 2 (April).
Webley, Radha. 2003. "Gacaca Courts in Post-Genocide Rwanda." University of California–Berkeley War Crimes Studies Center report, based on fieldwork conducted in Rwanda (Summer 2003).

19

Dialogue-Based Processes: A Vehicle for Peacebuilding

Edward (Edy) Kaufman

"Dialogue" is the kind of term with which most individuals—whether parties or conciliators to a conflict—can identify, and as such it has become a pervasive element in the field of conflict resolution. While accepting its many positive connotations as a vehicle for peacebuilding, we begin this chapter by clarifying the term's basic meaning within a conflict situation. We then complete this introduction to dialogue by filling in the remaining basic questions: when, who, how, which, and where?

Rather than concentrating on governmental or official dialogue, we will focus on peacebuilding by civil society, from Track Two dialogues among "influentials" all the way to people-to-people exchanges. Illustrating with examples from the five powerful stories that give substance to this chapter, this introduction puts the spotlight on practice rather than theory. Having lived most of my life in a region of violent conflict and having facilitated conflict resolution work in other areas, I will draw on my personal experience as a practitioner in making many of the following observations. Because of the wide global scope and diversity of the communal and national conflicts discussed, generalizations are to be understood as a flexible interpretation of numerous realities.

What? The Intrinsic Meaning of Dialogue

Bringing the concept down from the heights of theoretical model, the *Concise Oxford Dictionary* defines *dialogue* as a "conversation; piece of written work in conversational form." From this meaning, we see that dialogue is not necessarily a synonym of *negotiation,* defined as the process in which we "confer with another with view to compromise or reaching agreement." In our field of work, officials at best perceive dialogue as a prelude to informal negotiation by governments. However, at the level of civil society, negotiation is perceived as merely a more advanced stage of dialogue. Rather than take the proximity of both terms as a given, we should aspire to elevate dialogue into an effective tool of conflict prevention and management, toward settling disputes in nonviolent ways.[1]

However, to praise dialogue because "talking is better than shooting" may not be adequate if we take the victim's vantage point. If structural violence as described by Johan Galtung (1996) prevails, the dispute has not decreased through dialogue, it has just entered into another phase. Hence, it may be more useful to analyze dialogue as a conflict resolution tool in terms of costs and benefits, explicitly acknowledging its potential downsides. Both sides of a conflict may experience the negative aspects of dialogue. Typically, rejection of dialogue comes from the powerful. Even for a strong state actor that is seen as holding most of the cards, negotiating with the enemy can be seen as a sign of weakness; here, the state may prefer to avoid recognizing its struggling opponent as legitimate. One effective tactic exploited by the top dog to postpone dialogue is to accuse their opponents of using terror, without conceding that the tools of its own repression are perceived by this same opponent as "state terror." Although reluctance to engage in dialogue can be derived from the arrogance of power, many critiques of dialogue also come from the underdog. At times, the weaker party would rather wait until they can enter talks from a position of strength.

More worrisome, the refusal to engage in verbal exchange comes not only from those opposed to meeting with the adversary but also from those who have previously participated in dialogue and have become either frustrated or disenchanted. Jonathan Kuttab, a prominent Palestinian human rights lawyer, has articulated such counternegative effects (Kuttab and Kaufman 1988: 84–108). A summary of his list of pitfalls includes:

• The generation of a false sense of symmetry between the oppressor and the oppressed while the actual status between the parties is not that of equals; impediments to true equality within the context of dialogue include technical obstacles to participate (restrictions on freedom of movement, adequacy of preparation, levels of professional expertise and language skills, and availability of advisory services), as well as in power relations (the ability to exercise pressure, the language of diktats, and patronage).[2]

• The tendency to ignore basic conflict issues and, in the effort to reach agreement, the avoidance of tackling the most serious and divisive issues or postponing them indefinitely.

• The tendency to accept the status quo and take for granted the present constellation of forces, focusing more on bringing an end to violence and less on justice and its structural causes.

• In the name of pragmatism, parties engaged in dialogue are often pressurized into compromising legitimate principles and abandoning positions generally held within their own community.

• When meetings include participants closely associated with state military or security forces, there is a fear that dialogue can be used as intelligence gathering. There is uncertainty as to when the motivation of the powerful is "know your enemy" rather than "understand your neighbor."

• Dialogue as a device for "divide and rule." As a counterbalance to this tactic, the parties may adopt a tacit understanding to present a unified front when confronting the other side. Natural divisions within parties are, therefore, formally overlooked when facing a common enemy out of a simple fear that their opponent may take advantage of their lack of unity.

• Labeling those that participate in dialogue as "legitimate partners" thereby delegitimizing nonparticipants. Talking to some individuals or organizations may be a tactic used in order to avoid negotiating with more representative but problematic opponents.

• The intimidation of parties to dialogue may come from both sides. Within one's own camp, peer disapproval and even, at times of crisis, physical threats have kept many "towing the party line," while individually they may have been tempted to consider alternative positions, some of these more moderate and pragmatic than the group view.

• The "usual suspects" can monopolize participation in dialogue. Granted that talking may involve some risks, it also provides privileges, both tangible as well as elitist. The warm feeling of acquiring new friends from the adversary's camp may become an addiction in itself. As a result, the tendency has been toward exclusion and unwillingness to share access or widen the circles.

• Last but not least, the tendency to make dialogue a substitute for action to correct injustices. Dialogue can be seen as an academic exercise. Often, the organizers see dialogue as an end unto itself and declare themselves satisfied to repeat time and again this inconclusive experience with other groups.

In answer to Kuttab, I stress the positive elements of dialogue and its value as a necessary but not sufficient strategy for peacebuilding. For example, dialogue can validate the legitimacy of the "other" when recognition has been withheld as a bargaining chip. However, over the years I have come to agree that promoting dialogue instead of action can be used as an excuse for talking and talking without redressing the root causes of the conflict. The fear of normalizing an abnormal situation is real. At the same time, I believe that sustained dialogue diminishes misperceptions, prejudice, and stereotypes. Hence, we need to agree on some ground rules that ensure that talking is not a ploy to postpone action toward a just resolution of the conflict. Dialogue could be a step forward, but once that step is made, there is a danger of stagnation.

In short, dialogue should be a vehicle and not a destination. We need to understand why the expression "we have nothing to lose" is not always shared by the parties involved in the conflict, and that the suggested cost-benefit paradigm tells us that "we have a lot to gain" provided that we maximize the promising positive results of dialogue and minimize its potential negative consequences.

The goal of dialogue should be the transformation of participants into epistemic or "learning" communities in which both sides develop a shared understanding of each other's realities and are willing to invest a good chunk of their lives in changing it. A pioneering example is from the height of the Cold War when dialogue among Soviet and U.S. scientists evolved into the formulation of and commitment to "arms control" efforts (Adler and Crawford 1991).

When? Alternative Strategies for the Cycle of Conflict

In relation to official processes, three phases of civil-society "dialogue" can be distinguished: pre, during, and after Track One negotiations. Or, if lined up in terms of the level of conflict, we can focus on preventive work, Track Two negotiations, and postconflict activities. As a rule, we can argue that civil-society dialogue is relevant as long as it is one step ahead of official behavior. So, how does this principle translate into the different stages?

Stage One

When the effort is invested in prevention, before violence erupts or immediately afterwards, there is often a situation where official communication between the parties to the conflict has been severed. An example of *preventive* efforts in the absence of government action to redress conflict is civil society's resistance to cases of enforced segregation policies, such as in South Africa or the southern United States. In both examples, interethnic dialogue in itself was seen as a heroic and risky act. The joint marches and call for nonviolent means to redress discrimination encouraged change in the official governmental policies.

In the immediate aftermath of violence, the reinvigoration of stalled negotiations may also be possible, as described by an Egyptian intellectual in *When the Guns Fall Silent*.[3] The challenge for civil-society organizations is to show sooner rather than later that there is a partner to talk with. The therapeutic effect of mutual recognition is important to both sides, and particularly to the party who has been denied legitimacy as a partner. When governments have been reluctant to negotiate, "influentials"—who are separated nationally or ethnically across the divide but inspired by a common goal—can initiate a prenegotiation process, which holds the potential of pushing official representatives to overcome the barrier of sitting around the table together. Mutual recognition of partners to a conflict can be triggered by a Track Two dialogue, as was the case between Palestinians and Israelis when they met secretly in Oslo for close to a year. These side negotiations helped advance the official process toward dealing with the substance of the conflict rather than the form. In the aftermath of the 1995 Cenepa War between Ecuador and Peru, the official negotiations started only after prominent citizens from both sides convened at the University of Maryland and became known as a peacebuilding group (See Chapter 21.5).

Often the power asymmetries between the fighting parties lead one side to call for direct negotiations, while the other side will boycott any contact. Interestingly, calls for negotiations may come from the more powerful side when they believe they are well positioned to achieve their goals through negotiation,

The Geneva Accord

The Geneva Accord represents a comprehensive initiative for a permanent set-tlement of the Israeli-Palestinian conflict. This is a model for a permanent status agreement that puts an end to the conflict and to all mutual claims. Second, this is a detailed model. Until the signing of the agreement in Jordan on 13 October 2003, the detailed design of a permanent settlement, including a map, had never before been the subject of public debate. The official Israeli-Palestinian talks of 2000–2001 concluded with no success, and previous Track Two negotiations did not yield a document of comparable scope. Third, as opposed to earlier docu-ments, the Geneva Accord is a signed agreement. More than twenty people from each side signed the accord. These signatures created a personal commitment on the part of a large and respectable group of individuals, which, from the Palestinian side, included ministers, deputy ministers, Palestinian Legislative Council members (representatives of Fatah), senior officials, and academics. Although those holding official positions declared that they had signed the agreement as private individuals, they would not have been able to take such a dramatic step without the indirect authorization of the Palestinian administra-tion. Israeli signers included Knesset members from the opposition, peace activists, authors, security officials in the military reserves, economists, and aca-demics.

The Geneva Accord is formulated like a legal agreement between two states. In this way, it gives tangible expression to the idea of a permanent arrangement. Appended to the Geneva Accord is a cover letter which empha-sizes that the reference is to a model for an arrangement, not a binding docu-ment; to a document that complements the road map, not one meant to replace it; to a private initiative, not one that is representative—even in the case of those individuals who hold public office; to an appeal to public opinion on both sides in order to show that a permanent arrangement is attainable, not a pretense meant to create the impression of an accord between governments.

The goal of the Geneva Accord is to show public opinion on each side that there is a partner for peace and a way to reach the end of the historical conflict. The Geneva Accord constitutes an alternative to the policies of the central regime in Israel and the Palestinian Authority, to the ongoing deterioration resulting from the violent conflict, and to Israel's plan for unilateral disengage-ment from the occupied territories. The Geneva Accord was widely publicized immediately after it was signed and has become a focal point in the public debate on the diplomatic process both in the Middle East and beyond. Since it was signed the Geneva Accord has become the term of reference in every polit-ical and expert debate on the parameters of a permanent status agreement. The Geneva Agreement rests on the recognition of the need for a historic compro-mise. The perpetuation of the occupation of the 1967 lands is beyond Israel's capability and is destroying it. Instead of a lose-lose situation, the Geneva Accord offers a win-win alternative.

Note: Written by Dr. Menachem Klein. For more information, see: http://www.geneva-initiative.net

or from the weaker side when they assess that their aspirations cannot be achieved through alternative means, such as continued armed struggle. Furthermore, the preference for negotiation can shift depending upon its perceived usefulness, as well as evolving ideology. For example, from its establishment in 1948 Israel was interested in negotiations despite Arab refusals to acknowledge the so-called Zionist entity. Negotiation was the official declaratory policy of Israel from its independence until the peace negotiations with Egypt in 1978. By the time Palestinians had become more receptive to dialogue, Israel's policy had also shifted to a refusal to talk with "terrorist organizations." Facing stagnation in official negotiations or during periods of violent clashes, dialogue sponsored by nongovernmental organizations has been instrumental in breaking the ice and demonstrating that there is a partner for negotiation. This is the case with the 2003 Geneva Initiative launched by former Israeli minister of justice Yossi Beilin and Palestinian former minister of information Yasser Abed Rabo. This initiative was among the triggers for the Sharon government to undertake the initiative of pulling out from Gaza, first as a unilateral act and now as part of a negotiated process.

Stage Two

Once official negotiations begin, if peacebuilders are to keep a step ahead, they must be able to come up with creative solutions. At this stage, merely talking to each other is secondary and the need to embrace a problem-solving approach requires the parties to embark on more complex processes of negotiation. As in the Peru/Ecuador case, the impasses as identified in Track One were addressed by Track Two participants proposing ideas such as a transnational ecologic park in a border area under dispute. Numerous meetings took place between Israeli and Palestinian academics and NGOs to address the issues postponed for a later stage in official negotiations, such as borders, Palestinian refugees, Jewish settlements, and Jerusalem. With some issues, such as the allocation of groundwater resources, their recommendations were instrumental in shaping official agreements.

Sustained civil-society dialogue helps to show that no breakdown in official communication can stop the advancement toward peace, and at times, as in Northern Ireland, it provides the promise of a mutually agreed outcome. When third-party facilitated negotiations eventually led the officials to come up with a shared document such as the "Good Friday Agreement," the successful campaign of Catholic and Protestant peacebuilders was crucial in ensuring the wide popular endorsement through referendum.

Stage Three

The postnegotiation stage when a peace agreement is formally reached still leaves open many unresolved issues. Some of these issues are unmet interests but many are intangible needs. International or domestic formal agreements often remain totally or partially unfulfilled even a few years later. Particularly when growing expectations are not met in a timely manner, the recurrent cycles of violence can begin again. The gap that emerges when contrasting insufficient concrete achievements with persisting grim realities can produce setbacks and reversals. Hence transitions to peace or democracy need to be consolidated.

To be able to move from the management of conflict to a real transformation means addressing not only the symptoms but also root causes. A process that supports personal growth, an attitudinal change toward the "other," and the development of strong ties can strengthen its own sustainability.[4]

During the so-called postconflict period, one of the main challenges for peacebuilders is to help launch a process of reconciliation. Reconciliation includes numerous aspects, from material compensation to reducing impunity to justice. Among the intangible needs are healing wounds from the serious suffering produced during the violent conflict, with elements of acknowledgment, apologies, and forgiveness. In fact, a good process of reconciliation should start its planning stages during the negotiation period and then develop its implementation in the aftermath of the agreement. Later in this book, Hizkias Assefa explores in more depth the nature of reconciliation processes (See Chapter 23).

How? The Tools of Dialogue

We can identify a wide range of tools, some related to the technical aspects and others to the deeper meaning of mutual exploration. In terms of its complexity, dialogue can be as unstructured as a spontaneous "walk in the woods" or as systematic as a problem-solving workshop.

Spreading the word runs the risk of engaging peacebuilders in a one-sided communication, which may indeed be just a monologue. Still, perseverance in some cases has resulted in breakthroughs that eventually open up the authorities to new ideas. For example, the Oxford Research Group began a traditional process of letter writing to decisionmakers, spreading from a cluster of concerned scientists to citizens-at-large, with a shared concern with the need for nuclear disarmament (See Chapter 19.3).

Dialogue has also been developed through nontraditional techniques assisted by new technologies, such as Internet chats and the establishment of virtual communities of academics and intellectuals in regions of conflict. The use of videoconferencing can also enable peacebuilders physically separated by the confrontational policies of their respective governments to meet face-to-face through their computer screens.

Indeed, technology provides new avenues for communication. However, the connectivity is also dependent on the ability to deliver an effective message. For this, those involved in dialogue need to develop the skills of articulating their views as well as listening in a way that can maximize mutual understanding. Care is needed to prevent the clarity of the message from being distorted by the "noise" of intercultural obstacles, or by the uneven status of the partners in conflict (as is the case with gender differences in traditional societies or class inequalities in modern societies). It is important for us to be trained in how best to express our thoughts, choosing the sentences and words that not only are true to our feelings and positions but also maximize receptivity, and at the same time to ensure that our body language and the tone of our voices are not threatening to the receiver of our message. On the other side of the transmission process, we should train ourselves to become active listeners, a skill that helps us to put ourselves into the shoes of the "other." Furthermore, active listening also facilitates an introspection by the interlocutor, opening up to express his/her own needs beyond the known declaratory postures.

We also know that sustained dialogues produce better results than one-off encounters. There is no evidence to support the assumption that one-time contacts (such as mutual school visits or joint social events) can help to reduce stereotypes and are "better than nothing." In fact such exchanges may generate expectations for more and disengagement may result in the frustration of these expectations and an unwillingness to accept future invitations for interaction.

While objectives such as personal transformation and building intra- and intergroup relationships within and among the parties are meaningful in themselves, we should seek to maximize the investment. Dialogue is a step in the right direction, but over the years we have learned how to move forward from simply chairing and moderating meetings into facilitated processes that unite the adversaries in the search for common ground. Following the lead of Herbert Kelman (2003) and Edward Azar (2003), new approaches show that effectiveness depends on four autonomous but synchronized and progressive phases: an initial phase focusing on trust building among the stakeholders, the participants, the facilitator, and the methods used; a second phase developing both individual and group skills relevant for conflict resolution; a third stage building consensus on the identified agenda items; and the final phase addressing the challenge of reentry, in which the participants bring back home their shared commitment to working hard toward the implementation of their agreements.[5] This innovative form of citizens' diplomacy also needs to take into account the spiritual traditions across cultures, religions, and civilizations and include these dimensions in the dynamics of the process.

Who? The Partners for Dialogue

In identifying potential dialogue partners, it is useful to map the various linkages between civil societies and the parties in conflict. If we imagine a diagram, we would place civil society in the center as the dialogue initiators and draw arrows outward from the center indicating different interactions that occur: first, we direct arrows horizontally between the two civil societies across the divide, which seems to demand the largest number of interactions with the "other." Then, within each party's civil society, we draw arrows vertically upwards toward the decisionmakers and downwards toward the general public of their own society.[6] From our experience, most of the dialogue takes place across the divide between representatives of each others' civil society. Participants invest in these joint efforts with the hope of empowering each other and then influencing as agents of change their respective political and social processes.

The five stories in the following chapters provide us with interesting examples of partners in dialogue. An English team of researchers struggling for nuclear disarmament launched the Oxford Research Group. The group trained and mobilized about seventy teams to write sophisticated letters to decisionmakers in the United Kingdom and China. They then expanded to involve concerned citizens from other countries. This demonstrates a form of unilateral dialogue, in which active writers made contact with passive receivers. Eventually the percolation of ideas in the minds of the decision-makers allowed the unilateral action to evolve into a true exchange.

An interesting example of powerful intrastate dialogue is the transition in Georgia from an authoritarian regime to a democratic state. The organizers of large demonstrations were not only able to control violence, but also nonverbally communicated to aggressive law enforcement forces their peaceful intentions by offering thousands of roses to the police officers (See Chapter 19.4).[7] These gestures are as important as words, and both together can have a strong effect on reconciliation (Mitchell 2000).

The joint Israeli-Palestinian campaign "Hello Shalom, Hello Salaam" has generated close to a half million telephone conversations worldwide between

Inter-Tajik Dialogue

A combination of actors participated in the nonofficial Inter-Tajik Dialogue, which began in March 1993 when seven individuals from different factions in the civil war sat down around a table in Moscow. At that time, they formed a unique channel of communication across factional lines. Just past the peak of violence in a vicious civil war, they could barely look at each other. By the end of 2000, after twenty-nine meetings, the dialogue continued. The dialogue has helped to support a multilevel peace process that includes government negotiators, highly informed citizens outside government, and citizens at the grassroots level—all working in complementary ways that reflect these roles in their respective roles. Participants in the dialogue helped to start and then maintained the involvement with the inter-Tajik negotiations and engaged in activities in society a large. The dialogue had been convened six times before the UN-sponsored inter-Tajik negotiations began in April 1994. It continued throughout the period of official negotiations and then through the three-year transitional period after the 1997 General Agreement and beyond. Because most of the participants were citizens outside government, they were at the heart of Tajikistan "public peace process."

Kamoludin Abdullaev and Catherine Barnes. Introduction to "Politics of Compromise. The Tajikistan Peace Process." *Accord: An International Review of Peace Initiatives* 10 (London: Conciliation Resources, 2001). Online at: http://www.c-r.org/accord/tajik/accord10/index.shtml.

Israelis and Palestinians. Organized by a prominent NGO, the campaign connects the grassroots populations from both sides, often strengthening the dedication of those already committed to dialogue but also generating curiosity among newcomers to hear and thereby recognize the humanity of the "other" (See Chapter 19.2).

Which? The Models of Dialogue

We can borrow from Jay Rothman (1997) the classification of four dialogue types, categorized according to the nature of participants and objectives.

• *Positional dialogue,* adversarial in nature, focuses on articulation of positions, often in the presence of a foreign or local observing audience for the purpose of scoring points. Participants emphasize differences rather than commonalities. It becomes a dialogue of the deaf: we stop listening once the adversary is in the middle of his statement and start planning our retort. Even then, the exercise can have some positive results when participants role play in reverse, or come to the conclusion that dialogue serves as a first unavoidable step for speaking their truths (or half-truths) before moving into the search for common ground.

• *Human relations dialogue,* when differences of opinion on the substantive issues are relegated to a secondary status, gears its main efforts toward a better understanding of the "other." Methods of active listening help us to achieve this goal and even encourage introspection. It can lead to the sharing of some of the needs, fears, and motives that were not articulated previously, paradoxically helped by the expressed empathy of the once adversarial interlocutor.

• *Activist dialogue* occurs when "partners in conflict" have identified some common ground and plan joint action in implementation. Being an activist may not be a precondition for participation, but this inclination toward action may evolve within the participants as a result of the process dynamics. The dialogue process itself may move individuals from "knowledge" to internalized "act-knowledgement."

• *Problem-solving approach,* the most ambitious of all, maximizes and integrates the positives of the previous dialogue types and puts particular emphasis on how to implement the outcome of dialogue when returning to the participants' respective communities, which continue to mistrust and be hostile to the "other."

Mixing the models may create more challenges than we can handle. Sometimes we can transform participants from the first approach into the second and then move on. For transformation to occur, civil-society dialogue needs to take into account that conflict is typically not only between governments but also between the constituencies they represent. Hence inclusion of diversity of positions in the dialogue process is a priority for most types, avoiding the pitfall of simply "preaching to the converted." The limits of dialogue may exclude identified spoilers. However, when it comes to ideological and militant extremism, the challenge is indeed to move them away from being part of the problem to becoming part of the solution. Rarely can one hope for a conducive dialogue between extremes, such as the Islamic fundamentalists of the Palestinian West Bank and the militant Jews settled on the same land that they call Judea and Samaria. Provided that we know how to identify the type of dialogue that we can use, a gradual approach may include a peace activist or mainstream component on my side and an extremist group on the other. Or, as Mari Fitzduff (2004) explains, "there will be no stable peace until the extreme Catholic and Protestant military organizations are integrated into the negotiation process."

Third-Party Involvement

The role of third-party involvement needs to be carefully assessed. Although there are clear advantages in the parties conducting principled negotiations without a third party's involvement, the parties may choose to invite a third party when facing a high level of violence or complex issues. Under such conditions, third-party facilitators might even invite themselves. However, conflicting parties grow weary of an imposed dialogue by outsiders and such forced scenarios rarely lead to productive outcomes. Inviting also a variety of third-party participants makes a dialogue across purposes, like confrontations such as those that frequently occur in the UN General Assembly. On the other hand, third-party dialogue facilitators can be useful if they work to train and empower the parties to engage in direct dialogue.

Where? The Impact of Context on Dialogue

The particularities of a conflict's context influence the form and success of dialogue efforts. While we tend to prioritize dialogue, and rightly in areas of violent conflicts, we need to remember that *most* of the time *most* countries and communities live in peace with each other. During these times and in these places, the absence of violence is not because there are no conflicts but because the communities opt to deal with these conflicts by nonviolent means, including dialogue. As described below, the context can determine a dialogue's various main functions.

Dialogue is badly needed in *protracted communal conflicts*. Nowadays, the prevailing form of violent confrontation is within and not between states, or when one party is a nonstate actor. Recognition as a valid interlocutor is essential to get the dialogue process going, and often it is less problematic for nonofficial actors to deal directly with players who are unrecognized by formal authorities. The relative advantage of civil society over state actors is especially evident when parties to the conflict include those responsible for violence against innocent civilians, actors that are labeled illegitimate partners in Track One activities, and when governments are facing the dilemma of negotiating with terror, a major impediment for Track One. Once again, civil-society exchanges have a relative advantage.

The context of *transitioning democracies,* as has been the case in Latin America and Eastern Europe, introduces the dilemma of dialogue with regimes that have been involved in gross violations of human rights. Such authoritarian regimes have a history of crushing democratic opposition, including killing their leadership, members, families, and uninvolved bystanders. In some cases such as Argentina, Chile, and Uruguay, a *mesa de dialogo* (in the latter case, within military barracks) with the military regime was acceptable to some opposition parties but not to others. In such cases, the ground rules for who can participate in the dialogue and for what purposes are essential if not life-saving. When regimes were too oppressive and no domestic forces could lead the way to dialogue, we have seen the contribution of either a regional or international third party, as was used in facilitated dialogues in El Salvador and Guatemala.

In many developing countries, environmental, water, and other *common pool natural resources* have generated cross-border and domestic conflicts that cannot be resolved without the involvement of all stakeholders. While the technical and legal ramifications of environmental disputes demand that the negotiation itself be conducted by experts, it does not preclude a transparent participatory process in which grassroots constituencies are given an opportunity to be consulted from the early stages and to play a constructive role in the implementation of the resulting agreements.

For several decades, most countries in Europe and the Americas have been called "zones of peace" (Kacowicz 1998) without interstate wars. Hence, promoting a sustained dialogue as part of the political culture is a sound preventive of international conflicts as well as contributing to the decline of domestic riots and ethnic tensions. Institutionalized forums for dialogue—from debating societies in the old Oxford and Cambridge Universities to peer mediation in schools—provide long-term guarantees of constructive means for conflict resolution; such formalized practices should be expanded. Furthermore, approaching authorities through constructive negotiations is a useful addition to the protest tradition of many popular movements. Yet the promotion of a culture of dialogue should not only be the prerogative of one part of the world. It is no less relevant in the context of majority-minority protracted conflicts. Interethnic dialogue, like the one conducted in the nine centers of the Nansen Dialogue Network in the Western Balkans, stimulates renewed relationship building in divided communities and is a crucial step toward reconciliation. While at times dialogue is a process of rediscovering the good ties from the past, according to the West Balkan organizers, their dialogue is inventing a new partnership with the political culture of Western and Northern Europe. Dialogue rediscovers historically positive relationships and encourages building of new relationships (See Chapter 19.1).

Conclusions

Dialogue is a tool for advancing conflict resolution efforts, especially within the realm of civil society and unofficial contacts. We must emphasize, however, that dialogue in and of itself is not a universal panacea, but a means to an end. While it is typically Track One dialogue between leaderships that results in binding agreements, Track Two activities greatly enhance the feasibility of implementation, content, and commitment of the constituent populations to these formal agreements. Perfecting negotiation skills of Second Tracks can transform its inherent weaknesses into an asset. Citizen diplomacy provides room for flexibility, informality, and creativity that may be missing from official exchanges.

In-depth analysis of cases presented in the following chapters has shown that peacebuilders have not sufficiently employed approaching decisionmakers and engaging public opinion of the "other." Exceptional cases—such as the Oxford Research Group's contacts with Chinese authorities or Israeli academics providing stimulating feedback to Palestinian NGOs working to promote nonviolence—demonstrate the potential of outreach exchanges. Dialogue with the "other" at all levels seems to be more conducive to solutions than monologues in which each side tends "to play chess with itself." However, we should not neglect the need to bridge the gap inside our own camp, generating a consensus-building process in our own societies that strengthens the ability to negotiate with the adversary. Hence peacebuilding often requires promoting dialogue within and across the ethnic, religious, community, or national divide.

We should all engage in dialogue, even if only a few will be negotiators and influence changes in public policy. Dialogue should bring us one step closer to each other.

Edward (Edy) Kaufman is senior research associate at the Harry S. Truman Research Institute for the Advancement of Peace, Hebrew University of Jerusalem, and Center for International Development and Conflict Management, University of Maryland, College Park.

Notes

1. "In the conflict management field, the term *dialogue* refers to a method of getting people who are involved in an emotional, deep-rooted conflict to sit down together with a facilitator and to talk and listen, with the goal of increasing mutual understanding, and, in some cases, coming up with joint solutions to mutual problems" (Burgess and Burgess 1997: 78).

2. In the Israeli-Palestinian conflict, Palestinians often stress the "occupied-occupier" unevenness and ask for solidarity with the weak. However, some Israelis also

emphasize their weaker position when taken in the context of a small country surrounded by what are perceived as hostile neighbors and rising anti-Semitism.

3. The name of a pioneering book calling for Arab dialogue with Israel (Sid Ahmed 1975).

4. For a more detailed analysis of the different approaches in the field, see Ropers (2004).

5. Such an approach was applied in the Peru/Ecuador Track Two case study in Chapter 21.5. For a further presentation, see Kaufman (2003).

6. For a concrete use of this framework, see the "Lessons Learned and Best Practices" chapter in Kaufman, Salem, and Verhoeven (forthcoming).

7. In the political tradition, the idea was developed from the words of the first Georgian president, Zviad K. Gamsakhurdia, "We shall throw roses instead of bullets at our enemies."

Selected Bibliography

Adler, Emanuel, and Beverly Crawford, eds. 1991. *Progress in Post War International Relations* (New York: Columbia University Press).

Azar, Edward. 2003. "Protracted Social Conflicts and Second Track Diplomacy," in John Davies and Edward (Edy) Kaufman, eds., *Second Track/Citizens' Diplomacy—Concepts and Techniques for Conflict Transformation* (Lanham, MD: Rowman & Littlefield Publishers Inc.), pp. 15–30.

Burgess, Heidi, and Guy M. Burgess. 1997. *Encyclopedia of Conflict Resolution* (Santa Barbara, CA: ABC-CLIO).

Fitzduff, Mary. 2004. Lecture at Herzlyiah, Israel, September 7.

Galtung, Johan. 1996. *Peace by Peaceful Means: Peace and Conflict, Development and Civilization* (London and New Delhi: Thousand Oaks, Sage).

Kacowicz, Arie. 1998. *Zones of Peace in the Third World* (Albany, NY: SUNY Press).

Kaufman, Edward (Edy). 2003. "Sharing the Experience of Citizens' Diplomacy with Partners in Conflict," and "Towards Innovative Solutions," in John Davies and Edward (Edy) Kaufman, eds., *Second Track/Citizens' Diplomacy—Concepts and Techniques for Conflict Transformation* (Lanham, MD: Rowman & Littlefield Publishers Inc.), pp. 183–264.

Kaufman, Edward (Edy), Walid Salem, and Juliette Verhoeven, eds. Forthcoming. *Peacebuilding in the Israeli/Palestinian Conflict* (Utrecht, Netherlands: ECCP).

Kelman, Herbert C. 2003. "Interactive Problem Solving as a Tool for Second Track Diplomacy," in John Davies and Edward (Edy) Kaufman, eds., *Second Track/Citizens' Diplomacy–Concepts and Techniques for Conflict Transformation* (Lanham, MD: Rowman & Littlefield Publishers Inc.), pp. 81–106.

Kuttab, Jonathan, and Edy Kaufman. 1988. "An Exchange on Dialogue." *Journal of Palestine Studies* XVII, no 2 (Winter): 84–108.

Mitchel, Christopher. 2000. *Gesture of Conciliation* (New York: St. Martin's Press).

Ropers, Norbert. 2004. "From Resolution to Transformation: The Role of Dialogue Projects," in Alex Austin, Martina Fischer, and Norbert Ropers, eds., *Transforming Ethnopolitical Conflict: The Berghof Handbook* (Wiesbaden: Berghof Research Center for Constructive Conflict Management and VS Verlag), pp. 255–270.

Rothman, Jay. 1997. *Resolving Identity-Based Conflict* (San Francisco: Jossey-Bass Publishers).

Sid Ahmed, Mohammed. 1975. *When the Guns Fall Silent* (London: Croom Helm).

Resources

Lead Organizations

Berghof Research Center—Germany
Research Programmes on Dialogue and
   Conflict Management
E-mail: info@berghof-center.org
Website: http://www.berghof-center.org

Center for Humanitarian Dialogue—
   Switzerland
E-mail: info@hdcentre.org
Website: http://www.hdcentre.org

Coexistence Center—Uganda
E-mail: uganda@coexistence.net
Website: http://www.cecore.org

Initiatives for International Dialogue
   (IID)—Philippines
E-mail: davao@iidnet.org
Website: http://www.iidnet.org

Institute for Global Dialogue—
   South Africa
E-mail: info@igd.org.za
Website: http://www.igd.org.za

Institute for Multi Track Diplomacy—
   United States
Dialogue Initiatives
E-mail: imtd@imtd.org
Website: http://www.imtd.org/initiatives-
   dialogues.htm

Kettering Foundation–United States
The International–Civil Society
   Exchange Program
E-mail: info@kettering.org
Website: http://www.kettering.org

Nansen Dialogue Network
E-mail: nansen@sezampro.yu
Website: http://www.nansen-
   dialogue.net/

Publications

Abdullaev, Kamoludin, and Catherine Barnes. Introduction to "Politics of Compromise.
   The Tajikistan Peace Process." *Accord: An International Review of Peace Initia-*
   tives 10. London: Conciliation Resources, 2001. Online at: http://www.c-
   r.org/accord/tajik/accord10/index.shtml.
Barnes, Catherine, ed. "Owning the Process: Public Participation in Peacemaking."
   Accord 13. London: Conciliation Resources, 2002.
Davies, John, and Edward Kaufman. 2002. *Second Track/Citizens' Diplomacy—Con-*
   cepts snd Techniques for Conflict Transformation. Lanham, MD: Rowman & Lit-
   tlefiled Publishers, 2002.
Griffoli, Deborah Mancini, and André Picot. *Humanitarian Negotiation. A Handbook*
   for Securing Access, Assistance, and Protection for Civilians in Armed Conflict.
   Geneva: Centre for Humanitarian Dialogue, October 2004.
Reychler, Luc, and Thania Paffenholz, eds. "Dialogue and Listening," in *Peace-*
   building. A Field Guide. London and Boulder, CO: Lynne Rienner Publishers,
   2001, pp. 453–496.
Saunders, Harold H. *A Public Peace Process: Sustained Dialogue to Transform Racial*
   and Ethnic Conflicts. Basingstoke, England: Palgrave Macmillan, 2001.

19.1

Engaging the "Other":
The Nansen Dialogue Network in the Balkans

Steinar Bryn

A regional network of centers in the Western Balkans aims to stimulate dialogue in divided communities. In so doing, the goal is to break down enemy images and to increase understanding of the perceptions, interests, and needs of those on the other side of the divide.

In Kosovo, local political leaders and administrative municipal personnel came together to find solutions to the ethnic division in their municipalities. In Macedonia, twenty-five young politicians of different ethnicities gathered in October 2004 to discuss the current challenges of Macedonian society. In Croatia, teachers, parents, and official institutions cooperated on developing strategies to end the ethnic segregation in the school system. Journalists from several parts of Mitrovica, Vukovar, Mostar, Tetovo, Sandzak, and Sarajevo joined forces to address the challenges and responsibilities of the media in ethnically divided communities.

In each case, the organization behind the activity is part of the Nansen Dialogue Network. The network is attempting to make a contribution to peacebuilding in the western Balkans (Bosnia-Herzegovina, Croatia, Serbia-Montenegro, Kosovo, and Macedonia) by encouraging interethnic dialogue and reconciliation and by making available a neutral and open space where the different actors in a serious conflict can meet face-to-face in truthful and honest communication.

The overall goal of the project is to support the region's peaceful and democratic development by encouraging dialogue, and to thereby bring the region's political culture more closely into alignment with the dominant political culture of western and northern Europe. A secondary goal is to influence public discussions of politics and policy in the region. By applying the ideas and skills of dialogue, the Nansen Dialogue Network seeks to empower people who live in conflict situations to contribute to peaceful conflict transformation and the promotion of human rights. The facilitators try to stimulate the cognitive analysis of the conflict and the experience of the "other's" position.

The focus is not on who is right or most guilty, but on how to encourage respect for democratic principles, human rights, and peaceful conflict resolution as alternatives to national and ethnic chauvinism. The Nansen Dialogue Network differs from other international peacebuilding efforts in its emphasis on dialogue and reconciliation—just as essential to sustainable peace as are the issues of security, economic development, and democratization.

The network grew out of work initiated at the Nansen Academy in Lillehammer, Norway. Founded in 1938, the Nansen Academy's aim, throughout its history, has been to defend human dignity and human worth, and to serve as a meeting ground for people of different cultural, religious, and political backgrounds. Its Democracy, Human Rights, and Peaceful Conflict Resolution project was launched in 1995, and has since then gone through several different phases.

In 1997, on the initiative of previous participants at the seminars in Lillehammer, the project entered a second phase with the establishment of a "dialogue center" in Pristina, Kosovo. In the next two years this center organized a series of dialogue meetings between Kosovar Albanians and Serbs. Although the war in 1999 put an end to these activities, the experiences from these meetings inspired the establishment of other Nansen Dialogue Centres.

During 2000 and 2001, nine dialogue centers were set up in Skopje, Belgrade, Podgorica, Pristina, Sarajevo, Mostar, Banjaluka, Mitrovica, and Osijek. By 2004, sixty full-time staff members were engaged in promoting interethnic dialogue both locally and regionally. The core staff members were recruited from the Lillehammer alumni, thereby creating a network of people with a common dialogue experience.

The participants at dialogue seminars testify to a dearth of dialogue spaces where people from different ethnic backgrounds can come together and talk about political issues. The Nansen Dialogue Network's most important contribution has been the creation of such spaces, particularly in so-called microcommunities (Mitrovica, Presevo Valley, Sandzak, etc.) where new constellations and new ways of cooperation can develop, and where community development depends on personal relationships.

Dialogue as a Methodology

Existing literature on dialogue is limited, apart from certain classics such as Martin Buber's *I and Thou* (1922). The Nansen Dialogue concept is therefore mainly constructed from experiences in the field. It is simply a way of communicating that focuses on understanding the "other," rather than convincing him or her that you are right. This understanding is a prerequisite for successful mediations and negotiations. In the dialogue workshops we attempt to create a space of support and safety, where it becomes possible for the participants to honestly communicate their experiences, feelings, and more rational thoughts. In a dialogue on the status of Kosovo, for example, the aim is not to find the solution, but to explore the different standpoints and improve the understanding of why people have such opposing views. This means to practice tolerance and active listening, rather than to pass moral judgment on the "other's" position or to seek out weaknesses in his or her arguments. Then, as the next step, based on this deeper understanding of each other's position, one can attempt to find acceptable solutions for all parties involved.

Dialogue center staff members are cognizant of the fact that debate is an important part of the political world, and they are there to provide the very space for the important issues to be discussed. In fact the deficiencies inherent to political debate in many parts of the western Balkans are a fundamental problem. So the dialogue centers have taken the strategic choice to attempt to influence public debate over important issues, and specifically to attempt to influence the tone of the debate. When engaging in public debate, the centers will focus on bringing forward facts, providing space for all sides' arguments, and arguing in favor of mutual respect between disputants. In short, the centers argue that dialogue—an exchange of ideas and opinions—rather than diatribe is crucial to debate.

The very fact that the centers promote dialogue and reconciliation leads them to stimulate democratic thinking, respect for human rights (particularly minority rights), and awareness of modes of peaceful conflict resolution. As a result, the centers are becoming key actors in civil society. The dialogue perspective stresses an understanding of democracy as much more than an election and voting system. Indeed, a fundamental tenet is that the essence of democracy is the acknowledgment that one might very well be wrong, which is why public debate in open spaces is necessary. To paraphrase John Stuart Mill, you do not really know your own arguments before you have listened to the counterarguments to your own position.

In segregated societies, the information systems are parallel. It is possible to grow up on one side of the river exposed only to certain ethnic "truths." If there is no interaction with the people on the other side of the river who are developing "truths" diametrically opposed to your own, your worldview is unlikely to be challenged. In a dialogue space, people can simply compare notes, share the explanations they have of different events, and confront each other with alternative interpretive frameworks.

Dialogue can turn out to have a radical effect because it challenges the very self-image and worldview of the participants. We have observed that opposing parties believe they have the same set of facts. They believe that questions such "what happened?" and "who did it?" have unambiguous answers. Their perception is often that the "problem" is that the other side *denies* the facts. In a dialogue setting it becomes obvious that the parties have quite different interpretations of reality and possess different versions of the "facts"—totally different analyses of history and the present—and quite different hopes for the future. Dialogue groups provide the necessary cross-fertilization between the parallel systems of information; suddenly the "crazy" behavior of the enemy becomes more meaningful when interpreted within a different cultural and political framework of understanding.

If one can come to understand (if not accept) the other's perspective, then one comes to understand the "legitimacy" of a decision to fight for or against independence. One might argue that a political position is born of one's own situation in society. It is logical that an Albanian is in favor of an independent Kosovo while a Serb is in favor of Kosovo as a part of Serbia. Through the practice of active listening and tolerance it becomes possible to see that one's bitter enemy also perceives himself or herself as a victim of forces outside his or her control whose own political goals represent an escape from misery. This deeper recognition of the validity of each other's positions fosters mutual respect and makes it easier to enter negotiations. At this point dialogue partners may realize that despite their differences, their human needs and interests are often similar. A qualified facilitator can assist in shifting the focus from "position" to "interest" by making the participants realize that they have common interests in economic development, quality education, a reliable system of security, improved job opportunities, less corruption, more independent media, clearer separation of politics and business—and the simple pleasure of drinking a morning cup of coffee in peace.

When the focus is on that which we have in common, it becomes easier to embrace the thought of a civic state. Since politics most often is organized around ethnic principles, the notion of citizenship in a civic state offers a concrete alternative to nationalism. People are often very receptive to a clearer division between state and nation, where a civic state does not threaten the different nations, but rather allows them to flourish in the cultural sphere according to internationally recognized minority rights. Such a multinational state offers an alternative to the sort of thinking about a strong nation-state that leads members of each "nation" (ethnic Croats, Macedonians, Serbs, etc.) to believe they have more rights in their nation-state (Croatia, Macedonia, Serbia, etc.) than other citizens in the state.

A Range of Programs

The Nansen Dialogue Centres are involved in a range of activities to promote the dialogue approach, including seminars, interactive workshops (addressing topics such as human rights, mediation, negotiation, and strategic peacebuilding), regional network projects (e.g., the project directed toward journalists from nine different divided communities), conferences on topics related to conflict prevention and peacebuilding, and instant response activities (lectures, public debates and hearings, roundtables, and poster campaigns, organized in response to burning issues in society).

Impact

Before the Nansen Dialogue Centres were established, the physical spaces for dialogue were absent and the population groups had few opportunities to meet across ethnic divides. The centers themselves provide "space" for dialogue, as do the seminars, and these dialogue spaces are being used to address the challenges these societies face. In addition to this concrete infrastructure, lasting contact and relationships have been established across ethnic divides between political leaders, young politicians, journalists, academics, educators, government officials, activists within the nongovernmental organization community, and others who will take part in shaping the future of the region. A specific focus in 2004 has been on local politicians in municipalities, where "doing good" for the whole community is introduced as an ideal and alternative to ethnic struggle and competition. In conjunction with this program focus, the network organized a Regional Forum for Young Politicians in Ohrid, Macedonia, for six days in June 2004. More than forty young politicians from Croatia, Bosnia-Herzegovina, Serbia-Montenegro, Kosovo, and Macedonia participated in the forum. Such activities reflect one of the network's chief goals: to develop relationships across the borders, and to prepare young Balkan citizens to assume leadership roles. The effectiveness of these efforts can best be judged by the fact that many previous participants now occupy important professional positions as journalists, lawyers, judges, political advisors, or in government.

Challenges

Working to promote interethnic dialogue in an environment marked by ethnic violence, insecurity, and enemy images is not an easy task. It is a long-term investment, with unpredictable outcomes, requiring sustained commitment from the actors involved. Therefore, it is important to be able to cope with set-

---

Mitrovica: Interethnic Dialogue in a Divided City

In 2000, Kosovo was firmly divided resulting from decades of interethnic conflict and the horrors of the war in 1999. The city of Mitrovica was divided by barbed wire and international armed forces. The security precautions were keeping Serbs in the north and Albanians in the south of the city. Most international actors in Kosovo believed dialogue to be impossible, particularly in Mitrovica.

In this situation, Nansen Dialogue Network succeeded in transporting a group of twenty-five Albanians and Serbs to Struga, Macedonia, in December 2000. The aim was to discuss what had happened and why, and what could be done to rebuild society. Four of the participants in this first seminar became the core of the Nansen Dialogue group in Mitrovica, and organized ten new interethnic dialogue seminars in the year to come. In a seminar for journalists, two of the participants discovered that they had taken part in the same battle, trying to kill each other in April 1999. This was the first time they met face-to-face and they discovered that they liked each other. This is just one of many stories of meetings across the ethnic divide.

The dialogue work in Mitrovica was so useful that the United Nations Mission in Kosovo and Organisation for Security and Cooperation in Europe realized the need for a dialogue component in the repatriation work. Today, three Serbs and three Albanians are working full time on this. Dialogue did not fail in Kosovo. Dialogue had just never been properly tried.

backs, such as new episodes of ethnic violence and renewed political instability, and to maintain motivation under difficult circumstances. It is also a constant challenge to develop plans of action in an environment of insecurity and constant change.

In addition, the staff members have to keep in mind their personal security in relation to their work. Working with "the enemy" in multiethnic organizations in ethnically segregated societies implies a risk of being labeled a "traitor." It has repeatedly been a challenge to find the right balance between when to maintain a high profile and when to be more careful, how to be on the "cutting edge" challenging the public to enter interethnic dialogue, without undermining the network's credibility or endangering personal security.

All the staff members of the Nansen Dialogue Centres are locally rooted and subject to the flow of information from within their own community. Consequently, the different staff members adhere to different views about the political situation. A lesson learned is therefore that it is important to have multiethnic teams in all offices where the society is ethnically segregated, to ensure not only that the staff members are constantly challenged by each other in their perceptions of the day-to-day situation, but also that the centers are perceived as unbiased. Another challenge is connected to the regional dimension: since the causes of the ethnic conflicts in the different countries are interrelated, the solutions must also be explored on a regional level, not only in each state. The Nansen Dialogue Network regional reach is what makes the network unique and is therefore its greatest asset. Finding a balance between local and regional focus has, however, been a challenge.

A Model for Other Regions?

Not all divided communities end up in shooting wars, but whether the divisions result in mild segregation, general mistrust, open hostility, or outright bloodletting, they are, in general, accompanied by a total breakdown in communication and, as a result, a complete lack of understanding of the "other's" position and perceptions. The model provided by the Nansen Dialogue Network can be a useful one, then, for many divided communities where well-meaning individuals are willing to listen to what their counterparts on the other side of the divide have to say. The fact that the effort in Kosovo fell apart, at least temporarily, as the tensions in Kosovo turned into a hot war, should serve as a warning that one should temper optimism with a realistic appraisal of human nature. Nonetheless, the dialogue approach embraced by the Nansen Dialogue Network and the nine dialogue centers does indeed still serve as an example of one way to break down the invisible barriers that separate communities.

Steinar Bryn is the director of the Democracy, Human Rights, and Peaceful Conflict Resolution project at Nansenskolen (the Nansen Academy) in Lillehammer, Norway.

Contacts

Nansen Academy
Bjørnstjerne Bjørnsonsgate 2
2609 Lillehammer, Norway
Tel.: +47 61 26 54 08
Fax: +47 61 26 54 40
E-mail: steinar@nansen-dialog.no

Nansen Dialogue Network Office
Tordenskioldsgate 6b
0160 Oslo, Norway
Tel.: +47 22 47 92 32
E-mail: Ingrid@nansen-dialog.no
Website: http://www.nansen-dialogue.net

Nansen Dialogue Centre—Skopje
Tel.: +389 23 296 000
E-mail: ndcskopje@ndc.net.mk
Website: http://www.ndc.net.mk

Kosovan Nansen Dialogue
Tel.: +381 38 224 650
E-mail: knd@kndialogue.org
Website: http://www.kndialogue.org

Nansen Dialogue Centre—Montenegro
Tel.: +381 81 230 681
E-mail: info@ndcmn.org
Website: http://www.ndcmn.org

Nansen Dialogue Centre—Mostar
Tel.: +387 36 327 459
E-mail: office@ndcmostar.org
Website: http://www.ndcmostar.org

Nansen Dialogue Centre—Sarajevo
Tel.: +387 33 273 461
E-mail: office@ndcsarajevo.org
Website: http://www.ndcsarajevo.org

Nansen Dialogue Centre—Banjaluka
Tel.: +387 51 220 431
E-mail: office@ndcbanjaluka.org
Website: http://www.ndcbanjaluka.org

Nansen Dialogue Centre—Serbia
Tel.: +381 11 301 7024
E-mail: nansen@sezampro.yu
Website: http://www.bncserbia.org.yu

Nansen Dialogue Centre—Osijek
Tel.: +385 31 206 670
E-mail: office@ndcosijek.hr
Website: http://www.ndcosijek.org

Selected Bibliography

Aarbakke, Vemund. 2002. *Mutual Learning—Facilitating Dialogue in Former Yugoslavia.* International Peace Research Institute, Oslo PRIO Report 2.

Nansen Network Annual Reports. Various years.

Skjelsbæk, Inger, and Dan Smith. 2000. *Dialogue in Practice: Reflections on a Dialogue Project with Serbs and Albanians from Kosovo* (Oslo: International Peace Research Institute, August).

19.2

Building Trust, Promoting Hope: The Families Forum Hello Peace Project in Israel and Palestine

Aaron Barnea and Ofer Shinar

Contacts between ordinary Israelis and Palestinians are almost non-existent these days. Hello Peace allows both groups to contact each other—anonymously—simply to talk. In less than two years, close to five hundred thousand telephone conversations have been facilitated by the project, which aims to rebuild both trust and hope.

"The leaders on both sides refuse to talk, but through Hello Shalom, nothing can stop the ordinary people—precisely those who have to face the most crippling consequences of the conflict—from trying to understand each other, which may end up saving lives."
    —"Peace on the Line," Nick Taylor, *The Guardian*, 8 May 2004

In November 2000, the second Palestinian intifada had been raging for nearly two months, and relations between Israelis and Palestinians were at a new low. A young Israeli woman named Natalia Wieseltier picked up the telephone to call her friend. It was not with the intention of being a peacemaker, but things took a strange turn. "A man picked up and said I had a wrong number," she told Nick Taylor of the British newspaper *The Guardian*. "I said who is this, and he called himself Jihad and said he was an Arab living in Gaza. Instead of hanging up, I asked him how he was. He said he was very bad, his wife was pregnant and their town was under curfew, and we ended up talking for about 20 minutes."

With this serendipitous wrong number, a tenuous bridge between one single Israeli and one Palestinian was established, from which an impressive project to encourage dialogue between ordinary Israelis and ordinary Palestinians has developed. The project is called Hello Shalom/Hello Salaam (Hello Peace).

Hello Peace is perhaps the best-known project of The Parents Circle—Families Forum (hereafter the Families Forum), an organization of over two hundred Palestinians and two hundred Israelis who have lost children or other family members in the Israeli-Palestinian conflict. Members of the Families

495

Forum believe that "to move beyond silent despair and isolation, people must begin talking again—especially with people on the other side." For almost a decade, the Families Forum has attempted to play a crucial role in spearheading a reconciliation process between Israelis and Palestinians.

The Families Forum itself developed from the unique response of a father to the murder of his son. On 7 July 1994, the body of nineteen-year-old Arik Frankenthal was found in a village near Ramallah. Arik, an Israeli Defense Forces soldier and an Orthodox Jew, had been hitchhiking home on leave when he was kidnapped and murdered by members of Hamas.

No Revenge

Israeli society at the time was torn between hope and despair. On the one hand the government led by Yitzhak Rabin and Shimon Peres showed a profound commitment to the peace process initiated in Oslo. At the same time, the mass media fed the public a steady stream of images of terror, death, and bereavement.

Yitzhak Rabin's historic words of 13 September 1993, spoken from the White House lawn, still resonated with the Israeli public:

> Let me say to you, the Palestinians: We are destined to live together, on the same soil in the same land. We, the soldiers who have returned from battle stained with blood, we who have seen our relatives and friends killed before our eyes, we who have attended their funerals and cannot look into the eyes of their parents, we who have come from a land where parents bury their children, we who have fought against you, the Palestinians—we say to you today in a loud and clear voice: Enough of blood and tears. Enough.

Some Israelis were unable to embrace the words that followed:

> We have no desire for revenge. We harbor no hatred towards you. We, like you, are people who want to build a home, to plant a tree, to love, live side by side with you—in dignity, in empathy, as human beings, as free men. We are today giving peace a chance and again saying to you: Let us pray that a day will come when we will say, enough, farewell to arms.

After each incident of terror, for example, the Terror Victims Association called for vengeance against Palestinians. In response to the brutal murder of Arik Frankenthal, they raised the same cry. Then something new happened, something revolutionary. Arik's father, also an Orthodox Jew, faced the group and said, "You don't represent me and my family. My Judaism is not one of revenge and hatred. I know that violence against Palestinians, revenge and inflicting bereavement and affliction to Palestinians will not bring back my son, but will cause more pain, more bereavement to other families in Israel. I call all of us to stop the killings, to stretch our hands towards the other in search of reconciliation. This is my view of authentic Judaism: a profound thirst for life and peace."

Other bereaved Israeli families echoed his thoughts. These bereaved families became the core of the future organization—the Families Forum—which called for peace and reconciliation rather than vengeance. The forum was with

Rabin, Peres, and Arafat at the Nobel Peace Prize awards ceremony, and was at Rabin's side on the tragic night of his assassination by an Israeli extremist.

Message of Reconciliation

The Israeli group soon approached bereaved Palestinian families, who enthusiastically embraced its message of reconciliation. The joint appearance of bereaved Israeli and Palestinian families had a tremendous impact on individuals in both societies. An ambitious growing program was articulated and implemented, which included meetings in Palestinian and Israeli schools with kids aged sixteen to eighteen, bold public pronouncements, and support for peace rallies. Families Forum's actions attracted extensive media attention in the form of TV and radio interviews and numerous articles in the press.

Notably, Families Forum sees reconciliation not just as a process following conflict resolution, but as part of the process that helps to bring violent conflict to an end. Reconciliation allows each side to transform precisely those views about the other side that led to a self-perpetuating cycle of violence. This transformation creates trust between the two sides, a prerequisite for any peace process.

Empathy for those victims on the opposing side who have suffered loss is a key step in the process of reconciliation. Empathy can create the emotional change needed to undertake the transformation of beliefs that is inherent in genuine reconciliation; generating such empathy has been a prime focus of the work of the Families Forum.

The activities of the Families Forum focus on victims who, instead of seeking vengeance, choose to pursue dialogue with victims of the opposing side. The Hello Peace project of the Families Forum is, accordingly, a logical extension of this goal of pursuing dialogue and reconciliation.

Creating Contact at the Level of the Individual

According to the article "Palestinian-Israeli Hotline Melts Hate" by Deborah Blachor of the *Daily News,* 8 December 2002, Sammy Waed, a Palestinian user of Hello Peace, said: "Before, I thought Israelis didn't care at all when innocent Palestinians suffer and are killed, but now I know they do care. And now I have hope that there can be peace." "We are all people and want the best for our children and grandchildren. We have the power to make a change," said Miriam Inbal, an Israeli user of Hello Peace.

Hagit Ofran, an Israeli user of Hello Peace, said in a letter to the editor of *Haaretz* on 11 October 2002: "Instead of continuing to weep in frustration we should pick up the phone, hear the voices, and continue onward with renewed hope, knowing that there's someone to talk to, that the cycle of bloodshed can be brought to an end."

The Hello Peace project is an attempt to respond to the lack of trust and empathy between the Palestinians and Israelis that, scholars say, is one of the primary reasons that the cycle of violence continues. By getting thousands of Israeli and Palestinians to talk with each other, and by publicizing this fact, the popular belief that "there is no partner for peace" can be dispelled.

Camal Zaidan at Rabin Square (May 2004)

Hello Peace is the brainchild of Natalia Wieseltier and developed from that first errant phone call. Recalling that initial contact, she says, "We weren't making apologies to each other; I wasn't trying to make him feel better. We were just talking as individuals. At the end of the conversation, he said he was amazed that Jewish people were able to talk like that. He thought we wanted all Palestinians dead." After that phone call, Jihad discovered Natalia's phone number on his own mobile phone, called her back the next day, and left a message saying that the conversation had changed the way he thought. Then he gave her number to his brother. Soon, a circle of strangers from the two sides of the Israeli-Palestinian divide were talking to each other. Attitudes began to change. This gave Natalia an idea. The contact she had created by mistake led Natalia to approach the Families Forum with a proposal to set up a system to allow Palestinians and Israelis to talk to each other over the phone.

With Hello Peace, Israelis and Palestinians can call a special number— *6364—and a computer will automatically connect them to someone on "the other side" who has expressed a similar willingness to talk. Users do not have to leave their details or even their telephone number, ensuring that their privacy is protected.

From the moment of inspiration until the project was officially launched, it took two years of fund raising and preparation. In October 2002, the project started up with a massive media campaign under the same slogan in both Arabic and Hebrew: "You can talk about peace/pain/reconciliation." The publicity campaign leading up to the launch was undertaken on both sides of the divide in a similar manner and at the exact same time. This is crucial for success, which depends on the perception that Hello Peace is totally unbiased. A second media campaign was conducted in October and November 2003, coinciding, completely by chance, with the intensive media campaign to alert the international community to the independent peace initiative known as the Geneva Initiative. With the synergies of these simultaneous campaigns, peacemaking received a new impetus, and public interest in peacemaking was clearly apparent, suggesting a grassroots movement for peace was alive and well in both Palestinian and Israeli society.

Hello Peace endeavors to break down the psychological, if not physical, barriers between the two peoples. If numbers can serve as a measure of success, then Hello Peace has been a resounding success, and stands as proof that many Israelis and Palestinians are willing to engage in dialogue; between the project's inception in October 2002 and October 2004, more than 480,000 phone calls had been made. Hello Peace is probably the broadest peace project ever implemented regarding the Israeli-Palestinian conflict and its success suggests that many in both societies remain hopeful that peace is possible and are willing to communicate and learn more about those on the other side.

With Hello Peace a link has been established between the activities of the Families Forum promoting reconciliation over revenge among bereaved families, and the more general need among ordinary citizens on both sides to engage in a humanizing dialogue. As Roni Hirshenzon, a member of the Families Forum notes, sometimes the conversations initiated through the Hello Peace system begin with arguments, but quickly the parties will ask more personal questions, such as "Where are you from?" "How old are you?" "Do you have children?" and so forth, and then, often, the anger dissipates. The intimate nature of the contact that is possible with the Hello Peace system allows both sides to view the "other" as human beings rather than nameless members of an impersonal mass. By creating contact at the level of the individual, participants on both sides come to understand more of the complexity of the situation and learn more about the circumstances and difficulties of those on the opposing side. This knowledge, which is generated by all who are involved with the project, is the basis for the creation of trust between the sides.

Impact

While an independent evaluation of Hello Peace has yet to be undertaken, it can be said that its impact radiates out from the participants in three concentric circles: an inner circle that includes all those who have actively taken part in the project by talking with a person from the opposing side; a middle circle consisting of the friends and relatives of those who have used the system and who have heard about the project and its influence; and a third circle comprising those who have heard about the project either from news articles of from the media campaign. While the impact of Hello Peace on the inner circle is clear, the influence on those in the wider circles has also been notable. Those in the "middle" circle who have heard about the conversations of their friends or relatives have also grasped the significance of dialogue and are likely to feel more inclined to trust the opposing side as a result. Those in the outer circle may also be influenced, especially by the notion that so many have taken up the opportunity and used the system.

Challenges

Hello Peace now faces two challenges: first, how to increase the number of users, and second to create a sense of community, allowing the nascent dialogue to become a normative part of the lives of many Israelis and Palestinians. This will not only legitimize the project but will also give credibility to the opening of new and innovative channels of communication.

Currently, thousands of calls are being made each month. The Families Forum now aims, in the second stage of the Hello Peace project, to tie in other Families Forum activities to stimulate more extensive grassroots activities involving both Palestinians and Israelis. This second stage will focus on further development of the current telephone system, the launch of a new website, and a media campaign. Alongside the inventive use of traditional means of communication, it will exploit technology to allow more people to join in and participate in the dialogue, offering, for example, Palestinians and Israelis ways to expand their communication to the Internet as well as to continue talking over the phone. Already, the Families Forum, in collaboration with the international nongovernmental organization One to One Children's Fund, is setting up an Internet site allowing Israeli and Palestinian youth to communicate online.

Building trust between Israelis and Palestinians may seem to many to be futile after so much violence, but Hello Peace has proven that where ordinary people make contact with each other on a personal level, it is still possible to bridge the divide and rekindle hope, which had long seemed extinguished.

Aaron Barnea, who has lost his twenty-one-year-old son, Noam, due to the conflict, is the Families Forum international relations director.

Ofer Shinar, the Families Forum Reconciliation Initiative's director, has researched reconciliation between Israelis and Palestinians under the guidance of Alexander Boraine, the former co-chair of South Africa's Truth and Reconciliation Commission.

Contacts

The Parents Circle—Families Forum
Hayasmin 1 St.
Ramat-Efal, 52960 Israel
Tel.: +972 (3) 535 5089
Fax: +972 (3) 635 8367
E-mail: office@theparentscircle.org
Websites: http://www.hellopeace.net
          http://www.theparentscircle.org

Selected Bibliography

On Hello Peace: http://www.guardian.co.uk/prius/parttwo/story/0,14195,1214886,00.html.
On the Families Forum: http://www.theparentscircle.org/NewsArticles.asp.
Taylor, Nick. 2004. "Peace on the Line," *The Guardian,* 12 May. Online at http://www. guardian.co.uk/prius/parttwo/story/0,14195,1214886,00.html

19.3

Creating Expertise: The Oxford Research Group in the United Kingdom

By getting activists to enter into dialogue with those who make deci-sions about weapons, the Oxford Research Group opened up a new window in the struggle for nuclear disarmament. It took years, but gradually more and more decisionmakers became inclined to work with the group and other nongovernmental organizations on the chal-lenge to develop security through a collaborative approach, and to abandon the old Cold War thinking based on fear and distrust.

"When faced with a large system composed of many individuals, which is producing results you may want to change or influence, it is simply not true or realistic to believe that there is nothing one individual can do. With a small number of allies, the effects of the decision of one individual can spread dra-matically throughout the whole system, and thereby change the decisions it produces."

—Textbook of the Open University (U.K.)
Systems Theory decisionmaking course

Official Chinese banquets are highly formal affairs, especially when they involve very senior government and military officials. Scilla Elworthy was bowled over by the atmosphere when she led an Oxford Reseach Group (ORG) delegation to Beijing in 1995. Walking up the long red carpet into the Great Hall of the People at the head of such a delegation was, for her, the real-ization of a dream. She was brought down to earth when her Chinese host, walking forward to greet "Dr. Elworthy," went with outstretched hand straight toward the nearest male.

For the next three days, Elworthy and the ORG delegation engaged in a rare discourse. Seated around a huge square of tables, and with the help of simultaneous translation, military and civilian disarmament officials and inde-pendent experts from the West discussed with their Chinese counterparts the topic of nuclear disarmament in the context of "Global Security in the post–Cold War World."

Building Bridges

The visit to Beijing was a triumph for ORG. Since the early 1980s, the organization has made persistent efforts to do something about the dangerous nuclear arms race based on a simple idea: that the struggle against nuclear arms was best served by opening up channels of communication for face-to-face, nonconfrontational dialogue between antinuclear activists on the one hand and government decisionmakers on the other.

Operating as a body of independent researchers with support staff, ORG first identified who made the decisions on nuclear weapons in all the nuclear nations—the United Kingdom (U.K.), the United States (U.S.), Russia, China, and France—and within the Warsaw Pact and the North Atlantic Treaty Organization (NATO), and how the decisions were made. They then increased the level of knowledge among antinuclear activists about the issues at the center of their concern by providing information packets, and encouraging them to make contact directly by letter with one key decisionmaker each in the U.K. and in China. Traditionally, many of these decisionmakers—scientists in weapons laboratories, intelligence analysts, military strategists, defense contractors, and civil servants—operated behind firmly closed doors. ORG's approach was that by focusing on the personal and human relationships aspects of the arms race, they would foster a lasting process of informed dialogue and openness leading, eventually, to policy change.

Their approach effectively overcame some of the rebuttals commonly used by officialdom to put off critics: that the subject was too complicated for ordinary people to understand, for example, or that it should best be left to those in authority. In many instances, such responses would be just an excuse for maintaining secrecy and for hiding mistakes, accidents, and waste. The ORG wanted to remove this veil, and in so doing encourage greater public accountability for decisions on nuclear weapons.

ORG always stressed a collaborative, bridge-building approach involving "dealing with people, developing trust, finding common ground, [and] building confidence." In the early 1980s, when the organization started, the Cold War was at its height and discussions about disarmament amounted to a dialogue of the disinterested. Conferences held to discuss the issue were long on speeches, devoid of genuine dialogue, and short on meaningful results. The different sides of the divide held fixed positions and, with the atmosphere poisoned by Cold War thinking, there was no dialogue between official government and military representatives on the one side and nongovernmental and civil-society organizations (NGOs and CSOs) on the other.

The idea of trying to change this culture by using a fresh approach came out of an experience Elworthy had just had as a delegate to the Second UN Special Session on Disarmament in New York in 1982, where she had seen nearly a million people demonstrating against nuclear weapons in the streets without making any impression at all on the delegates inside the UN building. She came home, gathered friends around her kitchen table in Woodstock, near Oxford, England, and after several brainstorming sessions, ORG was born.

Getting Started

The direct-contact approach developed by ORG began with a pilot project that aimed to facilitate dialogue between seventy groups throughout the U.K. and nuclear-weapons decisionmakers. These included women's groups, Quaker organizations, doctors, teachers, church members, and others simply concerned about the buildup of nuclear arms, and at a loss as to what they could do about it. One thing marked out all these "pilot" groups: they were all willing to do their homework, and they were prepared to drop their traditional "confrontational" approach and learn the skills of dialogue. Each group "adopted" one British nuclear decisionmaker, and—in the interests of balance, and to ensure that the focus was widened beyond a narrow Western one—a counterpart from China.

Each group was provided with an information pack with contact details and background information on their British decisionmakers and his counterpart in China, and their specific area of responsibility. The pack also included a "How To" section, containing detailed guidelines on how to write the first letter, how to deal with a brush off, how to persist, and so on. Above all they were encouraged to write letters to their decisionmakers containing no angry polemics, but respectful, to the point, and designed to trigger a response. Just the seemingly straightforward act of writing a letter had an unexpected effect. Previously, some members of these groups had felt frustrated, helpless, depressed, or angry. Being able to address themselves directly to someone of influence, in appropriate language and citing hard facts, changed their attitudes and feelings: they began to feel empowered by the process.

The activists also learned the value of persistence. In one case, a group of musicians and actors opposed to nuclear weapons wrote to the U.K. chief of defense staff every six weeks, for three years, undaunted by the one-line response he sent to each letter. Eventually, when this man left government and was promoted to the House of Lords, his maiden speech to that chamber surprisingly included verbatim quotes from the letters he had been sent by the group.

Many activists became experts on the issues on which they worked, forcing officials to abandon the excuse that an issue was too "complicated" for the ordinary man or woman in the street. It was no longer easy for senior officials to merely pass the buck on to ministers, who would then instruct junior civil servants to send meaningless replies on their own. They felt challenged to provide substantial answers.

ORG made secrecy and accountability in defense decisionmaking the specific focus of its research. During the period of the group's dialogue project, the British Ministry of Defence imposed a ban on senior civil servants and military officers having any contact with ORG, but this did not prevent independent-minded officials from cooperating—thus reinforcing the underlying principle of ORG's work: that, ultimately, individuals can make the difference.

Spreading the Message

Very soon, helped by funds from Quaker charitable trusts, ORG was able to commission expert researchers to carry out research into decisionmaking structures and published the results in *How Nuclear Weapons Decisions Are Made* (Macmillan, 1986). By 1998, ORG had published thirty titles. In addition, it began to hold seminars and consultations bringing together policymakers and their critics, using the dialogue methods it had developed through the group's project. ORG eventually published these methods in a a handbook called *Everyone's Guide to Achieving Change: A Step-by-Step Approach to Dialogue with Decision-Makers*.

The group's dialogue project soon spread outside the U.K. In 1985, ORG launched a Nuclear Dialogue Project in the U.S., linking concerned citizens' groups with thirty U.S. decisionmakers. Five years later, a similar project was organized in Sweden involving professional groups of medical practitioners writing to French and British nuclear-weapons decisionmakers.

In time several professional organizations adopted what came to be known as the "dialogue approach" as a model, including the International Physicians for the Prevention of Nuclear War in their global Abolition 2000 campaign of 1999.

Meeting Critics Face-to-Face

One of ORG's most important roles came to be as organizer of international gatherings at which decisionmakers met their critics face-to-face. The conference in Beijing referred to at the start of this chapter is a case in point: it was cohosted by ORG on condition that substantial and challenging issues could be raised. For its delegation, the group invited knowledgeable independent experts and some of the military and defense science contacts it had developed over the years. The delegation to China was therefore a rich combination of physicists, security academics, high-ranking military officers, and peace activists.

Opening the seminar on the morning after the banquet, Elworthy caught some of the participants off-guard by asking for two minutes of silent contemplation. She asked each person in the audience to imagine his or her image of a world without nuclear weapons. Everyone complied.

In the ensuing discussion, the Western and Chinese participants enagagd in deep discussion about the doctrine of deterrence, the risks inherent in building stockpiles of plutonium, and a timetable for phased disarmament. The tone and content of the discussion pointed to the real and practical difficulties of disarmament. Soon the seminar participants began talking to each other as human beings, rather than adversaries, softening the serious tone with the occasional touch of humor.

On the final afternoon of their visit to China, the ORG delegation was invited to the key Chinese institute for nuclear weapons research, including arms control. In a remarkably informal roundtable discussion that lasted several hours, staff there answered detailed questions about subjects normally considered closed, such as a fissile material ban. ORG discovered later that these were the only bilateral discussions on nuclear weapons taking place between China and Britain at any level, even informally, during those years. "I left China having learned one thing clearly," notes Elworthy.

The manner in which most international relations are conducted is based on fear. The entire doctrine of nuclear deterrence is based on fear. This is consequent upon a hardware approach—we count weapons, we assess strength, we send spies out to discover enemy secrets, we compete to have the newest, cleverest weapons.

We are quite capable of adopting instead a software approach, even at the very top. Software would mean dealing with people, developing trust, finding common ground, and building confidence. It is what the best of tough leaders do; it's difficult, challenging work. It requires time. It requires flexibility and patience and savvy and wisdom. (Elworthy 2000: 58–59)

Changed Attitudes

When ORG started, back in the 1980s, there was practically no dialogue between NATO and the Warsaw Pact, and no dialogue between government and military officials and NGOs. Fear-based Cold War thinking polarized and poisoned the atmosphere. Such attitudes have changed.

Today, ORG—still a tightly run outfit with a small budget—adheres to the original idea that underpinned its creation, although its focus has widened over the years in response to changing demands and the altered social, political, and international security circumstances.

In 2002, it distilled its dialogue techniques developed over twenty years into an offshoot body called the Oxford Process. The Oxford Process offers consultancy services using skilled, experienced facilitators and the tried and tested methods of effective dialogue with decisionmakers, which combine expertise on political and technical issues with a recognition of the vital importance of building personal, human relationships.

Now, decisionmakers are much more open to working with the organization and other NGOs on the challenge of developing security through a collaborative approach, and to finally abandoning Cold War thinking based on the notion that, as one Chinese army general put it during the seminar in Beijing, "my security is based on your insecurity."

What enabled ORG to change attitudes to disarmament was its focus on putting research tools at the disposal of common citizens through education and training. By communicating directly with decisionmakers, it has shown them that they can make a difference, and from the decisionmakers' point of view, made them aware that entering into discussions with "ordinary" people can help them break out of outdated approaches and attitudes, and develop useful policies for a more secure future for all.

In 2003 the Japanese Niwano Peace Foundation recognized Elworthy's achievements by awarding her the prestigious twentieth Niwano Peace Prize. The foundation particularly mentioned ORG's work in "building relationships with policymakers from all the nuclear nations, and bringing them together with their critics to develop creative approaches to building down arsenals and exploring nonviolent methods as a force more powerful than weapons in resolving conflict."

Contact

Oxford Research Group
51 Plantation Road
Oxford OX2 6JE, UK
Tel.: +44 (0) 1865 242819
Fax: +44 (0) 1865 794652
E-mail: org@oxfordresearchgroup.org.uk
Website: http://www.oxfordresearchgroup.org.uk

Selected Bibliography
Elworthy, Scilla. 2002. "People Talking With Power," in Frederik S. Heffermehl, ed., *Peace Is Possible* (Geneva: International Peace Bureau).

19.4

Inside the Revolution of Roses: Georgia

Irakli Kakabadze

The peaceful Rose Revolution that took place in Georgia in November 2003 has started a new wave of political change in the former Soviet republic. This nonviolent shift of power brought hope to the local population, as well as to the members of the international community. I am deeply touched by the overwhelming desire of ordinary people to choose nonviolent approaches to change.

As the election period approached in November 2003, the party of Georgia's long-standing president, Eduard Shevardnadze, the Citizens' Union of Georgia, was divided into many factions. Most prominent among those factions was the National Movement for a Democratic Change, led by a young U.S.-educated jurist, Michael Saakashvili.

Saakashvili had served as the head of a judicial committee in the parliament of Georgia, as minister of justice, and finally as the head of Tbilisi's city council—the elected local government body of the Georgian capital. His outstanding advocacy and interpersonal skills had transformed him into a clear favorite to win the next presidential election. His party and allies had gained support throughout the country and was expected to gather the most votes in the parliamentary elections of 2 November 2003.

The first results of the exit polls showed that the party was leading in practically all regions of Georgia. However, the government resorted to fraud and the results published on 7 November by the election commission were false. They gave first place to Shevardnadze's party and second place to the party of the autocratic leader of the breakaway republic of Ajaria—both had been showing single digits in opinion polls and exit polls alike. This was a final blow to the disenfranchised citizenry of Georgia and they decided that dramatic civil disobedience was necessary.

Civil Disobedience

Some thirty to forty thousand people amassed at Liberty Square for several weeks in November to protest the election. Protests escalated and the government brought ten thousand armed police and soldiers to defend its headquarters.

Inequality as a Source for Conflict

After a long history of being an independent state, although at times occupied by different conquerors, in February 1921 Georgia was occupied by Soviet troops. As one of the republics of the Soviet Union, it soon became more centralized. Its resources and power were concentrated in Tbilisi, which was directly subservient to Moscow authorities.

The resulting unequal distribution of resources and power generated increasing dissatisfaction throughout Georgia. As a result, since the 1991 breakup of the Soviet empire, Georgia has faced a number of serious internal problems. Three civil wars in Georgia, between 1990 and 1993, each claimed thousands of victims. Russian forces were sent into the conflict to protect Soviet interests. They naturally sided with each region's self-declared government in order to maintain influence on the Georgian state.

President Shevardnadze returned to Georgia in March 1992 with overwhelming Western support, promising to build a democratic nation-state. He started peace negotiations with breakaway regions, but did not succeed in building conditions for peaceful conflict resolution. There were many reasons for this:

- Neither the regions nor the Russian leadership trusted Shevardnadze
- His style of leadership, although cosmetically changed, remained essentially based on the centralized Soviet government system
- Structural problems had grown and the social environment for creating conditions for positive peace were completely absent
- Widespread and systemic corruption resulted in massive draft avoidance
- Misappropriation of funds, salaries below the poverty level (when paid at all), and public officials profiting from drugs and arms naturally contributed to the popular loss of faith in the government

Georgia lacked favorable conditions for development and the creation of a truly democratic society. Georgian society enjoyed a relatively free press, but problems with corruption and mismanagement remained. Minimum wages were equal to roughly $20 per month, pensions $14 per month, and these were very rarely paid on time. While a few in the private sector prospered enormously, most of the population lived below the poverty level. The wealth and resources were concentrated in Tbilisi; government officials took huge kickbacks from various Georgian and foreign companies, whereas regional governments had very little. New capitalism proved to be good for only about 1 percent of Georgia's population. While people did not want to go back to the Soviet years, they longed for a democratic, capitalistic system that supported social justice and human rights for the whole population.

Despite, or perhaps because of, this economic inequality, the nongovernmental sector strengthened during the last six years of Shevardnadze's rule. Nongovernmental organizations (NGOs) made significant strides in educating the general public about their civil and human rights. Foreign NGOs, such as the National Democratic Institute for International Affairs, the Eurasia Foundation, CARE, and MerciCorps, together with the local Liberty Institute, the International Center on Conflict and Negotiation, and the Young Jurists' Association, managed to change the political climate. People's consciousness of their rights and duties as citizens of a democratic country grew. The time for a peaceful revolution in 2003 was ripe, but there were many challenges ahead.

The confrontation intensified after talks between the government of Prime Minister Avtandil Jorbenadze and Michael Saakashvili failed. Demonstrators demanded that President Shevardnadze resign, allowing for new parliamentary and presidential elections. He refused and the tension grew.

The other political parties were not powerful enough to challenge the president. The troops were ready to defend the "legitimate" government if the crowd attacked its headquarters. The political leaders of the opposition therefore appealed to the demonstrators to establish a nonviolent yet revolutionary Civil Disobedience Committee.

The committee was created on 10 November and included film director Goga Khaindrava, writers David Turashvili, Lasha Bughadze, and Defi Gogibedashvili, U.S.-educated lawyer Nicholas Rurua, Liberty Institute activists Giga Bokeria and David Zurabishvili, and Young Jurists' Association leader Tinatin Khidalsheli. The books of Gene Sharp, John Burton, Richard Rubenstein, John W. McDonald, Dennis Sandole, and Johan Galtung, together with works of Gandhi, the Dalai Lama, and Georgian activist Ilia Chavchavadze, a proponent of nonviolent social change, were our guiding voices for the peaceful revolution.

For a successful, nonviolent completion of the revolution, temporary dispersal of the demonstrating crowd was needed. Here creative thinking and decisionmaking proved to be crucial. The crowd had to disperse to allow the government to save face and to avoid confronting the soldiers who were, at that time, ready to fight. The organizers decided to encircle the government building for half an hour, giving a clear signal to the government to resign before starting their final action. They circled the building and handed a thousand roses to policemen and soldiers before returning to their homes. This changed the disposition of the armed forces toward the peaceful demonstrators and won their favor.

For the next five days, the Civil Disobedience Committee visited a vast number of universities, organizations, and regions, while opposition leaders continued working to convince the population that the resignation of the existing government was necessary for the good of the country. Saakashvili went to western Georgia and managed to bring in thirty thousand people from Samegrelo and Imereti. By 21 November, many people had also joined from eastern Georgia.

On the morning of 22 November, about one hundred and fifty thousand people assembled at Liberty Square. Opposition leaders and the Civil Disobedience Committee gave a final signal to the government to resign peacefully. It was clear that if the government used force, they would lose moral and legal power. The government refused once again and the leaders of the civic movement then made a direct appeal to the president: "If you do not resign, we will not obey you. We won't kill you and we will face death if your order is imposed upon the people. You can have our dead bodies, but you will never have our obedience again."

Those words of the great Mahatma Gandhi proved powerful. Thousands of people took to the streets to support the nonviolent change of power. Rock musicians played for the demonstrators in a musical protest that lasted all night, very much reminiscent of Woodstock. All parts of Georgian society became involved in the process, bringing together everyone from scientists, doctors, and teachers to farmers and students and all religious, ethnic, and sexual minorities—nearly 80 percent of Georgian society in total. Yet, the government remained unyielding.

How long would it be possible to hold peaceful demonstrations before somebody provoked the crowd? It was very important to leave a face-saving exit to the government, but at the same time to not give up. The people clearly wanted the president out, but they did not want to see blood. Not necessarily in support of one or another political party, people took to the streets, supporting the call for a nonviolent change of power. They spoke out against the corruption and structural dysfunction of the existing regime. The old-guard politicians, however, were not ready to act decisively.

In these tense moments, the young Saakashvili found enough resources within himself to conduct a very wise political campaign that would eventually lead to the unprecedented Rose Revolution. He borrowed the words of the first Georgian president, Zviad K. Gamsakhurdia, in saying, "We shall throw roses instead of bullets at our enemies," and drew on the experience of the so-called Flower Children during the 1960s peace and civil rights movement in the United States, as his guiding principles for action.

The first Georgian president failed in his attempt to use roses as a nonviolent weapon for progress and change—he did not have a well-trained, mobilized political team or the skills for waging a nonviolent campaign for change. Also, many people thought this was an overly idealistic approach, which eventually destroyed President Gamsakhurdia. However, Saakashvili proved that peaceful change was possible in Georgia. This was the lesson for Georgians and all liberation movements around the world: the ideals of Martin Luther King, Jr., Mahatma Gandhi, and the Dalai Lama could actually be implemented and sometimes they could be more realistic than realpolitik itself.

Independent media, especially the news channel Rustavi 2, played a major role in the success of the Rose Revolution as the media coverage contributed to the relatively high degree of transparency during the revolutionary events. The media's involvement was constructive, and their coverage of the tensions helped to prevent an outbreak of violence in many cases. The information and views forwarded by independent channels were on the side of prevention most of the time, rather than simply providing routine coverage of heated confrontations or violent events. They covered problems that could have led to the violence, supporting the nation's work toward peaceful solutions.

For example, Rustavi 2 showed a documentary about Mahatma Gandhi only six days prior to the revolution and aired a special program on *satyagraha*—nonviolence, the force that is generated through adherence to truth, or a way of life based on love and compassion. Throughout the days leading up to the revolution, Gandhi's word, *satyagraha,* became used more and more by revolutionaries who felt that being firm in truth and nonviolence did not represent a retreat or sellout of social justice.

At the same time, the government did not find a useful tool against Gandhi's philosophy. The rules of *satyagraha* were translated into Georgian, published in *Peace Times* magazine, and distributed to activists and demonstrators. Newspapers published articles while radio and TV stations aired programs educating the public about conflict resolution and the thinking of Gandhi, Johan Galtung, Richard Rubenstein, and other peacebuilders.

The Day of the Revolution

The events of 22 November were crucial for the revolution. Political and civic leaders assembled in Tbilisi's city hall to finalize their plans. As President Shevardnadze tried to convene his illegally elected parliament, the people stormed both the government and parliament buildings, giving the police hugs and roses on their way in. The demonstrators had established such good relationships with the armed forces through giving them food, supplies, and roses, that many of them laid down their arms, welcoming the spirit of change.

Moments later, Michael Saakashvili delivered a final rose to President Shevardnadze, who was then rushed out of the parliament through a back door. He did not resign immediately. The next day the Russian foreign minister, Igor Ivanov, came to Tbilisi and facilitated a dialogue that eventually led to Shevardnadze's resignation and a peaceful transition of power.

Irakli Kakabadze is editor in chief of Peace Times *magazine and South Caucasus Office coordinator for the Institute for Multi-Track Diplomacy. He was one of the leading members of the Civil Disobedience Committee during the Rose Revolution and is based in Washington and Tbilisi.*

Contact

Institute for Multi-Track Diplomacy (IMTD)
1901 North Fort Myer Drive, Suite 405
Arlington, VA 22209, United States
Tel: +1 (703) 528 3836
Fax: +1 (703) 528 5776
E-mail: imtd@imtd.org
Website: http://www.imtd.org

19.5

Taking the Constitution to the People: The Citizens Constitutional Forum in Fiji

Shoma Sharon Prasad

Against a background of political and constitutional turmoil, coups, and court cases, a Fijian nongovernmental organization is attempting to defuse a volatile, ethnopolitical struggle by providing a safe space for free and frank discussion of key issues within the community— whether the community is made up of the inhabitants of remote villages or recalcitrant politicians.

After nearly a century of British rule, Fiji achieved independence in 1970. The British decision to protect the indigenous population from exploitation by other Europeans through importing Indian laborers to work on their sugar plantations laid the ground for ethnic tensions that are still being worked out in the independent state. With many of the Indian laborers deciding to stay on in Fiji, the island now has a flourishing Indian population—some 44 percent of the total—while the indigenous Fijian population has fallen to around 50 percent.

The ethnic tensions first came to a head in 1987 when two military coups staged against the Indian majority government led to the drafting of a new constitution in 1990, which was then amended in 1997 along multiracial lines. Elections in 1999 returned a coalition government headed by the Fiji Labor Party under Fiji's first ethnic Indian prime minister, Mahendra Chaudhry. However, in May 2000 extreme nationalists under the leadership of failed businessman George Speight launched a coup and demanded the revocation of the multiracial constitution and the replacement with one that would allow only ethnic Fijians to hold the posts of prime minister and president. This coup, during which the prime minister and members of parliament were held hostage, ushered in a prolonged period of political turmoil. New parliamentary elections held in August 2001 returned a coalition government dominated by the nationalist Fijian United Party of Prime Minister Laisenia Qarase. However, he in turn faced a legal challenge from former Labor prime minister Chaudhry, on the grounds that the constitution guaranteed cabinet seats for his Labor Party.

It was in 1995 in this context, where constitutional debate expressed ethnic divisions established in the colonial period, that the Citizens Constitutional Forum (CCF) first emerged. Widely regarded in the Fiji Islands and beyond as the leading human rights advocacy nongovernmental organization (NGO) in Fiji, the CCF is supported by members of civil society in its fight for human rights, constitutional democracy, the rule of law, and the building of a multicultural Fiji.

Power to the People

After two preliminary consultations, the CCF began its activities in 1995 and from the beginning set about creating a space for dialogue and debate in order to achieve a sustainable constitutional solution of the tensions between the different ethnic groups. Initially this took the form of a series of workshops for political leaders, NGOs, religious and community leaders, and ordinary citizens on various aspects of constitution making, which inspired people to make submissions to the Constitutional Review Commission chaired by Sir Paul Reeves, the former governor general of New Zealand.

In this process, international experts and jurists assisted the CCF in national consultations on constitutional matters. Political and community leaders were invited to these consultations to encourage dialogue and discussion and help build consensus on a new democratic and nonracial constitution.

Having helped secure the adoption of the 1997 Constitution, the CCF has focused on educating citizens about the new "multiracial" constitution. A major instrument in this is a popular version of the constitution, "Your Constitution, Your Rights," a pamphlet that is published in English, Hindi, and Fijian. Besides its use in schools, it has been serialized in the *Daily Post* newspaper and has been widely distributed in the community. Through instruments such as this the CCF works at strengthening democratic institutions by ensuring the full implementation of the provisions of the 1997 Constitution, building multiculturalism and an understanding of human rights, and seeking a more proportional and fair electoral system.

However, the CCF has also taken a more direct role in the developments around the constitution. In the 1999 election, the architects of the 1997 Constitution—the Soqosoqo Ni Vakavulewa Ni Taukei government and the main opposition party, the National Federation Party—were defeated by a coalition led by the Fiji Labor Party (FLP). After one year in government, the FLP was deposed by a group of soldiers and some indigenous Fijian nationalist extremists under the leadership of George Speight. They held Prime Minister Chaudhry and members of his government hostage in parliament for fifty-six days. The Fiji military forces commander decided to remove the president, abrogate the constitution in response to the demands of Speight's group, and continue negotiations for the release of the deposed government.

As a vociferous and passionate defender of the 1997 Constitution, the CCF soon after these dramatic events took the bold step of supporting a human rights challenge by an individual, Chandrika Prasad, in the Supreme

Court and the Fiji Court of Appeals. Prasad contended that the commander of the Fiji military forces had not acted lawfully in abrogating the 1997 Constitution on 29 May 2000. The CCF led the NGO movement that organized the presentation of evidence in support of Prasad's litigation.

The Supreme Court decided on 2 November 2000 that the 1997 Constitution was merely suspended by the purported abrogation and came back into effect when the hostages were released. The court also declared that the interim administration led by Laisenia Qarase was illegal. The government appealed against the judgment. The five judges of the court of appeals upheld the Supreme Court judgment on 1 March 2001, declaring that the May 2000 revolution had been unsuccessful. The 1997 Constitution thus remained effective. Professor George Williams—one of the counsels involved in the Chandrika Prasad case—comments in an article in the *Oxford University Commonwealth Law Journal* (Summer 2001): "It was the first time ever that the leaders of a coup had voluntarily submitted to the jurisdiction of a court only months after taking power. It was also the first time ever in Fiji's history that a court decision has restored a constitution and the democratic system of government created by it."

Achievements

The response from the community at large was very encouraging. It appeared that people had very limited knowledge of the constitution and their rights. The impact of these educational workshops has not been measured and analyzed, but it is hoped that by providing people with accurate knowledge of the disastrous consequences of the 19 May coup, the nationalists will find it more difficult to mobilize these villagers in the future.

The workshops and discussions also covered other issues that were important to the communities, such as the meaning of human rights. In every workshop, the importance of democratic process and its institutions, the need to support the rule of law and the independence of the judiciary, and respect for human rights and other cultures were emphasized through discussions. Women and children actively participated in the workshops with local police representatives, who at the same time used the opportunity to educate them about crime.

All the workshop discussions were recorded and reported to the CCF's steering committee members. In 2002, the CCF hosted similar grassroots human rights educational workshops in towns and villages of the other provinces, attracting a total of two thousand participants. All the issues covered were directly related to conflict prevention and peacebuilding in Fiji after the coup. During these rural education visits, the CCF was able to identify a number of influential local people who have since been trained and are being maintained as part of this ongoing grassroots education project.

The CCF has also organized workshops that focused on constitutional issues in the urban centers. These provided opportunities for discussing the Bill of Rights, squatter settlements and evictions, land rights, indigenous rights, and the foundation of a coalition government, multiculturalism, tolerance, and peace-

Constitutional Awareness Campaign

Of all the work carried out by the Citizens Constitutional Forum (CCF) since its formation in 1995, the most effective has been its use of advocacy and public education to create awareness of constitutional and democratic issues among the wider civil societies ranging from grassroots communities to schools and religious groups. After the unsuccessful coup in 2000, the CCF has focused on building relationships between communities using the constitutional awareness campaign to encourage dialogue and reconciliation. This has been promoted through newspapers, radio, television, and a website that provides a forum for dialogue on important national issues.

The main aims of the CCF's educational workshops are to counter the misconceptions that the communities hold about the constitution and to inform them about their rights. In the rural areas, this is done mainly through village workshops and through the distribution of booklets and pamphlets about the constitution and rights, such as "Your Constitution, Your Rights."

Most of the CCF's activities are accomplished through volunteer efforts and respond to the needs of the moment. Educating people from different communities has required a major commitment. For example, between May and June 2004, a prominent tribal chief led a multiracial team to areas in Tailevu North and Lower Naitasiri Provinces, over a period of six weeks, and conducted thirty workshops in a total of thirty-three villages. Many of the supporters of the coup came from these areas.

A total of 943 people took part in these workshops. All households in the villages and settlements visited by the team now have a copy of the "Your Constitution, Your Rights" booklet. Important issues such as the entrenched constitutional protection of indigenous-owned resources such as land and fishing grounds, elections and the democratic process, the importance of following the rule of law, and good governance issues associated with development were discussed and debated.

The program has met some apparent resistance from the Ministry of Fijian Affairs through the provincial administration. A number of calls were received, allegedly from the Provincial Office, requesting that the team cancel its programs. However, the teams proceeded with their visits to the villages and were welcomed almost everywhere.

building culture.

More recently the CCF joined with other NGOs to make submissions to parliamentary committees on subjects such as information technology, the freedom of information bill, the defense review, and prison reform. The CCF has facilitated continued dialogue and consensus among the NGOs, civil society, and government.[1]

In 2002, the Fijian government, after a lapse of eighteen years, presented a report on Fiji to the United Nations Committee on Elimination of All Forms of Racial Discrimination. The NGO Coalition on Human Rights in Fiji, for which CCF provides the secretariat, presented a shadow report in Geneva.

After the two groups had presented their papers, a debate ensued in the national parliament on human rights issues and the legality of the present government. Ordinary citizens contributed to this debate through articles and letters in the three national newspapers. The debate continued in the newspaper columns for weeks.

The Multiparty Issue

The Citizens Constitutional Forum (CCF) has been deeply involved in the contentious issue of multiparty government in Fiji. The Fijian Constitution stipulates that after general elections, the leader of the party or coalition of parties that wins the election must invite parties with more than 10 percent of seats in the seventy-one seat House of Representatives to be part of the cabinet.

On forming his government after the 2001 election, Prime Minister Laisenia Qarase failed to invite the Fiji Labour Party (FLP) into the government, the only party with more than 10 percent of the seats. Consequently there has been litigation in the Supreme Court, which recently ruled that the FLP was entitled to a proportionate number of ministries.

The CCF tried to encourage politicians from both sides to discuss the agreement for the formation of the coalition government. A workshop on multiparty government was organized for the two main political parties and the minority parties to enable them to have open dialogue and raise differences. However, this was not achieved because the ministers and members of parliament in the current government declined to participate.

The members of the FLP and other opposition parties did share similar concerns about the country's progress and recognized the importance of working together for the betterment of the nation. Apart from observing the development progress between the two leaders of the political parties, the CCF has also encouraged dialogue and participation of other parties and civil-society groups on this issue.

In another area of conflict and peacebuilding, the CCF is involved in the Vatukola Goldmines trade union's twelve-year-old court case against Emperor Gold Mines Limited. The CCF provided legal aid to the union. Although the decision of the court went against the union, the CCF has continued its support in a study of the gold mines and the effect they have on their workers. Individual members and Oxfam Australia have assisted this.

CCF work has been reported widely in the news media, ranging from newspaper articles to radio talk shows. Overseas radio and television stations and Australian and New Zealand radio have frequently reported on the work of the CCF. Promoting and advocating the work of CCF has been a key feature in encouraging open dialogue among civil-society groups publicly.

The aim behind all this community work is to motivate and create a well-informed public that could, in the long run, become the most effective watch-

South and North Korean Women Reunite

After more than fifty years of partition on the Korean Peninsula, the scene on 17 October 2002, in Kumkang Mountain, North Korea, was a truly remarkable one: on that day, hundreds of women from the communist North Korea and capitalist South Korea were dancing and singing together. It was the closure ceremony of the South-North Women's Reunification Convention, with 357 participants from the South and 300 from the North. The conventions consisted of art and craft exhibitions, games, sports, joint banquets, cultural and musical performances, discussion groups, and small group meetings. Women came from different sectors of society including agricultural, religious, business, academic, nonprofit, and educational. Preceded by a smaller-scale Reunification Forum that was held one year earlier in the North Korean capital of Pyongyang, this was the first large-scale meeting of women from both sides. The South-North Korean women's interchanges substantially contributed to reducing the decades-old antagonism and tension between both sides.

Women Making Peace initiated the Reunification Exchange program between North and South Korean women in 1997, with a campaign called Sharing Love Sharing Food. During this campaign civic groups and public support in South Korea were mobilized to collect money for milk powder to send to the women and children in North Korea.

This was one of the first acts of cross-border engagement between the two Koreas since the partition and it became the spiritual and ideological basis of the "Sunshine" policy of the Kim Dae-Jung government, which resulted in the 2000 South-North Summit Meeting between the leaders of both Koreas.

The women from South and North Korea ended their 2002 convention with a resolution, declaring that they would keep peace together so that there would never be war again on the Korean Peninsula, and that women, the main victims of the division, should lead the way to reunification. When the South-North Joint Event for the Anniversary of the Independence Movement of 1 March was held in Seoul, North Korean women representatives joined with South Korean women to make a statement against war, and for peace and reunification, at their separate 8 March women's conventions. South-North Korean women's working-level meetings have continued after the conferences and have been held six times up to September 2004.

According to Women Making Peace, the North-South women's events and the continuous working-level meetings have had a major effect on peacebuilding in Korea and on the prevention of military conflict. South and North Korean women have offered an example of how to practice reconciliation and cooperation together. Women have recognized their core responsibility and have tried together to open the way to human security.

Contact
Women Making Peace
4th floor, The Women's House of Peace,
38-84 Jangchoong-Dong1ga, Joong-Ku,
Seoul, 100-391, Korea
Tel.: +82 2 2275 4860
Fax: +82 2 2275 4861
E-mail: wmp@peacewomen.or.kr
Website: http://www.peacewomen.or.kr/english/introduction.htm

dog for public finance, and would act as guardians of the constitution, democracy, and the rule of law. The program will enhance and foster tolerance, respect, and goodwill within the many different communities, cultures, and religious groups in Fiji.

Shoma Prasad is a student majoring in journalism/sociology at the University of the South Pacific. She has been a volunteer at CCF since 2002.

Contact

Citizens Constitutional Forum
P.O.Box 12584
25 Berry Road, Fiji
E-mail: ccf@coneect.org.fj
Website: http://www.ccf.org.fi

Note

1. Internationally, the Citizens Constitutional Forum's (CCF) work has been made possible by assistance from the European Union, AusAid (the Australian government's overseas aid program), Nzaid (New Zealand's International Aid and Development Agency), and Oxfam Australia. The CCF has also worked with International Partner NGOs such as Conciliation Resources in London and the European Centre for Conflict Prevention in the Netherlands, and overseas-based trade unions. High-ranking academics have paid regular visits and have supported the work of the CCF.

20

Campaigning to Create Awareness:
How to Influence People and Change the World

Rebecca Peters

Creating awareness and lobbying are interconnected campaigning tools. They are complementary; one supports the other. Awareness-raising mobilizes public opinion, which in turn softens decisionmakers who have previously been unreceptive to lobbying activity on that subject. They may change their attitude, becoming more willing to make time in their schedules, listen to lobbyists, and eventually to support the cause.

Nongovernmental organizations (NGOs) cannot change the world on their own. They can identify problems and what needs to be done about them. Governments are the ones who must make the changes. They are the ones who have the power to change laws, create new laws, and ensure that they are implemented.

NGOs have various tools at their disposal to influence government decisionmakers to take specific actions, including awareness raising and lobbying. Awareness raising is indirect, and aims to mobilize the power of public opinion in support of a cause. It aims to change public consciousness and arouse interest in an issue by providing information on the nature, extent, and complexity of a problem, as well as what can be done to solve it. Such information can have an impact on the decisions made by individuals on whether to buy a particular product for instance or whether to vote for a parliamentary candidate who supports a particular cause.

Lobbying specifically targets the policymakers: the people in society who have the power to change the laws under which we live. Classic lobbying consists of pressuring politicians to take specific decisions—such as whether to support or reject a certain piece of legislation—that will further a particular cause.

Making Use of the Media
One of the most important methods of raising the public's (and politicians') awareness of an issue is to make sure that it is represented in the media. This

means building relationships with journalists who work on that subject so that they cover a campaign's messages. They need information presented to them clearly and concisely: the most important information at the beginning and contact details at the end.

Relying on the statistics or dense policy reports that might impress politicians is not enough; journalists will not have time to read them. What they want is a story to tell. However good the information is, however important it is that it be made public, the first thing that a journalist will say is: "What's the story?" If campaigners have not provided one, the journalist is unlikely to be interested.

One of the best tactics is to illustrate a broad problem by putting a human face to it. Telling the story of one person, family, or situation—especially if it involves children—is very effective when it comes to raising awareness because it gives individuals something they can relate to. The public reads and sees so much bad news in the media that they can become desensitized; it can often seem to be happening to people far away, with whom they have little or nothing in common. Campaigners need to combat this by finding connections between the lives of the people who are suffering and the public and the decisionmakers. For example, during the war in Iraq in March and April 2003, a lot of the mainstream media coverage in Europe focused on the activities of the Coalition Forces and the bombs they were dropping. However when a twelve-year-old boy called Ali Abbas lost both of his arms and several members of his family in a U.S. missile strike, he came to symbolize the human cost of the war. The extensive coverage of his plight increased public awareness and sympathy for the victims of the war.

Identifying one message that is accessible and understandable to the public, then emphasizing it to the media, is a powerful way of getting a message across. Changing assumptions about one core issue among journalists can effectively turn them into amplifiers and spokespersons. Part of the success of the International Campaign to Ban Landmines (ICBL) was the fact that it could rely on sympathetic journalists to promote and amplify their core message: ban landmines. Excellent supporting research, concisely presented, plus an effective website that continues to be constantly updated, are crucial additional tools that the ICBL can employ when dealing with the media. The campaign has managed to alert public opinion and bring on board many governments all over the world.

Most media work by NGOs is done on a limited budget, so it is important to focus on gaining the coverage that will be most effective in raising awareness and support among as wide an audience as possible. Is there a radio program that is listened to across the country? Is there a morning newspaper that helps to set the media agenda for the rest of the day? Is there a particular publication that is read by politicians? This does not mean that coverage elsewhere, and at the local level, is not important, because coverage in any media outlet, as long as it communicates the message properly, can help to win new supporters to the cause. The point is that thinking about the audience can be more effective than aiming for sheer numbers of column inches.

Visibility of a cause in the media is a good start, but it does not mean that campaigners have won. It can even lead people to think that because it is being covered extensively in the media, that cause has already been dealt with. Activists also need to specifically target political decisionmakers. A private meeting with a minister can yield more results than copious national press coverage, although of course the press coverage might have helped to get the meeting with the minister in the first place.

Gaining Political Support

Like journalists, parliamentarians are also busy, with many concerns competing for their time. However, policymakers and politicians are here to serve the public, so there are usually clear mechanisms for community organizations to communicate with them. If a campaign group is headed by a high-profile community figure or public personality, the group can use them to set up a meeting with a relevant politician. However, essentially any group should be able to ask questions to parliamentarians and have the opportunity to meet them.

Organizations should think about which politicians are likely to support the change they are campaigning for, and then approach them for a meeting. Once they have the politician's time, they should ask them what would be helpful to them—they should not assume that politicians have all the materials they need to keep well-informed on their subject. People in government organizations would often like more information, so a crucial function that activists can perform is to keep politicians informed with research and information on forthcoming reports and events. While this benefits the politicians as they are kept informed, it also benefits the group involved as they gain a reputation as a reliable source of information—a crucial part of lobbying. Politicians may also reciprocate by keeping the group informed on topics such as forthcoming votes on their area of interest.

There are two more dimensions to gaining political support: constituency and the international context. Providing real solutions that actually will work is crucial in answering the all-time favorite question of politicians: Who do you represent? A constituency will form around workable solutions, not just theoretical ones. Additionally, and especially when working in countries that are less well-off, political support may also involve international donors and NGOs. This requires more diplomatic skills: establishing good relations with donors, having a trustworthy image, and keeping sound financial records are very helpful. Building what one activist calls "para-diplomatic" relationships with foreign NGOs, donors, and diplomats can even be a decisive factor in making real change in countries that have a more difficult political environment than developed democracies.

Tackling Opposition

Campaigning is fundamentally an adversarial business. Our work at the International Action Network on Small Arms (IANSA), for example, not only consist of persuading the public and politicians that we are rights; it is also about

---

The International Action Network on Small Arms (IANSA)

IANSA is the global network of civil-society organizations working to stop the proliferation and misuse of small arms and light weapons. World attention is increasingly focused on the humanitarian impact of these weapons, and IANSA brings together the voices and activities of nongovernmental organizations and concerned individuals across the world to prevent their deadly effects.

Founded in 1998, IANSA has grown rapidly to more than five hundred participant groups in nearly one hundred countries, with representation from many gun-affected regions. IANSA is composed of a wide range of organizations concerned with small arms, including policy development organizations, national gun-control groups, research institutes, aid agencies, faith groups, victims, and human rights and community action organizations.

IANSA aims to reduce small-arms violence by: raising awareness among policymakers, the public and the media about the global threat to human security caused by small arms; promoting the work of NGOs to prevent small-arms proliferation through national and local legislation, regional agreements, public education, and research; fostering collaborative advocacy efforts, and providing a forum for NGOs to share experiences and build skills; establishing regional and subject-specific small-arms networks; and promoting the voices of victims in regional and global policy discussions.

For more information, see http://www.iansa.org.

---

persuading them that the progun lobbies are wrong. This has the added drawback of making some politicians reluctant to support us, because it is simpler for them to ally themselves with a cause that has no opposition, such as a group raising money for cancer research.

When it comes to lobbying decisionmakers who are hostile to a cause, groups should start by finding out what their specific objections are, and whether there are any circumstances under which they could support their campaign. It is only by identifying obstacles that groups can hope to overcome them.

An unsympathetic politician or journalist may not be your only opposition; many NGOs have to campaign against another group with opposing aims. IANSA's work is a good example—our goals are difficult enough to achieve, yet in addition to facing the opposition of powerful governments, we also have to counter the arguments—and money—of arms-industry lobbyists.

In short, campaigners must think about what matters to the people they are trying to influence, and what their reasons are for not currently supporting the cause. Then they should identify what they can do to meet the needs of those opposing them. A politician may be reluctant to support a cause because of political pressure, such as not wanting to alienate a specific industry. While there are some factors that activists cannot influence, there are others they can—in this case, by offering a politician the opportunity to be publicly associated with a deserving cause, a benefit that may outweigh their political concerns.

For example, in Australia when gun control advocates were lobbying for stricter domestic gun laws in the 1990s, parliamentarians in some areas were uneasy about supporting the campaign for fear of losing votes in their communities. So the campaigners approached the politicians and offered them the opportunity to be photographed and thus associated with local supporters of the campaign who were also widely respected by communities, such as church leaders, the head of the emergency room at the hospital, and local police chiefs.

Lobbyists should remember that it is important to target those who are already sympathetic to a cause, as well as those who oppose it. Successful campaigns are those that build coalitions of NGOs and politicians. A parliamentarian might broadly support a cause, but it is important that activists keep him or her informed on the current debate to make sure that they share the same information and aims. The Fatal Transactions campaign is another example of how to build coalitions around a single core issue.

Societies in Transition

Awareness-raising and lobby campaigns face additional challenges when conducted in countries in conflict or transition. After war or a period of totalitarianism, those forces responsible for this negative policy environment are still there and new democracies (including the rule of law, respect for human rights, and much more) still need to be established. Besides, many countries have people within their borders whose main concerns are bread-and-butter issues, which is not to say that they do not care about larger issues—it is just not their main preoccupation. This is a hard situation to get out of. Politicians may not have the strength or even the will to deal with the problems that are the focus of the campaigns mentioned in this chapter, and NGOs need enormous amounts of effort, energy, and willpower to make politicians and the public at large listen to them. Here, establishing contacts with sympathetic media and other coalition partners is even more vital.

Lessons Learned

The harsh reality of campaigning is that supporting a deserving cause is not enough in itself. Activists need to be strong-willed and tough; being in the right does not on its own lead to winning the argument. There are lots of good

Fatal Transactions

The Fatal Transactions campaign is a consumer campaign consisting of four international human rights organizations (Global Witness, Medico International, the Netherlands Institute for Southern Africa, and Novib/Oxfam Netherlands) which was launched in October 1999 to alert the public of the links between the global diamond trade and the funding of conflict in African countries such as Angola, Sierra Leone, and the Democratic Republic of Congo. The aim is to pressure diamond companies to establish policies, controls, and management systems to ensure greater transparency and accountability in the procurement of diamonds. The campaign has attracted extensive media coverage around the world, raised consumer awareness, and helped to mobilize the diamond industry and governments into joint efforts to stop the trade in conflict diamonds.

One of the campaign's successes was the first international meeting of the diamond industry, including producer countries, that was held in Kimberley, South Africa, in 2000. The Kimberley Process Certification Scheme (KPCS) for rough diamonds is the result of three years of intensive negotiations that started there and then. A combination of innovative nongovernmental organization (NGO) investigation, an image-sensitive commodity, and a transnational company (De Beers) that realized the potential commercial risk posed by association with conflict got the process off to a good start.

De Beers, which controls some 60 percent of the world's uncut diamonds, responded from an early stage in the Fatal Transactions campaign. Although conflict diamonds represent only 4–10 percent of the world market, the company recognized the potential danger of an effective consumers campaign. In early 2000, De Beers announced that it would begin issuing written guarantees that the diamonds it sells do not come from any area in Africa controlled by forces rebelling against an internationally recognized government.

In November 2002 states, industry representatives, and NGOs managed to reach consensus on a document outlining the political as well as practical aspects of a worldwide certification scheme for rough diamonds. Implementation started on 1 January 2003. Although the United Nations is not a formal signatory, it has been essential to the process through its publication and dissemination of a panel of experts' report, through its leverage on governments, and through its formal endorsement of the KPCS from December 2000.

For more information, see http://www.fataltransactions.org.

causes competing for the attention of journalists, the public, and policymakers, so organizations have to work hard to sell their cause. This means that good research is also not enough. Research forms a core part of publicizing a cause and communicating the full extent of a problem. Too many campaigning groups conduct extensive research, then shy away from the adversarial arena of lobbying, which is where they could put that research to its most effective use. Awareness-raising and lobbying should be used in conjunction with research; the two methods complement each other. Research data should be

Publish What You Pay

Natural-resource revenues are an important source of income for the governments of over fifty developing countries. International oil, gas, and mining companies pay billions of dollars a year to the governments of many less-developed countries that are rich in natural resources, such as Angola and Nigeria. When properly managed, these revenues should serve as a basis for poverty reduction, economic growth, and development. Few of these countries' citizens benefit from this financial windfall, however, because of government corruption and mismanagement. Relying on companies to disclose information voluntarily has so far failed because they fear being undermined by less scrupulous competitors.

The Publish What You Pay campaign coalition consists of over two hundred nongovernmental organizations and civil-society organizations worldwide calling for a mandatory disclosure, backed by legislation, of payments made by oil, gas, and mining companies to all governments for the extraction of natural resources. The idea is that by knowing exactly how much revenue resource extraction is generating, communities can advocate with their governments for the productive use and equitable distribution of these funds. The campaign was launched by George Soros and founded by Global Witness, Catholic Agency for Overseas Development, Open Society Institute, Oxfam, Save the Children–U.K., and Transparency International–U.K. The campaign has led to the British government's launch of the Extractive Industry Transparency Initiative, which is a landmark approached in encouraging governments and companies to maximize transparency.

For more information, see http://www.publishwhatyoupay.org.

publicized to make use of it, while awareness-raising and lobbying activity must be backed up by comprehensive research.

It is vital that the information that activists provide be accurate. Research is crucial to helping an organization establish and maintain a reputation as a credible source of information. Campaigners should never be tempted to overstate a problem; the problems we deal with are severe enough in themselves. If journalists, the public, or policymakers feel a group has exaggerated a problem to gain support, they may withdraw their support, putting the campaign at risk.

The competitive campaigning environment also means that activists need to consider all of the potential tools at their disposal, such as getting celebrities or community leaders to speak up for their cause. When campaigners are absorbed in their own subject it is easy for them to presume that it is obvious that the need for action speaks for itself and so celebrity backing is not required. Yet the reason that the intervention has not yet happened, and they are still having to campaign, is precisely because it is not yet obvious to everyone, and if a celebrity can help to raise the profile of the cause, it may be worth considering. A word of warning, though—celebrities must be properly briefed, and committed to the cause themselves. Activists still shudder at the memory of a pop star who, on leaving a human rights fund-raising event during the late 1980s, was asked by a journalist what she thought about the situation in South Africa. To the horror of antiapartheid campaigners, she earnestly said that it was truly terrible that the rhinos were still being killed.

Rebecca Peters is the director of the International Action Network on Small Arms (IANSA). IANSA is the global network of civil-society organizations working to stop the proliferation and misuse of small arms and light weapons.

Resources

Lead Organizations

Coalition for the International Criminal Court—United States
E-mail: cicc@iccnow.org
Website: http://www.iccnow.org

Coalition to Stop the Use of Child Soldiers—United Kingdom
For contact, please visit website:
http://www.child-soldiers.org

International Action Network against Small Arms (IANSA)—United Kingdom
E-mail: info@iansa.org
Website: http://www.iansa.org

International Alert—United Kingdom
E-mail: general@international-alert.org
Website:
http://www.international-alert.org

International Campaign to Ban Landmines—United States
For contact, please visit website:
http://www.icbl.org

Hague Appeal for Peace—United States
E-mail: hap@haguepeace.org
Website: http://www.haguepeace.org

Fatal Transactions Campaign—Netherlands
E-mail: ft@niza.nl
Website: http://www.fataltransactions.org

Publish What You Pay Campaign—United Kingdom
E-mail:
coordinator@publishwhatyoupay.org
Website:
http://www.publishwhatyoupay.org

Publications

Cameron, Maxwell A., Robert J. Lawson, and Brian W. Tomlin. *To Talk Without Fear.* Oxford: Oxford University Press, 1998.

Chapman, Jennifer. "The Importance of People on the Ground in International Campaigns," in David Lewis and Tim Wallace, eds. *New Roles and Relevance: Development NGOs and the Challenge of Change.* West Hartford, CT: Kumarian Press, 2000.

Edwards, Michael, and John Gaventa , eds. *Global Citizen Action.* Boulder, CO: Lynne Rienner Publishers, 2001.

Fitzduff, Mari, and Cheyanne Church, eds. *NGOs at the Table: Strategies for Influencing Policies in Areas of Conflict.* Lanham, MD: Rowman & Littlefield Publishers, 2004.

Hubert, Don. "The Landmine Ban: A Case Study in Humanitarian Advocacy." Research policy report. Providence: Watson Institute for International Studies, 2000.

Hussein, Zahid. "Training of NGOs in Awareness Raising." Discussion paper. BICC, GTZ, InWEnt Capacity Building International and the German Federal Foreign Office, 2003. Online at: http://www.bicc.de/events/unconfII/paper_hussein.pdf.

International Alert and Saferworld. *Action Against Small Arms: Resource and Training Handbook*. 2003.

International Alert and Women Waging Peace. "Inclusive Security, Sustainable Peace. A Toolkit for Advocacy and Action." November 2004.

Wolf, Kristen, ed. *Now Hear This: The Nine Laws of Successful Advocacy Communications*. Washington, DC: Fenton Communications, 2001.

Yankelovich, Daniel. *The Magic of Dialogue*. New York: Simon & Schuster, 1999.

20.1

Never Again:
The Archdiocese of São Paulo and the
World Council of Churches in Brazil

During the period of military rule, Brazilian army officers kept detailed files of those that tortured, who they tortured, and even the methods used. They never imagined one day it would all come to light. It did, though, thanks to a project undertaken with zealous ecumenical passion by a team coordinated by the Reverend Jaime Wright, under the auspices and the protection of Cardinal Paulo Evaristo Arns of the Roman Catholic archdiocese of São Paulo, and the World Council of Churches.

In September 1973 Jaime Wright answered the telephone in his office in São Paulo, Brazil, and felt his world cave in. "Es caru," the voice at the other end said—"He is fallen." Then the line went dead.

The fallen was Jaime's younger brother, Paulo Stuart Wright. An assemblyman in the southern state of Santa Catarina during the early 1960s, Paulo was stripped of his position when the military took power on 1 April 1964. He fled the country but returned clandestinely and was organizing peasant cooperatives and rural networks when he "disappeared."

The body was never recovered. However, years later, Jaime Wright, a Presbyterian minister, uncovered the gruesome details of his brother's torture and murder. These were contained in one of the files of legal proceedings carried out in Brazil's military courts over the period 1964 to 1979. Thousands of such files were retrieved from the army archives under provisions of an amnesty law. Secretly copied and catalogued, they became a chilling parallel record of the military authorities' own torture archives.

In 1985, with the transition to civilian rule under way, the more than a million pages of documentation were synthesized into a best-selling book, *Brasil: Nunca mais—Um relato para a historia* (Brazil Never Again). This graphic but objective account of torture victims and their torturers, the instruments of torture, and the results was the most visible manifestation of a project undertaken with zealous ecumenical passion by a team coordinated by

Reverend Jaime Wright, under the auspices and the protection of Cardinal Paulo Evaristo Arns of the Roman Catholic archdiocese of São Paulo, and the World Council of Churches (WCC).

The project left another lasting legacy: a carefully assembled archive containing thousands of files detailing repression and torture that provided a window into the underside of Brazil during the years after the military took power in 1964. Such a detailed record has no parallel in Latin America.

What it amounted to was an indictment of the Brazilian military rule (1979–1985), a period when, under the guise of eradicating "communist infiltrators," the state waged an insidious campaign of terror on its own people. An era when anyone who voiced opposition to the regime became a target, including those fighting for the rights of the poor and landless, journalists, and members of the opposition political parties of the left.

A particular characteristic of the violence administrated by the state was the widespread and systematic use of torture. Thousands of people were subjected to acts of terror in order to extract confessions of wrongdoing or sometimes just to silence any dissent.

Highly Detailed Files

In 1979, fifteen years after taking office, the Brazilian military accelerated what up to then had been a slow stop-start process of liberalization, by offering an amnesty for both political prisoners, and state security agents who had carried out torture.

Human rights advocates representing victims warmly welcomed the amnesty for political prisoners, but the prospect of an amnesty for agents of terror deeply troubled many Brazilians. However, one particular provision of this amnesty provided a window of opportunity. In preparing amnesty petitions, lawyers for the political prisoners were permitted to view official state records of their clients. Crucially, they were also allowed to keep these files overnight, provided they returned them within twenty-four hours.

The files in question were extensive and highly detailed accounts of every person abducted, tortured, interrogated and killed by the security forces. Brazilian army officers were obsessive record-keepers. A group of lawyers realized that, though the process of accessing the files was ad hoc, the contents were valuable. Even a tiny sampling would offer unique insight into the use of torture in Brazil. They proposed the idea of acquiring such a sampling to Jaime Wright. Knowing there was little help or sympathy to be had from his own Brazilian Protestant churches, Wright went to his close friend, Cardinal Evaristo Arns, archbishop of São Paulo, who had become an increasingly vocal critic of the junta, and Phillip Potter, general secretary of the WCC in Geneva.

Within a matter of days, Cardinal Arns gave the idea his personal backing. The WCC agreed to provide funding and support. As the cardinal put it in an interview later: "What unites us, you see, is the Gospel—what the Word of God tells us to do. In concrete projects such as this one, there is no time to worry about the things that separate us." Catholic bishops, some Protestant leaders, as well as laypersons, worked hard to comfort the many victims of repression: twenty thousand citizens were imprisoned during military rule, many were tortured and killed, and others "disappeared" or were forced into exile.

Church opinion on the issue was by no means unified. Some characterized the reported incidents of torture as "isolated" and accepted that the alleged victims were "agitators" and "terrorists." They trumpeted the official propaganda about the "social reforms" undertaken by the military—literacy programs, highway-building programs, schools, a social security system, and housing projects.

In May 1971, a group of North American missionaries, meeting in Campinas, in the state of São Paulo, defended these reforms and condemned Church critics of the military such as Dom Helder Camara, archbishop of Olinda and Recife. Not only missionaries, but also broad sectors of Brazilian churches took this line, or were so far removed from the oppressed peoples they were in no position to reach a definitive conclusion. Given this situation, while Cardinal Arns provided a moral umbrella and some physical space, he could not use Catholic funds for the purpose, out of fear superiors—not all of whom were sympathetic to such an enterprise—would raise questions and compromise the project's secrecy.

In this regard, the role of the WCC was crucial. The WCC had already developed links within the ecumenical community in Brazil. It was involved in collecting reports of illegal detention and torture from the early 1970s. It circulated this information on abuses and torture to appropriate United Nations bodies and concerned governments worldwide. Through various ecumenical channels inside Brazil, the WCC also provided moral and financial assistance to detainees and prisoners.

In addition, working through La Coordinadora Ecuménica de Servicio (CESE)—the ecumenical service agency—the WCC launched a campaign across Brazil to publicize the Universal Declaration of Human Rights. Five million copies of the document were produced for churches in every single state. Each article of the declaration was accompanied by biblical and theological references. In the 1970s and 1980s, the world body had worked with Cardinal Arns to pressure the authorities for the protection and safety of union organizers from the military police.

Within a month after receiving the request, the WCC, through its Human Rights Office for Latin America, started covertly funding the Nunca Mais project. By 1980 the project was in high gear. It was carried out in utmost secrecy. Lawyers working with the team applied for the files under the pretext of preparing amnesty submissions. The documents were photocopied and returned without arousing the suspicion of the authorities.

The project was carried out from a nondescript office building in Brasilia. There was no sign on the door. Three photocopying machines were kept going ten hours a day, seven days a week, copying the files in time for the lawyers to return the originals on time. After the files were photocopied, they were transferred to São Paulo, microfilmed, and spirited out of the country to the offices of the WCC in Geneva. The courier who took the microfilm to Geneva brought back with him cash from the WCC stuffed into a money belt. In Geneva, the microfilm was analyzed and archived.

As Strong as Any Justice

In 1985, the organizers realized the entire archives amounting to one million pages had been photocopied. This material was condensed into a seven-thousand-page report detailing, sometimes in minute detail, the extent of state repression.

Still operating in the utmost secrecy, the organizers employed two Brazilian journalists to summarize this further into a readable and easily digestible narrative. Publishers were found in Brazil and the United States, and on 15 July 1985, without any advance publicity, the book *Brasil: Nunca mais* (Brazil: Never Again) appeared in bookstores in Brazil. It was a publishing sensation. Two weeks after publication, *Nunca mais* was the number-one best-seller in Brazil, a position it maintained for twenty-five weeks. It went on to become the biggest ever nonfiction title in Brazil, eventually selling two hundred thousand copies.

Brazilians had heard accounts of torture and repression before. Human rights groups and other organizations had reported these. Now they had a vivid account of the who, what, how, and why. The project also made available for public consumption duplicate archives with the complete record of Brazil's military courts during the height of the repression from 1964 to 1979. Preserved on 6,946 pages, complete with statistical tables, was an alphabetical listing of 444 torturers whose names were taken from official military court records, their 7,363 victims—people accused by the regime of one type of political activity or the other, and placed on trial—and methods used. As a corollary to the project, 10,170 publications that appeared during that period— published by almost fifty clandestine groups—were assembled in a library.

In September 1985, the recently inaugurated president, José Sarney, Brazil's first elected civilian president since 1964, signed the UN Convention Against Torture—a move many people argue was prompted by revelations in the book. Some months later, when the list of the 444 torturers was released, it was found that many held high positions throughout the country. Some were promptly fired; others had their career paths blocked. In 1999, Brazilian medical associations began hearings to revoke the medical licenses of doctors who took part in the torture of political prisoners between 1964 and 1985.

While the amnesty of 1979 still prevents criminal charges being brought by the victims of torture against their perpetrators, those implicated by the book are now publicly known for their crimes. The truth based in the revelation of the true horror of those crimes was for many people as strong as any justice.

The late Jaime Wright saw the Nunca Mais project as preserving the memory of years of repression. He said its great value was to provide the church and people of Brazil with an instrument for work and struggle on behalf of justice so that the horrors that were commonplace during the period never happen again. "It is only when the causes of repression are eliminated that its effects—torture among them—will disappear."

Torture Lessons

The majority of the trials on which the files collected in the Nunca Mais project are based—4,460 out of the total of 7,367—took place between 1969 and 1974, when Garrastazu Medici ruled Brazil. A total of 2,127 persons were imprisoned during the government of Castello Branco, from 1964 to 1966.

Some 38.9 percent of the victims were under twenty-five years of age. Ninety-one were below eighteen years of age when charged and imprisoned. Of the 7,367 trials, 1,918 accused swore, under oath, that they were tortured during detention—a significant number, given the likelihood that many were too afraid to make such a declaration.

Contacts

Charles Harper
2 Chemin des Aires
30210 Saint Hilaire D'Ozilhan
France
Tel.: +33—4 66 37 26 06
E-mail: CRoyHarper@aol.com

World Council of Churches
150 Route de Ferney
P.O. Box 2100
1211 Geneva 2, Switzerland
Tel.: +41 22 791 6111
Fax: +41 22 791 0361
Website: http://www.
    wcc-coe.org/wcc/english.html

Selected Bibliography

Lutheran World Information, Press release, 21 January 1987.
Matthews, Dylan. 2001. *War Prevention Works: 50 Stories of People Resolving Conflict* (Oxford: Oxford Research Group).
Weschiler, Lawrence. 1987. "A Miracle, A Universe." *New Yorker* (25 May and 1 June).

20.2

Making a Difference: The International Women Building Peace Campaign

Ancil Adrian-Paul

The goals of the international Women Building Peace Campaign have been to get its concerns about women in conflict situations onto the agendas of nations and international bodies including the United Nations and the European Union. Since the unanimous adoption by the UN Security Council of Resolution 1325 on Women, Peace, and Security, the campaign is focusing on the translation of the rhetoric of the resolution into gender-sensitive practice.

On 31 October 2000, the UN Security Council unanimously adopted Resolution 1325 on Women, Peace, and Security. It was the first time that the Security Council had so explicitly addressed the disproportionate and unique impact of armed conflict on women. It was, furthermore, the first time that the council acknowledged the underrepresentation of women in official conflict resolution activities and the special role women can play in building peace and security. The unanimous adoption of Resolution 1325 also represented an important success for a broad-based coalition of activists. Many of them supported the global campaign Women Building Peace: From the Village Council to the Negotiating Table, which was officially launched in May 1999 by International Alert (the U.K.-based international NGO with extensive experience in conflict resolution work).

The Campaign

The primary objectives of the Women Building Peace Campaign were to influence the policies of international bodies—especially the UN Security Council and the EU; to ensure that women's perspectives are integrated into peace and security issues, to develop a coalition of women's organizations working collaboratively to advance the issues highlighted by the campaign, and to stimulate the release of resources to support the work of women and women's organizations involved in peacebuilding, conflict resolution, and reconciliation.

Advocacy and lobbying for the resolution, along with a similar resolution at the European Parliament, represented tangible milestones the campaign established for itself. Such a resolution could serve as a "policy tool" setting out specific actions to be taken by governments, the UN system, and other organizations in support of women's inclusion in processes that affect their peace and security. The tool would also stimulate participating stakeholders to examine and adapt their own policies with respect to women's concerns and demands.

The Women Building Peace campaign was launched in response to five critical concerns articulated by women:

1. Lack of women's inclusion in decisionmaking processes
2. Women's absence from postconflict reconstruction and reconciliation processes
3. Lack of sufficient protection for refugee, displaced, and other war-affected women
4. The need to develop mechanisms to end impunity for crimes committed against women during armed conflict
5. Lack of sufficient and sustainable resources to support women's peace-building work

One of the main goals of the campaign has been to raise visibility about these issues. Beyond that, the campaign aims to "make women matter"—that is, to alter the processes of conflict resolution and peacebuilding in such a way that both the concerns of women and the often overlooked conflict resolution activities that they engage in become far more central to "mainstream" conflict resolution activities. As one observer, Rita Manchanda, remarked, referring to the role of women in Kashmir, it was often the case that, in the face of repression, "the women come out in their traditional roles as nurturers and as protectors of the community. It is an empowering experience. It is the women who negotiate with the security forces and the administration . . . it is both women's importance and weakness that gives them the right to access the powerful and say: Give me justice" (Anderlini, Manchanda, and Karmali 1999).

Key Stakeholders

In the forefront of this campaign was a loose grouping of nongovernmental organizations (NGOs),[1] calling itself the NGO Working Group on Women, Peace, and Security, which resolved to work together for the Security Council resolution. They quickly realized that support from UN agencies and key members of the Security Council would be critical in the process. Informed by research, the members of the group systematically and persistently engaged the member states in dialogue, providing information and analysis on the impact of armed conflict on women in different regions of the world, the positive role women play in peacebuilding, and the need to include women in peace processes and protect them from gender-related violence, including such abuses as sexual torture, rape, enforced pregnancy, and forced prostitution.

Items for discussion at the Security Council must be placed on the agenda by a member state. This was done by the Permanent Mission of Namibia, which had recently hosted a conference on Mainstreaming a Gender Perspective in Multi-Dimensional Peace Operations. Other member states such as Jamaica and Ireland offered support by convening what have become known as Arria Formula debates on the resolution—informal, unofficial meetings of the Security Council where nonmembers can speak about issues they wish the Security Council to address.

The involvement of many agencies and individuals within the UN itself was essential. In particular, the Fund for Women (UNIFEM) was especially key: for example, by identifying and facilitating the participation of women peace advocates from Guatemala, Zambia, Somalia, and Sierra Leone. These women electrified council members at Arria Formula meetings with their personal testimonies, reflections, and perspectives on women, conflict, and peacebuilding.

The Strategy

In order to ensure widespread and representative support for the initiative and to shape impact and influence policy at the global level, the campaign staff devised a multifaceted strategy.

Prior to the launch of the campaign an international conference brought together women from forty-eight conflict areas to share their experiences of armed conflict and their agency and positive role in peacebuilding. Key activities at the conference included discussing international mechanisms previously developed to promote women's advancement and empowerment, reflecting on the degree to which these mechanisms had been interpreted and entrenched into national laws, and examining strategies for future action. The women participating in the conference unanimously agreed on the need for a global campaign that would be a rallying point for women's demands and for increased visibility.

The launch of the Women Building Peace campaign followed in May 1999. Jordan's Queen Noor agreed to serve as the campaign's patron. (See her Personal Story in Chapter 7). Subsequent international events in 1999 afforded additional opportunities to launch the initiative internationally.

Organizationally, a nineteen-member, broadly based advisory committee was established, including representation from women and women's groups based in countries in preconflict, hot conflict, and postconflict situations. The advisory committee was supplemented with support from a myriad of local organizations that agreed to act as either local, national, or regional focal points for the campaign, and over 350 organizations that signed on as campaign supporters.

The organizers were cognizant of the fact that grassroots support was important for the success of the campaign, and accordingly held three separate regional consultations with grassroots organizers, including many from conflict regions. Parallel with these consultations, policy dialogues were organized with key UN agencies—not just those engaged with women's issues, but also development and security issues—focusing on such matters as language, key issues to stress, and identifying agencies that would be supportive of the campaign. Campaign staff engaged in policy dialogue with the governments of Namibia, Jamaica, France, and the United Kingdom (U.K.), and carried out desk research and mapping of the women and peace policies of the fifteen EU member states, to facilitate future campaign activities.

In order for the campaign to be truly inclusive and participatory, activities needed to take place at both the global and local levels. At the local level, women engaged in translating the campaign's information literature into local languages and distributing it in over 150 countries. They also launched advocacy campaigns locally in conflict regions including Nigeria and Sudan. At the global level, organizations produced leaflets, posters, and collected signatures, among other activities.

Tactics

The approach embraced by the campaign was to develop a well-founded, carefully researched understanding of the full range of issues related to women in peacebuilding, and to use that knowledge to generate policy documents and recommendations to disseminate to policymakers, parliamentarians, women's groups, church leaders, the media, and other interested constituencies. The campaign then followed up with personal contacts, as well as activities such as roundtable discussions and bilateral meetings to raise awareness and press for action.

It was also important to raise awareness about the campaign and the issues, and to share resources as widely as possible. One mechanism was the publication and distribution of a newsletter. Additionally, the initiation and delivery of a global petition addressed to UN Secretary-General Kofi Annan that listed the women's five demands contributed to raising the profile of women's organizations and their peacebuilding activities. Furthermore, the production of an interactive CD-ROM titled *Women and Conflict*, the establishment of the campaign's website, and the distribution of leaflets and other information also contributed to raising awareness.

Exploitation of the synergies made possible by the collaborative partnership with the broad coalition was invaluable for lobbying around Resolution 1325, monitoring campaign progress, and a range of other activities. The campaign also readily took advantage of the "leverage" that some of the participants enjoyed to advance the cause. For example, International Alert had a degree of leverage with the U.K.'s Department for International Development and the Foreign and Commonwealth Office because of its record of engagement in conflict resolution activities and its involvement with women in peacebuilding.

Outcomes

The Women Building Peace Campaign has succeeded, in cooperation with the many other individuals, organizations, and UN member states working on the matter, in placing issues affecting women's peace and security firmly on the agenda of the international community. In terms of policy impact—one of its main priorities—the campaign has contributed to steering the policy debate first to focus on concrete reasons why a gender perspective and women's views should be integrated into the policies of EU and UN organs, and subsequently, to focus on how this can be achieved. The participation at Arria Formula meetings—of which more are planned for the future—has been notable. The staff has, furthermore, had input into a range of initiatives, including, for example, the Brussels Afghan Women Leaders' Summit that focused on Afghanistan's transitional government and postconflict reconstruction. In addition, the U.K. and other governments specifically asked the campaign to provide assistance on the development of policies with respect to women, peace, and security.

There is no doubt that the campaign has succeeded in increasing visibility for women and peacebuilding, with its campaigns at the UN and the EU, its petition campaign and subsequent delivery to the UN of a hundred thousand signatures, and with additional activities such as the establishment, together with UNIFEM, of the Millennium Peace Prize for Women. The award of this prize to women and women's organizations from several conflict areas raised their profile, and accorded them a degree of protection from victimization and harassment.

The Resolution

Above all, UN Security Council Resolution 1325 stands as tangible proof of the campaign and all other women and groups who campaigned for it. Its unanimous endorsement by the members of the Security Council in October 2000 was swift and its incorporation of all the themes that underpin the campaign surpassed the expectations of those lobbying for its passage.

Undoubtedly, the resolution is a step forward for women and a tool that can be used for political negotiations, quiet diplomacy, and the mobilization of women and their organizations as well as UN agencies and other constituencies. Most importantly, it is a tool that provides those addressing the issues of women in conflict with leverage that they did not previously possess, and a rationale for demanding accountability.

Yet the binding nature of the tool is undermined by the weakness of the language—relatively cautious words such as "encourages" and "requests"—compared to the originally proposed language. There are also a number of substantive weaknesses. For example, it fails to address early warning and early response mechanisms and makes no mention of mechanisms, benchmarks, or success indicators that can be used to ensure state accountability. In addition, there are no mechanisms to ensure the protection and peace and security of women living in unrecognized states such as Abkhazia and South Ossetia (South Caucasus) and South Sudan in the Horn of Africa.

Follow-Up

The passage of UN Security Council Resolution 1325 now frames the second phase of the campaign's work. During this second phase, it is incumbent upon the campaign to strengthen and deepen its alliances with the broad coalition and other groups that have been involved in the first phases of the campaign. One important aspect of the second phase of the campaign should be to connect directly to individuals and organizations active in women's peacebuilding and conflict resolution activities, translating policy into practice and rhetoric into reality. One aspect of this continued work should be to conduct a "peace audit"—a mapping exercise of potential instruments and mechanisms that can enable the implementation of UN Security Council Resolution 1325 in each geographical area. This will be achieved by organizing consultations with relevant interested parties in and out of government. Additionally, campaign staff is working on a "know-how" project that will systematically document women's peacebuilding expertise, the steps they take, the challenges they face, and the lessons they learn in order to develop a body of evidence-based knowledge that can be shared with policymakers, women's groups, and other constituencies.

In this second phase of the campaign, crucial issues such as small arms, postconflict reconstruction, peace support operations, and early warning have been identified with the aim of carrying out further research to generate a more detailed gender analysis and develop recommendations for implementation. The follow-up advocacy and policy work is therefore focused on three distinct but interconnected aspects: linking the policy to women in the field, effective implementation of the tool, and highlighting emerging gaps and opportunities for further research. Simultaneously, the campaign is providing context-specific case studies of how the resolution could be implemented to benefit women in different regions and countries.

Conclusion

The Women Building Peace campaign has created opportunities and stimulated women's organizations to reflect on how they can become more involved in securing their own involvement in local, national, and regional decision-making processes that impinge on their peace and security. Engaging national and regional policymakers is essential for continued success. To date, the campaign has raised awareness of the special position of women as both victims of conflict and agents for conflict resolution. In so doing, it has also highlighted the need for constant engagement and continuous monitoring of the status quo. As this work continues, both formally and informally, civil-society organizations need to continually question the linkage between policy and practice and how this is being effectively mainstreamed to benefit women on the ground. It is one thing to articulate noble aims and to endorse an agenda embracing those aims. It is altogether another thing to alter the facts as they exist in the real world.

Ancil Adrian-Paul is program manager at International Alert.

Contact

International Alert
Gender and Peacebuilding Programme
346 Clapham Road
London SW9 9AP, U.K.
Tel.: +44 (0)20 7627 6800
Fax: +44 (0)20 7627 6900
Website: http://www.womenbuildingpeace.org

Note

1. International Alert, the Hague Appeal for Peace, the Women's Commission on Refugee Women and Children, Amnesty International, and the Women's International League for Peace and Freedom. Since then, Amnesty International has withdrawn from the group and the International Women's Tribune Centre and the Gender Caucus for the International Criminal Court have joined.

Selected Bibliography

Anderlini, Sanam, Rita Manchanda, and Shereen Karmali, eds. 1999. *Women, Violent Conflict and Peacebuilding: Global Perspectives* (London: International Alert).
UN Resolution 1325, English text, online at: http://www.peacewomen.org/un/sc/res1325.pdf.
UN Resolution 1325, text in other languages, online at: http://www.peacewomen.org/un/sc/res1325.pdf.
Women's International League for Peace and Freedom, online at: http://www.peacewomen.org/un/UN1325/1325index.html.

20.3

Fighting Corruption:
The Clean Election Campaign in Kenya

Joseph Karanja

In December 2002, Kenya made history when democratic elections were followed by a smooth and peaceful transition of power, the first in the country's history. Many individuals and organizations contributed to this success, but the Clean Election Campaign deserves special mention. After the elections the successful popular movement initiated a Clean Kenya Campaign and even a Clean Africa Campaign: "The dirt in our streets, the dirt in our hearts, the dirt in our minds all needed to be cleaned."

The international nongovernmental organization Initiatives of Change (or Moral Re-Armament, as it was called then) launched the first Kenya Clean Election Campaign in 1995, in preparation for the general election that was coming up in two years' time. Joseph Karanja, a twenty-six-year-old lawyer at that time, played a central role. Born into a humble African family, his story is not so much of rags to riches, but of rags to reforms; anticorruption reforms that have transformed his homeland, Kenya.

Karanja was born in a country that already had become a one-party state. Having gained its independence in 1963, it lost its democracy soon after when the opposition joined with the ruling party to form a stronger, harder rule. "I can remember as a small boy being sent to fetch water for my family from the communal water supply," Karanja said in an interview with the newspaper *Solomon Star,*[1] "and being sent away empty-handed because I didn't have a party-card."

The one-party system meant that the leaders went unchecked and were able to do whatever they liked with their young nation's wealth and people. "It was not that we didn't pay our taxes," Karanja says, "Everyone did, but those taxes went into the leaders' back pockets."

After studying law in India and an internship with the United Nations High Commission for Refugees, Karanja made a decision about his career: "Kenya had stopped working as a country simply because of corruption, and I wanted to do something for my country."

The First Campaign

After having heard of the effectiveness of a Clean Election Campaign project in Taiwan, he brought together ten friends for a weekend conference to consider the situation in Kenya. As a result, they decided to launch the Kenya Clean Election Campaign (CEC). "I was convinced that this was the right thing to address the corruption, violence, and apathy that had become a permanent feature in our elections," says Karanja. "We decided to start early because of the electoral process in my country; the government used to get the Central Bank to print money to fund the elections—not their operations but for the bribes. Either by intimidating people or bribing them, they would have the election tied up a year in advance."

The group first approached religious leaders. They talked with the heads of the Catholic, Anglican, and other churches and the religious leaders of the Muslims. Three points were put forward in these talks: (1) to ask people to commit themselves to accept no bribes, nor vote for anyone who offered a bribe; (2) to encourage people to take responsibility for the integrity of the voting process in the voting booths; and (3) to encourage honest men and women to stand for election to parliament.

The religious leaders gave their full backing to this and encouraged CEC speakers to address their congregations, which over the succeeding months the CEC did. This proved a most effective way of reaching the ordinary voter, because on praying days churches are always full in Kenya. A group of businessmen helped to finance advertising the campaign in the Kenyan press and a printer undertook to print hundreds of thousands of leaflets without charge.

The twenty-two Catholic bishops invited "all Kenyans, especially the eight million Catholics, to support the campaign by signing the pledge form." The pledge, which was part of the leaflets, consisted of the promises not to accept bribes, when possible to prevent and expose actions that would distort or rig the election results, and not to take part in any violence. In all, over seven hundred thousand pledges were signed and returned. The campaign leaflets also outlined fourteen qualities of a good leader, all of them nonpolitical qualities, as a background for voting choices.

The campaign became extremely popular and quickly grew into a national movement that many of Kenya's 33 million people took part in. Ordinary Kenyans invited campaign people to their homes to talk to various groups about the campaign. The people hosted campaigners wherever they went. "The entire country was mobilized to support the campaign," says Karanja. "It gave an opportunity to every Kenyan to play their part in curing the rot in our country."

Also the media and other organizations gave their support to the campaign. For the government, it was hard to fight against it, because they could not openly come out against a campaign that was fighting corruption. "We made the campaign wholly a positive one," says Karanja, "we were not seeking to blame any particular party or individual but launched an equal challenge to all leaders not to take part in corruption."

The apathy in the country, a result of the corrupt system, was broken. The campaign encouraged people to approach good leaders in their areas to stand as candidates. So they did. Thirty candidates, who probably would not have stood for election but for the encouragement of Joseph Karanja and his colleagues because of the perceived corrupt nature of politics, won office. Eleven government ministers and twenty-six deputy ministers lost their seats and President Arap Moi's majority in parliament was reduced to four. Some members of his own party were no longer simply yes-men and his dictatorial power was reduced.

Keeping Up the Momentum

The response that came following the 1997 elections was an encouragement to keep up the momentum. The campaigners started getting ready for the key 2002 presidential and parliamentary elections. This time, many other groups joined the Clean Election Campaign.

The Kenya Domestic Observation Programme invited the churches, the Hindu Council of Kenya, and the Supreme Council of Muslims to monitor the elections. Another partner was Transparency International's Kenya chapter. The operation—funded by the European Union—involved twenty thousand Kenyans acting as observers: one for each polling station. This helped in greatly reducing the election rigging.

Loopholes witnessed in the 1997 elections were sealed. This was done by fighting to have the votes counted at the polling stations rather than moving the ballot boxes, which would have increased the opportunity for them to be interfered with.

The team of Initiatives of Change managed to reach every region of the country; messages that would have jeopardized fair elections were neutralized by the CEC. The CEC activists distributed 140,000 leaflets and spoke on hundreds of occasions on radio and TV talk shows, in schools, and at public gatherings. "CEC called on the electorate to pledge that they would not be party to any violence or corruption and that they would report corrupt practices," Nairobi-based lawyer Francis Kimani commented in *For a Change* (April–May 2003). "I still remember how a congregation of about 3,000 people at the Christ the King Cathedral, Nakuru, was excited when Joseph Karanja of CEC talked to them for ten minutes. The congregation was left fully convinced that they could change things in Kenya" (Lightowler 2003: 107).

A Big Success

This time the Clean Elections Campaign did even better. It turned out to be the most peaceful and incident-free election in the history of Kenya. The power of corruption in elections was broken. The Kenya African National Union, the party that had been in power since independence, lost the election, as did the former president's preferred candidate. A new government was voted in on the basis that it was going to fight corruption. Despite the fact that there was no clear method of handing over power, the whole affair was a success. The new government immediately sacked many corrupt officials and judiciary. The chairman of the Kenya chapter of Transparency International was appointed by the new president to oversee and implement his anticorruption program.

The ethos against corruption continued after the elections, also with ordinary Kenyans. Since the elections the Clean Kenya Campaign (also initiated by Initiatives of Change) has been taking root in the country. The campaign asks Kenyans to speak up when acts of corruption occur, and has experienced notable success. Press reports speak of a growing number of cases where civilians forced police officers to return bribes. Karanja comments: "The people are now holding their government accountable by asking questions. The country is not clean yet, but at least something is happening. We won't stop until the job is done."

Spreading It Around

Based on the pioneering work done in Kenya since 1997, Clean Election Campaigns were mounted in Sierra Leone, at the first democratic elections since the war, and in Ghana. With the help of CEC, a Clean Africa Campaign was launched in 2003. A secretariat is already in place in Nairobi.

The Clean Africa Campaign will be spearheaded by a traveling faculty to train potential leaders in honest and unselfish leadership. Nigerian Amina Dikedi, initiator of the campaign, wrote:

> Experience shows that leadership which is not corrupt, but is unselfish and capable of reaching across historic divisions, receives an eager following. The Clean Africa Campaign aims to encourage such leadership throughout Africa. Working in partnership with churches, mosques, and other like-minded groups, it will make use of the extensive network of Africans committed to moral change in their continent, and build on the experience of the Clean Election Campaign in Kenya. (Lightowler 2003: 110)

Now the campaign is even moving outside of Africa. It was decided to launch a Clean Election Campaign following the Kenyan model for the municipal council elections for the Solomon Islands' capital, Honiara, which are due to be held in 2005. It is hoped that this will be a test for a nationwide Clean Election Campaign in 2006, thus transforming the original program from Kenya into a success with worldwide echos.

Joseph Karanja is a lawyer and the initiator and director of the Clean Election Campaign in Kenya.

Contact

Clean Africa Campaign Secretariat
(Joseph Karanja & Associates Advocates)
1st Floor, New Waumini House
Chiromo Road/Waiyaki Way

P.O. Box 14510 Westlands
00800, Nairobi, Kenya
Tel.: +254 (0) 20 445 2248/6349
E-mail: cleanafricacampaign@hkenya.org

Note
1. This and all other quoted material by Joseph Karanja that follows is taken from his June 2004 interview in the *Star*.

Selected Bibliography
Karanja, Joseph. 2004. "Fighting Corruption," interview in the *Solomon Star,* 25 June.
————. "The Clean Campaigns," unpublished manuscript.
Kimani, Francis. 2003. "Kenya Offers Hope Again." *For a Change* (April–May).
Lightowler, Brian. 2003. "Combating the Culture of Corruption," in Brian Lightowler, *Corruption: Who Cares?* (Caux, Switzerland: Caux Books and Grosvenor Books).

20.4

Rage Against the Regime: The Otpor Movement in Serbia

Milja Jovanovic

In 1998, Serbian students responded to new restrictions on academic and media freedom with a highly unconventional movement called Otpor ("Resistance" in Serbian). The movement was leaderless and its tactics innovative and elaborate. Otpor helped to mobilize the Serb population and break through a barrier of fear. In October 2000, in part because of Otpor's unusual brand of nonviolent activism, President Slobodan Milosevic was driven from power.

For those of us who grew up in Serbia in the late 1980s and 1990s, our world was one filled with war, economic and social disintegration, sanctions, bombings, political instability, ineptitude, and police brutality. We lived in a country whose institutions were manipulated by the ruling regime and where neither human rights nor the rule of law existed. Nationalism was the dominant ideology, and fear and suspicion of the outside world was such that many Serbians believed that the entire world was against us and wanted only to humiliate our people and destroy our country. The most negative of emotions prevailed: hopelessness, futility, apathy, and despair.

The options, then, were stark and limited. Most of us thought our best choice was simply to pack our bags, to somehow secure an invitation from some connection in a "prosperous" country, and get out of Serbia. Another option was to try somehow to get by, idling away the time, avoiding military service, attending university, or devising a scheme—any scheme—to earn some money, and then just wait patiently for the world to change. A third option was to choose not to wait, in spite of the hopelessness and skepticism of all those who could not imagine Serbia as a prosperous democratic country. The third option meant getting up every morning and doing something to change the way we lived and felt. It did not matter how small, but the important thing was to do something and work for a change.

President Milosevic and his regime ignored all three groups. He simply did not care if tens of thousands of young people left the country. It did not matter to him if we had no prospects for a decent life or a better future. As long as we were silent and obedient and did not cause trouble, and as long as he could continue to lure enough of us into the army to fight his "holy wars," he was satisfied.

We were not satisfied. That is why we created Otpor—the Serbian word for "resistance." Otpor was our way of saying, "Mr. Milosevic, enough. This is unbearable. And we hold you responsible, so you will pay." Otpor was created out of rage, frustration, and anger—three emotions that were part of the legacy that Milosevic bestowed on us. Those emotions became our weapons, and once we understood that we could use the very feelings that were destroying us in a positive, nondestructive way, we knew we would beat him.

Otpor was founded in October 1998 in response to two laws passed by the Serbian parliament. One of these was a new media law designed to silence independent media. The law allowed for immediate action, including closure and fines against media outlets that broadcasted or published anything that might undermine Serbia's constitutional order or integrity. The other was a law that completely violated our tradition of academic freedom, giving government-appointed deans the power to arbitrarily dismiss professors or order changes to the curriculum.

Many people might not understand why those two laws aroused so much outrage, but for us, it was a case, to cite a Serbian expression, of the "drops that caused the glass to overflow." The media and university were sacred to us. They represented knowledge and information, and those were two things we were not willing to sacrifice.

Otpor started as a small group of people who knew each other from earlier student protests, the Belgrade music scene, and the local nightclubs. Beginning with twenty or so people who came together in October 1998, we had grown to about one hundred by the end of the year. We called people we knew who shared our values and shared the goal of removing Milosevic, and those who we knew had the will, the time, and the energy to fight.

Something Completely Different

With the political opposition in Serbia in complete disarray, we made a firm decision to create a movement rather than a political party. We had seen how political leaders protected their own interests and fought among themselves instead of fighting Milosevic, so we also decided that we would have no leader—no president, no director, not even a spokesperson. What we wanted above all was to show Milosevic that we had strength in numbers and that he would have to deal with us as a mass movement. Every night on the evening news we saw the regime's relentless and shameless propaganda, so we said: "We will create a symbol that is stronger than their ideology, bigger than Milosevic, and goes beyond the symbols of the opposition parties." Our symbol would be a clear statement: "I am against this system; I am against Milosevic." The symbol that embodied that statement was a clenched fist.

We decided straightaway that Otpor would be open to all who wished to join, whether they were from the left or the right. The only conditions were that you believed that Serbia needed freedom, and did not need Milosevic. Our strategy was to spread the idea of nonviolent resistance through everyday activism on the streets, and to give every individual in Serbia who shared our opinions the opportunity to show resistance, to be a part of the movement, and to express his or her political opinion. Our goal was to force Milosevic to hold early elections and to defeat him when they took place.

Our first target group was the young people—mostly because we felt that our approach to politics and our attitude, strongly influenced by pop culture, and our concept of a leaderless movement would resonate within our own generation. Beyond that, we felt that young people had been the key "missing ingredient" in the past. Many, if not most, of the people born in the 1970s were against Milosevic but did not find a suitable representative in the existing political scene. So our thought was that they did not need representation but rather a way to express themselves. By inviting them to join Otpor, we would give them an opportunity to do just that.

Developing a Plan

We had an idea of what we wanted, but what we still needed was a plan. So that was the next step. We began by asking ourselves who among our friends and acquaintances could help us, and especially what journalists could write about us and how else we could make our ideas known to the public.

Then we began to talk about possible actions. In fact, we talked about actions constantly, because "doing" was important to us. We did not want a program that focused on writing speeches, sending out press releases, or preaching to the converted or those who would ignore us. We wanted to concentrate on "action," being out there on the streets and making ourselves visible. So we started by spray-painting graffiti on Belgrade's streets and facades. Everywhere you went you would see the spray-painted clenched fists on the walls, serving as a reminder of where you were living, who your president was, and what your life was like.

At first, people disapproved. They did not want to think about politics. All they wanted was peace, even if it was a false peace. Then we painted the provocative slogans and their disapproval turned to anger. Yet at the same time they began to ask themselves, "Who is this Otpor? What are they doing?"

In November 1998 the police arrested four of our activists during one of our "spraying sprees." They were each sentenced to ten days in prison, but the trials backfired, because soon the whole nation knew that Otpor was a movement of young people who were prepared to fight Milosevic's regime till the bitter end.

We decided to focus on the university and to try to reverse the restrictions on academic freedom. We started in Belgrade, urging a boycott of lectures and classes. Some of us were beaten up on the grounds of the university, but our action ended with our first small victory: the dean who had recruited the thugs to give Otpor members a beating resigned, and the state gave in to our demands to restore academic freedom.

Soon after that people from Kragujevac, Nis, and Novi Sad contacted us, saying they also wanted to start Otpor branches. We met with them and came up with a plan of action. Taking Otpor to places outside of Belgrade turned out to be a turning point in Otpor's history. We spread like the plague: everyone wanted an Otpor T-shirt or a small badge with the fist on it.

Our plan was very simple: ordinary people all around Serbia would participate in different kinds of actions on the streets in their own towns and use the media to send a strong message about what people really thought. We also decided that we were going to carefully monitor everything the regime did and openly ridicule and criticize it. A lot of our actions were humorous and witty. We knew people were afraid of Milosevic and afraid of the police. The best way to break through that fear and undermine Milosevic's power was to employ humor to make him look stupid, small, and insignificant.

We took advantage of every opportunity to mock the regime's stupidity and brutality. There definitely was no shortage of targets for our ridicule. We had plenty of opportunities to expose the government, make fun of it, and show the people its true nature.

Soon the police started arresting people who were taking part in the actions. During 1999 and 2000, there were more than two thousand arrests of Otpor activists. Still, Milosevic failed to understand: as the arrests continued and the repression grew, the resistance grew even more. For every Otpor activist arrested, many more approached us to join our movement. Our parents

Young Serbians protesting against Milosevic proclaiming, "He's finished!"

and our grandparents also took notice, angered by a regime that would arrest sixteen- and seventeen-year-olds. During 2000, our activists' base grew to ten thousand, and then thirty thousand, and by September 2000, we had eighty thousand Otpor activists.

The Otpor actions gave people, for the first time since the antigovernment protests of 1996 and 1997, a feeling of unity and solidarity. Our actions included continued graffiti campaigns, demonstrations in front of military tribunals held to try army deserters, circulating clandestine newsletters, and displaying an effigy of President Milosevic on the street and inviting passersby—for the price of one *dinar*—to punch it. We felt strong because we were all working together on something important—something that was going to change the course of Serbian history.

These were feelings that helped us to overcome the fear of change on which Milosevic had relied for so long—the fear that even though you have very little now, you would have nothing at all if he were to vanish from the scene. With that fear gone, and everyone in the Serbian opposition—Otpor, opposition parties, the independent media, nongovernmental organizations (NGOs), unions, professional organizations—working together for the first time since the end of one-party politics in Serbia, the pressure kept rising until, in July 2000, Milosevic announced early local, federal, and presidential elections for 24 September 2000.

On 2 August, Otpor began what was going to be the biggest campaign ever conducted in Serbia, the "Gotov je!" campaign, meaning, "He's finished!" Otpor produced more than sixty tons of material for that campaign—T-shirts, posters, brochures, flyers, and, most important of all, stickers. The black-and-white stickers with block letters declaring "He's finished!" were probably the most important part of the campaign. We usually placed them across Milosevic's own campaign posters—but they also appeared on road signs and garbage containers, and in shop windows. People put them inside their cars, on their notebooks, and on their doors. They were everywhere. We also returned to our early pastime—graffiti—spraying public-transport vehicles, construction sites, police cars, and building facades with the familiar stenciled fist and our bold statement: "24.9.2000. He is finished!"

On 8 August, Milosevic turned fifty-nine and we presented him with an ironic birthday card, thanking him for robbing us of our childhood and plunging our region into war. "May you celebrate the next one with your nearest and dearest on a deserved holiday in The Hague," we said.

Otpor activists went everywhere, even to the smallest little village in Serbia, campaigning door to door in a "get out the vote" campaign. We talked to people in person, organized public meetings, protests, and demonstrations, and handed out our materials, encouraging people to be active, to get involved, and to vote against Milosevic.

Everyone started to feel that the "He's finished!" message was real—that it really would happen. Milosevic was going to lose the elections. Which he did. On 24 September, the people voted him out of power, although at least for a few more weeks he refused to admit defeat. Otpor and other groups had sent out an army of election monitors, and the opposition parties had the data to prove that Vojislav Kostunica was the real winner. The entire nation mobilized against Milosevic's attempt to steal the election, and on 5 October, with hundreds of thousands of people gathered in Belgrade, he finally bowed to the inevitable and acknowledged what we all knew: Milosevic really was finished.

Latest Developments

5 October 2000 will be remembered as the day when Serbia succeeded with a nonviolent movement in replacing a totalitarian regime with a democracy. Otpor had played a vital role, using ingenious tactics, humor, and its unusual nonhierarchical organization. For the extraordinary contribution Otpor had made to the end of the Milosevic regime, it won MTV's Free Your Mind Award in November 2000. Then differences began to emerge within its membership about what strategies would be appropriate in the post-Milosevic era, and many of its activists left Otpor. Still, it waged a successful campaign to hold officials of the former regime accountable for corruption, and mounted a campaign against organized crime. In November 2003, it reorganized itself into a political party and polled sixty thousand votes in parliamentary elections. Finally, in 2004, following its merger with the Democratic Party, Otpor as a political party ceased to exist; the NGO does still exists, though, to resume activities when needed.

Sharing the Experience

When looking at recent developments in the Ukraine, the scene looks familiar. It brings back memories of similar images of Serbia and Georgia. The absence of violence, the almost joyful atmosphere, the lack of aggressiveness toward political opposition, the frivolous actions, the ironic posters, and the enormous persistence of the thousands of demonstrators. The protest is extremely well organized. Among the many reasons for this is the help of Otpor.

Otpor activists have set up the Centre for Non-Violent Resistance. After having helped youth movements from Tbilisi in 2003, they got in contact with Pora, the biggest Ukrainian youth opposition movement in the spring of 2004. In April there were even some eighteen young people that traveled to Serbia for a course on organizational and negotiation skills, street protest tactics, and how to monitor the elections to be able to fight possible fraud. Some of Otpor's members tried to travel to Kiev to join in the protest, but were stopped at the airport.

Still, their experiences have helped youth groups to act, both in Tbilisi and Kiev. Although attempts to do the same in Belarus and Ghana failed, Otpor believes it was because the time was not right for it, but that in the future the same familiar images will arise again.

Milja Jovanovic was an Otpor activist. She is currently an art director and head of the adult learning department in a PR/consulting/marketing agency based in Belgrade.

Contact

Otpor
Nusiceva 6/II
SCG-11000 Belgrade
E-mail: otpor@otpor.com
Website: http://www.otpor.com

Selected Bibliography

Chiclet, Christophe. 2001. "Otpor: The Youths Who Booted Milosevic." *The UNESCO Courier,* March. Online at: http://www.unesco.org/courier/2001_03/uk/droits.htm.

Mathews, Dylan. 2001. *War Prevention Works: 50 Stories of People Resolving Conflict* (Oxford: Oxford Research Group).

"Otpor." http://www.pbs.org/weta/dictator/otpor/.

"OTPOR Movement Ceased to Exist." One World Southeast Europe. Online at: http://see.oneworld.net/article/view/93868/1/3332.

"Otpor!—The Story of Mounting Resistance." Balkansnet: http://balkansnet.org/elect-otpor.html.

Pozun, Brian. 2001. "Planning for an Uncertain Future." *Central Europe Review* 3, no. 8 (26 February). Online at: http://www.ce-review.org/01/8/pozun8.html.

20.5

Protests Stop Devastating Nuclear Tests: The Nevada-Semipalatinsk Anti-Nuclear Movement in Kazakhstan

Established on the initiative of a poet, an antinuclear movement embarked on a successful people's campaign to stop nuclear testing in Kazakhstan. The movement sought inspiration abroad and developed tactics that turned out to be very effective in the former Soviet republic. Within months, testing stopped. The test site was closed permanently in 1991.

Bigger than Western Europe and the second-largest republic of the former Union of Soviet Socialist Republics, Kazakhstan seemed to be a perfect location for performing nuclear tests. The republic's remoteness, its relatively low population density, and the presence of uranium in its soil made Stalin's government chose the area as the place for nuclear experiments. The first Soviet atom bomb detonated here in 1949, and in 1953 the first hydrogen bomb was also tested in Kazakhstan.

The tests took place in the Semipalatinsk test range, an area of 18,000 square kilometers in the northeast of Kazakhstan in a region where the vast steppes, so typical for Kazakhstan, gradually give way to a mountainous area. Here, for decades the huge mushroom clouds that go with nuclear explosions would appear several times a year. Between 1949 and 1989, around 460 nuclear tests—some 340 underground and 110 in the atmosphere—were conducted at the Semipalatinsk test site. It would take decades before the painful consequences of the tests for the local population became clear. It would take even longer until the population of Kazakhstan found the courage and an opportunity to rise up against the tests and the people ordering them.

Changes in Health
The birth of the antinuclear protest movement in Kazakhstan took place during "perestroika," a period of considerable liberalization of political, economic, and other spheres, and in direct run up to the disintegration of the

Soviet Union. It was an opportune time for starting the movement, which was the result of an unusual step taken by one of the republic's most prominent writers.

As the years passed, the people in the Semipalatinsk region began to witness changes in their health. The number of birth defects increased, as did the number of cases of leukemia and other forms of cancer. New diseases never heard of before began to appear and to increase rapidly. Olzhas Suleimenov, a Kazakh poet elected as a People's Deputy, started to witness the suffering of the local people. He became more and more concerned as he saw an increasing rate of cancer. He informed his colleagues in the Supreme Soviet at the Kremlin that the nuclear testing resulted in serious health problems in Kazakhstan. No one paid attention to him. The region was far away from the Kremlin and very few of the People's Deputy had any knowledge of radiation diseases.

In February 1989, as a direct result of two underground tests at the Semipalatinsk test site, clouds containing huge amounts of radioactive gases passed over inhabited areas. A military pilot stationed at a base not far from the test site informed Olzhas Suleimenov that all the dosimeters in the town showed very high levels of radiation. The dosimeters had been installed in the kindergartens and schools for the children of the military officers. The pilot was very concerned about the future health of his children in Kazakhstan.

It was clear to those concerned about the tests and their impact that they would risk arrest by the Soviet police if they would protest publicly or seek to raise the issue in other ways. Discussing problems related to a military program that was considered to be top secret was a major taboo in the Soviet Union. Nevertheless, Olzhas Suleimenov decided to take action. He chose a resourceful, yet risky way to reach as many people as possible in one stroke. The poet, who had been accepted as writer by the authorities and was a member of the Writer's Union, in early 1989 was invited to appear on a television program. He was to speak about the cultural heritage of Kazakhstan and would read some of his poetry as the writer and the program producers had agreed. Unexpectedly, Suleimenov broke with the program's script while live on the air. With thousands of Kazakh viewers watching, he pushed the papers about history and poetry aside, looked into the camera, and addressed his audience about the nuclear devastation he said had been going on in Kazakhstan.

The poet said the tests were not harmless, contrary to what the authorities had been telling Kazaks for years, and urged citizens to raise their voices. Suleimenov also referred to recent international political developments when he pointed out that nuclear arms seemed no longer necessary as the Cold War was coming to an end. "Why continue testing when there is no enemy any longer?" he asked. He mentioned international protests that were going on in other countries, a phenomenon unknown to most inhabitants of the region. The poet in particular referred to activists in Nevada, counterpart of Semipalatinsk as the site of U.S. nuclear tests since the 1950s. It was clear to him that the example of activists in Nevada could be an inspiration for Kazaks, as well as a source of practical information about nuclear technology and its impact on health and the environment.

In his speech, Suleimenov told his audience that his interventions as a People's Deputy in Moscow had fallen on deaf ears. He stressed it was up to the citizens themselves to do something. He then called on viewers to come to his office at the Writers' Union the next morning and promised he would help them organize a people's movement against nuclear tests. More than five thousand people showed up, many more than Suleimenov had expected. They had to stand outside the building, and Suleimenov addressed them speaking from a balcony. Out of the mass meeting a committee was born, headed by a group of intellectuals. That very day, Suleimenov and others established what they called the Nevada-Semipalatinsk Anti-Nuclear Movement. The organization quickly came to include a broad range of people, as diverse as shepherds, doctors, housewives, and miners.

Three Types of Diplomacy

From the moment of its creation, the Nevada-Semipalatinsk Anti-Nuclear Movement embarked on a series of activities. It organized peace marches, demonstrations attended by thousands of people, and international and regional conferences.

The movement set itself five basic tasks: to bring a halt to testing, to restore the surrounding environment, to study the health of the population and win compensation for those who had suffered, to join in campaigns against testing in other regions, and to bring about the conversion of nuclear-testing facilities so that they would serve peaceful purposes.

Vladimir Yakimets, a Moscow scientist and one of the leaders of the movement, pointed out that the movement gradually adopted "a concept of three types of diplomacy." One he described as "people's diplomacy," meaning calling meetings and demonstrations. Another was "parliamentary diplomacy," aimed at getting deputies nominated in legislative bodies where they were in the position to propose legislation that was relevant to dealing with the issue. The third category was "expert diplomacy," consisting of liaising with experts and activists abroad who were campaigning against nuclear testing, such as in Nevada.

As a result of the protests, eleven of the eighteen tests planned for 1989 were cancelled. After a major test explosion in October 1989, 130,000 workers at the Karaganda coal mines declared that they would go on strike if the tests continued. Suleimenov raised the issue once more at the Supreme Soviet. This time it worked. In November the Supreme Soviet adopted a resolution in which it urged the government to discuss the issue to close the Semipalatinsk test site. A few weeks later, then-president Mikhail Gorbachev announced the first moratorium ending testing at the Semipalatinsk test site.

On 29 August 1991, President Nursultan Nazarbajev of Kazakhstan announced the formal, and permanent, closure of the Semipalatinsk test site. One of the major goals of the movement had been accomplished.

Extended Justice

The movement went on to acquire knowledge about radiation and its consequences for the region. "When our movement began its work, there were no reliable, independent studies of the medical consequences," Yakimets said. The movement established a committee to study the consequences of radiation on the environment and health. Focal areas were the contamination of groundwater and genetic mutations as a result of exposure to radiation. The group put significant effort into demanding access to archival material. It did obtain access to many of these documents and the group analyzed them.

The region is lightly populated. With about 330,000 inhabitants, Semipalatinsk was the largest population center and the test site was about 200 kilometers to the west of the city. Nonetheless, since the explosions and the radioactive clouds that were generated by them covered a vast territory, millions of Kazaks felt affected by them and were deeply concerned about the potential consequences once they realized what was going on and saw the first signs of mutilations and the proliferation of formerly unknown diseases.

It is now well established that the effects of the testing include sharp rises in cancer rates among the people of the region. This is especially true for the areas nearest to the test site. The incidence of lung cancer and digestive-tract cancers is particularly high. Birth defects occurring as a result of genetic disorders have also appeared. Maidan Abishev, another leader of the Nevada-Semipalatinsk Anti-Nuclear Movement, referred to a young woman, Renata, a bright-eyed, smiling seventeen-year-old who is just 55 centimeters tall because of exposure to radiation while in her mother's womb.

About 2 million hectares of agricultural lands also became radioactively contaminated. At three places in the area, contamination is especially grave; here the level of background radiation reaches a hundred times the permissible level. At one of these locations, a so-called peaceful test in 1965 created a new lake, as part of an experiment to find out whether the big nuclear explosions could be used to change the course of the northern rivers. "Not surprisingly, the lake is highly radioactive," scientist Yakimets said.

The group has been seeking a law to provide compensation to the victims. It also looked into the feasibility of clean-up measures aimed at undoing at least some of the damage caused to the environment and reducing the risk of genetic distortions in future generations. Chromosome tests were revealing damage among people in the Semipalatinsk region, Yakimets said. "The nation is in a state of stress," he commented in the early 1990s.

One of the strengths of the Nevada-Semipalatinsk Anti-Nuclear Movement was that it reached out to people abroad sharing a similar fate. The people of Kazakhstan did not limit their international outreach to Nevada. They also managed to forge ties with people in Japan, the only country that has experienced the devastation of nuclear bombs in wartime. Japanese experts and activists who have top-notch know-how about the impact of radiation on people's health came to Kazakhstan to investigate and provide advice. The Japanese team interviewed village people at schools and hospitals and learned that the nuclear tests affected virtually everybody in the vicinity of the site. Japanese activist Shunji Tsuboi, who visited the former test site in 2003, estimated that 1.2 to 1.5 million people in Kazakhstan have been affected by the nuclear tests. Tsuboi was quoted as saying in a press report on the visit:

> We saw the shocking ruins where the first nuclear test explosion took place in 1949. People think that the A-bomb in Hiroshima city is the only existing testimony to the damage caused by nuclear weapons. They should see the Polygon [Polygon is the Russian word for "test site"–ed.] ruins, which have been exposed to broad daylight. A mountain blown up, its remains lying around—it looked like a scene from hell. I am not exaggerating. (Sarwar 1998)

Ongoing Activities

Almost fifteen years after the movement launched its first protests and began its advocacy work, the Nevada-Semipalatinsk Anti-Nuclear Movement is still active, although with a new group of people. One of its focal points in the first years of the twenty-first century has been seeking to streamline the many national Kazakh projects aimed at alleviating the fate of victims of radiation and restoring the environment. The movement has also been an active member of the Global Anti-Nuclear Alliance. An important public awareness component of the movement's activities has been the organization of Anti-Nuclear Congresses (in 1990 and 1993 in Almaty, and in 2000 in Astana). The fourth congress is scheduled for May 2005 in Almaty, to look at the reemering nuclear threat throughout the world.

The organization is operating against the background of international developments that have been supportive of its goals. When the Soviet Union collapsed in December 1991, Kazakhstan inherited 1,410 nuclear warheads, in addition to the Semipalatinsk test site. Kazakhstan transferred all of these nuclear warheads to Russia. It began to destroy the nuclear-testing infrastructure at Semipalatinsk, a process that was completed in July 2000. Approximately 600 kilograms of weapons-grade enriched uranium was removed to the United States in 1994 under a joint U.S.-Kazakhstan operation known as Project Sapphire. Kazakhstan, as an independent nation, also is a party to START-1, the Nuclear Non-Proliferation Treaty, and the Comprehensive Test Ban Treaty.

However, weapons-grade nuclear material remains in Kazakhstan, including 3 metric tons of plutonium at a shutdown breeder reactor in western Kazakhstan and small amounts of highly enriched uranium at two nuclear institutes. To the Nevada-Semipalatinsk Anti-Nuclear Movement, it is clear that a lot of work still has to be done. According to figures of the state-run nuclear-energy company Kazatomprom, in 2001 only $1 million was devoted to cleaning up the country's massive radioactive-waste problem, a drop in the bucket compared with the more than $1.2 billion it says it needs to deal with the crisis. In 2003, the Nevada-Semipalatinsk Anti-Nuclear Movement protested plans by the government to begin importing medium-level radioactive waste from other countries. The government said it needed to do this in order to help finance the disposal of its considerable toxic-waste stockpiles. The group argues the move would worsen Kazakhstan's own massive radioactive-waste disposal problems by bringing more toxins into the country. The group said it was also concerned about transporting nuclear waste, especially in the context of an increased risk of nuclear terrorists using radioactive waste. Some activists pointed out that a country with rich oil resources and revenues from oil exports was not credible when claiming it lacked the money to deal with its own radioactive-waste problem.

Much work clearly remains; however, recognizing the enormity of what has been accomplished so far should give hope for even more progress in the future.

Contacts
The Nevada-Semipalatinsk Anti-Nuclear
Movement
85 Dostyk Ave.
480021 Almaty
Kazakhstan
Tel./Fax: +7 (3272) 912385

Selected Bibliography

Center for Nonproliferation Studies: http://www.cns.miis.edu. Based in Monterey, California, the CBS has extended documentation and up-to-date information available about developments regarding nuclear arms and nuclear waste in Kazakhstan.

Heffermehl, Fredrik S., ed. 2000. *Peace Is Possible* (Geneva: International Peace Bureau).

Sarwar, Beena. 1998. "Human Toll of Nuke Tests: A Lesson for South Asia," *Environment Bulletin Japan* (Hiroshima: Inter Press Service, September). Online at: http://www.ips.org/Çritical /Environment/Environ?env1209002.htm.

20.6

Lessons from Campaigns of the 1990s: Innovations in Humanitarian Advocacy

Don Hubert

A number of international campaigns that focused on the human face of war have met with varying degrees of success in the 1990s. Most notable success stories have been the International Campaign to Ban Landmines and the campaign for the establishment of the International Criminal Court. This chapter explores some of the critical factors in success or failure.

The 1990s witnessed a striking increase in both the scale of humanitarian advocacy and its effectiveness. In the face of public calls for action, governments and multilateral institutions launched a series of international missions designed to resolve violent conflicts and to reduce their human costs. This action on the ground was complemented by efforts to develop new international standards and institutions to enhance the protection for civilian populations. Of particular prominence were four major international campaigns: to ban landmines, against the use of child soldiers, to create an International Criminal Court (ICC), and to reduce the availability and misuse of small arms.

Were these campaigns necessary? As the UN secretary-general has argued, "The protection of civilians in armed conflict would be largely assured if combatants respected the provisions of international humanitarian and human rights law" (Annan 1999). There are, however, a number of areas—some relating to restrictions on weapons, others related to expanding protections for civilians—where the development of additional legal norms and standards can help to reduce the human cost of conflict. In this context, it is valuable to have a clear understanding of the reasons for the relative success of these four campaigns.

A comparative analysis of these four campaigns suggests that there are common elements to effective humanitarian advocacy, including: clear campaign messaging (advocating stringent provisions within an explicitly humanitarian discourse); effective coalition building (among and between nongovernmental organizations (NGOs), like-minded governments, and international organizations); and favorable negotiating conditions (a strong chairperson, access for NGOs, and decision by vote).[1]

Table 20.6.1 below sets out a rough assessment of these three broad dimensions across the four campaigns and highlights key factors that help to explain their relative degrees of success. The text that follows explains in detail the eight dimensions, and how they affected the specific campaigns.

Campaign Messaging

Campaign messaging includes the nature of the objectives sought and the way in which those objectives are framed. Recent humanitarian advocacy has privileged the development of stringent norms supported by strong majorities over lowest-common-denominator outcomes supported by all. These campaigns have also demonstrated the value of framing issues within an explicitly humanitarian discourse.

The strength of an international norm is dependent on both the stringency of the provisions and the breadth of support those provisions command. In multilateral negotiations, there is a strong preference for universal norms, and this leads inevitably to a tendency toward consensus decisionmaking. Yet the campaigns outlined above demonstrate a willingness among a solid majority of countries to pursue bold new standards. Both the landmine ban and the ICC were agreed to by more than 120 countries, while at the same time having only a few prominent opponents. The considerable support for a robust ban on child soldiers, while ultimately insufficient, further highlights the prospects for pursuing stringent standards rather than universal support.[1]

There are good reasons to assume that the tendencies demonstrated in the campaigns of the 1990s will be a routine part of humanitarian advocacy in the future. Existing universal standards such as the Geneva Conventions are already

Table 20.6.1 Comparing Humanitarian Campaigns of the 1990s

Dimension/Campaign	Comparing Humanitarian Campaigns of the 1990s			
	Landmines	ICC	Child Soldiers	Small Arms
I. Campaign Messaging				
Stringent Provisions	**	**	**	*
Humanitarian Discourse	**	**	**	*
II. Coalition-Building				
NGO Coalition	**	**	**	*
Government Coalition	**	*		
Grand Coalition	**	*	*	*
III. Negotiating Context				
Supportive Chair	**	*		*
NGO Access	**	*	*	
Decision by Vote	**	**	*	

The three main elements (and subelements) of successful humanitarian advocacy are listed on the left of the table. The relative strengths of each of these subelements are represented by asterisks (2* = strong; 1* = weak; 0* = nonexistent).

more stringent than current lowest-common-denominator positions. As a result, it is highly unlikely that negotiations based on consensus decisionmaking will be able to fill the gaps that exist in the international legal framework protecting war-affected populations.

Furthermore, there is no necessary correlation between universal acceptance of humanitarian norms and reducing the human costs of war. The destruction of landmine stockpiles in countries recovering from civil wars will greatly reduce the risk of these weapons being deployed in any future conflict, even when the acceptance of the universal ban on landmines is still not universal at all. Similarly, the ICC can proceed with investigations into atrocities committed in the Democratic Republic of Congo and northern Uganda even in the absence of U.S. support.

The second component of campaign messaging relates to how the issues are framed. While each of the four campaigns identified above has focused on a humanitarian objective—reducing the human costs of war—a humanitarian discourse has not always dominated or even been widely accepted.

The campaign against child soldiers was, from the outset, couched in explicitly humanitarian terms, but this was not the case for the other three campaigns. The crucial turning point for the campaign to ban landmines was shifting the discourse from disarmament (focused on the weapon, concerned with military utility, dominated by conservative negotiators) to humanitarianism (focused on victims, concerned with the human impact, engaging human rights and humanitarian experts). The ICC was first promoted in the early 1990s as a response to narco-traffickers but ultimately succeeded by focusing on the gravest violations of humanitarian law—genocide, crimes against humanity, and war crimes. To date, small-arms advocates have devoted much of their efforts to shifting the debate from illicit transfers to include state-state arms transfers. A more explicitly humanitarian approach is only now beginning to emerge.[2]

Framing issues in humanitarian terms plays to the strengths of nongovernmental organization (NGO) campaigners and to the weaknesses of their opponents. The landmine ban is instructive here, for although the landmines treaty is undoubtedly a "disarmament" treaty, campaigners rightly recognized that the disarmament discourse was inhospitable terrain. A humanitarian orientation not only lent greater weight to the scale of human suffering. It also justified avoiding politically charged disarmament venues and their relatively conservative government negotiators.

Observers often mistakenly assume that the success or failure of a campaign is due to the inherent characteristics of the issue in question. For example, landmines were inherently easy to ban, while small arms are inherently difficult. Yet there is compelling evidence that the way an issue is framed is more important than any "inherent" characteristics. Among the greatest assets that campaigners have is the ability to frame the issue in ways that make bold new directions in international action appear self-evident. An analysis of these four campaigns suggests that even where multiple discourses are available to campaigners, there are powerful benefits to situating the debate in an explicitly humanitarian context.

Coalition Building

Coalition building is fundamental to effective humanitarian advocacy. At best, cohesive coalitions are developed among and between NGOs, governments, and international organizations. Key to the success of the campaigns on landmines and the ICC were the strength and cohesiveness of both NGO networks and coalitions of like-minded governments.[3] In both cases, their overarching agendas were further legitimized by the active support of various bodies of the United Nations (UN) and the International Committee of the Red Cross (ICRC).

Shortcomings in coalition building also account for the limited successes of campaigns on child soldiers and small arms. In the campaign for a robust ban on the recruitment and deployment of child soldiers, the NGO Coalition to Stop the Use of Child Soldiers mounted an effective campaign and the UN and the ICRC provided valuable support, but a strong coalition of like-minded governments never emerged. In the case of small arms, the relative weaknesses in coalition building are striking. The International Action Network on Small Arms (IANSA) was designed more for constituency building and information sharing than strategic advocacy. On the government side, Norwegian efforts in the late 1990s to encourage the emergence of a like-minded group of states were unsuccessful. Progressive states did collaborate to salvage the 2001 UN Small Arms Conference, and a regular meeting of governments active in the international debate on small arms in Geneva may provide the basis for a proactive grouping of states in the future.

While credit for humanitarian advocacy tends to be directed toward NGOs, the successes and the failures discussed above suggest that strategic coordination among like-minded governments is frequently the decisive factor. With landmines, the profile of the NGO campaign obscures the importance of the core group of states, particularly in the final months leading up to the Oslo Conference. The like-minded group played an equally fundamental role in securing the ICC statute as its cornerstone positions in many ways predetermined the outcome of the negotiations. In the case of the campaign on child soldiers, the limitations of the negotiating conditions to be discussed below could have been overcome had there been an effective like-minded group committed to an outright ban.

If governmental coalitions are the key to the successful conclusion of humanitarian campaigns, NGO coalitions are the key to their emergence and development. NGOs are most effective at identifying the overarching objectives and at securing initial governmental support. In this context, one potentially counterproductive lesson that seems to have been drawn from the landmines campaign is the emphasis given to "partnership" between governments and NGOs. Although often called a partnership, "strategic collaboration" is a more accurate term.[4] This collaboration began only when a core group of states adopted the agenda of the International Campaign to Ban Landmines (ICBL) and was always conditional on governments remaining committed to a complete ban.

Negotiating Conditions

Once campaign objectives have been identified and coalitions built, negotiating conditions become a key determinant of success in securing new international standards. The campaigns on landmines and the ICC both benefited from three specific characteristics relating to the final negotiations: strong leadership from the chairperson, and rules of procedure allowing both access for NGOs and recourse to decision by vote. In both cases, provision for decision by vote was decisive. No vote was ultimately held on the landmine convention, but there were opponents who would undoubtedly have blocked consensus. In the cases of the Rome Statute on the ICC, seven countries voted to reject the agreement.

Shortcomings in negotiating conditions also help to explain the less satisfactory outcomes on child soldiers and small arms. Here, the pursuit of a consensus outcome significantly weakened the final outcome. The predisposition toward consensus decisionmaking within the UN Commission on Human Rights also substantially prolonged the negotiations. In the case of small arms, the principal multilateral negotiations—the Organization of American States (OAS) Convention, the Firearms Protocol of the Transnational Organized Crime Convention, and the 2001 UN Conference on the Illicit Trade in Small Arms and Light Weapons in All Its Aspects—have all represented a very traditional approach to diplomacy. The objectives have been defined by states, negotiations have taken place in closed-door sessions, and direct NGO involvement has been minimal. In particular, although the 2001 UN conference was never designed to produce a legally binding instrument, the negotiating context was extremely conservative. Access for NGOs and alternatives to consensus-based decisionmaking were rejected by a few recalcitrant states and lowest-common-denominator outcomes prevailed.

The stand-alone nature of the landmine negotiations has often been identified as a critical component of the success of the campaign. There is no doubt that working outside existing negotiating forums offered maximum flexibility. The example of the ICC, however, indicates that operating outside traditional venues is not essential for successful, fast-track negotiations. Whether within or outside formal institutions, the key to successful outcomes is strong leadership by the chairperson, recourse to voting, and NGO access. Formal negotiating venues where these conditions cannot be met should be avoided.

The International Campaign to Ban Landmines

Increasing awareness of the humanitarian implications of the use of antipersonnel landmines in battle led in 1991 to the formation of a broad-based international nongovernmental organization (NGO) coalition to call for a ban on antipersonnel landmines. Among the founding organizations were Handicap International, Human Rights Watch, Medico International, Mines Advisory Group, Physicians for Human Rights, and Vietnam Veterans of America Foundation. The actual International Campaign to Ban Landmines (ICBL) was officially formalized in October 1992.

The key message of the campaign comprised three core elements: an international ban on the use, production, stockpiling, and transfer of antipersonnel landmines; a call for increased international resources for humanitarian mine clearance; and the development of a mine victim assistance program.

The impact of this campaign was largely based on the strength and cohesiveness of NGO networks and coalitions of like-minded governments. The concrete result of the campaign was the adoption of the Mine Ban Treaty in 1997. However, the treaty did not mean the ending of the ICBL. Besides the treaty, they have managed to shift the debate from a focus on the actual banning of mines to a feasible model for disarmament and peace. The coalition still remains committed to working together to ban antipersonnel landmines, and to monitor the actual implementation of the treaty. Currently the ICBL network represents over 1,100 civil-society organizations and NGOs that work together locally, regionally, and globally for a world free of mines.

For more information, consult the ICBL website: http://www.icbl.org.

The Campaign to Establish the International Criminal Court

Even though the establishment of an international criminal court (ICC) was first considered by the UN General Assembly in 1948, it was not until 1989 that the International Law Commission was requested to resume its work on a draft statute, initially in response to narco-traffickers. However, the scale of atrocities committed in Rwanda and Yugoslavia during the 1990s demonstrated the need for international criminal justice, and the shortcomings of national justice systems and ad hoc tribunals pleaded for a permanent institution.

Halfway through the 1990s, nongovernmental organizations (NGOs), along with like-minded governments, formed several coalitions to advocate for the establishment of an international criminal court. Their purpose was the promoting and enabling of a diplomatic conference on the creation of an ICC in 1998. The result of these coalitions' work was not only a conference held in Rome in 1998, but also the agreement of coalition members on six substantive principles, all related to commitment to inherent jurisdiction over genocide, war crimes, and crimes against humanity, and to an independent and effective court that was not subordinate to the UN Security Council.

(continues)

The Campaign to Establish the International Criminal Court (continued)

Alongside this process, a handful of NGOs came together in early 1995 to form the NGO Coalition for an International Criminal Court. Their goal was mainly to coordinate the efforts to promote the creation of an effective and just court, and this resulted in various activities: facilitating the exchange of information among legal experts and NGOs; awareness-raising among a broader NGO constituency; providing research assistance and monitoring the negotiations during the Rome conference in 1998; and being part of numerous official delegations.

The quality and credibility of their work and presence at the conference was remarkable. Since then the coalition has grown to include over two thousand NGOs from all over the world and from all sectors of global civil society. These groups have all contributed to the entering into force of the Rome Statute of the ICC in 2002 and the further establishment of the court in The Hague. Their work still continues, especially in the area of worldwide ratification of the Rome Statute, implementing legislation in ratifying countries, monitoring and supporting the work of the court, and continuously generating international public support.

For more information, consult the coalition's website: http://www.iccnow.org.

The Coalition to Stop the Use of Child Soldiers

Leading international human rights and humanitarian organizations formed in May 1998 the Coalition to Stop the Use of Child Soldiers. Initiators were, among others, Amnesty International, Human Rights Watch, Terre des Hommes, World Vision, and Save the Children. The coalition was established to revitalize the negotiations over the process and press for raising of the age standard for children to be recruited into the armed forces to age eighteen. However, the coalition had a broader mandate than advocating raising the age standard. Over the past six years the coalition has been at the forefront of efforts to ban the recruitment and use of child soldiers, to secure their demobilization, and to promote their reintegration into their communities.

Key messages of their campaigns have been: advocating for the demobilization of all children being used as soldiers in armed conflict and the reintegration into their communities; awareness raising of child soldiers among the general public; and calling upon governments to adhere to international laws prohibiting the use of children under the age of eighteen in armed conflict.

In its fight to stop the use of child soldiers, the coalition achieved the adoption and implementation of the Optional Protocol to the Convention on the Rights of the Child on the involvement of children in armed conflict in 1998. It has also established national coalitions in thirty-five countries around the world and several regional coalitions.

(continues)

The Coalition to Stop the Use of Child Soldiers (continued)

Currently they are active in monitoring and researching the use of child soldiers worldwide, and they continue campaigning and advocating against child recruitment by armed groups.

For more information, consult the coalition's website: http://www child-soldiers.org.

Small Arms Campaign

The banning of landmines, one category of small arms, had throughout the 1990s led to increasing efforts to restrict the availability of the entire range of small arms. From the mid-1990s these efforts have been led and supported by nongovernmental organizations (NGOs), international organizations, and progressive governments. While government action has mainly been focused on stopping the illicit trade of small arms, the NGO community has become increasingly engaged in the security and disarmament perspective around the whole debate. Since the range of organizations involved is very broad, so are the objectives pursued. However, all these organizations were in 1998 embodied in the International Network for Small Arms (IANSA), the global network of civil-society organizations that works to stop the proliferation and misuse of small arms and light weapons. Additional roles in campaigning and advocacy are played by the United Nations and the International Committee of the Red Cross.

IANSA's campaigning focuses on the following issues: awareness raising about the threat to human security caused by small arms; promoting NGOs' work to prevent small arms proliferation through national and local legislation, regional agreements, public education, and research; fostering collaborative advocacy efforts; establishing regional and subject-specific small-arms networks; promoting the voices of victims in regional and global policy discussions.

The greatest progress has been achieved in the restriction of illicit trade, mainly because state consensus on this issue was more easily attainable. A lack of like-minded governments continues to hamper structural progress in the negotiations around restrictions on small arms. However, concrete achievements for IANSA so far have been the setting up of regional networks to counter gun proliferation and a leading role in the UN small arms conference process. IANSA continues to fuel the debate on small arms with research, campaigning, and advocacy.

For more information, consult the IANSA website: http://www. iansa.org.

Don Hubert is deputy director of the Peacebuilding and Human Security division of Foreign Affairs, Canada. He has a Ph.D. in social and political science from the University of Cambridge, and has held postdoctoral positions at the Centre for Foreign Policy Studies at Dalhousie University and the Humanitarianism and War Project at Brown University. He is a research fellow at the Centre for Foreign Policy Studies and is a member of the editorial board of the journal Global Governance.

Notes

This chapter is an abridged version of a more extensive analysis of the campaign to ban landmines, including a comparison with the campaign to ban dumdum bullets in 1899 and a comparison with campaigns on the International Criminal Court, child soldiers, and small arms. See Hubert (2000).

The views expressed in this chapter are not necessarily those of Foreign Affairs Canada.

1. The Coalition to Stop the Use of Child Soldiers sought a complete ban on the recruitment and use (both direct and indirect) of children below the age of eighteen. The Optional Protocol ultimately agreed prohibits the deployment of soldiers under the age of eighteen but does not address indirect participation in hostilities or raise the age of voluntary recruitment above the existing level of fifteen years.

2. A similar assessment underpinned the decision by the secretary-general's representative on the internally displaced to distill standards from existing human rights, humanitarian, and refugee law in the development of guiding principles rather than to pursue negotiations on a legally binding convention.

3. The International Campaign to Ban Landmines and the Coalition for an International Criminal Court both mobilized hundreds of NGOs in advance of the respective negotiations. On the government side, the thirteen members of the "core group" organized regional preparatory meetings, developed a draft text, and effectively steered the final negotiations, while the sixty-country like-minded group arrived at the Rome Conference having already agreed on five cornerstone principles to ensure an "independent and effective" ICC.

4. For the use of the term "strategic collaboration," see Atwood (1998).

Selected Bibliography

Annan, Kofi. 1999. Report of the Secretary-General to the Security Council on the Protection of Civilians in Armed Conflict, 8 September (New York: United Nations).

Atwood, David. 1998. "Tackling the Problem of Anti-Personnel Landmines: Issues and Developments," Study on Contemporary Issues in Arms Control and Disarmament, Zurich Security Forum, October.

Hubert, Don. 2000. "The Landmine Ban: A Case Study in Humanitarian Advocacy." An occasional paper published by Brown University, Providence, RI.

21

Civil Society:
Participating in Peace Processes

Celia McKeon

When people become directly affected by armed conflict, they develop a central interest in contributing to its resolution. Despite being confronted with harsh realities and huge dilemmas, civil-society actors can make significant contributions to peace processes. Their capacities may help to create the conditions for talks, build confidence between the parties, shape the conduct and content of negotiations, and influence the sustainability of peace agreements.

The nature of internal conflict in the post–Cold War era provides the most compelling argument for the participation of civil society in peace processes. It is not just that the consequences of brutal confrontation between competing military powers spill over to cause death and destruction among the civilian population; more gravely, we see the deliberate and sometimes systematic targeting of the most basic units of society by the conflict protagonists. Individual citizens, the family, and the community are violated, coerced, and subverted as part of the political, economic, and sociocultural strategies of the armed actors. This is the front line of modern warfare. As people become directly affected by armed conflict, they develop a central interest in contributing to its resolution. Living alongside the armed actors, they have greater need, and greater potential to take part in peacemaking efforts. As peace processes increasingly result in changes to political, economic, and social institutions and relationships in a society, people also have a right to participate in these decisions.

Contemporary peacemaking practice has to confront these realities and the challenges posed by them. Traditional diplomacy and conflict resolution approaches have largely focused on a narrow definition of a peace process—namely, the crucial task of bringing the political and military leaders of opposing groups into a process of dialogue and negotiation with the aim of exploring, reaching agreement on, and implementing measures to end violent conflict and create the conditions for peaceful coexistence. This approach is guided by the belief that the leaders have the power to reach decisions and bring along their constituencies in support of any resulting settlement. However, modern civil wars present strong arguments for a more holistic understanding of a peace process. Negotiations between the leaders of opposing groups do not take place in a social or political vacuum. They may sometimes be unable to adequately address the complex and dynamic interrelationships between these actors and other groups affected by and involved in the armed conflict, including the parties' constituencies, the wider public, and even the broader regional or international forces. People's independent initiatives in their towns and villages, as well as at regional, national, and international levels, therefore have the potential to become key elements in a broader peace process that is capable of addressing these complexities.

The roles of civil-society actors in peace processes are determined by a number of factors, including both external factors such as the attitudes of the warring parties and the degree of "political space" afforded to civic groups, and internal factors such as the resources and skills available for groups to draw on. The particular combination of opportunity and constraint in each context will lead civil society to assume a variety of possible roles. For the purposes of this short overview, these roles are clustered into four broadly distinct and complementary approaches.

Advocating Dialogue as an Alternative to Armed Violence

For noncombatant groups in society, the simple but courageous act of publicly declaring "no" to war and violence can have a powerful impact on the decisions of the warring parties about entering into negotiations. In many situations, an explicit withdrawal of support for the use of military force by sectors of the public will influence the parties' analysis of the options available to them. The public "mood" regarding the conflict and the desirability of a peace process is an important barometer for the leadership of governments and armed groups to take into account.

Civil-society groups can shift this mood by highlighting the unacceptable costs of the conflict and increasing the political stakes for peace. They can catalyze public mobilization for peace, whether through demonstrations, petitions, or media campaigns. Groups who may enjoy a certain degree of moral authority in a particular society, such as religious leaders or elders, can use their influence to add weight to public calls for peace. Advocacy can take diverse forms and benefit from creativity as well as from the richness of cultural traditions. Among some of the many powerful examples of such initiatives, it is worth mentioning the public demonstrations organized by the Acholi Religious Leaders' Peace Initiative in northern Uganda, and the 1997 Citizens' Mandate for Peace, Life, and Liberty (El Mandato por la Paz) in Colombia, which resulted in the participation of 10 million Colombians in a public vote in support of a negotiated settlement to the armed conflict. Across the world, women are frequently a powerful force in resisting war, through initiatives such as Women in Black, whose silent demonstrations on the streets of cities such as Belgrade and Jerusalem offer solidarity with the victims of violence and demand an end to killing and injustice. All of these acts communicate civilians' attempts to resist collusion and articulate alternative approaches to violent conflict. As such they contribute to shaping the social and political context necessary to underpin sustainable dialogue and agreement between the opposing groups.

Educational initiatives can also make a crucial contribution to the broader sociopolitical dimension of a peace process by challenging public perceptions about the conflict. This is particularly true in contexts where opposing groups promote divergent and mutually exclusive analyses of the social and political context. Against the backdrop of armed violence, the careful presentation of balanced and inclusive accounts of the causes and dynamics of the conflict can facilitate changed understanding of the "other side," encouraging fearful, divided communities to reassess the prospects of peaceful coexistence in the future. Moreover, in societies where violence has become the dominant mode of conflict resolution, civil-society groups can play an important role in educating their membership and wider public constituencies about the possibilities of nonviolent approaches to conflictual issues. Legitimizing dialogue as a viable and effective tool can encourage vital public support for political negotiations between the protagonists.

Finally, it is important to acknowledge the crucial role of the media in a peace process. Reporting of progress and obstacles at the negotiating table can have a huge impact on public support for the process, as can the format and content of debate about substantive conflict issues. Local or international media initiatives such as Angola's Radio Ecclesia or Search for Common Ground's Talking Drum program in West Africa (See Chapter 9.3) are just two examples of the many efforts to harness the power of radio and television to promote dialogue and understanding across the conflict divides.

Facilitating Dialogue Between the Parties

Traditional diplomacy has largely relied on governmental and intergovernmental actors to facilitate talks or mediate between the conflict protagonists. Certainly, the leverage exercised by an acceptable governmental or UN representative can have a significant impact on the prospects for agreement. However, in situations of protracted internal conflict, violence often penetrates through the social fabric, involving a larger array of armed actors (often with differing levels of autonomy and accountability), as well as a complex tapestry of interconnected and self-sustaining conflict dynamics at the community level. The state-based international system is comparatively ill-equipped to deal with the people involved in localized armed violence. In such situations, civil-society actors—whether indigenous or external—are arguably best-placed to complement state-driven diplomatic efforts at the leadership level, given their comparatively low-profile access within communities and greater flexibility than state or multilateral actors.

Civil society–led dialogue processes and mediation efforts can have a number of impacts: they can build trust and understanding between the grass-roots membership of divided communities; they can assist in identifying and resolving local-level conflicts, which can benefit the communities affected as well as build confidence between the conflicting parties; and they can create a safe unofficial space for middle-ranking members of the conflicting parties to engage in problem-solving exercises in advance of negotiations. In some cases, modest activities by civic actors can even lead to their acceptance by the leadership to mediate formal negotiations.

The experiences contained in the following chapters offer some specific examples of just such roles and impacts. In Mozambique, the opposing parties accepted the mediation of three representatives of the religious Community of Sant' Egidio, as well as the Catholic archbishop of Beira, Mozambique. Their identity as parties without any political stake in the outcome of the process—nor any of the leverage exercised by foreign governments or multilateral institutions—informed their commitment to finding an outcome that would be genuinely acceptable to both sides and therefore more likely to be sustainable (See Chapter 21.1). In Northern Ireland, Peace and Reconciliation Group's quiet mediation work between the British security forces and the Irish Republican Army led to a deescalation of armed conflict in the city of Derry/Londonderry and was an important opportunity for trust building between the parties (See Chapter 21.2). In the Andean region of Latin America, a dialogue process between members of civil society in Ecuador and Peru created opportunities for shared analysis and problem-solving in relation to the long-standing border dispute between the two countries. Their work created a foundation of awareness and understanding among the affected communities and contributed to the sustainability of the peace agreement reached between the leaders (See Chapter 21.5).

In some situations, civil-society actors may also become involved in providing assistance to one of the warring parties, to help them consider the potential benefits of engaging in a peace process and to assist them in their preparations. Where negotiations are taking place between a recognized government and a nonstate armed group, there may be particularly compelling reasons for this role; armed groups can often be deterred from the negotiating table because they fear domination by a government with superior resources, negotiating skills, and diplomatic support. While it is a delicate and often dangerous role to play, it may result in a greater chance of a sustainable and effective commitment to the negotiations by one of the parties. Again, and particularly given the sensitivities surrounding internal conflicts, civic actors are often more able to take up this challenge than governmental or intergovernmental representatives.

Monitoring Compliance and Violations

As well as causing devastating suffering to those affected, the perpetration of human rights violations by any of the parties to the conflict is often cited as the trigger for armed conflict or as a justification for escalating military engagement. Representatives of governments and armed groups frequently argue that their choice of violence is necessitated by the actions of the other side and that it is the only viable option for protecting "their" populations.

Whether unwittingly or quite deliberately, parties often blur the boundaries between civilians and combatants, resulting in the death, forced displacement, or mistreatment of civilian populations considered to be associated with the "other side." These violations further fracture communities, entrench fear and mistrust, and deepen the spiral of violence between the parties.

The collection of data on human rights violations is a vital task during armed conflict, and can also make a significant contribution to a peace process. Parties often begin talks without agreeing on a cessation of hostilities, and ongoing violations can therefore constitute one of the primary reasons for distrust between them, and ultimately for the breakdown of negotiations. While reliable and impartial data will not prevent these breakdowns, it is a first step in clarifying responsibilities. It is therefore important that it is seen to come from a reliable and impartial source and it is for this reason that civil-society organizations can have a particular role to play. International non-governmental organizations (NGOs) such as Amnesty International or Human Rights Watch are credited with providing accurate information on atrocities committed during armed conflict, and their work assists in putting pressure on the parties to engage in talks. It is frequently complemented by locally established human rights organizations who may document violations against their community or even across society more broadly.

This documentation becomes particularly important after the signing of agreements resulting in cease-fire arrangements. Such agreements increasingly contain provisions for monitoring, whether by international or national organizations. While this is sometimes conceived as a military mission, there is an increasing number of examples of civilian monitoring missions, including the international Peace Monitoring Group in Bougainville or the indigenous civil-society participation in the "local monitoring teams" in the province of Mindanao in the southern Philippines.

Finally, civil-society human rights advocates may play a particularly important role in ensuring that peace processes and any political agreements reached address the structural injustices that gave rise to the conflict, as well as advocating accountability of and effective sanctions against perpetrators of violations. By promoting respect for internationally agreed standards, civic actors can help to ensure that peace agreements do not perpetuate injustice, discrimination, or a climate of impunity.

Participating at the Negotiating Table

The notion that civil-society actors play an active part in the political negotiations to reach peace agreements is still a long way from being an established norm of peacemaking. As mentioned earlier, the dominant paradigm continues to focus on bringing together the leaders of the combatant parties to reach an agreement able to fulfill their minimum requirements and bring an end to violence. However, in a number of countries, civil-society groupings have mobilized to earn themselves an active voice in the negotiations—and made significant contributions to the peace process through their efforts.

One study has identified that there are at least three possible "modes" of civil-society participation in peace processes: mechanisms for consultation, representative decisionmaking, and direct participation (Barnes 2002).

Consultative mechanisms create spaces for noncombatant groups in a society to contribute their views on the substantive issues being discussed in the formal negotiations between the protagonists. In this way, Guatemala's Grand National Dialogue and Civil Society Assembly were able to identify the root causes of the conflict and propose "consensus" documents on the substantive themes being discussed in the negotiations. In the Philippines, the National Unification Commission created forums at provincial, regional, and national levels for different social sectors to offer their perspectives on the causes of conflict and possible solutions. In both cases, although the outcomes of these consultations were nonbinding on the parties, they made important contributions to national-level agreements on the conflict. They also created new spaces for discussion between groups with widely differing expectations and facilitated the involvement of previously marginalized sectors of society.

Representative decisionmaking mechanisms have offered opportunities for groups with an agreed level of public support to take their place at the negotiating table beside the warring parties. Thus in South Africa and Northern Ireland, the negotiations were designed to convene a broad range of political parties in addition to the active combatants. In Northern Ireland, this arrangement enabled ten political parties, and in particular a group of women called the Northern Ireland Women's Coalition, to have a place at the table and represent the interests and concerns of their constituencies. In South Africa, it brought together a range of smaller political parties alongside the African National Congress and the National Party. The subsequent constitution-making process opened the political process even further, inviting all South Africans to contribute their suggestions on its contents. In divided societies, these mechanisms are essential in creating sufficiently inclusive processes that can be "owned" by a broad cross section of the population, and thus less vulnerable to sabotage or breakdown.

Finally, direct participation mechanisms create spaces where all interested civilians can play a role in reaching political agreements to address violent conflict. For reasons of scale, these mechanisms often take place at a local or regional level to address the particular manifestations of the armed conflict in the immediate context. When the National Pact failed to bring an end to armed conflict in Mali, local civic leaders worked with an international NGO, Norwegian Church Aid, to facilitate numerous "intercommunity" meetings. These meetings convened thousands of people, and led to local-level cease-fires, trading agreements, and reconciliation processes. The format also facilitated greater participation by women and children, and prevented the domination of the proceedings by local politicians (See Chapter 16.1).

All of these examples indicate that space can be created for civil-society actors to make an active contribution to the political negotiations to reach peace agreements. They also suggest that broader public participation can contribute to widening the agenda of issues debated, ensure greater emphasis on structural causes of the conflict, enable broader ownership of agreements reached, and facilitate a degree of political reconciliation between participants—all factors that are likely to contribute positively to the sustainability of the process.

Challenges and Dilemmas

All the roles identified above present huge challenges and dilemmas to civil-society actors. First, there is often considerable danger in undertaking any of them, as promoting, facilitating, or participating in peace processes is often not a popular position to take. Governments or armed groups may resent the pressure to negotiate, or consider the pressure tantamount to support for the other side. Public information that deviates from the party line of one or other group may attract censorship or harassment. People or groups making financial profit from the armed conflict will have a vested interest in its continuation. Radicalized sectors of society may also be reluctant to concede anything to one or other of the warring parties through the inevitable compromise of negotiations. These interests represent considerable practical and political risk to unarmed groups of civilians promoting peace.

Ironically, once the parties do take a decision to engage in talks, these same unarmed groups of civilians may find themselves marginalized from negotiations. The warring parties frequently see themselves as the sole legitimate representatives of "their" people and may be reluctant to concede space or control of the negotiation process to a wider group of participants. The international community of interested governments and multilateral actors may compound this marginalization by confining civil society's role to the "post-conflict peacebuilding" phase—where there is important work to be done, but where the political frameworks have often already been determined.

In addition to these external pressures and constraints, civil society also faces its own internal challenges. The first relates to the heterogeneity of what is termed "civil society": the diverse array of interests, groupings, and agendas that are intrinsic to any large mass of people. Given the devastating effects of armed conflict on communities, building alliances across political divides and identifying points of minimum consensus can be a delicate task requiring time and a great deal of sensitivity. With the capacity for independent initiative and action, developing a helpful degree of coordination and complementarity between different sectors and initiatives can seem an almost insurmountable challenge.

Ultimately, however, these challenges are matched by the wealth of resources and diversity of skills that civil-society actors can bring to bear in peace processes. These capacities help to create the conditions for talks, build confidence between the parties, shape the conduct and content of negotiations, and influence the sustainability of peace agreements. By contributing to peace processes in this way, civil-society actors also play a part in long-term processes of change in how society deals with conflict, influencing social norms as well as the political culture of conflict resolution.

Celia McKeon is the program manager/series editor of Conciliation Resources' Accord program, which documents and promotes lessons from peace processes. Conciliation Resources supports groups working at a local level to prevent violence or transform armed conflict into opportunities for development based on more just relationships.

Selected Bibliography

Barnes, Catherine, ed. 2002. "Owning the Process. Public Participation in Peacemaking." *Accord* 13 (London: Conciliation Resources).

Resources

Lead Organizations

Conciliation Resources—United Kingdom
E-mail: conres@c-r.org
Website: http://www.c-r.org

Collaborative for Development Action—
United States
Reflecting on Peace Practice Project
E-mail: cda@cdainc.com
Website: http://www.cdainc.com

INCORE—Northern Ireland
Research on Peace Processes Programme
E-mail: incore@incore.ulst.ac.uk
Website: http://www.incore.ulst.ac.uk/

Publications

Abdullaev, Kamoludin, and Catherine Barnes, eds. "Politics of Compromise: The Tajikistan Peace Process." *Accord* 10. London: Conciliation Resources, 2001.

Baranyi, Stephen. *The People's Peace: Civil-Society Organisations and Peace Processes in the South.* London: Catholic Institute for International Relations, 1998.

Carl, Andy, and Sr. Lorraine Garasu, eds. "Weaving Consensus: The Papua New Guinea–Bougainville Peace Process." *Accord* 12. London: Conciliation Resources, 2002.

Cohen, Jonathan, ed. "A Question of Sovereignty: The Georgia-Abkhazia Peace Process." *Accord* 7. London: Conciliation Resources, 1999.

Curle, Adam. *In the Middle: Nonofficial Mediation in Violent Situations.* Leamington Spa, England: Berg, 1986.

Darby, John, and Roger Mac Ginty, eds. *The Management of Peace Processes.* London: Macmillan Press, 2000.

Doucet, Ian, ed. "Resource Pack for Conflict Transformation." London: International Alert, 1996.

Francis, Diana. *People, Peace and Power: Conflict Transformation in Action.* London: Pluto, 2002.

Garcia, Ed. *Participative Approaches to Peacemaking in the Philippines.* Tokyo: United Nations University Press, 1993.

García-Durán, Mauricio, ed. "Alternatives to War. Colombia's Peace Process." *Accord* 14. London: Conciliation Resources, 2003.

Guinard, Caroline. "From War to Peace. Lessons Learned from Achievements and Failures in Peace Agreements over the Past Decade. A Strategy for Peace Process Optimization." Nonviolence International and International Peace Bureau. Bangkok: December 2002.

Lederach, John Paul. *Building Peace: Sustainable Reconciliation in Divided Societies.* Washington, DC: United States Institute of Peace, 1997.

Lord, David. "Paying the Price: The Sierra Leone Peace Process." *Accord* 9. London: Conciliation Resources, 2000.

McCartney, Clem. "Striking a Balance: The Northern Ireland Peace Process." *Accord* 8. London: Conciliation Resources, 1999. Updated in 2003.

Meijer, Guus, ed. "From Military Peace to Social Justice? The Angolan Peace Process." *Accord* 15. London: Conciliation Resources, 2004.

Stedman, Stephen John, Donald Rothchild, and Elizabeth M. Cousens. *Ending Civil Wars: The Implementation of Peace Agreements.* London and Boulder, CO: Lynne Rienner Publishers, 2002.

Williams, Sue, and Steve Williams. *Being in the Middle by Being at the Edge.* London: Quaker Peace and Service, in association with William Sessions, York, 1994.

21.1

A Nonthreatening Approach to Peace: The Community of Sant' Egidio in Mozambique

Sant' Egidio, a community of socially engaged Catholic Italians, managed to achieve in the 1990s what superpowers and hardened professional diplomats could not: broker peace to end the civil war in Mozambique. The approach of the lay organization hinged on personal contacts and cultural understanding of both parties. "Unlike governments, we had no political or economic interests to promote."

Located in the old Roman neighborhood of Trastevere, hidden behind the church of Santa Maria Trastevere, lies the Piazza Sant' Egidio, a small square from which the Comunità di Sant' Egidio (Community of Sant' Egidio) derived its name and where it has its headquarters. The home of the lay community, a former sixteenth-century monastery, hosted the negotiations in the early 1990s that led to the signing of a peace agreement between the warring factions of the bloody civil war in Mozambique.

Sant' Egidio's approach to mediation has been taken as an inspiration by many individuals and organizations seeking to resolve conflicts. Word about the community's "intervention" in the Mozambican conflict spread quickly, leading to invitations from all over the world for the community to mediate peace, including in Kosovo, Algeria, Liberia, and Guatemala.

Although efforts to broker peace, as it did in the case of Mozambique, are one of Sant' Egidio's most notable achievements, this is certainly not its only core activity. Founded in 1968 by a group of deeply religious young students with a vocation to help the poor, Sant' Egidio chose prayer as one of its essentials, along with helping deprived people, often on a very personal basis. Until this day, the community focuses a lot of attention on its daily prayer sessions at several locations in Rome. Almost all members, most of whom have regular, often high-powered jobs, spend some hours a week to help children of poor families with their homework, provide food to homeless people, or in other ways help deprived persons in need. Over the years, especially after its successful contribution to making peace in Mozambique, the community became increasingly involved in seeking negotiated solutions to armed conflicts. In the perception of the organization's founder, Andrea Riccardi, this peace work is a natural continuation of its efforts to improve the lives of the poor. "War is the mother of all poverty, which makes everybody poor, even the rich," he once summarized the drive to commit himself to conflict resolution. Over the years, its activities have spread to other cities in Italy and to seventy other countries, and Sant' Egidio's membership has grown to over fifty thousand in 2004.

Sant' Egidio stresses that every conflict is different and requires its own approach. However, the story of the Italian organization's involvement in the Mozambican conflict indicates there are certain specific characteristics in the community's handling of conflict and mediation that could be called a "Sant' Egidio method." Developing personal relationships and understanding the culture of the belligerent parties are some of its most dominant features.

The War in Mozambique

Sant' Egidio's involvement with the Mozambican peace process originated from a personal friendship that started shortly after the African country had gained independence from Portugal in 1974. In 1976, a young Mozambican priest, Dom Jaime Gonçalves, was studying in Rome and became a friend of the community. A year later he was nominated bishop of the Mozambican port city of Beira. He shortly afterward returned to Rome for a synod and took this opportunity to discuss the suppression of Christian churches by the Marxist regime in Mozambique with his friends at the community. Sant' Egidio decided to start to work to enhance religious freedom in Mozambique. In 1981, it arranged a meeting between the then Italian Communist Party leader Enrico Berlinguer and Gonçalves. Berlinguer promised to use his influence to persuade the regime in Mozambique to soften its restrictions on religious organizations. This effort led to good contacts between Sant' Egidio and the Mozambican government. The community also managed to gain trust among the senior ranks of the rightist rebel movement Resistência Nacional Moçambicana (RENAMO), which had fought the leftist Frente de Libertação de Moçambique (FRELIMO) government since the mid-1970s. Thanks to its good contacts, Sant' Egidio in 1982 managed to negotiate the release of priests and nuns held captive by RENAMO. The community also had close ties to the Italian government and the Vatican, which increased its credibility in the eyes of the conflicting parties.

The war between the national army of the FRELIMO government and RENAMO was bloody and traumatic. RENAMO built up a gruesome reputation as the "Khmer Rouge of Africa," through a series of atrocities committed against the civilian population. The Marxist FRELIMO government, on its part, alienated large sections of the population through its oppressive politics. Its economic policies also did little to help the country. Mozambique's infrastructure and economy began to fall apart. This was one of the reasons why Sant' Egidio organized several humanitarian relief operations in Mozambique in the early 1980s.

After several failed efforts by foreign powers, including Kenya and the United States, to broker peace in the mid-1980s, RENAMO contacted the Vatican and Sant' Egidio in April 1989 with the request to help arrange a unilateral cease-fire in Nampula Province. Sant' Egidio invited rebel leader Afonso Dhlakama to Rome. He accepted, after some initial hesitation, and attended a few meetings set up by the community. At around the same time, the FRELIMO government made clear, in contacts with Sant' Egidio, that it was interested in direct negotiations with RENAMO. Sant' Egidio's leaders took this as a signal to move quickly. They immediately took steps to convene a dialogue in Rome. On 8 July 1990, representatives of the Mozambican government and RENAMO officially met for the first time at the Sant' Egidio's headquarters, after some officials from both parties had met informally at a World Cup match in Rome in June that year. The official meeting was the beginning of a peace process that would last twenty-seven months, consisting of eleven meetings under Sant' Egidio mediation, leading to the signing of a peace accord on 4 October 1992. The mediating team consisted of Mario Raffaelli, representing the Italian government; Matteo Zuppi, a priest and member of Sant' Egidio; Andrea Riccardi, founder-member of the community; and Bishop Jaime Gonçalves.

No Magical Solutions

The Sant' Egidio–steered peace process was treated with suspicion and apparent envy by some outsiders. Every negotiating session that did not produce the expected result, meaning peace on the ground or a cease-fire, was treated by the media as a failure. Political figures excluded from the discussions found it in their interest to say that the negotiations were going nowhere.

Prior to each meeting, a mediation team would talk with each side to find out what its delegation was thinking of the current situation, and to brainstorm about their possibilities and share information. This process was necessary to determine whether the time was right to actually get together and sit around the table again. Only with the explicit consent of the mediation team would the community organize a meeting between the parties. If the team refrained from giving the green light, a meeting would not only be a waste of time and money, the mediators reasoned, but could also have negative impact on the entire process. In some cases, the team decided it was better to hold a secret meeting, out of sight of the press.

The cautious and meticulous approach Sant' Egidio adopted contributed to the creation of an atmosphere in which close cooperation between the factions was possible. In addition to the two Mozambican parties, many states and non-state actors became involved as well, adding to the momentum and helping parties to move closer to one another.

There is no doubt that the negotiating process was complex. The final result followed a series of small steps gradually taken by the two parties in the conflict. There were no magical emotional solutions for resolving the war. The reason was simple: RENAMO would only lay down its arms if it would receive sufficient guarantees for the postwar period: guarantees of its members' physical security, guarantees that it would not face legal prosecution, guarantees of free political life, guarantees of access to a minimum of financial means in order to be able to set up its organization as a political party, and guarantees of being able to compete democratically for power. RENAMO operated with a high degree of mistrust, not only toward its adversary, the FRELIMO government, but toward everyone. RENAMO seemed to be convinced that a large part of the world was on FRELIMO's side, and that almost everyone was its enemy. For this reason, before giving up its arms, it wanted to accumulate all possible and imaginable guarantees.

It took the mediators time to understand this attitude and to get used to the exhausting negotiating tactics of RENAMO. They had hoped for a shorter and less unnerving peace process; yet they understood that the peace process could not be accelerated by handing ultimatums to RENAMO, but only by helping it to organize a political discourse and rationally formulate its fears and preoccupations about the postwar period. British ambassador Richard Edis later commented that much credit was due to the skill, persistence, and what has been termed the legendary patience of the Italian clerical and lay mediators, because these prevented the negotiations from breaking down.

The FRELIMO government, on its part, continually showed impatience with what it considered to be the tortuously slow pace of the negotiations. It frustrated the government that RENAMO seemed to deliberately slow down the negotiations from time to time. The apparent inability of the government, in the early stages of the process, to grasp the concerns of the rebel group provoked RENAMO to raise the stakes even higher, out of fear that the government would try to get around its requests or would try to deceive it once peace would have been reached. Experts Moisés Venâncio and Stephen Chan, however, remarked that the FRELIMO government also was partly responsible for the slow progress of the talks. "The Maputo regime expected the rebels to sign a peace agreement overnight," they observed in hindsight.

> Maputo assumed that its superior political sophistication and what was generally seen as its wide support in the international community would facilitate a quick agreement with RENAMO. All FRELIMO wanted was a cease-fire and then to iron out what it thought were a few of the rebels' political issues. In fact, Maputo may never even have expected the rebels to insist so constantly that the talks should touch upon so many political questions. [. . .] FRELIMO could not seriously have expected a movement with little or no political dimension to easily lay down its main negotiating weapon, military force, without getting some form of compensation. (Morozzo della Rocca and Riccardi n.d.: 6)

As the process continued, it became clear that the issue of a cease-fire should be dealt with in the later stages of the negotiations, after other issues regarding the postwar period would have been ironed out. The turning point in the process came with the signing of a preamble, a non-agenda document in which the government and the rebel group, having barely overcome their stubborn political stances and mental reluctance, finally accepted the necessity of reaching a mutual acknowledgment of the other's right to exist. With the preamble, the rebels recognized the legitimacy of the government within the existing legislative framework, and the government recognized the legitimacy of RENAMO's desire to maintain a political movement. According to the mediators, it opened the road to the final agreement reached in 1992, and signed by Dhlakama and Mozambican president Joaquim Chissano. The peace agreement turned out to be sustainable and was followed by democratic and free elections in 1994, which further stabilized the country.

Conclusions

It is not easy to deduce "rules" from the Mozambican experience that could be applied elsewhere. Peacemaking in all cases is constructed and shaped in specific conditions. "There is no standard formula for making peace," as the Sant' Egidio mediators remarked. Still some conclusions can be drawn from Sant' Egidio's experience. "In particular, the mediation of peace in Mozambique teaches us that cultural understanding of the conflicting parties—which obviously differs from conflict to conflict—is crucial for success," they said. Matteo Zuppi, one of Sant' Egidio's mediators, elaborated on the difficulties of the mediation work. He said the mediators were dealing with two systems of logic, going in opposite directions. They had to use both formal and informal, technical and less technical instruments. "I learnt that I had to join technique with intuition and patience," Zuppi said. The mediators needed the parties themselves to understand what they really wanted. They found a formula based on bringing together parties who are driven by completely diverging motives and considerations. He added that they relied heavily on personal relationships.

> I remember the U.S. State Department sent in a group of very good professional negotiators to help the peace process. They kept drafting documents and proposals that very much amused the delegations. In December 1991, they, quite rightly, tried to achieve a Christian truce. They were an officer and a lawyer, and they were very good, very professional, so we let them go on. After a few days they were desperate. They bumped into a wall of misunderstanding: technique could not substitute for personal relations with the parties. (Morozzo della Rocca and Riccardi n.d.: 3)

Another characteristic of Sant' Egidio's approach was to refrain from putting pressure on the parties or setting ultimatums. As it had no real power to back any threats, it would not have been able to do so convincingly. Therefore a "nonthreatening approach" was used. The inability of the mediators to promise any financial gains, simply because Sant' Egidio did not represent any donor or other body capable of disbursing loans or funds, is considered to be another cause of their success. The mediators did not have military or economic tools. They did not "buy" peace by offering money. Nor did they offer the individuals who were negotiating peace the sort of per diem honoraria that are characteristic of some of today's peace processes, which have the unhappy result of multiplying the number of participants and lengthening the duration of negotiations, as the talks themselves become a source of income for many individuals. The peace talks in Rome were a clear example of a "result-oriented" process, rather than a "process-oriented" one.

The Roman peace mediation was politically realistic, attentive to the many legal, strategic, and diplomatic elements. It explored several approaches, involving various bodies and actors, but it was also simply based on the dream that everyone can make peace.

Contact

Community of Sant' Egidio
Piazza S. Egidio 3/a
00153 Roma, Italy
Tel.: +39 06 585 661
Fax: +39 06 5800 197
E-mail: info@santegidio.org
Website: http://www.santegidio.org

Selected Bibliography

Edis, Richard. 1995. "Mozambique's Successful Peace Process: An Insider's View." *Cambridge Review of International Affairs* 2.

Hume, Cameron R. 1994. *Ending Mozambique's War: The Role of Mediation and Good Offices* (Washington, DC: United States Institute of Peace Press).

Morozzo della Rocca, Roberto. 1997. *Mozambique de la guerre à la paix. Histoire d'une médiation insolite* (Paris: L'Harmattan).

Morozzo della Rocca, Roberto, and Luca Riccardi, n.d. "The Sant' Egidio Peace Process: Unpublished Report" (Rome: Sant' Egidio).

Vines, Alex. 1996. *RENAMO: From Terrorism to Democracy in Mozambique?* (London: James Currey).

21.2

Facilitating a Mutual Deescalation Process: Quakers and the Peace and Reconciliation Group in Northern Ireland

Diana Lampen and John Lampen

By defusing tensions, a collection of unlikely but dedicated people succeeded in getting a peace process started in Derry/Londonderry that transformed relations between the opposing sides, making it less violent than any other city in Northern Ireland. It laid the basis for the cooperative relations that characterizes life in Derry/Londonderry today. Here is the personal story of John Lampen, who was, with his wife Diana, directly involved in this vital work.

On 24 October 1990, the Irish Republican Army (IRA) took the family of Patsy Gillespie hostage, tied him into a car loaded with explosives, and forced him to drive it into an army checkpoint on the border of Northern Ireland and the Irish Republic. The expolosion killed Gillespie along with five British soldiers. This had a deeply alienating effect on IRA supporters among nationalist (Catholic) people whose aspiration for a united Ireland provided the rationale for their campaign. (The IRA is a paramilitary group, and not the army of the Irish Republic.) They had repeatedly claimed that they were only at war with the British "occupation forces" and not the Unionist (Protestant) people of Northern Ireland—who of course saw it differently, since they wanted to remain part of the United Kingdom. Yet now the IRA was killing fellow Catholics too in the most callous way.

It was four years and many deaths later before the IRA declared a ceasefire. Yet these were the last soldiers to die at the hands of the Derry Brigade, and its level of military activity dropped by 60 percent afterwards in the city of Derry/Londonderry—the place where this round of civic unrest had started in 1969, the scene of "Bloody Sunday," and a city that had consistently ranked near the top in the statistics of bombings, woundings, and killings. This may have been partly due to the widespread disgust at the "human bomb" among those who had previously supported them. Nonetheless, its political party in the city, Sinn Féin, had two leading figures, Martin McGuinness and Mitchel McLaughlin, who were already looking for a way to shift the campaign from violence to a political process, and they were helped to do this by a collection of unlikely people, the Derry Peace and Reconciliation Group (PRG).

Gaining Trust

The PRG was the Derry branch of the Nobel Peace Prize–winning Peace People, but in 1978 it broke away because of the leadership's failure to consult the grassroots membership. It included several former members of the violent organizations on both sides, men who had decided to work for peace but still kept contact with their former associates. It also included members of the "respectable" part of the community, including the wives of a bishop and a high sheriff and also two English Quakers, my wife Diana and me, who had come to live in the city. The chairperson was Margaret O'Donnell, a nurse born in the Irish Republic.

The group ran a program of Protestant and Catholic mixed events, such as sports contests, youth contacts, pensioners' theater outings, and family holidays. It had quieter roles; one was befriending local people ordered to leave Ireland by the paramilitaries (in Northern Ireland, "paramilitary" always refers to the illegal organizations). Another was mediating between the nationalist community and the police and army when the security forces abused their powers. Margaret was appointed as a Catholic member of the city's Police Liaison Committee when no nationalist councilor would sit on it. She developed a keen sympathy for the young (mostly Protestant) policemen patrolling a hostile community; and she saw clearly that whenever a policeman or soldier got away with misbehavior and his seniors dismissed the complaint as "enemy propaganda," their task became harder, the public more hostile, and the IRA more eager to attack them.

Slowly the group gained some trust both with those who were harassed and with the police who began to make redress and to discipline their officers when needed. The ex-paramilitaries in the group made sure that their former organizations knew what the PRG was doing and why, and secured a grudging approval. For instance, I suggested to the British government that they appoint lay visitors, ordinary citizens with the right to visit police cells at any time of day or night to ensure that detainees were getting proper treatment. The police came to see that this protected them against false accusations, while the IRA agreed that it gave some protection to any of their members being detained. They promised not to target the visitors as "collaborators." Among others, Diana and Margaret from the PRG became lay visitors.

Tension Reduction

In 1989 the commanding officer of the Royal Hampshire Regiment, newly arrived in the city, asked the PRG how he could improve relations between his soldiers and the people of Derry/Londonderry. We asked if we could talk to the rank-and-file soldiers about the community's attitudes toward soldiers and explain that most nationalists were not hostile to them unless soldiers had been harassing people. A cold response usually meant that someone was afraid to be seen by neighbors as being friendly to a "Brit." The soldiers responded well to the Derry-born group members, seeing them as authentic members of their own class. The officers trusted Diana and me as English people who knew the Derry/Londonderry community well but could see both sides of a question.

Not everyone in authority liked the growing relationship with us; one police chief objected to "communication with the enemy." However, the local army commanders valued it greatly, and so did the government's security advisers. One brigadier said of the PRG, "We knew that they had contact with the IRA and the IRA presumably knew that they were in contact with us. There was an understanding, certainly on our part, and I suspect on theirs too, that the conduit could not be used for intelligence purposes, otherwise it would be undermined and destroyed." In 1991 the most senior British army officer in Northern Ireland assured the PRG that every new regiment posted to Derry/Londonderry would be told to renew the relationship.

The local army commanders increasingly consulted the PRG, particularly the ex-paramilitaries, about operational matters. Advice was given on public-order problems such as IRA funerals and political and traditional marches, and also on lesser matters such as whether people would respond better to soldiers if they wore berets rather than steel helmets and camouflage paint on their faces. Yet there was a danger that softer public-order tactics would make the police and army into easier targets for the IRA, unless the latter could understand and appreciate the changes. In thinking about this, the group was inspired by a U.S. theorist, Charles Osgood, who in 1962 formulated the idea of "graduated reciprocation in tension-reduction," conveniently called GRIT. He realized that an escalating conflict usually grows without (or despite) com-

Police marking off a suspected bomb area

munication; each party watches what the other is doing, and calculates what is the safest way for them to respond. This is how the stockpiles grow in an arms race. Osgood's insight was that this process could be put into reverse. Side "A" will not unilaterally disarm; but they can make a small reduction and wait to see whether there will be a response. If Side "B" reciprocates with a parallel concession, "A" can make a further move. Whereas complete disarmament requires a huge amount of trust, GRIT enables trust to grow as each side sees increasing evidence of the other's peaceful intent. Another beauty of GRIT is that the two sides do not have to negotiate until they are ready. Up till then deeds are speaking louder than words could. The outstanding example of GRIT was given by Mikhail Gorbachev when, after decades of fruitless Strategic Arms Limitation Talks, he simply made a large reduction in Soviet missiles and waited for Western governments to respond.

In Derry/Londonderry, the main source of violence was the conflict between the IRA and the British security forces. There were paramilitaries in the Protestant part of the community too, with whom the PRG had good relations; in fact the group had managed to secure promises of "no first strike" in the city from both sides. To bring peace, what was needed was an IRA response to the British moves. So an ex-paramilitary PRG member and I began discussions with them and found a much more open attitude than we expected. We were encouraged to draw up a list of moves that either side could make as they began to trust the other's intentions: for example, the army could stop indiscriminate house searches through a whole area, while the IRA could stop taking over people's homes as hiding places to ambush soldiers. The measures would at first be confined to the Derry/Londonderry city area, and made without publicity.

A possible problem was that British moves would often be obvious, such as dropping plans for a new police station on a contentious site; paramilitary moves, such as not attacking police when they were going to the assistance of the public, would be harder to identify—it could be due to voluntary self-restraint or more effective police tactics. Martin McGuinness raised another difficulty with me. He said, "You are talking about a bargaining process at the military level. But the IRA are not interested in that. They want to give up their violence, but they will only trade it for political gains. Otherwise their whole campaign would have been in vain." I responded by saying that without initial trust-building measures there could be no successful political bargaining, but I am not sure if I persuaded him.

GRIT began in Derry/Londonderry, and survived a dangerous time in 1991, when a Loyalist unit from another town went into the Republic and killed a Sinn Féin councilor. ("Loyalist" is the term for extremists and violent groups in the Unionist community). The IRA saw this as a breach of the "no first strike agreement" and murdered the Loyalist leader in the city, a good friend of the PRG who had been protecting his opponents from attack by his own men.

Yet violence continued to diminish and the death toll in Derry/Londonderry became very small. Army and police "mistakes" and misconduct became rare. The journalist Ed Maloney reviewed IRA operational statistics for the Derry Brigade, and found that between 1986 and 1989 they accounted for an annual average of 13 percent of all IRA activities; between 1990 and 1993, the average fell to just under 5 percent. Because publicity was avoided though, it was not easy to see whether this was an intentional process. At the end of 1992 I still felt unsure. I then asked Mitchel McLaughlin if there was a chance of a GRIT agenda being pursued, and he said, "What do you think we have been doing for the last two years?" He added that the army had been responding. On another occasion a Sinn Féin leader said, "We were looking for a way to move towards peace; what the PRG did was to show us the nuts and bolts of a possible process." A senior British officer said that once a Northern Irish peace process was clearly starting, and high-level discussions began on de-escalation, "it was possible to say that we have already done that in Derry."

Helping to Move Forward

This account may suggest that, provided the channels of communication are there, the process is easy. This of course is not true. In 1992 there was a "citizens' enquiry" on the way forward to peace in Northern Ireland, with an international commission of distinguished people who listened to submissions from many groups. In a private session the PRG told them about the GRIT process, and unfortunately rather too much of this was revealed in the subsequent *Opsahl Report* published in 1993 (Pollak 1993). Sinn Féin leaders reacted by angrily denying there had been any mediation process (which in a strict sense was correct—GRIT is not negotiation). They said about me in a newspaper interview, "He's either very flaky . . . or something more sinister." The PRG was sent a message saying I was now persona non grata with the people I had been talking to; it was not clear for a time whether Diana and I should take these remarks as a physical threat.

There are two possible reasons for this strong reaction. Ed Maloney believes that the Derry leaders had been acting without the sanction of the ruling group in the IRA, the Army Council—and also moving far ahead of the expectations of their members in other areas. It was thus embarrassing to have their moves exposed in a well-known book. I think the major reason was that there had been secret talks between Martin McGuinness and representatives of the British government since March of that year (also unknown to most of the members). These broke down in mistrust in September, and soon afterwards a journalist ran a story on the front page of the *Sunday Times* revealing the existence of the talks and (wrongly) pointing to me as the go-between. The *Opsahl Report* appeared at about the same time. It is hardly surprising that this mixture of disappointment, suspicion, untruths, and unwelcome revelation created a difficult and dangerous situation for Diana and me, who were "expendable." Luckily the other PRG members were able to maintain their trust and contacts.

What is remarkable is that despite this debacle, the GRIT process held, and a year later the IRA declared a cease-fire across Northern Ireland and asked for the start of the open all-party political negotiations that the British and Irish governments had offered. When this happened, a former commander of the British army brigade in Derry/Londonderry wrote to us: "I have thought so often that the roots of the initiative lay in Derry, which in some part showed the way (I think perhaps for the IRA as well as for the Army and others) and in that the PRG were central—in your philosophy and example and all you did to help us move forward."

Diana and John Lampen, since leaving Ireland in 1994, work as trainers and consult-ants in peace skills, both with children and adults. They work mainly in the U.K., but also in Bosnia, Croatia, Denmark, South Africa, Uganda, Ukraine, and the United States.

Contact

Diana and John Lampen
E-mail: lampen@hopeproject.co.uk
Websites:
> http://www.hopeproject.co.uk
> http://www. peaceprg.co.uk

Selected Bibliography

Lampen, John. 1983. *Will Warren: A Scrapbook* (London: Quaker Home Service).
Mallie, Eamonn, and David McKittrick. 2001. *Endgame in Ireland* (London: Hodder & Stoughton).
Maloney, Ed. 2002. *Secret History of the IRA* (Harmondsworth, England: Allen Lane).
Osgood, Charles. 1962. *An Alternative to War or Surrender* (Champaign: University of Illinois Press).
Pollak, Andy. 1993. *A Citizens' Enquiry: The Opsahl Report on Northern Ireland* (Dublin: Lilliput Press).

21.3

Engendering the Peace Processes in West Africa: The Mano River Women's Peace Network

Femmes Africa Solidarité

While rebels and soldiers traded bullets and political leaders talked tough, women from three West African countries promoted negotiations and reconciliation. With refugee flows reaching unprecedented levels, the women's network helped to prevent the outbreak of hostilities between the three countries by bringing their leaders back to the negotiation table.

In May 2000, at a meeting in Abuja, Nigeria, attended by women leaders and representatives of local nongovernmental organizations (NGOs), an initiative was launched linking women from Liberia, Sierra Leone, and Guinea in an effort to promote peace. The Mano River Women's Peace Network (MARWOPNET) adopted a mandate committing women from the three Mano River region countries to forget their differences and pursue a common agenda covering peace and sustainable development for their respective countries and the region as a whole.

Its formation marked the culmination of efforts facilitated, in the main, by Femmes Africa Solidarité,[1] which brought together women ministers, parliamentarians, journalists, lawyers, academics, researchers, and sympathetic individuals from the private sector.

MARWOPNET comprises roughly thirty umbrella organizations operating in diverse areas and focusing on promoting peace and development.[2] Within a relatively short period, MARWOPNET erected a network base that spread beyond the African continent to include national, regional, and international organizations. Its primary efforts focused on peace. This commitment was tested very quickly. With civil wars raging in Liberia and Sierra Leone, and tension on the rise in neighboring Guinea—a partner with the two West African nations in the Mano River economic alliance—the women of MARWOPNET launched a bold initiative in 2001 to get leaders talking to each other. It seemed a forlorn hope, given the depth of animosity among the presidents, but that was no deterrent.

Getting Them to Speak

A representative group of women from the three countries visited Liberia. On their arrival in Monrovia, President Charles Taylor was holding a cabinet meeting. He asked, "Are you telling me that women leaders from Guinea are here in Monrovia? And women from Sierra Leone?"

Struck by their courage, and impressed by the effort they had made to reach Monrovia, Taylor agreed to meet the women and assured them of his willingness to sit down with his counterparts from Guinea and Sierra Leone.

Encouraged, MARWOPNET sent a delegation to Conakry. Guinean president Lansana Conte received them. Mary Brownell, a member of the delegation, told the president: "You and President Taylor have to meet as men and iron out your differences, and we the women want to be present. We will lock you in this room until you come to your senses, and I will sit on the key."

President Conte laughed. "What man do you think would say that to me? Only a woman could do such a thing and get away with it." He agreed to attend a summit, declaring: "Many people have come before to try to convince me to meet with President Taylor and I have always refused them, but today I accept because I believe in you. You are not part of the problem. You have not brought war, but your commitment and appeal have convinced me."

Next, the women went to see President Tejan Kabba of Sierra Leone, who informed them he had already been contacted by President Conte and they had agreed to have their ministers of foreign affairs and defense meet to prepare the ground for the summit, including Taylor. Brownell, who was a veteran activist from Liberia, commented later that the leaders "know they have to listen because the women are not for war . . . [they] know that we don't want anything from them except peace."

Dialogue

These meetings between MARWOPNET delegations and the presidents took place between June and August 2001. In early March 2002, at a three-day summit in Rabat, Morocco, Presidents Taylor, Conte, and Kabba agreed to jump-start peace talks; initiate dialogue between the ministers of defense from the three countries; reopen borders between Liberia, Guinea, and Sierra Leone; rebuild diplomatic relations between the three countries; decrease the proliferation of small arms; and increase economic cooperation in the Mano River Basin.

By initiating dialogue among the three countries, MARWOPNET succeeded where many previous attempts had failed. The founders of the network followed through on their conviction that joint action would enable women to contribute meaningfully to the quest for regional peace and security.

Their efforts were not limited to forcing direct political action. MARWOPNET sent representatives on peace tours of the region, and participated in demonstrations by other women's groups. The network alerted the regional and international community to the situation in the region, and played a critical role as intermediary between the various factions involved in the Liberian peace talks in Ghana, where

Areas of Concern

Recognizing that peace, development, and security are interrelated, Mano River Women's Peace Network focused on five critical areas of concern. Each of the women's networks agreed to take a lead role in one area.

The areas, and their different components, were as follows:

- Peace process (involving provision of training; establishment of a dialogue; mainstreaming of gender; affirmative action; integration of a human rights approach)
- Peace mechanisms (increasing awareness; increased participation of women in international peace mechanisms; wide-scale education programs; greater interaction among women's groups and other stakeholders; establishment of a strong communication and information network and an effective early warning system; continued improvement in the transparent management of cross-border movements)
- Security (reduction and eventual eradication of arms in circulation in the subregion; increase of accurate information on the location of arms; decrease in and eventual end to recruitment of child soldiers; establishment of a more secure environment for development to take place)
- Reconstruction (physical and psychological rehabilitation of war victims; social reintegration of members of families and communities; restoration of basic welfare facilities in the region; restoration of women's self-confidence and desire to start afresh; empowerment of women to enable them to fully take part in the reconstruction and development of the region; training of trainers for each country; training to address psychological damage caused by war to child soldiers, other combatants, women, and refugees; training in housing reconstruction)
- Economic empowerment (revitalization of the economic capacity of women to stimulate economic development; promotion of gender equity and sensitivity in the policies of governments; strengthening the capacity of women to ensure their relevance and competitiveness in the global system)

it was invited as one of the signatories to the eventual agreement. During the two months of their stay in Ghana, the MARWOPNET delegation lobbied for inclusion of the peace agenda agreed in Abuja in 2000, as part of the Accra peace accord.

Sensitizing People to Peace

The network's success in bringing leaders of the Mano River Union to the negotiating table enabled women to secure access to decisionmaking structures—especially in regard to peace and development processes—and created effective programs to return and reintegrate refugees and internally displaced people to their homes.

MARWOPNET's concern for victims of conflict translated into a greater focus on projects to help reintegrate refugees and internally displaced people into their homes and communities. MARWOPNET's members visited refugee camps and drew attention to the plight of those sheltered there. They launched advocacy campaigns to give visibility to issues such as HIV/AIDS, economic empowerment, child soldiers, and disarmament.

Provisions were distributed to the needy and international organizations increased their lobbying efforts, highlighting conditions in the camps and urging more humane treatment and increased aid to refugees. There was particular focus on helping people heal both physical and psychological wounds, especially the thousands of women and young girls in the camps who were victims of sexual violence.

In its ongoing work in these areas, the network used specific strategies to achieve its objectives. MARWOPNET tried to sensitize people at all levels—from grassroots organizations to politicians—on peace issues, including advocacy, capacity building, the benefits of linking with other ongoing initiatives, networking, and partnership building. It carried out research and disseminated information on existing peace initiatives, and promoted best practices in peacebuilding among women.

At meetings with rebel groups, and during peace marches and demonstrations, the women demanded the destruction of small arms, the reintegration and rehabilitation of child soldiers, better treatment of refugees and displaced persons, and increased cooperation between the Mano River states.

In the area of capacity building, MARWOPNET's training sessions and workshops on peacebuilding focused on equipping women mediators from all walks of life with necessary skills in mediation, negotiation, and mobilization techniques and instilling in them the determination to work for peace and promote a culture of reconciliation. The women have taught conflict resolution and negotiation techniques to media NGOs and representatives of civil society.

Recognized Impact

The achievements of MARWOPNET earned the praise of UN secretary-general Kofi Annan who, in a report to the Security Council in April 2001, noted that MARWOPNET "aptly demonstrates" the multidimensional, coordinated and regional collaborative approach adopted by civil-society bodies in their struggles to promote peace. A similar endorsement came from the Organization of African Union that year. The network earned praise from the continental body for its "commendable efforts aimed at sustaining the peace process in Sierra Leone and bringing about peace, security, and stability in Mano River region."

In December 2003, MARWOPNET was awarded the UN Prize in the field of human rights by the UN General Assembly. This is an honorary award given to individuals and organizations in recognition of their outstanding achievement in human rights.

Conclusions

Despite the successes achieved by MARWOPNET, peace in the subregion remains precarious. There is an urgent need for the continuation and intensification of efforts to empower women and enable them to continue their role as effective advocates for peace. Although various international declarations and conventions call for increased involvement of women in peace negotiations, African women continue to be sidelined in this area. They have proven that they can negotiate through participation in the MARWOPNET and other regional peace processes, but even when organized and prepared they find it hard to secure necessary funds to attend negotiations. When they do obtain financial backing, they have trouble receiving accreditation. When they get accreditation, other participants tend not to take them seriously.

A number of crucial issues are on the table calling for the attention of women's caucuses involved in peace negotiations:

- How many women are participating in transitional governments?
- Will they participate in the drafting of new constitutions and thus be able to get gender issues into the mainstream?
- Will any war crimes tribunal take into special consideration violence committed against women?
- What protection will the international community provide to women who have taken risks?

One potentially powerful tool, whose implementation is vital to the rights of all women living in, or emerging from, conflict situations, is UN Security Council Resolution 1325 on Women, Peace, and Security. In order to effectively use this tool, African women must advocate for its implementation at the national level. The international community must support them, both politically and financially, in this endeavor.

The commitment expressed by the UN Department of Political Affairs to support the women of Mano River Women's Peace Network to participate in peace negotiations, as well as the UN Division for the Advancement of Women's support for creating national gender machinery in war-torn countries, are examples of positive responses. African women must build partnerships with other women and men from around the world who share similar interests, both in sustainable peace and gender equality.

The many obstacles to implementation of peace initiatives include the absence of a good communication network between the groups, and between them and their various constituencies. It is therefore important that an effective communication mechanism—including such tools as the Internet and e-mails—be set up and strengthened to ensure an easy flow of information among all concerned parties.

Women's groups have to seize every opportunity arising at the national or international levels. Recent initiatives in the area of postconflict peacebuilding by the United Nations, World Bank, Economic Community of West African

States, the African Union, and so on, offer the chance for women living in, or emerging from, conflict situations, to overcome the obstacles listed above, and pursue peace initiatives.

Femmes Africa Solidarité was created in 1996 from a brainstorming session with a group of women lawyers, judges, academics, and entrepreneurs, along with representatives from other nongovernmental organizations and international organizations, to promote, ensure, and give a voice to women in resolving conflicts and building peace. It functions within existing and emerging structures in Africa and as a communication network among African women.

Contacts

Femmes Africa Solidarité
8 Rue du Vieux-Billard
P.O. Box 5037
1211 Geneva, Switzerland
Tel.: +41 22 328 8050
Fax: 41 22 328 8052
E-mail: info@fasngo.org
Website: http://www.fasngo.org

MARWOPNET Secretariat
Freetown, Sierra Leone
E-mail: marwopnet@yahoo.com

Notes

1. With support from UN agencies, the African Union, Economic Commission of Africa, and the Economic Community of West African States (ECOWAS).

2. The largest members included the Coordination of Women nongovernmental organizations in Guinea, National Women NGOs of Liberia, Liberia Women's Initiative, and Sierra Leone Women's Forum. The network has six organs: a general assembly, board of directors, five multisectoral standing technical committees, three national country focal points, and a regional secretariat.

Selected Bibliography

"Africa Recovery." 2003. Vol. 16, No. 4. UN Department of Public Information, February.
Femmes Africa Solidarité. "Engendering the Peace Process in West Africa" Femmes
     Africa Solidarité online at: http://www.fasngo.org/en/publications/index.ht.
"Ford Foundation Report." 2002. Ford Foundation (Fall).

21.4

Small Steps Toward Reconciliation: The Joint Committee for Democratization and Conciliation in Moldova

Yuri Ataman

Most attempts to resolve the post-USSR conflict in Moldova have failed because of flawed processes and a lack of trust in the impartiality of the initiatives. The Joint Committee for Democratization and Conciliation, however, evolved from within communities on both sides of the conflict. It was the first local nongovernmental organization to facilitate conflict resolution attempts at all levels of leadership.

In September 1998 a week-long seminar, the second in a series, took place in Albena, Bulgaria, focusing on the unresolved conflict between the Republic of Moldova and the breakaway region of Transdniestria. The main aim of the meeting was to facilitate collaboration between governmental and nongovernmental sectors in Moldova and Transdniestria for the purpose of addressing the troubles of ordinary people. It also aimed to "kick start" the stalled processes of meditated negotiations and conflict resolution between the two governments, which had been initiated in 1993.

The seminar attracted a wide range of participants: nongovernmental organization (NGO) representatives, local and national authority leaders, journalists, businesspeople, students, housewives, lawyers, military personnel, Moldovan and Transdniestrian governmental officials, and mediating ambassadors from Russia, the Ukraine, and the Organization for Security and Cooperation in Europe (OSCE).

Interaction between all these levels of leadership was highly productive and there was a perceptible move away from entrenched positions. Two subsequent developments were attributed to discussions undertaken at the seminar: the resumption of the intergovernmental negotiations, and the reduction of peacekeeping troops in the security zone separating the two sides.

Perhaps the most remarkable aspect of the seminar was the diversity in leadership from both sides, engaging with one another, resulting in lines of interaction both vertically (within) and horizontally (between) the different camps.

The Moldovan/Transdniestrian Conflict

Moldova experienced severe problems following the disintegration of the USSR. In September 1990, as the result of a power struggle that had a significant identity-related dimension, the region lying east of the Dniester River, Transdniestria—where a majority of the population are of Russian or Ukrainian extraction—attempted to proclaim its autonomy. Armed conflict between the Moldovan authorities and the Transdniestrians broke out in March 1992. By July, when a cease-fire was imposed, hundreds had been killed and thousands had been forced to flee their homes. A security zone was created centered on the Dniester, policed by Moldovan, Transdniestrian, and Russian troops.

In 1993 the governments of Moldova and Transdniestria agreed to engage in political negotiations involving mediators from the Organization for Security and Cooperation in Europe, the Russian Federation, and Ukraine. Attempts to bring these negotiations to a successful conclusion, however, continue to be beset by seemingly insuperable difficulties.

Grassroots Efforts at Self-Help

Ordinary people were shocked and bewildered by the sudden outbreak of violence in their usually peaceful country. One cofounder of a locally based NGO expressed his feelings of incomprehension at one of the JCDC meetings:

> I could not imagine that people who had lived together for so many years, who had created so many "mixed" families, would divide on national lines, that events could lead to a violent military conflict. But our world proved to be fragile and ordinary people suddenly found themselves completely unprotected against violence. During the conflict many within the population were seized by a nationalist psychosis. Everyone was ready to go to fight against people who only yesterday had been their fellow-countrymen. We became enemies.

Many others were unable to make sense of the conflict and it was difficult to imagine what could be done to resolve it. Attempts at conflict resolution by grassroots organizations failed because of a lack of trust in the impartiality of the initiatives. Those programs that were initiated by local leaders helped distressed people, attempting to impose a code of conduct in their local regions.

An apprehensive Moldovan journalist invited Joe Camplisson into the conflict arena. Camplisson was a community development and conflict resolution specialist from Northern Ireland who had been assisting with community development needs in neighboring Romania. Shortly after Camplisson's arrival some people came together within a self-help process aimed at conflict prevention and development. They organized three conferences in 1992 held on neutral ground in the former Czechoslovakia. The first involved mainly Latin—Romanian-leaning—Moldovans; the second involved mainly Slav-leaning

Transdnestrians; and the third engaged participants from both sides of the conflict interface.

From both sides Camplisson and his associates received repeated requests for assistance with self-help attempts aiming at socioeconomic and political development and with the search for conflict resolution. Process participants from across the leadership spectrum of the divided society then initiated, individually and in groups, an extensive range of activities. In these, ordinary people engaged with political leadership and military commanders.

Meetings were also held with President Smirnov of Transdniestria and President Snegur of Moldova, both of whom made an official request to Camplisson for assistance with the resolution of the conflict. In 1994 they nominated six delegates to a conflict resolution process. (Years later, in 2004, as government ministers, some members of these delegations also represented their governments in the Pentagonal Bratislava Process of mediated negotiations.) Initial successes within this process included joint public statements by the main protagonists of their intent to treat their conflict as a problem to be solved rather than as a reason for war. They would, they said, employ only nonviolent means in the search for solutions, and pursue a win-win outcome for the conflict resolution process.

Camplisson and some of the specialists who had been assisting him formed the Moldovan Initiative Committee of Management (MICOM), and funding was obtained from Charities Aid Foundation (U.K.) and the C. S. Mott Foundation (United States). Simultaneously, Camplisson's local associates came together as the Joint Committee for Democratization and Conciliation (JCDC), drawing its membership equally from Moldova and Transdniestria.

These two organizations then began to consolidate their unique partnership. MICOM, acting as an "external third party," was able to bring a wealth of outside expertise to bear on the problems facing Moldova/Transdniestria. For its part, the JCDC, acting as a neutral "indigenous third party," brought the energy and commitment of ordinary people to bear on the search for solutions. Their capacity for initiating and facilitating meaningful self-help action was developed to a higher level.

A Multifaceted Program

In their programming, the JCDC and MICOM embarked on an ambitious program of activities that has been sustained ever since. Numerous mechanisms were utilized: facilitating workshops, study visits to Northern Ireland, seminars, and conferences. Some of these activities focused on the needs of a specific sector—NGOs, village mayors, local authority officials, and governmental representatives. Where possible, however, efforts were made to bring different levels of leadership together in a conflict resolution process to facilitate and share analysis of their most pressing problems and related needs.

The JCDC-MICOM seminar series held in Albena, Bulgaria, in 1997, 1998, 1999, and 2000 brought forward many governmental and nongovernmental initiatives. Among these were the setting up of an information center for NGOs, a mutual jazz festival in Bender, a program for assistance to unemployed people in Transdniestria, and a rehabilitation program that assists people who had been suffering from the Transdniestria conflict and the Afghan war.

Each of the seminars addressed the burning issues of the day as determined by different levels of leadership. The focus of each seminar was tailored to the specific needs of one particular sector. Working alongside that sector's leadership, however, were leaders from other levels. Participation in these seminars by the OSCE representative and the mediating Russian and Ukrainian ambassadors—at their request—became the norm. This was a clear indication of the growing importance accorded to the JCDC-MICOM program of work.

Bringing together participants with widely differing functions, positions, interests, ideologies, and backgrounds served to open many people's eyes to the breadth and scope of the problems they were confronting. It also provided an opportunity for them to develop their potential for dealing with everyday problems, as well as advancing the search for conflict resolution.

A striking feature was the clear evidence of a reversal in totalitarian perceptions and attitudes toward NGOs. This change of appreciation was identified by some of the governmental participants, one of whom remarked, "I now have a more favorable attitude to the activity of NGOs and I will try to support them." Another said, "I now have increased hope for the future knowing just how many dedicated, selfless people are striving for the good of their communities."

Governmental representatives listened to, and expressed their gratitude for, the clearly stated views of the NGOs during these seminars and workshops. NGOs on both sides of the conflict interface stressed the importance of cultural exchanges and "people's diplomacy" across the "peaceline" and between the various ethnic groups. One who was particularly enthusiastic about the work being done stated: "From now on I will strive to seek mutual understanding; I will have respect for the position of others." Another promised, "In my future work I will invite the participation of NGOs from the other side."

National and Local Impact

These seminars provided opportunities for informal meetings between governmental representatives where they could discuss issues in a manner not possible within the framework of the OSCE-mediated negotiations. In some instances, MICOM and the JCDC were able to use such meetings to overcome impasses in the negotiation process. Indeed, an increasingly productive working relationship developed between the OSCE-mediated negotiation process and the conflict resolution process being facilitated by the JCDC-MICOM partnership. Complementarity had effectively been established between the two.

The difference between these processes was evident in Moldova. The conflicting governments engaged in both processes, but each had a different influence on the resolution of the conflict. In the one, facilitated by the OSCE, they negotiated from positions of "power." It aimed at reaching a compromise agreement. In the other, facilitated by the JCDC-MICOM partnership, they had been engaging in a process of assisted analysis. It focused on sharing and explaining their respective "needs" within the circumstances. This process lent itself readily to the establishment of "parity of esteem" between the sides. In the field of conflict resolution this had not been thought possible because the one process was rooted in the "power theory" of conflict, the other in "needs theory." Some would say these are contradictory theories. The fact that complementarity between the processes nevertheless was consistently successful and demonstrably achieved has profound implications for similar situations in other countries.

Aside from successful efforts in bringing diverse levels of leadership together at a national level, the JCDC identified and enhanced local capacity for self-help through:

- Improved relationships between local people, and between them and soldiers on the checkpoints of the area. As a result, more small day-to-day situations began being resolved more easily.
- Facilitated analysis and constructive dialogue leading to collaborative action between local administrations from towns and villages on each side of the Dniester River.
- Initiation of a program in which mayors sought to clean up their respective stretches of the river and transform it into a nature preserve.
- Encouraging four towns (two from each side of the Dniester) to organize Christmas festivities involving four hundred children, who performed a concert in Transdniestria and then walked across a bridge over the Dniester to perform the same concert in Moldova.
- Organizing seminars that targeted the needs of marginalized sectors of society. One seminar, for example, endeavored to give a voice to young people and assisted in the building of a youth network. These seminars involved people from all three regions: Moldova, Transdniestria, and Gagauzia (another region of Moldova that has experienced war-related tensions).
- The JCDC was actively involved in work in the Commonwealth of Independent States (CIS) countries, being the chair in 2002–2003 of the assembly of NGOs from Belarus, Moldova, and the Ukraine dealing with conflicts, which is part of the working group of NGOs from the CIS on Prevention and Resolution of Conflicts—a network of NGOs working within the CIS.

Working Toward the Future

JCDC members are united and motivated to do something constructive about the situation. Coming together as the JCDC they found a common purpose. All members of the JCDC are volunteers. The JCDC chairman is its full-time executive director. With the support of two part-time staff he, in conjunction with MICOM's office in Northern Ireland, maintains an operational base in Moldova. The JCDC is continuously monitoring the most pressing issues of the day, while addressing the leadership needs of different sectors of society, mainly through assisted analysis and training. Whenever resources permit, the JCDC also seeks to consolidate and expand its community-development and conflict-resolution networking activities.

It is currently implementing two new programs: one entitled "Restoring the Integrity and Stability of the State—A Common Cause for All People of the Republic of Moldova," designed to assist different leadership levels in their attempts to determine their respective roles in relation to the processes of state reform and resolution of the conflict. The other, entitled "Strengthening Cooperation Between Local Authorities and Civil Society," is part of the Peacebuilding Framework Project involving Moldova, Transdniestria, and Gagauzia.

The work is not finished in Moldova, but as one member of JCDC pointed out to me:

> In the beginning I was not sure that the problems could be solved and I am not sure even now that they will be, but what the Committee [JCDC] does is to move us with small steps towards resolution. We can see results and this is positive. There was a time when the work of the Committee was in a dead-lock and there were even doubts if it would be able to exist, but the other members managed to allay my doubts.

Yuri Ataman is JCDC's chairman and executive director.

Contact

*Joint Committee for Democratization
    and Conciliation (JCDC)*
6 Botanica Veche Street, apt. 103
MD 2062 Chisinau
Republic of Moldava
Tel./Fax: + 373 (22) 530 751
E-mail: ataman@mdl.net

Selected Bibliography

Hall, Michael. 2002. *From Conflict Containment to Resolution: The Experiences of a Moldovan-Northern Ireland Self-Help Initiative* (Newtownabbey, Northern Ireland: Island Publications), online at: http://cain.ulst.ac.uk/islandpublications/.

Hall, Michael, ed. 2004. "The Search for Resolution: Lessons Drawn from a Community Development Strategy." Island Pamphlets No. 61 (Newtownabbey, Northern Ireland: Island Publications), online at: http://cain.ulst.ac.uk/islandpublications/.

Matthews, Dylan. 2001. *War Prevention Works: 50 Stories of People Resolving Conflict* (Oxford: Oxford Research Group).

Nan, Susan Allan. Unpublished thesis. George Mason University.

21.5

A Second Way:
Grupo Maryland Between Peru and Ecuador

Inés Cevallos Breilh and Sahary Betancourt

Civil-society leaders played an important role in the process that led to the signing, in 1998, of a peace treaty that settled a protracted border dispute between Peru and Ecuador. Their role in fostering conditions for wide acceptance of that agreement offers a model for dealing with such conflicts in the future.

In 1995, for the third time since 1941, Peru and Ecuador went to war over a disputed frontier region in the Amazon Basin. The skirmishes that took place in Alto Cenepa were the most serious of the three armed clashes. On this occasion, the confrontation triggered an intense process of diplomatic negotiations. There were calls for a ceasefire, a separation of forces, and negotiations to find a definitive settlement to the longest-running border dispute in the Western Hemisphere.

The diplomatic initiatives concluded, eventually, with the signing of a peace accord on 26 October 1998, in Brasilia. Running parallel to the diplomatic moves, was a process referred to as "citizen diplomacy"—an initiative in which civil-society groups discussed issues underlying the conflict, and ways of resolving it without official and diplomatic constraints. This took place under the auspices of a long-term program run by the University of Maryland from the United States called "A Culture for Democracy in Latin America." One of the projects included in this program got different partners, including the Pontificia Catholic University of Ecuador, to establish an Innovative Problem Solving Workshop under the theme "Ecuador and Peru: Towards a Democratic and Cooperative Conflict Resolution Initiative."

Finding Common Ground
The workshop took place in August 1997. Some twenty members of both Ecuadorian and Peruvian civil society, including academics, businesspeople, civic education and human rights specialists, journalists, and representatives of

environmental nongovernmental organizations, attended it. The aim was to help these individuals and groups establish their roles as stakeholders in the conflict and find and define a common ground from which to look for its resolution.

The dialogue between civil-society groups from Peru and Ecuador— referred to as Track Two diplomacy—centered around a series of workshops. Track One was the official diplomatic activity involving three Latin American nations—Brazil, Argentina, and Chile—and the United States, as the regional superpower. These countries were neutral guarantors of a 1942 treaty that settled the first border war.

According to Edy Kaufman and Saúl Sosnowski, in a background paper on the process:

> The peace treaty signed by Ecuador and Peru in October 1998 was not only the culmination of a successful and, at times, difficult diplomatic process; it was the faithful reflection of the transformation of society in both countries that shored up official diplomacy in order to achieve a bi-national consensus for peace. By this means, the longest-standing border conflict in the Western Hemisphere reached its end with a culture of peace, hopefully difficult to derail, and likely to become the norm between the two nations. (Kaufman and Sosnowski 2004: 175)

The input provided by the respective civil societies in the diplomatic process was indispensable to the eventual outcome. The direct involvement of the various groups, helped create useful lines of communication between official negotiations and nonofficial contacts. This made the negotiators aware of the sentiments existing among citizens—and ensured acceptance that the agreements, once signed, would be accepted by ordinary citizens, who were, in fact, the real actors who must deal with its implementation.

The Grupo Maryland, as the civil-society leaders were known, drew on a method developed at Maryland's Center for International Development and Conflict Management. Their efforts and ideas were carried out through a series of workshops. The first one, held in Maryland in August 1997, took place while diplomatic activity was in full swing, involving the foreign ministers of Ecuador and Peru and the guarantor countries.

Participants, designated "partners in conflict," were chosen because they shared common traits related to profession, gender, age, location, and the like. Efforts were made to understand what each group and individual wanted. What were their needs? What motivated them? Through a process of problem solving, common ground was sought among participants through written consensus. This involved getting them to personally accept their shared understanding of the roots of the conflict, and ways of resolving them.

The workshop format and methodology allowed participants to express themselves freely in a confidential atmosphere. In this atmosphere, fresh approaches and ideas were raised. The high status of some of the participants themselves was helpful. Several were prominent individuals whose views were respected by those involved in the Track One diplomacy.

The "partners" were divided into working groups dealing with their specific areas of expertise. Ten persons were invited from each country. They were encouraged to speak their minds. These working groups studied the role of civil society in the context of negotiations between the two countries, with the objective of getting them to discover ways in which they could contribute to the ongoing process between the two governments. Participants analyzed the origin of the conflict and explored fresh ideas for resolving it, without resorting to violence, and in a democratic context.

Most agreed the frontier conflict tended to resurface whenever there were problems between the civilian and military inside each country, or at times of significant political change. Others said the real reason for the conflict was the social changes under way within the two countries. Some traced the war attitudes to the education system of the two countries, which inculcated such ideas in children.

Using methods emerging from conflict resolution workshops held in other regions of the world, the participants followed a number of steps and engaged in various exercises, including trying to imagine an ideal for relations between Ecuador and Peru thirty years from now. Answers ranged from the existence of stronger political and economic ties to greater cooperation—including disappearance of the frontier; more efficient management of natural resources; integration of infrastructure such as highways, electricity, water, and the like, integration of the two populations; enhanced presence of civil society in governmental decisions; greater democratic participation; and creation of allied programs to fight the socioeconomic crisis and poverty.

They were then asked to change perspectives and imagine the worst possible scenario: What would happen if the conflict was not resolved for another fifty years? Some of the scenarios painted included continued confrontation and conflicts; slowdown in economic development and growth; irrational exploitation of the land and the subsoil, affecting the ecosystem of the zone in conflict; and violent colonization of each side of the frontier, leading to increase in poverty and displacement of the native communities.

Some participants pointed out that in polarized societies such as Ecuador and Peru, powerful people benefited from these confrontations, and that arms manufacturers were also beneficiaries. They concluded that the main question was how to create a culture of conciliation in educated societies to manage a conflict culture internally and externally.

Each member was asked to explain the official position of his or her government. Participants from the two countries painted two completely different realities—convinced it was the correct one. In the "reflective" stage of the project, they were encouraged to listen to one another and find ways of communicating. The groups were divided to discuss designated areas that could be seen as the foundations of the conflict, such as historical, cultural, economic, political, geographic, paradigmatic, and psychological root causes.

Members also pointed out that the press could be used to manipulate information to influence public opinion. The "rain of ideas," an elaboration of proposals and activities that could be undertaken by civil society, followed this step. Five work groups were set up to examine the environmental problems of the region, the role of the press, the role of businessmen in the development of the economy, and possible contributions of civil society to official diplomacy.

Mood of Optimism

By the time of the second workshop, which took place at the Pontificia Catholic University of Ecuador in Cashapamba—near Quito—in March 1998, progress in formal diplomatic negotiations created a mood of optimism, though there were still unresolved problems.

More participants were invited to this second meeting, including several representatives of the indigenous people living in the conflict area, and members of the Church, to provide real knowledge of the situation on the ground. Since some participants from the earlier workshop had, by this time, been invited to become official members of the diplomatic process, new participants replaced them.

The focus was on concrete actions that each member could take, given his own professional position. Goals set earlier were reviewed. Particular attention was paid to political order and psychological impact that could condition implementation of the ideas when presented in another context. Topics discussed included determining the actual border region.

The workshop featured a reflective phase during which subjects of a binational nature were raised. Participants were encouraged to examine "mutual confidence measures" that could reduce tensions and prevent confrontations. This whole exercise established the necessity of identifying common interests that could change conflict situations and opportunities for cooperation.

Many proposals from various work groups were presented to the press, citizens' participation groups, and businesses. A Declaration of Cashapamba was produced, and details of the proceedings were reported in a newsletter that was sent to media outlets in the two countries and presented to an Ecuadorian minister and the ambassador of Peru.

The presidents of the chambers of commerce of Lima and Quito signed a cooperation agreement. Looking back, one of them, Hugo Sologuren Calmet, president of the Lima Chamber of Commerce, commented:

> The academic exercise through which we presented our positions regarding the conflict, allowed for the mutual internalization of an issue that can only be resolved through negotiation. From this perspective, the business sector has already made progress. The chambers of commerce of Quito, Guayaquil, and Lima have recently subscribed to a treaty of cooperation. Business people from both countries have met on the border to reaffirm bonds of friendship and fraternity that join them. Delegations of Ecuadorean business people have traveled many times this year to Lima. (Latin America Center n.d.)

Continuing the Process

A third workshop, in 1999, in El Pueblo, a village center not far from Lima, the Peruvian capital, concentrated on reinforcing the new peace treaty drafted by officials in the Track One sessions, and ways of implementing some of the ideas raised by the participants themselves. The officer in charge of implementing the peace agreement was asked to join the group. The foreign ministers from both countries were invited to attend, in their personal capacities, and share their views with participants.

A Legacy of Colonial Rule

The border dispute between Ecuador and Peru is a legacy of colonial rule. Spain governed both countries; when they declared independence in the early part of the nineteenth century, their exact perimeters were not clearly defined. From the 1820s onwards, leaders of the two new republics of Ecuador and Peru used the threat of foreign invasion of sovereign territory as a convenient rallying cry whenever domestic and political upheavals threatened. This practice was facilitated by the rough and barren nature of the terrain in the disputed region, and the lack of clear documentary evidence as to its ownership.

In 1887, both countries agreed to submit the dispute to international arbitration under the King of Spain, without discarding the possibility of reaching a negotiated solution on their own. In April 1910, as the arbiter prepared to issue his ruling, the two nations mobilized their armies in the border region. The arbiter resigned, fearing his pronouncement would trigger a war.

Unable to reach agreement on their own, Ecuador and Peru continued to dispute ownership. In 1941, they went to war over it. Peru won. The Rio de Janeiro Protocol, an international treaty, established norms for a definitive solution. Four countries were named as guarantors—Argentina, Brazil, Chile, and the United States.

The treaty was never fully accepted by Ecuadorians—who, as the losing side in the 1941 war, were forced to accept conditions considered damaging. In 1981, there was another conflict, in which Peru again imposed its military superiority. This was followed by another, in 1995, in which Ecuador prevailed.

For the fourth and final workshop, in Cuenca, Ecuador, in August 2000, Grupo Maryland tried to strengthen planning and implementation of joint ventures between Peruvian and Ecuadorian institutions and people in the border regions. Participants felt it was essential that multiple steps be taken to "broaden fraternization among different social sectors." Further, it urged citizens to watch carefully what was done with funds destined for border development.

This workshop ended with the adoption of twelve recommendations for civil society in Ecuador and Peru. These covered areas such as greater citizen participation, supporting sustainable development projects in the disputed border region, paying attention to issues like health care, taking account of the interests of indigenous peoples, and the involvement of the press, trade unions, educational institutions, popular organizations, and other groups.

The experience taught that this "second way" or citizen diplomacy offered a new approach to conflict resolution in Latin America. It was possible to carry out such a program because of the high level of development achieved by civil society in Latin America over the last two decades, and the interest shown by professionals in alternative methods of conflict resolution.

Conclusions

Grupo Maryland has demonstrated that conflict resolution is an important component in efforts to reinforce democratic institutions and to create a democratic culture. An effective democracy cannot be defined only as having a representative government of the majority; it also means the existence of different ideas.

The ideas raised and discussed at the Grupo Maryland workshops were taken onboard during the diplomatic talks, and played an important role in the peace process that ended with the signing of an agreement between the two countries. Some of the projects proposed are developing slowly, consolidating union and confidence between the populations of the two countries.

These meetings generated new and creative solutions to the conflict and raised awareness and eagerness for peace within the civil societies of both countries. The relationship of cooperation and trust was maintained after the signing of the peace agreement, leading to improved relations between important sectors of the neighboring countries. It had not been the first such agreement, which taught that such documents alone do not hold guarantees. However, the active role of civil society before, during, and after the peace process might have been the key to holding onto the process this time.

The involvement of civil society represented a strong message for governments of the two countries that the people were truly in search of a common ground for peace. The fact that some participants at the first meeting were invited to become part of the official peace process not only shows that this message was heard, but also that it was appreciated and recognized as being of great importance.

Inés Cevallos Breilh and Sahary Betancourt worked at the Pontificia Catholic University of Ecuador and assisted both in organizing and researching for the Grupo Maryland activities. Inés Cevallos Breihl still works for Pontificia Catholic University; Sahary Betancourt now works for the Italian Embassy in Quito, Ecuador.

Contact

Inés Cevallos Breilh
Pontificia Universidad Católica del
    Ecuador
Tel.: +593 (2) 299 1582 or 09 70 99 549
E-mail: icevallosb@puce.edu.ec
Websites:
    http://www.puce.edu.ec (Pontificia
    Universidad Catolicá de Ecuador)

http://www.umd.edu/LAS (Latin
    American Studies Center of the
    University of Maryland, College
    Park)

Sahary Betancourt
E-mail: uffcont@ambitalquito.org

Selected Bibliography

"Ecuador and Peru: Toward a Democratic and Cooperative Conflict Resolution Initiative." Online at: http://www.inform.umd/edu/LAS/Publications/Newsletter/volVIII.1/peruador.htm.

Grupo Maryland Ecuador-Perú. Online at: http://www.inform.umd.edu/LAS/Projects/grupomaryland/relatorio3.htm.

Kaufman, Edy, and Sául Sosnowski. 2004. "The Peru-Ecuador Peace Process: The Contribution of Track Two Diplomacy" in Ronald J. Fisher, ed., *Paving the Way: Contributions of Interactive Conflict Resolution to Peacemaking* (Lanham, MD: Rowman and Littlefield, pp. 175–202).

Latin American Studies Center. n.d. "Grupo Maryland Ecuador-Peru, Conflict Resolution Initiative, 1997." Online at: http://www.informumd.edu/LAS?Projects?grupomaryland/conferencia.html.

22

Disarmament, Demobilization, and Reintegration: Not Only a Job for Soldiers

Sami Faltas and Wolf-Christian Paes

Former United Nations secretary-general Dag Hammarskjöld is believed to have said, "Peacekeeping is not a job for soldiers, but only soldiers can do it."[1] Over the years, this has become a cliché, quoted time and again in speeches and articles. How much sense does this paradoxical adage make today? In one way, it is still valid. Soldiers are still needed for peacekeeping, even though they are often poorly prepared for it. However in other ways, the old chestnut deserves a rest. Clearly, in the past decades, peacekeeping has become "a job for soldiers," but it has always been absurd to claim that "only a soldier can do it."[2] In these days, it is clear that there are also important roles to play for the nonmilitary actors such as the clergy, professionals of all sorts, and nongovernmental organizations. This chapter will examine these roles.

Military Preeminence

Since the end of the Cold War, peacekeeping has become a highly visible, increasingly familiar, and very important and honorable mission for the military. In a large and growing number of countries all over the world, military peacekeeping has become integral to defense and foreign policy. As peace operations multiplied in the 1980s and 1990s, the military enhanced their predominance. Increasingly, they were considered the professionals par excellence who are called in to do the job, even if ultimately the politicians remain in control. This is easy to understand. Nothing signals the will of the international community to preserve the peace as powerfully as the arrival of Hercules or Antonov troopships carrying large numbers of armed and presumably neutral peacekeepers. In the tense and uncertain conditions just before or after a war, military peacekeepers can potentially provide the stability that may preserve the peace.

So strongly is peacekeeping associated with the trademark "blue helmets" of UN peacekeeping units that one might overlook or underrate the essential roles played by civilians. Diplomats, politicians, civil administrators, observers, police officers, religious leaders, teachers, doctors, businesspeople, and many other civilians are usually needed to help consolidate the peace. No one would seriously claim today that civilians should keep out of peacekeeping, but there is a tendency to focus on the military element as the most important and to relegate civilian elements to supportive roles.

What do we mean by the predominance of the military in peace operations? The problem is not a lack of civilian control. The force commander of a UN peace operation reports to the head of the UN mission, the special representative of the secretary-general (SRSG). From the SRSG upward, the chain of responsibility is entirely civilian. The UN secretary-general is the servant of the UN Security Council, which comprises the representatives of fifteen national governments. In theory, and sometimes also in practice, these governments are accountable to elected parliaments. In many countries, independent media and civil-society groups also monitor their actions. Similar arrangements are made in peace operations that are not conducted by the United Nations (UN), but by regional organizations or national governments. As a rule, military peacekeepers are under civilian control.

Nor can one claim that military peacekeepers always get what they want. In many cases, they get much less than they need, with grave consequences. Some of the worst disasters of peacekeeping can be traced to the failure of politicians to give the military the troops, the equipment, the authority, and the guidance they needed to do the job properly.

The point we are making is that military perceptions, military requirements, military ways of doing things and military "facts on the ground" have a strong influence on peace operations. This may be due to the unique functions of the military, their high visibility, the resources they consume, and the risks to which they are exposed, compared with other actors. They dominate because they are the first in line, and no one else is taken equally seriously.

Soldiers are sometimes charged with tasks that would normally be done by civilians. Whether this is appropriate is always open to question. In 2000, Condoleezza Rice, soon to become George W. Bush's national security adviser and currently the newly appointed U.S. secretary of state, said with regard to Kosovo, "Carrying out civil administration and police functions is . . . going to degrade the American capability to do the things America has to do. We don't need to have the 82nd Airborne escorting kids to kindergarten" (*Washington Post*, 23 October 2000). Sending children back to school is important both in its own right and as a symbol of restored peace. The issue is whether this needs to be done by soldiers.

In this chapter we are concerned with the role of civil society in peacebuilding. We will focus on the removal of the tools of war from postconflict societies, as well as the demobilization and reintegration of fighters. We will not dispute that soldiers have a crucial key role to play in peace operations, but we will criticize the preeminence hegemony of the military and stress the need for civil society to assert itself, to be heard, and to actively involve itself in peacebuilding.

Building Peace After Conflict

When an armed conflict comes to an end as the result of a peace settlement or a military victory, this does not mean that peace has come to stay. In a sense, this is when the real trouble begins. People face a ravaged and volatile society. Repairing the physical infrastructure will be a big challenge. Treating the wounds, grievances, and traumas torn by years of violence and hatred will be even more difficult. One needs to remember that these changes are not linear. Building peace is not like building a wall, brick by brick. It is full of break-throughs and setbacks. In places such as Afghanistan, Angola, Colombia, Liberia, and Sierra Leone, all too often "after the war is before the war." Even after the fighting has stopped, the logic that led to war will persist until it is replaced by the logic of peace.

Unless the fundamental political and socioeconomic causes of the conflict are removed quickly, a return to warfare will remain a distinct possibility. This is particularly the case if "peace" is brought about not so much by a settlement among exhausted parties but rather by the intervention of the international community. In this case the superior military power might force groups to accept a peace agreement even though they feel cheated out of victory. The international presence might gloss over some of the grievances that drove the conflict, but this will not build a sustainable peace.

The most important actors in a peace process are the former enemies and their communities. If they are serious about turning their backs on war, this is the best foundation for peace. However, they often need external assistance. If this is not available in time, in adequate amounts, and in an appropriate form, the peace process may fail. Unfortunately, the countries that would be in a position to provide such help are not always willing to allocate sufficient funds, equipment, and troops for peace operations, especially if they have no strategic interest in the area concerned.

However, even when donor countries have shown a strong commitment—for example, in the Balkans, Afghanistan, and Iraq—winning the war has proved easier than winning the peace. International peacekeeping forces have great difficulties in combating armed groups employing traditional guerrilla tactics, particularly if their members enjoy some support among the civilian population. While these militia groups are unlikely to win an outright military victory, their actions can make a country ungovernable. If this is combined with the international reluctance to establish a permanent military presence and the onset of donor fatigue, it is often just a matter of time before the peacekeepers are withdrawn.

One of the key challenges of any postconflict situation is the disarmament and demobilization of the armed groups and the reintegration of their members into civilian society. Ex-combatants not properly demobilized form a pool of dangerous individuals, who can be easily tapped by politicians or criminals seeking recruits for new endeavors. Similarly, weapons and ammunition left behind after a conflict—or looted from state-run arms depots—often find their way into the hands of criminals or political opportunists. Given their physical nature, small arms and light weapons are particularly prone to be smuggled across regional borders. Following the end of the civil war in Mozambique in the mid-1990s, many AK-47 assault rifles ended up in the hands of criminals in neighboring South Africa, which was then at the peak of a crime wave. Similarly, when more than half a million firearms were stolen from police stations and military depots in Albania in 1997, Albanian insurgents and criminal groups all over the southern Balkans benefited from the sudden increase in supply.

The *R* Is Different from the *D*'s

There are two distinct phases in the disarmament, demobilization, and re-integration (DDR) process. During the first phase, often spanning a period of a few months to one year after the cease-fire, cantonment sites are established where fighters assemble, hand in their weapons, and receive medical attention. Often they are also offered financial incentives, vocational training, and trauma counseling. During this critical time period, peacekeeping forces provide security and mediate between the warring factions, while the actual imple-mentation of the demobilization process often rests with civilian organizations.

If disarmament is mostly a military function, demobilization is in essence a civilian operation (Gleichmann et al. 2004), and needs to be carefully attuned to subsequent reintegration. All too often, the people in charge of de-mobilization promise the ex-combatants benefits that the reintegration pro-gram is unable to provide.

The second (reintegration) phase of the process starts with the departure of the ex-fighters from the cantonment site and lasts until they have successfully returned to civilian life. Numerous studies (Pauwels 2000; Kingma 2000) have shown that this part of the process can easily take up to ten years. Its length is directly related to the duration and scope of the conflict: the longer the fighting took, the more difficult it will be for combatants to return to civilian life as a result of severed social ties and traumatization.

Similarly, it is easier for a society to absorb former combatants if the fighting directly affected only a comparatively small number of people, leaving the social fabric largely intact. Obviously, if the infrastructure has not been severely degraded, and the economy is growing, it will be easier for ex-combatants to find a new livelihood. Unfortunately, these favorable conditions are not often encountered in the aftermath of today's wars.

The countries that once formed Yugoslavia are, in that sense, luckier than most. Due to the short duration of their wars in Kosovo (Heinemann-Grüder and Paes 2001) and Macedonia (Matveeva et al. 2003), many former fighters were able to return to their families without the assistance of a formal de-mobilization program. The challenge is much greater in Afghanistan and Angola, where wars were raging for decades. Unfortunately, the challenges of this second phase are often underestimated by program planners, and inadequately funded.

Rehabilitation and emergency relief funds are usually highest immediately after the end of fighting (when the capacity of a country to absorb them is the lowest) and then dry up completely after a period of three to five years when international attention is captured by events elsewhere.

Bringing in the Civilians

One can identify several obstacles to the establishment of a sustainable peace following a period of armed conflict. Some of these may have already existed before the original conflict broke out, while others were caused by the fighting:

- Grievances, such as the distribution of power and resources between competing ethnic, religious, social, or political groups
- Mistrust and feelings of hatred toward parties that are held responsible for committing atrocities during the conflict
- Traumas and the establishment of a "culture of violence" whereby people who have experienced warfare themselves are accustomed to solve conflicts by violent means
- Destitution and lack of a perspective among former fighters who have often learned no civilian skills and who find it hard to return to civilian life
- The destruction of a country's infrastructure and public services, combined with a lack of economic opportunities

Frequently, these problems are compounded by slow, uncoordinated, and ill-advised attempts to help on the part of what is optimistically called the international community. Donors often engage in wishful thinking, basing their assistance projects on creating ideal outcomes instead of making a realistic assessment of possible scenarios and preventing the worst of them from happening.

Some or all of these factors might be experienced collectively or individually by former members of the armed factions. Returning to their villages after long periods of absence, they may find themselves less than welcome, their land and cattle lost, and family ties cut. Others might prefer not to return to their place of origin because they fear retribution for atrocities committed during the conflict. Without much of an economic perspective, the relief usually experienced after the cease-fire often gives way to new grievances— under these circumstances some may return to a life of violence. This is made easier by the fact that armed groups rarely ever demobilize completely. Usually substantial amounts of arms and ammunition are hidden in caches as a form of "life insurance," while many former fighters retain some informal contacts to their former comrades-in-arms.

In a nutshell, if peace is to become durable, the challenge for civil society is to overcome these obstacles by contributing to psychological and spiritual healing and by assisting the reintegration of former combatants. This is not, nor can it be, primarily a job for the military.

Some Western armed forces have started to complement their peacekeeping role with limited relief activities, such as the distribution of food assistance to refugees and the rehabilitation of wells, hospitals, and schools under the label of "civilian-military cooperation." For example, in Afghanistan the allied forces have established Provincial Reconstruction Teams in a number of locations that are supposed to integrate relief activities with peacekeeping duties. Many humanitarian and development agencies are very critical of such attempts to merge military and civilian functions (Heinemann-Grüder and Pietz 2004). Besides, there is reason to question the cost-effectiveness of using soldiers for such tasks.

Assisting in the healing of a nation is a task that rests squarely on the shoulders of civil society, most particularly religious leaders and bodies. Seeking reconciliation—for example, through the establishment of Truth and Reconciliation Commissions during the 1990s in South Africa and Guatemala—would be more difficult, if not outright impossible, without the leadership of the clergy. Elsewhere, the churches take the biblical word of turning swords into ploughshares literally by collecting weapons among the civilian population and handing out tools such as sewing machines and bicycles in return. The best-known project of this kind was started in Mozambique by the Anglican Bishop Dinis Sengulane in 1995. Called the Transforming of Arms into Ploughshares Project, it combines elements of civic education with the collection of weapons, some of which are then turned into pieces of art (Faltas and Paes 2004) (See Chapter 22.2).

Elsewhere, secular organizations such as the Patriotic Movement Against Crime (Movimiento Patriótico Contra la Delincuencia; MPCD) in El Salvador rose to the challenge of mopping up weapons left behind among the civilian population after protracted civil wars. With the support of the business community, which felt particularly threatened by the raise in violent crime following the end of the war, MPCD in 1996 launched a Goods for Guns program that provided agricultural tools and sewing machines in exchange for weapons. The organizers stress that this is not a buy-back program but that citizens would be compensated for their "contribution to the development of a peaceful and secure future for El Salvador." This underlines one of the often forgotten aspects of voluntary weapons collection—while removing a deadly weapon from society is important, the fact that people surrender weapons for a nominal reward can be even more beneficial by helping to establish trust between communities (Laurance and Godnick 2001). Unfortunately, in many postconflict countries, business is unable or unwilling to engage in such peacebuilding efforts.

Linking Peacebuilding to Development

It seems obvious that sustainable peace will be hard to achieve in the absence of economic opportunities and human development. It is equally clear that development can hardly be sustainable in conditions of violence and insecurity. At present, the realization is growing in circles of international development cooperation that in postwar societies, poverty reduction and improved security must go hand-in-hand. It is only recently that the development community has begun to overcome its aversion against engaging with former combatants in an attempt to assist their reintegration into civilian life.

In this context, program planners are often facing the following difficult question: Should we focus on former fighters in an attempt to steer them out of the way of future trouble (and in a way rewarding the perpetrators by offering privileged access to job creation and training programs)? Or should our programs focus on more vulnerable groups, such as women, children, and refugees (which would have little direct impact on the stabilization of a peace process)? One possible answer to this problem is to do both. Community development programs, which directly benefit larger segments of the population by rehabilitating the public infrastructure, can also serve to provide training, jobs, and rehabilitation for former combatants.

Something along these lines was attempted by the UN Development Program (UNDP) and the International Organization for Migration (IOM) in the Republic of Congo (Congo-Brazzaville), which experienced a bloody civil war during the 1990s. Unlike most other DDR programs, this one did not take part in the context of international peacekeeping and did not provide for collective "phase one" demobilization in a cantonment area. The program assisted some 7,250 ex-combatants and helped to collect and destroy more than eleven thousand weapons. In addition to very limited vocational training (one of the weaknesses of the project), the former fighters were helped to establish 2,270 microproject enterprises, which provide income-generating opportunities. Some established small businesses, while others took up paid employment in government agencies and private companies. The program was supplemented by a separate but related community-development project also run by UNDP that provided job opportunities in the reconstruction of the communal infrastructure. While this project benefited the whole community, it offered former fighters work experience and the opportunity to rehabilitate themselves in the eyes of communities affected by the war (Haden and Faltas 2004).

It must be added, though, that while micro enterprise is a positive intervention, the international community should not assume that all ex-combatants in developing countries (or elsewhere for that matter) are born entrepreneurs, the same way as many people in the developed world are not capable of running a business either. This kind of microeconomic activity is useful at an initial stage but it can in no way be a substitute for medium- and large-scale economic activity, be it industrial, agricultural, infrastructural, or any other type of upscaled economic activity that provides sustained employment.

Some of the first successful attempts to link community development with disarmament in a country that had not experienced recent armed conflict were the "weapons for development projects" run by UNDP between 1999 and 2004 in Albania. During the riots of 1997, the Albanian government requested UN assistance in retrieving some of these weapons. During a pilot project in the

Gramsh District, UNDP pioneered the idea of linking development grants to the surrender of weapons.

By using collective rather than individual rewards, it was hoped that the project would benefit the whole community (rather than just those individuals who had stolen the arms). It also wanted to encourage local people to apply peer pressure on their more reluctant neighbors to ensure that the weapons collection program would meet its goal. UNDP later introduced a nationwide competition for development grants. These were now awarded to those communities collecting the most weapons in relation to the population number. The development activities included upgrading the physical infrastructure, such as access roads, the urban lighting system, and telecommunications equipment, and renovating post offices, and constructing footbridges.

While the total number of arms that UNDP-sponsored projects have collected so far in Albania—some twenty thousand—pales in comparison with the number of weapons still at large, the projects have been extremely successful in raising awareness about the danger of civilian-held illicit weapons and by promoting a culture of peace (Faltas and Paes 2003).

Everyone's Job

Half a century ago, civilians such as Lester Pearson [3] and Dag Hammarskjöld helped to establish a clear and legitimate role for soldiers in peacekeeping. Today, we need to reassert the role of civilians and civilian organizations in the keeping and building of peace. No one will dispute that there is a need for civil-military cooperation in the quest for sustainable peace, but there is great uncertainty about how best to go about such cooperation.

Building peace is everyone's job. Soldiers are needed to provide the order that will allow a fragile peace to grow, and to disarm combatants. Their help is also required in demobilizing combatants, though that is mostly a job for civilian administrators, doctors, and trainers. In becoming civilians and members of communities, ex-combatants will again need the help of development workers, trainers, and other professionals. Religious leaders, traditional chiefs, and other people of influence will also have an important role to play. Yet most of all, the former fighters will need families and communities who are willing to open their doors and their hearts to them, despite all the problems that can be expected. Here lies the biggest challenge of all.

Sami Faltas runs the Centre for European Security Studies (CESS) in Groningen, the Netherlands. At CESS, his work includes research, consultancy, project evaluation, and training on the prevention of violent conflict, security-sector reform, the control of small arms and light weapons, and the disarmament, demobilization, and reintegration of combatants. CESS engages in research and training on transparency and accountability in the security sector.

Wolf-Christian Paes works as a senior researcher and project manager at the Bonn International Center for Conversion (BICC). His work is focused on disarmament and demobilization in sub-Sahara Africa and on the Balkans, and he currently manages BICC's research program on resource conflicts.

Notes

1. However, the UN Archives in New York, the Hammarskjöld archivist at the Royal Library in Sweden, several friends and colleagues of Dag Hammarskjöld, and the authors of this chapter were unable to verify the quotation.

2. It is obvious from Hammarskjöld's writings that he considered military-civilian cooperation essential to the success of peace operations.

3. Lester B. Pearson was president of the Seventh UN General Assembly and was in 1957 awarded a Nobel Peace Prize for his greatest diplomatic achievement, the proposal of sending a UN peacekeeping force to the Suez Canal.

Selected Bibliography

Faltas, Sami, and Wolf-Christian Paes. 2004. "Exchanging Guns for Tools: The TAE Approach to Practical Disarmament—An Assessment of the TAE Project in Mozambique" (Bonn: BICC). Online at: http://www.bicc.de.

———. 2003." 'You Have Removed the Devil From Our Door': An Assessment of the UNDP Small Arms and Light Weapons Control (SALWC) Project in Albania" (Belgrade: SEESAC). Online at: http://www.seesac.org.

Gleichmann, Colin, Michael Odenwald, Kees Steenken, and Adrian Wilkinson. 2004. *Disarmament, Demobilisation, and Reintegration: A Practical Field and Class-room Guide* (Eschborn: GTZ/NODEFIC/PPC, SNDC).

Haden, Philippa, and Sami Faltas. 2004. "Assessing and Reviewing the Impact of Small Arms Projects on Arms Availability and Poverty: A Case Study of the Republic of Congo's UNDP/IOM Ex-Combatants Reintegration and Small Arms Collection Project" (Bradford, England: University of Bradford).

Heinemann-Grüder, Andreas, and Wolf-Christian Paes. 2001. "Wag the Dog: The Mobilization and Demobilization of the Kosovo Liberation Army" (Bonn: BICC). Online: http://www.bicc.de.

Heinemann-Grüder, Andreas, and Tobias Pietz. 2004. "Zivil-Militärische Inter-vention—Militär als Entwicklungshelfer," in Christoph Weller, Ulrich Ratsch, Reinhard Mutz, Bruno Schoch, and Corinna Hauswedell, eds., *Friedensgutachten 2004* (Münster, Germany: LIT Verlag).

Kingma, Kees, ed. 2000. *Demobilization in sub-Saharan Africa: The Development and Security Impacts* (Basingstoke, England: Macmillan Press).

Laurance, Edward J., and William H. Godnick. 2001. "Weapons Collection in Central America: El Salvador and Guatemala," in Sami Faltas and Joseph Di Chiaro III, eds., *Managing the Remnants of War: Micro-Disarmament as an Element of Peace-Building* (Baden-Baden, Germany: Nomos Verlagsgesellschaft).

Matveeva, Anna, with Duncan Hiscock, Wolf-Christian Paes, and Hans Risser. 2003. *Macedonia—Guns, Policing and Ethnic Division* (London: Saferworld). Online at: http://www.saferworld.org.uk.

Pauwels, Natalie, ed. 2000. *War Force to Work Force—Global Perspectives on Demobili-zation and Reintegration* (Baden-Baden, Germany: Nomos Verlagsgesellschaft).

Resources

Lead Organizations

Bonn International Center for Conversion— Germany
E-mail: bicc@bicc.de
Website: http://www.bicc.de

Institute for Security Studies— South Africa
Arms Management Programme
E-mail: iss@iss.org.za
Website: http://www.iss.org.za

*Institute of Peace and Conflict Studies—
    India*
Disarmament, Arms Control, and
    Security Programmes
E-mail: officemail@ipcs.org
Website: http://www.ipcs.org

*International Action Network Against
    Small Arms (IANSA)—United
    Kingdom*
E-mail: contact@iansa.org
Website: http://www.iansa.org

*SAND Programme on Security and
    Development—United States*
Website: http://sand.miis.edu

*United Nations Institute for
    Disarmament Research (UNIDIR)—
    Switzerland*
E-mail: unidir@unog.ch
Website: http://www.unog.ch/unidir

*UNDP Bureau for Crisis Prevention and
    Recovery—United States*
Small Arms and Demobilization Unit
E-mail: bcpr@undp.org
Website:
    http://www.undp.org/bcpr/
    smallarms/index.htm

Publications

Alusala, Nelson, and Thokozani Thusi. *A Step Towards Peace: Disarmament in Africa.*
    Pretoria, South Africa: Institute for Security Studies, 2004.
Date Bah, Eugenia, ed. *Jobs After War. A Critical Challenge in the Peace and
    Reconciliation Puzzle.* Geneva: International Labour Office, 2003.
Faltas, Sami, and Joseph Di Chiaro, eds. *Managing the Remnants of War: Micro-
    Disarmament as an Element of Peace-Building.* Baden-Baden, Germany: Nomos
    Verlag, 2001.
Farr, Vanessa. "Gendering Demobilization as a Peacebuilding Tool." Paper 20. Bonn:
    Bonn International Center for Conversion, 2002.
Fischer, Martina. "Recovering from Violent Conflict: Regeneration and (Re)Integration
    as Elements of Peacebuilding," in Alex Austin, Martina Fischer, and Norbert
    Ropers, eds., *Transforming Ethnopolitical Conflict: The Berghof Handbook.* Wies-
    baden, Germany: Berghof Research Center for Constructive Conflict Management
    and VS Verlag, 2004, pp. 373–402.
International Peace Academy and UNDP. *A Framework for Lasting Disarmament,
    Demobilization, and Reintegration of Former Combatants in Crisis Situations.*
    New York: IPA and UNDP, 2002.
Spear, Joanna. "Disarmament and Demobilization," in Stephen John Stedman, Donald
    Rothchild, and Elizabeth M. Cousens, eds., *Ending Civil Wars: The Implemen-
    tation of Peace Agreements.* London and Boulder, CO: Lynne Rienner Publishers,
    2002, pp. 141–181.
UN Department of Peacekeeping Operations. Peacekeeping Best Practices Unit.
    *Disarmament, Demobilization, and Reintegration of Ex-Combatants in a Peace-
    keeping Environment: Principles and Guidelines.* New York: United Nations,
    1999.
World Bank. Multi-Country Demobilization and Reintegration Program. "Greater Great
    Lakes Regional Strategy for Demobilization and Reintegration." Report No. 2386-
    AFR. Washington, DC: World Bank, 2002.

PERSONAL STORY:
"The Importance of Civil Society in Arms Control"—Oscar Arias

During my term as president of Costa Rica from 1986 to 1990, I learned first-hand the devastating effects of arms transfers on poor and war-torn places. In Central America, the arms shipments that were supposed to resolve the region's ideological clashes in fact prolonged and exacerbated them. We would later learn that the civil wars in Guatemala, El Salvador, and Nicaragua had caused more than two hundred thousand casualties, mostly civilian. Conventional weapons imported from the Soviet Union and the United States were involved in the vast majority of these deaths.

Peace cannot take root unless the deepest causes of conflict are brought to light, examined, and publicly discussed. Arms betray this delicate process by adding to intolerance, deepening present grievances and making agreement more distant. Today, in troubled regions such as Sudan and Colombia, cheap and readily available weapons continue to poison efforts to establish peace for future generations.

By the end of my presidency, I was convinced that the arms trade represents the single most significant perversion of human priorities in our era. In talks at universities and political forums, I have emphasized that the arms trade, and its accompanying glut of military spending, exacerbates and prolongs wars, criminal activity, and ethnic violence; destabilizes emerging democracies; and inflates military budgets to the detriment of health care, education, and basic infrastructure.

I have not found this theme completely and utterly depressing over the years, thanks to a stubborn faith that speaking out will always galvanize at least one person in the audience to action. Also, I know that my efforts are not for the sake of rhetoric, but for publicizing and reinforcing an Arms Trade Treaty movement in close collaboration with members of civil society.

The Arms Trade Treaty (ATT), originally known as a Code of Conduct on Arms Transfers, was formulated in 1997 by eight Nobel Prize laureates: me, Ellie Wiesel, Betty Williams, the Dalai Lama, José Ramos-Horta, and representatives of International Physicians for the Prevention of Nuclear War, the American Friends Service Committee, and Amnesty International. The treaty

calls for a ban on transfers of weapons to governments that repress fundamental democratic and human rights, or that commit acts of armed international aggression. To date, over twenty Nobel Prize winners, a growing
group of governments and thousands of individuals and organizations have
expressed their faith in the ATT as both morally sound and politically necessary.

Since October 2003, a grassroots campaign to ratify this treaty into a
binding piece of international law has been advancing in seventy countries
around the world. Building consensus for international arms control implies
simultaneous action in a kaleidoscope of social, political and economic issues:
police training in human rights, and military accountability to democratic governments; anti-corruption controls at the local and federal level; better educational opportunities for children, and peace curriculums in the schools; gender equity and access to employment. Civil society groups have found
innovative and dynamic ways to combine the cause of arms control with
human development agendas. In Brazil, for instance, the nongovernmental
organization Viva Rio has advocated national gun control laws, while building
youth clubs and microcredit programs in poor neighborhoods affected by gun
violence. In Costa Rica, the Arias Foundation for Peace and Human Progress
has launched a public education campaign on the public health impact of small
arms, with a special component for peace training in the public schools.

The Arms Trade Treaty has roots in many different regions, historical
experiences and individuals; and this diversity is a great strength, driving the
movement's dynamic growth. Clearly, a campaign to regulate the global arms
trade brings us head to head with some very entrenched interest groups, and
it could take years, even decades, to move forward. In this struggle, the moral
and political leadership of civil society, from schools to church councils to
public action groups, is fundamental. It has been thrilling to watch in the past
decade as the ATT has gathered worldwide momentum, a rising tide that grows
out of the tiny ripples of every individual act of creativity and leadership.

---

*Dr. Oscar Arias Sánchez was president of Costa Rica from 1986 until 1990. Within this
capacity he initiated a regional peace process, which cumulated in 1987 in the signing of the Equipulas II Accord by all Central American presidents. It was for this work
he won the Nobel Peace Prize of 1987. He used the monetary award to establish the
Arias Foundation for Peace and Human Progress, from which he has continued his
pursuit of global peace and human security.*

22.1

Former Rebels Use Market Forces to Achieve Their Social Ideals: New Rainbow in Colombia

After deciding to demobilize, a group of Colombian former guerrillas found out the harsh realities of postconflict life. They decided to take their destiny into their own hands and founded a company with a social conscience. However, they found out that building peace is much harder than making war.

The dramatic developments that transformed Eastern Europe's political scenario in the 1990s turned the world leftist movement upside down. In Colombia, a large group of eight hundred rebels, set adrift by the breakup of the Soviet Union, broke away from Ejército de Liberación Nacional (National Liberation Army), one of the guerrilla groups engaged in nearly four decades of armed conflict against the government.

The former university students, who had been inspired by the Cuban Revolution, denounced violence at Flor del Monte on 9 April 1994 and demobilized. The event generated considerable publicity, and much excitement. "Flor del Monte, Flor de Paz" ("Blossom of Mountain, Blossom of Peace"), said one headline. Yet once it was all over, the former rebels faced a stark new reality. Their past associations left a stigma: no one wanted to employ them. At the same time, they faced hostility from former comrades.

In search for a way forward, they consulted experts and did research. Gradually, as the euphoria turned into doubts about future prospects, they entered into discussions with the government about the way and means of reintegration and examined carefully the methods used by other demobilized groups locally, and internationally. It became clear that they needed to find their own way.

With help from various European governments, including the Spanish, Dutch, and the European Union, they set up a corporation that would be, and would try to make, a difference. Nuevo Arco Iris (New Rainbow) was, at one level, a business: it was set up to make a profit. At another level, its founders wanted New Rainbow to fulfill the social transformation ideals for which they fought as rebels.

So while committed to making a profit, New Rainbow also supports projects that help promote peace and achieve social justice. It supports human rights, promotes negotiation and postconflict efforts, and other conflict resolution initiatives. Parts of the company statement, and some of the literature it produces, read more like that of a development agency or nongovernmental organization (NGO) than a business enterprise. As is stated in a background document: "For the Corporation Nuevo Arco Iris, a perspective of development compatible with an opening for peace and the reconstruction of a democratic state imply public and private elements that permit the full realization of the needs of population." The document goes on to highlight the corporation's determination to support "the settlement of employment and the integration of citizens; the guarantee of the economic rights, social, cultural rights for everyone; priority attention to people affected by poverty and internal conflict; and the creation of conditions favorable to regions and social sectors that enable them to reach national and international markets."

New Rainbow has accumulated substantial assets by Colombian standards. It owns a thirty-five-room hotel in downtown Bogotá, operates a construction firm that has built hundreds of homes, and runs an agricultural brokerage firm, among various other enterprises. It has offices around the country providing permanent jobs for 200 people, of whom about 115 are former rebels. While working according to a standard business model, it remains a nonprofit organization depending in part on funding. Proceeds from the businesses are used to channel money into social-change programs, including civilian actions to stop the civil war, environmental issues, and agricultural business sustenance to support improvement in public services.

A Highly Stratified Society

Colombia is a highly stratified society, separating traditionally rich families and the poor majority. This situation has fed the growth of left-wing insurgents who have been battling against the government for forty years. Right-wing paramilitary groups, sometimes in the pay of drug traffickers and large landowners, and backed by some within the armed forces, have entered the fray as well. More than thirty-five thousand people have been killed by the violence over the past decade. Many have been forced to flee their homes.

Security Is a Major Concern

"Building peace is much harder than making war," says Rodrigo Osorno, a former rebel who now is a member of New Rainbow's board. He notes that ex-guerrillas generally face hostility from comrades they left behind—and from right-wing paramilitaries who distrust them. Security is a major concern: fifteen of New Rainbow's members have been killed in recent years. Forty bodyguards are employed to protect employees.

"FARC—Colombia's largest rebel group—see us as traitors, the paramilitaries see us as part of a large guerrilla strategy; the military has us in their files; businessmen lack confidence in us," says Antonio Sanguino, chief executive of New Rainbow. "It has been a fight to win space in society, to win respect."

Both the commercial and public sides of the corporation's work are gaining trust. Its success is viewed by some as an example of how to disarm and demobilize more combatants and prevent them from sliding into organized crime. In 2003, almost 1,750 rebels deserted guerrilla armies; 1,300 did so in 2002. New Rainbow is just one of a number of demobilization and reintegration programs operated by former rebels.

The government's efforts to end the protracted conflict involve use of a two-pronged approach of military attacks and the olive branch of peace negotiations with Marxist rebels and right-wing paramilitary organizations. Integrating thousands of former combatants to make the transition from mountains to urban centers, from rebels to civilians, is not easy. Many could end up jobless and homeless—and drift into crime.

New Rainbow's executives say the corporation's commitment is to promote territorial alliances between public and private entities that increase disposable resources for productive investments; promote community organizations to support social actors that serve as vehicles for development programs, and facilitate social cohesion. It is engaged in microfinance, the provision of subsidies aimed at reducing extreme poverty, and supporting programs to improve conditions of communities in areas such as habitat and environment. The corporation helps with incorporation of technology for clean production and alternative production techniques. It carries out programs for entrepreneurial development including identifying and finding employment possibilities.

Further, it is committed to civilian efforts to promote peace, construct a good social order, and restore peace and reconciliation at the center of national life. It is involved in teaching children about conflict resolution and training human rights workers to run a crop-substitution program for coca farmers. One program, Jovenes en Accion (Youth in Action), involves more than 180 young people in Bogotá in various income-generating community activities.

The company identifies the internal armed conflict as "perhaps the major obstacle to the viability of Colombia as a nation . . . the armed confrontation . . . has generated a militarization of conflicts and civilian life, led to violations of fundamental rights of people and left many victims. The construction of a peace agreement and the promotion of mechanisms to resolve these conflicts, constitute areas of priority for the democratization of Colombia."

New Rainbow's activities also extend to the hotel sector—focused, in particular, on small and medium-sized hotels in Bogotá—and occupational health. Its programs also support self-employment projects for poor women in several towns. In this regard, one of its projects tested the viability of a School for Democracy, Peace, and Tolerance. This involved introducing eighty community leaders, demobilized fighters, and others to subjects such as local development, political culture, environment, and ethics. The project was carried out in several towns in the province of Sucre.

In Accordance with Market Forces

Overall, New Rainbow aims to combine business enterprises and development and peace initiatives to improve Colombian society, with special focus on ex-combatants.

These ex-comrades have no qualms about using the very system against which they fought in order to generate money to pursue their ideals. "We believe the market can generate wealth, which benefits people in the long run," says Sanguino, who runs the enterprise from offices in an old neighborhood of Bogotá.

A seven-member board of directors oversees New Rainbow's activities. "Our companies have to be competitive," says Sanguino. "They have to play in accordance with market forces. We have to offer services that people want." He notes that his experience and that of other combatants in this area shows the need for flexibility from various institutions, the public, and NGOs. "The transition that we have achieved is an engagement between public and private sectors. The technical and financial support of the international community was also critical."

Contact

Corporación Nuevo Arco Iris
Calle 39 # 17-26
Bogotá, Colombia
Tel.: 57 (1) 2871748—2872482
E-mail: nuevoarcoiris@etb.net.co
Website: http://www.nuevoarcoiris.org.co

Selected Bibliogaphy

Forero, Juan. 2004. "Bogotá's Social Capitalism, Led by a Marxist of Old." *New York Times*, 6 February.

22.2

Transforming Arms into Ploughshares: The Christian Council of Mozambique

Albino Forquilha

In Maputo, Mozambique, the artists work with an unusual material: the scrap of destroyed weapons. The small arms and light weapons leftovers they work with have been collected as part of the Transforming Arms into Ploughshares Project, a program that was launched in 1995, three years after the long-running civil war in Mozambique came to an end.

In 1992, after the signing of a peace agreement in Rome, the situation in Mozambique was still very unstable. The country had been torn apart by some sixteen years of civil war and a decade of independence struggle before that, combined with many natural disasters. The United Nations Operation in Mozambique (ONUMOZ) that followed was a success in many ways: it managed to help in preventing the combatants from again picking up their arms against each other, to demobilize most of the soldiers, and to assist in holding open, although delayed, elections.

Yet disarmament was never considered a big issue and even though some 190,000 weapons were collected, most of these leaked back into circulation after ONUMOZ left the country in 1995. Significantly more were never confiscated and remained in the hands of former combatants and civilians.

At the same time, in October 1995 the Christian Council of Mozambique (Conselho Cristao de Moçambique), an umbrella organization of Protestant churches and organizations, established a Department of Justice, Peace, and Reconciliation. The general aim was to strengthen democracy and civil society by encouraging the population to participate in active peacekeeping activities, while promoting reconciliation and facilitating the initiation of productive activities by the people themselves. It set out to focus on four primary activity areas, one of which was the Transforming Arms into Ploughshares or TAE Project (Transformaçao de Armas em Enxadas).

The moving force behind the project has been Bishop Diniz Sengulane of the Anglican diocese of Lemombo in Mozambique, who encouraged his compatriots to participate by warning them that "to sleep with a gun in your bedroom is like sleeping with a snake." Two other notable contributors in the early days of the TAE Project were Graça Machel—the widow of Mozambique's first president and wife of Nelson Mandela—and Masaru Kataoka, a Japanese advocate for peace and reconciliation.

The TAE Project developed several general and specific objectives. In general it set out to help build a culture of peace, to support and maintain a peaceful postwar transition in Mozambique, and to offer an alternative lifestyle to arms holders. All in line with the overriding aim of the Christian Council to establish a culture of peace. However, in relation to small arms and light weapons, it formulated much more specific targets, such as collect and destroy all weapons in circulation; to transform these arms into "ploughshares," i.e., offering useful tools in exchange for their weapons; to reduce violence and educate civil society about the results of arms and violence; and to transform the collected weapons into sculptures and other forms of art.

The primary device for stimulating people to cooperate with the program has been its use of incentives that were thought to generate income in the long run. Before, disarmament had often been promoted by giving out cash incentives, but problems with black-market stimulation and the short-term effect of this approach inspired the organizers of the TAE project to try something new. Common products handed out to people bringing in guns were bicycles, hoes, construction tools, sewing machines, cement bags, school equipment for children, various raw construction materials, typewriters, and wheelchairs. Although there has been criticism that much of the incentives were aimed more at rural necessities than urban desires, in general the products both in reality and symbolism gave the people a new beginning.

The TAE Project managed to tap into an apparent desire of people to disarm. Research has shown that while plenty of weapons were being collected, arms-related crimes were also rising in the country. The relative success of the program has hence been explained by pointing at the political momentum that was holding many Mozambicans in a spirit of hope for peace and democracy. The TAE Project in this context represented a known actor they trusted and that shared their desire for a culture of peace.

This theory is supported by the periods of successful collection that collided with hopeful developments in politics and the fact that at times when, because of lack of funding, the project could not offer incentives for the weapons handed in, there were still people bringing in their arms. Such does point to the complication, though, that with these types of weapons collection programs, it is very hard to reach those people that hold guns because of economic motivations.

Pieces of Art

Upon collection, weapons were immediately destroyed or at least made unusable. In the beginning the collection teams went from village to village bringing with them mobile bench saws. However, since this proved to be very

Artist displaying his chairs made out of decommissioned AK-47s
(Maputo, Mozambique)

expensive, people were later requested to bring in the arms to collection spots, normally churches. At the end of the day, in small public ceremonies, the weapons were sawn into pieces.

More importantly though, the program did not stop there. The feeling existed that something needed to be done with the scrap of these weapons. The ongoing battle against the circulation of small arms and light weapons needed stronger support. Therefore, it was decided to ask local artists to make pieces of art, monuments, or practical objects of the scrap. The monuments were placed in public places such as parks or squares. The art was combined into an exhibition that has toured both within and outside the country.

Hundreds of works of art have been made from arms fragments, which has resulted in sculptures of motorcycles, birds and animals, and a jazz player; traditional African statues; and functional objects such as tables and chairs. As Gonçalo Mabunda, the young artist who created a saxophone from the remnants of a bazooka and several AK-47s, comments, "I wanted to depict the opposite of what the arms were meant to do. I made an instrument that makes noise and gathers people for joyful celebrations, versus an instrument that makes noise and scatters people in a song of death."

This last part of the TAE Program has been seen by some as the most successful and most important aspect of the program. The monuments and the pieces of art give a strong symbolic message of peace. The transformation of weapons into objects of art stands as an important symbol to all of Mozambique's citizens. They represent the end of the war and of violence in general and are a reminder of how weapons created to kill can be transformed into objects of beauty and harmony for families. They call on a new generation, now assuming its place in steering the course of the nation, to articulate values and opinions rooted in peacebuilding rather than violence and destruction. Not just coincidentally, the program also gives young artists exposure that is beneficial, of course, to their own development and commercial success.

As mentioned above, the TAE artworks have been and continue to be exhibited in Mozambique itself and around the world, in Portugal, Germany, Zimbabwe, Namibia, Sweden, Belgium, Canada, the United States, Australia, France, South Africa, Japan, and the United Kingdom, and at the UN Building in New York during the Conference on Small Arms and Light Weapons in 2001. Such exhibitions have offered an example to other countries and organizations of the potential benefits of an innovative disarma- ment/demobilization program. In January 2005, a 3-meter-high work titled *Tree of Life,* the biggest sculpture created since the start of the project, is scheduled to be put on display for five years at the British Museum in London. The revenue of these exhibitions and the profit of selling some of the works are used to continue the project.

The Broader Picture

TAE also engages in an extensive civic-education program among those who participate in the weapons exchange, as well as members of their surrounding community. To secure the work they have done, the program conducts follow- up projects with weapons exchange participants to solidify the foundation upon which a culture of peace can firmly rest. In addition, at the national and international levels, TAE is involved in more generalized programs to promote peace and reconciliation.

To further promote a culture of peace, the TAE has set up a variety of other activities, ranging from demonstrations to theater pieces. The specific objectives of the educational initiative have included demonstrating the dangers of weapons circulation and their impact on crime; explaining the dangers of landmines and explosives; engaging in discussions on citizen responsibilities in civil society with regard to the ongoing project of peace- building and reconciliation; and follow-up activities to maintain contact with beneficiaries of the program following the initial weapons exchange.

The TAE Project's success has been, to a significant degree, a reflection of the establishment of a strong partnership and the building of trust among the chief players, including the government of Mozambique, the former adversaries Frente de Libertaçào de Moçambique (FRELIMO) and Resistência Nacional Moçambicana (RENAMO), and those within the Christian Council who are responsible for actual operations. Confidence in the Christian Council is in large part due to the fact that it played a role during the peace negotiations. Yet success has also been dependent on building confidence at the grassroots level; TAE has cultivated relationships and worked hard to build trust with local communities and with ex-belligerents.

Indications of Success

The TAE Project has continued for a very long time in comparison to similar weapons collection programs in other countries. The number of collected war artifacts is over 800,000, of which over 350,000 are weapons of different types (the rest is mainly composed of explosives). These are notable amounts, but with estimates of the total number of weapons in circulation running into the millions, they remain just a fraction of the work that still needs to be done. Even the combined efforts of the TAE Program, ONUMOZ, and the other ongoing disarmament program in Mozambique, Operations Rachel—a series of collection operations conducted by the Mozambican and the South African police forces—only have been able to collect a margin of the total numbers of weapons in circulation. Yet the quantity of weapons collected is only one way of looking at the success of the TAE Program.

TAE has identified several indicators that it views as significant for still seeing the program as a success, including the perceived achievement with which target-group members reintegrated into society, the revenue generated by new tools, the number of people affected by the exchange (directly and indirectly), the level of beneficiary satisfaction with the exchange, and the beneficiaries' perception on his or her involvement in the community before and after the exchange. Still, it is difficult to gauge the full impact of TAE. What is known is that over seventy thousand families have benefited directly from the project through the incentives they received, which enabled them to start small social projects in their communities. Another indicator is the yearly reduction of crime in Mozambique. There is also anecdotal evidence of the benefits realized through the weapons exchange program. Some of the most notable success stories include:

- A local woman who received a sewing machine in exchange for weapons has launched a successful business and she now employs eight people.
- A young man whose home was destroyed by the latest floods was able to begin the process of home reconstruction with the help of the cement he received in exchange for an AK-47 he kept in his home.
- A young university student received a copy of the *Oxford English Dictionary* in exchange for his weapon.
- A man who lost both his wife and his child during the war received zinc roofing sheets and was able to rebuild and secure his home. He has remarried and started a new family.
- The many bicycles that have been exchanged are now being used to deal with the difficulties encountered in taking care of daily needs such as water and firewood, transporting products to the market, and taking people to hospitals and clinics that would be difficult to reach otherwise.
- A Japanese partner donated a tractor to TAE, which was then offered as a prize in a competition to see which of two communities could collect and

hand over the most weapons. The winning community collected some five hundred weapons and ordnance and took possession of the tractor.

• The Anglican Church in Maputo initiated a civic-education program in which children were encouraged to follow the example of grown-ups by turning in toy guns, which would be destroyed, in exchange for new toys.

Yet obviously the true impact of the TAE Program is hard to measure. It is found in the people that see the monuments, the pieces of art, or the practical objectives and are reminded of the importance of peace and the necessity to continue to struggle against the circulation and misuse of small arms and light weapons.

Still Much to Do

It has become apparent to those involved in the TAE Project that the process of disarmament, demobilization, and reintegration is a long and difficult one. Former combatants do not simply and easily reintegrate into society and, to develop the necessary trust, programs must be established from the outset, and time must be allowed for their success. Even while the adversaries are first discussing the possibilities of peace, attention must be given to the challenges of the postconflict period, including the reintegration of combatants into society and the collection and destruction of their weapons and the ones in the hands of civilians.

Ultimately, the success of any disarmament initiative depends not on the number of weapons collected, but on the number of minds won over to the notion that peace is the only viable option. By providing a viable incentive to turn in the gun, the TAE Project may be stimulating more people to work toward their goal; in the end, the most important objective is to convince them they do not need their weapons anymore.

To quote Bishop Sengulane,

> We tell people: We are not disarming you. We are transforming your guns into ploughshares, so you can cultivate your land and get your daily bread. We are transforming them into sewing machines so you can make clothes. We are transforming them into bicycles so you don't have to spend money traveling to work and so you can collect the fruits of your fields to sell. The idea is to transform the instruments of death and destruction into instruments of peace and of production and cooperation with others (Christian Aid 2001).

Albino Forquilha is national coordinator of the TAE Project.

Contact

Department for Justice, Peace, and Reconciliation
Project TAE (Transformaçao de Armas em Enxadas)
Av. Marian Ngoaubi 704
C.P. 108, Maputo, Mozambique
Tel.: +258 (1) 419 979 / 414 980
Fax: +258 (1) 419 979/ 415 427

E-mail: forquilhatae@tvcabo.co.mz
Website: http://www.ccm.co.mz/abauttae.htm

Selected Bibliography

Bonn International Center for Conversion (BICC). Online at: http://www.bicc.de.

Chachiua, Martinho. 1999. "Records of Weapons Collection and Destruction in Southern Africa: The Mozambican Experience" (Pretoria, South Africa: The Institute for Security Studies). Online at: http://www.iss.org.za/Pubs/ASR/8No4/Chachiua.html.

Christian Aid. 2001. "Guns into Ploughshares" (London: Christian Aid). Online at: http://www.christianaid.org.uk/news/features/106mozam/story.htm.

Institute for Security Studies (ISS). Online at: http://www.iss.co.za.

International Action Network on Small Arms (IANSA). Online at: http://www.iansa.org.

"Mozambique Arms Amnesty Projects Goes Truly National." Online at: http://www.crosslinks.org/who/people/mp_reeve_TAE_article0311.htm.

Nucleo de Arte Website/ TAE Project Artwork (in Portuguese). Online at: http://www.africaserver.nl/nucleo/port/index.html.

"Small Arms Research and Consultancy Weapons Program TAE Mozambique" (Bonn: BICC).

Small Arms Survey. Online at: http://www.smallarmssurvey.org.

TAE Project detailed information and photo gallery. Online at: http://www.iansa.org/oldsite/documents/research/TAE/index.htm.

"Transforming Swords into Ploughshares." Christian Council of Mozambique.

Vines, Alex. 1998. "The Struggle Continues: Light Weapons Destruction in Mozambique." BASIC: Occasional Papers on International Security Issues, No. 25. Online at: http://www.basicint.org/pubs/Papers/BP25.htm.

"What Is the TAE Project?" Online at: http://www.fromeweaponstoart.org/eng/frame.html.

22.3

Fruits of War:
Homies Unidos in El Salvador
and the United States

Beverley Keefe

U.S.-style youth gangs have emerged as an unwelcome presence in Central America. Crime, intergang violence, and drug use are just some of the problems that have accompanied the rise of these gangs. Homies Unidos is a unique initiative, founded by former gang members, with branches in San Salvador and Los Angeles, that brings former gang members together and offers alternatives to the antisocial lifestyle of these gangs.

Empesando esto fue, como una semilla,
Trayendo como fruto la formación de pandillas.
Trataremos este tema con mucha seriedad,
Es algo sin sentido pero esto es realidad,
La realidad que se vive, como frutos de una guerra.[1]

(This started as a seed, and
Gangs were its fruits.
Let's deal with this topic with all its seriousness,
It's something that's senseless but it's a reality,
The reality we live, it's the fruit of a war.)

On 2 November 1996, twenty-two members of two of the largest rival gangs in the vicinity of San Salvador, El Salvador—most of them deportees from the United States (U.S.)—came together to turn a common vision into a reality: to build a movement to address the level of violence perpetrated both by and against their community. The result was the establishment of an organization called Homies Unidos.

Meeting in the home of Homies Unidos founder and international human rights activist Magdaleno Rose-Avila, it was the first time that many of the youth were in close quarters with one another. Even to this day, many scholars, governmental agents, and observers have failed to grasp the sensitivity of the exercise that afternoon. Each gang member present had taken a significant leap of faith by attending the gathering, not knowing for certain whether he or she would walk out of the meeting after it was over. Tension was high. At any moment a miscommunication or misunderstanding could have led to much bloodshed.

U.S.-Style Gangs

U.S.-style gang violence has, in recent years, spilled over onto the streets of several Central American countries. The spread of gangs from U.S. barrios to Central American cities has attracted the attention of law enforcement agencies, academics, and the media. It was also the impetus to establish Homies Unidos, an organization that aims to turn young people away from gang-related violence and drugs and offer hope for a better future through alternative education, leadership development, the building of self-esteem, and health education programs. A year after its establishment in El Salvador, an affiliate was launched in Los Angeles.

Homies Unidos, while by no means the only violence prevention organization in Los Angeles or in El Salvador, is the only such local organization that works in both cities to prevent conflict and violence and that also addresses systemic causes of violence so endemic to Central American immigrant youth and so disruptive to their families in both the U.S. and El Salvador. What also sets the organization apart from other social service or governmental agencies working to prevent violence is its status as the only program of its sort that is run by former gang members from rival gangs.

Homies Unidos adopts a unique approach to conflict and violence prevention. The organization strives to transform the gang culture from within, and to redirect the structures of solidarity and identification with gangs away from violent practices by building consciousness of human rights and human potential.

The Situation

The origins of youth violence both in Los Angeles and in El Salvador can be traced back, at least indirectly, to the Salvadoran civil war, which lasted from 1980 until 1992. Salvadoran refugee youth and their families who fled the fighting and settled in the U.S., primarily in Los Angeles, often faced a dearth of resources to ease their transition into U.S. society or to help them deal with the psychological effects of conflict and war. Abruptly removed from their homes and social networks, many families were torn apart by virtue of the move to the United States or through economic necessity, and many immigrant youth left to take care of themselves, sought out the familial comfort and protection provided by neighborhood gangs.

After the peace accords were signed in 1992, the U.S. began deportations of refugees back to El Salvador. The numbers were small at first, but following the 1995 Oklahoma City bombing and the passage of the Anti-Terrorist Act of 1996, repatriations of young Salvadorans increased significantly.

El Salvador's poverty rate is about 48 percent, and while its official unemployment rate hovers around 10 percent, unemployment among young males is estimated at about 80 percent. Combined with the accustomedness to violence that exists in Salvadorian society after the end of the civil war—some reports estimate that homicide rates were higher in the first years after the peace accord then during the actual war—has turned El Salvador in one of the most violent countries of Latin America.

For the young people returning to El Salvador, the absence of any type of repatriation program or support often led them to the only network they knew: gangs. The lack of socioeconomic and employment opportunities further drove youth to engage in criminal activities in order to survive.

Emergence of Alternatives

For some time prior to the founding of Homies Unidos, nongovernmental organizations and journalists in Central America had been observing and documenting the gang problem. Though it was not an altogether new phenomenon, the gangs proliferated as large numbers of refugees returned from the U.S. Estimates of the number of gang members have varied widely, from approximately twenty thousand to thirty-five thousand, in a total population of over six million. Although statistics indicate that these gangs have been responsible for some 10 percent of El Salvador's violent crime, the public sees it differently and attributes the majority of violent crime to gang activity. As a result, 45 percent of all Salvadorans polled in 1998 supported "social cleansing" of those elements deemed responsible for the violence—even if that meant a recurrence of paramilitary death squad activity. Eighty percent of the population wanted to see the military step in to suppress delinquency.

Several Central American agencies studied the rise of youth gangs, but with neither access to the gangs nor their trust, the accuracy of the findings was questionable, and the safety of the investigators could not be assured. Homies Unidos, however, did not face these impediments. So the first step they took in addressing the crisis of violence was to conduct their own study. Members of Mara Salvatrucha and 18th Street, the two largest rival gangs in El Salvador (and the U.S.) designed and executed a survey of gang members. It was the first-ever recognized study conducted by, for, and about gang members to examine the root causes and consequences of gang-related violence.[2]

The study provided the public with a vivid picture of gang culture and served to lay a foundation on which to build the organization. Perhaps most importantly, though, the study, entitled "Más Allá de la Vida Loca" ("Beyond the Crazy Life"), was effective in building solidarity and eliciting a commitment to pursue *calmado* (nonviolence) among gang members.

The results give cause for reflection:

- 51 percent of gang members had been hospitalized due to violence
- 69.3 percent had suffered the killing of a loved one

• 48.3 percent said that they had been beaten by a rival gang member (when asked if they had been on the receiving end of physical violence in the past thirty days)
• 26.9 percent had suffered at the hands of the police and rival gangs
• 10.8 percent had been beaten only by police

Their hopes for their future included a job (30.6 percent), stable family (25.5 percent), education (16.7 percent), to "be somebody" (7.6 percent), calmness (5 percent), self-improvement (4.8 percent), and finding God (2 percent).

Struggling Against a Culture of Violence

One of the most critical outcomes of the study was the picture that emerged of the pervasive culture of violence, conflict, and poverty from which the gang members came. The new organization took these findings and developed a series of programs based on the most pressing needs of the youth, including work force reentry skills, transnational family reunification through dialogue, and community dialogue.

Over the past seven years, the model has evolved and now addresses systemic issues relating to immigration, criminal justice—both in the United States and El Salvador—and most recently oppressive antigang laws passed by governments in El Salvador and throughout Central America. As a result of the study, policymakers have been more receptive to the view that community violence is a public health issue, and this has led to the acceptance of new approaches to conflict prevention and intervention based on a public health model rather than punitive and criminal-justice models.

Because El Salvador—and the rest of the region—had very little experience addressing violence and conflict stemming from the gangs, the efforts of Homies Unidos were essential in raising the collective awareness of gang violence to an international level. Through the development of a working model, these efforts provided a voice for gang youth and alternatives to gang involvement and violence. The results of the study also demonstrated to the international community that gang violence and related conflict does not occur in a vacuum, but is the result of years of poverty, lack of economic opportunity, and social inequality. Most significantly, the model examines systemic and socialized root causes of violence and civil conflict and seeks to head off violence by developing and targeting effective programs where they are needed most.

Among the most notable and effective have been the following programs:

• Assistance in reconnecting the former gang members with their families, also in cases where they have been deported and the family remains in the U.S.
• Sex education and health programs, focusing on prevention of HIV/ AIDS and addressing drug abuse

- An International Human Rights Campaign addressing the gang violence in Central America
- Vocational training workshops
- An arts and culture program that gives young people a creative outlet as an alternative to violence
- Lecture programs that take ex-gang members to schools and youth centers to highlight the risks associated with gangs and gang violence, and to encourage young people to stay in school

In Los Angeles, an alternative life skills program called the Epiphany Project offers help to gang members, including:

- Anger management and conflict resolution
- A tattoo removal program, which is offered free of charge on the condition the beneficiaries join the Epiphany Project
- An educational program to help high school dropouts to earn their high school equivalence diploma and find a job
- Special assistance to former gang members serving prison sentences, upon their release from jail

Most of these programs do not address violence directly, but by providing opportunities to escape from a dead-end lifestyle permeated by violence they offer hope for the individuals themselves and for society at large.

Since the first tentative days of Homies Unidos, the most prominent key actors have been the youth themselves, members of two of the most violent gangs in the Americas, who risked their own lives and the lives of their loved ones in pioneering a conflict prevention and violence intervention organization.

Strengthening Its Commitment

Entering its ninth year (as of 2005), the reasons for the development of Homies Unidos are as compelling as ever. Recent antigang laws in Central America have served only to heighten community violence and perpetuate civil conflict. In 2002, an update of the 1996 study conducted by the Homies Unidos and the Pan American Health Organization found that gang violence has worsened, and urged a greater commitment to effecting change in social and public policy.

As deportations from the United States continue, and the pattern of "circular migration" continues, fear escalates, and so too does violence and repression on the part of the government, in response to fear and media-fueled social hysteria. Gang youth and deportees have additional reasons to fear for their security. Beyond their own culture of violence, and the recent legislation, there have been death squad–style assassinations of deportees rumored to be gang members carried out by the Sombra Negra (Black Shadow). Under provisions of the *antimara* (gang) laws in El Salvador, more than 7,500 youth have been arrested, detained, or imprisoned, most reportedly without cause.

As the situation evolves, so do the efforts of Homies Unidos. Its transnational efforts are currently focused on supporting youth caught in the dragnet of antigang laws and spotlighting international human rights violations resulting from these laws.

It may be true that, as old problems are effectively addressed, new ones emerge. Still, Homies Unidos has at least shown that through dialogue and solidarity, the most marginalized individuals can leave hopelessness behind and begin to create a much more hopeful future for themselves and their communities.

Beverley Keefe is a Los Angeles–based writer and editor. A longtime activist in the arena of international solidarity, she has worked with Homies Unidos as a volunteer and consultant since its inception in 1996.

Contact

Homies Unidos
1625 West Olympic Boulevard, Suite 706
Los Angeles, CA, 90015
U.S.
Tel.: +1 213 383 7484
Fax: +1 213 383 7482
E-mail: homiesunidos@homiesunidos.org
Websites:
    htttp://www.homiesunidos.org
    http://www.libertadcondignidad.org

Notes

1. Verses from a song written by Marvin Bullet Novoa Escobar, San Salvador, El Salvador.

2. The survey was done with the support of the Pan-American Health Organization and the Institute of Public Opinion at the Central American University (Instituto Universitario de Opinión Pública, Universidad Centro Americana), and published through that university (see Giralt and Concha-Eastman 2001).

Selected Bibliography

Cruz, José Miguel, et al. 1998. *Solidaridad y violencia en las pandillas del gran San Salvador: Más allá de la vida loca* (San Salvador: UCA Editores).

Giralt, María L. Santacruz, and Alberto Concha-Eastman. 2001. "Barrio adentro: La solidaridad violenta de las pandillas" (San Salvador: Universidad Centroamericana José Simeón Cañas, Instituto Universitario de Opinión Pública).

Hayden, Tom. 2004. *Street Wars: Gangs and the Future of Violence* (New York: New Press, June).

Rodriguez, Luis J. 2001. *Hearts and Hands: Making Peace in a Violent Time* (New York: Seven Stories Press).

Vigil, James. 2002. *A Rainbow of Gangs* (Austin: University of Texas Press).

23

Reconciliation: Challenges, Responses, and the Role of Civil Society

Hizkias Assefa

Reconciliation is a process of restoring relationships between parties that have been deeply alienated from each other due to hurtful and destructive conflicts. Restoring such relationships involves multidimensional, complex, and far-reaching processes that aim at dealing not only with the past but also future relationships between the protagonists. Civil-society actors have a special role to play as catalysts and facilitators of societal reconciliation work.

Most approaches used to handle conflicts, such as force, adjudication, arbitration, or bargaining-type negotiation and mediation, tend to suppress or superficially treat problems that underlie conflicts. As a result, the same basic conflict tends to recur in different guises over time, sometimes increasing in intensity and destructiveness. Reconciliation, if handled properly, is a mechanism that can address root causes of conflict as well as mend deep emotional wounds and thereby produce more durable solutions and sustainable peace. In that sense it could be said that reconciliation is not only an effective approach for dealing with postconflict situations but is also a powerful crisis prevention mechanism.

Key elements of the reconciliation process are:

- Acknowledgment of harm done by either party to the other
- Genuine expression of remorse
- Asking for or granting pardon
- Remedying the consequences of the harm
- Defining a new mutually beneficial relationship that addresses the root causes of the past conflict and guarantees that past mistakes will not be repeated

Some have categorized these processes as truth telling, administration of justice, healing, and forging a new basis for future relationships that are different from the hurtful past. Translating this understanding of reconciliation into

637

practice—particularly where there has been large-scale social conflict—is not easy, to say the least.

Challenges

Long-Term View

Reconciliation is as much an affective process as it is cognitive and intellectual. It deals with feelings and emotions as much as reason. While it might be easier for bitter protagonists to rationally understand the need for reconciliation in their relationships, it is often more difficult for them to act on those realizations and come to terms with the conflict emotionally. The reconciliation process cannot be rushed or forced because it usually takes time for emotions to catch up with the rational mind. Moreover, we do not have many proven methodologies for ways to heal emotional wounds in large-scale social conflicts. Even if both sides think that restoring relationship is a good idea, it is hard to get offenders to overcome feelings of guilt, shame, pride, and denial, and adopt an attitude of acknowledgment, remorse, and humility. It is also very difficult to get victims to let go of their anger, bitterness, and fear and give their oppressors another chance in a new trusting relationship. Therefore, practitioners must have a long-term view and must be prepared to find ways to accompany the process over time, even if there may not be much to show for their efforts in the short term. How to continue to accompany such processes when resources and commitment are limited is one of the greatest challenges of reconciliation work.

Combining Justice and Reconciliation

Conflict parties may view the concept of reconciliation differently. In protracted conflicts, victims often insist on justice while offenders insist on forgiveness and amnesty. In fact, many victims resist reconciliation initiatives because they think it glosses over the guilt and responsibility of offenders. They insist on justice for past misconduct to safeguard them from being victimized again. In most societies working at reconciliation, there is a big debate with human rights activist and victims groups about the connection between justice and reconciliation and whether reconciliation is too easy on the perpetrators and therefore puts victims in jeopardy by encouraging impunity.

By the same token, offenders tend to cheapen reconciliation processes by focusing only on forgiveness, amnesty, and improving future relationships while ignoring accountability for the injury they have inflicted. They underestimate the long-term effect of past pain and abuse and how coexistence can stir up such painful memories. In general, offenders disregard the need for the truth to be told about the past, guilt to be acknowledged, the consequences of past misdeeds to be faced, and for the need to restore victims. They shy away from their obligation to convince victims that they have truly changed and that the past will not be repeated.

From this author's point of view, the apparent dichotomy between justice and reconciliation, though it appears in many discussions of reconciliation, is a false one. I believe it is not possible to have meaningful reconciliation without doing and being seen to do justice. Justice is at the core of reconciliation. The confusion seems to arise because people generally do not clarify what they mean by justice and how they aim to achieve it. For many, justice merely means the punishment of offenders. It implies administering proportionate suffering to those who have made others suffer. However, this is a narrow understanding of justice.

A broader concept of justice challenges people to look at what led to the unjust relationships and to undertake reforms in order to rectify the problems and remedy the victim's injuries. Making the victims as whole as possible is an important aspect of justice rather than just exchanging pain for pain. Sometimes punishment might be necessary to avert a culture of impunity or heal some emotional wounds. However, if the sole emphasis is on punishment, it will only perpetuate animosity, mutual fear, and a desire for future revenge. Justice should be concerned with the deeper needs of the victim and with the healing of the victims' past injury. It should leave the door open for the improvement of future relationships between victim and offender in an atmosphere of change.

When justice is approached in a more comprehensive sense, the compatibility between justice and reconciliation becomes apparent. On the other hand, when justice is viewed merely as punishment of the offender, it becomes more difficult to work on reconciliation. This is because it can feed the cycle of bitterness and resentment, especially when the punishment is done in the context of political conflict.

In situations such as Rwanda and the former Yugoslavia, where groups fought each other for control of the state and injury was committed not as an individual criminal action but in the name of one group in the struggle against the other, the trials and punishment of the wrongdoers, usually by the victor group, tend to be seen by the "offenders" and their supporters as "legal revenge." This reinforces the loser's desire to retaliate when opportunity arises.

Therefore, reconciliation must combine justice as well as forgiveness. It must deal with the past so that victims can minimize their fears and bitterness. At the same time it must deal with the future so that the protagonists do not foreclose the exploration of new possibilities for more mutually rewarding relationships. Reconciliation must work at the affective dimension to help the parties' attitudes of anger, bitterness, and suspicion turn into collaboration and ultimately trust. At the same time it must also involve the hard intellectual work of creating new commitments through policies, institutions, processes, and practices that show that the future will guarantee that past abuses will not be repeated.

Definition of the Victim and the Offender

Rigid definitions of the victim and the offender can detract from reconciliation. In many protracted conflicts one finds situations where victim groups have in the past been offenders, and offenders have been victims. Who is a victim and who is an offender might therefore depend on where one begins to analyze the relationship between the protagonists. Depending on how far back one looks at history, it is possible that it may not be only one side that has to ask for forgiveness and another to grant it; instead there might be a need for mutual acknowledgment of responsibility and mutual forgiveness. The more one encourages mutual acknowledgment, even if the wrongdoing of one side is proportionately smaller than the other, the easier it is to work at reconciliation. The more one side is presented as the sole offender and the other as the total victim, the more difficult it becomes to encourage the protagonists to engage in a reconciliation process. Of course this is not to deny the existence of cases where the guilt is totally one-sided and thus call for unilateral acknowledgment and responsibility.

The Peace Process in Nigeria

Two recent examples from the Middle Belt Region of Nigeria, where this author has been working for the past five years, illustrate the concepts and processes of reconciliation discussed in this chapter. In this region there have been a number of intertwined conflicts, some dating back to the early 1900s. In 2001, after a year and half of careful grassroots peacebuilding work, a preliminary peace agreement was signed between three ethnic groups in the Takum local government area to settle numerous issues of contention and outline actions for reconciliation. However, six months into the implementation of the agreement a new wave of ethnic violence erupted in a neighboring local government area that spread like wildfire in the region. The three ethnic groups in Takum stood firm and resisted being pulled into the violence despite it affecting their various ethnic groups. According to one observer, "Takum became a safe haven for fleeing people during the recent war in Wukari, and the fighting was stopped at the borders, saving millions of dollars in damage, and thousands of people from displacement." Not only was Takum an island of calm in an ocean of violence, but it also became an inspiration for the protagonists in the neighboring region to emulate the Takum peace process.

By August 2003, after an intensive process that was characterized by mutual contrition and forgiveness involving people from the grassroots all the way to the top leadership, an even more far-reaching agreement was signed in Wukari. At a reconciliation ceremony organized a year after the signing of the peace agreement, one observer remarked:

> The peace process was amazing. In spite of the painful moments when participants from the various communities took a hard look at what were the causes of these conflicts from their own and other group's perspectives, the negotiations were very constructive. It was heart-warming to see people who often had seen each other only through the barrel of the gun come together to find solutions together for issues that have been sources of conflicts and violence for decades. The extent to which participants went in order to accommodate each other was most remarkable. At the end, a twelve-point agreement was reached, which the parties signed. Those of us who witnessed what happened at the peace process rejoiced greatly. (Ali 2003)

Favorable Conditions

The approach societies take to deal with postconflict situations is influenced by the relative power position of the protagonists at the time that open conflict was brought to an end. For example, in Rwanda the conflict ended by the military victory of the minority group that experienced the genocide. Therefore, the predominant approach to dealing with the postconflict situation in that country emphasized punishment of offenders more than forgiveness. On the other hand, in places such as El Salvador where the groups who were accused of perpetrating human right violations still had the upper hand, the prevailing idea for how to handle the postconflict situation has tended to emphasize forgiveness and focus on the future. However, in situations such as South Africa's, where the conflict ended with a stalemate, the protagonists had to negotiate a balance between punishment and forgiveness. Out of this was born the Truth and Reconciliation Commission, which could grant amnesty to offenders if they told the truth and met some conditions.

In countries where one side has clearly won over the other, it is more difficult to influence the reconciliation process to incorporate either forgiveness or accountability as the situation might require. However, it must be recognized that reconciliation will not be effective if it is handled as an exercise in power politics. In order to work, reconciliation must be a genuine engagement where past mistakes and wrongdoings are named, regardless of who has the superior power. It must be an exercise of sincere soul searching with a genuine desire to take responsibility, to change, and to address the grievances of victims. Forced forgiveness or forgiveness by proxy on behalf of the victims will not create the necessary healing and trust to create new positive relationships. On the other hand, pursuing revenge in the name of administration of justice will only succeed in fueling hatred and violence. So, one of the challenges of reconciliation work in large-scale conflicts is to make the reconciliation exercise as genuine as possible regardless of the power position of the protagonists in the society.

Here civil society can play a crucial role as a balancer. In societies where the emphasis is on punishment, civil society can, through awareness-building programs, introduce different ways of doing justice in the society, and expand the options for handling past wrongdoings. In societies where the sole emphasis is on forgiveness and the future, civil society can work with perpetrators in order to encourage and support them to address the past. Many societies have been experimenting with adapting traditional conflict-handling mechanisms to bring about reconciliation between offenders and victims at the community and neighborhood levels. Most of these mechanisms have less cumbersome and fairly effective methods of encouraging acknowledgment and repentance, handling punishment, and rehabilitating victims, particularly where the wrongdoings committed are not heinous.

Political support and leadership are factors that can enhance societal reconciliation processes. The existence of prominent politicians or social leaders who demonstrate the values of reconciliation by their life and example can create a conducive climate for societal reconciliation. They can provide powerful inspiration for the rest of society to emulate their behavior. People who have the courage to admit past mistakes, who are willing to acknowledge responsibility and make necessary changes; or people who are willing to take courageous steps toward forgiveness and show that they are not chained to the past, can set a tone for how the postconflict situation in a given society is to be handled. The role of Nelson Mandela and Bishop Desmond Tutu in setting the tone for reconciliation in South Africa cannot be overstated.

Aside from lobbying for political support for reconciliation, civil society can play the role of inspirational leadership as a collectivity in situations where such prominent leaders may not be very noticeable in the community. I have worked with civil society in Sierra Leone where this leadership role was exercised in various ways. One was by creating and promoting a vision for societal reconciliation. The civil-society leaders first gathered together and developed their own strategy for how to work at reconciliation among themselves and then how to facilitate the development of a national reconciliation vision. They gradually proceeded step-by-step to involve all sectors of society (such as the military, business, victim groups, women's groups, students, traditional leaders, and the executive, legislative, and judiciary branches of government) in defining a collective vision of reconciliation and in agreeing on modalities for how to move toward that vision. The vision focused on dealing with the past but also envisaged a positive future that gave incentive for the protagonists in the society to temper their attitude of recrimination and revenge and be forward-looking.

In circumstances where reconciliation is not taking place at the higher echelons of leadership, civil-society actors can create momentum for societal reconciliation by starting to work at the grassroots. There are many examples where civil-society groups have facilitated trauma healing and reconciliation through psychosocial, relief, or development work between victims and offenders who have been forced by circumstances to live together in the same communities. Progress made at the community level can then be used to encourage reconciliation at the higher political levels.

Of course this is not to claim that it is easy for civil society to take on these roles. Civil society is a microcosm of the overall society and mirrors all the divisions and fault lines in the community. Therefore, it is inevitable that civil-society actors have their own biases and loyalties. They may lack the objectivity and distance to undertake the reconciler roles indicated above in ways that can be acceptable to all the protagonists. Civil-society actors themselves might need a reconciliation process before they can play reconciler roles. However, the fact that the role is a difficult one does not mean that it is impossible. I have worked in many conflict situations, such as Nigeria, Ghana, Sierra Leone, and to some extent Guatemala, where civil society have been catalysts and facilitators of societal reconciliation work and have exercised the objectivity and discipline needed to become effective players.

Finally, it must be acknowledged that societal reconciliation is not only the product of what transpires within that society. External influences (such as big-power interests, economic and cultural globalization forces) that are at times beyond the control of the protagonists could frustrate reconciliation efforts at home. Those that work on societal reconciliation therefore need to be aware of how their efforts could be frustrated by such external influences and should develop strategies to resist or mitigate those influences that undermine what their process is trying to accomplish. Sometimes such strategies for common action can even strengthen the bonds that reconciliation is trying to build.

Hizkias Assefa is professor of conflict studies at the Conflict Transformation Program, Eastern Mennonite University, Harrisonburg, Virginia, and senior special fellow with the United Nations Institute of Training and Research in Geneva. He is also the founder and coordinator of Africa Peacebuilding and Reconciliation Resources based in Nairobi, Kenya, and has been working on peacebuilding and reconciliation initiatives in many countries including Rwanda, Sierra Leone, Nigeria, Sri Lanka, Afghanistan, and Guatemala.

Selected Bibliography

Ali, Bulus. 2003 "Report on the Jalingo Negotiations between the Tiv and Jukun," Unpublished Report (Jos, Plateau State, Nigeria: Peace, Justice and Reconciliation Committee, 23 September).

Resources

Lead Organizations

Life and Peace Institute—Sweden
E-mail: info@life-peace.org
Website: http://www.life-peace.org

Centre for the Study of Violence and Reconciliation—South Africa
E-mail: info@csvr.org.za
Website: http://www.csvr.org.za/

Initiatives of Change—Switzerland
Agenda for Reconciliation
E-mail: afr@iofc.org
Website: http://www.afr-iofc.org

International Center for Transitional Justice—United States
E-mail: info@ictj.org
Website: http://www.ictj.org/

Coventry University—United Kingdom
Centre for the Study of Forgiveness and Reconciliation
E-mail: a.rigby@coventry.ac.uk
Website: http://legacywww.coventry.ac.uk/legacy/acad/isl/forgive

International Fellowship of Reconciliation—Netherlands
E-mail: office@ifor.org
Website: http://www.ifor.org

Website

http://www.ijr.org.za/pub.html
Institute for Justice and Reconciliation

Publications

Abu Nimer, Mohammed, ed. *Reconciliation, Justice and Coexistence: Theory and Practice.* Lanham, MD: Lexington Books, 2001.

Assefa, Hizkias. "Meaning of Reconciliation," in *People Building Peace: 35 Inspiring Stories from Around the World*. Utrecht, Netherlands: European Centre For Conflict Prevention, 1999.

————. *Peace and Reconciliation as a Paradigm: A Philosophy of Peace and its Implications on Conflict, Governance, and Economic Growth in Africa*. 8th ed. Nairobi: ACIS, 2003.

————. "Tools of Peace: Critical Perspectives on Peace Theories and Practice." *NewRoutes: A Journal of Peace Research and Action*, Vol 8, No. 3-4 (2003).

Bar-Tal, Daniel. "From Intractable Conflict Through Conflict Resolution to Reconciliation: Psychological Analysis." *Political Psychology* 21, no. 2 (2000): 351–365.

Bhargava, Rajeev. "Restoring Decency to Barbaric Societies," in Robert I. Rotberg and Dennis Thompson, eds., *Truth V. Justice*. Princeton and Oxford: Princeton University Press, 2000, pp. 45–67.

Bloomfield, David, et al., eds. *Reconciliation After Violent Conflict: A Handbook*. Stockholm: International IDEA, 2003.

Brounéus, Karen. *Reconciliation: Theory and Practice for Development Cooperation*. Stockholm: Sida, Department for Cooperation with Non-Governmental Organizations and Humanitarian Assistance, 2003.

Cullberg Weston, Marta. *War Is Not Over with the Last Bullet: Overcoming Obstacles in the Healing Process for Women in Bosnia-Herzegovina*. Stockholm: Kvinna Till Kvinna Foundation, 2002.

Hamber, Brandon. *Past Imperfect: Dealing with the Past in Northern Ireland and Societies in Transition*. Derry/Londonderry: INCORE, 1998.

Henderson, Michael. *Forgiveness: Breaking the Chain of Hate*. Wilsonville, OR: Book Partners, 1999.

Lederach, John Paul. *A Journey Towards Reconciliation*. Scottsdale, AZ: Herald Press, 1999.

————. *Building Peace. Sustainable Reconciliation in Divided Societies*. Washington, DC: United States Institute of Peace Press, 1997.

Minow, Martha. *Between Vengeance and Forgiveness: Facing History After Genocide and Mass Violence*. Boston: Beacon Press, 1998.

Müller-Fahrenholz, Geiko. *The Art of Forgiveness*. Geneva: WCC Publications, 1997.

Rigby, Andrew. *Justice and Reconciliation: After the Violence*. Boulder, CO: Lynne Rienner Publishers, 2001.

Tutu, Desmond. *No Future Without Forgiveness*. New York: Doubleday,1999.

Van Der Merwe, Hugo. *The Truth and Reconciliation Commission and Community Reconciliation: An Analysis of Competing Strategies and Conceptualizations*. Fairfax, VA: George Mason University Press, 1999.

PERSONAL STORY:
"A Force More Powerful"
—Desmond Tutu

We have seen quite breathtaking examples of "people power" within the past years. Citizens, often downtrodden for decades, have said "Enough is enough," as they have paraded and demonstrated in the streets, massing up against tanks and guns with empty hands, or with hands filled with flowers or food for those who could crush them with firepower. We have seen the Berlin Wall come down. We have seen nonviolence at work in the Philippines, Eastern Europe, South Africa, Haiti, and other places with the results that many, perhaps we ourselves, would have thought impossible. We have learnt that the most dangerous things a dictator, a tyrant needs to fear, is when people decide they want to be free. It has been an exhilarating experience, and one that nourishes hope.

There is much still to be accomplished. Shattered economies need to be rehabilitated, reconciliation between former enemies must be effected, shanties in the squalor of slums must be demolished, houses are needed in their thousands, communities cry out for help to help themselves, people who have grown up in one party totalitarian regimes need to be educated in the processes of democracy, in parliamentary procedure, government that is accountable to the people.

We need those who will defuse tense situations and to resolve conflict, and those who will tell us how to cultivate cultures of tolerance.

This is what active nonviolence and peacebuilding is about. It deserves the support of all who love our planet home and know that we have been created for interdependence. "Unless we learn to live together as brothers (and sisters)," said Martin Luther King, Jr, "we will perish like fools."

Let us strive together to make our world "peace friendly." Let us make it a world where humanity can survive and flourish and where justice flows like a river and tears are wiped away from eyes. For mourning and sorrow will be done away and peace and love, compassion and caring and sharing, laughter and joy will prevail. Because we are learning to see with the eyes of the heart, realizing that we are all members of one family—God's family.

Bishop Desmond Mpilo Tutu left his position as Bishop of Lesotho in 1978 to be the first black General Secretary of the South African Council of Churches (SACC). He started a crusade for justice and racial conciliation, which led him to win the Nobel Peace Prize in 1984. He also was the first black person to lead the Anglican Church in South Africa. After the fall of apartheid he headed the Truth and Reconciliation Commission. He is visiting professor at many universities around the world and is the author of several books.

23.1

From Saying "Sorry" to a Journey of Healing: National Sorry Day in Australia

John Bond

Every nation has cruelties in its history that it would rather forget. Nonetheless, these cruelties leave victims, who do not forget. When the federal government of Australia refused to apologize for the policies under which thousands of Aboriginal children were forcibly removed from their families, a million Australians apologized instead.

In Australia, for 150 years until the 1970s, many thousands of Aboriginal children were removed from their families to be raised in institutions, or fostered or adopted by nonindigenous families. The aim was to assimilate Aboriginal Australians into the dominant culture. The outcome was tragic. For many years, Aboriginal people agitated for an inquiry into this practice. In 1995 the federal government agreed. To chair the inquiry they chose a former High Court judge, Sir Ronald Wilson.

By the time the inquiry reported in 1997, an election had brought in the new federal government of John Howard. Their view was that Aboriginal interests had won too many concessions thanks to an undue sense of guilt among white Australians, and they took steps to "swing the pendulum back." Then Wilson's report, *Bringing Them Home,* landed on their desk. Its 680 pages told in heartrending detail of the agony endured by Aboriginals as a result of the forced-removal policies.

Stolen Generations

Australians had grown up believing that these children were altruistically taken out of wretched conditions to be offered the immense benefits of white society. Now a national inquiry described the immense harm caused by the policies. For eight months the government made no official response except to say that there would be no apology, and no compensation would be paid. Several government ministers attempted to discredit the report. When two of the "stolen generations"—as they have become known—went to court, the government spent over $10 million to defeat them, and won on a technicality.

Many in the Australian community responded differently, and *Bringing Them Home* sold in far greater numbers than any comparable report. This polarization of views was a gift to the media, and the stolen generations became a frequent media topic. In 1997, no other Australian story received more coverage in the world's press.

Sir Ronald Wilson spoke freely to the media. He had been profoundly affected by the inquiry.

> It was like no other I have undertaken. Other inquiries were intellectual exercises, a matter of collating information and making recommendations. But for these people to reveal what had happened to them took immense courage and every emotional stimulus they could muster.
>
> At each session, the tape would be turned on and we would wait . . . I would look into the face of the person who was to speak to us. I would see the muscles straining to hold back the tears. But tears would stream down, still no words being spoken. And then, hesitantly, words would come.
>
> We sat there as long as it took. We heard the story, told with that person's whole being, reliving experiences which had been buried deep, sometimes for decades. They weren't speaking with their minds; they were speaking with their hearts. And my heart had to open if I was to understand them. (Bond 1998: 11)

This was no easy challenge. "I was a leader of the Presbyterian Church in Western Australia at the time we ran Sister Kate's home, where removed children grew up. I was proud of the home, with its system of cottage families. Imagine my pain when I discovered, during this inquiry, that children were sexually abused in those cottages" (Bond 1998: 11). He and the Presbyterian Church apologized wholeheartedly to the Aboriginal people. Still, neither the Church nor the government has taken steps to help the victims of abuse. As a result Sir Ronald became a crusader, stumping the country at the age of seventy-five and drawing crowds in the hundreds. "Children were removed because the Aboriginal race was seen as an embarrassment to white Australia," he told an audience in Canberra, the national capital. "The aim was to strip the children of their Aboriginality and accustom them to live in a white Australia. The tragedy was compounded when the children, as they grew up, encountered the racism which shaped the policy, and found themselves rejected by the very society for which they were being prepared."

Saying "Sorry"

His words reached a responsive audience. Most of Australia's state parliaments and churches held formal ceremonies to hear from representatives of their Aboriginal communities and to ask forgiveness.

Eventually the federal government announced that it would make available 63 million Australian dollars over four years for counseling and family reunion services—a sum that is grossly inadequate to meet the need. They ignored most of the report's recommendations, including one that a Sorry Day be held.

"Sorry" is a potent word. It indicates understanding, a willingness to enter into the suffering, and implies a commitment to do more. In Aboriginal English it has a further meaning: "sorry business" denotes a time when Aboriginal people come together to grieve. So a Sorry Day would be deeply meaningful to both Aboriginal and non-Aboriginal Australians.

However, the federal government was not interested. Could a Sorry Day be held on a community basis? Sir Ronald Wilson consulted spokespeople for the stolen generations, and they jointly invited thirty of us, Aboriginal and non-Aboriginal, to meet and consider this question. At that meeting, in January 1998, we decided to try. We chose 26 May as the day, since the report had been tabled in parliament on 26 May 1997, and elected Carol Kendall, a widely-respected member of the stolen generations, as co-chair of our informal committee.

Heartfelt Response

First we developed a statement explaining the day's meaning. We described it as

> a day when all Australians can express their sorrow for the whole tragic episode, and celebrate the beginning of a new understanding. . . . Indigenous people will participate in a Day dedicated to the memory of loved ones who never came home, or who are still finding their way home. . . . Sorry Day can help restore the dignity stripped from those affected by removal; and it offers those who carried out the policy—and their successors—a chance to move beyond denial and guilt. It could shape a far more creative partnership between Indigenous and non-Indigenous Australians, with immense benefit to both. (National Sorry Day Committee 1998)

A former governor-general of Australia, Sir Zelman Cowen, accepted our invitation to be a patron. Then in March we launched the idea to the nation through the media.

The response amazed us. The Sorry Day Committee, so-called, was merely a group of people with almost no money, and no ability to organize events across the nation. It did not matter, because people organized their own events. Aboriginal and non-Aboriginal Australians met to plan. Artists painted, musicians composed, writers and playwrights wrote. A well-known actor created *Sorry Books*—manuscript books in which people could express their apology. More and more books were produced as demand grew from schools, public libraries, and town councils. Soon several thousand books were in circulation, and a million people wrote messages, many of them telling of personal experiences that prompted them to contribute to a *Sorry Book*.

When the day arrived, it was commemorated by thousands of events. There were theatrical presentations, cultural displays, and town barbecues. Universities, government departments, local councils, and churches held gatherings to hear from stolen-generations people. In many of them, the *Sorry Books* were ceremoniously handed to local Aboriginal elders. Over half of the thirty-minute national TV news that evening was devoted to Sorry Day events, and to the heartfelt response of Australia's best-known Aboriginal leaders.

Accepting the Blame

Why did Sorry Day touch such a chord? One person told me why he got involved:

> I thought back to my primary school classroom. I can name every person in that class except the four Aboriginal boys who sat at the back of the class, never asked a question, stuck with each other in the playground, never played with the rest of us. I looked on them as incredibly dull. When I read *Bringing Them Home,* I began to understand what they had probably endured, and why they acted as they did. And I felt ashamed.

Many Australians, like him, have encountered removed Aboriginal children, but few asked why they had been removed. One of the deepest human pains is that of a mother who loses her child, or a child its mother. Yet the gulf between Aboriginal and non-Aboriginal Australians was simply too immense for even this pain to flow across it. *Bringing Them Home* exposed this gulf, and many Australians were shocked. Sorry Day was a chance to accept blame, and to do something about it.

The federal government was taken aback by the strength of the day's message. They had no idea how to respond to a campaign that included many people active on their side of politics. So they stayed silent and aloof.

Toward Healing

The stolen generations were deeply moved. For the first time, they felt that the Australian community understood what they had gone through. Now the way was open toward healing. From across the country they met together. Out of their discussions came a decision to launch a Journey of Healing. A prominent stolen-generations woman, Lowitja O'Donoghue, became its patron.

The Journey of Healing's underlying concept is that, if the wounds are to be healed, both government and the community, Aboriginal and non-Aboriginal, have a vital role. It offers every Australian the chance to be part of the healing. Many have responded. Hundreds of events are arranged each year, bringing together Aboriginal and non-Aboriginal Australians, at which members of the stolen generations speak. When their local community understands the problems they face, some of these problems can be overcome. People who have felt alienated for years are experiencing the welcome of their communities. People who were hopeless, angry, or despairing now feel life is worth living.

One of them is a Sydney woman, Val Linow. In 2000, the Council for Aboriginal Reconciliation arranged a walk across the Sydney Harbour Bridge for all who wanted to show their support for reconciliation between Aboriginal and non-Aboriginal Australians. Many of the stolen generations walked behind a banner proclaiming the Journey of Healing. Still Val phoned me to

John Bond

Participants of a Journey of Healing walk, listening to a speech by the Minister of Aboriginal Affairs at the steps of parliament (Adelaide)

say that after all she had been through, there was no possibility of healing for her, and she would only walk with us if we got rid of the banner.

She told me her story. She had been removed from her family at the age of two, and had been cruelly treated and abused. So I understood how she felt. However, I urged her to walk, even if she could not come with us.

A quarter of a million people walked. It was the largest demonstration that had taken place in Australian history. As at Sorry Day, people made their views known in their own way. Some paid for a skywriting plane, which wrote "Sorry" in the sky above the bridge.

That night Val phoned me. "I went on the walk." she said. "I looked at the thousands of people who had come. I looked up at the word 'Sorry' in the sky. Suddenly, tears began to pour down my cheeks. I have found healing."

Today she is active in the Journey of Healing in Sydney.

Memorial

Walks took place in all cities that year, and a total of a million people walked for reconciliation. The federal government could not ignore such a demonstration. Prime Minister John Howard announced that a central area in Canberra would be set aside "to perpetuate in the minds of the Australian public the importance of reconciliation, and will include a memorial and depiction of the removal of children from their families."

The federal government still wanted control though, as they made clear when they refused to include those who had been removed in developing the memorial's design. This provoked demonstrations, and criticism even from party colleagues such as former prime minister Malcolm Fraser. The project ground to a halt.

We went to see the minister in charge of the project. "This memorial could be immensely healing," we told him, "if it comes out of genuine consultation. We are prepared to consult the stolen generations, former staff of the institutions to which they were taken, and those who fostered or adopted children, with the aim of reaching consensus on the design of the memorial."

Some months later the minister accepted our proposal. Quickly we organized consultation teams throughout the country, who met with several hundred people bursting with ideas. These ideas were brought together in three days of passionate meetings in Sydney. Through the heartache, people listened to each other, and shifted from hard-held points of view. By the end, we had agreement on a provisional text. Further consultation refined the text, and we presented it to the government.

For five months the government did nothing. So we let them know that Malcolm Fraser had accepted our invitation to give the 2003 Sorry Day address in the Great Hall of Parliament. Immediately we were invited to discuss our text. Our discussions enhanced the wording. Since we had reached consensus, we were able to resist attempts to remove words that the government found awkward. Eventually, a proposal went to the prime minister. His response reached us two hours before Malcolm Fraser gave his address. Our wording had been accepted.

Today the memorial stands between the High Court and the National Library, where hundreds of thousands of people each year stop and see it. The text begins: "This place honors the people who have suffered under the removal policies and practices. It also honors those Indigenous and non-Indigenous people whose genuine care softened the tragic impact of what are now recognized as cruel and misguided policies."

At the dedication ceremony in May 2004, our committee released a media statement. "As South Africa's Truth and Reconciliation Commission has shown," we said, "a public acknowledgement of shameful past practices is a crucial first step in healing the wounds caused by those practices. This memorial will inform Australians from all over the country and, we hope, will inspire a new determination to overcome the continuing harmful effects of the removal policies."

This is desperately needed. Today thousands of Aboriginal people struggle because their removal left them vulnerable to despair within themselves and abuse by others. Perhaps this is why Sorry Day has become a fixture on the national calendar, despite the federal government's lack of support. The Sorry Day gatherings that take place each year help the healing process. It takes immense courage and determination to break out of the despair in which many stolen-generations people exist. In many cases, an expression of empathy from their local community has helped them find that courage.

Still, there is a further step that we, as a nation, need to take. Our government must sit down with representatives of the stolen generations, and reach agreement on what needs to be done to end their grievance. Until this happens, many Australians will feel the need for a Sorry Day. Our sorrow means little unless it results in a serious determination to heal the wounds and address the continuing injustices. "Sorry" is not just a word, it is an attitude. When that attitude is felt widely enough across the Australian community, it will take hold of our government too. Then Sorry Day will probably fade away, or find another name. "Sorry" will have been said, in word and in deed.

John Bond is secretary of the National Sorry Day Committee and the campaign that it launched, the Journey of Healing. Patrons of the committee are former prime minister Malcolm Fraser and Doris Pilkington Garimara, author of the book and feature film Rabbit-Proof Fence.

Contact

*National Sorry Day Committee and
    Journey of Healing*
151 Kent St. Hughes
ACT 2605 Australia
Tel.: +61 (2) 6281 0940
Fax: +61 (2) 6232 4554
E-mail: johnbond@netspeed.com.au
Websites:
    http://www.journeyofhealing.com
    http://www.austlii.edu.au/au/special/rsjproject/sorry/

Selected Bibliography

Acting Aboriginal and Torres Strait Islander Social Justice Commissioner. 1998. *Social Justice Report 1998* (Australia: Human Rights and Equal Opportunity Commission). Online at: http://www.hreoc.gov.au/social_justice/sjreport_98/index.html

Bond, John. 1998. "Time to Say Sorry to 'Stolen Generations,'" in *For a Change,* Vol. 11, No. 1, Feb/Mar. (London: Initiatives of Change, p. 11).

Head, Mike. 1998. "The Politics of Australia's National Sorry Day." World Socialist website: http://www.wsws.org/news/1998/jun1998/aust-j2.shtml.

Henderson, Michael. 1999. *Forgiveness: Breaking the Chain of Hate* (Wilsonville, Oregon: BookPartners).

23.2

Listen to Understand:
The Listening Project in Croatia

Corinne Bloch

Berak, in Croatia, is a tiny village with extremely traumatic war experiences. In 1999, in order to open a space for dialogue and communication between the people, the Center for Peace, Nonviolence, and Human Rights in Osijek entered the community with the Listening Project. Five years later, the village has changed and one of its inhabitants may be nominated for the Nobel Peace Prize in 2005.

I shall never forget that day when they rang the bell for the first time. It was in autumn 1999, shortly after the tragic murder of a Serb in Berak. About one year after I came back to my village. I opened. Behind the door stood two people; they looked rather nice and smiley. Different. They introduced themselves as members of a Peace Team working for the Center for Peace, Non-Violence and Human Rights in Osijek (Center for Peace–Osijek). They said they just wanted to help. They were interested in my war experience, in my opinion about Berak today, in my ideas to improve life in that sad village. They just wanted to listen to me and let me tell what I had to say. Of course, I let them come in and I started to talk and talk, to cry and cry . . . I could not stop anymore to get rid of all the pain and questions I had inside myself for so long. They paid attention, taking notes. To understand what the presence of these people meant to us—even if we did not think about any peace or reconciliation as far—you have to know what Berak was at that time. You have to know how terrible the lack of communication between people was. You have to know how dark our future seemed.

Recounting the day she met the people working in the Peace Team still incites strong emotions in Dragica Aleksa. "They really brought something to me and to the community. They opened a way for communication and their commitment gave to some of us the motivation to get involved in the community. They made us feel responsible for our life and future."

Dragica has become one of the most committed people working for peace and reconciliation in Berak. Her work has been acknowledged as being of invaluable support to individual people in Berak, as well as to the empowerment of the community. Her story is illustrative for the big change and new spirit that the Listening Project, conducted by the Center for Peace–Osijek, has brought about, step by step, in several local communities in the eastern Croatian region of Slavonia.

In an atmosphere of great interethnic tension and negative attitudes of the public toward the idea of cohabitation, the center's Peace Teams were the first examples of ethnically mixed groups working to promote peace and to offer alternatives to violence. "Listen to Understand" was the project's slogan. Its approach of giving people ample opportunity to tell their stories was based on a specific method that was developed by the U.S. organization Rural Southern Voice for Peace. One of the major characteristics of the program in eastern Croatia was that it had been tailored to the specific needs of each community in the region. As a result, there are today a lot of "Dragicas" working for peace in Slavonia. Free from ethnic prejudice, they work to build a new society based on civil participation and sustainable peace.

Berak, September 1999

Situated on one of the few hills of predominantly flat Slavonia, Berak is a tiny village of some 350 inhabitants. Two small shops, two churches, and a little wood bench on the main street essentially compose its public life. Since the region has been reintegrated into the Republic of Croatia, an operation conducted between 1996 and 1998 under the control of the United Nations, displaced people, mainly Croats, have slowly come back to Berak. Dragica is one of them. After several years in a refugee camp, she and her fellow returnees have been in a hurry to go back to normal life. Those who lost their sons or husbands came back with the expectation that Serbs who stayed in the village during the years it was under Serbian control would tell them where the bodies of their loved ones were. In Berak, fifty-six people—or 10 percent of its population—were killed during the fights or in the village's concentration camp between 1991 and 1995. Dead bodies were thrown in wells or buried in unknown places; thirty of them are still missing.

The reality the returnees found did not meet their expectations. The village had changed. Many of the Croatian returnees are confronted with the silence of the Serbs, who claim that all those Serbs who might have information about missing people have left. The returnees hardly recognized their village. Dragica remembers, "I was looking at all the neighbor's houses, everywhere people were missing. Nothing was like before anymore."

She was unable to imagine any form of reconciliation, not even with her former best friend, a Serb woman. "When she came to me, asking why I still didn't visit her, I was just able to answer: 'Because you didn't come with us either when we had to leave.'"

Postwar tension in Berak was extremely high, because in this small community practically every family could be individually linked to the dramatic, violent events of the war. Most of the older Serbs living in the village are said to be parents of war criminals. Unlike bigger cities, such as Osijek, where neighbors maybe associated with traumatic events on a more anonymous level, as members of a specific ethnic group, in Berak the traumatic incidents are linked to individuals whose names are known to all villagers. Victims and perpetrators, or perpetrators' parents, are trying to live together.

Sometimes the horrors of the past incited new confrontations. Hate and tension suddenly flared up, at one time culminating in the murder of a Serb. The situation seemed out of control. In a move to stem violence, the Organization for Security and Cooperation in Europe (OSCE) stepped in and called on the Center for Peace–Osijek to help.

The center was founded in 1992 by a small group of intellectuals. It sought to explore and implement creative methods of problem solving and conflict resolution. The project's "Peace Building Model" involved the identification and training of local men and women, who themselves had been victims of war. Along with outsiders, recruited internationally, these locals were to become members of multiethnic and multinational Peace Teams throughout eastern Croatia. The teams' diversity was a powerful message to Serbs and Croats that they could work together on peace and community building. This turned out to be a courageous choice but did not make the work easier, especially not in a traumatized community such as Berak.

Open-Ended Interviews

The initiators of the project in Osijek took inspiration and used practical examples from Rural Southern Voice for Peace, an American organization working on the improvement of interracial relations in the United States. This organization developed what it called "Active Listening," a method based on conducting interviews consisting of open-ended questions. The approach provides space for people to openly express their feelings and concerns; to promote common beliefs and hopes; to encourage people to define their community problems; and to perceive these problems from the point of view of the person who is part of the solution.

"The fact that people could talk from their point of view, about their experience, their feelings and opinions, was a completely new approach," confirms the director of Center for Peace–Osijek, Katarina Kruhonja. "In the very urgent and difficult situation we had to face in the postwar period, compassionate listening was probably the only possible way to enter traumatized communities. Yet, for us, the Peace Team, it was also very challenging to give a peace message in this dark and even sometimes dangerous atmosphere. Just imagine; in Berak the Project was to respond to recent murders. In some villages, since the region had been reintegrated to Croatia, Serbs had even barricaded the streets to prevent Croats to come back. By listening to people without prejudice we helped to reduce the fear and, by doing so, we found a way to open communication where there was no one before. . . . This was crucial," Katarina Kruhonja adds. "Step by step, we could feel that the tensions and the hate were decreasing."

Nevertheless, the people running the project judged that the situation in Berak required a slightly different approach. They changed the questionnaire, which resulted in a list of twenty-one questions about five themes: experience of trauma; communication between Serbs and Croats; the problem of missing persons and recent murder of a Serb; guilt and war crimes; and perspectives for the future. Contrary to what had been standard practice in other communities, direct questions about the prospects of peaceful coexistence or reconciliation were avoided, since it was deemed too early for them. In addition, as some members of the Peace Teams feared that the interviews might give rise to confrontations, complementary training for Peace Team members was organized in dealing with conflict.

Eight teams, of two persons each, started to interview citizens of Berak. At least one member of each family in the village was represented among the sixteen interviewers. Vesna, a member of a Peace Team, admits:

> At the beginning, active listening seemed very unrealistic. Then I realized how important it was to investigate real needs of people. By listening to them, we made them feel respected because they had a chance to express their own needs. Listening helped us to build a relationship of trust with the inhabitants. They would stop us in the street and talk to us. At first, approximately 90 percent of the people let us enter their home; the others did it after we had an informal talk. In Berak, we were particularly afraid, but people welcomed us, delighted that there were someone was ready to listen to them.

In Berak, no one turned down an invitation to be interviewed. Most interviews lasted two hours and there were no incidents. An important feature of the Listening Program is analyzing and writing a detailed report on the stories heard, and giving feedback to the community. That is the first step that enables people to hear each other. The reports are impersonal and therefore can be easily accepted by both ethnic groups.

Additional Activities

Typically, the Listening Project is followed by activities aimed at solving the problems that have been identified during interviews. These activities are an essential part of the project.

It was clear from the interviews in Berak that mutual mistrust among neighbors of different ethnic origin was a major issue. Returnees resent the alleged role of those who stayed in the village during the war and the apparent inability to find the missing victims. The Serb inhabitants feel their fellow citizens have imposed a collective guilt on them, resulting in social isolation, discrimination at work, or loss of jobs. People also mentioned the difficult economic situation and the problem of unemployment, which created a sense of apathy and despair. There was consensus across all groups that there was a need for economic revitalization and improvement of the village's cultural and social infrastructure. Moreover, the Peace Teams noticed that several persons showed signs of posttraumatic stress disorder and that several families needed humanitarian or legal aid. The Center for Social Care, Caritas, and the UN High Commission on Refugees were informed about the humanitarian needs.

In order to build mutual trust, the Peace Teams tried to motivate inhabitants of Berak to participate in community activities. Dragica accepted an invitation to join a workshop for the empowerment of women."I had no idea what a workshop was, but I went. As I introduced myself, saying 'I'm from Berak,' a woman commented, 'The village where a Croat killed a Serb two months ago.' I immediately reacted aggressively: 'And what about the fifty Croats who have been killed during the war?' Today, this woman is one of my best friends and we fight together for peace."

Like others in her community, Dragica started slowly to feel that she could do more. First she started visiting people, opening a dialogue. Then she started to build bridges between the different ethnic groups. It took her almost a year before she had built sufficient trust to be allowed back into the house of Baba Savka, her old Serb neighbor. Today Dragica is one of these people who say "hello" to everybody, breaking the invisible wall between the groups. "I slowly understood to make a difference between 'the Serbs' and some particular 'Serbs.' You can start to forgive someone who burned your house if this person is an individual, with a name and a face. But you cannot enter such a process for a whole collectivity."

Step-by-step, more people got involved and more activities took place supported by Peace Teams. Almost all primary-school children participated in workshops for peacebuilding. A youth club was opened. Local people took part in constructing a house that would serve as a community center for the village.

After having worked for months to rebuild mutual trust, the project team decided that the time had come to start a dialogue about one of the most painful remaining problems in the village: the issue of missing persons and postwar justice. Most peace workers agreed that the healing process could hardly be successful as long as the bodies of people killed during the war were still unaccounted for. An ethnically mixed delegation from the village visited the president of Croatia to ask him to put more effort in finding their missing relatives. Serbs participated in the mission because they wanted the bodies to be found, realizing that there was not going to be any improvement in their position in the community until this issue has been resolved. The meeting was unsuccessful, but it opened a discussion in the community. This led to additional efforts aimed at finding missing persons.

Two years after the Listening Project began, independent evaluators and researchers have assessed that the peace activities empowered both the peace teams and the people who were listened to. Prejudices and fears with regard to the "other" ethnic group have decreased. More communication with members of different ethnic backgrounds has been taking place. Several villagers have become engaged in peace activities. Peace Team members said they learned a lot about themselves; about their fears and prejudices, but also about their inner ability to empathize and see somebody else's truth. However, the evaluators recommended putting in place additional education about debriefing techniques and self-protection against emotionally charged interactions for the Peace Teams, as some of them had burnout symptoms.

Berak, Summer 2004

According to the OSCE, the project was a breakthrough in the communication between divided populations. Even while graves were discovered, giving rise to deep emotions, the situation stayed calm. Since then, more bodies of missing war victims have been found. Although strong feelings of bitterness persist among many people, there are examples of cross-cultural communication at the individual level. In 2003, five members of the youth club chose for the first time to participate in an ethnically mixed summer camp; in the summer of 2004 ten members joined the group. In 2003, Dragica and Mile, a Croat and a Serb, succeeded in opening a milk-processing plant called Milk Association, operated as an NGO, which is being used by farmers of both ethnic backgrounds.

As of 2004, Dragica organizes workshops herself: poetry workshops to enter a process of dealing with the past through literature, and courses to train her neighbors to become peace workers. Asked what she considers to be her biggest achievement, Dragica answers: "My biggest success is not the work I did for the community but the work I did on myself." The time has gone when Dragica looked at her fields without seeing any future on the horizon. Her association, which was officially registered as an NGO this year, is called Luc ("small light"). A small light, but a big spark for the tiny village of Berak. A spark that is maybe going to get a prize. Dragica is nominated to be part of a group of one thousand women from all over the world that will be nominated for the Nobel Peace Prize 2005.

Corinne Bloch is a Swiss journalist who worked for various daily and weekly newspapers and magazines. After her studies at the Graduate Institute of Development Studies in Geneva, she came to Croatia in order to broaden her experience in peace-building. Since the beginning of 2004, she works for the Center for Peace, Non-Violence and Human Rights–Osijek in Bosnia and Croatia on different projects.

Contact

Center for Peace, Non-Violence and
    Human Rights—Osijek
Zupanijska 7,
HR-31000 Osijek, Croatia
Tel./fax: +385 (0)31 206 886 or 206 889
E-mail: centar-za-mir@centar-za-mir
Websites:
    http://www.centar-za-mir.hr
    http://www.listeningproject.info/media.htm

Selected Bibliography

Center for Peace–Osijek has published a wide variety of documentation and books related to its activities. Many of these publications can be downloaded from the center's website. Many resources are also available at the International Listening Project Training and Resource Center. A new publication on various Listening Project experiences is being prepared. It includes further information and results about the Listening Project conducted by the Center for Peace–Osijek in different communities in Slavonia and Croatia. The book will be available through the Rural Southern Voice for Peace's website.

Kruhonja, Katarina. ed. 2000. *I Choose Life: Building a Democratic Society Based on the Culture of Non-Violence: Post-War Peace Building in Eastern Croatia—Report on the First Project Phase (1998–2000)*. (Osijek, Croatia: Center for Peace, Non-Violence and Human Rights–Osijek).

Mathews, Dylan. 2001. *War Prevention Works: 50 Stories of People Resolving Conflict* (Oxford: Oxford Research Group).

23.3

The Spirit of Caux:
Moral Re-Armament/Initiatives
of Change in Switzerland

Michael Henderson

In 1946, a group of Swiss bought the run-down Caux Palace Hotel above Montreux to serve as a place where the combatant nations of World War II could meet. It was the fulfillment of an idea that had come to a Swiss diplomat named Philippe Mottu three years earlier: if Switzerland were spared by the war, its task would be to make available a place where Europeans, torn apart by hatred, suffering, and resentment, could come together. Mottu and the other Swiss were associated with a worldwide movement to promote reconciliation called Moral Re-Armament—known since 2001 as Initiatives of Change.

Moral Re-Armament (MRA) had been launched in 1938 by an American, Frank Buchman, who believed that selfish human nature lay at the root of national and international divisions. At a moment when the emphasis was on nations rearming militarily, he proclaimed the need for individuals and nations also to "rearm morally." He spoke of a "return to those simple truths which many of us have forgotten—honesty, purity, unselfishness, and love." Peacemakers had to begin the process of peacemaking by looking within themselves; apologies were central to the process of reconciliation. "Peace is people becoming different," he said. He stressed the importance of those from opposite sides of a political divide meeting in the right atmosphere.

The distinctively turreted hotel purchased by the Swiss, which was renamed Mountain House, is set in the midst of restful grounds with a panoramic view of Lake Geneva and the peaks of the Dents du Midi. In the years since Mountain House received its first guests, it has been host to several hundred thousand people from all over the world, many of whom met across contentious divides— whether they be Turks and Greeks from the two sides of the Green Line in Cyprus; Muslims, Christians, and Jews from the Middle East; or Cambodians attempting to move beyond the killing fields. In the early 1950s the reconciliation work taking place at Mountain House, particularly in helping to forge better relations between France and Germany, led to Buchman's nomination for the Nobel Peace Prize.

Philippe Mottu recalls the start. "On the day he arrived in Caux in July 1946, Buchman confronted us with a challenge. After meeting all those who had worked so devotedly to get Mountain House ready, he suddenly asked: 'Where are the Germans?' And he added: 'Some of you think that Germany has got to change; and that is true. But you will never be able to rebuild Europe without Germany.'"

His compassion for the countries that had suffered at the hands of Nazi Germany, and his understanding of Germany's own suffering in defeat, were matched by his realism. The material and moral ruins of six years of war formed the background to the first conference; national hatreds, class war, and personal vendettas were poisoning the atmosphere of Europe. "Neither international conferences nor grudging concessions could heal these wounds," says Mottu. "The peace for which Europe had so ardently longed was tragically incomplete, for there was no peace in people's hearts." In Germany, there was a vacuum that would be flooded by forces of anarchy and materialism unless the Germans were offered something more than just the end of war.

Approaches were made to the occupation authorities to permit a group of Germans to visit Caux the following year. A list of 150 possible participants was drawn up and, with the cooperation of the Swiss authorities, the Germans arrived in Caux in the summer of 1947. The group included survivors from Nazi concentration camps, widows of officers executed after the 1944 attempt on Hitler's life, and German personalities who were working with the Allies in the administration of Germany. Among them were prime ministers from West German states and two future chancellors of the Federal Republic of Germany. Hans Ehard, prime minister of Bavaria, told the international audience,

> It is a unique experience for Germans to find themselves received into a circle of so many different nations on a level of complete equality and in an atmosphere where they have every freedom to speak without previously set limitations on what they shall say and on what they shall remain silent, and where one can be sure that one will not be met by that hatred which is so strong in the world today.

Democracy at Work

In his autobiography, *Against Two Evils 1931–45*, Hans von Herwarth, West Germany's first ambassador to Britain, writes that most of the German personalities who played a role in the reconstruction of West Germany took part in Caux or its outreach. "At Caux we found democracy at work, and in the light of what we saw, we faced ourselves and our nation. It was personal and national repentance. Many of us Germans who were anti-Nazi made the mistake of putting the whole blame on Hitler. We learned at Caux that we, too, were responsible" (von Herwarth 1990: 59).

For the first time, wrote Hamburg's *Freie Presse*, "the question of the collective guilt of the past has been replaced by the more decisive question of collective responsibility for the future. Here in Caux, for the first time, Germany has been given a platform from which she can speak to the world as an equal."

Between 1948 and 1952 more than three thousand Germans attended Caux conference sessions, including most of the leading figures in German public life—future prime ministers, industrialists, educators, and opinion makers from all levels and occupations. The personal trust that developed among these men and women gave a decisive impetus to European unity at a crucial time.

At Caux, the Germans, like everyone else, had the chance to meet those from their own country and from other countries not only during plenary sessions and at meals but in walks together and in attending to everyday household chores. Scholar Edward Luttwak describes how, often, the German participants

> would give vent to expressions of self-pity upon their first arrival at Caux, recounting their own sufferings and those of their families as if they were unique, and with no apparent recognition that others had suffered far more at German hands. Later, having absorbed the "spirit of Caux," the tone and content of the declarations would change drastically, combining expressions of intense gratitude for being received as equals and even as friends by the other participants, avowals of guilt and repentance, repudiations of past belief in Hitler and his ideology, and promises that Germans would never again be guilty of aggression. (Luttwak 1994: 54)

The "spirit of Caux" was helped immeasurably by the willingness of some two thousand French participants, including cabinet ministers, members of parliament, industrialists and representatives of industrial workers, teachers, clergy, and journalists, to take account of their own country's part in the European tragedy. The French paper *L'Aube* reported that in Caux, Franco-German relations were dealt with "frankly and courageously." The Alsatian wartime resistance leader and French deputy Joseph Wasmer, for instance, asked forgiveness for his hatred of the German people. "I hated the Germans with everything in my power for what they did to my friends and my country," he acknowledged. "I rejoiced to see Berlin in flames. At Caux this hatred has left my heart. I ask forgiveness from the Germans. I want to make restitution to them."

The heart of the philosophy of Caux was the notion that if you wanted to bring a change in the world, the most practical way to start was with change in yourself and your country. Caux fostered the practice of spending time in silence, alone or in community, helping each individual find for himself or herself the right course of action. Even as sessions dealt with tough world issues, the concept of wanting the best for the other person took precedence over the desire to book political, social, or economic advantage.

Extending the Spirit

The work over the years at Caux was extended by international teams that crisscrossed Germany at the invitation of Germans who had been at the conference.

These teams helped to lay the foundation for the reestablishment of democracy and to heal the wartime hatreds. They included men and women who had survived the concentration camps, as well as veterans of Allied forces and the resistance movements.

In 1949 George Villiers, president of the French Employers' Federation, visited Caux as a representative of French foreign minister Robert Schuman. There he got to know one of the architects of the new Germany, Hans Boeckler, who was president of the German Trades Union Congress. Boeckler said to Villiers, "We ought to be enemies on two counts. I am a German, you are French; you are the head of the employers, I am a trade union leader." "Yes," Villiers replied, "and there's a third count: your countrymen condemned me to death, I was in a political concentration camp, and I saw most of my comrades die around me. But that is all past. We must forget it." With personal reconciliation came political reconciliation as well; Villiers announced that he would throw his weight behind the "moral and economic union" of France and Germany.

Six weeks after the essentials of the Schuman Plan—the framework leading to the creation of the European Common Market—had been agreed by France and Germany, Buchman was decorated with France's Legion of Honor for his "contribution to better understanding between France and Germany." Subsequently, he was also honored by the German government. Two months after the treaty creating the European Coal and Steel Community was signed in 1951, German chancellor Conrad Adenauer stated,

> The nations of the world will only have stable relations with one another when they have been inwardly prepared for them. During these last months we have witnessed the success of difficult negotiations and the signing of important international agreements. Moral Re-Armament has played an unseen but effective role in reducing the differences of opinion between the negotiating parties and has guided them toward a peaceful agreement by helping them to seek the common good.

"MRA did not invent the Schuman Plan but it facilitated its realization from the start," concludes Edward Luttwak. "That is no small achievement given the vast importance of every delay—and every acceleration—of the process of Franco-German reconciliation during those crucial, formative years."

The Continuation
In the more than fifty years that have elapsed since the arrival of the first Germans in Caux, Mountain House has continued to work on the principles learned and applied at that time—an emphasis on how to build the future rather than on assignment of responsibility for the past and a belief that caring for the individual's well-being and spiritual growth is as important as any diplomatic or political result. Historian Scott Appleby, writing on the role of Mountain House in *The Ambivalence of the Sacred,* observes that it embodies

MRA's conviction that "peaceful and productive change in hostile relations between nations or ethno-religious groups depends on change in the individuals prosecuting the war; that process, in turn, requires individuals representing each side to listen, carefully and at length, to their counterparts" (Appleby 2000: 225).

As a nongovernmental organization, Caux is today providing a forum for debate on a range of vexing issues, bringing together people from all corners of the world. A French member of parliament, Georges Mesmin, says that political figures find there a respect for all opinions, an openness, both to others and to the principle of forgiveness—even when one thinks another is wrong—and an atmosphere of friendship. Supplementing the work of individuals, which has always been the backbone of Caux, distinctive programs have been developed.

Agenda for Reconciliation, for instance, assists efforts in preventive diplomacy and nation building, and in recent years, has drawn to Caux men and women on opposite sides of conflicts in Somalia, Sierra Leone, and the Great Lakes region of Africa, as well as participants from Lebanon, Israel, and Palestine. In addition, encouraged by the Dalai Lama, who has twice been to Caux, sessions have brought together religious leaders in dialogue including, significantly, dialogue between Muslims and non-Muslims in 2002.

- Foundations for Freedom is fostering moral and spiritual values in newly democratic countries that have been undermined by decades of totalitarianism.
- The Caux Round Table has promulgated "Caux Principles," which have been described as the most widely distributed statement of business ethics in the world.
- The Caux Scholars Programme has, over more than a dozen years, graduated students from sixty-one countries from courses addressing practical aspects of conflict resolution.
- The International Communications Forum encompasses a network of hundreds of men and women in the media who are committed to restoring public confidence in their work
- Hope in the Cities works to create partnerships of reconciliation and trains dialogue facilitators in interracial community initiatives. In language that would have been as appropriate in 1946 as it is today, and which truly embodies "the spirit of Caux," it calls for honest conversation that "includes everyone and excludes no one, focuses on working together towards a solution, not on identifying enemies, affirms the best and does not confirm the worst, looks for what is right rather than who is right, and moves beyond blame and personal pain to constructive action."

Michael Henderson is a free-lance journalist and the author of nine books. He has been a TV presenter, a broadcaster, and for more than fifty years worked for peace and understanding in some thirty countries.

Contact

Caux Conference Secretariat
Mountain House
CH-1824 Caux, Switzerland
Tel.: +41 21 962 9111
Fax: 41 21 962 9355
E-mail: info@caux.ch or confsec@caux.ch,
    MichaelDHenderson@btinternet.com
Websites:
    http:// www.caux.ch
    http://www.michaelhenderson.org.uk
    http://www.uk.initiativesofchange.org

Selected Bibliography

Appleby, R. Scott. 2000. *The Ambivalence of the Sacred: Religion, Violence and Reconciliation* (Lanham, MD: Rowman and Littlefield).

Henderson, Michael. 2002. *Forgiveness: Breaking the Chain of Hate* (London: Grosvenor Books; Portland, OR: Arnica Publishing).

———. 1996. *The Forgiveness Factor* (London: Grosvenor Books).

———. 1994. *All Her Paths Are Peace* (West Hartford, CT: Kumarian Press).

———. 2003. "Initiatives of Change," in Abu-Nimer, Sampson, and Whitney Liebler, eds., *Positive Approaches to Peacebuilding* (Washington, DC: Pact Publications).

Initiatives of Change, http://www.iofc.org

Initiatives of Change—Agenda for Reconciliation, http://www.afr-iofc.org

Lean, Garth. 1985. *Frank Buchman, a Life* (London: Constable).

———. 1988. *On the Tail of a Comet* (Colorado Springs, CO: Helmers and Howard).

Life and Peace Institute, http://www.life-peace.org

Luttwak, Edward. 1994. "Franco-German Reconciliation: The Overlooked Role of the Moral Re-Armament Movement," in Douglas Johnston and Cynthia Sampson, eds., *Religion, the Missing Dimension of Statecraft* (New York: Oxford University Press).

Oxford Research Institute, http:www.oxfordresearchgroup.org.uk

Piguet, Jacqueline. 1986. *For the Love of Tomorrow* (London: Grosvenor Books).

Von Herwarth, Hans. 1990. *Von Adenauer zu Brandt—Erinnerungen* (Berlinn: Propyläen).

23.4

Dialogue Spices Peace: Baku Bae in Indonesia

The Baku Bae movement in Indonesia brought Christian and Muslim communities together by adopting bold conflict resolution and reconciliation methods. The initiators see these as a way of rebuilding social capital and restoring trust through dialogue and community focus.

In 2000, as fighting between Muslims and Christians in Maluku, Indonesia, spiraled out of control, peace activist Ichsan Malik began knocking on militants' doors. Neither side showed desire for reconciliation. "I was Si Buta Dari Goa Hantu," he admits, referring to a heroic figure from Indonesian fiction ("The Blind Hero of Devil Cave"). "They said I was a lunatic. It was, perhaps, my naivety that saved us."

Malik traveled first to Saparua Island, the Christian stronghold, to meet a group of priests. Then he visited Ja'far Umar Thalib, commander in chief of Laskar Jihad, the Muslim militia, in Yogyakarta Special Region. These approaches were met, initially, with suspicion.

The militants were used to military and government functionaries making such overtures and had doubts about Malik's motives. He pressed ahead nonetheless, and even arranged opinion polls among people from the two communities to convince their leaders that a sentiment existed in both camps for Christians and Muslims to engage in dialogue.

Malik was confident his bottom-up approach would work, that the key was to strengthen desire for peace at the grassroots (people actually involved in, and affected by, the conflict) before getting the authorities involved. That is the core idea of Baku Bae ("Reconciliation"), a movement formed in 2000 that became one of the most visible civil-society responses to the mass violence that broke out in Maluku a year earlier.

Peace Deal

The movement showcased an interesting alternative to normal conflict resolution methods. Its principles and methods were based on *baku bae*, which in

Molukan culture describes the peaceful spirit used in children's games to restore friendships after a quarrel.

Formally known as Institut Titian Perdamaian, the movement was started by civil-society actors from Maluku supported by a disparate group including activists from Jakarta (the capital), traditional and religious leaders, people from the women's movement, youth groups, intellectuals and educators, lawyers, and journalists. Malik, a former activist for nongovernmental organizations (NGOs) working to protect natural resources, was one of its founders.

The activities of this body helped reduce violence on Maluku and paved the way for the signing of a peace deal brokered by the central government, the Malino Declaration of 2002, signed by more than twenty Christian and Muslim leaders. This accord pledged to stop violence, support socioeconomic development, and undertake an independent investigation into what originally sparked the conflict. It urged unauthorized militia to surrender their weapons and called on groups from outside the Maluku Province to leave—a clear reference to the main armed Islamic group, which eventually returned its fighters to Java.

Physical divisions remained between the Muslim and Christian communities after this agreement, but the mass violence largely ceased and some of the armed groups disbanded. The army reduced its presence and Maluku settled into a period of uneasy calm, even if the traumatic memory of the bloodletting may never be fully erased.

A Five-Stage Approach

In the beginning, Malik and other initiators of Baku Bae carried out their work largely in secret. Tensions were running high and those within the warring factions interested in talking peace feared negative reaction within their communities to any disclosure of contact with opponents.

The efforts were divided into five main stages. In the first, the initiators invited leaders of parties directly involved in the conflict to meet. Twelve prominent members from both sides of the Maluku community attended in Jakarta. Owing to the security situation at the time, and disclosure fears, a neutral venue was chosen away from Maluku Province. Nonetheless, the tensions were evident inside the meeting. Each side blamed the other for the conflict. The mediators encouraged more general exchanges about common experiences, and tried to bring discussions around to the true nature of the conflict.

A follow-up session was held in Bali. Some forty people turned up. Twice that number attended the third meeting in December 2000 in Yogyakarta, including representatives of religious, *adat* (customary), youth, nongovernmental, and militant organizations. In a joint statement, the participants promised to continue using local traditions as a means of accommodating the interests of all the different parties. They proposed that "all local traditional leaders, or Bapa Radja, once again take the lead . . . but at the same time support state law and guarantee the acceptance of all migrants living in the province." This desire was tested at follow-up workshops involving various representatives of the Molukan people.

Deep-Rooted Fears and Years of Mistrust

Although they appear like dots on the map, the islands of Maluku Province in Indonesia, were once at the center of global commerce. Five hundred years ago, the spices they produced—nutmeg and cloves—cost more than gold. It was the quest for these riches that made European explorers sail around southern Africa to India for the first time.

Over the centuries, the islands changed hands between Dutch, Portuguese, and English traders, leaving an immensely diverse cultural and religious stamp. Muslim, Catholic, and Protestant religions blended into strong local customs.

During Dutch colonial rule, which lasted up to the late 1940s, Christians on Ambon—the main island—were recruited as soldiers to pacify the rest of Indonesia. In return, they received special benefits. Many Malukans converted to Christianity as a result. President Suharto (1966 to 1998) used social engineering to change this imbalance by selecting Muslims to fill vacancies. Suharto's removal from office in May 1998, after ruling for over thirty years, also marked the disappearance of a strong hand. The loosening of centralized rule brought many deep-rooted fears and mistrust to the forefront.

Violence between Christians and Muslims began on Ambon Island on 19 January 1999. It spread quickly to southeast and central Maluku. Entire villages were razed. At least five thousand people were killed. Several hundred thousand—out of a population of 2.1 million—became refugees.

The nature of the conflict changed in the middle of 2000 when a Java-based fundamentalist Islamic militia, Laskar Jihad, sent several thousand fighters to Ambon. With Christian militias on the defensive, and suffering heavy casualties, the government imposed a state of civil emergency in the two Maluku provinces. By 2001, the mass violence eased. The population was divided into Christian and Muslim zones.

During the third stage, entire communities—people from all walks of life, and different religions—were invited to general assemblies. The fourth step involved the setting up of neutral zones on the borders between communities where Muslims and Christians felt secure enough to undertake intergroup activities, including trade, sharing common health services, and the like. Inside these zones, meetings were organized between professionals from both sides, including Christian and Muslim lawyers, and journalists, who created a media center in one of these neutral zones. The involvement of security forces in the dialogue ensured security protection.

The last step in this stage-by-stage process saw the results of discussions and activities disseminated to people from the Christian and Muslim communities through workshops that encouraged the public at large to translate conflict urges into thoughts of peace. This stage was initiated when all the fundamental social structures aimed at stopping the violence were established, when people no longer wanted to be called "warring factions." In the Baku Bae philosophy, this final stage also involves carrying out activities to pave the way for legal action to redress grievances suffered by victims, and reinforce the rule of law—including, where necessary, independent investigation into the nature and roots of the conflict.

While the process evolved on Ambon, parallel activities were undertaken by civil-society groups like Ikrapati to promote dialogue between people from neighboring villages whose Christian members had fled during the violence. These dialogues were designed to get Muslims and Christians talking frankly about whether they wanted to live together again. Mediation skills were also taught. People from divided communities were encouraged to take the first steps at reunification.

Restoring Old Relations and Forging Alliances

Civil-society groups were not alone in pursuing peace. In the immediate aftermath of the outbreak of violence in January 1999, the Maluku provincial government secured pledges from community leaders to end the fighting. When mass violence continued, the minister of religion organized a meeting of Muslim and Christian leaders that produced a document outlining steps to stop the conflict and focus on rehabilitation. This did not go very far. Neither did an attempt, in early 2000, by a fact-finding team set up by the National Commission on Human Rights to foster mediation by bringing Muslims and Christians together at a course in Bali.

Baku Bae had its own difficulties, especially in removing the desire for revenge among people who had lost family or friends, and who were among the many forced to abandon their homes. Some of the problems were of a practical nature: with a state of emergency in place, movement was difficult and tensions remained high. There were also internal differences within the movement over approaches. What made it successful, in the end, was the benefits that people actually felt when they tried dialogue instead of fighting. Both the Christian and Muslim communities saw that embracing the simple method of Baku Bae—dialogue, cooperation, finding common ground in neutral centers—reduced the polarized atmosphere.

Old relations were restored and new alliances forged. Many partnerships achieved during reconciliation talks were carried over into sustained peace-building projects. This was evident when the *baku bae* dialogue encouraged between the regions of Lehitu (Muslim) and Baguala (Christian) and the Indonesian security forces spawned other local initiatives such as the establishment of joint community watches at neutral points along the road that runs through the two areas.

Individual contacts made during early activities later became partnerships between the organizations to which these people belonged. This was evident in collaborations forged between Muslim and Christian NGOs in various parts of Maluku. Dialogue helped to construct other bridges: within the Muslim community itself previously fractious groups buried differences and united.

The creation of neutral spaces in which Christians and Muslims shared health, education, and other basic services together without fear of attack was of major importance. This enabled the Masohi Hospital in central Maluku, for example, to resume its function as the main critical-care facility. Before that, patients were too afraid to spend the night there.

Workers from different NGOs, some former classmates and neighbors torn apart by the conflict, discovered that meeting in these spaces gave them the confidence to travel to each other's offices on either side. Soon, more and more citizens saw visits to the neutral space as their right; this was the place in which they felt safe after sunset.

By late 2000, Christians and Muslims were meeting openly at these locations without fear of reprisal and crossing into each other's neighborhoods. As more of these spaces were created, people began thinking of returning home to their villages. The conduct of economic activity—both Christians and Muslims set up sidewalk markets and opened stalls where they served customers from both communities—gave these spaces added importance.

The Alternative to War Is Negotiation

Ichsan Malik believes it was because of the Baku Bae movement that some of the vital issues eventually discussed by the parties at Malino were even on the agenda. He accepts that the presence of the army was important in reducing the violence, but says civil institutions are vital in ensuring a permanent solution, including socioeconomic development, law enforcement, and so on.

Baku Bae's activities, and especially the innovate thinking behind its methods, showed that people themselves need to build an agenda to reconstruct and rearrange their own future. Malik says:"We had to overcome enormous handicaps. We quarreled and swallowed many bitter pills, because our movement is a loose one. But we reestablished institutions . . . created an intellectual forum . . . and things like legal aid."

The initiators of Baku Bae see its methods as an alternative to traditional conflict resolution and reconciliation approaches: a way of rebuilding social capital and restoring trust through dialogue and community focus. As Malik says, "Of course we promote forgiveness. But by no means is what happened in the past forgotten. The alternative to war is negotiation."

In the Baku Bae approach, the need for credibility is central: establishing that you have a mandate, that people support what is being done. Establishing trust and solidarity between conflict parties is also vital, as well as ensuring that negotiation is carried out in a way that balances power among the parties. Patience, Malik stresses, is not just a virtue—it is vitally necessary.

In a background paper—written jointly with Hamdi Muluk, lecturer in social psychology at the University of Indonesia—Malik notes: "The success of the Baku Bae movement suggests the benefit of bottom-up approach and the role of civil society in strengthening and empowering survivors to make their own reconciliation processes." For negotiation to be successful, everything must be put on the table, including issues like multiculturalism and pluralism. Ordinary folk must be at the center, not the elite."There is no way to resolve the conflict in Maluku . . . without building a people's agenda and allowing them to reconstruct and rearrange their own future."

Contact

Ichsan Malik
Jl. Mendut no. 3
Jakarta Pusat
Indonesia
Tel.: +62 (213) 153 865
E-mail: bagjanet@indo.net.id or
     titian-damai@plasa.com

Selected Bibliography

International Crisis Group. 2002. *Indonesia: The Search for Peace in Maluku.* Online at:
     http://www.crisisweb.org/library/documents/report-archive/A400544_08022002.pdf.
Kirwen, Erik L., and Laurie I. Pierce. *Breaking Through Barriers: Rebuilding Trust
     and Social Capital in Maluku, Indonesia.* USAID DG Partners Conference. Online
     at: http://www.dai.com/publications/pdfs/maluku-indonesia-building-trust.pdf.
Malik, Ichsan. "A Peacemaker Visions." Online at: http://www.malukumediacentre.net/
     web/index.php?fuseaction=news.view&newsid=170920031846031&type=2&long
     =EN.
Muluk, Hamdi, and Ichsan Malik. "The Baku Bae Peace Movement as an Alternative
     Strategy to Conflict Resolution and Reconciliation in Indonesia."

Index

Aao Dosti Karein, 266–267
Aarhus Convention, 63
Aba women, 133
Abbas, Ali, 520
Abdul Karim Abdul-Kader Ghanchi, 414
Abishev, Maidan, 555
Aboriginal people in Australia, 647–651
Abu Sayyaf, 333
Acholi people, 348–353
Acholi Religious Leaders' Peace Initiative in
    Uganda, 568
ActionAid, 464
Active listening, 90, 488, 491
Activist dialogue, 482
Adenauer, Conrad, 664
Adult-youth partnerships, 152–153
Advocacy, effective humanitarian, 558–559.
    See also Awareness raising/lobbying;
    Civilian peacekeepers; Civil-society
    actors/organizations
Afghanistan: awareness raising/lobbying, 534;
    development aid, 398; diasporas, 341–343;
    disarmament/demobilization/reintegration
    process, 610; failure of military solutions
    for, 77; women's advocacy, 534, 537
Africa, West, 50. *See also* West African
    listings; individual countries
African (East) perspective on war on terror, 79
African National Conference (ANC) in South
    Africa, 321–324
Against Two Evils 1931–45 (Herwarth), 662
Agenda for Reconciliation, 665
Aggressive behavior, neurobiology of, 255
Aid, international, 21. *See also* Development
    aid
Aier, Wati, 220, 221
Albanians: civilian peacekeepers, 370;
    dialogue-based processes, 488, 493;
    Kosovar Youth Council in Kosovo, 167–
    172; television for children in Macedonia,
    187–192

Aleksa, Dragica, 654–655, 659
Al-Ghozi, Fathur R., 391
Al-Qaeda, 76, 399
Ambivalence of the Sacred, The (Appleby),
    664–665
American Association of Health Educators,
    278
American Friends Service Committee, 153,
    617
Amin, Idi, 349
Amnesty International, 17, 243, 384, 424,
    468, 617
Analytical capacity and warning signs/systems
    for timely intervention, 427
Anderson, Mary B., 401
Anglo American, 325
Angola: arts and peacebuilding, 289; civil-
    society actors/organizations, 569; diamond
    trade and civil wars, 399, 524;
    disarmament/demobilization/reintegration
    process, 610
Annan, Kofi, 63, 68, 536, 591
Antavi, Zahara, 141
Arbenz, Jacobo, 244
Argentina: Ecuador-Peru conflict, 604;
    women's advocacy, 98, 127–131
Arias, Oscar, 617–618
Arias Foundation for Peace and Human
    Progress, 618
Armenia, 316
Arms sales/proliferation: advocacy, effective
    humanitarian, 561, 562, 565; awareness
    raising/lobbying, 522; dialogue-based
    processes, 476; United Nations, 429;
    warning signs/systems for timely
    intervention, 444. *See also* Disarmament/
    demobilization/reintegration process
Arms Trade Treaty (1997), 617–618
Arts and peacebuilding: Bosnia-Herzegovina,
    301–308; Burkina Faso and Mali, 285–286;
    Ireland (Northern), 284–287; Mozambique,

624–626; Peace Festivals, 287–290; resources (informational), 291–292; Sierra Leone, 91, 288–289, 293–300
Arusha Accords, 159
Ashafa, Muhammed, 226, 227–228, 230
Asian (Southeast) perspective on war on terror, 80
Asoka (king), 175
Association of Southeast Asian Nations (ASEAN), 390
Association of Widows in Rwanda, 109
Athwaas Initiative in Kashmir, 111–115
Attitudes/patterns of relationships that generate conflict, 14–15
Atunda Ayenda in Liberia, 205
Australia: awareness raising/lobbying, 523; National Sorry Day, 647–651; terror (war on), 77, 80
Awareness raising/lobbying: Brazil, 528–532; Kazakhstan, 552–557; Kenya, 540–544; lessons learned, 523–526, 558–566; media (the), 519–521, 541, 553–554; opposition to, 522–523; political support for, 521, 523; resources (informational), 526–527; Serbia, 545–551; transitional societies, 523; Women Building Peace Campaign, 533–539
Azar, Edward, 480
Azerbaijan, 316

Baku Bae movement in Indonesia, 89, 667–672
Balkan Peace Team (BPT), 365, 369–374
Balkans and dialogue-based processes, 484, 488–494. *See also individual countries*
Bananas and local businesses/peacebuilding, 334–335
Bannon, Ian, 400
Bantay Ceasefire (BC) in Philippines, 365, 388–393
Baptist Peace Fellowship of North America (BPFNA), 220, 221, 223
Barak, Ehud, 145
Barasukana, 202
Barlow Rand, 323
Barnes, Catherine, 50
"Basic Agreement on the Search for Peace by Political Means" (1990), 244
Begin, Menachem, 176
Begovic, Nedzad, 306
Behavioral change and the media, 190
Belarus, 550
Belfast Agreement. *See* Good Friday Agreement
Ben-Dor, Rachel, 141, 143
Ben-Zvi, Linda, 145
Berghof Foundation, 354–361
Berlinguer, Enrico, 577
Bernassola, Marta, 195
Bernstein, Liz, 237
Berom people, 230

Best Choice, The, 159, 160
Betrayal of the Church, The (Robb & Robb), 385
"Beyond the Crazy Life," 632
Bickmore, Kathy, 277
BJ Coco Oil Mill, 337
Black Shadow group in El Salvador, 634
Boeckler, Hans, 664
Bokeria, Giga, 509
Bombande, Emmanuel, 285–286
Borama Conference (1993), 462–463
Bosnia-Herzegovina: arts and peacebuilding, 301–308; development aid, 398; Nansen Dialogue Network, 89; Noor's (Queen) personal story, 109–110
Bougainville:Bougainville Community Integrated Development Agency, 122; Bougainville Peace Monitoring Group, 365; and women's advocacy, 98, 122–125
Brady, Paul, 284–285
Brahimi Report (2000), 426–427
Brazil: awareness raising/lobbying, 528–532; Ecuador-Peru conflict, 604
Brazil Never Again, 528–532
"Breaking the Conflict Trap: Civil War and Development Policy," 397, 398
Brem, Iris, 251
Bringing Them Home, 647, 648, 650
British Department for International Development, 259. *See also* United Kingdom
Brownell, Mary, 589
Brussels Afghan Women Leaders Summit, 537
Bryant, Gyude, 137
Buchman, Frank, 661, 662
Buddhism, 213, 214, 234, 235
Bughadze, Lasha, 509
Burkina Faso and the arts/peacebuilding, 285–286
Burrowes, Robert, 237
Burton, John, 509
Burundi: arts and peacebuilding, 289–290; media (the), 180, 186, 200–204, 206–207; traditional/local conflict resolution, 451; youth, 91, 157–161
Bush, George W., 31–32, 77
Business activities feeding into or profiting from violence, 310. *See also* Economic/institutional structures that generate conflict; Local businesses, peacebuilding potential of
Business for Peace Alliance in Sri Lanka, 316
Business of Peace, The (Nelson), 330
Buttry, Daniel, 220–222, 224–225

Calmet, Hugo S., 603
Camara, Dom Helder, 530
Cambodia: faith-based intervention, 213, 233–238; youth advocacy, 150, 153
Cambridge University, 484

Campaign messaging and effective humanitarian advocacy, 559–561
Camplisson, Joe, 595, 596
Camps in Lebanon, summer peace, 272–273
Canada: development aid, 412; diasporas, 355, 359; landmines, 62
Canadian International Development Agency (CIDA), 397
Cardoso, Fernando, 64
Cardoso Panel. *See* Panel of Emminent Persons on Civil Society and UN Relationships
CARE International, 425, 508
Caribbean and regional networks/partnerships, 51, 53. *See also individual countries*
Caritas, 657
Carter Center in Venezuela, 181
Castillo, Cesar S., 129
Catholic Agency for Overseas Development, 525
Catholic Relief Services (CRS), 215
Catholic Reporter, 384–385
Catholic Women's Association, 122
"Caux Principles," 665
Cease-fire agreements, monitoring, 364, 388–393, 570–571
Celebrities and awareness raising/lobbying, 525–526
Celeste, Richard F., 278
Cell-structure network model, 57
Cenepa War (1995), 476
Center for International Development and Conflict Management, 601
Center for Peace, Nonviolence, and Human Rights in Osijek in Croatia, 90, 654–659
Center for Social Care, 657
Centre for Research and Popular Education, 379
Chain network model, 57
Chan, Stephen, 579
Charities Aid Foundation, 596
Chaudhry, Mahendra, 512, 513
Chavchavadze, Ilia, 509
Chavez, Hugo, 181
Chechnya: civilian peacekeepers, 364; terror (war on), 72, 78
Children in the Crossfire, 151. *See also* Education, conflict/peace; Youth
Children Like Any Other, 306
Children's International Summer Village (CISV), 266
Children's Learning Services (CLS) in Sierra Leone, 90, 257–263
Children's Movement for Peace, 162–164, 166
Children's Television Workshop, 189
Chile, 604
China: dialogue-based processes, 501–506; landmines, 62; terror (war on), 72
Chissano, Joaquim, 580

Christian Council of Mozambique, 623–629
Christian Health Services, 153
Christianity, 211, 214: Indonesia, 667–672; Nigeria, 89, 226–231; Philippines, 332, 336, 337. *See also* Faith-based approaches to conflict prevention/resolution
Christian Peacemaker Teams, 365
Christian Science Monitor, 226
Cilliers, Jacco, 397
Citizens' Constitutional Forum (CCF) in Fiji, 513–516
Citizens' Mandate for Peace, Life and Liberty in Colombia, 568
City Montessori School in India, 251, 264–268
Civic Forum in Northern Ireland, 330
Civilian peacekeepers: aim of, 363–364; best practices/lessons learned, 367; challenges for, 365–366; Colombia, 376–381, 385, 386; Croatia and Serbia/Kosovo, 369–374; Gandhi (Mahatma), 364; global initiative, 367; media relations, 366; military peacekeepers' relationship with, 366; Nicaragua, 382–387; Philippines, 388–393; protective accompaniment, 364; resources (informational), 368; United Nations, 365; volunteers *vs.* professionals, 366. *See also* Disarmament/demobilization/reintegration process; Reconciliation; Traditional/local conflict resolution
Civil-society actors/organizations in peace processes: challenges and dilemmas, 573–574; consolidating peace, 20–21; constituencies for peace, 17–18; defining civil society, 7–9; depoliticized initiatives of, 21; dialogue-based processes, 18, 476, 568–570; diasporas, 342–344; engaging with conflict and preventing war, 11–12; escalation of violence and emergence of war, 17; facilitating dialogue between the parties, 569–570; global civil society, 13–15; human rights violations data, 571; Ireland (Northern), 570, 582–587; lacunas in activities of, 32; limits of involvement, 21–22; Mano River Women's Peace Network, 588–593; modalities for engaging governments, 10; Moldova, 594–599; monitoring compliance and violations, 364, 570–571; Mozambique, 576–581; multiple arenas for prevention/peacebuilding, 12–13; negotiations involving, 571–573; overview, 567–568; partnerships for peace, 22–23; Peru and Ecuador, 600–605; polarized communities, 9–11; political negotiations/will and peacemaking, 17–20; principles that guide, 37–38; reconciliation, 641, 642; regional initiatives and, 48, 50–54; resources (informational), 574–575; specific conflicts responded to, 15–16; structural prevention and responding to conflict, 16–17; success-

ful activities, 1–2; violence reduction/peace monitors/zones of peace, 18; warning signs/ systems for timely intervention, 17, 425, 428; women's advocacy, 588–593. *See also* Disarmament/demobilization/reintegration process; Peacebuilding; Reconciliation; Traditional/local conflict resolution; UN-civil society interactions; *individual subject headings*

Clash of Civilizations (1997), 210

Clean Election Campaign (CEC) in Kenya, 540–544

Cleveland Municipal School District and dispute resolution/skills, 277

Cleveland State University, 280

Coalition building and effective humanitarian advocacy, 561–562. *See also* Partnerships, effective

Coalition on Human Rights, 515

Coalition to Stop the Use of Child Soldiers, 561, 564–565

Cold War: development aid in aftermath of, 396–397; dialogue-based processes, 476, 501; scientific cooperation during the, 255, 256

Colleges Collaboration Fund in South Africa, 325

Collier, Paul, 342, 398, 399

Colombia: civilian peacekeepers, 365, 376–381, 386; disarmament/demobilization/ reintegration process, 619–622; landmines, 109; outsiders serving as a deterrent to violence, 87; young population, 149; youth advocacy, 162–166

Colonialism's history hampering new methods of negotiation/mediation, 449, 604

Commission for Historical Clarification (CEH) in Guatemala, 239–240

Commitment declarations, 89

Common Ground News Service, 179

Commonwealth of Independent States (CIS), 598

Communication and encouraging dialogue, re-storing, 87. *See also* Dialogue-based processes

Community building and education in conflict resolution/peace, 247–249

Community Development Centre (CDC) in Northern Ireland, 436–440

Community of Sant' Egidio, 211, 576–581

Community Relations Council in Northern Ireland, 330–331

Comprehensive Test Ban Treaty, 556

Conditonality *vs.* transformative approaches, 32

Confederation of British Industry (CBI), 315, 327–331

Conference of Chief Justices of the World (2004), 267

conflictandpeace.org, 177

Conflict Humanitarian Assistance and

Peacebuilding, 405

Conflict Resolution Education in Teacher Education project, 280

Conflict Resolution Education Network, 278

Confronting War: Critical Lessons for Peace Practitioners (Anderson & Olson), 454

Consensus-based decisionmaking, 453, 562

Consolidating peace, 20–21

Constitutional Options and Their Implications for Good Governance and a Sound Economy, 325

Consultative Business Movement (CBM) in South Africa, 321, 323–326

Consultative mechanisms and civil society actors/organizations, 572

Contadora Group, 50

Conte, Lansana, 589

Contra rebels in Nicaragua, 382–385

Convention for a Democratic South Africa (CODESA), 324

Convention on the Elimination of All Forms of Discrimination Against Women (CEDAW), 106

Cooperation. *See* Partnerships, effective; Regional networks/partnerships

Coordinadora Ecuménica de Servicio (CESE), 530

Coordinadora Regional de Investigaciones (CRIES), 51

Coordinating Committees for the Cessation of Hostilities (CCCH) in Philippines, 388–391

Corporate social responsibility (CSR), 314

Corruption and awareness raising/lobbying, 540–543

Corti, Horacio P., 129

Côte d'Ivoire, 217

Crawley, Mike, 226

Creative Response to Conflict, 247

Creativity as a valuable resource, 90–91

Croatia: civilian peacekeepers, 369–374; Listening Project, 90; Nansen Dialogue Network, 89; reconciliation, 654–659

Cronkite, Walter, 176

Cross-conflict productions as peacebuilding media initiatives, 178

"Crossroads Radio" in Burundi, 207

Cry for Justice, 365

C.S. Mott Foundation, 596

CSO. *See* Civil-society actors/organizations in peace processes

Cuba: civilian peacekeepers, 386; faith-based intervention, 211; women's advocacy, 131

Cultural productions as peacebuilding media initiatives, 178

"Culture for Democracy in Latin America, A," 600

"Cure of Troy, The" (Heaney), 287

Daily Star, 144

Dalai Lama, 111, 509, 510, 617, 665
Daley, William, 328
De Beers, 524
Declaration of Cashapamba, 603
de Klerk, F. W., 322
Demobilization process, 610. *See also*
  Disarmament/demobilization/reintegration
  process
Democracies and dialogue-based processes,
  transitioning, 484
Democracy and the changing geography of
  politics, participatory, 61
Democratic Dialogue, 329
Democratic Republic of Congo (DRC):
  development aid, 398; diamond trade and
  civil wars, 524; diasporas, 341; exploitation
  by Western companies, 309; human rights
  violations, 560; media (the), 177, 201
Democratic states and civil society, interdependence between, 9
Democratization of information and UN-civil
  society interactions, 60
Department of International Development
  (DFID), 397, 406
Derry Peace and Reconciliation Group (PRG)
  in Northern Ireland, 583–587
Development aid: aggravating conflicts
  through, 395–396; Cold War aftermath,
  396–397; disarmament/demobilization/
  reintegration process, 612–614; India,
  414–420; long-term conflict prevention,
  403; mainstreaming conflict prevention,
  401–402; Mali, 401–402, 409–413; part of
  a package of foreign-policy measures, 403;
  preventive/ameliorative/curative development, 396–397; resources (informational),
  407–408; sensitivity (conflict), 87–88,
  404–405; trust in/support for peace
  processes, 403; violence (local) addressed,
  403; World Bank, 397–400
Development Assistance Committee (DAC) of
  OECD, 396
Development/diasporas and peace promotion,
  344–345
Dhammayietra Peace Walk in Cambodia, 213,
  233–238
Dhlakama, Afonso, 578, 580
Dialogue-based processes: China, 501–506;
  civil-society actors/organizations, 18, 476,
  568–570; context of conflict impacting,
  483–485; counternegative effects of,
  474–475; defining dialogue, 473–474; Fiji,
  512–517; Georgia, 481, 507–511; goal of,
  475–476; identifying potential dialogue
  partners, 480–481; Kosovo, 488–494; long-
  term process, 18; models of dialogue,
  482–483; Oxford Research Group,
  501–506; Palestinian-Israeli conflict, 91,
  474, 476, 481, 483, 495–500; resources
  (informational), 487; stages of, 476–479;

summary/conclusions, 485; tools of
  dialogue, 479–480; vehicle not a
  destination, 475
Diamond trade and civil wars, 399, 524
Diasporas: Acholi people, 348–353; civic-
  oriented involvement, 342–344; development and promoting peace, 344–345;
  negative aspects focused on, 339–340;
  Norway and, 356, 357, 359; positive
  political involvement, 340–342; resources
  (informational), 346–347; Sri Lanka, 342,
  354–361; summary/ conclusions, 345
Dibo, Amal, 274
Differences, act on the commonalities and
  understand the, 186
Digital technology, the good/bad of, 180
Dikedi, Amina, 543
Directorate General for International
  Development (DGIS), 397
Direct participation mechanisms and civil
  society actors/organizations, 572
Disarmament/demobilization/reintegration
  (DDR) process: Arias' (Oscar) personal
  story, 617–618; civilians need to be brought
  in, 611–612; Colombia, 619–622;
  development linked to peacebuilding,
  612–614; El Salvador, 612, 630–635;
  everyone's job, 614; military usually in
  charge of peacekeeping, 607–608;
  Mozambique, 612, 623–629; overview,
  609–611; resources (informational),
  615–616
Discourses on peace practices: cooperation
  and networking, 33–36; growth of conflict
  prevention field, 29–30; overview, 30–31;
  planning and assessment, 38, 40; professionalization, 36–40; self-understanding and
  guiding principles, 36–39; social change
  and justice, 31–33; summary/conclusions,
  40–42
Diseases, children dying from preventable, 80
Doe, Samuel, 285–286
Do No Harm (Anderson), 38, 40
Do no harm approach to development aid, 401
Do You Remember Sarajevo?, 306
Drugs and civil wars, 399
"Dublin Action Agenda on the Prevention of
  Violent Conflict" (2004), 54

Eastern Mennonite University, 223
East Timor, 398
Economic Community of West African States
  (ECOWAS), 17, 48, 425, 428–429
Economic empowerment and civil society
  actors/organizations, 590, 591
Economic/institutional structures that generate
  conflict: awareness raising/lobbying, 524,
  525; center/periphery and resource imbalances, 15; Colombia, 620; diamond trade
  and civil wars, 399, 524; diasporas,

344–345; disarmament/demobilization/ reintegration process, 611; El Salvador, 632; Georgia, 508; global civil society addressing, 13–15; Mozambique, 577; natural resources exploited in conflict zones, 309; Nigeria, 227–228; terror (war on) as more important than, 80–81; UN-civil society interactions, 60; warning signs/systems for timely intervention, 423, 428. *See also* Development aid; Local businesses, peacebuilding potential of

Ecuador: civil-society actors/organizations, 570, 600–605; dialogue-based processes, 476; Peru's border conflict with, 88, 570, 600–605

"Ecuador and Peru: Towards a Democratic and Cooperative Conflict Resolution Initiative," 600

Ecumenical Accompaniment Program, 365

Edis, Richard, 579

Education, conflict/peace: best practices, 251–252; civil-society actors/organizations, 569; community building, 247–249; defining peace education, 246–247; expressive arts as a means of conflict discovery, 249; India, 251, 264–268; Lebanon, 269–274; local businesses and peacebuilding, 325; Ohio Commission for Dispute Resolution and Conflict Management, 249, 275–276, 278, 280–281; overview, 245–246; Peace Boat, 250; peer mediation, 249; research symposium on, 252; resources (informational), 253–254; scientific community's role in preventing war, 255–256; sensitive (contextually/culturally) programs/ practices, 250–251; Sierra Leone, 90, 257–263; Students Offering Acceptance and Respect in U.S., 279–280; summary/ conclusions, 252; Winning Against Violent Environments Program in U.S., 277. *See also* Training programs/workshops; Youth

Education, U.S. Department of, 252

Educators for Social Responsibility, 247

Edutainment, 178

Egal, Mohammed I., 460, 463

Egypt: diasporas, 478; media (the), 176; terror (war on), 72

Ehard, Hans, 662

Elders (clan) as conflict mediators in Somaliland, 459–464

Elections and awareness raising/lobbying, 540–544

Elmi, Asha H., 117, 120

El Salvador: dialogue-based processes, 484; disarmament/demobilization/reintegration process, 612, 630–635; reconciliation, 641

Elworthy, Scilla, 501, 502, 504–505

Emotional/social skills to prevent conflict, providing children with, 246. *See also* Education, conflict/peace

Empowerment: arts and peacebuilding, 294; victim, 91; women's, 105

England. *See* United Kingdom

Environmental disputes and dialogue-based processes, 484

Equality Commission in Northern Ireland, 329–330

Equality Now, 119

Erigavo Conference (1993), 462

Eurasia Foundation, 508

European Centre for Conflict Prevention (ECCP), 3, 54

European Conference on the Role of Civil Society in the Prevention of Armed Conflict (2004), 54

European Union (EU): awareness raising/lobbying, 542; civilian peacekeepers, 365; coalition shifting emerging to counterbalance power of, 60; diasporas, 341, 355; Ireland (Northern), 329; women's advocacy, 537. *See also* Organization for Security and Cooperation in Europe

Evaristo Arns, Paulo, 528–530

Everyone's Guide to Achieving Change: A Step-by-Step Approach to Dialogue with Decision-Makers, 504

Exile communities. *See* Diasporas

Extremism and dialogue-based processes, 483

Faith-based approaches to conflict prevention/resolution: Brazil, 528–532; Cambodia, 213, 233–238; connecting with other stakeholders, 214–215; credibility and moral authority, 212–214; diplomacy, 210; disarmament/demobilization/reintegration process, 612; Guatemala, 239–244; India, 219–225; Kenya, 441–446, 541; Mali, 409–413; Mozambique, 211, 576–581, 612, 623–629; networks/networking, 214; Nigeria, 89, 226–231; nongovernmental organizations, 212; overview, 209; religion as an instrument of peace, 210–211; resources (informational), 217–218; summary/ conclusions, 215; World Conference of Religions for Peace, 216–217

Faith-Based Diplomacy: Trumping Realpolitik (Johnston), 211

Fatal Transactions campaign, 524

Federal Bureau of Investigation (FBI), 73

Festivals, Peace, 287–290

Fiji and dialogue-based processes, 512–517

Firearms Protocol of the Transnational Organized Crime Convention, 562

Fishnet network model, 57

Fitzduff, Mari, 483

Focus on Africa, 205

Fondation Hirondelle, 177

Fortune, Frances, 205–206

Forum on Early Warning and Early Response

(FEWER), 428
Foster, Lilibet, 194
Foundation for Tolerance International, 16–17
Fountain, Susan, 247
Four Mothers Movement in Israel, 141–146
France, 536, 663–664
Frankenthal, Arik, 496
Fraser, Malcolm, 652
Freie Presse, 662–663
Frente de Libertacâo de Mocambique
  (FRELIMO), 577–580, 626
Friendship Circle, Sri Lanka, 355, 358
"From Reaction to Prevention," 49
Fulani people, 230

Gabriel, Peter, 193
Gacaca traditional courts in Rwanda, 450,
  466–471
Gagauzia, 599
Galtung, Johan, 474, 509, 511
Gamsakhurdia, Zviad K., 510
Gandhi, Bharti, 264–265
Gandhi, Jagdish, 264–265
Gandhi, Mahatma, 215, 219, 223, 364,
  509–511
Garcia, Rodolfo C., 388
Gender mainstreaming, 102–105. *See also*
  Women
Geneva Conventions, 559
Geneva Initiative (2003), 478
Georgia: civilian peacekeepers, 364; dialogue-
  based processes, 481, 507–511; local
  business and peacebuilding, 316
Gerardi Conedera, Juan, 242
German Technical Service (GTZ), 356
Germany: development aid, 412; diasporas,
  354–355, 357, 358; reconciliation after
  World War II for West, 662–664
Ghana: awareness raising/lobbying, 543, 550;
  civil-society actors/organizations, 589–590;
  faith-based intervention, 217
Ghosananda, Somdet Phra Maha, 233–236
Ghozi, Fathur R. Al-, 391
Gillespie, Patsy, 582
Globalization: civil society (global), 13–15,
  46, 60; power balance in the world shaped
  by, 60; regional entities with new
  opportunities, 45–48, 50
Global Partnership for the Prevention of
  Armed Conflict (GPPAC): goals of, 84–85;
  overview of, 49; processes and challenges,
  3–4; regional and global civil-society
  linked, 47–48; resources provided by, 86;
  warning signs/systems for timely
  intervention, 428
"Global Security in the post-Cold War
  World," 501
Global Witness, 524, 525
Gogibedashvili, Defi, 509
Goldstone, Richard, 324

Goncalves, Dom Jaime, 577, 578
Good/evil division and the war on terror, 75
Good Friday Agreement in Northern Ireland
  (1998), 109, 328, 330, 345, 478
Gorbachev, Mikhail, 554, 585
Governor's (Ohio) Peace and Conflict
  Management Commission, 278, 280
Graduated reciprocation in tension-reduction
  (GRIT), 584–587
Grandmothers of the Plaza de Mayo in
  Argentina, 98, 127–131
Grassroots business actors, 315–316
Grassroots Initiative for the Protection of the
  Palestinians, 365
Great Britain. *See* United Kingdom
Grievance or greed as motivator of internal
  conflict, debate over, 33
Group of Friends, 50
Grupo Maryland, 88, 601–606
Guatemala: civilian peacekeepers, 365, 366,
  386; civil-society actors/organizations, 20;
  dialogue-based processes, 484; faith-based
  intervention, 239–244; Truth and
  Reconciliation Commission, 612; women's
  advocacy, 535
Guatemala: Nunca Más, 242, 243
Guinea, 217, 588–589
Gumbonzvanda, Nyaradzai, 120
Gusmâo, Xanana, 25–27

Habermas, Jürgen, 34
Haiti, 386
Hakena, Helen, 122–123, 125
Hall, John, 323
Hammarskjöld, Dag, 607
Handicap International, 563
Hatungimana, Rebecca, 200–201
Hawaii and traditional/local conflict
  resolution, 450
Heaney, Seamus, 287
Hello Peace in Israel and Palestine, 91, 481,
  495–500
Hezbollah, 142
High Commissioner on National Minorities,
  433–434
Hindu Council of Kenya, 542
Hinduism, 213, 265, 417
Hirschberg, Peter, 143
Hirshenzon, Roni, 499
HIV/AIDS, 151, 236, 399, 591
Holistic view of education, 260
Homies Unidos in El Salvador/U.S., 630–635
Ho'o Ponopono process in Hawaii, 450
Hope in the Cities, 665
Horjen, Stein E., 413
Hornstein, Caroline S., 307
Howard, John, 647, 651
Howard, Ross, 177
How Nuclear Weapons Decisions Are Made,
  504

Hozhooji Naat'aanii restorative justice process, 450
Humanitarian terms, awareness raising/lobbying and framing issues in, 560
Human relations dialogue, 482
Human rights: Balkan conflict, 371; Brazil, 528–532; civilian peacekeepers, 380–381, 384; civil-society actors/organizations, 571; dialogue-based processes, 484, 490, 515–516; the Grandmothers of the Plaza de Mayo, 127–131; humanitarian norms and reducing human costs of war, 560; Mano River Women's Peace Network, 591; Moscow Declaration (1991), 433–434; Naga people in India, 219–225; Reconstruction of a Historical Memory in Guatemala, 240–241; sexual abuse in Sierra Leone, 194–198; terror (war on), 72, 78; Uganda, 348, 350
Human Rights Commission in Northern Ireland, 329–330
Human Rights Watch, 72, 243, 424, 563
Hussein (King), 110
Hutu people, 109, 151–152, 157–159, 200, 203–204. See also Burundi; Rwanda; Uganda

I and Thou (Buber), 488
Immaculate Conception Parish in Philippines, 389
IMPACS, 177
Impact of Armed Conflict on Children, 147
Impartiality and local businesses/peacebuilding, 312
India: civilian peacekeepers, 365; development aid, 414–420; diasporas, 357; education in conflict resolution/peace, 251, 264–268; faith-based intervention, 219–225; landmines, 62; Pakistan's conflict with, 99, 101
Indian (Asian) people in Fiji, 512–517
Indicators and assessing impact of peacebuilding, 41
Individuals working together as a powerful force for positive change, 83–85
Indonesia: arts and peacebuilding, 290; Phillippine-MILF talks, 390; reconciliation, 89, 667–672; terror (war on), 78; and Timor-Leste, 25–27
Inequality gap between haves/have nots, 14, 429. See also Economic/institutional structures that generate conflict
Information, UN-civil society interactions and democratization of, 60
Initiatives for International Dialogue, 389
Initiatives of Change, 540, 542, 661–666
Inkingi y'ubuntu in Burundi, 201
Institute for Media, Policy, and Civil Society, 177
Institutional-bureaucratic dynamics and

warning signs/systems for timely intervention, 426
Intended-outcomes television, 189
Inter-Congregational Commission of Justice, 379
Interfaith Mediation Centre, 228, 230
Intergovernmental Agency for Development, 48, 428
Inter-Governmental Authority for Development (IGAD), 119, 120
International Action Network on Small Arms (IANSA), 522, 561, 565
International Alert (IA): discourse on social change/practice, 31; principles guiding, 36–37, 39; sensitive approach to conflict, 404, 405; traditional/local conflict resolution, 470–471; warning signs/systems for timely intervention, 424; women's advocacy, 100–101, 533, 536
International Campaign to Ban Landmines (ICBL), 62, 68, 562, 563
International Center for Religion and Diplomacy, 211
International Center on Conflict and Negotiation, 508
International Committee of the Red Cross (ICRC), 36, 561
International Communications Forum, 665
International Conference on War-Affected Children, 151
International Criminal Court (ICC), 558–560, 562, 563–564
International Crisis Group (ICG), 17, 31, 425
International Diaspora Workshop (2003), 359
International Peace Academy, 35
International Peace Research Institute, Oslo, 412
International Physicians for the Prevention of Nuclear War, 504, 617
International School-to-School Experience (ISSE), 266
International Service for Peace, 365
International Solidarity Movement, 365
International Student (IS) programs, 250
Internet and dialogue-based processes, 479, 500
InterNews, 177
Inter-Tajik Dialogue, 481
Iran-Contra scandal, 384
Iraq: awareness raising/lobbying, 520; faith-based intervention, 213; terrorism's roots ignored in favor of war on, 77
Ireland, Northern: arts and peacebuilding, 284–287; civil-society actors/organizations, 20, 570, 582–587; dialogue-based processes, 478; diasporas, 345; Good Friday Agreement, 109, 328, 345, 478; local businesses and peacebuilding, 312–315, 327–331; unemployment in, 328; warning signs/systems for timely inter-

vention, 425, 435–440; women's advocacy, 109, 535
Irish Republican Army, 435, 582–587
Islam: Christianity in conflict with, 211; India, 265, 417; Indonesia, 667–672; Kashmir, 213; Kenya, 542; Nigeria, 89, 226–231; Philippines, 332, 336, 337. *See also* Faith-based approaches to conflict prevention/resolution
"The Island," 284–285
Israel: arts and peacebuilding, 290; dialogue-based processes, 478; media (the), 176; women's advocacy, 141–146. *See also* Palestinian-Israeli conflict
Italy, 335
Ivanov, Igor, 511

Jackson, Jesse, 90
Jalampuri ni Chali Peace Committee (JPC), 414–419
Jama, Mohamud A., 463
JAMAA in Burundi, 91, 150, 157–161
Jamaica, 535, 536
James II (King), 435
Japan: awareness raising/lobbying, 555–556; diasporas, 357; nuclear issues/weapons, 555–556
Japanese Niwano Peace Foundation, 505
Jemaah Islamiyah, 80, 391
Jerusalem Center for Women, 109
Jerusalem Link, 99, 109
Jerusalem Post, 143, 145
Joint Committee for Democratization and Conciliation in Moldova, 594–599
Jorbenadze, Avtandil, 509
"Journey of Conscience" campaign in India, 222–224
Journey of Healing in Australia, 650–651
Justice combined with reconciliation, 638–639

Kabba, Tejan, 589
Kacoke Madit (KM) in Uganda, 348, 350–353, 450
Kaduna Peace Declaration (2002), 89, 229
Kamara, Emma, 90, 257–258, 262
Kane, Carol, 286–287
Karanja, Joseph, 540–544
Karim Abdul-Kader Ghanchi, 414
Kashmir: faith-based intervention, 211, 213; women's advocacy, 111–115
Kataoka, Masaru, 624
Katunga, John, 50
Kaufman, Edy, 601
Kazakhstan: awareness raising/lobbying, 552–557; terror (war on), 78
Kelman, Herbert, 480
Kendall, Carol, 649
Kenovic, Ademir, 306
Kent State University, 280

Kenya: awareness raising/lobbying, 540–544; development aid, 395; Mozambique's conflict, 578; terror (war on), 79; warning signs/systems for timely intervention, 90, 441–446
Khaindrava, Goga, 509
Kibaki, Mwai, 117
Kimani, Francis, 542
Kimberley Process Certification Scheme (KPCS), 524
King, Martin L., Jr., 215, 510
King, Rodney, 193
Kitenga, Yesu, 341
Kmitta, Dan, 252
Konare, Alpha O., 412
Kony, Joseph, 349
Kosovar Youth Council (KYC), 167–172
Kosovo: civilian peacekeepers, 369–374; development aid, 398; dialogue-based processes, 488–494; disarmament/demobilization/reintegration process, 610; Nansen Dialogue Network, 89; youth advocacy, 151, 167–172
Kostunica, Vojislav, 550
Kouyate, Kanja, 285–286
Kresevljakovic, Seadi H., 306
Kruhonja, Katarina, 656
Kumaratunga, Chandrika, 356
Kyrgyz Republic, 16–17

Ladies in White, 131
La Frutera, Inc., 334–335
Lakey, George, 237
La Memoria Subversiva (Galeano), 243
Lampen, Diana, 583, 584
Lampen, John, 582–587
Landmines, 62, 68, 109, 558–560, 562, 563
Langi people, 349
LaPierre, Wayne, 181
Laskar Jihad, 669
Latin America and regional networks/partners, 51, 53. *See also individual countries*
L'Aube, 663
Lawyers Committee for Human Rights, 193
Learning organizations, civil-society organizations as, 38
Learning process, peacebuilding as a, 86
Lebanon: education in conflict resolution/peace, 269–274; reconciliation, 665; women's advocacy, 141–146
Lederach, John P., 310, 360
Legal framework for traditional/local conflict resolution, 450, 466–471
Legislation: (Britain) Terrorism Act of 2000, 73; (India) Armed Forces Special Powers Act, 223; (Malaysia) Internal Security Act, 72; (US) Anti-Terrorist Act of 1996, 631; (US) Patriot Act of 2001, 76, 78
Legitimacy and local businesses/peacebuilding, 312

Legitimacy of CSO initiatives, 22
Leitana Nehan Women's Development Agency in Bougainville, 98, 122–126
Le Meilleur Choix, 159, 160
Lennon, John, 267
Letter writing and dialogue-based processes, 479
Liberalization and the ascents/descents pattern of development, 14
Liberation Tigers of Tamil Eelam (LTTE), 356, 358
Liberia: child soldiers, 147–148; civil-society actors/organizations, 588–589; media (the), 205–206; terror (war on), 78; women's advocacy, 98, 133–140; youth advocacy, 153
Liberian Women in the Diaspora, 136
Liberian Women's Initiative (LWI), 134–135
Linow, Val, 650–651
Listening, active, 90, 488, 491
Listening Project in Croatia, 90, 654–659
Local businesses, peacebuilding potential of: challenges for, 311–312; Colombia, 619–622; conditions contributing to promoting/sustaining, 310–311; core business, 313–314; Ireland (Northern), 312–315, 327–331; overview, 310; partnerships, 316–317; Philippines, 332–337; policy dialogue, 315; regional/grassroots business actors, 315–316; resources (informational), 319–320; social investment, 314–315; South Africa, 312, 313, 315, 321–326; summary/conclusions, 317–318. *See also* Civil-society actors/organizations; Reconciliation; Traditional/local conflict resolution
Local capacities for peace approach to development aid, 401
Locke, John, 34
London Sunday Times, 586
Lord's Resistance Army (LRA) in Uganda, 348–351
Lumad people, 332, 336
Lund, Michael, 423
Lutheran World Federation, 244
Luttwak, Edward, 663

Ma, Yo-Yo, 303
Mabunda, Goncalo, 625
Macapagal-Arroyo, Gloria, 391
Macedonia: arts and peacebuilding, 290; disarmament/demobilization/reintegration process, 610; media (the), 187–192; Nansen Dialogue Network, 89; terror (war on), 78
Machel, Graca, 162, 624
Mainstreaming conflict prevention, 31, 401–402
Malaria, 80
Malaysia: Phillippine-MILF talks, 390; terror (war on), 72, 80

Mali: arts and peacebuilding, 285–286; civil-society actors/organizations, 572; development aid, 88, 401–402, 409–413; faith-based intervention, 213; local communities addressing conflict issues, 20
Malik, Ichsan, 89, 667, 671
Malino Declaration (2002), 668
Maloney, Ed, 586
Manchanda, Rita, 534
Mandela, Nelson, 158, 321, 325, 642
Mano River Union Women's Network for Peace (MARWOPNET), 109, 136, 588–593
Mansaray, Binta, 194, 196, 197
Mansour, Anna, 270, 273
Marks, John, 185–186
Martín Beristain, Carlos, 240, 243
Martin Ennals Award for Human Rights Defenders, 380–381
Martin Luther King Jr. Law and Municipal Careers High School, 277
Mayan people, 239, 241
Mbeki, Thabo, 321
McDonald, John W., 509
McEnroe, Geoff, 329
McGuinness, Martin, 582, 586
McLaughlin, Mitchel, 582, 586
Media, the: added value from, 180; awareness raising/lobbying, 519–521, 541, 553–554; Burundi, 180, 186, 200–204, 206–207; challenges facing, 180–181; civilian peacekeepers, 366, 392; civil-society actors/organizations, 569; collaborative efforts, 181; dialogue-based processes, 498–499, 510, 513; diasporas, 340–341; "hate media," 176; historical peacebuilding examples, 175; impact assessment on, 179; Liberia, 205–206; Macedonia, 187–192; Marks (John), 185–186; news media, peacebuilding through, 176–177; non-news media, peacebuilding through, 177–179; overview, 175–176; ownership and content, 181; resources (informational), 182–184; Serbia cracking down on, 546; Sierra Leone, 193–198; summary/conclusions, 181–182; sustainability of projects, 179; warning signs/systems for timely intervention, 428
Media for Peace, 177
Medico International, 524, 563
Mega-FM, 179
Mennonites, 384
Mesmin, Georges, 665
Messaging in campaigns and effective humanitarian advocacy, 559–561
Mexico, 386
Middle East: arts and peacebuilding, 290; media (the), 186; terror (war on), 79. *See also* Palestinian-Israeli conflict; *individual countries*
Middle East Consortium for Infectious

Disease Surveillance, 186
Middle East Nonviolence and Democracy (MEND), 176
MILF. *See* Moro Islamic Liberation Front
Mill, John S., 490
Millennium Development Goals (MDGs), UN, 2, 65
Millennium Peace Prize for Women, 537
Milosevic, Slobodan, 545–549, 560
MindaLinaw (Peaceful Mindanao), 392
Mindanao conflict in the Philippines, 333
Mindanao Peoples' Caucus, 389
Mine Ban Treaty (1997), 563
Mines Advisory Group, 563
Mitchell, George, 109
Mobile Phones Network in Northern Ireland, 425, 436–440
Mohamed, Faiza J., 119
Moi, Daniel arap, 542
Moldova and civil society actors/organizations, 594–599
Moldovan Initiative Committee of Management (MICOM), 596–598
Moluccan people, 668
Monitoring cease-fire agreements, 364, 388–393, 570–571
Montenegro, 89
Montesquieu, Charles de, 34
Moral Re-Armament (MRA), 661–666
Moro Islamic Liberation Front (MILF), 333, 335, 336, 389–392
Moro National Liberation Front (MNLF), 388–389
Moscow Declaration (1991), 433–434
Moser-Puangsuwan, Yeshua, 237
Mottu, Philippe, 661, 662
Mountain House and reconciliation, 661–666
Mozambique: civil-society actors/organizations, 576–581; disarmament/demobilization/reintegration process, 612, 623–629; faith-based intervention, 211; youth advocacy, 164
MTV's Free Your Mind Award, 550
Muivah, Thuingaleng, 220, 221
Multitrack approaches to conflict resolution, 33, 85–86, 228
Muluk, Hamdi, 671
Musevini, Yoweri, 349, 350
Music. *See* Arts and peacebuilding
Muslim-Christian Dialogue Forum in Nigeria, 226–231. *See also* Islam

Naga National Council (NNC), 220
Naga people, 219–225
Naga Socialist Council of Nagaland (NSCN), 220, 221
Nahmias, Ronit, 141, 143, 144–145
Nairobi Peace Initiative-Africa (NPI-Africa), 50, 441, 443
Namibia, 535, 536

Nansen Dialogue Network, 89, 484, 488–494
Nashe Maalo in Macedonia, 187–192
National Agenda for Peace (NAP) in Kenya, 444
National Bank of Genetic Data, 129, 130
National Business Initiative (NBI) in South Africa, 321, 325
National Collaborative Network for Peace Building in Sierra Leone, 259
National Commission on Human Rights in Indonesia, 670
National Council of Churches of Kenya (NCCK), 90, 441–446
National Democratic Institute for International Affairs, 508
National Rifle Association (NRA), 181
Natural-resource revenues and awareness raising/lobbying, 525
Navajo people, 450
Nazarabajev, Nursultan, 554
NCCK Peace Program (NPP) in Kenya, 444–445
Ndabaniwe, Evariste, 201–202
Ndadaye, Melchior, 200
Negotiating conditions and effective humanitarian advocacy, 562
Negotiations involving civil-society actors/organizations, 571–573
Nelson, Jane, 330
Neocolonial import, conflict prevention seen as a, 449
Nepal, 406
Netanyahu, Benjamin, 144, 145
Netherlands, 357
Netherlands Institute for Southern Africa, 524
Networking: arts and peacebuilding, 299; benefits of, 88–89; faith-based intervention, 214; women's advocacy, 105. *See also* Partnerships, effective; Regional networks/partnerships
Network of Early Warning Monitors, 425
Networks of Effective Action (NEA), 36
Neurobiology of aggressive behavior, 255
Nevada-Semipalatinsk Anti-Nuclear Movement in Kazakhstan, 552–557
Nevo, Baruch, 251
New Rainbow in Colombia, 619–622
News media, peacebuilding through, 176–177, 179
New Sudan Council of Churches, 444
Nicaragua: Living in the Shadow of the Eagle (Walker), 384
Nicaragua and civilian peacekeepers, 364, 382–387
Nielsen, Zoe, 48
Nigeria: exploitation by Western companies, 309; faith-based intervention, 89, 226–231; reconciliation, 640; warning signs/systems for timely intervention, 425
Niyungeko, Abdoul, 157–158

Nkwe Microfinance Initiative in South Africa, 325
Nolan, Ed G., 385
No Man's Land, 306
Noncombatant injuries/deaths, 11–12
Nongovernmental organizations (NGOs): advocacy, effective humanitarian, 561–562; awareness raising/lobbying, 519, 521–523; camps (summer peace) in Lebanon, 272–273; civilian peacekeepers, 372–373; civil society is more than, 8; development aid, 396, 397, 401, 402; dialogue-based processes, 505; diasporas, 351, 355, 357, 360; faith-based intervention, 210, 212, 215; Georgia, 508; International Criminal Court, 563–564; local businesses and peacebuilding, 317; necessary/irreplaceable complement to governments, 2; Northern/Western *vs.* Southern/Eastern partners, 15; reconciliation, 671; traditional/local conflict resolution, 464; warning signs/systems for timely intervention, 422, 427. *See also* Civil-society actors/organizations in peace processes; *individual organizations*
Nonviolent wage conflict, women and, 98
Noor (Queen), 108–110, 535
North Atlantic Treaty Organization (NATO), 167
North Central Local School System (OH), 279–280
Norwegian Church Aid (NCA), 88, 213, 401–402, 409–413
Novib/Oxfam Netherlands, 524
Nuclear issues/weapons: awareness raising/lobbying, 552–557; dialogue-based processes, 501–505; graduated reciprocation in tension-reduction, 585; scientific community helping to cope with, 256
Nuh, V. K., 220

Obala Arts Center in Sarajevo, 306
Obote, Milton, 349
Ochola, Baker, 350
O'Donnell, Margaret, 583
O'Donoghue, Lowitja, 650
OECD. *See* Organization for Economic Cooperation and Development
Offender/victim definitions and reconciliation, 639–640
Ofran, Hagit, 496
Ohio Commission for Dispute Resolution and Conflict Management, 249, 275–276, 278, 280–281
Oil in Nigeria, 227–228
Okello, Tito, 349
Omaar, Rakiya, 463–464
One to One Children's Fund, 500
Open Society Institute, 525
Operational prevention strategies, 12
Operation Fine Girl: Rape Used as a Weapon

in Sierra Leone, 194–198
Oprah Winfrey Show, 198
Opsahl Report (1993), 586
Optional Protocol to the Convention on the Rights of the Child (1998), 564–565
Orange Order in Northern Ireland, 435
Organization for Economic Cooperation and Development (OECD), 396
Organization for Security and Cooperation in Europe (OSCE): civilian peacekeeping, 365; Croatia, 656, 659; culture of reaction *vs.* prevention, 2; Moldova-Transdniestria conflict, 594, 595; monitoring cease-fire agreements, 364; Moscow Declaration (1991), 433–434
Organization of African Unity (OAU), 591
Organization of American States (OAS), 48, 51, 562
Organization of Islamic Countries (OIC), 390–392
Osgood, Charles, 584
Oslo Declaration (2002), 356
Osorno, Rodrigo, 620–621
"Other" (the) transformed from enemy to another human being: dialogue-based processes, 480, 485, 488–494; media, 176, 178–179, 189; Palestinian-Israeli conflict, 91
Otpor ("Resistance") movement in Serbia, 545–551
Otvorene Oci, 369
Our Neighbors, Our Family in Burundi, 202
Outsiders' contributions need to be sensitive to local efforts, 87–88
Oxfam, 397, 401, 424, 525
Oxford Research Group, 385, 479, 481, 485, 501–506
Oxford University, 484
Oxford University Commonwealth Law Journal, 514
Oxygen Television, 196

Paglas, Datu, 85, 332, 334, 335–336
Paglas Corporation, 335
Paglas Rural Bank, 336
Pakistan: education in conflict resolution/peace, 266–267; India's conflict with, 99, 101
Palestine Liberation Organization (PLO), 270
Palestinian-Israeli conflict: civilian peacekeepers, 364, 365; dialogue-based processes, 91, 474, 476, 481, 483, 495–500; media (the), 176; reconciliation, 665; traditional/local conflict resolution, 474; women's advocacy, 99, 109
"Palestinian-Israeli Hotline Melts Hate" (Blachor), 496
Panel of Eminent Persons on Civil Society and UN Relationships, 49, 63–64, 66–67
Panos Institute, 178

Papua New Guinea and women's advocacy, 98, 122–126

Parents Circle–Families Forum in Israel and Palestine, 495–496, 500

Participatory democracy changing the geography of politics, 61

Partnerships, effective: adult-youth partnerships, 152–153; advocacy (humanitarian), 561–562; civilian peacekeepers, 377, 383–384, 389–390; cooperation discourse, 33–36; destructive dynamics in insider/outsider relationships, 22; education in conflict resolution/peace, 259, 260; faith-based intervention, 214–215; Governor's (Ohio) Peace and Conflict Management Commission, 278, 280; key to crossing the scale barrier, 22–23; local businesses and peacebuilding, 312, 316–317, 322, 333–334; media (the), 181; reconciliation, 670; terror (war on), 81; UN-civil society interactions, 65; warning signs/systems for timely intervention, 427–429, 444, 446. *See also* Networking; Regional networks/partnerships

Passive networks, 55–56

Pastor and the Imam, The: Responding to Conflict (Ashafa & Wuye), 227, 230, 231

Patrimonialism contrasted with civil society, 8–9

Patriotic Movement Against Crime (MPCD) in El Salvador, 612

Pax Christi-Netherlands, 379

Peace-A Challenging New Era, 327

Peace and conflict impact assessment (PCIA), 38, 40–42, 401

Peace and Reconciliation Group in Northern Ireland, 570

Peace and Reconciliation Project in Kenya, 443–444

Peace Boat, 250

Peace Brigades International (PBI), 87, 364, 366, 372, 376–381, 384

Peacebuilding: civil society roles in, 18–20; commitment declarations, 89; creativity as a valuable resource, 90–91; individuals making a difference, 85; local communities addressing conflict issues, 19–20; measuring impact of peacebuilding efforts, 41; multitrack approaches to conflict resolution, 35, 85–86, 228; networking, 88–89; "other" (the) transformed from enemy to another human being, 91; outsiders' contributions need to be sensitive to local efforts, 87–88; overview, 83–84, 86; peaceful processes for conflict engagement, 11–12, 29–30; positive visions/messages, 90; reconciliation, 92; safe places for self-expression/ reconciliation, 89; simple/effective actions, 90; successes identified, 41; tools for measuring impact of, 41; training programs and workshops, 88; victim empowerment, 91; warning systems for timely intervention, 89–90. *See also* Civilian peacekeepers; Civil-society actors/organizations; Disarmament/demobilization/reintegration process; Discourses on peace practices; Local businesses, peacebuilding potential of; *individual subject headings*

Peacebuilding Forum (2004), 35

Peace Clubs in Sierra Leone, 259–262

Peace Dividend Paper, 327, 328

Peace Education Working Group, 246

Peace Festivals, 287–290

Peacekeeping. *See* Civilian peacekeepers; United Nations

Peacelinks, 91, 293–300

Peace monitors, 18

"Peace on the Line" (Taylor), 495

"Peace Talks and Federalism as the Solution for the Conflict in Sri Lanka" (2003), 359

Peace Times, 511

Peace Update, 445

Peaceworkers, 367

Peaceworks, 314

Pedagogy and dispute resolution methods/skills, 276

Peer mediation, 249, 260, 275–281, 484

People Are Calling for Peace, 289

People Building Peace: 35 Inspiring Stories from Around the World, 3

Peramuna, Janatha V., 356

Peres, Shimon, 496

Perfect Circle, The, 306

Person-focused methodologies for alleviating social tensions, 16

Perspective taking as a conflict resolution education tool, 246

Peru: civil-society actors/organizations, 570, 600–605; dialogue-based processes, 476; Ecuador's border conflict with, 88, 570, 600–605

Phares, Gail, 382, 383

Philippine Business for Social Progress (PBSP), 332–334, 337

Philippines: civilian peacekeepers, 388–393; local businesses and peacebuilding, 315, 332–337; terror (war on), 72, 80

Physicians for Human Rights, 563

Pied Piper fairy tale and the arts/peacebuilding, 283–284

Pietragalla Corti, Horacio, 129

Poblicks, Nyeko C., 353

Podumljak, Munir, 304

Polarized communities and civil-society organizations, 9–11

Policymaking/politics: arts and peacebuilding, 295; awareness raising/lobbying, 521, 523; civil-society actors/organizations, 17–20; development aid, 395; diasporas, 340–342; lacuna in, 32, 61; local businesses and peacebuilding, 315; political role of civil society, 9, 17–20; reconciliation, 641–642; warning signs/systems for timely intervention, 423, 424, 426, 445–446. *See also individual countries*

Pol Pot, 233

Pontificia Catholic University of Ecuador, 600, 603

Positional dialogue, 482

Positive visions/messages/attitudes, 90

Potter, Phillip, 529

Poverty/conflict/aid, link between, 80, 396, 429. *See also* Development aid; Economic/institutional structures that generate conflict

Prahl, Susanne, 307

Prasad, Chandrika, 513–514

Pregnancy/childbirth, women dying as a result of, 80

Prevention of Armed Conflict, The (2001), 49

Prevention strategies, structural/operational, 12, 429, 433–434. *See also individual subject headings*

Principles, self-understanding and peacebuilding, 36–38

Proactive networks, 55–56

Problem-solving dialogue, 482

ProFemmes Twese Hamwe, 470–471

Professionalization discourse, 36–40

Professionals *vs.* volunteers as civilian peacekeepers, 366

Protective accompaniment and civilian peacekeepers, 364

Psychological dynamics and warning signs/systems for timely intervention, 426

Public participation in negotiated processes, 20. *See also* Civil-society actors/organizations; Local businesses, peacebuilding potential of

Publish What You Pay campaign, 525

Pugwash Conference on Science and World Affairs, 256

Qarase, Laisenia, 512, 514

Quaker Peace and Social Witness Group, 223

Quakers, 78, 384, 503

Rabin, Yitzhak, 496

Rabo, Yasser A., 478

Radio Ecclesia in Angola, 569

Radio Isanganiro in Burundi, 207

Radio Nederland in Sierra Leone, 299

Raffaelli, Mario, 578

Ramos-Horta, José, 617

Rape, the media used to confront, 193–198

Rapprochement approach, change through, 32

Reagan, Ronald, 383, 384

Recognition and dialogue-based processes, 483

Reconciliation: arts and peacebuilding, 294,

296–297; Australia, 647–651; Cambodia, 234; Croatia, 654–659; favorable conditions for, 641–643; Guatemala, 240–244; Indonesia, 89, 667–672; justice needs to be combined with, 638–639; key elements of, 637; long-term view, 638; Moral Re-Armament, 661–666; Nigeria, 640; overview, 92; resources (informational), 643–644; Sierra Leone, 195, 198, 217; South Africa, 214; Timor-Leste, 25–27; Tutu's (Desmond) personal story, 645–646; victim/offender defined, 639–640. *See also* Disarmament/demobilization/reintegration process

Reconstruction and civil society actors/organizations, 590. *See also* Disarmament/demobilization/reintegration process

Reconstruction of a Historical Memory in Guatemala (REMHI), 240–244

Recovering Memory (Jeffrey), 241

Reebok Foundation, 193

Reflecting on Peace Practice Project (2003), 32, 33, 41

Regional Coordination for Economic and Social Research (CRIES), 51

Regional networks/partnerships: bottom linked to the top: essential partnerships, 52–53; businesses and peacebuilding, 315–316; European Conference on the Role of Civil Society in the Prevention of Armed Conflict, 54; global dynamics changing, 45–46; how civil-society organizations fit in, 50–52; interregional cooperation, 53–54; local level working with, 45; regionness and civil society, 46–47; synergies created by linkages between civil-society initiatives at regional/global level, 47–48; thinking globally and focusing regionally, 48, 50; understanding networks, 55–57

Reintegration process, 610. *See also* Disarmament/demobilization/reintegration process

Relational orientation and traditional/local conflict resolution, 453

Religion, the Missing Dimension of Statecraft (Johnston & Sampson), 211

Religion as an instrument of peace, 210–211. *See also* Faith-based approaches to conflict prevention/resolution

Renne, Outh, 150

Report on the Prevention of Armed Conflict (2001), 3, 12

Representative mechanisms and civil society actors/organizations, 572

Research data and awareness raising/lobbying, 524–525

Resistência Nacional Mocambicana (RENAMO), 577–580, 626

Resource Network for Conflict Studies and

Transformation, 354
"Restoring the Integrity and Stability of the State-A Common Cause for All People of the Republic of Moldova," 599
Return to Happiness program in Colombia, 164–165
Revolutionary Armed Forces of Colombia (FARC), 378, 621
Rio de Janeiro Protocol, 604
Roberfroid, André, 270, 273
Root causes of conflict and traditional/local conflict resolution, 452–453
Rose-Avila, Magdaleno, 630
"Round Table Sri Lanka," 359
Rubenstein, Richard, 73, 509, 511
Rurua, Nicholas, 509
Russia: civil-society actors/organizations, 594, 595; landmines, 62; terror (war on), 72
Rwanda: development aid, 395, 398; faith-based intervention, 215; genocide in 1994, 421, 426, 466–471; reconciliation, 639; traditional/local conflict resolution, 450, 466–471; warning signs/systems for timely intervention, 421, 426; women's advocacy, 109

Saakashvili, Michael, 507, 509–511
Sadat, Anwar, 176, 215
Safe places for self-expression/reconciliation, 89
SaferWorld, 31, 424
St. Xavier's Social Service Society (SXSSS), 414–420
Salamat, Hashim, 335
Samanbal Centres in Kashmir, 114–115
Sanchez, Mayerly, 163, 164
Sandinistas in Nicaragua, 383
Sandole, Dennis, 509
Sant' Egidio approach to mediation, 576–581
Sarajevo Film Festival, 301, 303–308
Sarney, José, 531
Saudi Arabia, 335
Save Somali Women and Children, 117–120
Save the Children, 525
Sawa in Lebanon, 270–274
Sawyer, Junior, 147–148, 150
Schmeidl, Susan, 423, 427
School culture and dispute resolution methods/skills, 276
Schuman, Robert, 664
Scientific community's role in preventing war, 255–256
Search for Common Ground (SFCG): arts and peacebuilding, 288–290; beginning of, 185–186; civil-society actors/organizations, 569; media (the), 177, 188–192, 201; operating principles, 37; youth advocacy, 152, 159
Sebastian Castillo, Cesar, 129
Security apparatuses of the state and the war on terror, 75–78

Seeds of Peace, 108–109, 178
Sehested, Ken, 220
Sela, Miri, 141
Senegal, 178
Sengulane, Diniz, 612, 623–624, 628
Sensitivity, development aid and conflict, 87–88, 404–405
Serbia: awareness raising/lobbying, 545–551; civilian peacekeepers, 369–374
Serbians: dialogue-based processes, 489, 493; Nansen Dialogue Network, 89; reconciliation, 654–659; youth advocacy, 167–172
Sesame Street, 189
Sexually transmitted diseases (STDs), 195
Sexual violence: civil society actors/organizations, 591; media (the) used to confront, 193–198
Shadow globalization of illicit trade, 14
Shanti Sena (peace army) in India, 364
Sharon, Ariel, 478
Sharp, Gene, 509
Sherriff, Andrew, 404–405
Shevardnadze, Eduard, 508, 511
Shillong Accord (1975), 220
Shir (council of elders) in Somaliland, 460–461
Siad Barre, Mohamed, 118, 119, 459, 460
Sierra Leone: arts and peacebuilding, 91, 288–289, 293–300; awareness raising/lobbying, 543; civil-society actors/organizations, 588–589; development aid, 398; diamond trade and civil wars, 399, 524; education in conflict resolution/peace, 90, 257–263; faith-based intervention, 216–217; media (the), 193–198; reconciliation, 642, 665; women's advocacy, 535; young population, 149; youth advocacy, 91, 151, 293–300
Sindayigaya, Adrien, 201, 206, 207
Singhalese people, 354–361
Sinn Féin, 582
Situational dynamics and warning signs/systems for timely intervention, 424
Skidmore, Monique, 237
Slavonia, 369
Smailovic, Vedran, 1, 301–303
Smirnov, Igor, 596
Smyth, Nigel, 329
Snegur, Mircea, 596
Snyder, Tanya, 386–387
Social change/justice, discourses on, 31–32
Social/emotional skills to prevent conflict, providing children with, 246. See also Education, conflict/peace
Social investment and local businesses/peacebuilding, 314–315
Society for Conflict Prevention, Democracy and Minority Rights, 358, 359
Sologuren Calmet, Hugo, 603

Solomon Star, 540
Somalia: diasporas, 342; reconciliation, 665;
    Somaliland breaks away from, 460;
    traditional/local conflict resolution, 451;
    women's advocacy, 117–121, 535
Somaliland and traditional/local conflict
    resolution, 459–464
Somali Peace and Reconciliation Conference
    (2002), 117–119
Somdet Phra Maha Ghosananda, 233–236
Sommers, Marc, 246, 247
Somoza Debayle, Anastasio, 383
Soqosoqo Ni Vakavulewa Ni Taukei, 513
Sorry Books, 649–650
Sorry Day in Australia, 648–653
Sosnowski, Saúl, 601
South Africa: civilian peacekeepers, 365;
    faith-based intervention, 214; local
    businesses and peacebuilding, 312, 313,
    315, 321–326; peace monitors, 18; public
    participation in negotiated processes, 20;
    reconciliation, 612, 641, 642; Truth and
    Reconciliation Commission, 612, 641;
    vision for the future, 19; warning signs/
    systems for timely intervention, 425
South African Breweries, 325
South African Council of Churches, 322, 323
Soviet Union, the former, 2, 476. *See also*
    Cold War
Spain, 604
Speight, George, 512, 513
Speth, Gus, 396
Spider web network model, 57
Sri Lanka: civilian peacekeepers, 365, 367;
    development aid, 401; diasporas, 342,
    354–361; faith-based intervention, 213,
    214; local businesses and peacebuilding,
    312, 315; regional business actors, 316
Stakeholder power and UN-civil society
    interactions, 60
Standard Bank, 325
START-1, the Nuclear Non-Proliferation
    Treaty, 556
State security apparatuses and the war on
    terror, 75–78
Stern, Nicholas, 399
Stoel, Max van der, 433–434
Strategic Arms Limitation Talks (SALT), 585
"Strengthening Cooperation Between Local
    Authorities and Civil Society," 599
"Strengthening Youth Advocacy," 171
Structural prevention strategies, 12, 14,
    16–17, 21
Student Palava Managers in Liberia, 150, 153
Students Offering Acceptance and Respect
    (SOAR) in US, 248, 249, 278–280
Studio Ijambo in Burundi, 180, 200–204,
    206–207
Sudan: diasporas, 341; exploitation by
    Western companies, 309; Lord's Resistance

Army supported by, 349, 350
Suharto, Mohamed, 669
Suleimenov, Olzhas, 553–554
Sweden, 504
Sweeney, Frank, 286
Swiss Agency for Development and
    Cooperation, 40
SwissPeace, 356, 425
Switzerland: arts and peacebuilding, 307;
    development aid, 412; diasporas, 354–355,
    359
Systemic causes of war/conflict, 13–15
SyVorn, 237–238

Taif Agreement (1989), 270
Tajikistan, 481
Talking Drum Studio (TDS) in Liberia,
    205–206, 569
Talking things out and traditional/local
    conflict resolution, 452
Tamil people, 213, 354–361
Tamils Rehabilitation Organization (TRO),
    345, 355, 358, 359
Tanovic, Danis, 306
Tanzania: HIV, 399; media (the), 201; terror
    (war on), 79
Taylor, Charles, 133, 135, 137, 216–217, 589
Technology and dialogue-based processes,
    479
Television, Macedonia and children's,
    187–192. *See also* Media, the
Temple University, 280
Temporary International Presence, 365
Terror, the war on: African (East) perspective
    on, 79; Asian (Southeast) perspective on,
    80; conceptions of terror, 73–74; definitions
    of terrorism, 73–74; discourse on social
    change/justice, 31–32; effects of, 76–78;
    future for conflict prevention?, 78; good/
    evil division, 75; human rights and state
    security institutions, 72; nonterrorist
    violence, 79–81; reality in which we live
    overtaken by, 2, 80–81; soft power focus
    ended, 75; state security emphasized,
    75–76; summary/conclusions, 81–82; UN
    responses, 71–73, 77; warning signs/
    systems for timely intervention, 421
Terrorism as a byproduct of civil wars, 399
Thalib, Ja'far Umar, 667
Theory-gap discourse, 33
Thich Nhat Hanh, 213
Third-party involvement in dialogue-based
    processes, 483
Three-tier understanding of the peacebuilding
    potential of societies, 310, 311
Timor-Leste, 25–27
Tocqueville, Alexis de, 34
Today is Not Tomorrow in Liberia, 205
Torres, Gabriel, 377
Toure, Ahmed S., 285–286

Track One approaches, 230
Tract Two dialogue, 19
Trade, shadow globalization of illicit, 14
Traditional/local conflict resolution: appropriate situations in which to use, 450; best practices to be used with modest realism, 454; challenges to, 453–454; core essentials/experiences of, 452–453; integrating contemporary methods with, 451, 454–455; Kenya, 443; resources (informational), 458; Rwanda, 450, 466–471; serious consideration of, 455–456; Somaliland, 459–464; validity (contemporary), 449–450. *See also* Local businesses, peacebuilding potential of
Training for Change, 223
Training programs/workshops: arts and peacebuilding, 297; civilian peacekeepers, 367; Colombia, 164–165; dialogue-based processes, 480, 481, 483, 491–492, 514, 515; diasporas, 359; faith-based intervention, 222, 223, 234, 240–241; gender awareness, 104–105; local businesses and peacebuilding, 325; media (the), 177; overview, 88; warning signs/systems for timely intervention, 441; women's advocacy, 120. *See also* Education, conflict/peace
Transdniestria and civil society actors in peace processes, 594–599
Transformative approaches *vs.* conditionality, 32
Transforming Arms into Ploughshares (TAE) Project in Mozambique, 612, 623–629
Transitional societies and awareness raising/lobbying, 523
Transitioning democracies and dialogue-based processes, 484
Transnational and Diaspora Network for Development, 359
Transparency International, 525
Traore, Moussa, 410
Trauma counseling: education in conflict resolution/peace, 258–259; faith-based intervention, 240–244; women's advocacy, 104; youth advocacy, 159
Tsuboi, Shunji, 555–556
Tuareg people, 410, 413
Turashvili, David, 509
Tutsi people, 109, 151–152, 157–159, 200, 203–204. *See also* Burundi; Rwanda; Uganda
Tutu, Desmond, 214, 323, 642, 645–646
Tuyaga, Adrien, 157–158

Ubuntu-minded people (social caring/thinking), 451
Uganda: child soldiers, 149; development aid, 395; diasporas, 348–353; HIV, 399; human rights violations, 560; Joint Christian Council, 444; media (the), 179; partnerships that are effective, 444; Sudan People's Liberation Army supported by, 349; terror (war on), 79; traditional/local conflict resolution, 450; youth advocacy, 151
Ukraine: awareness raising/lobbying, 550; civil-society actors/organizations, 594, 595
Umbanyi Niwe Umuryango in Burundi, 202
UN-civil society interactions: conflicts tackled, 63, 65, 67; enhancing UN relations with stakeholders, 63–65; global changes of relevance impacting, 60–63; multilateralism reinterpreted to mean multiconstituencies, 64–65; overview, 59–60; Panel of Eminent Persons on Civil Society and UN Relationships, 66–67; partnerships and pooling complementary capacities of diverse actors, 65; summary/conclusions, 67–69
United Civilians for Peace, 365
United Kingdom: awareness raising/lobbying, 525; development aid, 397, 406; dialogue-based processes, 501–506; diasporas, 345, 348–353, 355, 357; education in conflict resolution/peace, 258, 259, 266; Extractive Industry Transparency Initiative, 525; local businesses and peacebuilding, 315, 327–331; terror (war on), 72, 77, 78; women, 536; women's advocacy, 536. *See also* Ireland, Northern
United Nations: arms sales/proliferation, 429, 562; Arria Formula, 535, 537; arts and peacebuilding, 290, 299; awareness raising/lobbying, 524, 536–537; Balkan conflict, 370, 372; civilian peacekeepers, 365; civil-society actors/organizations, 591; coalition building, 561; Colombia, 162, 165; Commission on Human Rights, 562; Committee on Elimination of All Forms of Racial Discrimination, 515; Conference on the Illicit Trade in Small Arms and Light Weapons, 562, 626; Convention Against Torture, 531; Department of Political Affairs, 592; Development Program, 79–80, 227, 613–614; dialogue-based processes, 481, 493; disarmament/demobilization/reintegration process, 613–614; Division for the Advancement of Women, 592; Economic and Social Committee, 66; Economic Commission for Europe, 63; Educational, Scientific and Cultural Organization, 264; education in conflict resolution/peace, 264; Fund for Women, 535; High Commission on Refugees, 657; International Criminal Court, 563; Iraqi conflict, 77; Israel-Lebanon conflict, 145; Liberia, 136; Mano River Women's Peace Network, 591, 592; media (the), 177; Millennium Development Goals, 2, 65; Mozambique, 623; Office for

the Coordination of Humanitarian Affairs, 17; Panel of Eminent Persons on Civil Society and UN Relationships, 49, 63–64, 66–67; Population Division, 149; poverty and disease statistics, 79–80; reluctance to get involved early in conflicts, 433; Resolution 1325, 533, 537–538, 592; Security Council, 66, 71–72, 77, 429, 533, 535; Sierra Leone, 195, 299; Somalia, 118; Somaliland, 460; Special Session on Children, 151; Tajikistan, 481; terror (war on), 71–73, 77; traditional/local conflict resolution, 451; warning signs/systems for timely intervention, 17, 426–427; women's advocacy, 100–101, 106, 533, 535–538, 592; youth involvement in conflicts, 151. *See also* UN-civil society interactions; United Nations Children's Fund

United Nations Children's Fund (UNICEF): education in conflict resolution/peace, 246, 247, 269–274; youth advocacy, 151, 162, 164, 165

United States: coalition shifting emerging to counterbalance power of, 60; contra rebels in Nicaragua backed by, 382, 384; dialogue-based processes, 504; diasporas, 357; education in conflict resolution/peace, 249, 275–281; landmine treaty not signed by, 62; local businesses and peacebuilding, 335; media (the), 181; Mozambique's conflict, 578; nuclear issues/weapons, 504, 556; terror (war on), 76–78, 80; traditional/local conflict resolution, 450

University of Maryland, 600

Unsung Heroes in Burundi, 201–202

Utstein Study, 33

Uzbekistan, 72

van der Stoel, Max, 433–434

Venâncio, Moisés, 579

Venezuela, 181

Victim empowerment, 91

Victim/offender definitions and reconciliation, 639–640

Video revolutionizing political advocacy, 193–194, 223

Vietnam Veterans of America Foundation, 563

Vietnam War, 185

Villiers, George, 664

Violence, costs (excluding war) of interpersonal, 281

Vision for the future, 19, 32–33

Viva Rio, 618

Volunteers *vs.* professionals as civilian peacekeepers, 366

Waed, Sammy, 497

Walker, Thomas, 384–385

Wall Street Journal, 380

War Art, 306

War Booty, 130

Warning signs/systems for timely intervention: challenges facing, 424, 426–428; civil-society actors/organizations, 17, 425, 428; critics of, 423; debate around various aspects of, 422–424; Ireland (Northern), 425, 435–440; issues at stake, 421–422; Kenya, 441–446; lessons learned, 428–429; overview, 89–90; regional networks/partners, 50; resources (informational), 430–432; summary/conclusions, 429; violence, occupational, 17

Wartorn Society Project International, 35

Wasmer, Joseph, 663

Weizman, Ezer, 144

Welcome to Sarajevo, 306

West African Network for Peacebuilding (WANEP), 134, 259, 260, 425, 428–429

West African Network for Women in Peacebuilding (WIPNET), 17, 99, 133–140

Westmoreland, Michael L., 1

When the Guns Fall Silent, 476

Wickramasinghe, Ranil, 356

Wiesel, Ellie, 617

Wieseltier, Natalia, 495, 498

Wilcox, Philip C., 74

Wilde, David, 303

Wilkinson, Paul, 73

William of Orange, 435

Williams, Betty, 617

Williams, George, 514

Williams, Jody, 68

Wilson, Ronald, 647–649

Winning Against Violent Environments Program (WAVE) in US, 249, 277

Winterbottom, Michael, 306

With Regards to the Doubt, 130

WITNESS, 193–198

Witness for Peace (WfP), 364, 365, 382–387

Wolfsfeld, Gadi, 145

Women: Bougainville, 98, 122–125; capacity building for ongoing peace work, 99; civil-society actors/organizations, 588–593; Cuba, 131; definitions of peace and security need to be changed, 101–102; empowering, 105; equality for, 102; gender mainstreaming, 102–105; grandmothers of the Plaza de Mayo, 127–131; Israel-Lebanon conflict, 141–146; Kashmir (Athwaas Initiative), 111–115; lessons learned and best practices, 103–105; Liberia, 98, 133–140; Mano River Union Women's Network for Peace, 109, 136, 588–593; need to involve, 99–100; nonviolent wage conflict, 98; Noor (Queen), 108–110; overview, 97; Palestinian-Israeli conflict, 99, 109; recent developments, 100–105; reducing direct violence, 98; relationships transformed by, 98–99; resources (informational), 106–107; Somalia, 117–120, 535; strengthening women's ability to contribute to peacebuilding, 105–106; traditional/local conflict resolution, 470–471; trained gender advisors, 104–105; West African Network for Women in Peacebuilding, 17, 99, 133–140

Women and Conflict, 536

Women Building Peace Campaign, 533–539

Women in Black, 99, 568–569

Women in Security, Conflict Management, and Peace (WISCOMP), 99, 111–116

Women's Commission for Refugee Women and Children, 148, 151, 170

Women's Initiative for Peace in South Asia (WIPSA), 99

Women's International Peace Service for Palestine, 365

Women's Mass Action for Peace, 98

Working Group on Women, Peace and Security, 534

Workshops. *See* Education, conflict/peace; Training programs/workshops

World Bank, 259, 397–400

World Conference of Religions for Peace, 216–217

World Council of Churches (WCC), 528–532

World Health Organization (WHO), 281

World Methodist Peace Award, 130

World Peace Prayer ceremony, 267

World Vision, 214–215

Wright, Jaime, 528, 529, 531–532

Wright, Paulo S., 528

Wuye, James, 226–228, 230

Xeer (law) concept and traditional/local conflict resolution, 459–460, 464

Yakimets, Vladimir, 554

Young Jurists Association, 508

"Your Constitution, Your Rights," 513

Youth: arts and peacebuilding, 293–300, 306–307; Burundi, 91, 157–161; challenges ahead when working with, 153–154; Colombia, 162–166; diseases (preventable) killing the, 80; facilitating the participation of, 151–152; gang violence spreading from U.S. to Central America, 630–635; Kosovo, 151, 167–172; lessons learned when working with, 152–153; media (the), 187–192; overview, 147–148; protecting their own rights and promoting peace, 149–150; resources (informational), 155; Sierra Leone, 91, 151, 293–300; soldiers (child), 147–149, 558–562, 564–565, 591; television for children in Macedonia, 187–192; Uganda and human rights, 350; victims of war, 148–149; violence alternatives created by, 150–151. *See also* Education, conflict/peace

Youth for Peace (YFP) in Cambodia, 150, 153

Yugoslavia, Former Republic of (FRY), 639. *See also* Croatia; Kosovo; *Serb listings*

Zaher Shah (king), 343

Zaire, 395. *See also* Democratic Republic of Congo

Zalica, Pjer, 306

Zambia, 535

Zelizer, Craig, 305

Zimbabwe, 78

Zones of peace, 18, 50, 237, 484

Zuppi, Matteo, 578, 580

Zurabishvili, David, 509

About the Book

Individuals can make a difference working for peace worldwide. That is the message of *People Building Peace II*, an inspiring collection of stories of how "ordinary" men and women have played a crucial part in conflict prevention and peacebuilding.

Thematic chapters, illustrated with compelling case studies, present new trends in the role of civil society in conflict transformation. The cases reflect the variety of activities initiated and sustained by a broad range of actors, including women's groups, youth groups, and faith-based organizations. Such topics as reconciliation, dialogue, networking, and traditional methods of conflict resolution are among the topics throughly explored, as are the successful initiatives of lesser-known NGOs.

The resulting rich tapestry, an outcome of the Global Partnership for the Prevention of Armed Conflict, is an invaluable compendium of best practices and lessons learned, and at the same time a stirring call to action.

Paul van Tongeren is the founder and executive director of the European Centre for Conflict Prevention (ECCP). In 2002 he initiated the Global Partnership for the Prevention of Armed Conflict, an international network of organizations working in conflict prevention and peacebuilding worldwide. Together with the Global Partnership he organized a global process that resulted in a Global Action Agenda, presented at the global conference called "From Reaction to Prevention: Civil Society Forging Partnerships to Prevention Conflict and Build Peace," which took place in New York, from July 19 to 21, 2005.

Malin Brenk works as a project officer for the Research Unit at the European Centre for Conflict Prevention (ECCP). She has a masters degree in Political Science from Lund University, Sweden, with a specialization in conflict theory, and her thesis examined NGOs strategies and ability to influence the UN. Prior to joining the ECCP she spent six months at INCORE (Centre for International Conflict Research) in Northern Ireland and at the Norwegian Peace Alliance in Oslo, Norway.

Marte Hellema works as a research officer at the European Centre for Conflict Prevention (ECCP). She has a masters degree in international relations from the University of Amsterdam, the Netherlands, and wrote her thesis on disarmament programs for small arms and light weapons. Before joining the ECCP, she spent several months at both the Centre for Security Analysis, Granada, Spain, and at the United Network of Young Peacebuilders, the Netherlands. She is also active in youth movements, like the SF2000.

Juliette Verhoeven is senior staff member of the ECCP and coordinates the research unit and the programs related to the Middle East . She has an academic background in peace and conflict research at Uppsala University and holds a master degree in international relations from the University of Amsterdam. She has co-edited several publications on issues related to conflict prevention and peacebuilding, including the first edition of *People Building Peace*.

European Centre for Conflict Prevention
Korte Elisabethstraat 6
PO Box 14069
3508 SC Utrecht, The Netherlands

Tel.: + 31 30 2427777
Fax: + 31 30 236 9268

info@conflict-prevention.net
www.conflict-prevention.net
www.gppac.net

About the Global Partnership for the Prevention of Armed Conflict

The Global Partnership for the Prevention of Armed Conflict (GPPAC) is an international network of organizations working in conflict prevention and peacebuilding worldwide. Initiated in 2002 in response to a call from the UN Secretary-General, the Global Partnership has embarked upon a worldwide civil society–led process to mobilize a shift from reaction to prevention in the way violent conflict is dealt with, particularly focusing on the role of civil society and its interaction with local, regional, and international organizations. It is organized through fifteen regional processes, coordinated by regional initiators who collectively govern the Global Partnership through the International Steering Group. This book is one of the main outcomes of the Global Partnership and was launched at the global conference "From Reaction to Prevention: Civil Society Forging Partnerships to Prevent Violent Conflict and Build Peace," organized at United Nations Headquarters in New York in July 2005.

GPPAC aims to support a shift from reaction to prevention through the following goals:

1. To create a sustainable network of individuals and groups efficiently and effectively trained in prevention and peacebuilding at global, regional, national, and local levels. This network will include multi-stakeholder partnerships involving diverse civil society organizations, governments, regional organizations, and the United Nations to enable effective engagement.

2. To develop and work toward the implementation of a policy change agenda, as articulated in this Global Action Agenda and Regional Action Agendas, that will strengthen the long-term effectiveness of conflict prevention and peacebuilding through new formal and informal mechanisms of interaction between CSOs, governments, regional organizations, and the UN.

3. To raise public awareness around the world and generate constituencies who actively support human security as an alternative to militaristic approaches that privilege state security over the human rights and safety of individuals and their

communities and are informed about prevention and peacebuilding and the important role of civil society in achieving it.

The International Secretariat is hosted by the European Centre for Conflict Prevention.

About the European Centre
for Conflict Prevention

The European Centre for Conflict Prevention is a nongovernmental organization, based in the Netherlands, that promotes effective conflict prevention and peace-building strategies, and actively supports and connects people working for peace worldwide. It currently holds the secretariat for the European Platform for Conflict Prevention and Transformation and for the Global Partnership for the Prevention of Armed Conflict.

European Centre for Conflict Prevention
Paul van Tongeren, Executive Director
Korte Elisabethstraat 6
PO Box 14069
3508 SC Utrecht
The Netherlands

Tel.: + 31 30 2427777
Fax: + 31 30 236 9268

info@conflict-prevention.net
www.conflict-prevention.net
www.gppac.net